A SPIRITUAL HYPOTHESIS

AN INQUIRY INTO ABNORMAL AND PARANORMAL BEHAVIOR

DANIEL PUNZAK, P.E.

authorHOUSE®

AuthorHouse™
1663 Liberty Drive
Bloomington, IN 47403
www.authorhouse.com
Phone: 1 (800) 839-8640

Published by AuthorHouse 03/31/2017

ISBN: 978-1-5246-5237-1 (sc)
ISBN: 978-1-5246-5238-8 (hc)
ISBN: 978-1-5246-5236-4 (e)

Library of Congress Control Number: 2016919646

Print information available on the last page.

CONTENTS1

Chapter 1

SPIRITUAL ANALYSIS IN THE AGE OF MATERIALISM

A. Introduction

That humanity is the product of multiple evolutionary steps—beginning with nonliving molecules conjured into living matter—has been a pervasive mode of thought for over 150 years. This mode of thought is known as physicalism, materialism, or the mechanistic view of life. In this book I will demonstrate that a spiritual perspective of human consciousness and behavior has more evidence to substantiate it than does the mechanistic paradigm.

B. Spiritual, Spirit, and Soul

The word *spiritual* is evocative. It is frequently used in religious contexts, bringing to mind the thought of someone praying or meditating. The phrase *spiritual values* is often used to describe intangibles such as honesty, truth, justice, and compassion for others. Another form of the word is *spirited*, as in a spirited person or animal. The term *human spirit* implies a sense of hope or determination for achieving an objective or overcoming a challenge. The above perspectives are universal, even to those with no hope that a human being can survive after death.

   I use the word *spirit* as the name for an immaterial duplicate human being that resides (overlaps and penetrates) inside an individual's physical body during life and continues to exist after the body dies. I will often use the term *spirit body* to indicate that this spirit has a form. This spirit body may also appear to briefly leave the physical body prior to death. By *death*, I do not mean the total cessation of life, as would a materialist. I mean, more properly, the shedding of the physical body, since the spirit or spirits of a person live on. One of the key chapters of this book will examine near-death experiences (NDEs). One phase of an NDE is

1

frequently called an *out-of-body experience* (OBE), in which the person believes that his or her spirit body has left his or her physical body.

The word *spirit* is a translation of the Greek word *pneuma*, for "breath." Another Greek word related to the nonphysical part of humans is *psyche*, for "soul." Thus, the word *psychology* means "study of the soul," and *psychiatrist* means "doctor of the soul," although many such doctors do not believe in a nonphysical soul.

Much of the Western view of nonphysical life comes from the Bible, especially from the New Testament. Primarily written in Greek, it uses distinct terms for denote spirit and soul. One of the basic premises of this book is that humans consist of more than one spiritual component. Consider the following verses from the New Testament:

- "May the very God of peace sanctify you wholly; and may your spirit and soul and body be preserved without blemish to the coming of our Lord Jesus Christ" (1 Thessalonians 5:23, LT).
- "For the word of God is living and powerful and sharper than any two-edged sword, piercing even to the point of division between soul and spirit, and between the joints and marrow and bones, and is a discerner of the thoughts and intents of the heart" (Hebrews 4:12, LT).
- "And Mary said, My soul magnifies the Lord. And my spirit rejoices in God my Savior" (Luke 1:46–47, LT).

The Old Testament usually uses the word *spirit* in reference to the Spirit of God, but there is one verse that clearly states that humans have a spirit: "Truly, there is a spirit in men; and the breath of the Almighty gives them understanding" (Job 32:8, LT). Some translations indicate that the "spirit in men" referenced above is the spirit of the Almighty and not the individual's own spirit, as I would interpret it. But here, Isaiah 26:9 clearly distinguishes between the two: "My soul has desired thee in the night; yea, with my spirit within me will I seek thee early." The Hebrew language differentiates between the two incontrovertibly. The word for soul is *nephesh*, and the word for spirit is *ruah*, although the latter sometimes refers to the Spirit of God. In the above verse, Isaiah specifies both "my soul" and "my spirit," terms distinct from "the Spirit of God." These Hebrew terms will be discussed in a later chapter.

In addition, the word *spirit* is frequently used in reference to other nonmaterial beings, such as angels and ghosts, which may or may not be friendly to humans. Although I may use *spirit* in this manner, it is not my primary focus. Only when these other spirits relate to the spirit body of humans will they be relevant to this discussion (e.g., *beings of light* observed by a person having an NDE). Likewise, the term *ghost* will not be used except in the sense of a person in a spirit-body form being observed by another person, as in an apparition.

Of particular interest in this book is the relationship between concepts of spirit or soul and behavior. Psychologists may say that you have the right to believe in a soul or spirit and its survival after death, but they may interject that such a belief does not conform to reality. This book will provide evidence that spirit and soul are better explanations than the purely neurochemical ones for explaining much about abnormal behavior as well as creative inspiration. Citing some experienced therapists, I will identify the root of abnormal behaviors and show how these behaviors can be remedied without psychoactive medications. Awareness of the causes of abnormal behavior may enable people to avoid these causes in the future or to correct a current situation before the complications become severe. I maintain that the principal cause of abnormal behaviors is trauma in its many forms, with its consequent effect on the connection of the soul to the physical body.

C. Materialism

Many people who believe only in the biological basis of sensing and thinking are vocal atheists or agnostics. Some may have religious beliefs that they hold apart from their materialistic view of consciousness. Although I do not know if he has any religious views, one of the chief proponents of the mechanistic viewpoint is the late Sherwin B. Nuland (1930–2014), an American medical doctor and author of the books *How We Die* (1992) and *The Wisdom of the Body* (1997). On the topic of spirit in the latter book, Nuland states, "Organic structure and function are the essential starting points for any exploration of humanity and spirit" (p. 69). Earlier in the book, Nuland explains that until the middle of the nineteenth century, many authorities believed that living things possessed a "vital force" or energy; these believers were called *vitalists*. Such belief was not necessarily connected to religion or the supernatural.

Nuland's vivid explanation of human nature is as follows:

> Nevertheless, I do not hesitate to propose that man is in some as-yet-undiscovered way more than the sum of his biological parts, that a thing greater than the innate has somehow been crafted from the innate—that we have taken nature's endowment and made with it the stuff of spirit and all that implied by my use of the word. How indeed, it might justifiably be asked, can such a formulation escape the charge of being another form of vitalism?

> Actually, vitalism has nothing to do with the case. My formulation does not require the existence of any "energy"—nor any substance, either—beyond what is already well known from the study of physics or chemistry. I propose a human body each of whose constituents follows, as do all living things, the well-researched principles of biophysical systems that are amenable to study by standard scientific methods. I am not postulating a uniqueness within human tissue that presupposes the need to discover new natural laws to understand it. The human spirit of which I speak depends for its elucidation on principles already explicated. In the battle of vitalists versus mechanists, I stand squarely in the center of mechanist camp. My concept does not involve a "nonmaterial" source.

> The quality I call spirit is in its very essence the product of the organization and integration of the multiplicity of physical and chemical phenomena that is us. It has to do with the way the various parts of the human body communicate and are coordinated with one another under the control of the evolved masterwork that is the human brain. That such a complex multicellular organism functions with a unity of purpose is the result of a myriad of messages of various sorts and of integrative capacities that in themselves originate in *nature's* purpose, which is merely to keep the organism from dying, at least until its reproductive capacity is spent. (pp. 68–69; original italics)

What Nuland has called a mechanistic concept has also been called *materialistic*—the idea that each person has only a physical body. In the context of this book, the word *materialism* will refer only to this philosophical premise. People who accumulate wealth, cultivate impressive lifestyles, or are hedonists are often called materialistic, but not in the sense here discussed. Another term for a materialistic or mechanistic view of humans is *physicalism*. In general, I will use the terms *physicalism*, *materialism*, and *mechanistic* concept interchangeably. A term that writer Raymond Tallis, whom I will cite extensively, uses is *biologism*. Biologism may imply, among other things, that the laws of physics and chemistry are somewhat altered in all living things—that the laws of biochemistry could be different from those of inorganic chemistry.

Previously, I discussed various meanings of *spirit*. Sometimes languages other than English elegantly encapsulate a complex term in a single word. One such word is the German *zeitgeist*. The English translation I prefer is "spirit of the times." I would call the last one and a half centuries the age of materialism, in the sense that Will and Ariel Durant refer to certain historical periods as "the age of faith" and "the age of reason." Even some philosophers during the axial age, including the ancient Greeks, would be considered materialist thinkers. Today's materialists often claim that all phenomena of the mind will eventually be shown to be brain-based. Those opposed deride this philosophy as "promissory materialism."

Mechanists normally view the human body and brain as the apex of the evolutionary scale. Thus, they believe that any spiritual concepts of God arose through an evolutionary process because ancient people who had those views were more likely to survive. A recent book took the dualist approach, gathering data on brain function and human behavior that do not appear to be explainable through materialism. This included original research by the lead author, who views the mind as separate from the brain. This book, *The Spiritual Brain: A Neuroscientist's Case for the Existence of the Soul* (2007), by Mario Beauregard, PhD, and Denyse O'Leary, has two interesting, and related, glossary terms.

Evolutionary psychology: The branch of psychology that maintains that human brains, including any component that involves religion or spirituality, comprise adaptations or psychological mechanisms that have evolved by natural selection to benefit the survival and reproduction of the human organism. (p. 345)

Neurotheology: An approach to religious, spiritual and mystical experiences that seeks a neurological and evolutionary basis for spiritual experiences. (p. 346)

It should be noted that although they disagree with evolutionists on these particular points, Beauregard and O'Leary do not deny that evolution applies to plant and animals. I agree with them on this point and also on their point that spirituality is not a product of evolution; rather, we have spirit components in addition to our physical bodies.

One question frequently raised by evolutionists is when to properly differentiate between two species, either as a matter of degree or of kind. Obviously, major differences such as invertebrate versus vertebrate, cold-blooded versus warm-blooded, and nonmammal versus mammal indicate a difference of kind. Less significant differences between mammals, for example, between canines and felines, would be a difference of kind. However, differences between breeds of canine would be a difference of degree. Even evolutionists debate whether humans are different by degree or in kind from great apes. The spiritual concept I posit makes humans different in kind from the great apes.

Although many other researchers in the field of consciousness examine the relation between brain function and the physical body, researchers who study NDEs pose a fundamental question: If a human being can perceive and think when the brain is not functioning (i.e., when there are no brain waves on an electroencephalograph [EEG]), then what is the nature of consciousness? A few years ago, the prestigious magazine *Science* published a list of the 125 most important questions for which science was seeking answers, including "What is the biological basis of consciousness?" In other words, how do biochemical reactions in the brain result in sensing and thinking, memory, and a sense of self? For the physically nonfunctioning brain, spiritual realities are the only explanation for individuals' ability to record visions and spoken words as well as to think rationally.

It should be noted that when an EEG reports no brain waves, the EEG is generally measuring "higher"-level brain functions. The "lower"-level brain activities, such as those in the brain stem or amygdala, could still be functioning. However, these parts of the brain are not responsible for color vision or rational thought, the latter being exclusive to humans.

A problem with a discussion of a spirit or a soul within humans is that we consider these things to be associated exclusively with humanity. If each human has a soul and a spirit, and possibly other spirit forms, then could not one of these be in plants or animals? Could not these forms be a functioning part of the plant's or animal's biophysical system? Although Nuland's explanation of a vital force or energy unique to living organisms will only be briefly mentioned in this text, the concept of nonphysical forms and their functions will be the primary issue presented in this book. Animals may have some nonphysical forms, but they do not have a form that is unique to humans.

D. Mind, Brain, and Psi Phenomena

If use of the words *spirit* and *soul* appears to reflect a religious view, despite the fact that Nuland, a mechanist, uses the word *spirit*, some nonreligious people present an alternative. These philosophers and scientists study the issue as a mind/brain problem. The issue is similar to that previously discussed, of a person's being able to perceive and think when the brain is not functioning. In this case, the mind is separate from the brain, although the two normally function concurrently. People who believe that the mind and brain are separate are called *dualists*. A recent book entitled *Irreducible Mind: Toward a Psychology for the 21ˢᵗ Century* (2007), written by multiple authors, addresses many of the phenomena that I will discuss. With the term *irreducible mind*, the authors connote that the mind cannot be reduced to the biophysical activities of the brain.

Earlier, I mentioned a mechanistic view of humans and an Out-of-body experience (OBE) that can occur during an NDE. I believe that NDEs are spiritual experiences, although those who uphold the mechanistic view have been very outspoken in trying to present mechanistic explanations. In the previously cited book *The Spiritual Brain*, the authors note how quickly the news media present speculative research that "explains" NDEs as physical, brain-based phenomena. The general news media tend to demonstrate a friendlier attitude toward NDEs, as they know it often brings higher viewer ratings. The scientific press, after presenting its physical explanation of NDEs, is then reluctant to present evidence that refutes the original research when newer evidence shows that the original research was poorly done or that the conclusions of the research went beyond the scope of the observed phenomenon. *Irreducible Mind* notes that many scientific "explanations" are not true explanations, but rather a restating of a phenomenon in scientific linguistics. *Irreducible Mind* calls upon scientists to explain the explanation.

Scientists or well-educated laypeople interested in parapsychology, or psi phenomena, often refer to scientists who immediately reject these psi phenomena as "fundamental scientists" or as those practicing "scientism," defined by Tallis in his book *Aping Mankind* (2011) as "the mistaken belief that the natural sciences (physics, chemistry, biology and their derivatives) can or will give a complete description and even explanation of everything, including human life" (p. 15). These are scientists who uphold the unproven assumption that only information that comes from the senses or from scientific instruments (devices that magnify or extend sense impressions) is valid.

Another explanation for scientism is that it happens when scientific opinion becomes rigid dogma. One example is a short question-and-answer section in the Newsmakers section of *Science* (vol. 315, February 23, 2007, 1061) about the closing down of the Princeton Engineering Anomalies Research laboratory. Its director had been Robert Jahn, an aerospace scientist and the former dean of the School of Engineering and Applied Science at Princeton University. Among the lab's controversial claims was that human thought can influence physical reality. Here are two questions posed to Dr. Jahn, along with his replies.

> Q: Do you think these phenomena will ever be proved in a way that will satisfy these skeptics?
>
> A: That raises the whole question of where the skepticism comes from. I have to tell you that I was not totally prepared for the intensity of recalcitrance we have encountered. ... For skepticism to be useful, it has to be informed. It doesn't

help if the people haven't read your papers or visited your laboratory or talked with you personally.

Q: What's the worst snub you ever received from a scientist?

A: [One wrote,] "It's not worth my time to inform myself [about your research] because it is so obviously impossible." This is not a scientific attitude.

Apparently, the writer of that snub and most other materialists are unfamiliar with a comment by John Stuart Mill (1806–1873) in his book *On Liberty* (1859). In it, he states that a person who knows only his own side of a case (or issue), knows little of that.

By claiming that they are doing "true" science, fundamental scientists claim that they hold or have seized the high moral ground. I believe my writings will show that many scientists are actually holding the opposite position. Many "scientists" in recent years have engaged in outright fraud in their investigations. The public may sometimes hear about it when the perpetrators are exposed, but this practice could be much more prevalent than reported. Advocates of scientism employ a logical fallacy when they cite frivolous examples of anomalous data to debunk an entire phenomenon.

Often, when a scientific person uses the term *faith*, he or she is using it in a derogatory manner about people following a previously written book, like the Bible, that conflicts with other, "hard" evidence gathered by scientists. I posit that people who believe only in sense-based input to the brain hold this opinion on faith, as the same cannot be validated by the viewpoint itself. To some extent, everyone, including scientists, uses faith every day, although not necessarily in a religious sense. The writer of the book of Hebrews includes the following in his definition of faith: "Faith is ... the evidence for things not seen" (Hebrews 11:1, LT). Much of this book will be such evidence that a spirit-body-based concept of behavior and brain function is a better model for explaining behavior than is the standard medical model or the mechanistic approach currently employed in psychological research. Davis (2010) attributes the following quote to R. Buckminster Fuller, but provides no reference to Fuller: " You never change things by fighting the existing reality. To change something, build a new model that makes the existing model obsolete." Whenever I use the phrase *I believe*, I mean that evidence, not any one authority, person, or book, has led me to the stated conclusion.

E. An Interesting View on the Paranormal

I will be using the word *paranormal* regularly in this book. My interpretation of *paranormal* has little to do with the Hollywood version but instead draws from the work of psychologist Lawrence LeShan (1920–), a popular writer on the subject of psi phenomena and their relationship to standard science. LeShan is the author of *How to Meditate* and numerous other books on alternate realities, and more recently on a book about how to deal with cancer. The parapsychology he writes about that is most relevant to this discussion is presented in *The World of the Paranormal: The Next Frontier* ([1984] 2000). Although the term *paranormal* is used in the title of his book, he maintains that it "is a perfectly normal part of human potential" (p. 11). He refers to communication using the senses as "Type A" perception. "Type B" perception is that not involving the senses but instead paranormal/extrasensory perception (ESP).

LeShan frequently discusses different metaphysical systems, or "realms." Type A events are in the Realm of Sensory Experience, while type B events are in the Realm of Consciousness and the Realm of Meaningful Behavior. Modern science, especially physics, has little to do with human experience, meaningful events, or consciousness. Scientific methodology is only applicable in the Realm of Sensory Experience, based on *ceteris paribus* (other things being equal). Furthermore, the scientific method is based on 19th-century theories of physics (a mechanical model) and not today's quantum mechanical (QM) model. Indeed, the most influential 19th and early 20th-century academic precepts, by Sigmund Freud, Karl Marx, and Charles Darwin, were all mechanistic.

To state that type B perception is impossible is to base one's view on 19th-century physics. LeShan notes that when theory and facts disagree, it is the theory that needs to be discarded, not the facts. He quotes St. Augustine: "There is no such thing as a miracle which violates natural law. There are only events which violate our limited knowledge of natural law" (p. 47). LeShan maintains that consciousness has no material qualities; it is not located and has no bounds. As an example, mystic Jacob Boehme, when asked where the soul went at death, replied that it was not necessary for it to go anywhere. Heaven is not a "place" that occupies physical space. However, when a soul is in a physical body, it roughly corresponds to the shape of the physical body.

Different types of experiences require different metaphysical systems. Faith and reason can disagree but still remain valid within their own metaphysical systems. These differences in metaphysical systems are also noted by Michael Harner, an author to be discussed later, in his discussion of shamanic states of consciousness.

Closely related to these realms of experience are two terms infrequently employed in the social sciences and psychology: nomothetic science, which deals with objective phenomena (the natural sciences), and "idiographic" (or ideographic) science, which deals with individuals and subjective phenomena. In essence, the same laws that govern inanimate matter do not explain human behavior. Each of these areas of study uses different metaphysical systems (models or reality), and the experimental methodology of one science cannot be used to prove or disprove claims made in another realm.

To further delineate these concepts, I have developed the following table from LeShan's explanations of the differences between the two types of perception and two sciences.

TABLE 1.1. Differences Between Two Types of Perceptions

Variable	Realm of Consciousness Type B Perceptions Idiographic Science	Realm of Sensory Experience Type A Perceptions Nomothetic Science
Space, distance, and location	No	Yes
Purpose	Yes	No
Causation	No	Yes
Processes	Yes	No
Death	No	Yes
Common sense	Not applicable	Applicable
Physical theory	Quantum model	Newtonian model
Repetition	Rarely repeatable	Usually repeatable

Relationships	Histories, stable	Physical properties
Mathematical laws	Rarely	Frequently
Examination	May change the subject	Steady/independent
Applicable theories	Communication (transaction or interaction model)	Information

LeShan also discusses three types of truth: empirical, analytic, and scientific. He argues that there can be no scientific truth concerning annihilation of consciousness at the death of the physical body because the annihilation of consciousness cannot be observed. Additionally, LeShan provides interesting insights and questions regarding assumptions made by parapsychologists in their study of paranormal events such as telepathy, clairvoyance, and precognition. For instance, a number of parapsychologists have performed rigorous studies demonstrating that the accuracy of telepathy (communication between two people's minds) is not affected by distance and that the experimental subjects can be inside cages that prevent communication via electromagnetic radiation. Early parapsychological research used card-reading experiments to provide evidence that some people could tell which card another person was viewing (telepathy), or to demonstrate clairvoyance (no other viewer) or precognition (which card will be selected before the selection is made).

LeShan maintains that it does not make sense to perform such experiments, because they are in different realms of experience. A purely statistical analysis of this research can be misleading. The difficulty is that coin tosses or card guesses are not really relevant to most humans, especially when done multiple times. Some studies have shown that accuracy decreases the longer an experiment of this type lasts, as it has no meaning to the test subject. Hearing messages from an injured or deceased person at the moment of injury or death has human meaning but is not repeatable for a statistical analysis. The same is true for greeting deceased relatives during an NDE. A complex sensory definition for type B perception cannot be developed, as there is no known physical explanation.

Eastern religions often speak of the material world as the illusory maya. LeShan would probably prefer to explain that the material world is not an illusion in the sensory realm but is an illusion in the Realm of Consciousness. This is similar to Michael Harner's noting the difference between an ordinary state of consciousness and a shamanic state of consciousness.

LeShan discusses several types of consciousness, referred to here as altered states of consciousness (ASCs). I will not go over his four types here (sensory reality, clairvoyant/unity reality, transpsychic reality, and mythic reality), for the sake of brevity. Normally, when the word *consciousness* is used, it implies waking consciousness, but sleep is an ASC as are hypnagogic and trance states. Mystical consciousness is very rare, and the paranormal phenomena that occur during it or during NDEs are much deeper—and different from telepathic communication. A reader should see close parallels between the realms of consciousness that LeShan discusses and spiritually transformative experiences (STEs). STEs are similar to NDEs, except that the person is not near death. Still, LeShan classifies STEs as ineffable experiences, indescribable with sense-based language.

LeShan surmises that there should be a sign above the doorway of the cathedral of science that states that it is a dangerous and unstable structure that is undergoing major renovation and may be torn down at any moment for complete rebuilding. He maintains that when scientists are asking questions about consciousness and cannot find an answer, they are asking the wrong questions and making incorrect assumptions, such as doubting the existence of telepathy. Type B perception is the study of how individuals cannot be fully separated from each other. My book is about how behavior can be better explained if a proper understanding is reached regarding plural spiritual entities within humans.

F. Psychology and Spiritual Factors

When I use the term *psychology*, I use it in a broad sense, to include perception and other concepts not limited to sense-based perception. Within the parameters of paranormal behavior, I include a variety of items such as telepathy, clairvoyance, precognition (seeing the future), retrocognition (seeing the past), communication with a deceased person, time distortion, unusual healing abilities, bilocation (physically appearing in two locations at the same time), and other anomalous phenomena.

Society often thinks of the role of psychology as developing motivation for desired behavior. While psychology is not the primary focus of this book, I will delve into changing abnormal behavior into socially acceptable behavior. By *abnormal behavior*, I mean mental illnesses as defined in the *Diagnostic and Statistical Manual of Mental Disorders*. My primary focus will be auditory and visual hallucinations, especially pathological ones that are threatening or undesirable. People who heard voices encouraging them to go on shooting sprees have committed numerous public shootings. I will explain spiritual factors of this phenomenon, although many of these hallucinations may be a combination of physical and spiritual forces. I will often mention posttraumatic stress disorder (PTSD) and explain how trauma can activate abnormal behavior by way of the manner in which it affects a person's spirit body.

By *spiritual factor*, I do not necessarily imply that abnormal behavior is the result of sin. For example, substance abuse and addiction are defined mental disorders, which, many religions would assert, are the result of moral error. My preferred definition of *sin* is "to miss the mark." In other words, the behavior in question is a waste of time and energy but is not necessarily offensive to a deity. Such unacceptable behavior can often appear in various "victims," for instance, those who were abused as children. Even some problems that seem to be purely physical may have a spiritual influence. For instance, epilepsy was once called *the sacred disease*. Needless to say, some of the concepts discussed here are more speculative than other areas of study.

Many scientists engage in speculative theoretical science, but their results are implied to be absolute. Most common scientists so engaged are astronomers or physicists. For instance, there is no way on earth to replicate the nuclear reactions occurring at the center of stars, what happens in a supernova, or a gamma-ray burst, so astronomers or physicists speculate on what is happening to explain the observed phenomena. To a great extent, I have speculated similarly, but I believe that my speculations are able to reduce some seemingly disparate observations of behavior to a common cause, for example, the effects of trauma through abuse or injury.

Another important area of my inquiry is the spiritual origins of creativity. As with pathological hallucinations, people's creative aspects can come by way of voices, music, visions, or guidance. But these, unlike pathological hallucinations, are considered to be appreciated communication.

G. Metaphors and Spiritual/Physical Interactions

Although this book seeks to relate consciousness and behavior to a spirit body, there have been attempts by physicists to explain such brain function using discoveries of modern physics. For instance, some have adopted quantum theory to explain the brain, especially its role in memory. According to quantum theory, memory could use the brain but not necessarily be stored there, being active when the brain is not. Another common explanation is that the brain can behave like a hologram. Although I consider these to be valid discussions, I regard them as metaphors for explaining spiritual realities, as there is no holographic device in a person's brain.

One of the terms used by NDErs (near-death experiencers) is *ineffability*. This term refers to their difficulty in conveying their feelings in words. Quantum and holographic terms help us to relate these spiritual phenomena to a physical explanation. Some physicists have gone beyond simply using them as metaphors. Physicist Itzhak Bentov (1923–1979) developed the following concepts: (1) The universe and all matter is a mode of consciousness in the process of developing to higher levels; (2) Our brains are thought receivers, not the source of thought; and (3) According to Bentov, the universe is a hologram and the brain is a hologram interpreting a holographic universe. These concepts could be compatible with my concept of the spirit body, but they could also be materialist thinking if taken beyond analogy.

One of the vital issues raised by the concept of a spirit body is its relation to a physical body. If the two never interact, then the spirit body is not the mind. However, I maintain that they do interact and that spirit is the basis for mind, as separate from the brain. NDErs often state that when their spirit body is out of their physical body, it can pass unimpeded through doors, walls, and other people. Although many NDErs report that despite their having spoken when out of their body, no one could hear them, although many NDErs could hear what a person in a physical body was saying.

The film *Ghost* (1990) depicted much of the phenomenon that occurs during an NDE. In the film, Sam Wheat (Patrick Swayze) dies and attempts to communicate with his grieving girlfriend, Molly Jensen (Demi Moore). He initially fails but then discovers that he can contact her through Oda Mae Brown (Whoopi Goldberg), a usually fraudulent medium. In a later scene, Sam needs to type on a computer, but his spirit body's fingers keep passing through the keyboard. The spirit of another deceased person explains to Sam that to interact with the physical world, he must have a strong emotional desire to do so. This interaction between spirit and matter is very important, perhaps explaining why materialists have difficulty understanding how spirits, if they even exist, could be important if they simply pass through physical matter.

Metaphors or analogies from the physical world further help to explain my point about spirit bodies. Biologists and physiologists have made great strides recently toward understanding infectious diseases and pharmaceutical drugs (hereafter just "drugs") and the latters' interaction with the human body. Infectious agents such as bacteria and viruses (hereafter just "agents") have proteins on their surface. Unless these proteins match up with receptors on an animal's cells, they cannot enter, or interact with, the animal cells to infect or destroy them.

There is a similar mechanism for drugs. An effective antibiotic must have the ability to enter the agent. Agents can develop resistance to antibiotics by changing their receptors. The same is true of an individual's immune system. It must recognize the foreign agent and develop a countermeasure that recognizes and neutralizes the intruder.

I think that the spirit body may have nonphysical receptors so that, in general, only the spirit body that belongs with that physical body can interpenetrate and interact with it. Each person's nonphysical receptors may have a different vibration frequency. Another spirit body can pass through the normal spirit body. For example, when an NDEr in its spirit body passes through a physical body, it also passes through the normal spirit body. Generally, the spirit body prefers to remain in its designated physical body, but trauma can cause it to depart. This trauma can be physical pain associated with a heart attack, childbirth, injury, anesthesia, or shock (e.g., the result of an allergic reaction or loss of blood). Emotional trauma (e.g., child abuse) or depletion of energy can also cause the spirit body to depart the physical body. Under any of these circumstances, the spirit body may become fragmented and may not completely return. The spirit body does not normally depart, and it can return after an NDE. However, if the physical body is beyond repair, the spirit cannot return and the physical body dies. It is possible that the spirit body temporarily leaves the physical body during sleep (especially when the person is dreaming) but then returns without the person's having a memory of where the spirit body went.

H. Sources and Validity of Data

Regarding research of spiritual phenomena, it is important to note a few words of caution. Some of my information comes from fields of inquiry that in the past were called the occult or spiritualism. The word *occult* simply means "hidden." *Spiritualism* usually refers to contacting the dead through a medium. Most religious texts warn against such exploration. In Leviticus and elsewhere in the Bible, one finds warnings against diviners, soothsayers, and various means of contacting the dead through witchcraft. Perhaps because of the association of the word *occult* with problem areas of human nature, the term *New Age* has come into vogue. This term is so broad that it is largely useless for purposes of this book.

While I agree that precautions must be taken when researching spiritual phenomena, this does not mean that all investigation is dangerous or that valid data cannot be obtained. Perhaps some of the people who became involved in this area of study fell under the influence of dark spirits, but that does not necessarily mean that everyone does, or that the concepts of the spiritual nature of humanity are incorrect.

I do believe that there can be a dark side to the occult. In the film *Raiders of the Lost Ark*, the character Indiana Jones stated that the National Socialists (Nazis) studied the occult extensively. In reality, the practice had been going on in Germany (as well as in other parts of Europe and in the United States) years before the Nazis came to power. Some of their racially based theories came from the occult, but I believe this dark side of human nature was more closely related to social Darwinism, the overapplication of evolution to humanity.

In addition to the occult and spiritualism, I will discuss some concepts from Eastern thought. Just as the spirit and the soul are mentioned in the Bible, Eastern religions have a concept of human nature. I will be emphasizing this nature of humanity, rather than the nature of divinity, in those religions.

I will usually describe a concept presented by an author without comment about the author or publisher's viewpoint, with some exceptions. For instance, I may say that this particular publisher has primarily published books from a religious, New Age, or skeptic's viewpoint. Skeptics are so called because they question nonphysical explanations of behavior.

Throughout this book I will be citing findings or "research" by other people. If the person has a special degree or an academic credential, I will list it. However, I may not cite any academic degree if the information is from a research publication, as it is understood that the writer in all likelihood has an advanced degree. The research in the area of study with which this book is concerned is often a collection of gathered anecdotal information. Many people would say this type of data is not valid, but in some cases it is difficult to obtain the real thing. For instance, no research committee would approve deliberately bringing people close to death in order to study NDEs. It is up to you to decide if the findings I present are appropriate. In some cases I may give my opinion, such as stating that a finding is unique and unconfirmed but consistent with my hypothesis. Much of my information is anecdotal, not the results of experiments.

I. Hypothesis

I am presenting the hypothesis that spirituality is a better explanation than physicalism to explain consciousness and behavior, but a definitive conclusion about spirituality is not yet available. As the invention of the telescope helped verify that the earth circles the sun, it also raised more questions about the solar system. More powerful telescopes answered those questions but then raised even more profound questions. Likewise, my hypothesis for a spiritual explanation of behavior may raise other questions about spirituality. An inquisitive person (or an inquisitive society) may never reach a final conclusion, as each answer raises greater questions.

In the title of this book, I have used the word *hypothesis*, defined by the *Encarta Dictionary* as a "tentative explanation for phenomena." Paranormal phenomena have been around for a long time, and some may conjecture that they indicate God's intercession in the physical realm or that the person around whom one of these phenomena occurs is spiritually gifted. Some skeptical scientists may contend that a certain spiritual phenomenon does not even exist and is an impossibility according to physical laws. Others may maintain that the phenomenon is so unique or infrequent that nothing can be learned from it since it is not repeatable. In writing this book, I am suggesting a tentative explanation of abnormal and creative behavior. If other researchers further study the concepts presented, then human behavior can be better understood and modified to improve life for all.

J. Goals and Perspective

There are two specific goals of my research, the first being to achieve a better understanding of abnormal behavior and to attempt to correct serious cases of abnormal behavior without the use of expensive, ineffective, or harmful medications. When I discuss correcting abnormal behavior, I mean the possibility of preventing and curing various mental illnesses and criminal behavior, not just the continuous use of pharmaceuticals to combat the symptoms. People with mental illnesses often commit crimes and are also victims of crime. If my hypothesis provides improved methods for curing mental illness, perhaps our society can reduce the economic and social cost of crime and incarceration and the security apparatus to prevent crime. The second goal of my research is to better understand the spiritual origins of creativity so that it may be more readily accessed for the benefit of all. Although not the primary or secondary focus of this book, the importance of maintaining healthy family relationships will also receive significant attention.

I have included information that I have discovered over the last 45 years or so, although some of the references were written well before this period. Overall, I have an eclectic approach. In discussing behavior, sometimes psychological concept A may be best, while in seemingly similar circumstances psychological concept B may be more appropriate.

Finally, I would like to make a statement about my own perspective. I have had virtually no psychic experiences in my life. In one sense, I think it is good that I am simply evaluating data. This enables me to provide an objective third person view of others' concepts. However, some may ask that if these experiences have not happened to me, how do I know they exist?

Since my background is in the technical field of science and engineering, so are my concepts of creativity. I also have an interest in literature and music. I enjoy reading about how various composers wrote their musical works. Although I do not know if the creative ideas for a symphony or a novel spring from the same creative impetus as scientists' works, I do know that writers often have a special ability to explain human nature. For example, the 20th-century American writer Thornton Wilder (1897–1975) offers a fantastic description of humanity in the words of the narrator in the third act of *Our Town* (1938):

> Now there are some things we all know, but we don't take'm and look at'm very often. We all know that *something* is eternal. And it ain't houses and it ain't earth, and ain't even the stars … everybody knows in their bones that *something* is eternal, and that something has to do with human beings. All the greatest people ever lived have been telling us that for five thousand years and yet you'd be surprised how many people are always losing hold of it. There's something way down deep that's eternal about every human being.

Unfortunately, and tragically, the views of scientism have preempted this once universally accepted concept.

I believe it was Carl Sagan who first asserted, "Extraordinary claims require extraordinary evidence." While I agree that some skepticism is necessary, perhaps the preeminent physicalism or evolution is the true extraordinary claim. Many types of parapsychological phenomena have been shown in laboratory experiments. Scientism refuses to accept the data since they do not fit into its paradigm. However, stories about many parapsychological phenomena come from anecdotal sources. How does one perform an experiment verifying that the instructions from a deceased relative's voice saved one's life?

One of the consequences of a mechanistic/evolutionary concept of humanity is that those who adopt it believe that life is the survival of the fittest. There is no purpose in life other than to keep an organism from dying (at least until after reproduction). One of the primary messages I hope to convey with this book is that there is a purpose for each person's life. Some people may have a seemingly grander purpose, but each life has a purpose, even if it is only to help one other person. However, this does not imply that each person actually fulfills his or her purpose.

K. Outline of the Book

The following is an outline of concepts I will be discussing in this book to support my spiritual basis for explaining consciousness and human behavior. In chapter 2, I will introduce the concept that humans have multiple spirit bodies, a concept that was developed from shamanic peoples. In chapter 3, I will relate how one of the spirits mentioned in chapter 2, the High Self, is the real source of much creative expression. I will then refer to this spirit form as *Spirit*, to distinguish it from generic usage. In this chapter, I will begin discussing how mental disorders relate to spirit bodies. In chapter 4, I will relate historical perspectives on studies of psychic phenomena.

In chapter 5, I will review NDEs and their relation to the concept of multiple spirits in humans, show how one of the spirits can leave the physical body, and offer great evidence for a life after death. This information will include the nature of a transcendental realm and spirit beings other than human spirits. In chapter 6, I will discuss dissociative identity disorder (DID) and demonstrate a strong correlation with the Spirit, expanding the concept that the Spirit, or the High Self, can assist in healing processes as well as contribute to creativity and our concept of self. I will also explain how alternate personalities result from the departure of the person's designated or birth soul, which is replaced by an intruding soul as a result of trauma.

In chapter 7, I will review the phenomena of end-of-life experiences and after-death communication. In chapter 8, I will discuss concepts of multiple spirits in humans from an Eastern viewpoint on human nature, showing how these support, rather than contrast with, Western thought. In chapter 9, I will discuss shamanism in greater detail. In chapter 10, I will discuss various mental disorders related to deceased people whose spirit form (soul) may have missed entering the world of *light* mentioned by NDErs and, instead, intruded on the lives of the living.

In chapter 11, I will discuss mystical experiences and some unusual/ paranormal phenomena that happen to people who have these experiences. I will also explain how those experiences are related to the same transcendental realm that NDErs enter. In chapter 12, I will bring the previous concepts together, explaining how they support my hypothesis of separate spiritual bodies in each human being. I will also discuss the serious problems that have resulted from the use of psychiatric medications to cure what is really a spiritual problem. In addition, I will present some alternate explanations for human behavior. These explanations will include secular and spiritual models. Chapter 13 will consist of conclusions.

MULTIPLE SPIRITS WORKING TOGETHER

A. Introduction

About 45 years ago, I was looking through books at a public library. I came across one with an interesting title: *The Secret Science Behind Miracles (SSBM)*, by Max Freedom Long, published in 1948. The ideas Long presents are very intriguing. Over the past 45 years I have read many books that support the ideas presented in *SSBM*. In this chapter, I will summarize the concepts in *SSBM*. Much of the remainder of this book will provide information that either directly supports these concepts or agrees with them in sufficient part. The main thesis of Long's book is that humans have multiple spirits and that behavior can best be understood by knowing the function of each. Long uses the term *magic* to describe this type of phenomenon, defined as "getting something from supernormal sources."

B. Kahuna Concepts of Human Nature

Max Freedom Long (1890–1971) went to Hawaii in the early twentieth century and frequently heard stories about the kahunas, Hawaii's native shamans. (Chapter 9 is devoted to shamanism, but this material serves as an introduction.) Long was ready to dismiss most of the stories as legends, but then he visited Dr. William Tufts Brigham, the director of the famous Bishop Museum. The elderly Brigham had lived on the islands for a number of years before Hawaii was well settled, when kahunas practiced openly. Before Long's arrival, the kahunas were forced to go underground, their activities outlawed as sorcery or witchcraft. Despite this, Brigham viewed them as genuine and described to Long some of the phenomena he witnessed or heard about. Brigham reported that two kahunas enabled him to walk across lava that was just cool enough to support his weight. His shoes were destroyed, but his feet were not burned. The kahunas who accompanied him wore only ti leaves on their feet and were not burned.

The word *secret* in the title of Long's book comes from *huna*, which means "secret," and *kahuna*, meaning "keeper of the secret." The knowledge the kahunas hold is usually passed on to familial descendants, not to the general public. Men and women can be kahunas. Also, some kahunas' abilities are specialized. A kahuna might have only one ability. Although Long uses the term only for knowledge and spiritual powers, *kahuna* is also used for people of various occupations, like canoe builders, temple builders, agriculture specialists, and wood carvers.

Long wrote an earlier book, *Recovering the Ancient Magic*. Subsequently, a retired English journalist told him he had encountered similar abilities to those of a kahuna when he was a young journalist among a Berber tribe in the North African Atlas Mountains. The journalist persuaded a woman magician to adopt him and to train in her methods along with her daughter. Shortly after beginning training, the magician was killed by a stray bullet. Despite her death, the magician had demonstrated control over animals and the weather. The journalist reported that many of the words used by his teacher were similar to words of the kahunas.

Long surmised that shamans in many cultures have the same abilities as the kahunas. But as they became more involved with other cultures, especially Western society, their abilities were eventually lost or greatly diminished in power. The isolation of the Hawaiian Polynesians helped preserve the purity of the knowledge. As the training system was rigorous, many children of the kahunas chose not to undertake it after Westerners arrived.

Long tried to learn the secret of the kahunas' abilities by analyzing the words of their chants and prayers. Unlike in the English language, each Hawaiian syllable has meaning, and complex words use a combination of many meaningful syllables. Long was familiar with Theosophy and New Thought as well as with other spiritual thought. Thus, some of his explanations of kahuna concepts were molded to explain these spiritualties and were not a direct interpretation of kahuna thought.

According to Long's analysis, humans consist of three selves: the low self, the middle self, and the High Self. The low self roughly corresponds to our subconscious or animal nature; the middle self describes our rational or thinking conscience; and the High Self refers to what could be called our superconscious. Each of these selves has a "shadowy body," or what I would call an invisible spirit body. The low-self body corresponds to the shape of the physical body, perhaps extending slightly beyond it. The middle-self body is concentrated in the forebrain. The High-self body is outside the physical body but is connected to the physical body via a thread from the low self. As people have a shadowy body of each self, so thoughts have shadowy bodies, becoming thought forms. Long states that inanimate objects have shadowy bodies, but theirs are different from those of animate beings.

The kahuna/Hawaiian words for these selves are *unipihili* (low self), *uhane* (middle self), and *Aumakua* (High Self). *Aumakua* translates as "older parental utterly trustworthy spirit" and consists of a male–female pair. It is not worshipped but loved. It should be noted that if these spiritual selves are a natural part of our human anatomy, then the phenomenon is natural, not requiring a higher being to explain the phenomena. Long referred to huna as an advanced form of psychology, only minorly religious.

Almost all shamans speak of a vital force or energy that people possess. Anton Mesmer's concept of animal magnetism explored this subject, but these conclusions have been generally renounced by established science (e.g., by the vitalists cited by Nuland in chapter 1). The kahunas believe that each self—low, middle, and High—has its own vital energy (mana, mana mana, and mana loa) that it uses for its activities, although this energy may be converted to another type. I will use only one kahuna/Hawaiian word, *mana*, for vital energies. Mana's symbol is water. Like water, mana can flow, can fill things, or may leak away. For instance, by the laying on of hands, one person can transfer mana to another.

According to Long, the low self has elementary thought like animals and cannot reason, though it has beliefs, instincts, and memories. It easily responds to suggestion if the suggestion does not contradict current beliefs. The middle self thinks rationally but cannot remember something once that thing moves out of its center of attention. It obtains memory from the low self. The middle self has willpower. The High Self has no limits, but since it is connected to the person through the low self, the irrational beliefs of the low self can interfere with communication between the middle self and the High Self. When the High Self communicates, it is often through symbols, archetypes, or metaphors, as in dreams, when the middle self sleeps. The High Self's symbol is *light*. (Note that I will italicize the word light when it is associated with any light associated with what I refer to as Spirit, unless within a quote.) Although each person has a High Self, Long asserts that all High Selves are connected to all other High Selves. In addition to humans, a group High Selves watch over groups of animals by locale and/or species. A High Self can be responsible for various aspects of this planet, such as localized winds and weather. Many Hawaiian stories exist about the kahunas' involvement with powerful weather phenomena.

C. The High Self

The High Self has complex healing powers and can observe or change the future. Only the High Self possesses such abilities. The High Self takes an individual's thoughts, fears, deeds, hopes, and dreams (as thought forms) and creates a future for the person. The High Self creates or crystallizes the circumstances that will lead to those thoughts, deeds, and dreams. The High Self can see the crystallized parts of the future that it has created. Prior to crystallization, the future is not set. If requested to do so, the High Self can view the future and change it. Long describes how he once felt he wanted a major change in his life and went to consult a kahuna about the situation. Long maintains that the kahuna was able to break down his future as it had been crystallized and create a new future for him. However, it is possible that some events or circumstances of an individual's life cannot be changed. There are world events that are beyond an individual's control, and these may be crystallized farther in advance than the future of an individual. In chapter 5, on NDEs, I discuss the notion that each individual has a purpose in life, and thus circumstances that lead to fulfillment of that purpose would be more difficult to change than unrelated circumstances.

According to Long, the kahunas conceptualize that the ideal situation for a fulfilling human life would be one that sought the aid and guidance of the High Self. The High Self acts in agreement with any life purpose. The High Self wishes to help us but does not interfere unless a person believes he or she has a High Self and requests its assistance. However, the message to the High Self has to be very clear, without conflicts or doubts.

It would be best if these thought forms came from the middle self, but often people let their low self take the lead. The low self changes plans frequently based on what it feels. Long believes the low self contacts the High Self during dreams, and the future may be contained in the dream symbols. However, the dreams that are usually remembered or interpreted correctly are often of ordinary or insignificant events.

Since the low self is constantly receiving messages from the middle self, some of these messages are contradictory whims. Long claims that the best way to communicate with the low self (which the low self then conveys to the High Self) is by logical appeal combined with mild suggestion and physical stimulus. The low self is impressed by real, tangible things. This can be something like a spoken suggestion. For instance, placebos for ailments can be effective as long as the person does not remind him- or herself that the substance is only a placebo. Another form of stimulus is to transfer mana to the person while making a suggestion. Other possible stimuli include massage, heat, and bathing.

Communication with the High Self via a prayer or telepathy is often avoided by the low self because the person has a sense of guilt brought about by social and religious teachings. The High Self cannot answer a request if it has not received the message. The kahunas said that this guilt causes a blocking of the path preventing transmission of the message. Lesser guilt may be removed by techniques like fasting and prayer.

Although a person must often contact the High Self to request certain action, the High Self may act alone. For instance, the High Self may intercede to avert a disaster through what might be considered divine intervention. I believe that this intercession may be of at least four types. The first is a seemingly miraculous incident to avoid death, like being thrown from a vehicle before it falls off a cliff or burns. A second might be "missing" a plane, bus, or train (through the High Self's intervention) that goes on to be in a major accident. After the events of September 11, 2001, several people were interviewed after they had missed work at the World Trade Center for various reasons and on account of various unusual events. I believe this could have been the result of their High Selves acting for their benefit. A third type of intervention may be rescue by a spiritual being that manifests physically but then disappears after the rescue. In the chapter 5 addendum, I describe the *Third Man factor*, a term used by mountain climbers in perilous situations. A fourth type is a resource with unusual abilities called an Inner Self-helper, which intervenes in the therapy process for people afflicted with dissociative identity disorder (DID; see chapter 6).

Long emphasizes the practical nature of huna and asserts that its methods are not rigid. If a person feels that he or she has an effective method for contacting his or her High Self, then this method should be used, even if it is not previously discussed here. It is important that the three selves work together. One is not "low" in the sense of being less important. The low self is as vital as the High Self.

Because circumstances can be requested from the High Self, this emphasizes that it is not a god. The kahunas believe in spirits above the High Self. The High Self knows how to contact those still-higher spirits, and the individual does not need to communicate with them. The kahunas also believe that humans cannot offend higher spirits; the latter are too strong and powerful to be bothered by our behavior. Thus, sins only hurt other people. Although the "good" kahunas taught this, their society often had taboos and idol worship, which unscrupulous kahunas used to control people. The good kahunas knew that idols were only wood and feathers, unnecessary to effect change.

D. Abilities of the Kahunas and Application of Their Concepts

So what abilities do the kahunas possess? Let us begin with a rather simple phenomenon: telepathy (mind-to-mind communication). One person's low self's shadowy body can be connected to another person's shadowy body (most connections are to people with whom one has previously interacted), and the connection, called an *aka cord*, can be stretched any distance. Information can be passed along the aka cord with undiminished clarity, because the aka cord is a perfect conductor of mana. The information carried can be in the form of thoughts, words, voices, or visions. Connections can also be made to another space, as in remote viewing where a viewer's eyes can see from the aka thread projection to another site. To send a message along the aka cord, the low self needs instruction from the middle self. Even if a message is received from another person's low self, it must be brought to the attention of the middle self.

Earlier, I discussed fire walking and vital energy. According to the kahunas, this vital energy can be transferred to another person and then act as a shield of protection. Long alleged that a kahuna could transfer mana from himself to an object or to another person. For instance, the kahunas could charge wooden sticks with mana in battle and throw them at an enemy. When struck, the enemy would be temporarily rendered unconscious.

A complex problem, explainable by the kahuna concept of mana, is the death prayer. A kahuna is capable of either finding a wandering low-self spirit of a deceased human or keeping an enslaved spirit around indefinitely, even sending that spirit to a person whom the kahuna wants to die. For the death prayer to work, the dying person is required to feel guilty about offending another. When the low-self spirit reaches the intended victim, the spirit can attach itself to the living person if that person feels some guilt. Once attached, the low-self spirit steals mana from the living person, eventually causing death. The mana is first taken from the legs, making the person unable to walk. Mana is then sapped from other parts of the body until the person grows weaker and finally dies. After stealing all of the mana, the spirit returns to the kahuna and expends the extra mana in poltergeist activities, like throwing objects. (In German, *poltergeist* means "noisy ghost.") In Brigham's experience, the local hospitals could recognize such a weak (undiagnosed) person entering the hospital and then dying within a few days. No known medical intervention could prevent death.

Brigham even had personal experience with a death prayer. He once hired a native Hawaiian as a guide on a naturalist expedition. The local kahuna had previously informed the native not to interact with Westerners. Angry that the native had disobeyed his advice, the kahuna sent a spirit to kill the guide. Typically, the kahuna needs an object connected to the intended victim so that the spirit has a "scent" to follow. Brigham, through his own partial knowledge of what was happening, was able to convince the robbing spirit that the native did not deserve death. Normally, a kahuna would perform a cleansing prayer (*kala*) to protect him- or herself before sending out a spirit. In this case, the kahuna did not expect the spirit to return without accomplishing its goal and so had not performed the cleansing prayer. When it returned, the robbing spirit killed the kahuna. If a death prayer has been requested by a third party, and if the enslaved spirit returns without performing the kill, the kahuna may send the spirit to the person who requested the death prayer.

In general, though, the kahunas Brigham encountered were not routinely praying people to death. Long notes that kahunas teach the people a very simple philosophy: "No hurt, no sin." If a person is not doing something deliberately to hurt another person, then the person does not need to feel guilty.

The kahunas are also capable of instant healing, although they do not always achieve it. Long relates a story he had heard from a trusted friend. The friend had been at a party when someone fell, causing a compound fracture visible just above the ankle, although the skin was not pierced. An elderly kahuna was there and manipulated the area while chanting a prayer. Shortly thereafter, the kahuna said that the healing was complete, and the injured man could walk normally. Long explains that healing a person this way is done with the aid of the High Self and its mana. The healing is performed by dissolving the injured tissue into ectoplasm and reforming it into the shape of the uninjured low-self shadowy body. The reshaped ectoplasm is then solidified to conform to the uninjured shadowy body. *Ectoplasm* is a term used by Spiritualists to depict an ethereal mist (I think that Long simply could not think of another word to use). It is not necessarily the same ectoplasm that Spiritualists encounter in séances.

Regarding other kahuna healing powers, Brigham told Long of a kahuna who brought a drowned person back to life. Although Brigham was not a medical doctor, he was quite sure the person was dead. Before attempting to restore a person to life, the kahuna determines if the person's low and middle selves are still attached by aka cords to the body. The restoration is done by warming the body so that the selves feel comfortable returning. The kahuna energizes the body with mana and then summons back the wandering selves. It is simpler to bring back the spirit if there is no severe tissue damage, as in drowning. Various shamans often attribute illness to "soul loss," and shamanic healing involves retrieval of the departed part of the soul. The kahuna accomplished this retrieval in bringing the drowned man back to life.

Since mana is a necessary energy, kahunas pay attention to the possible theft of mana by spirits of the dead. If the spirits steal enough mana, the normal resident pair (the low and middle selves) may leave, and then the spirit of a formerly dead person may enter or influence a living person. This may result in the living person's becoming insane. A discussion of abnormal psychology in several other chapters will discuss specific mental diagnoses. Guilt may make a person more likely to have vital energy taken by a discarnate entity, thus allowing these entities to influence behavior. Long refers to these discarnate entities as darkly evil beings that stalk and prey upon the living. Long also describes dark forces that have never been incarnate, as well as *beings of light* other than the High Selves.

Long illustrates several cases of a person's becoming sick as a result of participating in an activity he or she learned was sinful when younger, such as dancing or drinking a moderate amount of alcohol. Essentially, the middle self educates the low self as to what is right or wrong. If the low self comes to believe the person is performing a prohibited activity, it may bring about physical injury to the person as punishment, even if the middle self no longer believes that the activity is improper. Long calls these *guilt complexes*. Long contends that a person can try to reeducate his or her low self to see that a certain activity is not a sin, but if the problem does not cease, then one should discontinue the activity. Long believed it was important to eliminate guilt complexes before dying.

Long discusses life after death and how huna concepts explain it. The shadowy bodies retain many of the beliefs they had when physically incarnated and tend to gravitate to a level commensurate with these beliefs. It is difficult to think new thoughts when discarnate, as that requires mana, very little of which is carried over from life. In the event of a low self's separation from a middle self while alive, a living person may become obsessed, as the low self cannot reason. This will be important when I discuss abnormal psychology later. In *SSBM*, Long also conveys what happens when ghosts or spirits of the dead become involved in the lives of humans. He believed that a disincarnated low self could occupy a second body; that a middle self could do the same; and that both selves could occupy a second body.

Long offers an example of how discarnate spirits may cause problems for the living. In one case, a son told his mother that his first daughter would be her namesake. Forgetting his promise once he became busy, he did not often visit his mother. She grumbled to her departed relatives in an effort to correct the situation. The son and daughter-in-law had no guilt, so the avenging departed spirits began to take mana from the granddaughter. Some kahunas heard about the sick child and were able to psychically detect the theft of mana. Interviewing the family, the kahuna determined the ultimate cause. The family reconciled, and the child made a rapid recovery.

Long also mentions some situations in which a profound or extremely knowledgeable personality was encountered in cases of multiple personality disorder, now called DID. (Dissociative disorders became more prevalent about forty years ago, and there is more clinical information now available than when Long wrote.) I believe this was contact with the High Self. When this personality was asked about itself, it replied that the body was under its care and guardianship. Long concludes that this superconscious mind used a form of thought higher than memory or reason that he calls *mentation*. This mentation could see into the part of the future that had been crystallized.

The kahunas' method for treating insanity is to transfer a large quantity of mana to the patient, along with a willed command that the invading spirit leave. He also states that the High Self could be employed to handle intruding low selves, as low selves have a natural fear of higher beings. In chapter 10, I discuss intruding spirits and various therapies for removing them.

E. Others Who Found the High-Self Concept

Long also describes other Westerners he believes found the High Self. One was Phineas Parkhurst Quimby (1802–1866), a man who made both clocks and watches, and who later developed a healing ministry. Before his healing work, while studying mesmerism (named after Anton Mesmer, a healer who practiced in Austria and France), Quimby met an entity he called Wisdom, which accomplished things using the Power (possibly mana). His simple healing mostly involved speaking with a patient. He allegedly had hundreds of crutches and wheelchairs left behind by healed patients. He accepted only donations and is often considered the intellectual father of the New Thought movement. One of his cured patients was Mary Baker Patterson (Eddy) (1821–1910), the founder of Christian Science.

Long believes that Quimby found out how to contact and employ the High Self for healing. He may have relied upon his own High Self or may have had his patients contact their own High Selves. In kahuna lore, when a kahuna requestsd aid for a patient through the kahuna's High Self, the message automatically goes to the patient's High Self, per the connection of all High Selves.

Another person whom Long believed had contact with her High Self was the writer Mary Hunter Austin (1868–1934). She grew up in Carlinville, Illinois, about 40 miles from where I am writing. She later moved to California where she did most of her writing, frequently about Native Americans and the California desert. She had a spiritual experience at the age of five, after which she could communicate with an inner personality she called "Inknower," "Genius," or "I-Mary." This entity—her High Self—would assist her in her writing.

F. Criticism and Support for Long's Concepts

If you look up information on huna, you will find various criticisms of Long's concepts. For instance, in *The Kahuna Sorcerers of Hawaii, Past and Present* (1979), Julius Rodman states that he cannot swallow Long's "huna stuff." Rodman maintains that Long "means well but, being a *haole* [not a native Hawaiian] ... is unable to comprehend the inner meaning of kahuna philosophy." For instance, Long almost never discusses herbs, a frequent shamanic healing tool, as healing agents.

In his book *Witchcraft, Oracles and Magic among the Azande* (1937), English anthropologist E. E. Evans-Pritchard (1902–1973) illustrates the difficulty of translating shamanic or indigenous peoples' thought into Western words. The Azande are an indigenous tribe in what is now southern Sudan. Evans-Pritchard would often end up using the word *soul* to describe a nonmaterial essence in humans, but that one word was insufficient. Evans-Pritchard describes two souls, one he called "body-soul" and the other "spirit-soul." This indicates that this shamanic culture believed that humans have more than one spiritual component. Other shamanic cultures will be mentioned later in chapter 9.

While not necessarily associating souls with spirit bodies as Long has done, psychiatrist George Makari (2015), in his book, *Soul Machine: The Invention of the Modern Mind,* comments on the views of the soul by a prominent ancient Greek philosopher.

> Aristotle divided the soul into two forms that were material and one that was immortal. The vegetative soul was required for all life and passed away with it. The sensitive soul was the force that caused animal movement and action; it too was of matter. Only the rational soul, equated with the intellect, was eternal and divine (p. 6).

The functions of Aristotle's three souls do not correspond with the functions of Long's three selves.

Much of the discussions to follow agree with Long's concepts of the three selves, but some are contradictory. I am merely presenting Long's information as an introduction to the concept that people have multiple spirits. This assists in explaining human behavior better than the notion of one spirit or the materialistic concept of isolated physical bodies. Other important huna concepts supported by my research are thought forms and the spirits of deceased people affecting the living.

In the next chapter, I will discuss further findings that can best be explained by the concept that each person has a High Self.

Chapter 3

SUPPORT FOR THE CONCEPT OF SPIRIT

A. Introduction

In chapter 2, I introduced the concept of the High Self. In this chapter I will introduce the term *Inner Self-helper*, or ISH, and present a theory that the ISH and High Self are one and the same. I present ways in which the ISH / High Self intervenes in individual lives, such as during a crisis or through a gift of heightened creativity.

B. Other Names for the High Self

In chapter 2, I briefly mentioned that in the *Secret Science Behind Miracles* (*SSBM*), Max Freedom Long contends that dissociative identity disorder (DID) occurs when a middle self or low self of one deceased person takes control of another person's body. There was an epidemic of DID beginning in the mid-1970s. In one case, Long surmises that one extremely intelligent personality was actually the patient's High Self. Psychiatrist Ralph Allison encountered it enough to call it the *Inner Self-helper* (ISH). Other therapists employ the same term or use *internal self-helper*, *center*, or *hidden observer*.

The following list provides a brief summary of some of the recently discovered functions of the ISH. I provide a therapist's description of the ISH (compiled from various therapists' descriptions), and in parenthesis I relate the descriptions of Long's "High Self." Long cites only one case of DID (then known as multiple personality disorder [MPD]) wherein there was a probable High Self presenting itself. I believe these additional powers of the ISH would fit well with his concept of the High Self, since he put no limits on its power.

1. The ISH is the state of conscious awareness.

2. The ISH is very logical, is often gender neutral, and does not usually show emotion. (Long claims the High Self is a male–female pair.)

3. The ISH seeks to guide the patient toward mental health but cannot simply remove the alter personalities. It cares for all of the personalities.

4. The ISH is an entity rather than a personality.

5. The ISH is the source of love, appreciation, truthfulness, coping ability, and artistic talent. It is also mannerly, tasteful, optimistic, outgoing, serious, nonaggressive, and self-controlled.

6. Therapists have found the advice given by the ISH very helpful, and in some cases essential, in the treatment of their patients. The ISH expects to be a working partner with the therapist.

7. For the most rapid healing, both the patient and the therapist need to know the patient's ISH.

8. The ISH can accelerate healing, but it is not always attuned to the physical body. (Long discusses healing by the High Self.)

9. The ISH is always present but is distinct from the other personalities. (Long would say the High Self's shadowy body is outside the physical body but simultaneously connected to it.)

10. The ISH can grow tired and can only function for short periods of time. (Long would say that the High Self requires mana generated by the low self.)

11. Some ISHs regard themselves as agents of God. (Long would say there are spiritual levels above the High Self and that the High Self is able to contact those higher levels if necessary.)

12. The ISH can predict the future. Although it is not specified, I would suspect it only predicts the future of the patient. (Long asserts that the High Self can see the future and can participate in the creation of the individual's future.)

13. One therapist I came across believes that the patient's ISH can telepathically communicate with the therapist's ISH. (Long asserts that all High Selves are connected.)

14. The ISH can communicate by a voice that seemingly, to the patient, is from "nowhere."

15. Additional descriptions of the ISH include: a unifying element, hyperintellectual and inhuman, an invincible part of the human

spirit, one's own spirit or soul, guardian of the spirit, aspects of the Spirit of God, and a part of the patient's unconscious that is in touch with higher helpers.

In chapter 1, I mentioned that the Bible makes distinctions between spirit and soul. I believe that this spirit part of humanity mentioned in the Bible is the same as the High Self / ISH. In the future, I distinguish this meaning of *Spirit* by capitalizing it. Uncapitalized, *spirit* will imply a nonmaterial human aspect. Occasionally, I may specify Holy Spirit, the third part of the Christian Trinity.

I will present much more detail on the role of the ISH / High Self in chapter 6, on DID. Here, I will identify some circumstances of the ISH / High Self / Spirit intervening in an individual life. Although the Spirit cannot *directly* act itself to prevent a personality from attempting suicide, it can use a helper personality (see chapter 6) to try to prevent the suicide or to contact emergency personnel. If a person without DID is discouraged and there are no helper personalities, the Spirit can speak directly to the person contemplating suicide (i.e., the Spirit can be "a voice from nowhere"). The following provides an example from the life of a famous American designer R. Buckminster Fuller (1895–1983). This incident occurred after his child had died.

> In 1927, on the shore of Lake Michigan, an unemployed and possibly drunk US inventor contemplated suicide. Then, according to a legend he later spun he had an out-of-body experience. He felt he was floating above the ground, surrounded by celestial light. A voice spoke to him: "You do not have the right to eliminate yourself," it said. "You do not belong to you. You belong to Universe." (*Nature 454*, August 14, 2008, 828)

This type of spiritually transformative experience (STE) does not seem unusual for a person familiar with near-death experiences (NDEs), except that in this case Fuller's physical body was not close to death. I do not believe that he was drunk or that he made up the story of the voice, but rather that his Spirit spoke to him.

While DID is the complete, albeit temporary, replacement of the original personality by foreign personalities, I believe that the High Self,

ISH, or Spirit can affect an individual in conditions less severe. Bill Wilson, one of the cofounders of Alcoholics Anonymous (AA), reports that the following incident happened to him during his deepest alcoholism. This information is from *Getting Better: Inside Alcoholics Anonymous* (1988) by Nan Robertson. Bill checked himself into Towns Hospital, began the belladonna treatment, and repeated the Oxford Group's (a predecessor to AA) formula.

Bill said that he thought, *I'll do anything, anything for release.*

The effect was "electric," he wrote in the book *Alcoholics Anonymous* (often referred to as the Big Book).

> There was a sense of victory, followed by such peace and serenity as I had never known. There was utter confidence. I felt lifted up, as though the great clean wind of a mountain top blew through and through. God comes to most men gradually, but His impact on me was sudden and profound." He cried out, "If there be a God, let Him show Himself!" He told Lois (his wife) how the room blazed with light, how he was filled with a joy beyond description.
>
> [Robertson states,] In recent years physicians and pharmacists have analyzed the drugs involved in the Towns treatment of alcoholics and theorized that Wilson's visual and auditory experiences in the hospital room in 1934 were delirium precipitated by toxic psychosis (pp. 44-45.) [Note: Belladonna is known to cause hallucinations.]

Later in life, Bill Wilson referred ironically to the episode as his "hot flash," but he never took another drink. He founded AA two years later. Although the organization is still known as Alcoholics Anonymous, it will sometimes be called Friends of Bill W. Many other twelve-step programs for dependency employ the formula he developed for alcoholism. I believe Bill Wilson's High Self / ISH / Spirit intervened in his life to enable him to recover.

C. Spirit and Creativity

The list of the ISH's attributes, above, includes the idea that it is the source of artistic talent. I believe that composers of the highest order are able to hear music from their Spirit. Robert Jourdain provides the following information about musical inspiration in *Music, the Brain and Ecstasy: How Music Captures Our Imagination* (1997). Mozart reported that music just flowed into him and he wrote it down. He could not force the flow. Beethoven asserted that his music came unbidden. Handel wrote *Messiah* in a 24-day mania period and commented, "I thought I saw all of heaven before me, and the Great God himself." Puccini claimed, "The music of this opera was dictated to me by God. I was merely instrumental in putting it on paper and communicating it to the public." Brahms reported, "I felt that I was in tune with the Infinite, and there is no thrill like it." A recent portrait in words of J. S. Bach is titled *Music in the Castle of Heaven* (Gardiner, 2013). There is a French language expression, *tout ensemble*, for these phenomena, i.e., the sudden appearance of a complex finished product.

George Gershwin considered writing a symphony using jazz music, which was a fairly new type of music in the 1920s. One day on a train ride, he found his mind was wandering (possibly in a hypnagogic state). He heard the music to *Rhapsody in Blue* in his head and simply wrote it down. Lest we think that all the composers who do this are from the past, in recent years a teenager named Jay Greenberg composed music by writing down what he heard in his head, as he explained on the CBS program *60 Minutes*. One of his symphonies (No. 5) was played by the prestigious London Symphony. Greenberg can reportedly multitask, listening to one symphony while composing another.

Jourdain contends that the best ideas come when the composer is "off guard." He also comments that many great musicians suffered from psychosis, primarily manic depression (bipolar disorder). Among these musicians were Hector Berlioz, Anton Bruckner, Edward Elgar, Mikhail Glinka, George F. Handel, Gustav Holst, Charles Ives, Gustav Mahler, Modest Mussorgsky, Sergei Rachmaninoff, Gioachino Rossini, Robert Schumann, and Peter Tchaikovsky. In her diary, Robert Schumann's wife, Clara, depicts how Robert heard "music that is so glorious, and with instruments sounding more wonderful than one ever hears on earth." However, she also wrote that the angels that delivered that music could also turn to devils and sing horrible music. In his book *Musicophilia* (2007), Oliver Sacks reports that Schumann eventually went insane, hearing a very loud A note continuously. Sacks also describes how a medical doctor with very little musical training began to hear music after an NDE, the result of a lightning strike when he was on the telephone. That doctor, Tony Cicoria, referred to his music the same way Mozart did, as if it were from heaven. He named the piece of music that he heard in his head *Lightning* Sonata, and eventually learned to write it, as he was musically untrained and could not recognize the notes.

Mozart did not write down every finished note from memory of what he had heard. Writing music that way may have accounted for only a fourth of Mozart's creativity. He had to fill in the rest using his training. Creative inspiration usually comes to those who have prepared themselves for it. The fact that it appears suddenly and in (nearly) complete form is why I believe it comes from the Spirit.

In addition to composers, I surmise that other gifted individuals, like scientists and mathematicians, receive inspiration from their Spirit. Nikola Tesla (1856–1943), a famous electrical inventor, is often considered a cult hero by New Age groups. Born in Croatia to Serbian parents, he developed a practical method for generating alternating current (AC), although he was told by professors that it was impossible. Tesla also made major contributions to radio (the Supreme Court said the radio patent that went to Marconi should have gone to Tesla), radar, fluorescent lighting, and the one thing named after him, the Tesla coil. Magnetic flux density is measured in units called teslas. He was allegedly working on a particle beam accelerator at the time of his death. When Tesla came to the United States, he worked in New York City. One of his early biographers was a New York newspaper writer named John J. O'Neill. O'Neill's biography, *Prodigal Genius: The Life of Nikola Tesla*, was written in 1944, a year after Tesla's death.

If Tesla could conceive an invention in his mind, he could visualize the solid object before him. One day in 1882, while looking at a Budapest sunset, he was reminded of lines from Goethe's *Faust*, and he visualized a workable AC system employing a rotating magnetic field. He was unable to convince anyone in Europe to build his design. A few years later he came to the United States and persuaded George Westinghouse that an AC design would work. O'Neill writes:

> The mental constructs were built with meticulous care as concerned size, strength, design, and material; and they

were tested mentally, [Tesla] maintained, by having them run for weeks—after which time he would examine them thoroughly for signs of wear. (p. 51) ... Tesla could project before his eyes a picture, complete in every detail, of every part of the machine. These pictures were more vivid than any blueprint and he remembered exact dimensions which he had calculated mentally for each item. (p. 55)

Tesla's visions often seemed so real that he thought he was observing a physical object. I believe that such visions are the visual equivalent of the musical composers' aural inspirations received from Spirit.

Jourdain used the word *ecstasy* in the title of his book about musical inspiration; this word is often synonymous with mystical experience. O'Neill mentions mystical experiences and relates the following story about Tesla (Tesla is speaking):

I have been feeding pigeons, thousands of them, for years; thousands of them, for who can tell—

But there was one pigeon, a beautiful bird, pure white with light gray tips on its wings; that one was different. It was female. I would know that pigeon anywhere.

No matter where I was that pigeon would find me; when I wanted her I had only to wish and call her and she would come flying to me. She understood me and I understood her.

I loved that pigeon.

Yes, he replied to an unasked question, Yes, I loved that pigeon, I loved her as a man loves a woman, and she loved me. When she was ill I knew, and understood; she came to my room and I stayed beside her for days. I nursed her back to health. That pigeon was the joy of my life. If she needed me, nothing else mattered. As long as I had her, there was a purpose in my life.

Then one night as I was lying in my bed in the dark, solving problems, as usual, she flew through the open window and stood on my desk. I knew she wanted me; she wanted to tell me something important so I got up and went to her.

As I looked at her I knew she wanted to tell me—she was dying. And then, as I got her message, there came a light from her eyes—powerful beams of light.

Yes, he continued, again answering an unasked question, it was real light, a powerful, dazzling, blinding light, a light more intense than I had ever produced by the most powerful lamps in my laboratory.

When that pigeon died, something went out of my life. Up to that time I knew with certainty that I would complete my work, no matter how ambitious my program, but when that something went out of my life I knew my life's work was finished. (pp. 316–17)

The solitary Tesla was too eccentric for many financiers and had trouble raising funds. He died at the age of 86, materially poor but certainly not spiritually poor. I believe his mystical experience was the culmination of living his life in tune with his Spirit.

Another example of a person who received intellectual information from his Spirit is the mathematician Srinivasa Ramanujan (1887–1920). He was born in India. After English mathematician G. H. Hardy heard about him, he arranged for Ramanujan to come to England. Ramanujan made contributions to mathematical analysis, number theory, infinite series, and continued fractions, but he may be best known for several formulas for calculating pi. So interested in math that he would not study other subjects, he had little formal education. Some of his formulas for pi were not used until the computer was invented, and his formulas proved the best to calculate pi to thousands or millions of decimal places. He called every integer a personal friend.

Ramanujan told people that he did not intellectually develop his formulas or other theorems but that they came to him in dreams from the Hindu goddess of Namakkal. The value of his work was not based on divine authority, but the formulas arrived at the correct answer. My point is that rational thinking was not used in Ramanujan's formula creation, although he used standard mathematics to prove that his formulas were correct. Like the composers and Tesla, Ramanujan received his formulas as spiritual gifts, which came when he was off guard.

D. Spirituality and Mental Disorders

It would be nice if all of my writings were simply about examples of Spirit. As explained in the introductory chapter, much of this book will be about mental illnesses and their relation to spirituality. I agree with Long's theory that DID is often caused by the displacement of the low self and/or middle self by spirits of the deceased. There may be more than one of these invading spirits, alternating based on which personality is in charge at any given time.

While DID is an extreme mental disorder, as the original personality is completely displaced, I believe that many other types of mental illnesses, and abnormal or criminal behaviors, are caused by spirits of the deceased. The influence may induce criminal behavior or merely interfere with normal functioning. For example, I believe that schizophrenics are listening to voices of deceased humans and/or other, dark, inhuman spirits. Not all of this abnormal behavior may result from invading spirits. Long discusses the concept of thought forms, and these also can affect behavior. In several future chapters, I will review a number of writers who present evidence for these spirits or thought forms that affect behavior. I will also explain various methods for their removal.

In chapter 4, I will review some historical investigations into psychic phenomena, discuss the reality of psychic phenomena, and explain why physicalism or mechanistic concepts of the human brain cannot explain the phenomena.

HISTORICAL PERSPECTIVE

A. Introduction

According to the previously cited book *Irreducible Mind*, the mind is separate from the brain although they often function together. In one sense, *Irreducible Mind* is a historical book. It compares modern findings with a theory of personality proposed by F. W. H. Myers (1843–1901) in his two-volume book, published posthumously in 1903. The title of the book referenced is *Human Personality*, but its full title is *Human Personality and Its Survival of Bodily Death*. I believe it is important to realize that these issues of the mind were important to people in the past. Materialist reasoning, which overwhelmed these ideas in the late 19th century, continues to stifle the true understanding of human nature. I am convinced that this has had disastrous consequences for individual lives and for society in general.

B. Psychic Research and Types of Psychology

In 1882, F. W. H. Myers helped found the Society for Psychical Research (SPR) in England. The words *psychic* and *psychical* are not used as frequently as they once were. The preferred terms today are *paranormal*, *parapsychology*, and *psi phenomena*. SPR continues in existence and has not changed its name. Many accomplished and eminent people have served as president of this organization, including Arthur Balfour (before he became prime minister), Sir William Crookes (chemist and physicist), Sir Oliver Lodge (physicist and mathematician), Sir William Barrett (physicist), and Charles Richet (French physiologist and Nobel Prize winner). Although not a scientist, one famous founder of the SPR was Sir Arthur Conan Doyle, author of the *Sherlock Holmes* books.

Dr. William James (1842–1910) was a famous American psychologist and onetime president of the SPR. Dr. James was also a founding member of the American Society for Psychical Research (ASPR) in 1885. The ASPR, too, boasts a number of distinguished founders and past presidents. James was the brother of noted writer Henry James. William James authored *Principles of Psychology* and *Varieties of Religious Experiences*. His brand of psychology is sometimes referred to as pragmatism.

James held that one of the main functions of the brain is to act as a filter to eliminate extraneous thoughts. This concept of a filter or eliminated function of the brain was first proposed by philosopher Henri Bergson (1859-1941). For example, near-death experiencers (NDErs) often communicate with the deceased, and there can be after-death communication outside of an NDE. For functioning in normal consciousness, there must be a method to prevent continuous contact between the living and the dead. If the dead are attempting to communicate and the living do not desire the communication, then the brain acts as a filter. In this respect, schizophrenia may simply be the condition of people who have lost this ability to resist communication from deceased spirits. Psychiatrist E. Hartmann, who has written about the boundaries of the mind, states that the critical question is not why people hallucinate, but what keeps us from hallucinating most of the time.

In *Irreducible Mind*, Emily Williams Kelly divulges that views of human nature that included psychic phenomena were common in the early part of the 20th century. Myers's concept has been called a *tertium quid*, or a third way between two other concepts, namely the religious concept of a soul and the evolutionary concept of behavior and morality. In 1913, psychologists began to move away from psychic phenomena when John B. Watson published a book on behavioral psychology that became the "scientific" method for psychological studies, but which I believe to be scientism. The behavioral school believes that if desirable behavior is rewarded, it will prevail. Behaviorists are generally concerned with outward behavior and not with inner motivation. A well-known behavioral psychologist who followed Watson was B. F. Skinner. It is important to note that proofs for human behavioral concepts are often demonstrated with animal experimentation.

Another school of psychology that gained notoriety a century ago is psychoanalysis, although it is associated more with psychiatry. One of the main concepts of psychoanalysis is that all humans have subconscious motivations. Consequently, human behavior centers on resolving inner conflicts between the conscious and subconscious minds. This is in contrast to the behavioral school, which is not concerned with inner thoughts.

Both the behavioral and psychoanalytical schools drew psychological studies away from the psychic realm. However, in recent years, two new schools of psychology have been developed, ones that I consider very relevant to these topics. One is humanistic psychology, or the third force (behaviorism and psychoanalysis being the first two). This school emerged when a number of psychologists became convinced that neither behavioral theories' emphasis on animal experimentation nor psychoanalysis' subconscious motivations could explain much of human behavior. Humanistic psychology may have its philosophical basis in existentialism. To some extent, humanistic concepts arose from Abraham Maslow's hierarchy of needs, particularly his concepts of self-actualization and peak experiences. ("Peak experience" is Maslow's term for mystical experiences, as he was not religious and wanted to avoid religious terminology.) Maslow's theory holds that humans can be motivated for reasons that are higher than physiological needs. Other well-known developers of humanistic psychology are Carl Rogers, Rollo May, R. D. Laing, and Erich Fromm.

Humanistic psychology is a recognized field by the American Psychological Association. It emphasizes a qualitative approach, rather than the quantitative studies undertaken by behaviorists. Encounter groups and self-help concepts are usually associated with humanistic psychology. My concepts are humanistic in the sense that studies of the concepts are not based on animal experimentation. One of the major criticisms of the humanistic approach is that its theories lack predictive power and hence cannot be considered scientific. However, I believe that one could call such a theory speculative science, and someday an experiment of its validity may be possible. Physical scientists often develop speculative explanations for the material world that cannot be tested on earth, for example, conditions at the center of the sun. My book may be classified as speculative; thus, I use the word *hypothesis* in the title.

Supporting the idea of speculative science, Kelly includes two interesting quotations from Myers: "Science, while perpetually denying the unseen world, is perpetually revealing it" and "Science cannot conjecture beforehand how many distinct but coexisting environments may now surround us. ... Her (i.e., science) own history has been one of constantly widening conceptions" (p. 69). Two centuries ago, we could not have contemplated ultraviolet rays, infrared rays, x-rays, microwaves, and other parts of the electromagnetic spectrum, yet these are part of the physical universe. How then can scientists claim that the human aura does not exist and deny that it is seen by other people (or by a special camera), or that vital energy (mana) does not exist and may be transmitted from one person to another?

Transpersonal psychology is another recent innovation within humanistic psychology that specifically mentions spiritual aspects of humanity. This method particularly addresses phenomena that arise from the fields of shamanism, cross-cultural studies, meditation, consciousness research, transcendental states, parapsychology, addiction recovery, guided imagery and visualization, near-death and end-of-life experiences, Kabbalah, kundalini awakening, Eastern religions, and Christian mysticism. It can also include psychedelics, ethnopharmacology, and psychopharmacology. Ethnopharmacology includes substances such as certain mushrooms that are used by some indigenous peoples in sacred rites (the active ingredient in these mushrooms is psilocybin). Psychopharmacology would include the use of LSD in therapy, a practice now illegal. If an NDEr has complications when trying to readapt to society, it is recommended that the person consult a transpersonal psychologist, although there are not many of them in practice. Transpersonal psychology has many commonalities with the New Age movement, and it is also connected to Perennial philosophy and Jungian psychology.

There is a transpersonal section within the British Psychological Association, and one edition of *The Diagnostic and Statistical Manual of Mental Disorders* (*DSM-IV*) now has a category called "Religious and Spiritual Problems." The field of transpersonal studies is attempting to apply its principles to such diverse areas as business studies and art. To the extent that it succeeds, it will demonstrate that the field is not just a theory.

C. Clinical Findings and Automatisms

Kelly points out that in the days of F. W. H. Myers and William James, psychological concepts were often developed from patient counseling and not necessarily with experimentation. This was also true for Freud. It was not until the early 1900s that behaviorists developed the concept that psychology is only a science if there is a testable hypothesis of behavior and an experiment developed to prove or disprove the hypothesis. Drawing from their clinical work, psychologists of Myers's and James's period developed the word *automatism*, of which mediumship is one example. Current psychological publications rarely mention automatisms.

According to Kelly, James's studies included the use of alleged mediums. In his day, most mediums were often trance mediums. James found many frauds in this field, but he believed one medium in particular to be authentic: a Mrs. Leonora Piper (1859–1956), a medium living in Boston. Some who observed Mrs. Piper over many sessions thought the information she supplied was very good on some days but not very good on other days. Thus, opinion of her based on one observation of her ability could be influenced by the ability she exhibited on that day.

Other examples of automatisms cited by Kelly include dreams, secondary personalities, hypnosis, automatic writing, trance speaking, and creative inspiration. In another example of automatism, James witnessed one person who, with his face in the crook of his left elbow, wrote out an entire sheet of paper with his right hand and with the pencil never leaving the paper, so that the words ran together. This automatic writer could then go back to the top of the page and dot each *i* and cross each *t* very precisely while still not looking at the page. Another automatic writer could write with both hands simultaneously and on different subjects.

Like automatism, *hysteria* was a term frequently used in the time of Myers and James. Hysteria was considered to be more prevalent in women because it was thought to be related to the uterus. Hysteria covered a variety of mental symptoms, some of which can be converted to somatic symptoms, which now have specific criteria. These included hallucinations, somnambulism, amnesia, anesthesia without drugs, fear, and panic. At times, the word *hysterical* was put before a word to distinguish the condition from an organic problem. For instance, there can be hysterical blindness or hysterical paralysis, both of which are temporary. Some of these hysteria symptoms are now considered to be dissociative phenomena, a critical point to which I will return in a later chapter.

Neurosis is another example of a term used then but not now. General symptoms of neurosis were anxieties or phobias. Although hallucinations are usually classified as a symptom of a mental disorder, Myers claimed that about 10% of people with no other symptoms of mental disorders experience hallucinations. This would concur with concepts presented in this book thus far. I believe that schizophrenics receive undesirable (i.e., both frequent and unfriendly) communication from deceased people or other spirits, though a person can experience after-death communication (ADC) that is both friendly and helpful. Both friendly and unfriendly communication would be classified as hallucinations, as the communication is from a nonphysical being. A hallucination is sometimes described as perception without any corresponding sensory input.

D. Creativity and Newer Theories of Mind

According to Kelly, Myers believed that creative inspiration comes from the subliminal regions of the mind. Myers's concept of human personality was composed of a unity and multiplicity. The unity is your individuality or self (which he capitalized: "Subliminal Self"), and it is permanent. Within this unity are the transitory parts of the personality including the supraliminal self, or ordinary waking consciousness.

Kelly states that Myers observed that genius and madness would sometimes occur in the same person. He attributed this to the permeability of a psychological boundary, as both genius and madness are subliminal phenomena. Using Max Freedom Long's terminology, it could be conjectured that madness occurs when only the low self is in control of behavior. However, the High Self is contacted through the low self, and since I suggest that creativity/genius often comes from the High Self (Spirit), it is easy to see how genius and madness could occur in the same person. This topic is discussed further in chapter 12.

Kelly often references the work of Myers and James, and she uses modern research findings to support their concepts. She also refutes many concepts that have arisen since. One example is the computational theory of mind (CTM), or artificial intelligence (AI). The authors of *Irreducible Mind*, including Kelly, believe that the mind is different from the brain. Supporters of CTM claim that the mind is the software and the brain is the hardware. However, Kelly asserts that the accomplishments of CTM lag behind its achievements by a wide margin; that the claim that the brain is a computer is not false but incoherent; and that supporters of CTM believe that unless human beings are proven to be computers, something terribly important about human nature will be lost. However, Kelly states that it is satisfactory to model a particular cognitive function using CTM, but not a fundamental theory of mind. Kelly believes that psi phenomena are important because they cannot be accounted for by any CTM, or by any biological or behavioral theories of brain function. Here, Kelly touches on the concept of volition, or the will to do something. It is possible to conjecture how memory storage in the brain could be similar to electronic storage of data, but how does one account for making a decision to consciously perform a task?

According to Kelly, Myers did not believe in miracles, although he did use the term *supernormal*. If the word *miracle* does not seem appropriate, another religious term often used is *theophany*, meaning "a divine manifestation." Unexplained phenomena are in accordance with the laws of the universe but not necessarily the physical universe. These higher laws belong to a more advanced stage of evolution. I believe that Max Freedom Long would agree, arguing that there is a secret science of the High Self that explains miracles. Myers considered supernormal phenomena to be evolutive, something toward which humanity is moving. In contrast, he considered pathological states to be dissolutive. Myers conjectured that the greatest advances would come not from studying normal psychological states but rather from studying subliminal phenomena, whether pathological (abnormal) or supernormal. Myers also thought that the beliefs among indigenous people would be important in expanding psychological concepts.

E. Mind as Separate from the Brain

Kelly presents a number of psychophysiological changes that she does not believe can be explained by a brain-only model of behavior. Kelly concludes that the mind, or a mental state, can be an initiating cause and that a change in a physical state is the result. She notes that there have been numerous studies demonstrating a relationship between physical health and the following factors: spirituality, religion, personality, stress, depression, bereavement, humor, imagery, meditation, and the use of a placebo.

The following examples present some information from select cases that Kelly believes demonstrate a model of the mind operating as a separate unit that controls functions to cause a physical change in the body. All of Kelly's cases are referenced from technical journals or books by professional authors.

One author described a voodoo-like death in a Western man who had asthma. All of his asthma attacks came after an encounter with his mother. On the day this man died, a doctor determined that he was in excellent health at 5:00 p.m. At 5:30, the man's mother called, and by 7:00 p.m. he was dead. To me, this would indicate that his mind, independent of his brain, made the decision based on his relationship rather than on a physical problem. (Later in this book, there will be an extensive review of a myriad of health problems that resulted from family interactions, including those involving deceased members of the family.) In another case, a man was told he had incurable cancer and would probably die shortly thereafter. He did die, but an autopsy revealed only a small cancerous growth that could not have caused physical death. However, his mind believed he would die, and hence he did die.

The previous examples Kelly cites demonstrating that the mind can affect the body are seemingly uncontrolled situations. Kelly also discusses physiological effects that a person (i.e., the person's mind) can deliberately induce. For example, a yogi confined to a small underground space stopped his heart for five days, as verified by a monitoring device that was checked to make sure it was not malfunctioning. Another yogi showed a difference of 11°F between the left and right sides of the palm of one hand while employing learned concentration techniques.

A second set of examples Kelly discusses regarding the mind's effect on the body involve changes induced by hypnosis. These include physiological changes associated with a person's autonomic nervous system. Hypnotic analgesia (reduction of pain) has been known for a long time. Hypnosis can also reduce the symptoms of allergic reactions, control bleeding, increase the healing rate after being burned, remove warts, and initiate multiple other effects on the skin. Kelly reviews a number of attempted behavioral explanations for the above phenomena and concludes that the behavioral explanations fall short, that only the mind separate from the brain is an acceptable concept. In *The Sanctified Body*, a book by Patricia Treece (1989), there is mention of a psychiatrist who interviewed a German woman classified as a mystic with stigmata, Therese Neumann (1898–1962), who could survive without eating anything (a condition called *inedia*) other than daily Eucharist during Mass. She even knew if an unconsecrated host had been given to her. The evaluating psychiatrist concluded that Neumann was a "complex neurotic," as if this explains how a person can survive without any physical food. Inedia and other unusual phenomena will be discussed in chapter 11 on mysticism.

Kelly also discusses how a brain process in one person can result in a physical expression in another. Kelly explains how one woman doubled over, clutching her chest in severe pain, and immediately knew something had happened to her daughter. At a distant location, her daughter had died in an automobile accident when the steering wheel of her automobile pierced her chest. I will provide more information similar to this particular case provided by Kelly in chapter 7, entitled "End-of-Life Experiences and After-Death Communication."

Although I have generally not cited Kelly's references, an important reference for Kelly was a published paper by J. B. Rhine, who coined the term *ESP* (extrasensory perception) in the 1930s as he applied experiments and statistics to psychic phenomena such as telepathy. Rhine analyzed 169 cases of people who had a "somatic experience" corresponding to an injury or illness in a person who was not nearby. Of the 169 cases, 58 were related to a death, 52 were nonfatal accidents, 33 were illnesses or operations, and 26 were for childbirth.

Kelly was an associate of the late Dr. Ian Stevenson at the University of Virginia. In one of his publications, Stevenson reviewed fifty cases in which a pregnant woman had been injured or had viewed another person who had an unusual injury—and the child that was born from that pregnancy had a similar injury. Stevenson is a very thorough researcher who, in most cases, interviewed the woman and/or her physician, her child, and the person with the injury whom she had seen, in order to verify important facts of the case.

Kelly also covers an extremely controversial area—birthmarks and birth defects in cases of purported reincarnation. Stevenson originally began studying children, usually younger than ten years old, who allegedly remembered incidents from the life of a person whom they had never met. These cases usually took place in India, where belief in reincarnation is strong, but there were cases from many other countries, including the United States. Typically in these cases, the parents would listen to the child for a period of time and then decide to take the child to the home of the person whom the child claimed to be formerly. The child would allegedly know the former person's relatives, many features of the house, and events in the person's life that would be difficult for the child to have learned on his or her own. Kelly cites Stevenson's work not simply because she believes in the correctness of reincarnation, but rather because the birthmarks on the child often corresponded to the method of death of the person whose life the child remembered. Frequently, the person died a violent death, which gave rise to the birthmarks. In one case, a man was shot in the chest at close range with a shotgun, and the child had multiple hypopigmented spots on his chest in the same area as the gunshot wounds on the decedent. These birthmark cases were only a small fraction of the total reincarnation type cases Stevenson studied.

Kelly also includes an extensive review of the placebo effect and of its counterpart, the nocebo effect. Most people are familiar with the placebo effect and its use as a control in drug-effectiveness tests in which a similar number of experimental subjects are given a sugar pill as are given the real drug. The nocebo effect is this: if the experimental subjects are given a list of possible side effects of the drug, a number of those given the sugar pill will experience those side effects. Another example of the mind affecting the body is false pregnancy (pseudocyesis). If a woman who is hoping for a child is told she is pregnant, she may develop many of the symptoms of pregnancy, even if it is later determined that she was never pregnant. On rare occasions, men will also experience false pregnancy.

Kelly also points out that each personality in a patient who has dissociative identity disorder (DID) may have different physical conditions, a topic I will discuss later in chapter 6, on DID. For instance, each alter may have different eyeglass prescriptions or no glasses, or even experience blindness. The alters may also have different medical conditions and thus different needs for, or responses to, various medications. Different languages may be spoken by alter personalities. Within one physical body, there may be some male alters and some female alters. Almost always one alter will be a child personality. Some of the differences encountered in each personality are measured by instruments and cannot be accounted for by citing the subject's feigning or pretending. In some studies, professional actors pretending to be different people were used as controls.

Kelly concludes, and I would agree with her, "Phenomena suggesting that mental activity in one person can produce physiological effects in another person clearly contradict the prevailing materialist conception of the mind-body system as a closed unit" (p. 238). Also, these phenomena "lie beyond the reach of current neurophysiological understanding, and seem likely to remain so" (p. 238). Most of the information presented in this book also contradicts the materialist conception.

In the next chapter, I will cover the topic of the near-death experience (NDE). I believe the NDE has aspects of both a spirit temporarily departing the physical body (an out-of-body experience) and encountering a realm of *light* or *beings of light*. Some near-death experiencers (NDErs) also encounter spirits of the deceased, usually relatives. These are spirits that have passed on into the *light*, not spirits that have remained on the earth plane and are able to communicate with or adversely affect the behavior of other people.

Chapter 5

NEAR-DEATH EXPERIENCES

I can live without my body, but apparently my body cannot live without me.
—Near-death experiencer's comment to researcher Pim van Lommel (2010, p. 318)

A. Introduction

Although there are many fads that quickly become passé, one media interest that has not abated is near-death experiences (NDEs). The book that seems to have triggered this interest and to have coined the term *NDE* is Dr. Raymond Moody's *Life After Life* (1975). Dr. Moody has a PhD in philosophy and is also a medical doctor. The question of life after death has been a part of religion since prehistoric human beings existed, but the concept that science may be able to contribute to the debate is fairly new.

I previously stated that NDEs are considered to be dissociative phenomena. Unlike with dissociative identity disorder (DID), which is now recognized as a significant disorder, NDEs seem to occur in people who are psychologically (and even perhaps healthier than) normal. Although there are different events in each individual's NDE, some events are common to what may be called a mystical experience. This chapter will present information on what occurs during an NDE, how an NDE changes the life of those who experience it, and why materialistic interpretations all fall short of a satisfactory explanation.

Moody lists ten different phenomena that frequently occur when a person is near death. He emphasizes that no one person experiences all ten of these events. To make Moody's list, each event must have occurred in more than one person. The events are as follows: hearing the news; having feelings of peace and quiet; hearing the noise; seeing the dark tunnel; being out of the body; meeting others; seeing a *being of light*;

undergoing a life review; seeing a border, or limit; and coming back. In a second book, *Reflections on Life After Life* (1977), Moody adds three additional events: seeing cities of *light*, having visions of knowledge, and being supernaturally rescued. However, these events occur less frequently. In addition to these events, Moody mentions "ineffability," the inability afterward to express what has occurred in common words. For instance, the peace, calmness, or tranquility that engulfs an NDEr surpasses any peace felt in the physical body. When the NDEr describes the experience, she soon realizes that the listener cannot possibly understand it.

Although Moody states in his book that his information is not scientifically gathered, his method of simple classification is similar to the first step often taken in a scientific endeavor. He collected this information by interviewing about 150 people, and another 100 in the later book. By his third book's (*The Light Beyond* [1988]) publication, he had interviewed over 1,000 near-death experiencers (NDErs).

After Moody's original book, several researchers took up the challenge to conduct NDE investigations under more controlled conditions. The two primary scientific follow-up studies were done by Kenneth Ring, PhD, and Michael Sabom, MD. Kenneth Ring, author of *Life at Death* (1980), was a psychologist at the University of Connecticut when he performed his study. Michael Sabom, author of *Recollections of Death: A Medical Investigation* (1982), was a professor of medicine at Emory University when he wrote his book, a member of Phi Beta Kappa, a fellow of the American College of Cardiology, and a fellow on the Council of Clinical Cardiology of the American Heart Association. Each confirmed and quantified many of Moody's basic findings.

Both Ring and Sabom started from completely different viewpoints and methodologies. Ring believed Moody's information to be correct but wanted to quantify it, learn more about the conditions under which it occurred, and understand more about the backgrounds of the NDErs. When he first learned about the information in Moody's book, Sabom attempted to disprove it. Sabom surmised he could pit his knowledge of resuscitation procedures against those accounts of NDErs who claimed to have observed (from a position outside their bodies) their bodies undergoing resuscitation. Sabom speculated that they were just guessing or fabricating visions from conversations they could hear while appearing comatose. During their studies, these researchers were attentive to any medication the NDEr may have been taking. These investigators, along with John Audette and Bruce Greyson, MD, founded the International Association for Near-Death Studies (IANDS) in 1981. It is the premier organization in the world for promoting and disseminating knowledge about NDEs. I have been a member of IANDS for over 25 years and have had an article and a number of detailed book reviews printed in their research journal, the *Journal of Near-Death Studies*.

There have been several other studies since Ring's and Sabom's books. One of the most formal studies was by Pim van Lommel, MD, and his associates, published in *Lancet* (2001), one of the most prestigious medical journals in the world. Van Lommel followed up that journal article up with a book titled *Consciousness Beyond Life: The Science of the Near-Death Experience* in 2010 (originally published in Dutch in 2007), in which he addresses explanations for the findings described in his earlier journal article. Many medical and psychology journals have published articles on specific areas of near-death studies relevant to their audience, for instance, areas such as suicidal behavior, children's NDEs, and emergency medicine. Several other areas of study have arisen since Moody's general overview, including NDEs in children, "empathic" or "shared" NDEs, "negative" or "distressing" NDEs, and NDEs in non-American cultures.

Another frequent researcher and writer on the topic of NDEs is Bruce Greyson, MD, and now retired psychiatrist at the University of Virginia. He has not written a complete book, but he is a frequent contributor to relevant publications and fields. He has published numerous articles about NDEs in various psychiatric and health journals.

One of the more prolific writers in the field, writing from an insider's perspective, is P. M. H. Atwater. She had three NDEs in 1977 and was informed during one of her NDEs that her earthly assignment was to write about NDEs. Her research is broad in scope and is not as formal or as academic as that of some of the other writers, but she gathers data on the aftereffects of NDEs, which few other researchers mention. She began when these aftereffects were happening to her, desiring to know if she was not alone. By the time she finished writing numerous books over a 30-year career, she had interviewed close to 4,000 NDErs, including about 275 children. She has been a popular speaker at conferences on NDEs and broaches subject matter rarely discussed by others, such as her finding that people who die unexpectedly may act as if they know death is approaching for up to a year in advance of the actual death. Cherie Sutherland, another prominent contributor on the topic, is from Australia and had several books about NDEs published in Australia.

Most of the original writers on the subject have had follow-up books published. Here is a list I have compiled, sometimes listing the year published. The list may not be complete.

- Moody: *Glimpses of Eternity: Sharing a Loved One's Passage from This Life to the Next* (2010)
- Ring: *Heading Toward Omega: In Search of the Meaning of the Near-Death Experience* (1984), *The Omega Project* (1990), *Lessons from the Light: What We Can Learn from the Near-Death Experience* (with Evelyn Elsaesser Valarino, 1998)
- Sabom: *Light and Death* (1998)
- Melvin Morse (with Paul Perry): *Closer to the Light: Learning from the Near-Death Experiences of Children* (1990), *Transformed by the Light: The Powerful Effect of Near-Death Experiences on People's Lives* (1992), *Parting Visions: Uses and Meanings of Pre-Death, Psychic, and Spiritual Experiences* (1994), *Where God Lives* (2000)
- Atwater: *Coming Back to Life* (1988; reissued in 2001), *Beyond the Light* (1994), *Children of the New Millennium* (1999) (reissued and revised as *The New Children and Near-Death Experiences* [2005]), *Future Memory* (1999), *The Complete Idiot's Guide to Near-Death Experiences* (2000) (reissued and revised as *The Big Book of Near-Death Experiences* [2007])
- Greyson: "Near-Death Experiences," chapter 10 in *Varieties of Anomalous Experience: Examining the Evidence* (2000); "Unusual Experiences Near Death and Related Phenomena, chapter 6 (with E. W. Kelly and E. F. Kelly) in *Irreducible Mind: Toward a Psychology for the 21ˢᵗ Century* (2007); *The Near-Death Experience* (co-editor with Charles Flynn, 1983)
- Peter Fenwick: *The Truth in the Light: An Investigation of Over 300 Near-Death Experiences* (1995)
- Sutherland: *Transformed by the Light: Life After Near Death Experiences* (1992), *Reborn in the Light* (1995), *Within the Light*

(1993), *Children of the Light: Near-Death Experiences of Children* (1996)

In addition to research-based works like those above, there have been hundreds of books written by individuals just describing their own experiences. Among the more well-known of these individual authors are Betty Eadie and Dannion Brinkley. Dr. Yvonne Kason wrote a book that included her own experience and NDEs' relation to other areas of spirituality, like kundalini and mystical experiences. There have also been collections of stories of NDEs without the analysis of the research studies above.

The approach for this chapter will consist of three levels. First, a summary of a complete NDE from Ring's book will be presented. (Moody also constructed an NDE with all the events, but it should be emphasized that very few NDErs have encountered all of these events.) This will be followed by a brief discussion of each of the events. (When I am describing a specific phase of an NDE, I may give some examples. The example may include other parts of the NDE unrelated to the specific phase for which I chose that example.) Then, I provide a discussion of research methodology, some historical work, research findings related to nearly dying, some information on the above-mentioned specialty areas, and a discussion of potential physiological and psychological interpretations of an NDE. I will give a spiritual explanation for these events, but even at the end of this chapter my spiritual explanation may seem incomplete. It is only after reading about other areas of study, such as mental disorders, shamanism, and mystical experiences, in the remaining chapters that a complete pattern emerges.

B. Overview, Including Ring's Prototypical Summary of an NDE

Before further discussion of NDEs, it is useful to read a description of a complete NDE. The following is Ring's prototypical summary of an NDE.

> The experience begins with a feeling of easeful peace and a sense of well-being, which soon culminates in a sense of overwhelming joy and happiness. This ecstatic tone, although fluctuating in intensity from case to case, tends to persist as a constant emotional ground as other features of the experience

begin to unfold. At this point, the person is aware that he feels no pain nor does he have any other bodily sensations. Everything is quiet. These cues may suggest to him that he is either in the process of dying or has already "died."

He may then be aware of a transitory buzzing or a windlike sound, but, in any event, he finds himself looking down on his physical body, as though he were viewing it from an external vantage point. At this time, he finds that he can see and hear perfectly; indeed, his vision and hearing tend to be more acute than usual. He is aware of the actions and conversations taking place in the physical environment, in relation to which he finds himself in the role of a passive, detached spectator. All this seems very real—even quite natural—to him; it does not seem at all like a dream or an hallucination. His mental state is one of clarity and alertness.

At some point, he may find himself in a state of dual awareness. While he continues to be able to perceive the physical scene around him, he may also become aware of "another reality" and feel himself being drawn into it. He drifts or is ushered into a dark void or tunnel and feels as though he is floating through it. Although he may feel lonely for a time, the experience here is predominantly peaceful and serene. All is extremely quiet and the individual is aware only of his mind and of the feeling of floating.

All at once he becomes sensitive to, but does not see, a presence. The presence, who may be heard to speak or who may instead "merely" induce thoughts in the individual's mind, stimulates him to review his life and asks him to decide whether he wants to live or die. This stocktaking may be facilitated by a rapid and vivid visual playback of episodes from the person's life. At this stage, he has no awareness of time or space, and the concepts themselves are meaningless. Neither is he any longer identified with his body. Only the mind is present and is weighing—logically and rationally— the alternatives that confront him at this threshold separating life from death: to go further into this experience or to return to earthly life. Usually the individual decides to return on the basis, not of his own preference, but on the perceived needs of his loved ones, whom his death would necessarily leave behind. Once the decision is made, the experience tends to be abruptly terminated.

Sometimes, however, the decisional crisis occurs later or is altogether absent, and the individual undergoes further experiences. He may, for example, continue to float through the dark void toward a magnetic and brilliant golden light, from which emanates feelings of love, warmth, and total acceptance. Or he may enter into a "world of light" and preternatural beauty, to be (temporarily) reunited with deceased loved ones before being told, in effect, that it is not yet his time and that he has to return to life.

In any event, whether the individual chooses or is commanded to return to his earthly body and worldly commitments, he does return. Typically, however he has no recollection how he has effected his "reentry," for at this point he tends to lose all awareness. Very occasionally, however, the individual may remember "returning to his body" with a jolt or an agonizing wrenching sensation. He may even suspect that he reenters "through the head."

Afterward, when he is able to recount his experience, he finds that there are simply no words adequate to convey the feelings and quality of awareness he remembers. He may also be or become reticent to discuss it with others, either because he feels no one will really be able to understand it or because he fears he will be disbelieved or ridiculed. (Ring, 1980, 102–103)

Moody took the first step in a scientific investigation of NDEs by simply listing the phenomena. Science then tried to group or classify phenomena into broader categories. Ring divided the events of an NDE into five stages, as seen above in his prototypical summary: peace, body separation, entering the darkness, seeing the *light*, and entering the *light*, each with characteristic events. Sabom refined the categorization of NDEs into two phases: the autoscopic NDE and the transcendental

NDE. For purposes of this book, the two distinctions of Sabom will be emphasized. However, the reader should keep in mind that in each phase there are still distinct events. The reason I prefer Sabom's two phases is that they rather closely correspond to my designation of multiple spirits. Being out of one's body and observing the scene around one's body correspond to one spirit form, and encountering the transcendental world and the *light* would correspond to the realm of Spirit.

There are also aftereffects following the NDE proper. The aftereffects on the individual having the NDE are important in demonstrating their reality, so these will be discussed in great depth. While Moody discussed some psychological problems NDErs encountered when readapting to life in their physical body, other researchers have found profound physiological changes, such as healing more quickly.

Although Sabom divides the NDE into two phases, there are aspects of the NDE that occur prior to these divisions, such as feelings of peace and love that arise throughout the experience. While Moody and others refer to an out-of-the-body experience, Sabom uses the term *autoscopic*. Autoscopic, meaning "self-visualizing," refers to someone's seeing his body and possibly the scene of an accident or a hospital room from a position outside the body. Often the person describes himself as looking down upon the scene from the ceiling or an upper corner of the hospital room. The NDEr may leave the immediate site, in which case the action is no longer self-viewing and is classified as an out-of-body experience (OBE).

Since some of these events occur in a fairly short period of time, it may be difficult to determine in which part of the overall NDE they occur. For instance, Moody lists hearing the news as one event of the NDE. "Hearing the news" usually refers to hospital situations in which a doctor realizes a patient is in imminent danger of death and comments aloud that the patient "is gone." At times, however, the NDEr may not hear this until after she has left her body. Some NDErs, rather than hearing other people comment that they are dead, simply get a subjective impression that they have died.

Moody reports that some people hear strange noises (such as a buzzing or ringing) early in their NDE, but this is infrequent. Some of the sounds are pleasant (i.e., beautiful music), but these are more likely to occur in later stages of the NDE. Feelings of peace, calm, tranquility, and quietude can occur without the person's feeling like he or she has ever left the body. However, these feelings continue as the person enters the autoscopic state.

When entering the autoscopic state, some people report that they feel like they are in a second type of body. Others do not notice this second body at all. Nevertheless, the visualizations of the two groups are very similar. Most people report seeing resuscitation being performed on their physical body from a corner near the ceiling of the emergency room or wherever they are located, such as the scene of an accident. People with corrective vision feel they can see well even though they are not wearing their glasses. Some report leaving their room and going to other areas inside or outside the hospital. To move, all they have to do is think about doing so. These visualizations add a convincing note to NDE reports. If they occur in the hospital, there is rarely any doubt that the body is unconscious and the eyes are closed. The NDEr may report equipment readings that cannot come from hearing alone. Although some information could be heard and inferred, no near-death researcher has reported information from an NDEr that has later proven patently false.

Moody's events generally follow a chronological order. Based on more recent investigations, there is one event, the tunnel, that appears to be out of sequence. Moody lists this event before the autoscopic event. It now appears that the tunnel is most often a transition from the autoscopic experience to the transcendental experience. A small percentage of experiencers felt that they returned to their body through this tunnel, and others felt that while in the transcendental stage they could look back through the tunnel to see their physical body.

My overall impression of NDEs is that all autoscopic events are fairly similar; the NDEr is simply seeing what is happening to her body from an outside position. The further or deeper the NDEr goes into her experience, the more subjective her impressions become. For example, the tunnel is open to many different interpretations. Some report a funnel rather than a tunnel; others experience a dark area with no walls. Some NDErs feel they are moving through the tunnel at an extremely high speed, while others do not feel any movement. Some feel lonely, while others feel they are not alone. Finally, the next stage, seeing the light, is begun by most while still in the tunnel.

At this point, according to Ring, each chronological step occurs less frequently. This makes sense if the transcendental experience is considered to be deeper. Those who have the deeper experience are more likely to have had the earlier events of the NDE experience. Sabom found that more respondents experienced the transcendental NDE than the autoscopic NDE, but this may be the result of a sampling error, as he employed a retrospective approach. If both phases occurred, however, the autoscopic phase almost always came first. Deeper experiences were more likely to occur if the person was clinically dead instead of near death.

The final two stages are called transcendental experiences by Sabom because they contain descriptions of objects and events that transcend or surpass earthly limits. Again, the events that occur here are more subjective, but they may include meeting with deceased people, usually relatives; meeting a *being of light* or feeling a presence; reviewing the events of one's life; observing scenes of spectacular beauty; approaching a border; and finally, deciding to return to life.

The meeting with deceased people provides some means of corroboration of the NDE. For example, one particular case involved an NDEr who did not recognize one of the spirits she observed, but she felt it was a relative. When she described the person to her family, she was informed that she had described her grandmother. When shown a picture of her grandmother, she was able to confirm that she had seen her grandmother, although she had never met her. The deceased person seen always appears healthy and whole. If the deceased person had died in old age, he or she appears younger, without any infirmities. One young child who had an NDE reported seeing her dead brother. Her brother had died prior to her birth, and she had never been told of his existence. A few people have seen people who were still living, but the NDEr could clearly distinguish the living from the dead. In most cases, the person saw only deceased relatives and possibly some friends.

Dr. Elisabeth Kübler-Ross, the well-known writer on death and dying, has written on NDEs, but her work consists of individual cases and not formal research. She has also written introductions to others' books on the subject. In her writing, she usually states that she can confirm the phenomenon discussed by the main author. She has reported that when there is a family with a seriously injured child who is close to death, the child knows if his parents are dead. Even if the child has not been told of his parents' deaths, the child has told Dr. Kübler-Ross that he has seen his parents in an NDE vision and knows they are dead. If the child has not been able to see both parents and only one is deceased, the child knows which one is deceased. No child has ever been incorrect, reporting that his parents were dead when they were still alive. Adults may have the same experience. If husband and wife are both in an accident and one dies while the other has an NDE, the survivor knows the other has died. NDErs have reported seeing a deceased relative who died just a few hours earlier at another location, but the NDEr in question did not know that the person was sick or near death.

The being-of-*light* event reported by Moody is very subjective and may reflect the experiencers' religious upbringing. Ring found a similar event, but the *light* phenomenon in his survey did not present itself as a being. His experiencers felt they could see a *light* and possibly enter it or encounter an unseen presence. The feelings during this state were very similar to those who saw a *being of light*. While peace and calm were felt by most during the first events of the NDE, in or around the *light* there was the additional emotion of love. If the peace and calm mentioned earlier were ineffable, then the love felt from the *light* was even more indescribable. The importance of love, and acting with a motive of love toward other people when living, is often explained by the presence. Another factor impressed on the NDEr during this event is the importance of gaining knowledge during life. Many NDErs believe that this quest for knowledge continues in the afterlife.

It is usually during this time of the NDE that the person may undergo a life review. During this phase, the person witnesses scenes from her life. This often includes inconsequential events as well as highlights. The *being of light* or the presence does not judge the person's actions but lets the person judge herself. NDErs report they feel the emotions of the scene at the time of its occurrence, even the pain or joy of another person in the scene viewed. What is interesting is that the person appears to visualize these events as if watching a film at a normal rate of speed, but a lifetime is compacted into perhaps only a few moments. Some people even preview future events. Many of the NDErs who reach this transcendental phase observe scenes of great beauty. Most often the scenes are pastoral ones, such as meadows or fields with flowers. In his second book, Moody adds that some scenes are cities of *light* where the buildings glow.

Finally, the NDEr makes the decision to return to life. This may take several forms. One form is an apparent dividing line in the NDEr's vision. For instance, if the NDEr is in a beautiful pastoral scene, there may be a fence or a stream, and the NDEr knows that if he crosses it he will not return. Several people have seen themselves on a boat headed toward a distant shore, and they suspect that if they reached the shore they would not return. Other NDErs may have one of their deceased relatives or the presence of *light* tell them that they are not ready to die and must return to life. The information from the *being of light* is often an unspoken understanding. While the foregoing cases do not involve a decision, some NDErs have encountered a decisional or bargaining situation. A decision means that the NDEr could have chosen to die and proceed with the spiritual journey, never returning to the body. Moody suspects that many people who died during operations with good prognosis for survival were given a choice and simply chose not to return. One man "bargained" his way back to life by explaining how important it was for him to help another person on earth.

When the decision is made to return to life, the NDE effectively ends. Some people quietly return to their body and wake up hours later (or much later, as some NDEs occur during a coma that continues after the NDE ends). Many feel a jolt as they return to their physical body. Others may feel the pain in their body, either from the accident or illness that put them near death, or from a medical procedure.

Although frequent media coverage and the cited writings have made NDEs well-known, much of the research I cite was done when the topic was not in the news. When patients recovered and tried to tell their doctor, nurse, or clergyman what they had experienced, they were usually scorned. They may have been told they were hallucinating. Some people had not informed anybody, including their spouses, for over 20 years. Moody would sometimes ask a group he was addressing if anybody had had an unusual experience when near death and, if so, to come and discuss it with him. Therefore, he initially had no statistics on how frequently the experience occurred. Ring and Sabom began their studies shortly after Moody's book was written, when most people were not yet familiar with the subject. When they asked people who had been near death if anything unusual had happened during that time, the NDErs were suspicious and wanted to know why the doctor was interested, as the NDErs may fear ridicule.

Finally, there are the lifetime aftereffects of an NDE. I believe that these are important because they demonstrate that something spiritual has happened. Generally, there are major changes in people's lives, usually toward being more spiritual, believing in life after death, and acting with more care and concern for others. The experiences themselves seem to be independent of prior individual religious beliefs, though those beliefs may affect an interpretation of the events. For instance, a Christian is more likely to report the *being of light* as Jesus even if the being did not say he was Jesus. In addition to psychological changes, Atwater found a number of physiological changes in the NDEr, such as an increase in allergies. In some cases, spouses are questioned about the NDEr's behavioral changes.

Ring found that people who had these experiences fell into two groups. Some tried to read all they could about the subject so they would know that they were not unusual. Others refused to read anything about NDEs because they were afraid that their memory of their own NDE might be contaminated by what others experienced.

C. Research Methodologies

Most of the formal studies described are classified as retrospective, data collected from people who are identified as having had an NDE after questioning. Control groups for the studies are difficult to establish. For instance, a typical control group may be people who have nearly died but did not have an NDE. Another difficulty can be coming up with the definition of "nearly dying." In contrast to a retrospective study, there can be prospective studies, in which everyone who has a cardiac arrest in a hospital (or hospitals) is interviewed to determine who among them had an NDE. The difficulty with this type of study is that people who experience cardiac arrest in a hospital are often people who are elderly or are people who die. Although an investigator may find the typical phases or events of an NDE in this elderly group, it is difficult to assess changes in lifestyle of someone who never leaves the hospital.

Ring was interested in comparing NDErs who came close to death from illness, accident, or suicide attempt. He was unable to find enough people who were hospitalized after accidents or suicide attempts. He therefore put advertisements in newspapers and wrote letters to several psychiatrists. No mention was made of his interest in NDEs. His total sample was 102 people, 21 of whom were contacted through advertisements. This method of collecting information classifies the study as a retrospective one.

In addition to learning about the NDE, Ring was interested in demographic information to determine if gender, marital status, educational level, religion, and age were contributing factors to the likelihood of an NDE occurring or of particular events happening. In addition, he wanted to discern if there was any change in religious beliefs or belief in an afterlife as a result of the NDE. Of the 102 people interviewed, 60 had their NDE less than 2 years prior to the interview. To determine who had an NDE, Ring developed what he called a Weighted Core Experience Index (WCEI). For each type of event that may occur in an NDE, he developed a point score ranging from 1 to 4. For instance, having a subjective sense of being dead had a score of 1, while entering the *light* had a score of 4. The maximum possible score was 29. The highest score obtained by any participant in his sample was 24. Ring used the cutoff score of less than 6 to indicate a participant who was not a "core experiencer." Those with scores of 6 to 9 were labeled "moderate experiencers," and those with a score of 10 or above were labeled "deep experiencers." These last two divisions were not as important, but people in both groups were classified as core experiencers when Ring made comparisons between experiencers and nonexperiencers. In his follow-up book (1984), Ring primarily discusses people who had very deep experiences.

Michael Sabom, a cardiologist, took a much different approach. Since he was a medical doctor interviewing people whose treatment he guided or who were patients in the hospital where he was working, he did not need any special clearance. Sabom had worked in hospitals for six years and had never heard of an NDE, but he only had to interview three people before finding a person who had had an NDE. As a doctor, he wanted to know the medical details of the crisis that led to the NDE. He developed a set of six questions:

1. Was the participant near death?
2. Was the content of the NDE comparable to those NDEs described in Moody's book?
3. How common were NDEs for people near death?
4. Was the NDE influenced by the person's background?
5. Was the NDE affected by medical details?
6. Was a reduction in fear of death the result of the NDE?

Sabom was intrigued by the fact that NDErs could observe their resuscitation being performed. He wanted to compare his knowledge of what usually occurs during resuscitation, or of what the medical report said actually occurred, with what the individual NDEr reported. Were the NDErs making educated guesses, or could they actually see what was happening?

In his book, Sabom discusses the differences between clinical death, biological death, and brain death. Clinical death occurs when external signs of life, such as consciousness, reflexes, respiration, and cardiac activity, are absent. Brain death occurs when there is a flat EEG. Biological death is final and irreversible and thus cannot be included in any study. The criterion for inclusion in his study was anybody who had suffered any physiological catastrophe that had put him or her physically near death, not distinguishing between the first two above. Sabom interviewed a total of 116 people. Excluded from the study were 10 people who were under general anesthesia at the time. Of the 106 remaining, 78 were interviewed on a prospective basis

P. M. H. Atwater began writing about NDEs after she had three NDEs herself. In interviews, she tried to elicit detailed information with different questions to determine if she received contrasting answers. Her research uncovered such interesting phenomena as post-NDE synesthesia, something that occurs when one type of sense stimulation evokes another sense. A common example is when a musical tone appears as a color or a taste sensation. She also discusses many aftereffects other researchers have not mentioned. In addition, she writes about how readapting to the world after an NDE may take years.

Atwater divides the NDE into four types (Atwater, 2007, 26), as follows:

1. Initial experience—sometimes referred to as the nonexperience (an awakening). Usually involves only one—maybe two or three—elements such as a loving nothingness, the living dark, a friendly voice, a brief out-of-body experience, or a manifestation of some type. Usually experienced by those who seem to need the least amount of evidence for proof of survival, or those who need the least amount of shake-up in their lives at that point in time. Often, this becomes a "seed" experience or an introduction to other ways of perceiving and recognizing reality. Rarely is any other element present. Incident rate: 76% with child experiencers, 20% with adult experiencers.

2. Unpleasant and/or hell-like experience—sometimes referred to as distressing (inner cleansing and self-confrontational). Encounter with a threatening void, stark limbo, or hellish purgatory, or scenes of a startling and unexpected indifference (like being shunned)—even "hauntings" from one's own past. Scenarios usually experienced by those who seem to have deeply suppressed or repressed guilt, fear, and anger, and/or those who expect some kind of punishment or discomfort after death. Life reviews common. Some have previews. Incident rate: 3% with child experiencers, 15% with adult experiencers.

3. Pleasant and/or heaven-like experience—sometimes referred to as radiant (reassurance and self-validation). Heaven-like scenarios of loving family reunions with those who have died previously, reassuring religious figures or beings of light, validation that life counts, affirmative and inspiring dialogue. Scenarios usually experienced by those who most need to know how loved they are, how important life is, and how every effort has a purpose in the overall scheme of things. Life reviews common. Some have previews. Incident rate: 19% with child experiencers, 47% with adult experiencers.

4. Transcendent experience—sometimes referred to as a collective universality. Exposure to otherworldly dimensions and scenes beyond the individual's frame of reference; sometimes includes revelations of greater truths. Seldom personal in content. Scenarios usually experienced by those who are ready for a "mind stretching" challenge and/or by individuals who are more

apt to use (to whatever degree) the truths that are revealed to them. Life reviews rare. Collective previews common (such as the world's future, evolutionary changes). Incident rate: 2% with child experiencers, 18% with adult experiencers.

As a psychiatrist, Greyson divides the NDE into its phenomenological components: cognitive, affective, transcendental, and paranormal. For each of those components, Greyson has four questions to ask a person who is near death in each of the above categories. For each question, the answers can be "no," which is assigned a value of 0, "somewhat," which is assigned a value of 1, and "yes" or "definitely," which is assigned a value of 2. The maximum score is 32. If the score is above 7, a person is deemed to have had an NDE. The questions, in each category, are as follows:

- Cognitive: Did time seem to speed up? Were your thoughts speeded up? Did scenes from your past come back to you? Did you suddenly seem to understand everything?
- Affective: Did you have a feeling of peace or pleasantness? Did you have a feeling of joy? Did you feel a sense of harmony or unity with the universe? Did you see, or feel yourself to be surrounded by, a brilliant *light*?
- Paranormal: Were your senses more vivid than normal? Did you seem to be aware of things going on elsewhere, as if by ESP? Did scenes from the future come to you? Did you feel separated from your physical body?
- Transcendental: Did you seem to enter some other, unearthly world? Did you seem to encounter a mystical being or presence? Did you see deceased spirits or religious figures? Did you come to a point or border of no return?

While many studies include a control group, when Morse (1992) performed his study he included five different groups. These were as follows: child NDErs, child illness, psychic / New Age, out of body (OBE), normal control, and a vision (or dream of *light*). His study included four ethnic groups: whites, blacks, American Indians, and Hispanics. It also included multiple religions. For those interviewed, the NDE was at least ten years prior.

George Gallup Jr., the well-known pollster, collected information on American people's belief in an afterlife and NDEs. The information was collected in 1980–81 and published in 1982. The actual number of people polled was not stated. Gallup reported that a surprisingly large number of people have had an NDE experience. The book based on this information, written with William Proctor, is titled *Adventures in Immortality*. In addition to information about NDEs, the book includes reports of religious and mystical experiences. Much of the information was not obtained from simple typical polling questions. People who reported having NDEs or mystical experiences were asked to describe their experiences in depth and were then asked additional questions.

Dr. Maurice Rawlings is a cardiologist who often resuscitated people who were near death. He published a book titled *Beyond Death's Door* in 1977. Most other researchers interviewed people sometime after the near-death incident. Rawlings believes that his perspective of reviving the patient contributes additional information. Rawlings states that many patients when interviewed afterward could not remember what they said or saw when they were near death. If the person cannot remember the NDE, then the experience cannot classified as an NDE. Moody comments that he could not find anyone with a "hellish" experience, but Rawlings found many distressing NDEs, confirmed since the time of his report. Rawlings's book is mostly anecdotal (and evangelical), and he is a strong believer in conservative Christian interpretations of Hell. Although best known for his reports of distressing NDEs, he does report many positive ones as well as combination NDEs (which consist of a distressing phase and then a heavenly phase).

Although there have been a number of personal NDE stories published by Christian publishers, some books with fundamentalist Christian views attack NDE researchers. One of these, by cult researcher Richard Abanes (1996), is titled *Journey into the Light: Explaining Near-Death Experiences*. Abanes claims that most NDE researchers are New Agers whose studies are flawed and not in agreement with his interpretation of the Bible. Abanes is well versed in the literature on NDEs, and he believes that NDErs are deceived when they feel that anything paranormal has happened to them.

One of the verses that Abanes and other fundamentalist writers quote in order to discredit NDEs is 2 Corinthians 11:14 (LT), which reads,

"If Satan disguises himself as the angel of light." Thus, these writers feel that any message of peace and love that does not agree with their interpretation is a deception by Satan. Even Moody, in his early writings, questioned why Satan would teach people about the importance of love. Many of these fundamentalist writers believe there cannot be any valid communication with the dead. However, some Christian publishers have published books in which the NDEr claims to have met deceased relatives in heaven.

It is also interesting that these fundamentalist writers are willing to accept materialist explanations of NDEs, such as brain chemistry. I believe that most NDE researchers have shown those explanations of NDEs to be inadequate. One of the most detailed materialistic explanations for NDEs is provided by English psychologist Susan Blackmore (1993). She believes that the NDE *light* is generated by a natural phenomenon, of dying brain cells. Her book is titled *Dying to Live: Near-Death Experiences*. These materialistic explanations will be discussed in the "Alternative Explanations" section of this chapter.

One Christian group that does promote NDEs is the Mormons. One Mormon from the Salt Lake City area, the late Arvin Gibson, wrote extensively about NDEs. He mostly recounted interviews with NDErs and did not perform a formal study. I found the NDE examples he gives to include the same events as Moody, Ring, and Sabom, although in a few instances he does endorse some views that only a Mormon would recognize, such as a salute from an angel.

There have been a number of writers about NDEs from countries outside the United States. Dr. Peter Fenwick, a psychiatrist in England, has collaborated with his wife, Elizabeth, on a book about NDEs (Fenwick and Fenwick, 1997). They also collaborated on phenomena at final death in a book titled *The Art of Dying* (Fenwick and Fenwick 2008). The latter book will be discussed in chapter 7. Margot Grey is a psychotherapist and a humanistic psychologist in England. She is one of the few writers in the field who has had an NDE. She had her NDE in 1976 and published her book *Return from Death* in 1985. Her sample of 41 people consisted of people who had an illness, people who were in an accident, or people who had attempted suicide. Her goal was to see if the nature of an NDE in England was similar to that of an NDE in the United States. Her methodology was similar to Ring's, but it was not as elaborate. She used the same five stages. She does not compare experiencers and nonexperiencers; however, she includes distressing experiences in her study.

D. Historical Perspective

Much of the early writing on the possibility of life after death has come from the area of psychical research, now sometimes referred to as parapsychology or the paranormal. William James had a strong interest in psychical research and was one of the founders of the American Society for Psychical Research (ASPR). Noted works about this area of study include F. W. H. Meyers's book *Human Personality and Its Survival of Bodily Death*, published posthumously in 1903, and William F. Barrett's book *Deathbed Visions*, published in 1926. Continuing in that tradition is a work by Karlis Osis, PhD, director of research for the ASPR (in 1977), and Erlendur Haraldsson, PhD. In 1961, Dr. Osis authored a book called *Deathbed Observations by Physicians and Nurses*. This and the 1977 study are discussed in chapter 7.

As previously stated, it was medical doctor Raymond Moody's book that aroused a great interest in the topic of NDEs. *Life After Life* was dedicated to Dr. George Ritchie, author of *Return from Tomorrow* (1978), which was not published until after Moody's first two books. Ritchie's NDE occurred during a noncombat illness during World War II. Moody knew of Ritchie and his experience, and that spurred his early interest in the subject. Moody's medical specialty is psychiatry, as is Ritchie's. Moody stated in his first book that he was raised a Presbyterian but later joined the Methodist Church. He expressed that he was not familiar with literature on paranormal phenomena in *Life After Life*, but I believe he became familiar afterward.

A year prior to Moody's book, 1974, a book titled *Glimpses of the Beyond*, by Jean-Baptiste Delacour, was published in the United States. This book, a translation of a book published in Germany the year before, is a collection of stories about NDEs and other stories about life after death. These accounts include some well-known Europeans' experiences.

Weiss (1972) also published a collection of similar stories in a book titled *The Vestibule*, which includes Ritchie's account and an article by Emmanuel Swedenborg about life after death. Swedenborg was a famous scientist born over 300 years ago. Later in his life, he turned his attention to spirituality. He claimed he could see into the spiritual world. In chapter 10, I discuss a therapist named Wilson Van Dusen, who maintains that some findings he made while treating mental patients closely resemble Swedenborg's views of the spiritual world.

Writers of fiction have also incorporated narratives that describe experiences similar to NDEs. Leo Tolstoy (1828–1910), sometimes considered a mystic, related such an episode in *War and Peace*. Ernest Hemingway (1899–1961) came close to dying in World War I and described an incident similar to an NDE in his novel *A Farewell to Arms*. Moody touches on the ancient Greek concept of life after death, recounting Plato's story of Er, who "died" on a battlefield but recovered ten days later and then told others of what he saw (as discussed in *The Republic*). Much of the information is similar to what is reported about NDEs. One of the closest similarities to the accounts Moody collected appeared in a book called *The Tibetan Book of the Dead*. Though written many centuries ago, the book was not translated into English until early in the twentieth century.

In 1892, Albert Heim wrote an article titled "Remarks on Fatal Falls" (original in German), which appeared in the yearbook of the Swiss Alpine Club. His work was partly autobiographical, as he had fallen off a cliff while mountain climbing and thereafter experiencing what is now called a *fear-death experience* (FDE). He landed in a snowbank and survived. This type of experience is called "fear-death" because the person involved believes he is about to die but in most cases has no severe injuries. Heim interviewed a number of other fear-death experiencers, who all had the same positive experience, often including a rapid life review.

Carol Zaleski wrote a book titled *Otherworld Journeys* (1987), in which she discusses views of life after death beginning with ancient times, continuing through the Middle Ages, and including the modern works of Moody and those following him. She details some near-death accounts from the Middle Ages, some of which had profound effects on church thought. Although she teaches religion at a major university, her interpretation of an NDE is more mythological than spiritual.

Julian of Norwich (ca. 1342–ca. 1416) and John Newton (1725–1807) are historical figures whose lives changed after they nearly died. Julian did her writing (*Sixteen Revelations of Divine Love*, 1393) after the Black Death ravaged Europe in the 14th century. Many people at that time thought the illness was God's punishment for some unspecified evil the people had done, but Julian informed people that God only wanted to shower his love on people and that the Black Death was not a punishment. She nearly died of a fever in 1373, at which time her revelations began. Incidentally, the book may have been the first in the English language written by a woman.

Another person who greatly influenced history after having one or more NDEs was John Newton (1725–1807), composer of the song "Amazing Grace." He was an English sea captain of some ships involved in the slave trade. After several near-death incidents (nearly drowning and experiencing a violent fever), he greatly changed his lifestyle, became a minister (later an abolitionist), and convinced William Wilberforce, a member of Parliament, to persuade the rest of Parliament to have England stop its involvement in the slave trade. The Slave Trade Act was passed in the year 1807 (Newton died shortly thereafter), well before the Civil War in the United States ended its practice of slavery. Newton's story was part of a 2006 film by the name *The Amazing Grace*. In the film, Wilberforce also was shown as having a mystical-like experience, but he was convinced by others that he could do more good for humanity in Parliament than by becoming a member of the clergy.

E. Peace and a Sense of Death

What Moody (1975) calls "hearing the news" about one's own death, and what Sabom (1982) labels a "sense of death," appears to be the transition encountered when the person's spiritual body moves from being in the physical body to being out of the body. A person may still be able to hear even while apparently unconscious. This is probably the case when the person hears someone say that she is dead. This occurs prior to out-of-body visualization. Leaving her body is a sensation a person has never experienced (or at least does not remember), and so her first thought when it occurs is that she must be dead.

The feeling of peace is probably a facet of being out of the body, but an NDEr may report this feeling prior to being able to visualize from outside his body. The feeling continues through the entire NDE, both autoscopic and transcendental, but may be less thought about when sight develops. When an NDEr sees a resuscitation team frantically working on his physical body, he may wonder what all the concern is about since he feels so great.

Gallup and Procter (1982) classify all these types of feelings under the category of "peace and painless." It should be kept in mind that many, if not most, of these people who experienced NDEs were in extreme pain just prior to this experience. Sabom (1982) states that one man felt no pain even though one of his ribs was cracked during a resuscitation procedure.

F. The Autoscopic NDE

The autoscopic NDE is the case in which the person is able to view his own body and surroundings, or even depart the immediate area. It is sometimes referred to as an out-of-body experience (OBE).

1. Separation and a Second Body

The feeling of peace appears to be the first stage of separation from the body, but it may occur prior. Ring (1980) found that 60% of his total sample had experienced the feeling of peace, but only 37% reported body separation. Sabom reports that 33% of his sample had experienced only the autoscopic elements, 48% had experienced only the transcendental elements, and 19% experienced elements of each. Thus, over 50% experienced the autoscopic elements. These figures of Ring and Sabom cannot be directly compared, because Ring's 37% figure is a percent of his total sample, including nonexperiencers (as determined by the WCEI discussed in the "Research Methodologies" section of this book), and Sabom's percentages are from experiencers only. Ring's figure would be about 75% if only experiencers were considered.

The sensation of being outside the physical body is described by some as light, airy, and weightless. An interesting element of these reports is the existence of a second body. Moody (1975) states that a few NDErs felt that they definitely did not have a second body but were "consciousness" only. The majority did find themselves in a "new body," and each individual used different words to describe it. Moody refers to this second body as a "spiritual body" and reports that it has a form, even parts analogous to arms, legs, and a head. Moody (1988) states that when one NDEr studied his hands during his NDE, he saw them to be composed of *light* with tiny structures in them. He could see the delicate whorls of his fingerprints, and tubes of *light* up his arms (p. 8). Moody (1988) adds that most NDErs regard their body as a house for their spirit. Some have difficulty recognizing their own physical body over which they are hovering.

Grey (1985) states that most of her respondents were not aware of a second body. One person told Grey that she realized that she was neither woman nor man, just pure spirit. However, Grey says her respondents were still conscious of being themselves. Similarly, Ring reports that most of his sample felt they consisted of mind only and were not aware of a second body. However, one person described a second body and said he wore clothing but had bare feet. His body felt light, but he could feel his face. Another person told Sabom (1982) that he wore a white robe. Sabom estimates that 93% of those having the autoscopic experience perceive their "separated self" to be an invisible, nonmaterial entity that is their conscious identity. Two from Grey's sample reported a silver cord connecting their spiritual body to their physical body. Morse (1990) describes a case in which a boy named Ben had an out-of-body experience (OBE) and was viewing his body, linked to him by a silver cord attached to his foot.

In the NDE literature, I found a number of cases in which a living person saw a spirit form leaving the body of a dying person. Some examples of people reporting that they saw a spirit form leave a dying body come from Moody's stories of shared death experiences. Those descriptions are in section L of this chapter.

2. Location and Movement

Generally when NDErs leave their bodies they remain close by, but there are exceptions. Moody's examples occur near the vicinity of the actual body. Sabom, whose sample includes mostly people in hospitals, states that in all but three of his cases the "separated" body was located at ceiling height, above the physical body. The three exceptions viewed their bodies from great heights. These NDErs did not explain how they saw through the walls or roof of the hospital.

Some NDErs do recall traveling. Sabom refers to this as "thought travel." One experiencer told Moody, "When I wanted to see someone at a distance, it seemed like part of me, kind of like a tracer, would go to that person." This same woman compared herself to a zoom lens; as soon as she thought of a person, she was immediately with that person. When one is having an NDE, physical objects are no barrier to any movement, as the spiritual body can pass through any physical object. Another person interviewed by Sabom said he went around the hospital parking lot, boiler room, and cafeteria. This same man said that several months later he visited the hospital cafeteria and found it exactly as he had visualized it. Perhaps not many NDErs attempt movement outside their vicinity, since the idea of going through a door or wall does not occur to them.

In a separate section of this chapter, I summarize the entire lengthy NDE of George Ritchie (1978). It includes an extensive OBE phase with a view of a building far from his body that he was later able to verify. He passed this building when he thought of his hometown of Richmond and immediately found himself flying toward Richmond.

3. Perception and Thought

A person's simply saying he felt like he was out of his body may not carry much credence. But when out of their bodies, NDErs can see and often hear. In the next subsection, the accuracy of these reports is reviewed. Here, a description of the NDErs' general sight, sound, and thought impressions during an NDE will be discussed. Taste and smell are rarely noticed.

Almost all researchers report that out-of-body sight is unusually keen during an autoscopic NDE despite, in most cases, the physical brain's being starved of oxygen. Moody states that vision and hearing seem heightened, more acute than in physical life. Dr. Kübler-Ross describes one woman who was totally blind when in her physical body but who could see when out of her body (Seligson, 1981). Grey states that her sample of NDErs report clearer and sharper perception and a heightened intellectual process when out of body. Ring (1980) also states that NDErs felt they had heightened sensory awareness and mental clarity.

Sixteen of Sabom's patients could also hear during their NDE. Eight of these attempted communication, without response. Moody (1975) claims that most of his NDErs did not hear physical voices or sounds but picked up the thoughts of the people around them. Moody (1988) describes a case of this reported to him by a physician in South Dakota. The physician had rear-ended a car just prior to reporting to work at an emergency department. He was worried about being sued. Part of his work that day involved resuscitating a man who had experienced cardiac arrest. That patient accurately described the resuscitation to the doctor the next day (not unusual), but he added that the doctor did not have to worry about the accident in which he was involved. The patient read the doctor's mind during the resuscitation and possibly saw that in the future there would not be any legal action.

Sabom (1982) also emphasizes that his NDErs felt alert, fully awake, mentally acute, and in full control of their minds. It can be noted that no NDEr thought his autoscopic NDE could have been a dream or hallucination. A number of researchers have noted that during clinical compromise of the physical body, it would be expected that perception would be diminished rather than enhanced.

4. Accuracy of Autoscopic Sight/Veridical Perception

The word *perception* is used to indicate what an NDEr reports he or she saw or heard, as this information normally only comes by sensory means or is deduced from logical inference. An example of an inference would be when an unconscious person hears a doctor mention an instrument reading and then that person's mind decides what the instrument may look like. This is sometimes referred to as fabrication or gap filling. There is also the possibility that the NDEr's eyes came open during or prior to surgery. A patient is likely to have been under a general anesthetic during surgery, and many anesthetics prevent memories from forming. Some NDE researchers speculate that people who exhibit the aftereffects of an NDE but do not remember the NDE may have failed to form a memory of the NDE.

The reason I think it is important to have some verification of alleged perception is that it demonstrates that something capable of perception departs the physical body during an NDE. This something is one of our spiritual components. Many times NDE patients are relieved to find that what they heard or observed is actually true. Thus, what could have been considered to be a subjective experience actually corresponds to objective reality. One of the alleged debunkers of NDEs, Susan Blackmore, reports that she once thought she was out of her body during an illegal drug trip and that what she observed was not the actual situation. From this drug-induced experience, she concludes that all OBEs during NDEs are similarly hallucinatory and invalid.

Like Susan Blackmore, physicalists hold that consciousness cannot exist apart from the physical brain. Although NDErs are only near death, if this spiritual component is capable of perceiving when temporarily away from the physical body, why could this feature not continue after irreversible death? This would also give validation to the messages with which NDErs return, namely the importance of love and of acquiring knowledge.

Without going into detail, I will say that there have been some scientific studies in which a computer monitor, facing upward and only visible from near the ceiling, is placed above an operating room. The specific object on the monitor is not known until the person being operated on is questioned as to whether or not he or she observed anything during the operation (normally only if the individual had a cardiac arrest). There might be five possible objects and five variations in color on the monitor. If a person claims to have seen the object, there is only a 4% ($^1/_{25}$, or $^1/_5$ × $^1/_5$) chance of guessing correctly both the object and the color. These studies are few, with inconclusive results. Thus, science, using a prospective format, has not been able to affirm or deny out-of-body visualization.

In his study, Sabom (1982) performed an evaluation on the NDE claims of resuscitated people. Because he was a cardiologist and most of his NDErs were resuscitated after having heart failure, Sabom was able to assess the accuracy of the NDErs' reported observations of the resuscitation procedure. For controls, he asked people who did not report an NDE to explain what they thought had been done to them. Of 23 controls who attempted an explanation, 20 made a major error. Of 32 who had an autoscopic NDE, only six paid much attention to the medical details. The other 26 had their attention directed to the pleasant qualities of the experience. Those 26 were asked to reconstruct what they thought was happening, and 80% made at least one major error. The six who were concentrating on the details of the resuscitation procedure gave extremely accurate accounts. Sabom asked them many detailed questions. These questions, along with their responses, appear in his book. Their descriptions led Sabom to conclude that the NDE accounts were not likely to be a subtle fabrication based on listening or prior knowledge.

An interesting case was reported by Kimberly Clark (1984), a social worker at a hospital. A migrant worker patient had a heart attack, and during her out-of-body NDE she found herself above the hospital emergency department's driveway. The patient reported to Clark that on the third floor's ledge of the hospital there was a tennis shoe with a worn place on the little toe—and the shoelace was under the heel. Clark went into all the rooms on the third floor and had to press her face against the glass in order to see the ledge. She finally found a room from which she could see the tennis shoe. From the window, she could not see the worn spot or the lace under the heel. That could only be seen by a person floating outside, close to the shoe. Clark retrieved the shoe and gave it to the patient.

Moody (1975) says that many NDErs have described activities they observed when outside the body, some later confirmed. However, Moody could not personally confirm the anecdotal reports, such as being able to identify the doctor who performed the resuscitation, even though the subjects were unconscious when wheeled into the room. Moody (1988) reports that one NDEr observed her brother-in-law in the lobby and heard him make an unkind remark about having to be a pallbearer. When she told him what he said, the man turned so pale that there was little doubt the NDEr was correct. One NDEr saw a nurse break a glass vial in her hand in the next room and told the nurse to be careful, that she could cut herself. Moody (1988) also writes that one 70-year-old woman had an NDE and described in vivid detail her resuscitation. She described the instruments, their colors, and the color of the doctor's suit. This is not unusual, except that the woman had been blind since age eighteen.

In his second book, published in 1998, Sabom describes and verifies one highly detailed OBE. In 1991, the late Pam Reynolds underwent what is referred to as standstill surgery for a basilar artery aneurysm deep in her brain. To do this, it is necessary to stop the heart completely and drain the blood from the brain. First, though, the body is cooled to about 60°F so the brain can survive longer. Cooled, the brain was drained of its blood, and then the rest of the body was placed on cardiopulmonary bypass. Reynolds' eyes were taped shut, speakers were inserted into her ears that played 100-decibel sound, and an EEG confirmed that no sound was reaching her brain. Despite the blockage of sensory input and general anesthesia, Reynolds was able to accurately see and hear what the medical personnel were saying and doing during the processes of preparation and surgery. She felt like she was sitting on the surgeon's shoulder. She described her vision as "more focused and clearer than normal vision" (Sabom, 1998, 41). Pam is a musician and described the sound of the "saw" used to open her skull as having a natural D sound. At some point, Pam went into a transcendental NDE. During this phase, she observed a number of her deceased relatives. When it was time for her to return to her body, her uncle took her back through the tunnel.

Another very controversial case of veridical perception is the report of van Lommel (2010). Although a majority of the NDEs in van Lommel's study were cardiac arrest cases in which the patient was already in the hospital, this case involves a person brought into the hospital after being found comatose and in cardiac arrest. When he awoke about a week later, he identified the nurse who had attended him when he was brought into the hospital. The patient also told this nurse that she knew where to find his false teeth, as he "saw" her place them into a drawer. What van Lommel considers to be unusual is that 15 seconds after cardiac arrest, there is no blood supply to the brain and the brain essentially shuts down. The brain is not expected to be recording information without blood supply.

In *The Handbook of Near-Death Experiences: Thirty Years of Investigation* (2009), Janice Miner Holden describes having performed a voluminous search of anecdotal NDEs in various systematic research literature that involved corroborative perceptions during an NDE. Some cases were prior to 1975. She excluded cases mentioned in popular press articles and those that appeared in autobiographical books. She "found 107 such cases gleaned from 39 publications by 37 different authors or author teams" (p. 193). She listed them all in a table. Although there were some cases of minor errors, and not all cases had strong verifications, overall Holden agrees with Ring and Valarino that "the cumulative weight of these narratives is sufficient to convince most skeptics that these reports are something more than mere hallucinations on the patient's part" (Ring and Valarino 1998, quoted in Holden 2009, 197).

Holden also reviewed cases including transmaterial information claimed by the patient. This involves information received during the transcendental phase of an NDE. In these cases, the information involves unknown family matters conveyed to the NDEr by a deceased relative met in the transcendental realm. In some cases, it is simply the identity of the person met. For instance, a child's grandparents may have died years before the child was born and the child has never seen their photograph. When the child NDEr returns to life, she is shown an old family photo, she child identifies the person in the photograph as the person she met. The following cases may involve the autoscopic phase, the transcendental phase, or both.

A three-year-old girl in Britain named Vivien had an incident reported by St. Clair (1997). Vivien had a fever. During what was seemingly an NDE, she met her auntie Rita, speaking the latter's name while the former was delirious. Vivien and Rita "danced on a cloud." When Vivien recovered, her mother would not talk about her alleged sister Rita. Fifteen years later, when the mother was dying, Vivien asked about Rita. The mother said her sister Rita had run away with a married man many years earlier. Consequently, the family disowned her and refused to talk about her. The mother heard that her sister Rita had died. She had an old photograph of her sister, and Vivien identified the woman in that photo as the person she had seen during her NDE. Vivien went for a walk along the shore and felt the presence of Rita, who then told Vivien to get back to the house. When she got back home, the mother had a predeath vision of Rita welcoming her to the afterlife. In difficult times, Vivien still feels Rita's presence.

Atwater (1999) reports the case of a nine-year-old boy named Johnny who "drowned" in his family's pool. He recovered and told his parents that he had seen his brother while unconscious. They told him that he did not have a brother. He said that the child had been removed him from his mother's stomach. It turns out that his mother had had an abortion a number of years earlier and had never told her husband. The boy was happy to meet his brother in the other world, but the situation resulted in a divorce for the parents.

The following was conveyed by Minnesota resident Patti Harvey to Dr. Janis Amatuzio, a local coroner. Patti had a 17-year-old stepson named Danne Lynch who died in an automobile accident in Salt Lake City. He had been driving under the influence of alcohol and did not have his seat belt on. A fellow passenger, who had been wearing his seat belt, suffered only minor injuries. On his recently renewed driver's license, Danne had stated he wanted to be an organ donor. In Salt Lake City, a man named Mike was a 32-year-old father with three children and a wife, Kim. He had had diabetes since childhood and required a kidney and pancreas transplant. Mike received Danne's organs. As soon as he awoke in the postanesthesia recovery room, he told Kim that his donor's name was Danne. Kim's sister was there, and she recognized the name Danne Lynch as belonging to someone who died at the hospital.

A few days later Mike explained to Kim what happened during the surgery. He first had an autoscopic NDE, where he observed the operating room, and then felt a wave of love and gratitude. He said to himself that he wanted to see his donor, and immediately he passed through a wall to see Danne's body. Mike then reported that he was sucked up (like a vacuum) into the *light* and heard the sentence, "Danne died, and you are going to live" (Amatuzio, 2006, 116). Mike observed three luminous beings. One was his deceased aunt; the second was Danne; and he did not identify the third. Kim read the obituary for Danne Lynch, which listed his stepparents' names and revealed that they were from Minnesota. She obtained their address and sent a letter to Patti Harvey. The Harveys decided to fly to Salt Lake City to visit with Mike. He was able to verify that the photo of Danne they brought with them was the likeness of the person he had seen twice, first his physical body in the hospital and then in spirit with his aunt.

To demonstrate that NDEs can be cross-cultural, St. Clair (1997) reports the case of Durdanda Khan. She was living in Pakistan, and at age two and a half she died at home for about 15 minutes from an unknown cause. When she recovered, her mother asked her where she had been while "dead." She replied that she had been to the stars. She also saw a beautiful garden with various fruit trees, along with her dead grandpa and the grandpa's mother. She heard her father ask her to come back, and she told her grandpa that she had to go back. The grandpa said they would first go and ask God, after which time

God said that it was okay for Durdanda to go back. She said God was blue. Several months later, Durdanda and her family were visiting some other relatives, and she correctly identified a person in a photo as her grandpa's mother. The family later moved to England, where St. Clair does her writing. Durdanda is now an accomplished artist and has painted a picture of the garden she was in during her NDE.

One of the best-selling books of 2011 was *Heaven Is for Real: A Little Boy's Astounding Story of His Trip to Heaven and Back* (Burpo and Vincent, 2010), which is about an NDE in a four-year-old boy named Colton Burpo. (The story in the book was told by Colton's father, Todd, and was penned by a professional writer, Lynn Vincent.) The father is a part-time Methodist minister (his church is not large enough to support a full-time minister) who lives in a small town in western Nebraska. The book is not a single retelling of the boy's entire NDE, but rather it is about how the boy would, out of the blue, make strange comments about what he learned while sick and undergoing surgery for a ruptured appendix and the resulting infection. One day after he recovered, he said he had two sisters. On earth, he only had one sister. Colton's parents had never told him that his mother had had a miscarriage before he was born. He also told his parents what they were doing while he was in surgery. During his NDE, he also met his great-grandfather named Pop, who had died 24 years before Colton was born. The family had photos of Pop as a young person and then some of when he was an older man. In heaven, Pop looked like he did in the photos where he was younger. In the photo of Pop as an older person, he was wearing glasses, and Colton said no one in heaven wears glasses. These meetings of Colton's miscarried sister and of his grandfather more likely happened in the transcendental phase of his NDE.

Gloria met her brother during her NDE. She hadn't known that she had a brother who died before she was born (Rommer, 2000, 7). The brother was with her father and another brother whom she did know, both deceased. There were not any family photos of her brother, but her mother confirmed his existence. The unknown brother identified himself to Gloria, but in some other visitations of this type the person does not identify himself.

G. Transition—The Tunnel

A tunnel or darkness appears to signify the transition from an autoscopic NDE to a transcendental NDE. Ring (1980) employs the phrase *entering the darkness*, something that was experienced by 23% of his total sample, or about 50% of core experiencers. Other researchers have found entering the darkness to be less frequent. Moody (1975) refers to this darkness as a tunnel, but other terms his NDErs used to describe it include *cave, well, trough, enclosure, funnel, vacuum, sewer, valley, cylinder,* and *a void.* Around the year 1506, Dutch painter Hieronymus Bosch (ca. 1450–1516) painted a classic example of a tunnel similar to what an NDEr encounters. The title of his painting is *Ascent into the Empyrean.* Empyrean is considered to be the highest level of heaven. Moving through the tunnel may be a fast or slow process, the tunnel's walls may be *light* or dark, and the person traveling through the tunnel may be alone or with other spirits.

While a stairway is distinctly different perceptually from a tunnel, Moody (1988) states that an NDEr may proceed up a stairway instead of through a tunnel. Although we normally think of tunnels as long and straight, Morse (1992) writes about one NDEr who described the tunnel as curved around like a seashell, but there was still a *light* at the end. If the NDEr hears a strange sound, it is usually at the same time he or she travels through the tunnel (or up the stairway). Sounds heard by NDErs include buzzing, ringing, clicking, roaring, banging, whooshing, and whistling. Most people report not liking the sounds. Some people did hear pleasant sounds, but those may have occurred in the preliminary part of the transcendental NDE.

Moody (1988) provides information on NDEs in several children. He describes in detail the discussions he had with the children, and in all three cases the child traveled through a tunnel. One nine-year-old girl was accompanied through the tunnel by a pretty lady. An eleven-year-old boy was accompanied by two people. This child also returned to his body through the tunnel. Another boy reported that he was moving upward very rapidly before entering the tunnel.

In a later section of this book, the NDEr decision to return to the body will be discussed. While there is usually not much description provided for the mechanics of returning, Grey (1985) reports a case in which a woman returned to her body by rushing down a long black tunnel. She could see a light and her daughter's face at the end of the tunnel. This was not the light associated with the transcendental phase or a deceased daughter; she saw her living daughter and probably the light in the hospital room.

H. The Transcendental NDE

The tunnel or darkness is often a transition into a "deeper" NDE. Sabom used the term *transcendental* because the scenes seemed to transcend the earthly environment.

1. Seeing the Light

Moody uses the term *being of light* because that is the way many of his NDE interviewees referred to it. This *light* is usually formless. Ring uses two terms to describe this aspect: *seeing the light* and *entering the light*; there is not a specific dividing point between the two. As Moody explains, the *light* is dim at first, and either white or clear, but it rapidly becomes brighter until it reaches unearthly brilliance. This warm, vibrant, living *light* does not hurt the NDEr's nonphysical eyes.

In Ring's study, about 16% of his total sample reported seeing the *light*. These NDErs usually described the *light* as golden. Some could see a variety of vivid colors. Although many NDErs who reach this stage have had the autoscopic experience, some have not. The latter may feel peace at this time. Some saw the *light* getting brighter after the period of darkness, but several others remained in an earthly environment. In other words, the room they were in became intensely illuminated; the *light* was very different from normal room lighting or sunlight. There may be minor variations in the color of the *light*, from white to golden, and occasionally a pastel color. Ritchie (1978) describes a similar situation where his room filled with *light*.

I also discuss this concept of light in some specialty areas of NDEs, such as children who have NDEs, empathic NDE experiences, and even distressing NDEs, later in this chapter.

2. Entering the Light or Encountering a Being of Light

At some point after first seeing the *light*, the NDEr actually enters into it. According to Moody, the love and warmth coming from the *light* are indescribable. The person is completely attracted to and surrounded by the *light* and love. This subsection will concentrate on communication with the *light*, and some identification will be given to the *being of light*.

Moody states that a person's communication with this *being of light* is often made without audible sounds or language. Transference of thought occurs, leaving no possibility for misunderstanding or lying. One person described the *light* as being full of compassion and perfect understanding. Another person described it as having a voice and a sense of humor. Grey quotes a man who stated that an NDEr's thought waves are read, regardless of language, and thus the message cannot be misunderstood. The first message is, "Relax. There is nothing to fear."

During their experiences, some NDErs were asked general questions about their lives. The questions, however, were not intended to condemn, accuse, or threaten but simply to make the person think about his or her life. Moody states that these questions were directed toward two main ideas: the NDEr's life accomplishments and his or her preparation for death. Moody compares these questions to a Socratic question in the sense that they are meant to uncover the truth. One person interpreted the question as conveying, "If you love me, go back and complete what you began in your life."

Some Christians called this *being of light* Christ, but other Christians did not. In three cases of NDEs in children reported by Moody (1988), the children all referred to the *light* as God or Jesus. One reported that the beings who accompanied him in the tunnel were wearing very white robes. Grey recounts a man who reported he saw Jesus Christ, including the imprint made by the nails in his hands and feet. For others, the presence also appeared as a religious figure, but some sensed it rather than saw it. Grey states that respondents often claimed to have a special relationship with this presence, which is sometimes understood to be God and sometimes the High Self of the individual; some felt the two could not be separated.

3. Scenic Beauty and Harmonious Music

In addition to mentioning feelings of love and warmth amid the *light*, NDErs often describe a heavenly, yet often earthlike, environment. The most common descriptions include a flowery garden or a meadow. Some NDErs see *cities of light* with buildings that glow. Almost all say that the colors are much more vivid and intense than in the physical world.

Ring's NDErs cited many examples of scenic beauty. One woman saw soft, bright, high golden grass that swayed. One saw beautiful blue lakes, bright flowers, and pure white angels. Another person saw beautiful flowers and heard birds singing. One woman saw a lane winding through a beautiful meadow and heard pleasant music. The woman who had the deepest experience, based on Ring's numerical measurement technique, described everything around her as looking like marble but being filled with *light*. Grey's examples include landscapes with beautiful grass, trees, and flowers; some did mention buildings. A few heard preternatural harmonies, regarded as the music of the spheres.

Rawlings (1978) describes several cases of NDErs seeing *cities of light* similar to what Moody described. In one case, as the NDEr flew out of a black tube, below which he saw a river and a city with streets made of shining gold. The people were happy, and he thought he saw his parents. He awoke in the hospital and wished he had not returned. When the next episode of chest pains occurred, he died. One item I find interesting in reading about this and other scenes is that there is no overhead light source, like a sun. All of the objects that were observed emitted their own *light*.

4. Life Review

The scenic beauty aspects of the transcendental NDE and even the love and warmth are interesting, as they appeal to our aesthetic sense of what the afterlife may be like. However, the event called the life review judgment is more philosophically pleasing for learning about the meaning of life here on earth. Although many NDErs feel they have learned much about life from the love they felt from the *light*, many of the changes these people have made in their lives since their recovery may be a result of their life review. However, no researcher has attempted to determine which phase of an NDE was responsible for the changes in people's lives after the NDE.

There are two different types of life review. This discussion appears in the section titled "The Transcendental NDE" because most reviews occur in the presence of the *light*. However, some reviews occur without the presence of the *light*. Still others occur without injury or being near death.

The life review phenomenon has been reported by every major researcher who has written on the subject of NDEs. In a previous section I mentioned the quality of timelessness, which can be dramatically seen in the life review. It appears that many NDErs had only been unconscious for several minutes, yet they reported reviews of their entire lives completed at normal speed. Some people have had a life review in the seconds between falling and landing without injury in what could have been a life-threatening accident.

Moody states that some reviews occur in chronological order while others happen with no temporal order. For the latter, everything appears at once. These reviews are similar to watching a movie screen. Some people felt that all aspects of their lives were in the review, even seemingly insignificant events. Others felt that only the highlights of their lives were included. All indicated that the review was in vibrant color and three-dimensional. The emotions and feelings associated with the images were reexperienced. The NDEr seemed able to recall sometimes forgotten events in lifelike detail. Moody says the life review was primarily an educational experience for the NDEr, one devised by the *being of light*. During the life review, it was stressed that the two most important activities in life were learning to love other people and acquiring knowledge. The importance of love can be demonstrated in a positive or negative fashion in an NDE. The NDEr may see how an unkind or selfish act could hurt another person, or she may see how an act of kindness created satisfaction for both her and the recipient. According to Moody (1988), the NDEr, in effect, became the consciousness of the person acted upon, feeling that individual's sadness, hurt, or regret. If the *being of light* is involved in the review, the feeling is more intense and the emphasis is not on judgment but on learning from the experience. The *being of light* knows all of the events of an NDEr's life. NDErs report that judgment seems to come from the self.

In his statistical analysis, Ring found an interesting point concerning the life review. The life review occurred in 55% of his accident victims but in only 16% of respondents who had had an illness or who had attempted suicide. This difference is statistically significant. Not a result of random chance, the life review is seemingly orchestrated by a higher power. About one-fourth of Ring's group who had had an NDE underwent a life review. Several felt they saw millions of frames of pictures. Some felt that they were detached, like a spectator watching pictures, rather than being a participant. Ring also found that some people had what he calls *flash-forwards*, that is, seeing future events in their lives with the life review simply going beyond the current time. These people also had flashbacks. One young man who had his review following an accident had the reason for his accident explained. Though no details were given, the reason was most likely not mechanical failure; that is, the accident happened for a reason. No feelings of guilt were imposed. He also had some flash-forwards. One woman reported that if parts of her review seemed boring, she could skip over them. Grey reports on one person who said he felt embarrassed about some of the stupid things he did in his life, but the presence reminded him that he was now learning from these. Another man commented that in his life review, he could see how all the parts of his life fit together like a jigsaw puzzle. This theme will be shown in other parts of this book.

Flynn (1982) states that one NDEr told him that he was overwhelmed when he realized that a person is responsible for every single action he or she takes in life. During this NDEr's life review, he relived not only every thought and word he had thought and spoken but also observed the effect of every thought, word, and deed. In the section on distressing NDEs, I examine this concept.

Although Ring never identifies the real name of any of his NDE subjects, later on one of them identifies himself. Tom Sawyer was quite athletic and qualified to participate in the US Olympic Trials in bicycling, but because he had injuries, he did not make the Olympic Team. He had his NDE in 1978 when he was 33 years old and the pickup truck he was working underneath slipped off its jacks and fell onto his chest, arresting his breathing for several minutes. His life review is an excellent illustration of some of the unusual perspectives afforded by the life review. In observing one incident during the summer when he was eight years old, Tom said he could count the number of mosquitoes in his vision. Of course, when the incident actually occurred he hadn't counted them, but this illustrates the accuracy and details of the review.

Another episode of Tom's life review provides insight into the review process. When Tom was nineteen years old, a pickup truck was his pride. When a man stepped out in front of Tom's truck, Tom would have hit him had he not swerved. Tom was mad and said some swear words to the man. The man in turn reached inside Tom's truck and slapped him. Tom felt that this offered him a justification for retaliating in any way he could. He got out of his truck and began pummeling the man with his fists. During his review, Tom had three perspectives of the incident. He could remember his own anger and the adrenaline rush he felt at the time, and his vindication for being able to strike back. He could also view the incident from a position outside his body. But mostly, he could experience what the man he was striking felt:

> I also experienced seeing Tom Sawyer's fist come directly into my face. And I felt the indignation, the rage, the embarrassment, the frustration, the physical pain. ... I felt my teeth going through my lower lip—in other words, I was in that man's eyes. I was in that man's body. I experienced everything of that inter-relationship between Tom Sawyer and that man that day. I experienced unbelievable things about that man that are of a very personal, confidential, and private nature. (Farr, 1993, 33)

As a result of being in the man's body, Tom came to know the man's name, the man's age, and the fact that he was in bereavement over his wife's death and had turned to alcohol as an escape. Tom hit the man thirty-two times, and he could feel the man's humiliation and helplessness at being struck. Tom even checked with the police after the accident to see if the man may have died, but the incident was never reported to the police.

Tom could also feel his interaction with other objects during his review. On one hand, he could experience the joy of a tree after he noted that he loved the appearance of the tree. However, on another occasion, after he had gone to the woods and maliciously chopped down some trees for no purpose, Tom could sense the trees' sadness. He could also sense his own feelings and those of his mother when he was only several months old. Tom believed that the Christ figure beside him during his review was not judging him but was giving him unconditional love. Tom was raised to attend church, but at the time of his NDE he described himself as an atheist.

In the next chapter, I will be writing about child abuse. The following NDE, reported by Rommer, happened to a woman named Priscilla and contains interesting insight about recovery after abuse. She had been sexually abused as a child by an older brother and had a lot of guilt and shame about the abuse, even after undergoing many types of therapy. Her review was only about her abuse.

> She was shown the sexual abuse. She relived it. The Supreme Entity, who facilitated this, lovingly said to her only one sentence, telepathically: "My child, it was *not* your fault!" That one sentence from that loving, nonjudgmental presence did what all those years of therapy couldn't do. It liberated her from her fear, liberated her from her guilt, liberated her from her shame, bathed her in unconditional love, and gave her back her self-esteem. Her healing was instantaneous! (Rommer, 2000, 187)

In reading probably thousands of NDEs, I have never come across one in which an NDEr admitted he was a former or active child abuser, saw the abuse or the consequences of his action during the life review, or lost the propensity to be an abuser. Alcoholics and drug users often lose the desire for the substance of their choice following their NDE. This missing behavior in a review appears conspicuous by its absence.

Rommer (2000) mentions a life review that more or less went backward in time. The individual incidents may have been going forward, but the woman's review included incidents that happened before those when she was young. The woman was named Kari. She was able to recall her life in the womb just before birth and her mother's apprehension of the upcoming birth.

5. Meeting Others

The life review may be the event most likely to change a person's way of living, and the meeting of deceased relatives is greatly responsible for the NDEr's belief in life after death. One man told Gallup and Proctor that during an NDE "conversations with deceased relatives are always constructive, never destructive" (p. 103). Some NDErs who see deceased relatives mention only the people, but most comment on the environment in which they meet them. This environment is frequently similar to those described in the subsection on scenic beauty, but there may only be *light* with no background. In some cases, NDErs may meet others while in the autoscopic NDE.

Moody explains that some people encountered "guardian spirits" or "spiritual helpers." One person reported that he sensed people around him but could not see them. Whenever he had a question, he received an answer. Deceased relatives are often instrumental in informing the NDEr that the return is necessary. Such examples will be addressed in the subsection on the decision to return. One man changed his priorities in life from acquiring money and improving his social position to focusing on family, friendships, and knowledge as a result of meeting deceased relatives during an NDE (Moody, 1988).

Ring came across cases in which the NDEr became aware of the spirits of deceased loved ones, primarily relatives. With the exception of one person whose impressions were very weak, Ring found that in his sample, an encounter with the presence is almost mutually exclusive to an encounter with deceased relatives. The NDEr is usually surprised but happy at the reunion. There are several examples of these meetings. One woman saw her two deceased aunts sitting on a rail in a meadow, and they started calling her. According to Ring, the woman who had the deepest experience saw her mother and father, as well as other people she had never seen before, but somehow she recognized them as familiar people. The mother spoke Hungarian, the language she had spoken when alive. The woman's father asked her if she had brought her violin. Her father could play the violin, but she could not.

These visions appear to be genuine excursions into a spiritual world that mortals enter after deciding to leave their physical body. The variations in scenery can be, and definitely are, affected by wishful thinking. An example of this, combined with seeing others, is reported by Grey. She recounts that a woman near death found herself in front of a prefab, a dwelling used for bombed-out victims in World War II; there were nasturtium on either side of the path. The NDEr said she always wanted a prefab and loved nasturtium. She went to the door and talked to her mother. She could see her uncle Alf, someone she had not cared for in life. She asked to enter but was told it was not her time to stay. She noticed that her mother and uncle were expecting someone, so she asked who. Her mother said that the NDEr's aunt Ethel was expected shortly. When the NDEr awoken in the hospital, she was told that her aunt Ethel had died unexpectedly.

During these visits with the deceased, any infirmities (e.g., missing limbs, blindness, or deafness) the deceased had while alive are gone and the deceased appears as he or she may have looked as a healthy young adult.

6. Borders and the Decision to Return

This subsection presents some of the more unique aspects of an NDE. In addition to having a deceased relative informing an NDEr that she must return, there are many variations on how a person returns to her physical body. Some people may not even be aware of any decision; their NDE simply ends. Most of the information presented here comes from people who experienced the transcendental NDE. If a person returns from an autoscopic phase, he may have less chance for a decision.

Many NDErs say that if they saw a border or limit, they understood that if they reached it or crossed over it, they would not be able to return to their physical body. The border might be a body of water or a shore, a mist, a door, or a fence across a field. The person may or may not have made an active decision not to cross the border. For instance, one man was in a beautiful green field and saw a fence across the field. As he walked toward the fence, a man on the other side appeared to be walking toward him. The NDEr wanted to reach the other man but was irresistibly drawn back. The other man also turned around and walked away.

The boundary separates the borderland, or transcendental realm, from the celestial realm, from which there is no return. Grey discusses five phenomena said to occur at the boundary: encountering a barrier, encountering the presence, meeting with deceased spirits, having a life review, and making a decision to return. Seventeen of her 32 respondents could actually describe their decision to return.

Several types of barriers were encountered by Grey's samples. One man saw that behind a door in a garden was a long corridor, and he was aware that he should not reach the end of the corridor. Another man saw a dark curtain that he thought would open to a new experience, but it never opened. One man did open a large, illuminated white door and started through it when there was a flash of *light* and he returned. This could have been the beginning of a transcendental experience rather than a barrier at the end.

Some people in Sabom's sample also perceived a definite border or limit. These included a stream, a barbed wire fence, and a mountaintop where the NDEr heard a voice say, "You can't go yet. You have unfinished business." One woman saw her deceased husband wading across a stream and coming toward her with outstretched arms. She felt that if he had reached her, he would have carried her across. She did not feel that it was her decision to return, but she returned nonetheless. Sabom said that some NDErs did not have a concluding event. Instead, in the middle of transcendental phase of the NDE, they just blacked out.

Rawlings reports on an NDE in which the man tried to get over a fence. The NDEr first went through a long corridor and then found himself in an area filled with a brilliant *light*. He was then in a meadow and saw his brother, walking arm in arm with him through the meadow. They reached a split rail fence. When the NDEr tried to get over the fence, an unknown force kept him from getting over it. He could not understand why he could not get over. He did not see anybody on the other side, and he did not comment on what happened to his brother.

The border may simply represent a mechanism of the decision process. Moody (1975) also describes reasons that NDErs give for the decision to return. Many would prefer to stay with the *being of light*, but one woman felt she must return to her husband and three children. Another person wanted to complete his or her college education. One person did not go into detail about the decision to return except to state that he thought he could do something good on earth. He credits this decision to the effective stopping of the bleeding that would have resulted in his death. Some people recalled consciously desiring to return, but when they thought of other people in their lives, the decision was made for them. This happened to two women with children and to one man who thought of his wife and her drinking problem. The latter NDEr reported that his wife had overcome her problem with his assistance upon his return. One woman felt she was pulled back by the love of her sister and her husband. Another woman reported to Moody that her elderly aunt had told her that she had been to the beauty of the other side several times when she stopped breathing but that her family's prayers kept calling her back. She asked them not to pray for her return. They stopped praying for her, and shortly thereafter she died. When praying for an elderly person, perhaps a person should pray that the Lord's will be done rather than praying outright for a continuance of the person's life.

All borders may not represent a transition to death of the physical body. One man found himself surrounded by a brilliant and calming white *light*. He was asked if he wanted to die. He replied that he did not know what death was. The white *light* said he would understand if he crossed a line. He crossed the invisible line and experienced the most wonderful feelings of peace, tranquility, and loss of worry. In other words, the first light was not the final "heaven" that a dying spirit reaches.

An example from Moody (1988) involved bargaining. When the *being of light* told the NDEr that it was time to die, she complained that she was too young. The being did not budge until she said, "But I'm young. I haven't danced enough yet." The being laughed heartily and permitted her to return to earth. Thirty years later, during a cardiac arrest, she again met the same being, who again said it was time to die. This time she argued that she had to raise her children. She was again allowed to return but was informed that next time she would have to remain.

Ring gives several examples of making a choice. One man had been in a motorcycle accident at the age of 18 and had a conversation with a voice (but he saw no *light*). He was given a choice to live or die but was told that if he chose to live, there would be some real pain. He did experience much pain during his year of recuperation. Another case with an interesting reason for returning is reported by Grey. This NDEr had a friend named Jerry, who was also a priest and had administered the last rites to him. The NDEr was very comfortable (on the other side), but Jerry's hand was extended through the tube (tunnel), and he insisted the NDEr take hold of it. The NDEr maintained that it was Jerry's insistence that brought him back.

Closely related to a decision to return is that many NDErs felt they still had a purpose to accomplish in their life. For example, a woman who gives birth but then nearly dies may simply be shown her child, after which she realizes that she must return to raise the child. However, a majority of NDErs are not informed of a specific purpose for their return. A few years after an NDE, a person may find himself in a situation in which his assistance is invaluable to another person. For example, Rommer (2000) found that 25% of the positive NDErs knew why they had come back, compared to 44% who experienced the distressing type of NDE. Of course, whether an NDEr remembers or forgets the reason for his return could depend upon the length of time after the NDE that he was interviewed. If interviewed within a few weeks, the NDEr may not know the purpose for his return. For example, an NDEr named David later found out why he was allowed to come back. His brother and sister-in-law died in a plane crash, and David and his wife raised their four children. Another man felt he had returned to care for his aging parents, but that was a number of years after his NDE. In the many anecdotes of NDEs in this chapter, I have placed a comment about the purpose for the NDEr's return.

7. Visions of Knowledge and Flash-Forwards

From speaking to NDErs and discovering the view of life they gained from their experience, Moody believes that acquiring knowledge is an important goal in life. In his second book, he delves deeper into this subject. His explanation of knowledge acquisition is derived from his philosophical training. He states that two Greek words can be translated into the word *knowledge*. When emphasizing knowledge, the NDErs do not mean the Greek word more properly translated as "technology" or "technique," such as one's "knowing" how to ride a bicycle, as that is not the type of knowledge discussed by the NDErs. Moody believes that the NDErs refer to factual and theoretical knowledge. However, technology can also imply theoretical knowledge about the laws of matter as it can knowledge of a technique. Moody cites one example in which the NDEr had the impression that learning is continuous and that it even continues after death.

Moody (1977) says that several people told him they had a vision of knowledge during their NDEs in which they knew everything about the past, present, and future. One of his respondents, a woman, designated this knowledge "the secret of the ages" and "the universal secrets." She said that she was told that if she returned to life she would have to forget the knowledge; that is, it would be erased from her memory. The communication of the information is by done by means of sights, sounds, and thoughts. Some compared the experience to having access to a library where they could immediately absorb anything they desired to know. The people who had these impressions did not feel that gaining knowledge in this earthly life was any less important even though a person would know it all later.

Rommer (2000) mentions that a man named Jarod went to what he called a universal library during his NDE. In the library, he could get any information on many topics depending on what he thought might be interesting, but there were no books. The building could change from transparent to translucent. There was also an entire city of *light.*

Ring (1982) does not report NDErs having any visions of knowledge like this. However, he does report that some people were able to see into the future. These future visions can take two forms. One is a personal flash-forward, in which an individual sees some future events in her life. These flash-forwards may occur in conjunction with a life review. One good example is a woman who was able to skip through boring parts of her life and then continue the review five years into the future, the time when she had two children. She did not have two children when she was interviewed by Ring. Ring discusses a young man who fell while attempting suicide and who was then sent back to life against his wishes. During his NDE, a voice mentioned his daughter, though he was not married. He could see the daughter in the arms of his current girlfriend, so he concluded that God must want him to marry her. At the time of the interview, shortly after the man's NDE, the couple had not married.

The cases above relate to flash-forwards that occurred during an NDE. Ring states that some people who had deep NDEs developed various psychic abilities after their NDE. Ring attempts to explain this by stating that perhaps the NDE is a spiritual experience that serves as a catalyst for spiritual awakening and development. One of the psychic abilities is the flash-forward. The second form of ability to see into the future regards not just the NDEr's personal life but also what Ring describes as prophetic visions about the planet. Unlike personal flash-forwards, which only the individual can verify, prophetic worldly visions can someday be verified. The short-term planetary forecast of NDErs was not very optimistic (this was in his 1982 book). Of Ring's sample, 96% of deep-NDE experiencers claimed that they were more in touch with an inner source of knowledge or wisdom than they had been before the NDE. Having this psychic ability develop as a result of an NDE is an aftereffect. I will discuss it further in the section of this chapter titled "Aftereffects."

8. Supernatural Rescues

In the one case of a supernatural rescue cited by Moody (1977), a man seemed on the verge of dying in an industrial accident when a voice guided him to his only escape route. In the addendum to this chapter, I discuss similar situations. The addendum consists of a review of one book, *The Third Man Factor: Surviving the Impossible* (Geiger, 2009).

Morse (1992) discusses guardian angels that seem to provide protection to people when they are in mortal danger. Guardian angels do not have to appear as winged creatures. For example, one four-year-old boy was falling from a tree when he saw a little girl floating in the air next to him. She told him to look up and not to move his neck. When he landed, his collarbone was broken, but the doctor said if his head had been turned in any other direction, his neck would have been broken.

In his book on children's NDEs, Morse (1990) relates the story of how David Young and his wife were armed with an arsenal of weapons, went into a school in Wyoming, and detonated a gasoline bomb that destroyed the school. Some children were injured, but none died, possibly because a number of the children reported that various "people of *light*" were leading them away from the blast area. Some children did not see anyone but heard voices directing them to the safe areas.

I. Rapid Healings Following NDEs

Grey (1985) reports several cases of people who, after returning from an NDE, were cured of the illness that caused them nearly to die. One man had leukemia and encountered a being in front of the *light*. This NDEr believed the *light* to be Christ, although the being did not match his idea of how Christ should look. The *light*-man said, "That's enough. It's done. It's gone." When the NDEr awoke, his leukemia was gone. After six years, it had not recurred. One woman reported that during her NDE four or five men in white coats stood around her and then appeared to perform "psychic" surgery on her. They said that they needed to adjust something and to reactivate something. One of the white-coated men stayed behind after the others had left. He put his hands on the woman's head. After she awoke, the doctor told her a gland spontaneously reactivated after it malfunctioned, putting her in great danger.

The case of Anita Moorjani's rapid healing from cancer is a non-Western example. Her book is titled *Dying to Be Me: My Journey from Cancer, to Near Death, to True Healing* (2012). Although ancestrally from India, she was born in Singapore and then moved to Hong Kong as a small child, where she currently resides. She is multilingual (Indian dialect, Chinese, English, French), having attended British schools in Hong Kong. She felt that most of her life she was pushed to conform to cultural and religious traditions of the Indian community, although she did refuse a marriage arranged by her parents. During her NDE, she realized she was suppressing her own intelligence and creativity in order to please others. She had not followed her own beautiful heart or spoken her own truth, and the fear of doing so had resulted in her developing cancer.

She was diagnosed with cancer (lymphoma, eventually stage 4B) in 2002 and "died" from the cancer in 2006. Although there may be brief, transient periods of recovery, a multiyear decline certainly indicates a shutdown of a cancer victim's entire body, in Anita Moorjani's case from malnourishment and organ failure typical of end-stage cancer. She was given only hours to live, yet after her NDE, she left the hospital in five weeks with no trace of cancer. The cancer was actually undetectable in a few days, but she had to undergo physical therapy and renourish her body in the hospital. Moorjani also had some lesions on her body that promptly healed without reconstructive surgery. Several doctors reported to her that they had never before encountered such a swift recovery.

Although I have placed the information in this section on rapid healing, many events during and surrounding Moorjani's NDE relate to other NDE information. When she entered the hospital, she was comatose. During her NDE, she met her deceased father, who informed her that she had a choice to continue on to the spiritual world or else return to life on earth. Either decision would be the right decision. She felt she had something to accomplish if she returned. She also saw a boundary, knowing that if she crossed it she could not return.

Her brother lived in India. Although she did not know it when she entered the hospital, he was flying to Hong Kong to be with her. During her NDE, she could see him in the plane, which would indicate that OBE travel can occur to a person in an unexpected location as well as to an expected place. Although in a coma, Moorjani was able to identify a doctor who came into her room to drain fluid from her lungs so she could breathe. This same doctor had told Moorjani's husband in a separate room that she had only hours to live, and Moorjani "heard" that conversation. She could also "see" her family's reaction to her death, but that would only happen if she chose death, so she was really observing a possible future sequence of events.

One comment she made about information received on the other side cannot be verified. When she entered the hospital the final time, the medical team took some of her blood and body fluids for examination. This was before her NDE began. She was informed during her NDE that if she chose to live, the test on those fluids would indicate that her organs had begun to function properly again. If she chose not to return, the test results would show total organ failure.

Observing a reaction to her death and having test results dependent on the future decision is similar to the concept promoted by quantum mechanics (QM). According to QM, in many systems there are two possible alternatives (probabilities) until an observation of the system is made. At that point, one probability becomes fact (100%) while the other, previous possibility has a 0% chance of happening. In Moorjani's circumstance, the final probability was dependent on her decision rather than an observation. QM in relation to the paranormal will be discussed later.

Another interesting reflection during Moorjani's NDE was how everything in her life was interwoven. As Moorjani recounts,

> I became aware that we're all connected. This was not only every person and living creature, but the interwoven unification felt as though it were expanding outward to include *everything* in the universe—every human, animal, plant, insect, mountain, sea, inanimate object, and the Cosmos. I realized that the entire universe is alive and infused with consciousness, encompassing all of life and nature. Everything belongs to an infinite Whole. I was intricately inseparably enmeshed with all of life. We're all facets of that unity—we're all One, and each of us has an effect on the collective Whole. (p. 70)

Later, I will review several other sources that continue with this theme of interweaving and connections.

Long and Perry (2010) discuss a case of rapid recovery from an advanced stage of Burkitt's lymphoma in a 13-year-old girl named Geralyn. She was not expected to survive, as she had numerous tumors in her spleen, liver, and intestines. She was sent to surgery to remove a tumor that was blocking the passage of food into her intestines. In this surgery, which removed two and a half feet of intestines, she had an NDE and felt that all the mysteries of the world were revealed to her. She also had an OBE and could see people outside the operating area. Later, she accurately described the medical procedures to the surgeons. She rose to be with what she referred to as a bright white cloud in which she felt love, safety, and warmth. Angels were attached to the cloud. A large, nonthreatening hand came toward her, and a voice stated that she had to go back, for there was work she still had to do. After waking up, she protested against receiving her one chemotherapy treatment because the tumors were gone. She was still living 33 years later.

Another example includes a New Zealand woman named Rene Turner, who incurred massive head injuries in an auto accident at age 35 (Cohen, 2006). She was not expected to survive, and her parents were told she would be "a vegetable" if she lived. Thus, no repair surgery was performed, and her parents were asked if she could be an organ donor. In her NDE, Rene first entered "an explosion of glorious light" (p. 79). She referred to the being she met as "the gatekeeper." She also met her deceased grandfather, who looked younger than when she had known him, and he said her grandmother would be joining him soon. This would happen even though the grandmother's terminal cancer had not even been diagnosed at the time. Rene did not feel judged during her life review, but she did feel some guilt. For instance, once as a child she had insulted her teacher, and she could see and hear her teacher crying from the hurt hours later when out of Rene's presence. When she went into a second coma, this one the result of meningitis, she was given less than 24 hours to live, but Cohen interviewed her 24 years later. She has never been able to determine what her "task" is for her life. This case was only a miracle of survival, as Rene had numerous medical difficulties in her life as a result of her traumatic brain injury. She did unsuccessfully attempt suicide in order to return "home" and be with her grandfather.

At age three, James Eldridge became ill, but it was three years before he was diagnosed with Hodgkin's lymphoma (Cohen, 2006). The doctors expected him to live for only a few more days when they found a softball-size tumor in his neck. He lost vision in one eye and was put into hospice care with no further medical intervention. James entered a coma and went to a dark place, where he found himself on a narrow ledge. He was afraid of falling into an abyss. He then saw a star in the distance, walked toward it, and—after going through rolling hills and grass—ended up inside the *light*. He then became the *light*. He saw no human spirits or spiritual beings. He was told he had to go back. He said later, "Nothing was explained to me because I already understand the reasons for everything" (p. 188).

James returned to his body to see his mother, who began crying. His cancer was in total remission, and the medical specialists called his recovery a miracle. James said, "All I know is that I went into a coma riddled with cancer and, when I came out five days later, it was gone" (p. 189). Having been in the *light* helped him survive the humiliation of being bullied for having only one eye. He has premonitory dreams, but usually not of significant things. He believes he can pick up on the emotions of others, and he believes we are all connected, "that they are me and I am them" (p. 191). He has a troubled stepbrother the same age who tried to commit suicide by hanging himself, but the rope broke. He told James that "he'd seen riders on flaming motorcycles coming to get him" (p. 192). James had an interesting perspective on his brother's distressing situation: "Wherever we go next, we take ourselves with us" (p. 192). It does appear that James's own NDE began as a distressing situation, which is unusual for children, before he went to the *light*.

Morse (1992) describes a case in which a disease caused an NDE, but the NDEr was also cured of an unrelated, but probably fatal, illness. A 35-year-old woman named Kathy was diagnosed as having cancer of the thyroid gland. The cancer metastasized to the point that she was given only six months to live. She developed viral pneumonia, and one day her breathing and heart stopped. After seeing a beautiful valley and feeling a *being of light* touch her, her whole body was filled with *light*. She was told she could not enter the wonderful valley. She recovered from pneumonia, and a few weeks later she realized her cancer had also disappeared.

Morse also provides a case of a vision that resulted in an unusual healing unrelated to an NDE. A woman had a difficult delivery of her child, and the baby boy began hemorrhaging, resulting in cerebral palsy and a seizure disorder. She stayed with the boy in the hospital for several months. Late one night, she reported that a *being of light* came into her room and told her that her son would be all right. She felt love being poured into her body from this being. The next day, she asked for another EEG test for the boy, and the results came back showing that he was now normal.

When she was a child, a woman named Loretta was cured of scarlet fever within several days of undergoing an NDE that involved an OBE, a tunnel, and love from a *light* permeating her. When she was looking at her own body from above it, her body appeared ivory/translucent (Morse, 1992).

While I agree that in many cases a person may not have survived without advanced medical care, Morse (1990) supplies an interesting case in which the medical team gave up but the NDEr survived. A 14-year-old boy named Ben with rheumatic fever went into cardiac arrest. He had an OBE and was viewing his body, which was linked to him by a silver cord attached to his foot. His pain was gone. While he watched the medical team frantically work on him, including injecting his heart with epinephrine, two *beings of light* stood at his side. They asked if he wanted to stay or to go with them, and he chose to stay. The *beings* left. The medical team gave up and pulled the sheet over Ben's face.

The *beings of light* reappeared and told Ben that he could return to his body. Back in his body, Ben threw the sheet off, pulled the needle from his chest, and shouted that he was alive.

Rommer provides a list of some illnesses cured after the NDE, although the speed of the people's recoveries is not specified. Rommer is a doctor and was able to view the medical records of these healings, which include legal blindness, pneumonia, and cancer. One patient named Rudie had kidney failure and end-stage liver failure reversed during his NDE, which began with a distressing episode (a topic to be discussed later). The kidney and liver failure was the result of AIDS (before antiretroviral therapy). Rudie was informed during his NDE by his former partner, then deceased, that he had to return to earth for a purpose. Although this former partner was emaciated when he died, he appeared healthy when speaking with Rudie. The partner also knew that Rudie had a grandson that was born after the partner died. Also, one NDEr whom Rommer interviewed was in a morgue when he came back to his body, and another person was at a funeral parlor. One NDEr I heard give a testimony reported that he was triaged after a military accident into the category of "slim chance of survival" and was not administered any medical assistance.

Another case of unusual healing during an NDE is Kacie (Rommer, 2000). Kacie was diagnosed with kidney disease and aplastic anemia, in which the bone marrow stops producing blood. Her red blood cell count was very low. She was in the hospital, but when she awoke after her NDE she was in the morgue with a name tag attached to her toe. During her complex NDE, she was told she could choose to live or die, but she feels she came back against her will. When she regained consciousness, her kidney disease and blood problem were gone. She believes that the imaginary playmate that she had as a child and also saw in her NDE is now her spiritual guide.

Jarod was healed of atrial fibrillation during an NDE. Rommer (2000, p. 151) said that Jarod had three NDEs, but he did not specify during which one the healing occurred. A man named Charles was healed of kidney problems and Crohn's disease during his NDE (Rommer, p. 160).

In her 2015 book *Miracles from Heaven* and the 2016 film of the same title, Christy Beam narrates the story of the miraculous healing from serious and painful digestive disorders of her nine-year-old daughter

Annabelle after Annabelle's NDE in 2011. The disorders were pseudo-obstruction motility disorder and antral hypomotility disorder, for which she was then taking ten medications daily. Annabelle's NDE came as a result of falling 30 feet into the hollow interior of a dead tree. It took rescuers several hours to remove her from the tree but there were only minor bumps and bruises from the fall, which considering she fell headfirst, the fall could have been fatal by itself. Annabelle visited a beautiful garden during her NDE. The family was religious and the family and their church prayed for her to heal, but their prayers were not answered until the NDE happened. Shortly after the NDE, Annabelle stopped taking all of her former medications and is now symptom-free from the previous life-threatening disorders.

In this section, I have emphasized healings that happened much more quickly than a normal healing and, in many cases of illness unrelated to the situation (e.g., an accident), that resulted in the NDE. Many NDErs survived accidents that left them with injuries from which they were expected to die.

J. Important Lessons about Life Learned during an NDE

While I have created this special section on life lessons learned during an NDE, many of the previous and later examples of NDEs include similar lessons. In some cases the lesson was significant for the respective NDEr, but the following examples have lessons that I believe are valuable for all people.

I have previously read about behaviors prior to an accident that enabled a person to survive death in order to have an NDE. John Owen Jones had a rather unusual cause for his NDE. He accidentally took an alcoholic drink containing GHB (known as the date rape drug) that was intended for a woman at a party while he was on vacation in Ibiza. GHB can cause respiratory failure and death. When he passed out later in the evening, he entered a white room with lots of mist. Apparently familiar with NDEs, he, when neither God nor a deceased relative showed up, figured he had to have a life review to proceed to the next level. He reported that he reviewed hundreds of his previous lives and noted how he died in nearly every one. He mostly remembered the violent deaths. In these deaths, he mostly felt forgiveness. In discussing his current life, he understood "that each person I came across was there to push me onto a different kind of path, that each stranger affected my life in some way ... [and] at any time, anyone can be a guide or a messenger in your life, even these strangers in the street" (Cohen, 2006, 214).

John went back to the white room. There he saw white glittery things he called angels and realized that he could go with the angels or return to his earthly friends. He screamed. His friends heard the scream. He had been unconscious only for a minute. He passed out again and was in the white room, especially reviewing the times in his current life when he could have died. In one of these scenarios, he saw himself nearly dying from a fall, but then he saw the possible scenario of his living in a wheelchair. He also relived being born and recalled how he couldn't breathe during his birth. He told this to his mother, and she froze when she remembered that a midwife had to stick a straw in his throat to clear his airway. During his NDE, he heard a voice with which he struck a deal; the deal was that he had to share the knowledge he had been given. His main message is twofold: each person who crosses your path can make a difference in your life, and there are no coincidences.

The following is an example of a rapid healing and an important lesson grasped while in the *light*. Not everyone who experiences the *light* is healed quickly, but Morse (1992) provides an example of a woman named Janet who had a basal cell carcinoma and had this experience without being near death. She was awakened from sleep two nights before surgery. A sphere of *light* appeared in front of her. She was filled with unconditional love, and the *light* went through her. She further describes it as follows:

> I asked that my cancer would be removed. I prayed actually. And the light said that what we think of his prayer is more like complaining and we are frequently begging to be punished for something that we are simply going to do it again in the future.

> He asked me to think of my own worst enemy and I did. Then he said to send all of my light to my worst enemy. I did and the sudden burst of light when out of me and returned as if it had been reflected back from a mirror. I became aware of every cell in my body. I could see every cell in my body.

It was the sound and sight of light coming from my being. I was crying, laughing, shaking, trying to hold still and trying to catch my breath. When I finally recovered, the being of light said, "Now you have prayed for the first time in your life." (Morse, 1992, 139)

Janet's carcinoma disappeared. Morse believes that the experience with the *light* produces the greatest changes, regardless of whether the person was near death or even if the *light* experience was very brief. "The trans-formative powers are in the light" (Morse, 1992, 163). Those who experienced the *light*, even if they were not near death, scored high on the Greyson NDE Validity Scale.

How life can change as a result of an attempted suicide. The lesson learned is illustrated by Beverly, who made her attempt at age seven because of her abusive home situation in a poor neighborhood. The NDE conveyed some interesting messages. She attempted suicide by running her sled into a concrete bench—an unusual method, but perhaps not for a child of seven. After she hit the bench, she left her body and saw that no one came to her aid. Then, what looked like a big umbrella without a handle enfolded her, and she was in a warm, loving, bright *light*. A voice in the *light* told her she had made a mistake and had to go back. When she argued that no one cared, the voice replied, "You're right. No one on this planet cares about you, including your parents. It is your job to care for yourself" (Morse, 1990, 159).

Beverly returned to her body. She had a lot of pain, including a broken neck, and she wanted to try to kill herself again. However, she was engulfed by the umbrella once more. She was first shown snow on a nearby tree and the same tree, this time with apples on it. Even at age seven, she was able to grasp the metaphor that she was temporarily in the winter of her life and that summer was ahead. She was willing to return to her body. She was in a coma for several months, and she still has some physical problems as a result of her injuries. "The experience immediately transformed her. After her coma, she spoke up more for her rights, becoming a self-advocate instead of the dispirited victim of child abuse" (Morse, 1990, 160). She eventually was happily married. She now has three children and wears an umbrella on a charm necklace.

In another suicide attempt, this one by an 11-year-old named James, James heard a voice in the *light* that was kind, but it was not sympathetic to his reason for wanting to kill himself. The voice told him he would have to stick around and see what he could do with his life. For years afterward, he thought he might be insane, but he still learned that he had to create his own possibilities. Although not necessarily feeling insane, some childhood experiencers, whether as a result of suicide or not, have had many difficulties in life, even after their NDE (Morse, 1992). Counseling with a psychologist familiar with NDEs may reduce some of the difficulties.

A woman I met through IANDS had an NDE as a result of a depression-induced suicide attempt. The message she received from the *light* was, "You are wasting your time thinking you are not loved." At the instant she heard that message, she felt an incredible influx of love from the *light*.

Members of the Church of Jesus Christ of Latter-day Saints believe in a premortal world. A number of Mormons have written books about NDEs. Betty Eadie, author of the popular book *Embraced by the Light*, is a Mormon, and her book reflects some NDE views exclusive to Mormons. Mormons believe that a soul exists before coming into a body and that this soul can make choices. However, this preexistence before the current life is not between reincarnate lives.

The Eternal Journey: How Near-Death Experiences Illuminate Our Earthly Lives (1997) was written by Craig Lundahl and Harold Widdison, both Mormons. They discuss an NDE in which a man named DeLynn reports that he made a decision in a premortal world. An "instructor" in that world explained that when coming to a physical life, a person can learn lessons slowly through certain experiences or learn the lessons very rapidly through pain and disease. DeLynn volunteered to come to this world with cystic fibrosis. As a result of this insight received during his NDE, he had the following to say:

> No longer did I consider myself a victim. Rather, I was a privileged participant, by choice, in an eternal plan. That plan, if I measure up to the potential of my choice, would allow me to advance in mortal life in the fastest way possible. True, I would not be able to control the inevitable slow deterioration of my mortal body, but I could control how I chose to handle

my illness emotionally and psychologically. The specific choice of cystic fibrosis was to help me learn dignity in suffering. My understanding in the eternal sense was complete—I know that I was a powerful, spiritual being that chose to have a short but marvelous, mortal existence. (p. 32)

For this example, I do not see how DeLynn could discern whether he had had a premortal spirit or whether he had been between lives. A believer in reincarnation would view the decision as a rapid elimination of any karmic debt.

K. NDEs in Children

NDEs in children create a dilemma. On the one hand, children are considered less culturally influenced, particularly if the NDE occurs before age seven. The parents are not likely to have educated their children in specific beliefs, religious or irreligious, especially about life after death. The child may describe an OBE without ever having heard the term. However, because children often fantasize or have imaginary playmates, noticing major changes in their behavior after the NDE is more difficult. A parent is unlikely to describe a five-year-old child as less materialistic after an NDE. However, by the time a person who had an NDE as a child reaches age twenty-five to thirty, there are definite characteristics he or she exhibits that are the result of the NDE.

The earliest writer in the field of children's NDEs is Melvin Morse, a pediatrician whose first encounter with a child NDEr occurred when he was working as a physician in an emergency department. He first wrote about this incident in a medical journal (Morse, 1983), but then he described it again in his first book, *Closer to the Light* (1990). A nine-year-old girl named Katie Merzlock (a pseudonym) drowned in a swimming pool and appeared profoundly comatose when she reached Morse in the emergency department. He did not expect her to survive because she had massive brain swelling, no gag reflex, fixed and dilated pupils, and an inability to breathe on her own. She was clinically dead for nineteen minutes. Her family prayed for her while Morse was doing his medical procedures. Within three days, she had a full recovery with no serious consequences from her trauma.

When Morse visited her on the third day, the girl noted that he was one of the doctors who had treated her when she was comatose. She also described the other doctor, indicating that she had had an OBE. Morse asked her what had happened, intending to find out how Katie ended up underwater. She, however, answered, "Do you mean when I visited the heavenly Father?" I give Morse credit for not disparaging her remark and for, instead, asking for more details. Katie described whom she met during her coma, including two boys named Andy and Mark who were "waiting to be born." In the original medical journal, the phrase used is "waiting to be reborn." Katie is a Mormon, and Mormons do not believe in reincarnation. Katie also described a woman named Elizabeth who accompanied her in a tunnel before going to the heavenly Father and Jesus. Several times, Katie asked to see Andy and Mark. She would be around 45 years old now, and I wonder if she ever met Andy and Mark here on earth. She also told Morse that heaven was fun. I have placed a number of children's NDE incidents by Morse (1990 and 1992) in appendix B, as I do not want to place too many individual narratives in the main text.

As part of his research, Morse (1990) interviewed 121 children (the control group) who had serious illnesses but had not nearly died. None of them had an NDE, although some were hypoxic (had low oxygen levels in the blood) or hypercarbic (high CO_2 levels) or had acid-based disturbances. Morse also reviewed various mind-altering medications that a control group of children were taking. None of those children described an experience that resembled an NDE, which verifies a conclusion made about adult NDErs, namely that medications do not cause NDEs. Morse concluded that a child had to be very close to death (usually involving cardiac arrest) in order to have an NDE. The child who experienced the NDE very likely would have died without medical intervention.

In this chapter, I will cite other cases in which a child apparently had an NDE even though he or she was not close to death. When Morse published his final paper on this project (1986), he did not claim that his study was a proof of life after death. Rather, Morse contends, "It isn't important for the medical establishment to accept near-death experiences as proof of a life beyond this one. It is important that they not dismiss them as deathbed fantasies or categorize them as bad dreams. They are real to the person who has them and should be used accordingly as a healing tool" (Morse, 1990, 91).

While most of Morse's NDE cases list a first name only, Morse (1992) does tell the story of Olaf Sunden, which is not a pseudonym. Olaf had his NDE when he was given too much ether in preparation for a tonsillectomy (around 1930). During his NDE, he "felt [he] had a total comprehension which made everything understandable" (p. 12). The *light* he experienced was bright orange. Prior to his NDE, he had been an average student, but the insight into the universe he received during his NDE (a "cosmic gift") enabled him to obtain hundreds of chemical patents as an adult. When I made an inquiry for his name on the Internet, I found some writings of his on the topic of time—space oscillation, which is in the realm of theoretical physics. Although I often describe NDEs as spiritual experiences, Olaf's NDE aftereffect demonstrates his desire to understand the physical world. A number of other NDErs developed the same desire.

1. The Light

Morse maintains that one aspect of the NDE that cannot be accounted for by neuroscience is the *light*, the key element of the NDE. The *light* does not have an anatomical basis. NDErs who discussed with Morse what the *light* represents mentioned terms such as *unconditional love, all-knowing, all-forgiving, peace, happiness,* and *joy.* One patient named Terry, after her encounter with the *light,* felt that she "could see how everything in the world fits together" (Morse, 1990, 117).

Morse (1990) questions where this *light* may be coming from. Is it inside the brain/body or outside it? He concludes that it may be outside of the body's area when he relates the story of an eight-year-old girl named Cher who fell from her father's fishing boat and was on the murky and sandy bottom twenty feet below the surface of Puget Sound. A friend on the boat dove down to rescue her. On the first three dives, he could not see anything. On the fourth dive, he saw her body because it was illuminated from within by a soft, bright *light.* Despite being underwater for twenty minutes, Cher survived. The Puget Sound is fairly cold. People can survive longer without oxygen if the core body temperature is lowered. Morse says the rescuer may have seen the same *light* that Cher saw during her NDE, but the NDE was not described. A few days later, the diver who rescued her dove down to see if anything was visible from natural light, and he concluded that no, it had to be a *light* generated by the girl.

Morse (1992) relates how one childhood NDEr was in the garden with intense colors. The *light* in the garden did not cast a shadow. The NDEr could also hear the sounds of flowers blooming. Such sensory confusion is referred to as *synesthesia*, which will be discussed later. In a number of other sources, this perception of a *light* that does not cast a shadow is common.

2. Transformation Study and Transformations

In his second book, *Transformed by the Light* (1992), Morse emphasizes changes in people's lives as a result of the NDE they had as a child, such as a reverence for life and the interconnections among all living things and even with the inanimate world. Many of the changes resulting from the NDE simply included a better perspective on life. Most of the people with major transformations encountered the *light*. Without describing particular NDE features, the following are a few one-line comments about what NDErs learned from their experiences. In some cases, I list the age at which the NDE occurred, but most answers are the result of a perspective on the NDEr's life many years later. Most are quotations, but some are paraphrases from Morse (1990), except as noted.

- Rick, age five. Life is precious, and we are all born with all the knowledge that we need to solve life's problems.
- Warren, age ten. Very little in life is worth getting upset about.
- Jim, age six. There is something greater out there. I have experienced it.
- Love your neighbor and cherish life.
- Clean up your own mess.
- Be the best you can be.
- Contribute to society.
- Be nice, kind, and loving.

- James, age nine (raised in poverty). Life is not to be played with. I want to better myself.
- Life is for living, and the *light* is for later (Morse, 1992).

Morse (1992) reports that nearly all of the people who had childhood NDEs had psychic experiences afterward, about four times as many as in the normal population. Many of these psychic experiences were rather simple, such as knowing who will be calling when the phone rings in a few minutes. Sometimes the information comes in dreams. Other psychic impressions are of people who were either just experiencing an injury (not near the NDEr) or were about to be injured. One woman took prescription drugs to prevent the unsolicited information from coming to her.

Although Morse (1992) believes that these anecdotal stories are not necessarily proof of life after death, he thinks the standards of proof are irrationally high. He states that medical advances are often based on less documented evidence that his studies have for life after death. He says that the standard is high because having proof of life after death would require many people to alter their worldview. I would describe this as rejecting the current materialistic paradigm or altering the prevailing reductionist viewpoint.

Some type of trauma often got the person into the medical situation that resulted in an NDE. But instead of labeling what NDErs experience after the NDE as posttraumatic stress disorder (PTSD), Morse (1992) refers to it as a *posttraumatic bliss syndrome*.

3. Very Early Childhood NDEs or Dreams of Them

Morse (1992) mentions two cases of children having NDEs before the age of one (at four months and nine months). These two NDErs gave some typical details of their NDE years later. He also remarks that one person claimed to have had an NDE prenatally. Morse did not list any details about that NDE. He also did not specify if he gave any of the numerous tests that indicate that a person had an NDE or mention the lifestyle changes that indicate the person had an NDE to those three individuals two infants and one prenatal child.

Although theoretically the following research does not prove an NDE is possible at as early an age as four months, Morse does quote from two books about birth and prebirth incidents that at least indicate comprehension of information prenatally or during birth. In psychologist David Chamberlain's book *Babies Remember Birth* (1998), the author discloses how he hypnotized people between the ages of nine and twenty-three, regressed them, and asked them to describe their birth and specific events during and immediately after birth. He separately asked these people's mothers the same questions. He found a very good correlation between the two descriptions and very few contradictions.

4. Cultural Similarities of NDEs

Although the studies Morse (1992) conducted on NDEs were done in the United States, he did discuss the studies of NDEs that Dr. Nsama Mumbwe conducted among fifteen subjects in Lusaka, Zambia. Although the core elements of the NDEs were similar to those in the United States, half of the participants thought that the NDE indicated they were bewitched or that it was a bad omen. In some cases, it was not the patients who thought they were bewitched, but their families who expressed that opinion.

L. Empathic, Shared, or Simultaneous Near-Death or Death Experiences

My title for this section has three modifier words to describe differing circumstances. While my modifier words are not perfect fits, these experiences do confirm NDE phenomena. Other possible nomenclature include the words *conjoined* and *mutual*. The following events may occur to the following people under various conditions, all of which involve one person's death:

- A healthy individual physically near a dying person, whether the latter person actually dies or not.
- A healthy person undergoing an NDE or a near-death-like experience who observes another dying person but does not go or cannot proceed to where the dying person departs
- Other situations, but involving a dying person, a tunnel, or *light-filled* destiny

For example, Sir Alister Hardy (1896–1985) was a prominent British scientist (a zoologist and marine biologist) and a fellow of the Royal Society who later in life began a study of the religious/spiritual nature of humans. He formed the Religious Experiences Research Centre in 1969 at Manchester College / Oxford University, where researchers collected people's descriptions of deep religious feelings. He published his material in 1979 under the title *The Spiritual Nature of Man: A Study of Contemporary Religious Experience*. He placed one such case under the topic of "sense of timelessness" in a chapter on the varieties of spiritual awareness. The case involves a woman holding the hand of her dying husband. She describes the experience as follows:

> I felt he [the woman's dying husband] might be aware of my presence although unconscious, and I took his hand and closed my eyes. Immediately my surroundings disappeared from my conscious mind and I was aware of two distinct things at once: reverence for the presence of God on my left side, powerful in its effect, and then I was swiftly being propelled into a vast current into space that is almost indescribable. It resembled the ecstasy of a beautiful symphony. It was out of this world of feeling. Love was its force. The speed of it was as though I were traveling a million miles a second. I felt this involved my husband's being as it did my own, and I was closer in love and spirit with him than ever in our actual lives. The energy of this vast stream of upward and outward spatial experience finally frightened me as I was aware that if I held onto my husband's hand too long I should be unable to return. I dropped it and opened my eyes to look for God. But he wasn't there. I looked at the officers in the room, and my son, and asked them if they had seen anything; they had

not. When I closed my eyes my son was in the act of putting the telephone back on the receiver: when I opened them his hand had just placed it there. (Hardy, 1979, 59)

It was not stated if the husband actually died at that moment, but I suspect he did. Hardy's study will be discussed further in chapter 11, on mystical experiences.

Carl Becker is an American philosopher who has lived and taught at a university in Japan for many years. He says the Japanese also have an interest in NDEs. At an NDE conference, Becker presented a film made about an NDE in Japan. A man who was injured in an accident perceived himself traveling rapidly toward a *light* with two other men. At one point, the man telling the story saw one of the other men slow down, so he decided to stop and assist him. The third person continued the journey toward the *light*. The storyteller then awoke in a hospital bed. The man he stopped to assist was alive in the bed next to him, as was the deceased body of the man who continued the journey toward the *light*.

Observing other spirits was discussed in great detail in the section on transcendental NDEs; however, this can also occur during the autoscopic phase of a shared NDE. Delacour (1974) describes an NDE that occurred to singer Serge Lama following an auto accident. In his separated body, Lama viewed the accident scene and saw, in ghostly silhouette, the woman who had been next to him in the automobile. He started to follow her, but she retreated. He was prevented from catching up to her by an invisible barrier he could not cross. He remained behind this mysterious barrier. The woman's form completely disappeared. He survived, but the woman and another person who had been in the auto did not. I classify this as an autoscopic experience since Lama could see the accident scene, but being held back (encountering a barrier) is more commonly associated with a transcendental experience. A similar example, which was reported by my local newspaper, *The State-Journal Register* in 1986, occurred in a hospital. A man suffered cardiac arrest and left his body. His separated body went into the hall and was joined by another spiritual body. The two of them walked into a tunnel to the hereafter. When they reached the point of no return, the original man's spirit turned back and the other spirit went on. Afterward, the man found that at the same time he had gone into cardiac arrest, another patient on the same floor died.

In 2010, Moody and Perry authored another book, this one about empathic NDEs. The title is *Glimpses of Eternity: Sharing a Loved One's Passage from This Life to the Next.* Some of the accounts contained therein are one that Moody obtained shortly after his original book, so it is clear that he had been collecting them for a number of years. His notoriety on an unusual subject was an asset, as most of the subjects would not have told their stories to a stranger. He heard a number of them when appearing as a speaker at a conference.

Moody and Perry list the various elements that may happen in a shared experience. These are as follows:

- Change of geometry (i.e., the shape of the room may change)
- Mystical light
- Music and musical sounds
- Out-of-body experience
- Coliving a life review
- Encountering unworldly or "heavenly" realms
- Mist at death
- Difficulty describing the experience to others; ineffability
- (Moody and Perry, 2010, 80–104)

One of Moody and Perry's examples came from a faculty member of a medical school, a Dr. Jamieson. (Assume that all people referred to by a single name have been given pseudonyms; in one example I do not cite, the authors used a first name and a surname. I know that person, so I assume that first and last names appearing together are not pseudonyms.) Her mother had gone into cardiac arrest. After administering CPR for about 30 minutes, the daughter realized that her mother was dead. Dr. Jamieson then felt herself lift out of her body. She then observed her own body and that of her mother. She could also see her mother in spirit form next to her. She related that the following occurred:

> I looked into the corner of the room and became aware of a breach in the universe that was pouring light like water coming from a broken pipe. Out of that light came people I had known for years, deceased friends of my mother. But there

were other people there as well, people I didn't recognize but I assume they were friends of my mother's whom I didn't know.

As Dr. Jamieson watched, her mother drifted off into the light. The last Dr. Jamieson saw of her mother, she said, was her having a very tender reunion with all of her friends. Then the tube closed down in an almost spiral fashion, like a camera lens, and the light was gone, she said. (Moody and Perry, 2010, 7)

Just as Dr. Jamieson observed some of her mother's friends whom she did not know, a woman named Susan witnessed scenes from her son's life as he was dying from cancer. Some of the scenes from his early childhood she recognized, but many places from later in his life when he was away from home were unfamiliar to her. She later visited some of those places she had seen in the shared vision / life review. She said she was never embarrassed by what she saw, so perhaps in a final life review a person is not shown scenes that serve as a learning tool (ones in which a person is embarrassed by his or her behavior), since the person can no longer apply the knowledge of how each of us affects other people in our interactions (Moody and Perry, 2010, 9–10).

One day a paramedic named Ted was called to the home of a man who committed suicide. Ted realized that the victim was a psychologist at the nearby hospital whose wife had recently left him. Ted perceived that the man was dead, but he observed the spirit of the deceased man, with regret on his face, looking at his own body. A neighbor came over and, when he saw the dead man, made a disparaging remark about him. Ted recalls the spirit's reaction: "The spirit seemed to shrink, as though shriveling from the hurt caused by the comment. ... It was as though the life was sucked out of him ... drained" (Moody and Perry, 2010, 28).

One of the more unusual cases found in Moody and Perry (2010, pp. 30–32) is that of a Canadian doctor named Gordon. He was treating a Mr. Parker for chronic obstructive pulmonary disorder at a hospital, but he let him go home for the Christmas holidays. A few days later Gordon saw Mr. Parker in the hallway of the hospital, and the latter seemed "lit up," with a clear *light* coming from him. Parker was looking at a gurney with a sheet covering a body. Gordon pulled the sheet back, and on the gurney was Parker's body. By thought transference, Mr. Parker insisted that the body was not his. Gordon could sense some other unseen presences around them. Suddenly, Mr. Parker disappeared into a golden *light*. Gordon did not tell his medical colleagues about the incident, but they often comment on how composed he appears around people who have died.

When people who are believers in life after death say they see *light* of something else unusual near a dying person, skeptics consider them to be fantasizing about what might be a minor observation. A doctor named Tom did not have much of a belief in life after death and thought that NDEs were dreamlike experiences. However, as his mother lay dying, the room filled with *light*, and he "saw this film or transparent envelope of light close up and lift off her body going upward and out of sight" (Moody and Perry, 2010, 24). For Tom, it turned what could have been be grief into a moment of joy. Now, when patients of his says he wouldn't believe what happened to them, he stops and listens.

Moody holds that, while not empirically verifiable, shared experiences provide better evidence of life after death than do NDEs because the skeptics cannot claim it is the physiology of a dying brain that causes the events of the shared experience. I discuss brain chemistry later in this chapter, in a section titled "Alternate Explanations."

Rommer (2000) describes an unusual form of an empathic experience. A woman named Kari, during her life review, underwent the earlier death of her first husband, who died from an accidental gunshot. She experienced him at first being mad at himself for letting the accident happen and then worrying about Kari and their daughter living without him. This phase was before he left his body; after he left his body, she viewed him having a warm and beautiful crossing over, similar to what NDErs describe.

Near-death-experience investigator P. M. H. Atwater (2007, p. 47) often contributes interesting perspectives and cases on NDEs. She wrote about the following case concerning shared experiences. She employs the term *surrogate* in this situation, since the experience involved the physical pain of the dying person. A woman named Barbara Ivanova witnessed a man stabbing a woman on a street in Moscow. She went over to assist and began saying, "Help me," words the victim was most likely nonverbally expressing. Barbara, who saw scenes she did not recognize, believes she had a partial life review of the victim. Barbara also had a pain in her solar plexus, the location where the victim was stabbed, and the pain lasted for several weeks.

Atwater (pp. 49–50) explains that there are often precursor signals that precede a full shared death experience, such as music, odor, a glow around the dying person, or a sense of an unseen presence. At the point where precursors appear, a healthy relative or friend can choose to participate in the event by doing the following:

- Consider your role as being that of a helper.
- Telepathically "tell" the dying individual that you are a helper if he or she cannot respond.
- Hold his or her hand, if possible.
- Reassure the individual that it's okay to "leave."
- Be in touch with your own feelings and inner promptings.
- "See" yourself "walking" the person into the light if it feels right to do so.
- Allow subjective imagery to arrange itself by itself.
- Withhold any tendency to force or control the situation or to go farther than the initial entry into the light.
- Offer a prayer or some form of positive upliftment.
- Share on whatever level feels right, and then let go and release. (Atwater, 2007, 50)

The healthy person may also perform guided visualization similar to an NDE, as follows:

- Pace your breathing with that of the dying individual. Should his or her breathing be erratic, calm things down with your own steady breaths.
- Talk softly, saying that the individual is now leaving his or her body and floating upward. Speak of how easy and effortless this is, how good to leave the heaviness and the pain of the physical body behind.
- Acknowledge the gathering of simple shapes and forms in the air, dark or light, as if something were coming together. The body

may still be seen down below, but the fascination now is with what seems to be forming in midair.

- Affirm the presence of a special light that is slowly growing brighter and brighter but does not hurt the eyes to see.
- Mention that any sudden sense of speed is okay, that it's all right to go faster and faster and to feel a wind brushing your face.
- Prepare the individual for an abrupt stop and an increase in light, and for the presence of strangely familiar but melodious music and sweet smells.
- Greet anyone who might appear, be it a loved one, an angel, a being of light, a religious figure, or a pet or other type of animal.
- Encourage engagement, dialogue, talking, or a question-and-answer session, to whatever degree feels right.
- Remain for a while, and then return as you came. Go back to earth and back to the individual's body.
- Linger with the feeling of being back, continuing to talk softly to the individual in a reassuring manner until he or she opens both eyes or when you sense that sleep (death) has come.
(Atwater, 2007, 50–51)

M. Distressing NDEs

1. Early Cases

This section involves a discussion of experiences that are different from the peacefulness and joyfulness of those NDEs previously discussed. In this section, distressing experiences will be considered. Grey (1985) defines two types: negative experiences and hell-like experiences. In some cases, the NDErs appeared to view confused spirits or observe a hell-like environment without participating in it themselves. Moody comments in his first book that he never uncovered an NDEr who had had a vision of hell.

Moody (1975) presents some of his information regarding distressing NDEs as answers to questions. One question concerns whether the NDEs of people who attempt suicide are any different from those of people who are in an accident or who suffer from illness spectrums. One man attempted suicide after the death of his wife. He said, "I went to an awful place. ... I immediately saw the mistake I had made. ... I wish I hadn't done it" (Moody, 1975/2001, 131). His wife was not there. Other respondents of Moody who experienced this unpleasant environment felt that they could have remained there a long time. They believed the unpleasant environment was the penalty for breaking the rules and not fulfilling a certain purpose in life. Moody also states that many NDErs' overall impression was that if a person leaves this life with conflicts, the conflicts will still be present when the individual becomes disembodied. In addition, if the person is unable to resolve the conflicts when disembodied, he will also view the unfortunate consequences of his actions.

Moody (1988) quotes an incident from the Evergreen Study (Lindley, Bryan, and Conley, 1981), in which a man "mistakenly" reached hell. The NDEr went "downstairs" and observed millions of miserable, hateful people asking for a drink of water (p. 21). Then someone informed the NDEr that he had to go back because he was not mean enough. Moody also reports on a case provided to him by Michael Grosso, a philosophy professor with an interest in NDEs. The NDEr described images of some horrific beings clutching and clawing at him. It was something like descending into the hell described in Dante's *Inferno*. He had a claustrophobic, hostile, nightmarish NDE, without the slightest positive experience (Moody, 1988, 118). The NDEr had been a ne'er-do-well, and a drug overdose precipitated the experience. His life was totally transformed afterward; especially noteworthy was his new sense of self-determination.

The man who actually began the controversy about distressing or hellish NDEs was Dr. Maurice Rawlings (1978). His book is titled *Beyond Death's Door*. Rawlings is a cardiologist who has resuscitated many patients. He does not provide as much systematic information as some other researchers do, so it is difficult for readers to evaluate his information. He does say that as many as half of the people who have NDEs may have distressing ones, but this is only his impression. No figures to substantiate that claim are presented in his book. Most of Rawlings' NDE reports are different from other reports in that they are accounts of people speaking while being resuscitated.

The first distressing NDE that Rawlings witnessed occurred in 1977. While resuscitating a man, Rawlings heard the man comment about being in hell and pleading to the resuscitation team not to let him die.

He said, "I am in hell," and had a terrified look on his face. Each time the doctor stopped his external heart massage, the man would report that he went back to hell. He asked the doctor to pray for him. Two days later Rawlings went to see the patient; the patient could not remember any hell. Rawlings met several other forgetful distressed NDE patients.

Rawlings provides information on two types of distressing NDEs. One type is similar to Moody's cases, in which the person acts as observer. One case of this type concerns a man who fell into a lake and was underwater for at least 45 minutes. He found himself standing by a turbulent, rolling lake of blue fire and brimstone. He was not in the lake, and neither was anyone else. He saw two deceased people he had previously known. They both seem bewildered and confused. The NDEr commented that there was no escape except by divine intervention. He then saw the compassionate face of Jesus, who looked at him just before passing out of sight. Then the NDEr returned to his body. Rawlings read this case in a booklet published by the experiencer. The experiencer had been severely injured by the fall into the lake and was rapidly healed of his resulting injuries.

In the second type, the NDEr is involved. For example, a woman dying from a heart attack left her body and found herself in a gloomy room. Through the window she saw a giant with a grotesque face. The giant beckoned her to come outside, and she could not resist. Outside it was dark. She could hear people moaning, and she could feel creatures moving at her feet. She began crying; the giant turned her loose; and she returned to life. Another person experienced his distressing impressions while in a tunnel or cave. He heard awful sounds and smelled a terrible odor. The workers in the darkness were only half human and talked in a language the NDEr did not understand. Another case involved a tunnel lined with fire, its lower half opening into a second fiery world of horror. The NDEr saw some of his old friends, who exhibited blank stares of apathy; they were going nowhere and carrying useless loads. They did not stop for fear of "the main drivers," who were beyond description.

In the previously reported first incident of Rawlings, of the man standing by the blue lake, the man later went on to have a positive experience with both autoscopic and transcendental phases. This NDE occurred during the same resuscitation as the distressing one. The patient remembered seeing the resuscitation team working on his physical body.

He then went to a gorge with beautiful colors, lush vegetation, and brilliant illumination. He saw his mother and other deceased relatives. His mother had died when he was 15 months old. He had never seen her photograph, yet he was able to pick her out of a group of family photographs.

Many researchers do not agree with Rawlings's reports of distressing NDEs, partly because the book is written from a "biased" fundamentalist Christian perspective. Since the time of the book's publication, distressing NDEs have been confirmed by numerous investigators, such as Margot Grey (1985). Her book and views are not religiously oriented. She discovered eight people with this type of experience, representing about 12% of her respondents.

Grey divides negative experiences into two categories, negative experiences and hell-like episodes. Negative experiences are usually characterized by extreme fear or panic. People report being lost and helpless, and there is often an intense feeling of loneliness during this period, coupled with a great sense of desolation. The environment is described as being dark and gloomy, or it can be barren and hostile. People sometimes report finding themselves on the brink of a pit or at the edge of an abyss, and they state that they needed to marshal all their inner resources to save themselves from plunging over the edge (p. 58).

Several such examples from Grey are as follows: During an operation, one man found himself in an unintelligible river of sound. He was afraid he would be overcome by the ever-growing mass of noise. He heard the voice of his sister, and then he heard a quiet, unemotional voice say to him, "Not until the end." Another case raises the possibility of the physical environment's having an effect on the nature of the NDE. One woman was overcome by heat from cookers in an institutional kitchen, and thus she was probably not near physical death. She went outside but found herself in a place surrounded by a mist. There was a big pit with arms and hands coming out, trying to grab her. She was afraid they would pull her in. Another woman, while undergoing a hysterectomy, found herself looking down into a large pit full of swirling gray mist, hands and arms reaching out to grab her and pull her in.

Grey also reports one experience that was a combination of positive and negative aspects (not one experience following another). The woman found herself in an environment she did not like; she saw dazzling *light*.

There were some dark creatures around that tried to grab her, but she saw a *being of light* stop the dark figures.

Grey's examples of hell-like episodes include both heat and cold. One man who was contemplating suicide felt himself be enveloped in a blue flame, float out of his body, and then float down into a black vortex. He said the place reminded him of the place described in Dante's *Inferno*. The people seemed gray and dreary, and there was the smell of decay. The cold case involved a man who had a cardiac arrest. He felt himself descending into the earth with snarling voices all around, and he saw two beings. One he believed to be the Devil, who was trying to pull him in deeper. The other being was Jesus, but the man could not shout to Christ because of the screaming in the former's head. He rushed through a black void on his return.

Delacour (1974) describes the experience of ballerina Janine Charrat after a fire on the stage on which she was performing in 1961. Unlike many who forget negative experiences, Charrat can remember hers many years later, though hers was a combination negative–positive experience. She found herself in a strange and unfamiliar world with high flames that seemed to be coming out of the earth. The ground consisted of lavalike, boiling mud. She was determined to leave the place and said a few prayers. The flames appeared to decrease, and a woman in a silk dress appeared, identifying herself as Janine's deceased grandmother. The grandmother said, "In the land of the dead everything is written down—the past, the present, and the future too" (p. 19). Janine and her grandmother went to a big garden with a pond. The pond was like a mirror filled with *light*. Janine looked into the pond and first saw two nurses. These turned out to be the nurses who helped her learn to walk again. She looked again into the pond and saw herself being married to a man named Michel on a South Sea Island. Years later she married a man named Michel on a South Pacific island. This would be classified as a personal flash-forward. Delacour was writing before the term *NDE* was developed and well before the terms *distressing NDE* and *personal flash-forward* were in vogue.

Delacour also describes another distressing NDE that turned positive. This NDE happened to the late actor Curt Jurgens (1915–1982) during heart surgery. Jurgens was looking at a big glass cupola over the operating room. Twisted faces began staring down at him. A fiery rain began falling, and from the splattering around him came tongues of flame. Out of the tongues of fire he saw the black silhouette of a slender woman with a black veil and a lipless mouth. Her eyes were empty holes, but she was still staring at him. Curt asked her who she was, and she replied, "I am death." He thought, *I will not follow you,* and he concentrated on living. The phantom of his wife (living) appeared, and the death woman disappeared. Curt and his wife left the realm of shadows and approached the great *light*. The *light* became so bright he had to close his eyes.

Another good example of an NDE that began as a distressing event and then turned positive is the autobiographical NDE of Howard Storm, recounted in his 2000 book *My Descent into Death*. Storm was a professor of art at the University of Northern Kentucky when he had his NDE on a trip to Paris. In Paris, he was hospitalized for a perforated duodenum and was ill-attended, as it was the weekend. He was in severe pain when a number of voices, both male and female, young and old, asked him to follow them. He followed these creatures through a fog or mist with no walls. He could look back and see his body on the hospital bed and his wife sitting beside him. These beings kept encouraging him to follow but would not indicate where they were going. At some point, the scene became very dark, and this mob of unfeeling people began to insult and attack him. It felt like a game of cat and mouse as they were tearing off pieces of his flesh while laughing at, howling at, and tormenting him. The beings who attacked Storm had sharp nails and long teeth. "The all-consuming physical pain was secondary to the emotional pain. Their psychological cruelty to me was unbearable" (p. 25).

Although at the time he described himself as an atheist, Storm heard his own voice give the message to pray to God. He was raised in a churchgoing home, so he began reciting the Twenty-Third Psalm, the Lord's Prayer, the Pledge of Allegiance, and "God Bless America," with the words intermixed. The cruel and merciless beings became even angrier at him, but they began to back away from him and eventually retreated. With the tormented beings gone, Storm thought of the innocent childhood song with the lyrics "Jesus loves me." Then began a *light-filled* experience. Afterward, he became a pastor in the United Church of Christ, retiring 25 years later. Although Storm reveals that he had a change of heart when he proceeded from a distressing to a blissful experience, not everyone who goes from negative to positive seems to do so by conscious thought.

2. A Systematic Study

The first systematic study of distressing NDEs began with an article in *Psychiatry* by Greyson and Bush (1992) entitled "Distressing Near-Death Experiences." In this frequently cited article, the authors employ the term *distressing* in place of *negative* but may also use *frightening*. In their study, they found three distinct phenomenological accounts of distressing NDEs. The most common type is a terrifying loss of control, possibly during a normal NDE. For instance, a person may feel he is going too fast through the tunnel, not concentrating on the *light* at the end of the tunnel. Some of the NDErs may describe this as a frightening vortex. In the second type, the NDEr finds herself in an inescapable void, overcome with feelings of total isolation. It is possible that the void is also the tunnel, but the experiencer is alone and not moving, and again cannot see the *light*. Those who go from a distressing NDE to a positive one may eventually observe the *light* at the end of the tunnel. The third type, much less frequent, involves graphic hellish symbolism. This type of NDE is described as inverted, as a void, and as hell-like. From reading some cases, I speculate that one possibility for being frightened is that the individual is not completely disengaged from the physical body while involved in the trauma of the situation.

Zaleski (1987), in her book *Otherworld Journeys: Accounts of Near-Death Experience in Medieval and Modern Times*, points out that frightening NDEs were often used by the premodern church to convince people that hell was waiting for those who did not obey certain teachings. I do not have a problem with asserting that there can be distress after death, but it may depend on religious context. Certainly, one of the perennial NDE lessons is to do to your neighbor as you would do to yourself, a biblical proscription. But I would never say that church attendance is required to avoid distress after death.

There can be agreement between a biblical statement and some modern distressing NDE accounts involving duration. St. Peter comments in his second epistle (2 Peter 3:8) that a day with the Lord is like a thousand years, and perhaps the same applies to the distressing world.

A brief view by an NDEr of a hell-like environment could possibly seem like an eternity.

Bush summarizes the Greyson and Bush article and other, later research in chapter 4 of *The Handbook of Near-Death Experiences* (2009). Bush also discusses several other studies on distressing NDEs that found wide variations in percentages when it came to how many were having the distressing variety, some as high as 50% of total NDErs. As Bush notes, ignoring distressing experiences or diminishing their impact does not make their reality go away. After thinking about her own distressing NDE, combined with reviews of other NDEs, Bush developed three responses to a distressing NDE. The first response is a conversion or repentance, in which the person realizes that his or her previous behavior was improper and seeks to change it. The second response is to accept the reductionist explanation, determining that the experience has no meaning. The third response is to think about the existential implications of the distressing NDE. People who follow the last type may never lose their fear of death. They frequently seek counseling, often to no avail.

Bush (2009) has some conclusions about radiant and distressing NDEs and shows a comparison between the two types. I have edited her list.

- Radiant and distressing experiences belong to a family of NDEs of the deep psyche.
- Radiant NDEs represent the height of spiritual experience, whereas distressing NDEs represent the depth.
- Their similarities include a sense of movement, intense emotions, encounters with nonmaterial beings, life-changing messages, and ineffability.
- Post-NDE interpretations are more culturally derived than the content of the NDE itself.
- Distressing NDEs are underreported due to fear, shame, or social stigma.
- Distressing NDEs, like blissful ones, may occur in non-life-threatening situations.
- "There is no evidence that these experiences [distressing NDEs] are punishment for wrong beliefs are unacceptable or evil

behavior, nor does evidence show that [distressing] NDEs happen only to bad people" (p. 81).

There have been no systematic studies to prove or disprove the last point, but in general, distressing NDEs seem to happen to ordinary people. The people who report them are not normally drug addicts or drug dealers, child molesters or rapists, or violent criminals or terrorists. I do not know of any major studies of NDEs among prison inmates, but I have heard of some prisoners who had blissful NDEs that changed their lives to include remorse for the harm they have done to others.

3. Rommer's Study

In another systematic study, the late Barbara R. Rommer, MD, interviewed about 300 NDErs for her book *Blessing in Disguise: Another Side of the Near-Death Experience* (2000). She reported that 17.7% of her sample had distressing NDEs. She agreed with the three classifications of Greyson and Bush, but she added a fourth type, in which the NDEr felt that there was some judgment during his or her life review, although it may have been self-judgment. As already discussed, in positive NDEs, the NDErs did not perceive that their actions were judged as sinful or evil, but they were to understand the consequences of their actions, that is, the effect they had on others. Rommer goes into detail on the long-term benefits that result from distressing NDEs. Her term for them is "less than positive," or LTP. She has found that these LTP experiences usually result in the person's rerouting of the life journey that he or she had been on. Her view is that "it is the person who causes the LTP to happen, but he or she is also responsible for the type of imagery that occurs in the experience and the total content of it. In the LTP, we see what we need to see, hear what we need to hear, and feel what we need to feel in order to do those re-evaluations" (Rommer, 2000, xxii). These determinations may be made unconsciously long before the event occurs.

According to Rommer, what we need is more important than what we want when it comes to NDEs. Rommer also mentions that an LTP experience can occur if the person is unloving or fearful just prior to the event. Based on this, I speculate that physical circumstances may also be a factor. In earlier-cited cases, the surroundings of the woman who was working in a hot kitchen and the ballerina who was on the stage that caught fire may have affected their LTP NDEs. Rommer also considers the possibility that a person's being programmed to visualize fire and brimstone as an after-death image may result in the person's fulfillment of that expectation. Rommer's book was published by a New Age publisher. From her contacts in that field, I have heard that entities from the lower astral plane may also facilitate an LTP NDE.

In Rommer's study, 28% experienced the void, but the rate was much higher for self-induced circumstances, such as suicide, that resulted in the NDE. Rommer did not find any of this type (experiencing a void) progressing to the *light*, but some proceeded to the hellish experience. One of Rommer's subjects described a phase similar to Storm's (2000) account: one filled with emotional, psychological, and spiritual pain. Although this person felt that he was judged for the way he was leading his life (he had an NDE after overdosing on a drug), to me it did not seem to be a panoramic review of his life like those who have a blissful experience. It seemed to be more of a reminiscence. He changed his lifestyle afterward, but he does fear death and believes that human beings continue to live after death. Still, having a fear of death is not uncommon among LTP types. A person named Dennis, an alcoholic, was hospitalized during detoxification and had a ruptured appendix. His life review seemed more like a blissful one in that he was reviewing scenes of his life. However, it is also an LTP NDE because there did not seem to be a friendly guide beside him—and he judged that his life was a waste.

An example of a person who changed her life after experiencing this void type of distressing NDE is a lawyer named Keeley. She had her NDE while using cocaine. She was in total blackness, heard bad noises, and had a "negative" life review. Afterward, she stopped using cocaine. One man named Anthony, who attempted suicide, found himself in a void and heard a message that seems similar to one a person may hear in a blissful NDE, but it also included a warning: "If this is what you're going to do, this is where you're going to be" (Rommer, 2000, 44). Those who had their distressful NDEs during a failed suicide attempt afterward believe that suicide is not an option.

Rommer discusses the psychological concept that people have three main modes of processing information. These are visual, auditory, and kinesthetic (feeling). She believes that a distressing NDE often corresponds to the individual's method of processing information or its corresponding opposite. For example, a visual person may see misery or may experience darkness. An auditory person may hear threatening voices or be in a state of total silence.

The third type of LTP, hellish imagery, makes up the largest percentage of Rommer's group of LTP experiences. Some of these actually began as peaceful but then progressed to the third type (13.3%), but a higher percentage (46.7%) began as the third type and proceeded to the peaceful type. A smaller percentage (18%) of this type had self-induced their death, and many of those thought their action was responsible for the experience. It is interesting that some who were atheists before their experience felt that their nonbelief was the cause of that form of experience, so they changed their beliefs afterward. But others who were brought up in a fire-and-brimstone childhood religious atmosphere felt that their upbringing may have been responsible for that imagery, given that they were programmed to see what they had done as a sin. Although the individuals in each group may have attributed the experience to past belief, this connection is not solidly established.

Although I find it difficult to put a specific number or percent to it, and given that Rommer did not provide a figure, a number of LTP NDErs, for which she provided a summary of their NDEs, did return to attending religious services after their distressing encounter. This seemed especially true for those who had attempted suicide or were leading self-destructive lives. My impression is that after their NDE, they felt they were active participants in fulfilling their religion and not simply attending an obligatory service.

While being in a void or a dark space and being terrified is enough to change some people's lives around, Del had a different set of experiences. He died a number of times from drug overdoses. Finding himself in a dark space but still feeling peaceful, he kept on using drugs. Finally, he had an experience in which he became terrified upon seeing a tattooed man and a big dog after descending a downward spiral staircase. He also had a life review, but it was not peaceful. He then sought treatment for his drug addiction. While Del's fearful animal was a big dog, some others associated an animal with Satan; for one woman it was a gorilla.

Earlier, I mentioned that many atheists are not in the mind-set of atheism after having an LTP experience. This was true of Bess, but she believed she had had an NDE (no details remembered) when she flatlined as a baby. She feels that her NDE gave her some psychic abilities. It seems unusual for a person with psychic abilities (she claims to see auras and the "inner being" of other people) to be an atheist, as most atheists are believers in physicalism. However, after an LTP experience in her twenties, Bess stopped being an atheist. Some people wonder how there can be a God when there is so much evil in the world. Bess's concept is that God does not make it happen but lets it happen. He lets life take its course. She thinks her multiple illnesses made her stronger. Bess has had multiple physical problems since she was born, even after several of her NDEs, so healing does not occur to everyone who has an NDE.

Rommer holds that LTP experiencers undergo life changes similar to those of people who have blissful NDEs. These changes include trying to express unconditional love, not judging others, forgiving others and oneself, experiencing a decreased fear of death (blissful type only), having a thirst for knowledge and wisdom, having veneration for all life, and caring about people rather than objects or prestige. NDErs also frequently change their lifestyle so that the physical container will last longer.

While most people have a distinct change from a distressing to heavenly experience, a woman named Stephanie had a reverse direction. She went through a tunnel to a beautiful valley and then saw a beautiful woman coming toward her. As the woman got closer, her features began to change to resemble one animal and then to another, the final one being very scary before Stephanie returned to her body.

Rommer comments that when the NDEr felt judged by anyone but him- or herself, it was always in cases in which suicide was contemplated or attempted. However, it almost always resulted in a change in the person's life afterward. It also appears to me that in most cases in which there was self-judgment (which would be similar to those with heavenly NDEs), the scenes were only those in which the person behaved badly, whereas in heavenly NDEs, the person is also shown scenes in which he or she was amicable to other people. Perhaps in describing his or her life review to Rommer, the NDEr did not desire to go into sufficient details, but in the cases I read, the NDEr never mentioned the unusual effect of "being the other person" in social interactions. In heavenly NDEs, the NDEr may feel the harmful effects he or she has on the person with whom he or she is interacting. Rommer does mention the ripple effect that some actions do have. With that statement, she may have been commenting on life reviews in positive NDEs as well as in distressing ones. Also unusual, one person was shown what he should have done in certain circumstances, that is, the proper choice he should have made.

In the Rommer study, about 40% experienced a dramatic increase in psychic ability. The percent was about the same for a heavenly NDE and an LTP. Many NDErs also increase the amount of reading they do after an NDE. The percentage increase was 50% for LTPs and 32% for heavenly NDEs. The reading was often in the metaphysical area of study. Rommer says there was an increase in belief in reincarnation, especially for those who had something specific in their experience that confirmed the occurrence of reincarnation. "A few subjects have had reviews of apparent previous lifetimes and a few were shown apparent future lifetimes" (p. 11). No percent was provided. Rommer could not determine if a "shorter" versus a "deeper" experience affects life changes the most, but truly psychically gifted people did have profound experiences with the *light*.

Rommer also mentions the electrical phenomenon of watches ceasing to operate around NDErs after their NDE. All of her examples were from people with positive NDEs. It would surprise me if this phenomenon happened only around LTP experiences, as I believe it is an encounter with a *light* (a transcendental experience) that makes NDErs electrically sensitive. It may happen if the person had a combined positive and LTP experience.

While Rommer almost always found positive changes in people who had LTP experiences, Atwater (1994) determined, "Of those who experienced unpleasant and/or hellish near-death scenarios, a little over 50% in my survey had the exact same aftereffects as a universal pattern; the others exhibited traits that range from numbness you find with people who are in a state of shock to avoidance and denial, confusion, and/or occasional bouts with fatigue and depression" (p. 123).

Atwater also found that "men were less willing than women to view an unpleasant and/or hell like scenario in a positive fashion and take steps to make constructive changes in their lives because of it" (p. 112).

4. Other Findings

Atwater (2007) has a good table comparing aspects of a blissful NDE and a distressing NDE. The table is presented below.

TABLE **5.1.** Comparison of Blissful NDEs and Distressing NDEs

Element	Considered Heaven-Like	Considered Hell-Like
Beings	Friendly and supportive	Lifeless or threatening
Environment	Beautiful and lovely	Barren or ugly
Voices	Conversations and dialogue	Threats, screams, indifference
Feelings	Total acceptance and love	Discomfort, danger, or dread
Sensations	Warmth, and a sense of having found one's true home	Cold (or of temperature extremes), and a sense of loneliness, separation

Although it may apply to any type of NDE (heavenly or distressing), it probably applies more to the distressing type when Atwater (1988) surmises that the response to the NDE is more important than the NDE itself. If an NDEr holds that the NDE happened solely on account of a chemical in the brain, he or she may not experience profound aftereffects. However, there are some children who do not even remember they had an NDE and still have major aftereffects.

Atwater (2007) reports that Judith Werner had what I would classify as an inverted type of distressing NDE, which is notable given the subject's young age. This happened during surgery for a staph infection when she was only nine days old. Judith observed white-clad zombies that she was afraid of. The voice she heard, referred to as the "Inner Stranger," sounded threatening and demanding. When she was old enough to be verbal, Judith tried to explain her experience to her parents and others, but they dismissed her story. It was not until she was twenty-eight that she had a positive NDE and the reason for her childhood experience was explained to her. Judith is highly intelligent, like many childhood NDErs.

Gracia Fay Ellwood performed an analysis of what she calls "painful NDEs" in her book *The Uttermost Deep: The Challenge of Near-Death Experiences* (2001). Other than a few personal communications, she did not interview NDErs, but she still contributes to the discussion of distressing NDEs.

I have previously discussed empathic NDEs. In these, a person not near death seems to undergo the death experience of a nearby dying person (this is similar to an NDE from which the dying person does not recover). What Rommer calls a life review involving judgment, Ellwood refers to as an empathic life overview (ELO). I have already discussed some life reviews that demonstrate how one individual's action may affect others, but here are some that Ellwood mentions. Although in these cases the NDErs felt they were the judge of their own behavior, the anguish they caused in others generated their own consternation and was, therefore, painful. For some of Ellwood's excerpts, I have gone back to original sources, but for others I am citing Ellwood. One such source is the popular best-selling autobiographical book *Embraced by the Light*, by Betty J. Eadie (1992). In Eadie's words:

> I not only reexperienced my own emotions at each moment, but also what others around me had felt. I experienced their thoughts and feelings about me. There were times when things became clear to me in a new way. "Yes," I would say to myself. "Oh, yes. Now I see. Well, who would have guessed? But of course, it makes sense." Then I saw the disappointment that I had caused others, and I cringed as their feelings of disappointment filled me, compounded by my own guilt. I understood all the suffering I had caused, and I felt it. I began to tremble. I saw how much grief my bad temper had caused, and I suffered this grief. I saw my selfishness, and my heart cried for relief. How could I be so uncaring?
>
> ...
>
> I was judging myself.
>
> ...
>
> I was shown the "ripple effect," as they described it. I saw how I had often wronged people and how they had often turned to others and committed a similar wrong. This chain continued from victim to victim, like a circle of dominoes, until it came back to the start—to me, the offender. The ripples when out, and they came back. I had offended far more people than I knew, and my pain multiplied and became unbearable.
>
> The Savior [Jesus] step toward me, full of concern and love. His spirit gave me strength, and he said that I was judging myself

too critically. "You're being too harsh on yourself," he said. Then he showed me the reverse side of the ripple effect. I saw myself perform an act of kindness, just a simple active unselfishness, and I saw the ripples go out again. The friend I had been kind to was kind in turn to one of her friends and the chain repeated itself. I saw love and happiness increase in others lives because of that one simple act on my part. I saw other happiness grow and affect their lives in positive ways, some significantly. My pain was replaced with joy. (Eadie, 1992, 112–14)

Atwater describes her life review as more of a reliving rather than a review. It also demonstrates the ripple effect.

For me, it was a total reliving of *every* thought I had ever thought, *every* word I had ever spoken, and *every* deed I had ever done; *plus* the effect of each thought, word, and deed on everyone and anyone who had ever come within my environment or sphere of influence whether I knew them or not (including unknown passersby on the street); *plus* the effect of each thought, word, and deed on everyone and anyone who had ever come within my environment... .

It was a reliving of the total gestalt of me as Phyllis, complete with all the consequences of ever having lived at all. No detail was left out. No slip of the time or slur was missed. No mistake nor accident went unaccounted for. If there is such a thing as hell, as far as I am concerned this was hell.

I had no idea, no idea at all, not even the slightest hint of an idea, that every thought, word, and deed was remembered, accounted for, and went out and had a life of its own once released; nor did I know that the energy of that life directly affected all it touched or came near. It's as if we live in some kind of vast sea or soup of each other's energy residue and thought waves, and we are each held responsible for our contribution and the quality of "ingredients" we add. (Atwater, 1988, 36–37)

Elwood (2001) discusses the ELO of a prisoner with a pseudonym of Starr Daily, who wrote a book titled *Release* in 1942. Needless to say, as a career criminal he had done harm to many people and had to relive their suffering in his ELO. Daily had multiple NDEs, including positive ones, and turned his life around as a result. He was befriended by George Ritchie, whose NDE is recounted in the section titled "A Unique Journey." Thus, it is possible to understand how a life review or an empathic life overview can be considered to be distressing to the NDEr.

Ellwood also mentions the case of an NDEr named Cathy Baker, who, during surgery, entered a tunnel with a strong headwind and first heard hideous laughter and moaning before she saw a vast pit with people who tried to grab her. Then, a benevolent woman urged her to go to the end of the tunnel without looking back. She then had a heavenly NDE. The headwind she encountered is rather unique for a tunnel experience.

Ellwood divides the hellish experiences into several categories: entity-centered tormenting beings, sexually charged gang violence by the beings, and visions of hell. The entity-centered case she provides actually comes from Greyson and Bush (1992) and involves an interesting outcome. The man who encountered these entities was attempting suicide by strangulation. From a position outside of his body, he saw his body hanging and demons trying to drag him down to hell. In his spirit body, he ran to the house to tell his wife, but he had to enter into her body in order for her to hear him. Able to understand what was happening, she grabbed a knife before running back to cut him down.

The gang violence case involved a battered wife who shot herself as a "cry for help." Her vision was of grotesque creatures shooting holes in her and putting excrement or vomit into the holes. She could hear a heavy creature (with a horrible stench) approaching her, and when she called out to God she was back alive. Although the specific details vary, this case is eerily similar to the previous description of Howard Storm.

Atwater (1994), in her book *Beyond the Light: What Isn't Being Said about Near-Death Experience*, notes that the word *hell* is actually Scandinavian (Norse mythology) and comes from Hel, the queen of the underworld. The word *Hades*, considered one of the underworlds of Greek mythology, actually is the name of the ruler of that domain. The lowest level of the underworld in Greek mythology, which is closer to our vision of the fiery pits of hell, is ruled by Tartarus.

N. Aftereffects of an NDE

1. Introduction

Although the aftereffects of an NDE are being discussed prior to the section on alternate interpretations, the findings of this section may have major implications for that section. For example, everyone dreams at night, but rarely do the dreams affect the way people lead their lives. If an NDE were just a dream (or a hallucination), it would not produce the profound effects seen in people's beliefs and in the way they lead their lives afterward. Those who say they better realize the importance of love and knowledge after an NDE have had their view of life changed even if actual implementation of their new view is difficult to measure. This section addresses attitude and perspective changes, as well as observable behavioral changes.

The changes in people's lives occur in several areas. One essential area is a person's belief system. Documenting changes in this realm is not always easy, because everyone has a belief system prior to his or her NDE. Therefore, an attempt must be made to measure changes. The most obvious question concerns whether an NDEr's view of life after death changed as a result of the experience. Closely correlated with this would be a change in the NDEr's fear of death.

Some aftereffects have also been discussed as part of the experience itself. Although some personal flash-forwards may have occurred during the NDE, some NDErs felt after the NDE that they had an ability to see future events, both personal and planetary. A specific example of a correct premonition after an NDE is supplied by Malz (1978) in a book about her own NDE. Of course, it cannot be proved that she would not have had the premonition without her previous NDE (transcendental type). During a storm she heard a sudden voice tell her to get out of one room. She and her daughter quickly went to a bedroom, and the room she had been in was totally destroyed by a tornado. Afterward, Malz said she was surprised at how calm she was at the loss of all her personal possessions. Another effect of her NDE was a loss of fear of high places.

2. Early Findings

Moody found major changes in people's lives as a result of their NDEs. He believes the experiences are genuine and not fabricated. Almost all NDErs have told him that they no longer fear death. However, they are not seeking death and they disavow suicide as a means to experience their NDE again. Persons who were not previously religiously involved also expressed that after their NDE, they believed in life after death. Some felt death was just a transition; one person compared it to a homecoming. NDErs felt that their lives had been broadened and deepened by the experience. One person emphasized that the NDE made her live in the present instead of worrying about the future. None, however, took a "holier than thou" attitude. Three people in Moody's group of experiencers felt they had developed psychic abilities, but the ability involved being able to intuit other people's feelings and moods. They were able to use this ability to help others.

One example of an extremely long and rewarding life following a conscious return from an NDE is provided by Brandt (1988). Brandt's article is about people who are a century old. A woman named Lila Hoover told Brandt that she had had an out-of-body experience:

> During the great influenza epidemic of 1918. I was burning up with fever and couldn't move or speak. Suddenly, I felt an extraordinary surge of energy, heard exquisitely beautiful music and felt my spirit begin to part from my body. I had never felt so blissfully free. But the thought of my husband and small son held me back. I believe I made the conscious choice to return to the world and continue my work. Since that day, I've had the feeling that nothing can really harm me and have lived completely without fear.

Moody (1988) reports that some NDErs "sense that everything in the universe is connected." Moody also emphasizes that all of the transformations that occurred in their lives after the NDE were positive and were accepted willingly, not as a result of their being told during the NDE that they had to change. The NDErs felt more responsible for the course of their lives and their actions. Little things in life are as important as the big decisions, many NDErs believe. Moody also states that psychiatrist Bruce Greyson determined that NDErs who had their NDE as a result of attempted suicide rarely attempted suicide again.

Sabom administered two tests to a group of NDErs and to a group of survivors of a near-death crisis. The two tests were the Templer Death Anxiety Scale and the Dickstein Death Concern Scale. NDErs exhibited lower scores on both metrics, at a rate not ascribable to chance (*p* less than 0.01 and 0.005). A *p* of 0.01 would be interpreted as meaning that the chances are less than 1 in 100 that the difference is due to chance. Sabom also asked both groups to classify their fear of death and their belief in an afterlife as a result of their near-death-crisis event. The results are shown in Table 5.1 below. The NDErs said that their reduced death anxiety was a result of their NDE.

TABLE 5.2. Fear of Death and Belief in Afterlife Changes Resulting from the Near-Death Experience

Fear of Death	With NDE (61 Subjects)	Without NDE (45 Subjects)
Increased	0	5
No Change	11	39 $p < .001$
Decreased	50	1 $p < .001$

Belief in Afterlife	With NDE (61 Subjects)	Without NDE (45 Subjects)
Increased	47	0 $p < .001$
No Change	14	45 $p < .001$
Decreased	0	0

Many believed their NDE represented a glimpse of the moment of final bodily death. Some described the NDE as a "peak" event that did more to shape their life goals and attitudes than did any prior experience. Sabom says that the religious views of people who had an NDE were commonly strengthened, but no basic changes in religious views occurred. No agnostics in his sample became believers. The changes in people's lives as a result of their NDEs, such as being more caring, were noticed by others. Moody also reports that an NDE researcher named Robert Sullivan, who specializes in combat NDEs, told Moody that he thought NDErs give off a special kind of energy that he could feel when around them.

Grey (1985) found that people who had NDEs changed in three primary ways. First, they found themselves more loving, compassionate, and tolerant toward others; second, they had a desire to attain more knowledge; and third, they had an urge to develop inherent gifts and talents to be used for the benefit of others. However, any given change does not occur to every NDEr. Grey presents two tables, which I have combined to show the percentage of NDErs who had various life and attitude changes. This is shown in table 5.2.

TABLE **5.3.** Life and Attitude Changes Resulting from the Near-Death Experience

	No. changed	(%)	No. unchanged	(%)
More positive attitude toward life	24	59	17	41
Life lived more fully	19	46	22	54
Sense of rebirth	14	34	27	66
Renewed sense of purpose and meaning	22	54	19	46
Enhanced sense of self-worth	16	39	25	61
More personal power	20	49	21	51
More disinterested	12	29	29	71
More loving and compassionate	23	56	18	44
Less attached to material possessions	13	32	28	68
Fewer expectations	12	29	29	71
Greater empathy	21	51	20	49
Greater understanding and discrimination	15	37	26	63
Decrease in fear of death	26	63	15	37
Increase in belief of life after death	31	76	10	24
Concept of heaven	14	34	27	66
Concept of hell	23	56	18	44
Belief in God	11	27	30	73
Concept of God	15	37	26	63

Source: Grey (1985)

Grey also discovered many people who developed paranormal abilities. Grey reports what NDErs told her and has not substantiated the claims. A number became clairvoyant, and others developed the ability to heal. One woman found herself to be in telepathic rapport with people. Another woman became able to see future events. When the ability manifested itself, she felt she was overtaken by a power or force greater than herself. One person's predictions came through automatic writing. For some, future events came only as part of the life review, which extended into the future and was not a lasting ability. Grey reports a number of people who developed the ability to heal others as a result of their NDE. Methods of healing include the laying on of hands or the sending of healing power from a distance. One NDEr stated that death, unlike many illnesses, is not necessarily contrary to God's will for humankind. He claimed he healed many people but that two people who were in great pain and who expected to live for weeks or months died within hours after he had laid hands on them. One NDEr found that he was not injured on several occasions when he might have been; for example, he put his hand and arm in boiling water and was not burned.

Ring found three major changes associated with NDEs. These were an increase in conviction of belief in life after death, the loss of a fear of death, and an increase in religiousness. These conclusions were based on statistical analyses of tests, not just subjective impressions. Ring asked the NDErs and nonexperiencers to rate their religious attitudes before and after their near-death situations. The scores of experiencers when compared to nonexperiencers indicated a significant increase in religiousness. Ring also asked his sample to evaluate whether their religious attitudes increased, decreased, or remained the same. Woman experiencers had a significant increase as compared to nonexperiencers, but the difference was not significant for men.

Although there was an increase in belief in God among experiencers as compared to nonexperiencers, the difference was not significant at a p less than 0.05. The test for belief in life after death was administered by asking the subject to make pre- and postexperience evaluations of their view on life after death. Their six choices were as follows: completely convinced, strongly convinced, tend to believe, not sure, tend to doubt, and no belief at all. The increase in belief was very significant, with a p of less than 0.001. Ring also asked his sample about their fear of death and whether it changed. Almost 80% of the experiencers had no fear, lost their fear, or saw their fear decreased. Some stated that they completely lost their fear of death. For nonexperiencers, changes occurred for only 29%. This difference is significant at p less than 0.005.

Noyes (1980) describes the changes in people's attitudes following exposure to life-threatening danger. The respondents were 138 people of the same group described by Noyes and Kletti (1977b). They identified five attitude changes resulting from their NDE and four more changes associated with a heightened awareness of death. These are grouped together.

1. A reduced fear of death
2. A sense of relative invulnerability
3. A feeling of special importance or destiny
4. A belief in having received the special favor of God or fate
5. A strengthened belief in continued existence
6. A sense of the preciousness of life
7. A feeling of urgency and a reevaluation of priorities
8. A less cautious approach to life
9. A more passive attitude toward uncontrollable events

Three of these changes seem to be related, though Noyes does not comment if the same people responded positively on all three or at least two. For instance, a feeling of destiny (commented on by 21%) relates to invulnerability, because those who feel a special destiny are more likely to feel invulnerable. Recall that more of Noyes's respondents were involved in accidents than were the respondents of other NDE researchers. These factors may also relate to a special favor from God in order for the NDEr to complete his or her destiny. This helped some people's self-esteem. Others (25%) experienced almost the opposite of special destiny in that they became aware that death could occur at any time. Though Noyes listed a strengthened belief in continued existence, this was only reported by 10% of those sampled. Noyes (1982) discusses these findings more completely, such as noting NDErs' describing themselves as experiencing their own death and rebirth. He believes this could have great therapeutic value if it could be applied.

In the previously cited transformation study by Morse (1992), the overall conclusions about people who had an NDE as a child are that these people have the following things:

- A decreased death anxiety
- An increase in psychic abilities
- A higher zest for living and
- A higher intelligence (opinion, no test methodology).

The childhood NDErs do the following:

- Eat more fruits and vegetables
- Take fewer medications
- Have fewer psychosomatic complaints
- Miss less time at work
- Spend more time in meditation and contemplation
- Perform more community and volunteer work
- Donate more to charities
- More likely to be employed in helping professions.

3. Unusual Aftereffects

The above findings were typical and fairly uniform until Atwater began writing on NDEs. As I stated earlier, she had three NDEs and was probably attempting to confirm that other NDErs were having some of the aftereffects that she had. She began describing some changes that others ha never mentioned. Since many of these findings have been confirmed, possibly the early researchers never thought to ask about other unusual changes in the post-NDE life, the NDErs being reluctant to broach the subject. Atwater provides some statistics within her sample group, but she rarely had a control group for comparison.

Atwater (2007) lists the positive and negative immediate reactions people have as a result of an NDE. Positive reactions include feeling ecstatic, thrilled, grateful, in awe, evangelistic (about God and love, not necessarily about religion), and humbled. Negative reactions include feeling anger at being revived, guilt over past behavior, disappointment, horror (if a frightening experience), dumbfounded (afraid to discuss the

NDE), and depressed. She states that in her large sample of NDErs, 21% claimed no discernible changes; 60% reported significant changes; and 19% stated they had radical changes in their lives. If possible, Atwater interviews spouses, siblings, children, or significant others in conjunction with her interview with an NDEr. In some cases where NDErs contended there were no noticeable life changes, the co-interviewee disputed this contention. The divorce rate is rather high (65% to 75%) for NDErs, possibly because the spouse loves the "old person" rather than the "new person." A later marriage may be more successful, as the new spouse admires the qualities in the "new person." Some NDErs describe their NDE as a death—rebirth event.

Atwater (2007) lists the characteristics found in NDErs under the terms *psychological* and *physiological*.

Psychological

Most Common (80–90%): loss of the fear of death; more spiritual/less religious; more generous and charitable; handles stress easier; philosophical; more open and accepting of the new and different; disregard for time and schedules; regards things as new even when they are not (boredom levels decrease); form expansive concepts of love while at the same time challenged to initiate and maintain satisfying relationships; become psychic/intuitive; know things (closer connection to Deity/God, prayerful); deal with bouts of depression; less competitive.

Quite Common (50–79%): displays of psychic phenomena; vivid dreams and visions; "inner child" issues exaggerate; convinced of life purpose/mission; rejection of previous limitations/norms; episodes of future knowing; more detached and objective (dissociation); "merge" easily (absorption); hunger for knowledge; difficulty communicating with language; can go through deep periods of depression and feelings of alienation from others; synchronicity commonplace; more or less sexual; less desire for possessions and money; service-oriented; healing ability; attract animals (good with plants); aware of invisible energy fields/auras; preference for open doors and windows/shades; drawn to crystals; laugh more; adults younger afterward/children more mature (wiser) afterward.

Physiological

Most Common (80–95%): more sensitive to light, especially sunlight and to sounds (tastes in music change); look younger/ act younger/more playful (can be the opposite with children); substantial changes in energy levels (can have energy surges); changes in thought processing (switch from sequential/selective thinking to clustered/abstracting, with an acceptance of ambiguity); insatiable curiosity; lower blood pressure; brighter skin and eyes; reversal of brain hemisphere dominance; heal quicker.

Quite Common (50–79%): reversal of body clock, electrical sensitivity, heightened intelligence, metabolic changes (doesn't take that long to process food, bowel movements can increase); assimilate substances into bloodstream quicker (takes less for full effect); loss of pharmaceutical tolerance (many turn to alternative/complementary healing measures— holistic); heightened response to taste/touch/texture/smell/ pressure; more creative and inventive; synesthesia (multiple sensing); increased allergies; preference for more vegetables, less meat (adults)/more meat, less vegetables (children); latent talents surface; display indications of changes in brain structure and function (changes in nervous and digestive systems, skin sensitivity). (Atwater, 2007, 101)

I will expand on some of the above. With regard to psychic phenomena, Atwater describes "future memory." When an event occurs in a person who previously had an NDE, he or she may recall the event as similar to a memory but see it as a view of the future. Atwater does not like Ring's term *personal flash-forward*, but I think that what she describes is similar. Atwater holds that these flash-forwards are not vague impressions that an event may occur, but actual specific scenes of the future.

Atwater (2007) lists some specific actions that people took after their NDE:

- Dan Rhema developed an unusual form of artistry.
- Donna DeSoto founded an organization called Sav-Baby to find new homes for helpless abandoned babies.
- Dannion Brinkley (author of *Saved by the Light*) started an organization called Compassion in Action to assist the dying.
- An Australian NDEr named Jan reported that people were surprised when she did not overreact when a doctor's mistake resulted in the death of her son or when a motorist killed her daughter.

4. Other Findings

Another example of a major change in life, not from Atwater, is from popular writer Oliver Sacks, MD. It comes from his book *Musicophilia: Tales of Music and the Brain* (2007). He begins his book with the interesting story of Dr. Tony Cicoria, an orthopedic surgeon in upstate New York, when he was struck by lightning through a pay phone in 1994. He first had an autoscopic NDE when a woman gave him CPR. He also saw his children, who were not with him. He was then surrounded by a blue *light*, reviewed his life events, and then returned to the pain from the burns to his face. He took several weeks off work as he was experiencing some memory problems. In two more weeks, his memory recovered, but he developed an insatiable desire to listen to piano music. Cicoria had a few piano lessons thirty years earlier as a child, but now he had a desire to play the piano. Just at that time, his child's piano teacher asked if she could store her piano in his house. He would wake up at four in the morning and play until he went to work.

Then he began to hear music in his head. It came in torrents. He had trouble writing it down, as he did not know how to notate music. He borrowed a phrase used by Mozart to describe where this music came from: "from heaven." Cicoria attended a camp for students and gifted amateur musicians. One of the instructors had a knack for finding a perfect piano for each client. Cicoria had just bought a new one, and the instructor said it was the perfect piano for him. Cicoria began composing and gave his own concert. Two of the titles he chose were "Lightning Sonata" and "Rhapsody." He also began to see auras around people's bodies, a subject that will be delved into in chapter 8.

Synesthesia is one of the more interesting occurrences following an NDE and is sometimes called *multiple sensing*. One of the more common forms is to see colors when the sound is heard, but the synesthesia can involve other senses. Atwater (2007) also lists "hearing" paintings, "smelling" sounds, and "tasting" sights. She cites research and a book by Richard Cytowic, MD, holding that synesthesia is a product of the limbic system in the brain. Atwater maintains that there are many other changes in brain structure and functions following an NDE.

I have already mentioned that a number of NDErs have electrical sensitivity, but perhaps it would be better to say that electronic equipment, such as microphones, watches, and computers, malfunction in the presence of some NDErs. It is the electrical equipment that is sensitive to the NDErs, but other NDErs sometimes have unusual feelings in the presence of lightning and storms. Morse (1992) found a number of NDErs who could not wear watches because the watches would stop running. In those who had not had an NDE, he listed the figure as 4%. Morse believes that an NDE permanently alters the electromagnetic force field around a person. He also maintains that the NDE changes our "'I am' ... the aspect of ourselves we consider to be unique" (Morse, 1992, 134).

Noyes et al.'s (2009) summary of the aftereffects in *The Handbook of Near-Death Experiences: Thirty Years of Investigation* provides a detailed list of various paranormal experiences that was first published in 1983 in a now defunct journal. The table has been modified by Noyes et al., and I have dropped the *p* value listed by them.

TABLE 5.4. Paranormal Experiences in Percent Reported by Sixty-Nine NDErs Prior to and After Their NDE

	Before NDE	After NDE
Psychic Experiences		
Waking extrasensory perception	24.6	55.1
Extrasensory perception "agency"	10.1	29.0
Extrasensory perception dreams	18.8	33.3
Psychokinesis	11.6	18.8

Psi-Related Experiences

Out-of-body experiences	11.6	43.5
Encounters with apparitions	13.0	44.9
Perception of auras	11.6	33.3
Communication with the dead	11.6	27.5
Memories of previous lives	14.5	29.0
Déjà vu	48.5	60.3

Psi-Conducive Altered States of Consciousness

Mystical experiences	23.2	59.4
Lucid dreams	25.0	55.4
Weekly dream recall	36.8	63.2
Weekly vivid dreams	26.5	48.5

Psi-Related Activities

Dream analysis	33.8	72.1
Meditation	21.7	50.0
Visits to psychics	7.2	25.0
Psychedelic drug use	17.6	20.9

Source: Noyes et al. (2009, 50)

Noyes et al. interpret these findings as follows: "The altered consciousness during an NDE sometimes remains or reoccurs afterward, either voluntarily or involuntarily" (p. 49). Some NDErs welcome these changes, but others try to suppress them. My opinion is that people from a fundamentalist religious background who feel that these new experiences are the work of the Devil are the most likely to suppress them.

Greyson has paraphrased a scientific paper with, "If you ignore everything paranormal about NDEs then it is easy to conclude that there is nothing paranormal about them." Another way of paraphrasing this statement is as follows: "If you ignore all that data that do not fit (into your preconceived notion), then the data that remain fit very well." Of course, the promoters of physicalism would claim that I have a preconceived notion about spirituality into which I fit my data, but I argue that information about the paranormal is valid evidence that is purposefully ignored by the reductionists. My new paradigm is able to account for this evidence.

5. Continuation of Meetings with Others

I have already discussed that as part of their transcendental NDEs, many people meet deceased relatives, deceased friends, and spiritual beings. Many NDErs contend that they continue to maintain contact with the spirits. I have previously mentioned some examples throughout this chapter. Noyes et al. (2009), in discussing the findings of Greyson and Liester (2004), state that up to 80% of NDErs hear "inner voices," or have nonpathological auditory hallucinations, after their NDEs, and about a half of them had that type of communication before their NDE. They welcome this contact and consider the voices to be sources of inspiration, guidance, and comfort. This is unlike schizophrenics, who are distressed by a majority of the voices they hear. Morse (1992) reports that about 12% of child NDErs who first encountered a *being of light* or a guardian angel during their NDE had contact with this *being* later in life. About 10% of NDErs see ghosts or apparitions after their NDE, but Morse does not have any data to compare to the incidence among a population of nonexperiencers.

Another person who encountered this type of a helper is a man named David, who had his NDE during a childhood bout of infectious hepatitis. A woman of light appeared. David feels she is still with him, although she is invisible. David is an author, and the woman of light appears during periods of stress and also assists him during difficult stages in his writing of stories. The style of writing during those periods is different, and sometimes he does not remember doing the writing. David feels he has more powerful imagery during these periods. David's wife can circle items in his manuscripts that are not his regular writing (Morse, 1992).

6. Other Features

Noyes et al. (2009) also discuss the finding of Greyson (1993) that after their NDE some NDErs had physical and mental changes that resembled a kundalini awakening. Kundalini is thought to be a force or energy that, when activated, brings on a spiritual awakening. This energy allegedly travels from the base of the spine to the top of the head. Yvonne Kason discusses her NDE and later kundalini experiences in her book *Farther*

Shores (1994) and in the later, revised version of that book. Mystical and kundalini experiences will be discussed further in chapter 11. Greyson (1993), as reported in Noyes et al. (2009), lists the following as typical phenomena of a kundalini experience that may occur after an NDE: "assuming strange positions, becoming locked into position, changes in breathing, spontaneous orgasmic sensations, ascending sensations, unexplained hot or cold sensations, internal sounds, intense positive emotions, watching oneself as if from a distance, and changes in the speed of thought" (p. 51).

Noyes et al. also cite a study by Ring and Rosing (1990) as part of the Omega project, concluding that NDErs had higher incidence of childhood trauma than a control group and thus exhibited higher values on measures of dissociation. Other researchers have not agreed with this finding. I think it is possible that Ring and Rosing are correct because those who have dissociated are more experienced at departing the physical body and thus, when traumatized by the events that precipitate an NDE, follow the accustomed path of dissociation. In the next chapter, I discuss dissociation in detail, especially with respect to childhood abuse. At least now, the *Diagnostic and Statistical Manual of Mental Disorders* has a section called "Religious and Spiritual Problems," and thus these categories are not necessarily considered disorders but something that can be addressed by a psychiatrist.

O. Discussing the NDE

In this section, two types of reactions to NDEs will be discussed. The first type is the skepticism that many people exhibited to the reports when the early NDErs revealed their experience. The second type is the reaction to Moody's first book.

Moody cites examples of many NDErs who, when they told their doctor, nurse, or minister about what had happened, were told they had been hallucinating or imagining the experiences. Parents were skeptical when their children told them what happened. When told by one person that she had hallucinated, the NDEr will rarely tell anyone else her story of being near death. (Hallucinations as a possible cause will be discussed in the section on alternative explanations.) Moody states that the people he interviewed had functional, well-balanced personalities.

When Moody told them that many people had similar experiences, they were glad to hear it, as they knew they were not going crazy. Some NDErs would not tell anyone because the experience was ineffable.

P. Demographic and Frequency Findings

In this section I will review some facts that are best expressed as statistics, demonstrating that NDE phenomena are consistent between demographic groups. Studies may be based on age differences, religious beliefs, or reasons for the near-death occurrence. Most of the information is from Ring, Sabom, and George Gallup.

Ring's Weighted Core Experience Index (WCEI) is a method to mathematically measure the depth of an NDE. Ring discovered an order of higher WCEI scores with illness, the next highest scores with accidents, and the lowest scores with suicide attempts. The difference was not significant if both sexes are grouped together, but it is significant if men and women are separated, because women have higher WCEI scores for illnesses. Men have opposite scores: suicide is the highest and illness is the lowest. The latter does seem surprising, because no suicide attempter reached stage IV or V (seeing the *light* or entering the *light*).

Ring then developed a numerical rating for how close a person was to death. He then correlated this score with the WCEI. The correlation was very significant for females: that is, the closer to death, the higher the WCEI. A high WCEI is more likely to occur if a person reaches stages IV and V.

Ring discovered there was no difference related to religious affiliation between those who had a core experience (WCEI score of 6 or greater) and nonexperiencers. In addition to religious affiliation, he asked his respondents about the strength of their religious convictions. A person could be classified as a member of a religious denomination and never attend services or follow the beliefs. In addition to religious beliefs, Ring inquired about belief in God, life after death, and belief in heaven. He also asked respondents to compare themselves before and after the time they were near death. There was no correlation found between the strength of religious conviction and the likelihood of an NDE.

Since Ring conducted his work after Moody's book had become popular, he inquired if the respondents had become familiar with NDEs by reading about them. He concluded that nonexperiencers were more likely to have had previous knowledge of NDEs than were experiencers (37% to 19%). Core experiencers, however, are more likely to acquire knowledge about the phenomenon after the experience. Prior knowledge does not increase the likelihood of an NDE. Ring also compared the WCEI to prior knowledge and found that the depth of the experience (i.e., the WCEI score) is also not affected by prior knowledge. Ring found that the life review occurred in 55% of his accident victims but only in 16% of respondents in the other two categories combined (illness and suicide attempts).

Sabom's conclusions were based on sample of 78 people who were near death. Of these, 33 (43%) had NDEs and 45 (57%) did not. Since some patients were near death more than once, he found 42 NDEs during 156 near-death-crisis events (27%). Almost his entire sample was made up of illness victims, so no comparisons could be made to other causes for being near death. There were no major differences between those who had an NDE and those who did not in age, sex, size of residential community, education level, occupation, religion, or frequency of church attendance. There were not enough minorities for a comparison of racial differences. A much higher percentage (60%) of the nonexperiencers had previously heard of NDEs than did those who had had the experience (12%). The NDErs were significantly more likely to have been unconscious for longer than a minute and were more likely to have been resuscitated. However, there was no significant difference in NDE elements as a result of differences in time or resuscitation method.

Gallup reached some rather extraordinary conclusions. He found that 15% of Americans have had a verge-of-death or temporary death experience (statistical table in Appendix).

Q. A Unique Journey

One of the most detailed NDE accounts is provided by the late George G. Ritchie (1923–2007), who underwent an NDE at a Texas army training base in 1943. After the war, Ritchie became a psychiatrist. The first NDE ever described to Raymond Moody was Ritchie's, and Moody dedicated his first book to Dr. Ritchie. Much of the information from Ritchie's book *Return from Tomorrow* (1978) is important to later concepts presented in my book, especially my conviction that the spirits of the dead can enter the living and the manner/circumstances in which such a thing happens. All of the information to follow is from that book.

Ritchie had been attending college and, after some basic training, planned to go to medical school on a special military program. Just before he was to report to medical school, he caught double lobar pneumonia and "died." During his death, he underwent an NDE unlike most others. What is unique about Ritchie's NDE is the combination of autoscopic and transcendental events. Actually, very little of his NDE was autoscopic. It was during the early part of this first phase of Ritchie's NDE that he found himself outside a restaurant in Vicksburg, Mississippi, a fact he was able to verify later. After Ritchie realized he did not have a body, he decided to return to the army camp. Unlike many NDErs who find themselves immediately in their bodies when thinking about it, Ritchie had difficulty locating his body. After his decision, he quickly returned to the army camp but was unsure in which of the two hundred similar barracks to search first. Eventually he found his body by identifying the ring on his finger.

At this point, the second phase of his NDE began. As he was examining his body, a being of light entered the room. This being, whom Ritchie identifies as Jesus, the Man of Light, or the presence, accompanied him on another journey. What is unique about this journey is that a being of light is normally encountered in the transcendental stage of the NDE, in which the scenes are celestial rather than earthly. The first half of Ritchie's journey with the being of light appeared to consist of earthly scenes. This earthly phase may be further subdivided into two subphases, one in which spirits of the dead interact with the living and the other in which there are only spirits. Both of these are extremely important for understanding intrusion and release (see chapter 10), that is, cohabitation in the same body with a living person and removal of these spirits. Finally, in the third phase, Ritchie left the earth plane to undergo a more traditional transcendental experience. The following narration begins as Ritchie finds his physical body.

Ritchie tried to pull back the sheet covering his body, but his attempt failed. He realized that his spirit body did not affect matter. Quite suddenly the room became much brighter. It occurred to him that if he had physical eyes he would have been blinded. Ritchie then realized the source of the brightness—"a Man made out of light" had entered the room. This thought, with much authority, came to him: "You are in the presence of the Son of God" (p. 49). Ritchie knew with certainty that "what emanated from this Presence was unconditional love" (p. 49). Then Ritchie saw, appearing as murals on a wall, every single episode of his life, beginning with his caesarean birth in which his mother had died.

He considered his boyhood days and becoming an Eagle Scout, but the presence reminded him that he was only glorifying himself. He thought about his desire to help people by becoming a doctor and realized that the occupation would enable him to afford an expensive car. Ritchie then fabricated the excuse that he had not accomplished anything worthwhile because he had not had the time. He then realized that death can come to anyone at any time and that a person is always responsible for his own life. He also realized that he was judging himself and that the condemnation he experienced was not coming from the glorious *being* beside him.

Ritchie and the *Man of Light* then began moving at tremendous speed, high above the earth, toward a pinprick of *light*, and then they descended to a large city beside a body of water. The two of them traveled through the city, where Ritchie often noticed people who were unaware of other people right beside them. One man was instructing another man, but the latter could not see or hear the former. Some assembly line workers were gathered around a coffee machine, and one begged another for a cigarette. After one lit a cigarette, the other greedily snatched at it yet was unable to grasp it. Ritchie then realized that the "people" who were being ignored were spirits of the deceased, the same as he. In another scene, he observed one woman following a man who was oblivious to her existence. She told him how to take care of himself because his wife was not doing a proper job of it. Ritchie concluded that the woman must have been the man's mother. Since the two appeared to be the same age, she had apparently been wrapped up in the affair of watching her son for many years. In another city, Ritchie observed a young man constantly apologizing to an older couple. After viewing another similar scene, Ritchie asked the presence why those people were sorry. He realized they were suicides chained to the consequences of their actions.

Ritchie noticed that the living people were surrounded by a faint, luminous glow, "like a second skin made out of pale, scarcely visible light" (p. 59). His own body did not have this glow. The *Man of Light* beside him then drew Ritchie to a bar and grill at a naval base. Spirit beings without an aureole surrounded the bar. Although the spirits could not be seen by the living, they could see each other and would often bicker over glasses they could not raise to their lips. Ritchie mentions the following:

> I thought I had seen heavy drinking at fraternity parties in Richmond. But the way civilians and servicemen at this bar were going at it beat everything. I watched one young sailor rise unsteadily from a stool, take two or three steps, and sag heavily to the floor. Two of his buddies stooped down and started dragging him away from the crush.

> But that was not what I was looking at. I was staring in amazement as the bright cocoon around the unconscious sailor simply opened up. It parted at the very crown of his head and began peeling away from his head, his shoulders. Instantly, quicker than I'd ever seen anyone move, one of the insubstantial beings who had been standing near him at the bar was on top of him. He had been hovering like a thirsty shadow at the sailor's side, greedily following every swallow the young man made. Now he seemed to spring at him like a beast of prey.

> In the next instant, to my utter mystification, the springing figure had vanished. It all happened even before the two men dragged their unconscious load from under the feet of those at the bar. One minute I'd distinctly seen two individuals; by the time they propped the sailor against the wall, there was only one.

> Twice more, as I stared, stupefied, the identical scene was repeated. A man passed out, a crack swiftly opened in the aureole round him, one of the non-solid people vanished as he hurled himself at that opening, almost as if he had scrambled inside the other man. (pp. 60–61)

Ritchie concluded that the aureole of light around the living was apparently a shield against these disembodied beings.

Ritchie surmised that the spirits lurking in the bar must have developed a dependence on alcohol that penetrated beyond the physical, even to their spiritual component, and that the loss of their bodies did not stop the craving. It appeared to Ritchie that this could this be a form of hell on earth. Ritchie wondered why the disembodied could not see the *Man of Light*, more brilliant than the noonday sun, beside him. Perhaps their attention was so focused on the physical world that they simply could not see Him.

Ritchie's journey then switched to an earthly plane where there were no living persons. Prior to this, the living and the dead coexisted. On a wide, flat plain, discarnate beings were engaged in war; they were the most frustrated, angry, miserable beings Ritchie had ever seen. They had no weapons but were fighting to the death with only bare hands, feet, and teeth. They hurled themselves at each other "in a frenzy of impotent rage" (p. 64). However, since they were already dead, they could not be killed. At times these discarnate beings also performed perverted sexual acts. Their thoughts were instantly apparent to those around them; such thoughts were usually an expression of their pride in possessing superior knowledge or abilities. The presence beside Ritchie had compassion for this group, and Ritchie perceived it was not His will that they were there.

Ritchie observed that there were no fences to impede their departure. Perhaps the only consolation for these discarnate beings was to exist with beings as loathsome as themselves or with those who, like them, had fled the *light* and chosen darkness. Over the entire plain hovered beings who appeared to minister to the bickering spirits, although the spirits were unaware of them. Ritchie believed that the *light beings* were angels and that they had been present in the previous scenes, only he had not noticed them. He concluded that three conditions can prevent a person from seeing Jesus at death: a physical appetite, an earthly concern, and absorption with self.

Ritchie, accompanied by the presence, then began traveling again and soon entered a more typical transcendental realm. The *light* itself became different, and he was aware of peace. Standing in a beautiful sunny park were large buildings, and inside them were people studying. Faces could not be seen nor age or sex determined, because all were wearing long, flowing, hooded cloaks. These "people" appeared absorbed in thought, preoccupied with a purpose beyond themselves. Some were looking over charts; others sat at consoles with flickering lights. In another building, music more complex than anything Ritchie had ever heard was being composed and performed. As he entered a vast library, it occurred to Ritchie that the important books of the universe were assembled there. After several more dazzling scenes, he asked the *Man of Light* beside him if this were heaven. He did not receive a direct answer but realized that on earth these people had grown and were continuing to grow.

Withdrawing from the immediate scene, Ritchie observed in the distance a bright, glowing city. Two bright figures approached Ritchie. Despite their incredible speed, Ritchie and Jesus moved away from them even faster. They arrived back at the army hospital. Ritchie observed a figure beneath a sheet, and he realized Jesus was informing him that he belonged in that body. After crying to Jesus not to leave him, he awakened in his body for an instant and then fell asleep. This was the end of Ritchie's NDE.

After his NDE, Ritchie described his difficulty in adjusting to the real world. Later at the war front, when others died, he wondered why he could not have died. After a while, however, he began to realize that he had been absorbed in himself and not in Jesus. Ritchie seemed to have developed one of the best perspectives on life and death when he surmised, "I believe that what we'll discover there [i.e., in the afterworld] depends on how well we get on with the business of living, here and now" (p. 122).

In a previous section, I had mentioned rapid healings following an NDE. This certainly applies to Ritchie's case. He had no pulse, no respiration, and no blood pressure; his weight had dropped from 178 pounds to 119 pounds; his temperature was 106.5°F; and he had been covered with a sheet as dead. A ward boy (a private) suggested to the doctor (an officer) that a shot of adrenaline be given directly to Ritchie's heart. The doctor accepted the suggestion and administered the adrenalin, and Ritchie's heart began pumping again. After Ritchie's recovery, and his brief and unsuccessful enrollment at medical school, he had to return to the same army base. A commanding officer described Ritchie's recovery as "the most amazing medical case I ever encountered ... virtual call from death and return to vigorous health has to be explained in terms of other than natural means" (p. 81).

R. Could Have Died

This section concerns the findings of a psychiatrist who studied people who were near or threatened with death. A frequent term for this is *fear-death experience* (FDE). Some of the people he interviewed fall within the traditional near-death situations previously described, but most are different. Many of the situations reported occurred during falls or accidents wherein the subjects believed they were about to die. However, in many cases they were not even injured, and some never lost consciousness or required hospitalization. A range of spiritual experiences are related to physical and psychological trauma. Fear of imminent death is a psychological trauma. The section on supernatural rescues earlier in this chapter could be discussed here, but this section mainly concerns the psychological aftereffects, while the earlier section concerned the unusual assistance the person received in order to survive.

Many people who undergo an FDE encounter phenomena similar to others whose physical bodies are close to death. Dr. Russell Noyes, with collaborators, is the major contributor to the area of FDEs. This description of his work appeared in *Omega, Journal of Thanatology*, and various other psychiatric journals from 1971 to 1982. Most of the articles were written or researched prior to Moody's 1975 book, and thus the term NDE is not used. Most of Noyes's research involved interviews with people who had had these experiences, but his early work involved analysis of reports by others. Perhaps Noyes could have received the recognition that Moody had if he had published a book for popular reading rather than only reporting in scientific journals. Noyes does not imply that these fear-death experiences may be indicative of an afterlife. That emphasis probably increased sales of Moody's book.

Noyes and Kletti (1972) present a translation of an article by Albert von St. Gallen Heim titled "Remarks on Fatal Falls," originally published in 1892 in the *Yearbook of the Swiss Alpine Club*. Heim was a geologist and mountain climber who almost died in a fall. He gathered information on similar incidents (potentially fatal falls). During his own accident, Heim experienced a life review ("my whole past life") as if seeing himself on a stage in a performance. Everything became transfigured as though by a heavenly *light*; he heard magnificent music; and he was very calm. All of this happened prior to his landing in the snow and losing consciousness. He suffered no major injuries.

Heim summarized his findings after speaking with other people in similar situations. According to Heim, there is no grief, no paralyzing fright (as can happen in lesser danger), no anxiety, and no trace of despair or pain during the fall. There is a calm seriousness, a profound acceptance, a dominant mental quickness, and a sense of surety. There is little confusion, and time is expanded. Many have life reviews and hear beautiful music. Some aspects are more difficult to explain or include as brief examples, but he does mention several people who had bones broken or a skull fractured and yet felt no pain.

Noyes's (1972) interpretation of the experience of dying has three parts: resistance, review, and transcendence. His initial explanation of resistance is typically the response of a person struggling to survive. However, according to Noyes, when the person surrenders, tranquility and calm replace the fear of dying. Noyes and Kletti (1976a) quote one person who reported that when he realized he could not rescue himself, indescribable calmness and serenity came to him. Noyes (1982) discusses death—rebirth experiences and how they bring changes in the individuals who have them. He mentions that people who are only involved in attempting to survive are less likely to report a reduced fear of death afterward. This attitude of surrender is also common in religious conversion, in alcoholism recovery programs such as Alcoholics Anonymous, and for the mystical-like experiences that may occur to people who are under the influence of LSD.

Noyes and Kletti (1976a and 1976b) began a separate set of investigations of FDEs by sampling a number of people who were involved in near-death or life-threatening situations. The psychiatric explanation they provide for the similarities to an NDE is based on depersonalization, a psychiatric term used to describe other problems. In Noyes and Kletti (1976a), they describe their research and findings, and in Noyes and Kletti (1976b) they give an interpretation.

Noyes and Kletti (1976a) had 85 people complete a questionnaire, and others were also interviewed. In total, they obtained 114 accounts of NDEs from 104 people. They selected their sample in a variety of ways.

For instance, 38 responded to an advertisement in a mountaineering journal. The circumstances responsible for the life-threatening situations, along with the number of people who experienced them, were as follows: falls, 47; drowning, 16; automobile accidents, 14; serious illnesses, 10; battlefield explosions, 6; cardiac arrests, 5; allergic reactions, 4; and miscellaneous accidents, 12. About two-thirds of the sample were men. The questionnaire asked the respondents if they had believed they were about to die. The results of their questionnaire are shown in table 5.3 (along with the results of a similar test reported in Noyes and Kletti [1977a].) Although the responses were similar, any given phenomenon was always more frequent in those who believed they were about to die.

Grouping together of answers provides some useful information, but in reading the examples Noyes and Kletti present, it is easier to make comparisons to NDEs reported by Moody, Ring, or Sabom. What is interesting is that in many cases there was no actual physical injury, or the injury was minor and the person did not lose consciousness. The experience happens during the few seconds when the person thinks his life could end. For instance, a race-car driver whose car was thrown thirty feet into the air had an autoscopic experience. From a position outside the car, he could see the car tumbling. He felt he was

TABLE **5.5.** Subjective Phenomena Experienced during Life-Threatening Danger

Subjective Phenomena or Effects	Percentage of Subjects					
	Noyes and Kletti, 1976a			Noyes and Kletti, 1977a		
	Yes*	No*	Total	Yes	No	Total
	N = 59	N = 26	N = 85	N = 59	N = 42	N = 101
Altered passage of time	80	65	75	78	63	72
Unusually vivid thoughts	71	62	68	65	55	61
Increased speed of thoughts	69	68	68	68	50	61
Sense of detachment	67	56	64	61	38	52
Feeling of unreality	67	54	63	81	60	72

Automatic movements	64	52	60	63	50	57
Lack of emotion	54	46	50	57	55	56
Detached from body	54	38	49	36	31	34
Sharper vision or hearing	49	38	46	34	37	35
Panoramic memory	47	12	36	42	12	30
Colors or visions	41	24	36	32	17	26
Controlled by external force	37	25	32	39	32	36
Objects small or far away	36	33	35	44	31	39
Vivid mental images	36	12	29	19	7	14
Voices, music, or sounds	25	14	23	24	15	20
Great understanding	43	24	37			
Sense of harmony or unity	39	24	35			
Unreality of world				29	32	30
Disbelief regarding incident				28	31	29
Thoughts blurred				16	7	12
Vision or hearing dull				14	19	16
Body parts changed in size or shape				17	17	17
* "Yes" is believed about to die; "No" is did not believe about to die						

floating. His vision was very clear, and he saw flashes of color. The car landed upright. Similarly, a woman whose car was about to hit an abutment felt very peaceful and had a life review of hundreds of her past experiences. These scenes were superimposed onto the scene of the ready-to-crash car. These two incidents show that an OBE and a life review can occur in a few seconds' time and that they are not dependent on actual injury to the body. Thus, they are not the product of a "dying brain." The subjective phenomena found by Noyes and Kletti closely resemble the findings of numerous other NDE researchers.

Depersonalization is considered a dissociative disorder, and its definition is discussed further in the next chapter, on dissociative identity disorder. In general, it implies that an event is not happening to the individual self. The person may think, *I cannot be dying. I am up here. That body down there [actually his or her own physical body] must be the person dying.* Some of the findings do fit into the symptoms of depersonalization. To some extent, though, Noyes and Kletti contradict their own theory that life-threatening phenomena are examples of depersonalization, as their data show vivid and increased speed of thoughts, sharper vision or hearing, and vivid mental images. These are almost exact opposite qualities of depersonalization. Noyes and Kletti do not believe the life review (what they call *panoramic memory*) to be an aspect of depersonalization; they consider it to be a separate process. Detachment is one of the symptoms of depersonalization, and Noyes and Kletti believe the person psychologically detaches him- or herself from his or her impending fate.

Noyes and Kletti (1976b) discuss various explanations for the phenomena shown in the previous table, reviewing how others have explained depersonalization or some particular aspect of the NDE. The four areas of explanation they cover are biological, psychological, spiritual, and rebirth. For example, under spiritual explanations, they state that two people found themselves in hell. One description was much different from any discussed under the subhead "Distressing NDEs." As one woman was coming out of anesthesia, she found herself in a brilliant white *light*. She saw an eye looking at her but recognized it as her own. The idea of an eye searching her life forever seemed to her like hell. This experience could be classified as an inverted NDE; that is, it becomes distressing when the brilliant *light's* normal message of peace and love is misinterpreted.

Noyes et al. (1977) compared the responses on a questionnaire from a group of accident victims to a those of a group of psychiatric patients. Both groups, each about a hundred in number, consisted of people who had consecutive admissions to a hospital either for injury in accidents or for psychiatric problems. Of the psychiatric patients, twenty-five had schizophrenic tendencies; twenty-five had depression; sixteen had neuroses; fourteen had personality disorders; and twenty fit into the miscellaneous/other category. Noyes et al. then compared the percentage of subjects in each group reporting specific phenomena similar to phenomena in Noyes and Kletti (1976a; see Table 5.5, p. 164). They used a chi-square analysis to determine if the difference was significant. For a series of factors on alertness, there was no significant difference. The accident victims showed increased alertness, while the psychiatric patients demonstrated intensified emotion and déjà vu (a sense of increased familiarity). In the category of depersonalization items, there was no significant difference. The psychiatric patients scored significantly higher in the categories of thoughts; visions; hearing or images blurred or dull; thoughts disconnected or slowed; and dreaminess. Noyes et al. (1977) conclude that depersonalization appears very similar in normal people who are exposed to danger and in psychiatric patients during the symptomatic periods of their illness. These similarities could be due to trauma experienced by both groups. Although both may have some similarities, overall there is a major difference between the two groups. This will become apparent after other forms of trauma are described in a later chapter of this book.

Noyes and Kletti (1977a) wrote about depersonalization in a group of 101 people, 62 of them men and 39 of them women. The results for this 1977 report were presented on the earlier table (5.3). Some examples from their report will be given here. Three people involved in vehicle accidents had autoscopic experiences. In all three cases, the autoscopic experiences began prior to the actual collision; that is, the person, from a position outside his or her vehicle, saw the vehicle collide (as in the doppelgänger phenomenon, a German word that translates as "one's double"). One man said he felt helpless, as though something or someone were in control. Several claimed that their observing self seemed to resign itself to its fate while another self maintained rescue efforts. The explanation of Noyes and Kletti is based on depersonalization, which "appears to be an adaptive mechanism that combines opposing reaction tendencies, the one serving to intensify alertness and the other to dampen potentially disorganizing emotion" (p. 382). They present a diagram from another researcher (Arlow, 1966) showing a split of the self into a participating and an observing self. This diagram is shown in table 5.6.

TABLE **5.6.** Splitting the Self

Participating Self		Observing Self
Thoughts, movements speeded	Time	Thoughts, movements slowed
Intensified emotions, fears	Emotion	Reduced or absent emotions; calm
Heightened perception, mental imagery	Sensation	Perception, mental imagery dulled
Increased control of movements, thoughts	Volition	Movements, thoughts automatic
Sense of increased familiarity (déjà vu)	Reality	Feeling of strangeness, unreality
Revival of memories (panoramic memory)	Memory	Loss of memory
Heightened awareness of body	Attachment	Detachment from body
Objects large, close at hand	Space	Objects small, far away

* Source: Arlow (1966) as referenced by Noyes and Kletti (1977a)

Although the above divisions do not necessarily correspond to expected actions according to my divisions into two spiritual aspects, they do show that humans can have different "selves" that view the world dissimilarly.

S. Suicide Attempts and NDEs

In the section called "A Unique Journey," I related how Ritchie observed a man who was apologizing to his family for committing suicide. Several other researchers have commented on suicide in relation to NDEs. In the section titled "Important Lessons," I recounted the story of a child who attempted suicide and what she learned from the *light* during her NDE. One NDEr told Morse (1992), "Suicide violates everything that I believe about the values and importance of human life. I can't condemn someone else's decision, but I know that it's not for me" (p. 65). Another childhood NDEr described suicide as a crime against nature. This same NDEr also reported that everyone's purpose is to serve the entire community of humankind. My opinion is that this does not preclude a person from having a singular purpose not related to all of humankind.

Morse (1992) also cites an unlisted study in which people who attempted suicide by jumping from the Golden Gate Bridge. After having an NDE, these people did not attempt suicide again. More than 25% of those who did not have an NDE did attempt suicide again. A similar result was found by psychiatrist Bruce Greyson, but it was unrelated to the Golden Gate Bridge.

In another suicide attempt, by an 11-year-old named James, the boy heard a voice in the *light* that was kind to him but not sympathetic to his reason for wanting to kill himself. The voice told James that he would have to stick around and see what he could do with his life. For years afterward, James thought he might be insane, but he learned that he had to create his own possibilities. Other childhood experiencers, whether as a result of suicide or not, have had many difficulties in their life (Morse, 1992). These difficulties may not have happened if the child had been to a therapist who was knowledgeable about NDEs.

A teenage girl attempted suicide using barbiturates and alcohol at a party. Her mother had committed suicide a few years earlier. The girl was a frequent user of alcohol and drugs before the attempted suicide. In her NDE, she met a nonsolid being to which she referred as her guardian angel. She felt love and peace, and it was communicated to her that her body was a gift and to be cared for, not killed. When she came back, she gave up drugs and alcohol. She now has an inner energy that never leaves her (Morse, 1992).

T. Alternate Explanations

This section is very significant. I interpret the NDE as a spiritual phenomenon in which a spirit body leaves the physical body and/or encounters the spiritual realm. If an alternate physical explanation seems more plausible, then my hypothesized spiritual rationale is not likely to be accepted. Ultimately, each individual has to be the judge of the evidence.

Drs. Moody, Sabom, and Ring each address issues of alternate explanations and the reasons that each of these seems to fall short of explaining the NDE. Explanations are usually divided into two main categories: psychological and physiological. Each of these can then be subdivided. For instance, physiological explanations may result from administered drugs or from naturally produced neurochemicals in the brain. Psychological explanations may be either a fabrication or an altered state of consciousness. Psychiatrist Bruce Greyson has provided good summaries of these alternate explanations, either alone or in conjunction with other writers.

I will address physiological explanations first, since they would appear to most closely relate to the reductionist thesis that anything that happens in the brain is caused by a chemical in the brain. However, promoters of psychological explanations are basing their concepts on an altered type of reductionism by maintaining that these NDE features are interpretations by the brain rather than by specific chemicals in the brain.

1. Physiological Explanations

a. Pharmacology

Many drugs can cause delusions and hallucinations. For example, Moody (1975) points out that one anesthetic is classified as a dissociative anesthesia because it seems to induce an out-of-body sensation, similar to that reportedly occurring in an NDE's autoscopic phase. Moody also describes the experience of a patient under the effects of nitrous oxide, another anesthetic. Some parts of the description are similar to an NDE, but in general this description is much less real. However, I have heard some NDErs state that their "real" NDE began when they were administered nitrous oxide.

Sabom (1982) also discusses the possibility of drugs causing or affecting NDEs, arguing that some people in his study were under the influence of morphine or a similar narcotic at the time of their near-death-crisis event. He then describes the hallucination of a person under sedation with opiates and evinces that the hallucination is much different from an NDE. Several persons who had NDEs reported that earlier in their lives they had hallucinated during one illness but could clearly distinguish between that encounter and their NDE. Osis and Haraldsson (1977) found that drugs are more likely to prevent visions near death rather than cause them. Sabom says that many NDEs have occurred without any medical hallucinating agents; thus, the drug-induction hypothesis is not valid in those situations.

Ring points out that most of his respondents who had attempted suicide used a combination of drugs and alcohol in an attempt to kill themselves. A lower percentage of NDEs occurred among people who had attempted suicide than among people with illnesses or people injured in accidents. More discussions of hallucinations will appear in the subsection on psychological explanations, because it appears that if NDEs are hallucinations, they are not caused by administered drugs.

b. Endorphin Release and Other Neurochemical Explanations

Carr (1982) discusses the possibility of endorphins and limbic lobe dysfunction as the cause of NDEs. Sabom similarly reviews the possibility that endorphins may be the cause of one aspect of NDEs. Endorphins are chemical substances released by the brain that reduce or eliminate pain. They have been discovered in the last 50 years. Absence of pain during an NDE is quite common, and severe pain may be what sometimes causes the spirit body to leave the physical body. The endorphins appear to attach themselves to the same chemical receptors that morphine attaches to. The problem with this explanation is that the effect of endorphins, when tested by injecting them into the cerebrospinal fluid of a person with intractable pain, lasts for 22 to 73 hours, while NDEs may last for only several minutes. The severe pain returns as soon as the NDEr returns to her physical body, often within seconds or minutes. In addition, endorphins tend to reduce pain, but there is still some feeling. NDErs usually have no feeling of pain. Third, endorphins usually induce somnolence or sleep, not the hyperalertness or clarity of vision and thought that NDErs report.

c. Other Chemical Explanations

Under his section on altered states of consciousness (ASC), Sabom discusses the issue of hypoxia and hypercarbia and why they are inadequate explanations for NDEs. Hypoxia is a lowered oxygen level in the brain. Hypercarbia is an elevated level of carbon dioxide (CO_2) in the brain. These conditions may occur at the same time. If the flow of oxygen-rich blood to the brain is cut off, then the oxygen in the brain is reduced and the CO_2 levels increase. Sabom refers to some studies that have been conducted on the effects of hypoxia and hypercarbia. The hypoxic condition resulted in mental laziness, slowness in reasoning, difficulty in concentrating and remembering, and irritability. These are almost the opposite of conditions during an NDE.

One way to induce hypoxia in the brain is with a flight simulator. As part of their training, pilots are placed in a spinning flight simulator to observe their reaction to g-forces, sometimes referred to as accelerator-induced hypoxia. When an airplane makes a sharp turn, the inertial forces make it difficult for the heart to pump blood to the brain; unconsciousness may result. Prior to unconsciousness, pilots report some impressions that are similar to NDEs, such as pleasurable sensations, tunnel vision, bright lights, fragmented visual images, floating, and perhaps a sense of leaving the body (Whinnery, 1997, in Greyson, Kelly, and Kelly 2010). However, they also report many symptoms of acceleration that do not occur in NDEs, such as "rhythmic jerking of the limbs, compromised memory for events just prior to the onset of unconsciousness, tingling in extremities and around the mouth, confusion and disorientation upon awakening, and paralysis" (p. 217). NDE researchers have noted that NDEs have occurred with normal blood gases and that studies with abnormal blood gas levels only infrequently will induce an NDE. Blood gas levels are unlikely to be abnormal during the a few brief seconds of a fear-death experience.

These abnormal blood gas levels will typically include some features of an NDE, but other features are rarely or never encountered. I would also opine, in conjunction with the spiritual concept I am presenting in this chapter and book, that even if all the features of an NDE did occur, they may simply represent impending death and the spirit body of the individual departing the physical body, comparable to what happens during trauma from an accident or a heart attack. It is not the altered blood gas level that directly causes the NDE-like features, but rather the fact that the spirit body is no longer in the physical body.

Another possibility is that it is not the level of oxygen in the blood that is important to NDE phenomena, but the amount of oxygen that reaches the neurons. When the heart stops beating, as in a heart attack or when blood pressure to the brain drops, the oxygen in the blood may not be able to reach the neurons in the brain. However, measuring oxygen levels in the neurons is very difficult. There are methods to measure oxygen activity in specific areas of the brain, for example, by measuring glucose activity using a positron emission tomography (PET) technique, but this complicated device is unlikely to be connected to the person during emergency resuscitation.

The reports Sabom cites on hypercarbia would not show a simultaneous low O_2 level, as the experimenters used a mixture of 30% CO_2 and 70% O_2 for their study. Some of the phenomena reported by the experimenters closely resembled an NDE (primarily the transcendental phase), including perception of a bright *light*, a sense of bodily detachment, revival of past memories, ineffability, telepathic communion with a religious presence, and a feeling of cosmic importance and ecstasy. Some phenomena were not similar to NDEs: perception of brightly colored complex geometric figures or patterns, animation of fantasized objects, compulsion to solve mathematical puzzles or enigmas, polyopic vision, and frightening perceptions. The hypercarbia explanation comes the closest to resembling an NDE, but it is not completely adequate. Grof and Halifax (1977) (as discussed by Ring) believe that oxygen deficiency induces an ASC that becomes an NDE. In chapter 1, I proposed that physiology and spirituality have been separated too much. If there is a spiritual body that resides in the physical body and that departs at true death, there has to be one of several physical measures triggering the departure. One may be hypercarbia. Another may be simply too much mental or physical trauma. The departure is gradual. If the physical situation is relieved, the spiritual body can return.

One other chemical whose effects come close to resembling the experiences during an NDE is ketamine. It can be used as an anesthetic, but in very few cases of NDEs was it actually used. Ketamine acts by occupying receptors on the neurons. It is classified as a psychoactive drug, and some of its side effects include patients' seeing a tunnel, entering a *light*, undergoing a life review, and communicating with spirits. However, ketamine also produces frightening and bizarre imagery. People who had those experiences would rather not repeat them, although some described them as real. Once again, I maintain that as an anesthetic, ketamine causes the spirit body to temporarily depart and allows phenomena similar to those that are part of an NDE to occur. Later in this book, I will be discussing mental illnesses. Ketamine has been found useful by some people to relieve their depression, though it is not yet approved for that use. However, the effects of any Ketamine-like drug may depend on dosage and individuated personal responses.

Another psychoactive/psychedelic drug that can produce effects similar to an NDE is dimethyltryptamine (DMT). DMT was investigated by psychiatrist Rick Strassman, and the results are presented in his book *DMT: The Spirit Molecule: A Doctor's Revolutionary Research into the Biology of Near-Death and Mystical Experiences* (2001). Strassman theorizes that DMT is released by the pineal gland when we die or nearly die. He speculates, "If outside administered DMT replicated features of the NDE, it would strengthen my hypothesis that endogenous DMT mediates naturally occurring NDEs" (p. 221). Because DMT is classified as psychoactive, it was very difficult for Strassman to obtain permission to perform his study and to acquire the necessary DMT.

In his studies, Strassman administered varying levels of the drug to volunteers. One of his requirements for volunteers was that they had to have previously used psychoactive drugs so that they would be somewhat familiar with what events unfold. Strassman summarizes the experience of one of his test subjects, a woman named Willow, under the influence of DMT as follows:

> While it's never a good idea to call anyone's experiences on DMT "classic," I think that it's not too far afield to use that term in describing Willow's near-death experiences. Her consciousness separated from her body, she moved rapidly through a tunnel, or tunnels, toward a warm, loving, all-knowing white light. Beings helped her on the way, and some even threatened to drag her down. Beautiful music accompanied her on the early stages of the journey. Time and space lost all meaning. She was tempted not to return, but realized she needed to share the incredible information she received with this world. There were spiritual and mystical overtones to her joining with and basking in the white light. (p. 226)

Strassman drew similarities between Willow's experiences and the *bardo* states discussed in *The Tibetan Book of the Dead (TBD)*. Other NDE researchers have made comparisons to *TBD*. I will not go into details about the descriptions in *TBD*, but monks who have spent many years in meditation may be able to mentally go to the edge of death and return, similar to those who have shared NDEs. Strassman did not investigate if these DMT-induced experiences resulted in some aftereffects akin to the aftereffects of a medical- or accident-related NDE.

One of the better attempts at explaining the chemical basis for NDEs and alleged contact with deceased people was made by UCLA psychologist Ronald K. Siegel. Interested in the field of psychopharmacology, he has published numerous scientific articles on the effects of hallucinogenic drugs. He endeavors to refute the concept of a life after death in a chapter of the book *Science and the Paranormal: Probing the Existence of the Supernatural* (1981), edited by Abell and Singer. This book is a collection of articles written by skeptics who attempt to debunk various supernatural topics such as biorhythms, ancient astronauts, UFOs, the Bermuda Triangle, and psychic healing. Most of those topics are unrelated to the subject matter of my book. One topic that may appear related is Kirlian photography, which some people claim is a photographic technique for observing the human aura. Although Siegel's chemical explanation is not outdated in itself, when he mentions NDEs his background information is dated in the 1970s and thus does not include significant findings since then.

While he does not do so in depth, Siegel traces the origins of belief in an afterlife ("postmortem survival") to as far back as some behaviors of Neanderthal and Cro-Magnon beings, such as burial rites. He also discusses some science fiction writers delving into the topic of life after death. He believes that some writers in the field of life after death, including Raymond Moody, employ a "quasi-scientific orientation" that "gives the appearance of valid scientific thought and testing" (p. 165). I assume he might say (but did not) that the science he uses is valid thought, but science cannot prove a negative, for instance, that unicorns do not exist. I would classify his reasoning as scientism.

Siegel's overall hypothesis is that he has encountered a great majority of the findings of NDE studies during his investigations into hallucinogenic drugs. In his chapter of the book, he directly compares statements made by NDErs to those made by individuals who are under the influence of hallucinogenic drugs, discerns no difference between the two, and thus concludes that NDEs are chemically induced and not an indication of postmortem survival after death of the physical body, which he refers to as an "abstraction." Among the items from Moody's prototypical NDEs that have correlates in drug-induced hallucinations are the following:

- A bright *light* in the center of the visual field
- A tunnel
- Cities and lights with many bright colors
- Pleasant surroundings such as meadows with flowers or various friendly animals
- Life reviews appearing as motion pictures (which he classifies as "retrieved memory images")
- The descriptions of the hallucinations are ineffable

Siegel believes drug-induced hallucinations can include transcendence of space and time; awe, wonder, and a sense of sacredness; a deeply felt positive mood, often accompanied by intense emotions of peace and tranquility; a feeling of insight into or illumination of some universal truth or knowledge (the noetic quality); and changed attitudes and beliefs that pass into an afterglow and remain as a vivid memory (p. 180).

He does not address how the body produces these phenomena when the NDEr has not taken any hallucinogenic drugs. He would probably claim that a brain near death ("massive cortical disinhibition and autonomic arousal" [p. 180]) can produce unspecified chemicals, such as the previously discussed DMT (dimethyltryptamine, the "spirit molecule"). In addition, he says that sensations of *light* can be produced by phosphenes being discharged by neurons in the eye. However, he does not address how the brain can process those images from the eye when the brain itself exhibits no electrical activity within 15 seconds of cardiac arrest.

Siegel also discusses states of excitation and arousal of the central nervous system. Stimuli that can trigger these include "psychedelic drugs, surgical anesthetics, fever, exhausting diseases, certain injuries and accidents, as well as by emotional and physiological processes involved in dying" (p. 181). In long-term situations (a type including very few NDEs), Siegel postulates a mechanism similar to Geiger's (2009) concept that boredom (minimal sensory input) can result in the mind's fantasizing. The reduced sensory input causes the individual to turn her attention inward to self-reflection, reminiscence, and thoughts of approaching death. There is even a term used by psychologists for preoccupation with death, *meditatio mortis*. I would argue that Siegel's two possible mechanisms are to a great extent contradictory. A state of excitation or arousal, possibly from drugs, appears to be the opposite of minimal sensory input and self-reflection.

In regard to visions near final death, Siegel claims that a person can hallucinate while otherwise appearing to be in a state of clear consciousness. Previous writers on the subjects of end-of-life experiences and after-death communication (two subjects to be discussed in chapter 7) maintain that these visions are not hallucinations but are insight into another reality to which ordinary consciousness does not have access. Grieving is one mechanism that allows access to this other reality. Even if a person can hallucinate a deceased family member, Siegel does not explain how an NDEr can communicate with someone whom he or she did not know was deceased or whom he or she never even knew, such as a child, without having seen a photograph of the grandfather, who sees a deceased grandfather who died years before the NDEr was born. While not providing data from drug-induced hallucinations, Siegel maintains that a vision of a deceased relative does not prove the relative is alive and well in the hereafter. He speculates that hallucinations are similar to waking dreams, often with elaborate embellishments of retrieved memory images. He also compares hallucinations to mirages. I would argue that psychedelic drugs can induce an altered state of consciousness (ASC) that enables a person to peer into the spirit world.

Siegel criticizes people who claim to see apparitions and ghosts, noting that one investigator into life after death states that "we must free ourselves from the tyranny of common sense" (p. 172). In other words, the investigator is not rational and his claim should be dismissed by scientists. In chapter 1, I discussed a viewpoint of LeShan (1984), that common sense only applies in the Realm of Sensory Experience, not in the Realm of Consciousness or Meaningful Behavior.

I mentioned that Siegel's information on NDEs is outdated. He accumulated his data before the term *negative NDEs* and *distressing NDEs* were developed. I am sure that someone who has studied descriptions given by people on hallucinatory drugs would have no difficulty finding numerous examples of "bad trips" that are very similar to distressing NDEs. This is especially true of the frightful/hellish type of NDE. I maintain that psychedelic drugs allow access to an extensive variety of ASC. Siegel did not address the significant life changes that occur as a result of an NDE. He does mention changes of attitude, but these most likely result in simply giving up a drug after a frightening reaction to it, not a complete change of lifestyle and a sense of the meaning or purpose of life gained from an NDE.

Although many scientists who attempt to debunk NDEs and other phenomena I have labeled paranormal describe themselves as skeptics, they actually are not that in light of the classical elucidation of the term by Greek philosophers. According to the Greeks, a person is a skeptic when he or she holds that there is not enough information for him or her to make an unambiguous decision. These alleged debunkers have already made their decision that only the material world exists, and no amount of evidence will alter that decision. A true skeptic is similar to an agnostic. Modern skeptics more closely parallel atheists. They have made up their mind, and there is nothing left to debate or discuss.

d. Other Physiological Explanations

Although chemicals are not believed to cause them, temporal lobe seizures are a possible explanation for NDEs. This explanation may be considered a neurological cause, but neurology is a part of physiology. Sabom (1982) reviews the phenomena that occur during artificially induced seizures. Though some aspects may be similar to NDEs, such as detachment, most aspects are very different. The environment brought on by a temporal lobe seizure is more distorted than NDErs report; the person having the seizure is more likely to feel fear instead of calm and peace; and the sufferer's memory of events is likely to be a single event instead of many, as in an NDE.

While I will not be going directly into the chemistry of the situation, others have proposed that temporal lobe epilepsy or electrical stimulation of the temporal lobes may cause effects similar to an NDE. However, Greyson, Kelly, and Kelly (2009) conclude, "The net result of electrical stimulation, as with epileptic seizures, is a poorly controlled, poorly characterized, and spatially widespread pattern of abnormal electrical activity" (p. 219).

A researcher named Michael Persinger claims that transcranial magnetic stimulation (TMS) of the brain may cause some of the features of an NDE. His device for the stimulation has been referred to as a "God helmet," for the alleged peace and OBE it occasionally induces. However, when Swedish researchers attempted to duplicate his study with a double-blind format, they were unable to achieve the same results. They believe that Persinger was suggesting to his subjects what may happen.

2. Psychological Explanations

a. Semiconscious State

Sabom comments that hearing is often the last sense to go before a person loses consciousness. He speculates that messages heard during a semiconscious state could be converted to visual descriptions. However, he notes that hypnotized patients could remember words but could not convert them to visions. Auditory descriptions rarely have as much detail as autoscopic ones. None of Sabom's NDErs could hear while apparently unconscious prior to the NDE; when they had their NDEs, they could not hear (others have heard during an autoscopic NDE). Sabom also notes that some NDErs have had their NDE while no one was present, and therefore there was no one to listen to.

b. Conscious or Subconscious Fabrication

Sabom recalls that when he first read *Life After Life* he thought the respondents were fabricating the stories to take advantage of Moody. Based on the fact that so many people were reluctant to discuss their NDEs with Sabom because of fear of ridicule (see the section titled "Discussing the NDE"), he does not think fabrication is likely. Sabom notes that many people's lives change for the better following an NDE. People who would fabricate a story are unlikely to change. Although it may appear that many different features occur during an NDE, there really are only a few features with individual variations, such as being in a *light* tunnel or a dark tunnel. Sabom says that when he originally began his study of NDEs, he expected a much wider variety of responses. Finally, Sabom was able to verify the accuracy of autoscopic descriptions, thus making it less likely that the NDEs were fabricated. As for subconscious fabrication, Sabom thinks it unlikely that someone would subconsciously fabricate two completely different stories, one transcendental and the other autoscopic, on two different occasions of being near death. Sabom feels that the NDE is not so much a protective response of the subconscious mind as it is a basic human experience.

c. Prior or Psychological Expectations and Wishful Thinking

Some have argued that an NDE is simply the result of prior expectations or wishful thinking. To address this issue, Sabom asked many of his NDErs if their experiences were what they expected. Most said no. If they had previously heard about NDEs, they were the ones who had disbelieved those stories. Moody says that nobody ever saw pearly gates (our culture often says that pearly gates are the entrance to heaven). Until our society became familiar with the use of the word *tunnel* in conjunction with NDEs, encountering a tunnel would not have been expected either. Descriptions of NDEs since Moody's book have not changed.

Ring comments that the similarity of experiences seems to preclude wishful thinking, as presumably people would have a wider variety of wishes. He also states that Dr. Elisabeth Kübler-Ross has argued that children would be expected to fantasize their parents, but they rarely do so unless their parents are deceased. Furthermore, Sabom and Ring both found that prior religious belief is not a factor in determining the likelihood of an NDE. It may, however, affect the interpretation of the NDE. Atheists and agnostics have had these experiences; this hardly conforms to their belief that death is simply an annihilation of life.

d. Depersonalization

Dr. Russell Noyes and his colleagues attribute the NDE (or closely related phenomena) to depersonalization. In the broadest sense, depersonalization means that in traumatic situations a person believes that what he senses is not really happening to him as an individual. It has already been pointed out that some phenomena appear to be the opposite of depersonalization. Many people who experienced depersonalization described it as unreal, while NDErs characterized their experience as real.

In discussing this explanation, Sabom notes that the explanation is based on the person's perceiving that he or she might die. For many of Noyes's respondents, that was true, for example, one who fell and thought he might die but was not even injured. The explanation is based on the person's being psychologically near death. Sabom states that the NDErs in his study were physically near death, but most were not psychologically near death. Their experience was also different according to Sabom. With the exception that much fewer of them had the transcendental NDE, the experiences are not much different. However, many people who are not psychologically near death have NDEs. Sabom also describes cases in which a person went into surgery fully expecting to recover. Sometime during surgery an unexpected complication occurred, and the patient came close to dying. At times it may not even take a complication. In either case, the person had an NDE. Since the complication occurred after being anesthetized, the person was not psychologically near death.

In an article about the history of dissociation, Carlson (1986) lists a table of the phenomena of dissociation recognized today. See table 5.7. In a later chapter, I will be show that this list in table 5.7 should be expanded.

TABLE 5.7. The Phenomena of Dissociation Recognized Today*

A. Varieties of Religious Dissociation
    1. Shamanism
    2. Asceticism and the limits of individual identity
    3. Possession
    4. Revivalism and conversion
    5. Glossolalia or speaking in tongues
    6. The spiritualistic medium
    7. Near-death experiences
    8. Crystal gazing, imagery, visions, and hallucinations

B. The Secular and Medical Dissociations
    1. Spontaneous trances: ecstasy, catalepsy, and somnambulism
    2. Induced trances: animal magnetism
    3. Amnesias
    4. Fugue states
    5. Multiple personality

C. The Dissociations of Everyday Life
1. Dreams and other sleep-associated phenomena
2. Reverie
3. Absentmindedness and inattention
4. Habitual actions
5. Automatisms, the planchette, and the Ouija board

---

* Source: Carlson (1986)

This chapter has not fully discussed how NDEs relate to other spiritual topics. Much of that discussion will be presented later in this book. NDEs are a form of dissociation, but a form that occurs in psychologically healthy people—and intruding spirits cannot take over the body while an NDE occurs. Since depersonalization is also a symptom of some dissociative disorders, both may be caused by trauma.

e. Dreams

While some may insist that NDErs experience just another dream, NDErs feel that their experience is too real to be a dream. Most people know their dreams are not real. Sabom points out that dreams are extremely variable in their content whereas NDEs are rather limited to the various aspects previously discussed. In addition, most people quickly forget their dreams, while some NDErs can vividly recall their NDE decades after it occurs.

Researchers Nelson et al. (2006) propose that NDEs may be caused by REM intrusion. REM, short for "rapid eye movement," is found during vivid dreams when the eyes are darting back and forth beneath closed eyelids. Nelson's group surveyed NDErs and a control group of medical center personnel and found that the NDE group had more symptoms of REM intrusion, thus predisposing them to NDE phenomena. These symptoms include visual and auditory hypnagogic and hypnopompic hallucinations, sleep paralysis, and cataplexy.

There are many reasons for dismissing this research. Sleep paralysis often brings fear, something infrequent in NDEs. Anesthetics often inhibit REM, and although NDEs may be less frequent when a person is anesthetized, they do occur. Also, the Nelson et al. control group had hypnagogic and hypnopompic hallucinations at a lower rate than in the general population, so that group may not have been a good choice. Finally, the study was conducted retrospectively, and it is possible and very likely that REM may increase as a result of an NDE.

After the original Nelson et al. research, Nelson (2011) followed up with a complete book on the subject titled, *The Spiritual Doorway in the Brain: A Neurologist's Search for the God Experience*. He developed the following table for contributing factors to the NDE.

TABLE 5.8. Contributions to NDEs Briefly Encapsulated

NDE Feature	Physiological Explanation
Tunnel	Low blood flow to the eye's retina
Light	Ambient light and REM visual activation
Appearing "dead"	REM paralysis
Out-of-body	Temporoparietal REM deactivation
Life review	Memories (hippocampus) from fight-or-flight
Bliss	Reward system
Narrative quality	REM dreaming and the limbic system

There is website called yourlogicalfallacyis.com that lists numerous logical fallacies people employ in making a case for their viewpoint. One of them is black-or-white in which a person lists only two or three possibilities, when in fact there are many more possibilities. Nelson asserts, without proof, that there are only three possible brain states: waking consciousness, REM sleep and non-REM sleep. Most neuroscientists would assert that there are many more possibilities, such as various trance states. With the limit Nelson has imposed, I believe his research is easily dismissed.

In chapter 9 on shamanism, there is discussion of how a shaman-in-training must learn to distinguish between ordinary dreams and spiritually significant dreams. Shamans consider dreams to be a door between the physical and spiritual worlds. Since NDEs are momentous spiritual experiences that occur during an OBE, NDEs may have dreamlike qualities but be much more than a dream.

f. Hallucinations

Hallucination is a very broad topic. In fact, many of the previous alternative explanations can be viewed as reasons for developing hallucinations, such as psychoactive drugs. If at during the time of an NDE a person sees a person, place, or object that has no physical reality, then the NDE is a hallucination. However, I maintain that transcendental NDEs are visions of a spiritual reality not physical reality. Autoscopic NDEs are visions of physical reality truly seen by the spirit body from a position outside the physical body.

The physiological explanation is based on some chemical substance, whether administered or natural, causing the person to see something that has no physical reality. In this subsection, hallucinations will be discussed in which no drugs or natural substances are specifically named but are only implied.

Sabom reviewed the phenomenon of autoscopic hallucination. The example he provides is of a waking person who sees herself as if looking in a mirror. Sabom says autoscopic hallucinations are not like autoscopic NDEs in that the double has a physical body; there is an interaction between the two, for instance, a conversation; the situation seems unreal to the experiencer; and the experiencer has a negative emotion about the situation. Autoscopic hallucinations are rare, but they usually occur in patients with depression, epilepsy, or schizophrenia. Therefore, it can be argued that the autoscopic hallucinations of this type are the result of a pathological dissociative disorder. An autoscopic NDE is a dissociative phenomenon but not a disorder.

Ring contends that he has known NDErs who have hallucinated at some time in their lives, and they could clearly distinguish the NDE from a hallucination. Delusions and hallucinations are less likely to occur in emotionally stable people. Moody, whose medical specialty is psychiatry, states that the NDErs to whom he has talked are emotionally stable.

Moody also discusses isolation research. When a person is without sensory stimulation, unusual events can happen, including hallucinations. Moody says some hospital rooms with a quiet atmosphere, drab surroundings, and no visitors may result in isolation, which can cause hallucinations. The problem with this as an explanation for NDEs is that many NDEs begin within seconds or minutes of high activity and awareness of the surroundings. As Moody conjectures, "Isolation, therefore, may very well be, along with hallucination drugs and a close call with death, one of several ways of entering new realms of consciousness." To this, I would add a realm of awareness of an individual's own spirituality.

Dr. Ronald Siegel works in the UCLA Department of Psychiatry and Behavioral Science and has written books and articles in medical journals about hallucinatory drugs. In 1980 in *American Psychologist*, he published an article titled "The Psychology of Life After Death." This article has been reprinted in books supposedly debunking the paranormal. Siegel, who assembled a vast number of references for his article, addresses some issues not previously discussed in another article of his, which I reviewed earlier. His article was written prior to the work of Sabom and Ring.

Siegel's premise is that aspects of an NDE are very similar to the hallucination reports he has encountered in his study of psychedelic drugs. The similarities occur in the phenomena of tunnels, *light* and cities of *light*, memory (i.e., life review), perceived reality, and meeting others. Siegel explains that some of these phenomena can be explained by entoptic phenomena (structures within the eye) or electrical activity in the visual system. They can also occur when the electrical activity in the brain is altered in such a way that the threshold for perception of phosphenes (electrical activity in the visual system) is lowered. Hearing voices is particularly common with dissociative anesthetics such as nitrous oxide, ether, and ketamine, each of which permits sensory input into the brain.

The examples Siegel gives about statements made under the influence of drugs are very short, so it is hard to compare those experiences to NDEs. The two can have similarities, since drugs could bring on an awareness of spirituality. Grey (1985) reports that one person, a psychotherapist familiar with dreams and hallucinations, had previously taken LSD and also had an NDE. This person maintains that his NDE was not anything like the hallucinations he had while on LSD. He believes that LSD interferes with free will, whereas in an NDE one is totally free (all NDErs may not agree with that statement). Grey claims, as do others, that medication is likely to interfere with an NDE rather than cause it. Drs. Moody, Ring, and Siegel all reference a book titled *The Center of the Cyclone*, by Dr. John C. Lilly, who performed isolation, ketamine and LSD research and concluded that the resulting phenomenon of LSD is spiritual reality and can be experienced without the use of drugs.

Siegel's explanation is filled with much speculation. Rather than assuming that a drug permits sensory input to the brain, is it not just as reasonable that the dissociative drug forces a spirit body out of the physical body to a place where it can hear or see? Certainly the possibility exists that psychedelic drugs activate the body into believing it is dying.

Although Siegel's explanation is mostly geared toward phenomena of a transcendental NDE, he does say that out-of-body experiences are common in a wide variety of altered states and hallucinations (presumably under drugs). Although he should not be expected to have addressed issues that arose after his article was written, his explanation does not address much of the phenomena of an NDE. For one, he does not explain the accuracy of autoscopic NDEs as evidenced by the detailed work of Sabom. Another thing he neglects to touch on is why the meeting of others is almost exclusively with deceased people, in some cases people who had died before the NDEr was even born. Stating that the electrical activity of the brain is somehow stimulated is just an unprovable assertion. Siegel would also have to demonstrate that people who hallucinated under the influence of drugs have had their lives change positively as a result of their experience, as has happened to NDErs. Psychedelic drugs usually have the opposite effect. As Moody states in his second book, there is a big difference between explaining a theory and explaining it away.

3. Other Explanations

Dr. Carl Sagan (1979), the famous astronomer, proposed that the tunnel followed by the vision of *light* can be attributed to the birth experience (traveling down the birth canal). However, people born by caesarean section also have NDEs and the tunnel does not happen in all people born vaginally.

Michael Grosso (1983), in an article titled "Jung, Parapsychology, and the Near-Death Experience: Toward a Transpersonal Paradigm," provides an explanation of NDEs utilizing Jung's concept of archetypes. He classified the transcendental NDE as meeting "the Archetype of

Death and Enlightenment." Jung himself once had an NDE, but Grosso, not Jung, named the archetype. Since Jung's ideas are based on a spiritual concept of humans, details of Grosso's explanation will not be discussed. His concept is more psychological, whereas my theory is based on a spirit in humans that can leave the body. These are two different approaches, but they are not mutually exclusive.

Some researchers have compared an NDE to an OBE. In one sense the two phenomena are similar, but the comparisons are often made to poor examples of OBEs. Even brain researchers as early as Wilder Penfield (who worked in the 1950s) had some patients state that they felt they were leaving their body when the brain was electrically stimulated. However, none of them claimed to see anything from outside of their body. Similar to that, Blanke et al. (2002 and 2004) determined that patients with a neurological pathology also felt they were leaving their body when the junction between the temporal cortex and the parietal cortex was stimulated. Again, none were able to describe the local environment away from their body as NDErs do; they only felt like they were leaving their body. However, unlike Blanke et al's patients, most NDErs do not have neurological problems and thus Blanke's alleged explanation is invalid.

At the end of his book, Ring discusses a parapsychological–holographic hypothesis of the NDE. His research does not prove this hypothesis. His explanation is spiritually based, as he discusses a second body's existence outside the physical body. He shows how the five aspects of an NDE, which he identifies, can be explained by his model. This explanation is compatible with mine. I have taken a method of explanation based on similarities from completely different phenomena and have shown that they are consistent, rather than basing any conclusions only on NDEs. The conclusions of my book will address this.

Morse (1990) studied the work of Wilder Penfield, MD, an early Canadian neuroscientist. Penfield's most well-known work was titled *The Mystery of the Mind: A Critical Study of Consciousness and the Human Brain* (1975). Morse quotes Penfield as follows: "I came to take seriously, even to believe, that the consciousness of man, the mind, is not something to be reduced to brain mechanism" (Morse, 1990, 100). Morse states that Penfield (and some other researchers) determined that stimulating certain areas of the brain, in particular the Sylvian fissure in the right temporal lobe, produces phenomena similar to an NDE, such as leaving the body, seeing a tunnel, hearing beautiful music, seeing deceased friends and relatives, seeing God, and experiencing of a life review. While this may appear to support the reductionist claim that these NDE stages are within the brain, it does not explain the accuracy of visual descriptions during OBEs when the patient is in a coma or not conscious and the eyes are closed. Morse concludes that "the simplest, most logical way to explain our current knowledge of man's consciousness is the hypothesis that there is actually a soul within each of us, independent of brain tissue" (Morse, 1990, 169). Morse does not use this term, but perhaps it could be said that these NDEs *mediate* through the right temporal lobe rather than originate there. Some NDErs have told Morse that locating an area in the brain is similar to debunking them as valid spiritual expereinces, but that is not his purpose. Morse maintains that the healthy transformations he recognizes in NDErs are proof of the reality of NDEs. He also asserts that the *light* people see during an NDE does not originate in the right temporal lobe, which is genetically coded for NDEs and mystical experiences.

4. My Explanation

In chapter 1, I proposed that human behavior can better be understood if we assume that humans have more than one spiritual component. In chapter 2, I summarized Max Freedom Long's description of the three spiritual complements of humans as elucidated by the kahunas of Hawaii.

How do these ideas relate to NDEs? I maintain that one of these components (soul, mind, or lower or middle self) can depart the physical body during trauma (near or temporary death) and is able to view the physical world with this component. At some point, when away from the body, the soul may become aware of its own Spirit, or High Self. The latter has always been a part of the human makeup, but it is rarely perceived by the soul when a person is conscious. The Spirit may be perceived by the soul in many different manners. Frequently, it is simply a *light* or a *being of light*. It may be a beautiful setting (meadow, mountainside, lake); it may act as a contact with deceased relatives; or it may be a futuristic or brilliant city. Which one of these manifestations appears will depend on the "needs" of the person involved. The person may need to understand how his behavior affects others (a life review) or that he still has a purpose to fulfill on earth. These are the primary options when a person becomes aware of his own Spirit or High Self. After having made contact with his own Spirit, the person returns to his physical body and his life is unlikely ever to be the same.

5. Conclusions on Alternate Explanations

Although the explanations above, other than my own, may approximate some events that occur during an NDE, none of them can address all of the events and the broad variety of circumstances that initiate the NDE. In addition, none of the previous explanations have attempted to address the aftereffects of an NDE. I maintain that my spiritual concept can accommodate all of the phenomena during the NDE, the happenstance that caused the NDE, and the aftereffects.

U. Some Good Quotes and Other Tidbits of Information

I frequently employ quotations from researchers, but I also like to find quotes by NDErs, or others closely connected to death or to spiritually transformative experiences, that summarize some of the important lessons of NDEs. Those that follow without explanation are understood to be from NDErs and contain widely applicable or inspirational sayings.

The first of these is, "Oh, wow! Oh, wow! Oh, wow!"—the last words of Steve Jobs to his sister, who was beside him when he died.

In the book *The Spiritual Brain*, by Beauregard and O'Leary (2007), the authors conclude, "People who attempt suicide and have an NDE abandon thoughts of suicide because 'losing the fear of death seems to mean losing the fear of life itself'" (p. 159).

From the book *Consciousness Beyond Life* (2010) by Pim van Lommel:

- "Dead turned out to be not dead, but another form of life" (p. xiii).
- "When the power of love becomes stronger than our love for power, our world will change" (p. 347).

Another quote is from Albert Einstein, commenting to a family on someone else's death: "He has departed from this strange world a little ahead of me. That means nothing. People like us, who believe in physics, know that the distinction between past, present, and future is only a stubbornly persistent illusion" (p. 229) (reference to Einstein's original writing not provided by van Lommel).

From Chris Carter's book *Science and the Near-Death Experience: How Consciousness Survives Death* (2010): "We can easily forgive a child who is afraid of the dark; the real tragedy of life is when men are afraid of the light" (unnumbered page opposite of contents page; reportedly said by Plato, but no reference provided by Carter).

The last sentence in the book *The Bridge at San Luis Rey* by Thornton Wilder reads as follows: "There is a land of the living and a land of the dead, and the bridge is love, the only survival, the only meaning." (British Prime Minister Tony Blair used this quote when speaking at the site of the World Trade Center shortly after September 11, 2001.) Some background on this quotation: Thornton Wilder came medically close to death, but I believe it was after he wrote the above-cited book. However, he had a twin brother who was stillborn. I am not sure how long Wilder was in the womb next to the dead body of his brother. I employed another interesting quotation of his in chapter 1 of this book.

Another expression of Wilder's that can easily be thought ascoming from a deep spiritual insight is: "Love is an energy which exists of itself. It is its own value." Found in brainyquote.com but no reference to Wilder's writings.

V. Music and NDEs

I think musical composers and/or their compositions sometimes have an interesting relationship to death or NDEs. One of these composers is Richard Strauss (1864–1949). Some of his compositions are referred to as tone poems, stories told by music instead of words. An interesting one is *Death and Transfiguration*, composed in 1889. The story, as conceived by Strauss, is that of an older composer reviewing his life as he is about to die. To me, this sounds similar to the life review that some NDErs encounter. When Strauss died sixty years later, his daughter was beside him, and he allegedly said to her that it was just like he imagined in that composition.

Symphony No. 2 of Gustav Mahler (1860–1911), often called the *Resurrection* Symphony, was composed after the death of a conductor whom Mahler knew. It contains the themes of redemption and resurrection and a transcendent renewal after death. The *Requiem* of Giuseppe Verdi (1813–1901) includes the famous term for a piece of music called the "Dies Irae" (Day of Wrath), which is sometimes incorporated into other music with a theme of sorrow and death.

American composer Morten Lauridsen (b. 1943) composed a choral symphony called *Lux Aeterna* (*Light Eternal*) in 1997. He reportedly said it does not relate to the light seen around the time of death, but some NDErs report that his composition sounds similar to music they heard during their NDE.

W. Uncategorizable Incidents

During her mononucleosis infection at age fifteen, a girl named Cindi left her body (i.e., she had an OBE). To her, this event proved that there is life after death, but since she did not see God she does not believe in God.

A man named Sam tried to relive his NDE through hypnosis. However, he would always break out of his trance before entering the *light*. He concluded that the experience happened when he needed it, not because he wanted it (Morse, 1992).

Morse could not find any support for the idea that people who have been abused are more likely to have NDEs, though he did not cite the most prominent research in this area by Ring (1990). My interpretation is that abuse is a form of trauma that may result in one of the spiritual aspects of a person leaving the individual's physical body. In most cases, though, the trauma that causes the NDE may be sufficient to cause departure of this spiritual aspect; the person does not have to have undergone previous trauma.

X. Conclusions

In this chapter, I have tried to demonstrate that there are two different aspects of an NDE. One aspect is being able to depart the physical body and usually remaining nearby (above the body) to view the earthly situation. However, this spirit aspect may leave the area and may typically visit living relatives. The second aspect is encountering *light*, or *light beings*, in a transcendental world. I maintain that this world is, in reality, an encounter with the NDEr's own Spirit, or nonhuman spirits with whom the Spirit can commune.

Although Morse (1992) believes that these anecdotal stories are not necessarily proof of life after death, he thinks the standards of proof are irrationally high. He states that medical advances are often based on less documented evidence than his studies have for life after death. He says the high standard exists because proof of life after death would require scientists to change their worldview. I would describe this as rejecting the current materialistic paradigm or altering the prevailing reductionist viewpoint.

After reviewing a book that relates to supernatural rescues but that is not directly related to NDEs, I will then turn to a discussion of how psychotherapists in the last thirty-five years have found in dissociative identity disorder patients what they called the *Inner Self-helper*. Like Long, I believe that the Inner Self-helper is the patient's High Self, and I explain that this relates to creativity as well as healing.

Y. Addendum: The Third Man Factor

1. Introduction

Earlier in this chapter, I mentioned a concept related to NDEs called *supernatural rescues*. Raymond Moody introduces that term in a second book about NDEs, *Reflections on Life After Life* (1977). As previously discussed, a supernatural rescue is an incident in which a person is in a very dangerous situation and could easily die, but "aid" seems to appear from nowhere so that the person does not perish. In most cases, there is no physical injury, but a person can become emaciated if a lack of food is involved in a long-term ordeal. Being seemingly trapped in a burning building and being unsure where the safest exit is, but being led by a nonphysical presence, serves as an example. I have placed this information in an addendum, as the phenomenon discussed does not directly relate to NDEs—but it does occur when a person could possibly die.

I now cover a topic from a recent widely acclaimed book that I believe relates to supernatural rescues and spirit helpers. The book is *The Third Man Factor: Surviving the Impossible* (2009) by John Geiger. Geiger, a senior fellow at Massey College at the University of Toronto, is a mountain climber. Many of his examples arise from other mountain climbers, including a term, *extreme and unusual environments* (EUEs), devised by one of the informants in the book. EUEs are divided into "three broad categories: environments in which survival depends on advanced technology (space, deep ocean); environments that require special equipment and techniques but can be a natural habitat for some human groups (the Arctic, mountains, desert); and environments transformed by disaster (earthquake, hurricane, war, terrorist attack). Other EUEs include traumatic environments, such as those experienced by shipwreck survivors adrift in the ocean" (p. 83).

I classify Geiger's book as especially interesting because he reviews multiple explanations for the phenomenon, ranging from guardian angels to imaginary friends to brain/neuron functioning (or malfunctioning). He reviews explanations from clerics, psychologists, and neurologists. He questions if it is a who or a what that is assisting people in these situations.

2. How the Term Third Man Factor *Originated*

Geiger did not coin the term *the Third Man factor*. The phenomenon has been known by mountain climbers for over a century, but the term received a name when writer T. S. Eliot (1888–1965) employed it in a touchstone poem, "The Waste Land" (1922). The idea came to Eliot after reading Sir Ernest Shackleton's description of what happened to him as he crossed South Georgia Island in the Antarctic Sea in 1916. As a result of the poem, the term is entrenched. There were actually three people in Shackleton's party, so the extra man each of the three described was a fourth person. Shackleton would sometimes refer to him as a "Divine Companion." When a minister heard of this fourth man, it reminded him of a verse from the book of Daniel, 3:24–25, in which three men were bound and cast into a hot furnace. The next day, when the king who condemned the three men looked in the furnace, he observed four, with the form of the fourth like the Son of God. Eliot's poem is 434 lines long, but the part that uses a third entity is as follows:

Who is the third who walks always beside you?
When I count, there are only you and I together
But when I look ahead up the white road
There is always another one walking beside you.
Gliding wrapt in a brown mantle, hooded
I do not know whether a man or woman
—But who is that on the other side of you?

It is rather a coincidence (or not) that in 1922 Shackleton was on a return journey to the Antarctic and stopped at South Georgia Island. He suffered a fatal heart attack and was buried on the island.

Although an overwhelming majority of the episodes in *The Third Man Factor* are incidents in which the person lives to disseminate the information, Geiger does impart one event in which others found a diary of an Everest climber's last days mentioning that a presence was with him. This concurs with some NDErs who, after their experience, believe that no one ever dies alone. However, it also demonstrates that the person does not always survive. I opine that the Third Man may provide encouragement to a person to survive, but the individual always has the option or free will to choose to give up and die. Geiger states that the Third Man needs a willing partner. In the above case, the climber who died went farther up the mountain despite his circumstances. In his diary, the climber did not state if the presence advised him to return rather than go forward.

In this section, I will relate only incidents in which an unidentified presence or simply a voice imparted the assistance to the person in arduous circumstances. In chapter 7, I will discuss after-death communication (ADC), situations in which the helpful advice or encouragement was definitely identified as coming from the voice of a deceased relative.

3. An Initial Incident, and Departure of the Presence

Geiger begins his book with the account of Ron DiFrancesco, a man who was on the 84th floor of the World Trade Center South Tower when the

North Tower was struck by an airplane on September 11, 2001. At first, he remained at work, but when a friend called, he agreed to get out. He was in the stairwell when the second plane struck the opposite corner of the building. At first, because he encountered smoke, he went back up, but then he resumed his downward trek. When he was not sure what to do, he heard a male voice giving him instructions and encouragement, and he felt a hand leading him, even running with him through a fire. After five minutes, he reached the seventy-sixth floor, which was below the impact zone, and there was no smoke or fire. At that point, the "angel" left Ron. Near the exit, he heard the building collapsing. He then went unconscious, later awaking in a hospital. He was the last man out alive from the South Tower and was only one of four survivors working in an office above the impact zone. He attributes his being alive to divine intervention.

In a number of circumstances similar to the above, this Presence or Third Man leaves the distressed person as soon as the latter is out of danger. This departing may be temporary, such as when a very serious situation is alleviated, but then the Presence may return for another serious situation or a final departure when the entire ordeal is over. Quite frequently the person(s) in a desperate situation will receive both encouragement and critical advice to reach safety, although in some situations it will only be one or the other. In one situation, a mountain climber had to carry another injured climber and sensed that someone lent a hand. The Presence offers "a sense of protection, relief, guidance, and hope, and the person convinced he or she was not alone" (p. 14). The Third Man also only guarantees safety and not necessarily freedom. In one instance, three men, captured while fighting in a foreign country, escaped and were protected from death while fleeing, but they were eventually recaptured.

Geiger points out that there are five basic rules that govern the Third Man's appearance. These are "the pathology of boredom, the principle of multiple triggers, the widow effect, the muse factor, and the power of the savior" (pp. 17–18).

4. The Pathology of Boredom

Geiger notes that in scientific tests performed employing sensory-deprivation chambers, the test subjects would begin to fantasize. Although there may be some sensory information, landscapes such as snow-covered areas, deserts, and the ocean present a very uniform input to the brain, or, in other words, stimulus-hunger, monotony, or a pathology of boredom. Thus, one explanation for the Third Man is that it is "an attempt by the brain to maintain a sufficient level of stimulation in a monotonous environment" (p. 103). Although Charles Lindbergh was above the ocean, not on it, he nevertheless may have found the inside of his small plane boring, especially with the din of an engine. Lindbergh did not originally mention his "phantoms" or ghostly presences in 1927; it was not until his 1953 book about his journey that these phantoms were publicly mentioned. He reported that they seemed familiar and were transparent forms in human outline. He also said that they spoke to him. This is one of the few instances in which a plural form was used in the description. The presences appeared at a point of Lindbergh's sleep deprivation (twenty-two hours into the flight, late at night or early dawn) and informed Lindbergh about navigation problems. When he passed over Ireland, he was only three miles off course, much better than he expected, so perhaps his phantoms assisted in correcting his flight path. He only had a compass for navigation. (Note: I have placed Lindbergh's entire description of the event in appendix C. I classify it as a profound metaphysical discourse.) As evidenced by Lindbergh's experience, the Third Man can, and frequently does, occur when a person is alone, as the latter's sensory input is reduced by not having a physical companion. Of course, a boring environment would not apply to the previously discussed World Trade Center survivor story.

While some skeptics assert that the people who sense the Third Man are embellishing their reports, Geiger mentions that some individuals, if they were on an exploration trip financed by others, were more likely not to report the phenomenon, as it may have made them sound like they were eccentric or mentally unstable.

Although many people who experience the Third Man know it is only as a Presence, one mountain climber offered to share his food with his "companion." Joshua Slocum was attempting to circumnavigate the globe by himself over a century ago. He had a "strange guest" navigate his sloop through some very rough waters when he was seriously ill below deck. Slocum commented that the guest was a seaman of vast experience. The guest also woke him when it was necessary to avoid a disaster. Another solo ocean traveler referred to "we" when discussing surviving a harrowing part of the journey. One man who was forced onto the ice from a research ship in the Arctic had this to say:

> Once again I became aware of what I can only describe as a Presence, which filled me with an exaltation beyond all earthly feeling. As it passed, and I walked back to the ship, I felt wholly convinced that no agnostic, no skeptic, no atheist, no humanist, no doubter, would ever take from me the certainty of the existence of God. Whatever hardships the future might hold, whatever fate the North had in store for me, I felt supremely glad I had come. (p. 54)

This incident more closely resembles a mystical experience than do many of the other examples in Geiger's book. Mystical experiences are discussed in chapter 11. Another term referenced by the solo ocean traveler was "the presence of an ineffable good" (p. 238). The word *ineffable* is also frequently used in describing NDEs.

Geiger reports that Macdonald Critchley studied various cases of British sailors cast adrift on the ocean during the Second World War. He was writing before the phases of NDEs were known, so Critchley simply described some as having bioscopic fantasies, such as having "past events from a person's life flash before them at incredible speed" (p. 64). This was in Geiger's chapter titled "The Guardian Angel," which primarily addresses religious explanations for the Third Man. Although a scientist, Critchley believed this intangible presence is proof of the existence of angels. Geiger also mentions that around the fourth century, many Christian hermits spent time in the desert, where there is reduced sensory input, and they often fasted. These practices would often result in visionary experiences, as would similar practices during a Native American spirit quest. Geiger reviews what St. Thomas Aquinas (1225–1274) wrote about angels. Aquinas held that "angels are not primarily security guards or safety experts" (p. 77). However, they may appear visibly to humans and "save people from dying before they have done their work in life" (p. 77). Thus, this eight-century-old view is in agreement with many NDErs' beliefs that they survived because they still had some purpose to fulfill on earth. Another religious reference to the phenomenon in the book is "a kindly Providence."

Brian Shoemaker, a helicopter pilot, lost navigational radio contact in the Antarctic and observed a field of white in every direction. He felt lost but sensed a "guiding presence," which first said that his direction was correct and which later spoke and had him turn 20 degrees to the right. He arrived safely. He later mentioned the incident to a chaplain at the Chapel of the Snows at McMurdo Station. The chaplain disclosed that what had happened to the pilot was not uncommon.

Geiger discusses "imaginary playmates" experienced by children that are always benevolent. These playmates occur in about 30% of children, usually between ages three and six. The children do not seem to be pretending; instead, they actually see and hear these imaginary playmates. These playmates are more common in single-child families and thus may be a coping mechanism to ward off loneliness. One woman, when under stress, found that her childhood playmates returned—and they had also grown up.

5. The Principle of Multiple Triggers

The principle of multiple triggers delves into physical effects that may act in conjunction with monotony. Since the Third Man frequently occurs in mountainous or polar regions, one view is that the Third Man could be a cold-stress-induced hallucination. Another view is that there could be inadequate nutrition, as cold weather and demanding physical effort burn a very high number of calories. Other factors include hypoxia, thirst, injury, exhaustion, sleep deprivation, and fear. However, many people do not feel that their reasoning ability was impaired when they encountered the Third Man. One example of the extreme limits to which the physical body endures is one man who was on a raft for 32 days on the ocean; he weighed 56 pounds when rescued.

Geiger recounts that the previously mentioned Critchley reported that a phenomenon similar to the Third Man occurs in epileptics, narcoleptics, schizophrenics, and people with brain injuries. These cases are more likely to fall within the category of visual hallucinations. One researcher referred to some presences among psychiatric patients as "the accompanier." However, Critchley noted that many of these encounters have a "beneficent quality," not like the unreality of many hallucinations. The advice of the Third Man always appears useful and supportive. Some people in situations comparable to those in which the Third Man appears do encounter delusions, but these can easily be distinguished from the benevolent companion.

6. The Widow Effect

Geiger discusses the possibility that the Third Man could be a deceased spouse, another relative, or a friend. He calls this *the widow effect*. He cites one study that found that 50% of widows sensed the presence of their deceased partner. Ten percent felt that their dead spouse was always with them, especially in the first three months after the death of the spouse. While part of this book (chapter 7) supports the concept of after-death communication, and I have included incidents from this book, in almost all of these cases the person definitely knew if the voice or presence was that of someone he or she knew. There were a few cases in *The Third Man Factor* wherein the person thought the presence had a semblance of familiarity. In one incident, an Antarctic explorer thought the presence might be the spirit of Robert Scott, an explorer who died in his attempt to be the first person to make it to the South Pole.

7. Consciousness Theories

One of the more interesting possible explanations for the Third Man is provided in Geiger's review of the theory of controversial psychologist Julian Jaynes. Jaynes wrote a book with a rather intriguing title, *The Origins of Consciousness in the Breakdown of the Bicameral Mind* (1976). He believed that up until about 1000 BCE, the right side of the brain was a "'god-side' which appeared like an omnipotent being or authority figure, dispensing admonitory advice and commands by way of visual and auditory hallucinations" (p. 158). The left side of the brain listened and obeyed. Jaynes arrived at this concept from studies of "neurology, anthropology, archaeology, theology, and the classics" (p. 160). Thus, the explanation for the Third Man based on Jaynes's theory would be that during periods of being in a monotonous environment and experiencing high stress, the mind reverts back to its bicameral status.

Another potential explanation, partially related to Jaynes's concept, is found in the research of Michael Persinger of Laurentian University in Ontario. He developed a device "dubbed the 'god-helmet,' because it is said to induce religious experience by stimulating the brain with low doses of complex, low-intensity magnetic fields" (p. 167). Thus, when normal consciousness is significantly altered, bicameralism would emerge again and the helmet wearers might sense a presence. Persinger believes that these presences have been the basis for gods, spirits, near-death experiences, and extraterrestrial entities. Swedish researchers were unable to duplicate his results, inferring that Persinger was giving suggestions as to what may happen when activating the magnets in the helmet. Persinger counterclaims that the Swedish researchers altered his research protocol and says that their results are invalid.

8. The Muse Factor

Although it does not explain the nature of or what the Third Man is, Geiger discusses a psychological variable he surmises is very important. He refers to it as the muse factor, but then he employs the term *openness* to describe it. He states, "Openness to experience distinguishes imaginative, independent individuals from the unimaginative conformists, and is based on a person's 'willingness to explore, consider, and tolerate new and unfamiliar experiences, ideas, and feelings,' ... and a need for stimuli derived from exploration" (p. 188). Geiger also identifies a second important variable, "a state of heightened awareness called 'absorption'" (p. 189).

Geiger reviews the findings of a neuroscientist, Peter Brugger, who proposed that the Third Man is a full-body equivalent of the phantom limb effect. This is a phenomenon in which an amputee feels pain in his or her amputated limb. This happens in up to 90% of amputees. A frequently used term, employing a foreign-language word, for the full-body phantom is *doppelganger*.." A full-body phantom can be compared to an autoscopic (self-viewing) NDE, discussed earlier in this chapter, but in many cases the person is not near death. Therefore, Geiger would say that the Third Man is actually an aspect of the person having the experience. Geiger relates some examples that may appear to fulfill that explanation, such as the Third Man's moving in tandem with the person who is having the experience.

9. Geiger's Own Experience

Although it is not an incident involving the Third Man in the sense previously discussed, Geiger had his own personal narrative that, when I read it, I immediately identified is as a doppelgänger phenomenon. When Geiger was a seven-year-old child, he was walking with his father near a river in a wilderness area in Alberta. He saw a coiled rattlesnake that was between him and his father. Then suddenly he was observing his father and a child (himself) from "an impossible angle." Very quickly his father grabbed the boy and pulled him out of danger. Geiger reports that there were three people there: the father, Geiger the observer, and Geiger's physical body being pulled to safety. This incident that happened to Geiger would also be a fear-death experience, a term previously introduced earlier in this chapter. In the next chapter I will discuss a related phenomenon called *the hidden observer.*

Some of the previous examples of the appearance of the Third Man were in Geiger's chapter on the power of the Savior. I could not find an explanation for the term, but I did find the question of why it happens to some people but not others.

10. Other Theories and the Switch

Geiger discusses some other theories of the Third Man that I do not perceive necessary to review, as I discredit them as too simplified. These include REM sleep and sleep paralysis; physical stimulation during brain surgery in which the person being operated on felt a presence; and perceptual dysfunction. However, one writer speculated that the Third Man may be related to a collective unconscious, a term employed by Carl Jung. That explanation could be classified as being related to a spiritual explanation.

Although I did not go into details of physical stimulation of the brain inducing a presence, I have no qualms with Geiger's stating that it is simply a "switch." In other words, there is some unknown variable that activates the phenomenon. Geiger refers to this as an "angel switch," although he does not infer that it is a spiritual angel. Even from a spiritual perspective, I cannot augur a detailed explanation of why it happens to some people and not others, just as I cannot explain why approximately only one out of seven people who are clinically dead has an NDE.

Geiger references another writer, who speculates that perhaps someday in the future we will be able to contact the Third Man anytime during periods of loneliness. Geiger also comments that one physician and mountain climber who had experienced the Third Man perceived that even a "biological explanation does not preclude a benign metaphysical origin—an explanation of 'how' does not answer the question of 'why'" (p. 253). I posit that the angel switch could be biologically based but not the actual appearance of the Third Man.

Chapter 6

DISSOCIATIVE IDENTITY DISORDER

Allen, one of the personalities in Billy Milligan, replied to a suggestion as follows: "They're not personalities, they're people."

Psychiatrist: "Why do you make the distinction?"

Allen: "When you call them personalities it's as if you don't think they're real."

—Keyes (1981, p.61)

A. Introduction

Dissociative identity disorder (DID) is one psychiatric disorder with which the general public is loosely familiar. A number of popular books and films on the subject are widely known, using its former name multiple personality disorder (MPD). The term is likely to be recognized by a nonprofessional since the term is, in itself, fairly descriptive. Of course, the psychiatrist's diagnosis of DID is much narrower than the public's conception, which is informed by popular books or films like *The Three Faces of Eve* and *Sybil*. There have been other popular books written for the general public, such as *Minds in Many Pieces* by Dr. Ralph Allison with Ted Schwarz, *The Minds of Billy Milligan* by Daniel Keyes, *The Five of Me* by Henry Hawksworth with Ted Schwarz, and *Katherine, It's Time* by Kit Castle and Stefan Bechtel.

This chapter includes descriptions of the general characteristics of a person (or people) with dissociative identity disorder (PwDID). It also covers frequently encountered types of alternate personalities (APs) and their psychophysiological differences. A short history of DID, its causes, its diagnosis and treatment, and some case histories are also included.

Note that I prefer to use the term *alternate personality* rather than *alter personality* (the latter is used by many therapists). *Alternate* is defined as "occurring or succeeding by turns," which I believe represents what spirits are doing in people with DID. Recently, therapists further obscured this difference between alternate and alter personalities by referring to them as *alter identities*. These alternate personalities correspond to the spirit form that leaves the body during the autoscopic phase of an NDE. The Inner Self-helper (ISH) closely corresponds to the transcendental phase of an NDE, that is, the inspirational and otherworldly aspect of an NDE, and it does not depart from the physical body except at death.

Although in one sense DID is one of the most severe mental disorders, there is a good prognosis for a willing patient who has a good therapist. There is a chance for complete recovery (cure) without the continued use of medications, unlike many disorders in which only symptoms are relieved and medications may be required for the remainder of the patient's life. DID is not an epiphenomenon of other psychiatric disorders or of abnormal neurochemical activity.

The information I present in this chapter has been gathered from articles in professional journals, usually written by psychiatrists and psychologists, and based on observations during PwDID treatment, as well as the aforementioned popular books. The observations speak for themselves. At times it seems the researchers are so amazed by the information that they do not attempt to interpret it (which is often commendable). Some researchers attempt explanations by using existing psychiatric terms, although at times they develop new terms. These terms are usually limited to forces or drives coming from within the individual.

Another principal reference will be *Dissociative Identity Disorder: Diagnosis, Clinical Features, and Treatment of Multiple Personality Disorder* by Colin A. Ross, MD. It is a second edition, published in 1997; the first edition was published in 1985 under the title *Multiple Personality Disorder*, because the fourth edition of the *Diagnostic and Statistical Manual of Mental Disorders* (DSM-IV), which changed the name of the disorder to DID, had not yet been published. Ross's book is a summary of relevant research findings, including his own, and his insight from treating a number of patients. Generally, I will not cite the sources of information he cited. Ross's book was written 20 years ago; since he continues to treat clients, his views may have metamorphosed since then.

I will also be discussing a book coauthored by Ross with psychologist Alvin Pam: *Pseudoscience in Biological Psychiatry: Blaming the Body* (1995). The book plays on the fact that many scientists claim that any concept of spirituality or the paranormal is pseudoscience. Ross and Pam hold that such reductionism is an incorrect ideology and, therefore, a pseudoscience. People with a materialistic viewpoint often disparage parapsychological (or paranormal) phenomena because they realize that there is no physical explanation for such things. They know that it would require a paradigm shift in their understanding of human nature, in fact of all of nature, to explain these phenomena. Many more details will be discussed later.

In a previous chapter, I distinguished between two separate phases of an NDE: an autoscopic (self-viewing) or out of-body-experience phase and a transcendental phase. Although the phenomena may seem superficially different, I believe there are two distinct aspects involved in DID that correspond to the above distinctions in an NDE. The first involves regular APs that take control of a PwDID at stressful times. The second aspect is the ISH, which I consider to be unlike personalities that take control of the body. The ISH was briefly introduced in chapter 3, where I explained it as having similarities to Max Freedom Long's concept of the High Self. In this chapter, I will describe in more detail the various aspects of the ISH, especially those related to therapy, that may not have been relevant when comparing it with the High Self.

The thesis of my book is that behavior, memory, brain waves, activities of the senses, and outward manifestations of health are affected by a spiritual body, which inhabits or permeates the physical body. Personality is a reflection of this spiritual body and its activity. (See especially chapter 8 for a discussion of various spirit bodies and their relationship to health and behavior.) For psychologically normal people, this spiritual body does not leave the body; changes are typically made slowly. The rapid changes that occur in PwDID are due to invasion by an alien spiritual body, usually that of a deceased person who was formerly outside the physical body of the victim. The victim, or patient/client if in therapy, is often referred to as the host, original, or birth personality. If the first departure of the spiritual body has not occurred before the age of seven (the time of teething), but possibly as late as the age of 14 (the time of puberty), it is unlikely to completely depart later. The first departure is usually caused by a traumatic event, often involving childhood sexual abuse, but it can be the result of psychological abuse or other trauma. Typically the abuse is frequent and inflicted by a family member. According to Ross, in other cultures the form of the trauma may be war, famine, religious persecution, or natural disaster, and the symptoms may be different. One of Ross's multiple definitions of DID is that "it is a poly diagnostic disorder of childhood onset, arising from childhood trauma, at least on its primary pathways" (Ross, 1997, 181).

Less severe mental disorders often involve discarnate spirits, but the spirits only attach themselves to a living person and do not completely displace the original spirit body. Although in some cases the person who has a spirit attached to himself may have no control over the circumstances, in most cases the person left himself open to the attachment (or spirit intrusion) because of his own activities. One example of such an activity would be substance abuse. The section in chapter 5 on NDEs titled "A Unique Journey" is about how this very thing happened to a man while he was under the influence of alcohol. However, some abnormal behavior may be the result of thought forms the person has created. An attached spirit can influence behavior but does not have all of the aspects of a personality. Ross even has a term, *copresence*, for what I consider to be spirit attachment. He describes it as follows: "Copresence occurs when an alter personality in the background takes joint control of the body without displacing the primary personality, or when it influences the primary personalities mental state from the background" (Ross, 1997, 30). Although Ross and I differ on where the APs originate, I think his book on DID is excellent. He employs the term *reify* when discussing APs, which is defined as regarding or treating an abstraction as if it had a concrete or material existence. He cautions against considering the personalities as real, and certainly not as the "spirits of deceased people." Ross states that there is only one person, and this person imagines other people in order to survive. "Alter personalities are highly stylized enactments of inner conflicts, drives, memories, and feelings" (p. 144). However, Ross does recognize that parapsychological phenomena are a "normal" aspect of many PwDID. Although a reductionist would disparage this, Ross notes that many PwDID claim that they had left their body (i.e., had an OBE) when they were children, especially during abuse.

Ross considers DID to be a survival strategy gone awry, often creating more problems than it solves. He believes it is not possible to have more than one person or personality in the same body. He compares it to hallucinations. I, on the other hand, believe that a person can have more than one spirit in the same body, but only one can be in control at any given time. Ross esteems Myers's book *Human Personality*, which I discussed in chapter 4. I hope that my book will provide the impetus for that paradigm shift away from reductionism.

In line with my argument, the previously mentioned book by Ross and Pam (1995) is notable in that it opposes the brain chemical theory of abnormal behavior (i.e., reductionism). The authors state that childhood abuse is a major precipitator of abnormal behavior that occurs later in life. Many therapists, especially those in academia performing pharmaceutical research, do not accept the connection between abuse and DID because of the few cases involving "false memory syndrome" (FMS), that is, where the recalling of abuse occurred under hypnosis and was later shown to have falsely resulted from the therapist's suggestion. Ross has shown that the abuse information can be garnered without hypnosis or any type of suggestion and that, in most cases, it has been corroborated by other family members or disinterested parties. FMS will be discussed later.

The title of this chapter is "Dissociative Identity Disorder," but there are other forms of dissociation that are not as severe as DID. Dissociation is defined in the *DSM-IV* as a disruption in the usually integrated functions of consciousness, memory, identity or perception of the environment. Ross employs a secondary definition: "DID is a complex dissociative disorder, in which dissociation occurs in virtually all psychic functions, including sensation, memory, motor function, feeling, and cognition" (Ross, 1997, 118). In fact, anyone can experience normal dissociation, which is neither a disorder nor unusual. In other words, dissociation is not intrinsically pathological.

Within the general classification of dissociative disorders, as listed in the *DSM-IV-TR*, there are five separate categories, from least to most severe (often referred to as a spectrum): depersonalization disorder, dissociative amnesia, dissociative fugue, dissociative disorders not otherwise specified, and DID itself. The term *not otherwise specified*

(NOS) appears in a number of cases without clear-cut diagnoses. The criteria for DID in *DSM-IV-TR* are as follows:

1. The presence of two or more distinct identities, each with its own relatively enduring pattern of perceiving, relating to, and thinking about the environment and the self;
2. At least two identities that recurrently take control of the person's behavior;
3. The inability to recall important personal information that is too extensive to be explained by ordinary forgetfulness; and
4. The disturbance is not due to the direct physiological effects of a substance.

According to Ross, there can also be personality fragments that can only remember one incident or memory fragment. If there is more than one fragment, then this condition is referred to as *polyfragmentation*. There are also "special-purpose" fragments, which have only one minor function. For instance, in one case a male personality fragment only appeared when a female personality was the controlling personality in a PwDID, in apparent sexual pursuit of the female personality. I suggest as part of my theory that personality fragments are spirit intruders connected to one of the APs. Ross also discusses shamanism and mentions that although a shaman may temporarily enter a trance state (a form of dissociation), shamans are psychologically normal when not in the trance state. I devote chapter 9 to indigenous peoples and shamanic concepts of spirituality.

The terms *false-positive* and *false-negative* are often used for an incorrect diagnosis. A psychiatric diagnosis is a false-positive if a person is informed that he or she has a specific disorder but in actuality does not. A psychiatric diagnosis is a false-negative if a person is informed that he or she does not have a certain disorder but in fact does have it. Thirty years ago there were many false-negatives for DID, but now that it is being diagnosed more frequently, there are probably some false-positive diagnoses.

B. History

The first semimodern case of DID was reported in Pennsylvania in the early 1800s. The patient's name was Mary Reynolds. There was only one AP, and the switch lasted a considerable length of time, in contrast with frequent switching in modern cases of DID. Up until 1979, the Cumulated Index Medicus listed information on DID under the heading of "Dual Personality" because many of the cases reported listed only two personalities, as in the case of Mary Reynolds. Several other famous cases in the United States include Miss Beauchamp, as reported by Morton Prince in 1905, and the Ansel Bourne case, as reported by William James. Around the turn of the 20th century, French psychiatrists were prominent in analyzing and reporting DID, but they rarely do so now.

One reason it is difficult to analyze older reports of DID is that the knowledge of childhood abuse is a helpful criterion for diagnosis and older case reports rarely discuss the subject of childhood abuse. In the Mary Reynolds case, her diagnosis was determined after her death and was written by people who did not know her. Prince and James were experienced psychiatrists, so it is difficult to believe they would fail to mention child abuse if they knew it had occurred. They probably did not inquire about it.

Ross divides the phases of the history of DID into five periods:

- Period 1, up to 1880, hazy beginnings
- Period 2, 1880 to 1910, establishment and elaboration of DID
- Period 3, 1910–80, full maturity and rapid decline of interest
- Period 4, 1980–84, resurgence of interest in DID
- Period 5. 1984–present, modern scientific study of DID

Except for DID's relationship to child abuse, modern findings often verify the same symptoms that the original students of behavior found a century ago.

At first, Freud considered some of his patients with symptoms of hysteria to be suffering from the aftereffects of real childhood abuse. However, he later repudiated this seduction theory and concluded that the patients only imagined the abuse (calling them "incestuous fantasies").

In 1910, a psychiatrist named Breuer introduced the term *schizophrenia*, which means "split brain," and the diagnosis of dissociation practically disappeared. Split mind is not the same as split personality, which could be a description of DID. Schizophrenia is in the category of psychotic disorders, not a dissociative disorder.

In 1944, Taylor and Martin published an article summarizing all known previous cases of DID that could be found. Of the 76 cases, 49 were dual personality and only six had more than five APs. The average number of APs was 2.9, and the median was 2.0. In contrast, in several studies in the late 1980s, the mean was 13 to 16, and the median was 8 to 9. Taylor and Martin did not discuss sexual abuse or other traumas. The main causes of DID were considered to be head injuries, intoxication, fatigue, and conflicts (Ross, 1997).

The separation of dissociation into a separate category in the *DSM-III* in 1980 made it much easier to make the correct diagnosis of DID (Ross, 1997). The formation of the professional organization the International Society for the Study of Trauma and Dissociation (ISSTD) also brought more attention to DID in the early 1980s. There were an estimated 500 identified cases of DID in 1979, 1,000 in 1983, and 5,000 by 1986. There were probably many more earlier cases of DID, but these were frequently misdiagnosed as other mental disorders.

A recent book, *Sybil Exposed*, by Debbie Nathan (2011), claims that the original book titled *Sybil* (1973) was a cooperative hoax between the patient Sybil (real name Shirley Mason); her psychiatrist, Cornelia Wilbur; and *Sybil*'s author, Flora Rheta Schreiber. The three are now deceased. The book was made into a two-part television special in 1976. Nathan holds that the 1973 book was instrumental in bringing about the rise in interest in DID/MPD. Nathan contends that Shirley Mason did not have childhood trauma that resulted in DID but generated the personalities as a result of subtle and coercive pressure by Wilbur. According to Nathan, the patient, psychiatrist, and author at some point all knew that the personalities were not real, but they proceeded anyway on account of emotional dependence, ambition, and financial incentives. I have gathered this information from a detailed book review of *Sybil Exposed* by Carol Tavris (2011).

The book posits that Shirley Mason did have emotional problems but agreed to have the cost of her treatment covered by the book's royalties.

Treatment included many medications, including sodium pentothal, and these resulted in many memories, often either false or misinterpreted. Shirley admitted that she had lied about her personalities, justifying it by mentioning that she was addicted to her medications and could not afford to pay for past therapy if the book was not completed. The psychiatrist and author both realized their efforts would be for naught, but they published the book with the claim of the integration of the personalities and the end of Shirley's dissociation. An interesting aside, a sibyl (*i* and *y* reversed; adjective: sibylline) was a woman in ancient Greek and Roman folklore considered to be an oracle or prophetess.

Nathan agrees with psychiatrists who maintain that DID is a culture-bound syndrome and comes from suggestion by the therapist, i.e., that it is iatrogenic. She also holds that psychologists have scientifically discredited the assumptions underlying DID, especially the assumption that abuse causes dissociation. I went through the extensive list of reviews of *Sybil Exposed* on *Amazon*'s website. The majority of those reviews are very critical of Nathan's analysis. I do not agree with Nathan and other discreditors of the connection between trauma and dissociation. Many therapists who treat DID have obtained outside confirmation of the abuse and do not base the allegations solely on the patient's memories of it.

Ross states that he has been involved as an expert witness in six cases of iatrogenically caused DID. He claims that in those cases, the DID symptoms remit rapidly once the patient is away from the offending therapist. In most cases, the patient had a psychiatric illness that could be confused with DID. Ross claims that if groups of people with APs created by hypnosis or true DID patients were presented to him, within five minutes of interviewing them he could determine with 100% accuracy to which group each person belonged. People acting like they have an AP cannot approach true clinical symptoms of DID but could fool some clinicians.

C. Description and Diagnosis

Because DID is difficult to diagnose, for many years it was not considered a major category of illness and was classified in a minor category, under the subcategory of neuroses (namely, hysterical neuroses), a term virtually unused by the psychiatric community today. Not until the 1980 issue of the *DSM-III* were DID and other dissociative disorders defined as separate illnesses. The next volume of the *DSM* was issued in 1994 and revised in 2000, but since this latter volume was not considered totally new, it is titled *DSM-IV-TR* (*TR* for "text revision").

The American Psychiatric Association (APA) has issued a new volume, *DSM-5*. Various committees of the APA have sent out proposed revisions for comments by psychiatrists or other interested parties. Ross recommended, and I agree, that a special category be created called "Trauma-Related Disorders." This new section would include all current dissociative disorders and also posttraumatic stress disorder (PTSD), acute stress disorder, and borderline personality disorder (BPD). As Ross states, "The trauma disorders could be subdivided into acute and chronic trauma, childhood and adult onset, and dissociative or non-dissociative, bearing in mind that dissociation occurs on a continuum" (Ross, 1997, 184).

The *DSM* is used only in the United States. In Europe and many other parts of the world, the *International Classification of Diseases* (*ICD*, short for *International Statistical Classification of Diseases and Related Health Problems*) is employed for diagnosis, and the current volume is *ICD-10*. The illness with symptoms similar to DID in the *ICD-10* is classified as a conversion disorder.

DID almost always coexists with other psychiatric disorders. It is not unusual for a DID patient to have had 15 different diagnoses prior to being diagnosed with DID. The presence of two or more disorders is referred to as *comorbidity*. When Ross was writing his book in the mid-1990s, it was common that a patient may have been in treatment for six or seven years for various diagnoses before being diagnosed with DID. Here is a list of other disorders that were often diagnosed prior to a final DID diagnosis:

1. Mood disorders (depression and bipolar disorder [formerly manic depression])
2. Anxiety disorders (panic disorder, phobias, and obsessive-compulsive disorder)
3. Psychotic disorders (schizophrenia and schizoaffective disorder)
4. Substance-abuse disorders (alcohol or other drugs)
5. Somatoform disorders (somatization disorder, pain disorder, and hypochondria)

6. Eating disorders (bulimia and anorexia nervosa)

Although not another mental disorder, severe headaches were mentioned by virtually all DID patients. Some patients who were eventually shown to have DID were also diagnosed with physical disorders rather than mental disorders. Among the physical diagnoses were epilepsy (both temporal lobe epilepsy [TLE] and grand mal epilepsy), brain tumors, and learning disabilities.

Two other frequent behaviors in a PwDID are self-destructive behavior and suicide (attempted and/or successful). In one study, 92% of patients in therapy for DID had attempted suicide. Making a threat of or actual attempting suicide is one of the main grounds for hospitalizing a patient after a failed attempt. Ross states that people often make suicide attempts on account of internal disputes and hostility among the APs, not to cry for help, as they often are in depressed patients. To give an idea of how confused the various APs are, a persecutor personality (more often male) may believe he can convince the host personality to commit suicide, not realizing that the host lives in the same physical body in which the persecutor dwells. Ross regards this as a cognitive error commonly made by people who dissociate. Those who attempt suicide usually have more Schneiderian first-rank symptoms of schizophrenia and usually have more personalities. I once read that a confused AP was falling in love with another AP, not realizing that the two lived in the same body. This would verify my belief that APs believe that they and other APs are actually separate people.

According to Ross, 48% of PwDID had had imaginary companions in childhood. In PwDID the imaginary companions may persist into late adolescence, even into adulthood, and some may evolve into alter personalities. Some imaginary companions seem to shift back and forth from inside to outside.

Ross conceives of these multiple diagnoses as a hierarchy, with DID at the apex ("hierarchically superior"). If a therapist treats a lower disorder, such as depression or substance abuse, the results may be unsatisfactory. However, if the DID is treated, the lower disorders often go into remission. In fact, although substance abuse is one of the most common features of DID (usually one or two of the APs are responsible for it), the substance abuse is virtually eliminated after integration (along with many other lower disorders). Ross refers to these lower disorders as subdiagnoses, while DID is the most inclusive.

Ross believes that many of the above disorders with which a PwDID is first diagnosed should often have a subtype description for them using the phrase *with dissociative features*. In other words, a patient who is depressed may have pathological dissociative moments but does not have a dissociative disorder. There are several types of depression, and one of these could be referred to as the dissociative subtype. State-dependent learning is an example of dissociation occurring in another disorder. A very specific example is that an alcoholic may hide a bottle when she is drunk and be unable to remember the location when sober but will remember the location when drunk again.

Although it is considered a neurological illness and not a mental disorder, temporal lobe epilepsy quite frequently has dissociative symptoms, meaning that DID patients could be referred to as having a dissociative subtype of TLE. True DID patients never respond to anti-epileptic medication. Note that it is possible that the diagnosis of TLE may not be incorrect. In a later section on psychophysiology, I will discuss physical and psychological differences between APs. It is possible that one personality did have TLE and may have had an EEG evaluation to verify it when that particular AP was in control. In this case, the personality with TLE should respond to anti-epileptic medication.

The most common mental illnesses or syndromes in the *DSM* are referred to as Axis I disorders. This includes dissociative disorders. There is a second group, referred to as Axis II, that includes personality disorders and developmental disorders. The rest include Axis III—general medical conditions that may contribute to mental functioning; Axis IV—psychosocial and environmental conditions that may contribute to mental functioning; and Axis V—global assessment of functioning.

In addition to having the specific Axis I mental disorders listed above, many PwDID in Ross's book were diagnosed with Axis II disorders. Someone once explained personality disorders to me in the following way: Axis I disorders are mental problems that may occur suddenly or be chronic, but they often are correctable. For instance, a patient may have depression for a while and then achieve full recovery. The same applies to phobias, substance abuse, and eating disorders. Axis II personality disorders, however, are usually a description of an individual's long-term personality traits, and they rarely get completely better; rather, they reach a certain plateau. A person who is correctly diagnosed as schizophrenic has less likelihood of regaining full capabilities, but many of that person's symptoms can be minimized with medications. Some psychiatrists believe that Axis I disorders belong in the realm of biology (i.e., are best treated with medications) and that Axis II disorders belong to the realm of psychodynamic treatment. Given my theory that spirituality is a factor in many mental disorders, I do not agree with this as I believe they can all be treated, and most cured, with psychodynamic treatment. Ross has treated many DID patients (with an Axis I disorder) to complete recovery without medication, thus demonstrating the statement to be incorrect. However, Ross does prescribe medications for temporary relief of some problems during therapy for DID.

Ross discusses other disorders that may be related to dissociation. One Axis I disorder is called organic brain dysfunction: something physically wrong with the brain or its neurochemistry. Within that category is a syndrome called intermittent explosive disorder (IED). Ross states that he has never treated a patient with IED exclusively, but he has met a number of intermittently explosive APs. Ross also considers alcohol idiosyncratic intoxication, where a small amount of alcohol can cause intoxication, to be a symptom of partial or full DID. Ross holds that when the patient goes for substance-abuse treatment, the responsible AP is in the background, not in control, and therefore learns nothing from the treatment. Although depression and bipolar disorder are not necessarily APs, Ross says there may be dissociative mechanisms involved in these two illnesses. For instance, he mentions a case in which a woman was in a catatonic state with psychotic unipolar depression. She recovered within five minutes of being administered sodium amytal. "Such dramatically effective interventions arise from looking at the world through dissociative colored glasses" (p. 214).

Although there are about a dozen personality disorders defined in the *DSM*, sometimes they are grouped into clusters on account of their having some similarities. Cluster A personality disorders include paranoid, schizoid, and schizotypal personality disorders. People with these disorders are often odd or eccentric, with traits of distrust, suspiciousness, or social detachment. Cluster B personality disorders include histrionic, narcissistic, antisocial, and borderline personality disorders. People with these disorders tend to be emotional, erratic, and dramatic. Cluster C personality disorders include avoidant, dependent, and obsessive-compulsive personality disorders. There are three additional personality disorders that are not in a cluster. These are depressive personality disorder, passive-aggressive personality disorder, and personality disorders not otherwise specified (PDNOS). Borderline personality disorder has symptoms most closely resembling DID. The term *borderline* describes a patient being on the border between a neurosis and a psychosis.

When the number of DID cases began to increase in the 1970s with many misdiagnoses, it was prior to the development of specific criteria to recognize DID. Perhaps many people are unaware of the large number of "tests" that are now available for assisting in various diagnoses of mental disorders. For DID disorders, the simplest test is the Dissociative Experiences Scale (DES). This is a series of questions that ask about having memory loss, missing time, or finding things in your closet that you do not remember purchasing. The DES is only a screening tool. According to Ross (1997), the average score on this test for a DID patient is in the 40s, but the standard deviation is about 20. Only 17% of those with a score above 30 had DID, and some PwDID had a score below 20. A second available test is the Dissociation Questionnaire (DIS-Q), an expanded version of the DES. If either of those tests indicates the possibility of a dissociative disorder, an interview called the Dissociative Disorder Interview Schedule (DDIS) can be administered. The interview takes about forty-five minutes when administered by a trained person. This may only indicate a dissociative disorder and may not be specific for DID.

However, according to Ross, some patients' situations and histories automatically suggest the necessity of a DID screening. As he writes, "Chronic self-destructive behavior and a woman with a long psychiatric history and childhood trauma should always prompt a thorough diagnostic evaluation for DID" (Ross, 1997, 126). Another good prompt for administering the above tests, according to Ross, is if a patient under evaluation refers to himself or herself as "we" or "us."

Furthermore, although the personality that originally presents itself for therapy is assumed to be the "host" or birth personality, it is possible, and perhaps frequent, that the presenting personality is actually one of the APs. Atlas (1988) reports a case in which a woman who was diagnosed as learning disabled actually had DID, and the primary AP that presented itself to the therapist acted ignorant and uncomprehending. A well-known therapist and researcher in the field of DID named Richard Kluft (1984) states that the classic host personality, which often seeks treatment, is depressed, anxious, somewhat neurasthenic, compulsively good, masochistic, conscience-stricken, and constricted hedonically, and suffers both psychophysiological symptoms and time loss/distortion.

It is very difficult for therapists to reach a decision of DID without actually having an alternate personality appear during therapy. However, this is unlikely, since an AP switch normally occurs only under stress. A therapy session may not be stressful enough to provoke a switch. Kluft (1985), however, states that a PwDID will almost always dissociate if the interview lasts for four hours, but this is rather unlikely as most therapists are unwilling to spend that amount of time with one patient.

Therapists often have to discuss symptoms with family members because the host personality of the PwDID is usually unaware of the activities of the other personalities when in control of the body. This is why amnesia is often listed as a requirement for a definitive diagnosis of DID. Typically the host personality is unaware of personalities that follow, but an AP may be aware of the host personality and some or all of the other APs. (There is one entity called the Inner Self-helper [ISH] that is aware of all the other personalities and that has complete recall of the activities of the PwDID, including which personality [original or AP] was in control when each activity occurred. There is a separate section in this chapter titled "The Inner Self-helper.")

While I disagree with Ross on the origin of the APs, and despite my thinking of them as intruders, I agree with Ross when he states that it is incorrect to view the primary personality as desirable and normal and the secondary personalities as "bad" or undesirable. The APs often perform a necessary function for the host personality. Until the host has learned to cope with the life situation that induces a switch to an AP, that AP should remain as a resource. However, in chapter 10 I will discuss spirit intrusions in which it is acceptable to remove the spirit intruder, seeing as it is only an attached spirit and normally not necessary for functioning.

As discussed earlier, Ross believes there are dissociative subtypes within many mental disorders. Schizophrenia is one of these. The differentiation of schizophrenia from DID is interesting. There are usually chronic auditory hallucinations in both. What is also striking is that the hallucinating voices in DID are generally described as coming from inside the head, while in schizophrenia the voices come from outside the head. Ross speculates that perhaps the voices heard in the dissociative subtype of schizophrenia could be engaged in conversation. The psychotic voices in "normal" schizophrenia cannot be engaged in conversation because they are incoherent and irrational, whereas hallucinatory voices in DID often seem similar to those one hears when listening to a normal conversation between several other people. According to Ross,

> Psychotic voices tend to be associated with thought disorder and acute phases of a psychotic illness, whereas dissociative voices tend to be chronically present even when the patient is functioning well. All these distinctions are only general rules of thumb. The distinction between psychotic and dissociative voices may be semantic. Psychotic, in this regard, may be a subset of dissociative, because dissociation must occur in some form for a mind to hear part of itself talking and to experience that as nonself talking. (Ross, 1997, 199)

The finding that voices are internal in DID, and external in schizophrenia, is consistent with my spiritual theory. In DID, the alien spirits have further penetrated the physical body of the host personality and are thus "internal." In schizophrenia, a spirit is only attached to the victim and therefore is "external." I would agree that it isn't the affected person talking, but the voice of a discarnate spirit. Recent research with modern brain neuroimaging, such as positron emission tomography (PET) and functional magnetic resonance imaging (fMRI), indicates that speech-production areas of the brain are activated rather than speech comprehension (hearing) when voices are being heard. In other words, the brain is creating an internal voice rather than hearing something that is not there. However, either distinction of being internal or external is not critical to my theory. Dissociative voices can sometimes be engaged in conversation, as they are less chaotic than schizophrenic voices (Ross).

Schizophrenics who are also dissociative are more likely to have ESP experiences and borderline criteria. A German psychiatrist named Kurt

Schneider (1887–1967) developed what he called *first-rank symptoms* for schizophrenia. If a number of these are present, a person is very likely to have schizophrenia. Patients who have schizophrenia are more likely to display dissociative features if they have a history of trauma or abuse.

Schizophrenia also has what are called positive and negative symptoms. Positive symptoms are behaviors that a psychologically normal person does not have, such as hallucinations and delusions. The negative symptoms are deficiencies in functioning, such as flattened emotions, asociality, apathy, anhedonia (inability to experience pleasure), and poverty of speech. There are also disorganized symptoms such as bizarre behavior and disorganized speech. The positive symptoms of schizophrenia are dissociative in nature and are actually more common in DID than in schizophrenia itself.

Although this chapter is primarily about DID, since DID is sometimes misdiagnosed as schizophrenia, Ross's following comment about schizophrenia is important: "Of all the diagnostic errors in psychiatry, a false positive diagnosis of schizophrenia is probably the most dangerous and most difficult to reverse. It can lead to a self-fulfilling prophecy of lifetime medication, and deteriorating function in the absence of correct treatment" (Ross, 1997, 129). I believe it is important to distinguish between the two conditions before proceeding with therapy. As mentioned above, an attached spirit with its concomitant voices may be sent away, but a DID patient must be taught to cope without passing behavior onto an AP.

One of the difficulties in reaching a conclusion of DID is that the personality that appears for the first therapy session (i.e., the host personality, sometimes called the original or presenting personality) may have its own problems in addition to being dissociated from the body. The therapist may become overly involved in analyzing those problems. For instance, the host personality could easily have depression, or any one of a myriad of problems that PwDID are characterized as exhibiting, without that disorder being caused by an AP's having taken control. The host personality may also be a substance abuser, which creates even more complexity. Some problems, such as suicidal tendencies and anorexia nervosa, may be life-threatening.

The following are characteristic signs used to suggest careful scrutiny for DID. This list comes from Kluft (1985), who condensed them from several previously articles:

1. Prior treatment failure
2. Three or more prior diagnoses
3. Concurrent psychiatric and somatic symptoms
4. Fluctuating symptoms and level of function
5. Severe headaches
6. Time distortion or time lapses
7. Being told of disremembered behaviors
8. Others noting observable changes
9. Discovery of productions, objects, or handwriting in one's possession that one cannot account for or recognize
10. The hearing of voices (greater than 80% experienced as within the head), experienced as separate, urging toward some good or bad activity
11. The use of we in a collective sense
12. The elicitability of other alters through hypnosis and/or amytal

While substance abuse by PwDID will be discussed in a later section, since this section concerns diagnosis and chemicals that can produce dissociative symptoms, further comments are appropriate. Fawcett (1985) states that among the chemicals that can produce dissociative states are alcohol, marijuana, cocaine, phencyclidine, sedatives, and hallucinogens. Although these can produce dissociative states, it is unlikely—unless there had been an abuse factor prior to the age of seven, as previously discussed, or if use of these chemicals had begun prior to that age—that these chemicals would result in a case of true DID. A dissociative state or symptom is not the same as DID. There is a good chance that the use of these chemicals could result in personality fragments or partial intrusion. This will be discussed in chapter 10, on spirit intrusion and release.

D. Hypnosis

Hypnosis is a term so frequently encountered when discussing DID that it is necessary to explain some aspects of the phenomenon. Therapists use hypnosis in diagnosis and treatment. A demonstration of hypnosis may involve loss of pain, loss of memory, or performing feats of strength. Many people are also aware that hypnosis can be used to help a person stop smoking, reduce his or her weight, and/or eliminate fears. Observing some of the unusual phenomena that can occur in hypnosis with "normal" people is what leads many professionals to believe that DID either is caused by hypnosis or that the similarities in phenomena (e.g., loss of memory) demonstrate that the APs come from within the individual.

In addition to the relationship of hypnosis to DID, the overall relationship of hypnosis to other branches of psychiatry and other parts of this book is important. Ellenberger (1970), in his book *The Discovery of the Unconscious: The History and Evolution of Dynamic Psychiatry*, discusses the metamorphosis from primitive healing to (animal) magnetism, magnetism to hypnosis, and hypnosis to psychoanalysis and the newer dynamic schools. Thus, hypnosis has made a contribution to many schools of psychiatry except for those based on behaviorism and biochemical theories of behavior.

Adam Crabtree is a therapist who is considered very knowledgeable in the history of mesmerism, from which hypnosis was derived. In his book *Multiple Man: Explorations in Possession and Multiple Personality*, Crabtree (1985) gives a history of hypnosis from the time of Anton Mesmer (1734–1815), who named his curing method "animal magnetism." While attempting to cure someone of inflammation using the so-called magnetic passes, Marquis de Puységur (1751–1825), a student of Mesmer, induced what he called *magnetic sleep*. An English doctor, James Braid, began using the method in the 1840s; he used the term *neurohypnosis*, which means "nervous sleep." This term was later shortened to *hypnosis*.

Crabtree divides the phenomena of hypnosis as discovered by early experimenters into what he calls lower and higher phenomena. The lower phenomena consist of the following:

1. A sleepwalking kind of consciousness
2. Double consciousness and double memory
3. Loss of sense of identity
4. Suggestibility
5. Heightened memory
6. Deadening of the senses
7. Insensibility to pain
8. Rapport between operator and patient

Crabtree states that the lower phenomena are unusual but do not defy belief. He contends that the higher phenomena, listed below, are difficult to accept by reductionists as genuine.

1. Physical and sense rapport between hypnotist and patient
   a. Sensation
   b. Muscular action
2. Mental rapport between hypnotist and patient
   a. Read thoughts of anyone put in rapport
   b. Hypnotize at a distance (once established)
3. Clairvoyance
   a. See at a distance, even around the world
   b. See into the body—medical clairvoyance
   c. Clairvoyance back through time
4. Ecstasy—visions of afterlife and communication with spirits of departed

Most modern hypnotists rarely try to get involved with the higher phenomena, which may be just as well until the phenomena are better understood and the side effects are identified. Ross notes that there seems to be a connection between dissociation, ESP experiences, and hypnosis.

Whereas Bliss (1983) believes that APs are created by autohypnosis (self-induced hypnosis), many have cautioned about the possible creation of APs during hypnosis. For example, Braun (1984) states that he has made a diagnosis of DID 59 times and that in only four cases was hypnosis employed prior to diagnosis. He believes a personality fragment can be created by hypnosis, but these fragments do not have a full history or full range of effect. These fragments can be easily integrated. Full APs have been verified by family members and others long before the PwDID experienced therapeutic hypnosis. Putnam et al. (1986) gathered information on a hundred cases of DID. They found that there was no difference between the patients diagnosed or treated with hypnosis and those who had not been treated with hypnosis with regard to clinical presentation of symptoms, AP phenomenology, or past history. In 23% of the cases, hypnosis was used to facilitate the initial meeting of an AP. In 51% of the cases the AP appeared spontaneously, and in 16% of the cases the therapist simply asked to speak to any other personalities. In the Ross et al. (1989) study, 82.2% of the subjects had been hypnotized at some point in therapy, but of those hypnotized, 48.3% were hypnotized only after diagnosis. However, therapists do recommend caution when using hypnosis. They also find that they can call upon APs without using hypnosis. If hypnosis is used during therapy, one sign of successful fusion is being unable to find the APs while utilizing hypnosis. If hypnosis created the AP, then that AP would likely continue to appear during later hypnosis. Because hypnosis is frequently used in treatment or therapy, it will be discussed in this section as well as in the section titled "Case Histories."

As mentioned in the "Description and Diagnosis" section, there is a strong correlation between DID and susceptibility to hypnosis. In fact, perhaps ease of hypnosis directly correlates with dissociation. Measurements in this field are, of course, imperfect. Hypnotic-susceptibility tests most likely have a wide margin for error. When susceptibility to hypnosis is correlated with a diagnosis of DID, which is partly subjective, potential error is compounded. Ross comments that it is possible that DID patients, but only those that undergo severe trauma form DID, are born highly hypnotizable and have a higher ability to dissociate. However, the ability to be hypnotized may be the result of the trauma.

Correlations similar to this may be extended a step further. For instance, since most PwDID have been subject to child abuse, perhaps susceptibility to hypnosis might be used to measure likelihood of child abuse. Nash and Lynn (1986) found that physically abused subjects evidenced a greater behavioral response to hypnosis than did nonabused controls. However, behavioral response to hypnosis is not necessarily the same as susceptibility to hypnosis, although there is probably some connection.

Another term often encountered when studying hypnotism is the *hidden observer* phenomenon. This was discovered by psychologist Ernest Hilgard (1904–2001) during some hypnosis experiments. Hilgard was performing experiments with pain suppression by having subjects put their hands in ice-cold water, which normally is very painful. With the subjects under hypnosis, Hilgard told them that they would not feel the pain, and that was the result he got on the conscious level. However, by going into deeper hypnosis, he was able to elicit a response that the cold water actually made the subjects' hands feel very painful. He referred to the entity making the observation as the hidden observer. The hidden observer remains quiet unless called upon. Some researchers consider the hidden observer to be similar to the Inner Self-helper discussed in the next section of this chapter. This is possible, but other than memory, there is not much evidence that the hidden observer has the capabilities of the ISH.

E. The Inner Self-helper

1. Introduction

In chapter 3, I introduced the concept of the Inner Self-helper. I focused on its spiritual nature rather than its role in therapy, an important aspect I will explore here in much greater detail.

During treatment of PwDID, many therapists have discovered a "personality" they have come to call the Inner Self-helper (ISH). This personality is able to assist the therapist (as a cotherapist, peer, or consultant) in defining the patient's major problem areas and assisting with other aspects of the therapy process. The ISH will not dictate orders to the therapist nor blindly follow them. While many of the personalities are amnestic about other personalities, the ISH knows of the existence of all the personalities, is cognizant of which one is in control of the patient at any given time, and cares for all of them. Though some therapists have slight disagreements on the characteristics of the ISH, generally the ISH is found to be rational rather than emotional, to have no gender, and to be able to produce customized dreams for the patient. It also claims it is able to contact entities higher than itself. Some therapists who believe that unitary persons (people who do not have DID) also have an ISH further believe that there can be patient—ISH-to-therapist—ISH communication. The ISH does not act but can create helper personalities to assist itself. There is only one ISH, but helper personalities are sometimes confused with the true ISH. Many therapists have had an ISH present itself spontaneously, but experienced therapists may simply call upon the ISH, similar to asking to speak to an alternate personality. While some therapists believe the ISH is iatrogenic or a modified AP, many others strongly disagree.

In a questionnaire survey about the ISH conducted among therapists who have been treating people with DID, Adams (1989) provided the following operational definition of the ISH:

> Internal Self Helpers: Portions of psychic energy within the MPD person which primarily serve as helpers in the MPD system. Unlike host or alter personalities, the ISHs demonstrate objectivity and possesses information which frequently spans the entire lifetime and experiences of the MPD person. The ISHs are said to possess mental capabilities which far surpass that of the host or alter personalities. ISHs have also been referred to as the "Centers" or "Centrals," and have been found at times to be beneficial in the healing/therapeutic process. In this investigation, ISHs were to be differentiated from other "helpers" or "helper personalities" who are more limited in knowledge and capabilities than the ISH. (Adams, 1989, 138)

Fraser (1987) also lists characteristics and features of the ISH. Characteristics are more general and almost always true, while features occur less often and are variable.

Characteristics of the ISH:

1. It is the observer or monitor of the other personalities, the therapist, and the therapy.
2. It is a memory trace of all personalities. (This is a requirement. Without it, the ISH has not been found).
3. It is the state of conscious awareness that is buffered by the personality. It is the sense of being one has while the personality determines the kind of being one is.
4. It is very logical but compatible with the basic IQ and learning of the core personality.
5. It is psychologically minded and can interpret concepts like motivation.
6. It is neutral with regard to the many personalities and is concerned about and connected to each of them.

7. It can act as advisor or cotherapist, but it can also learn from the therapist.
8. It remains in the present time even if the personalities are progressed or regressed.

Features of the ISH:

1. It usually has the same sex and age as the birth personality (note that others have described it as gender neutral; I use the identification *it*).
2. It often has no name or body image (the names used here are often assigned by the therapist).
3. It may present itself spontaneously.
4. It may not be aware of its ability to relate to the therapist. This may have to be explained.
5. It may possibly be a preview of what the fused or integrated personality will be like at the end of therapy.
6. It may not want to have its existence revealed to some of the APs.
7. Some of the personalities may be aware or co-conscious with the ISH; that is, there may not be an amnestic barrier.
8. It works for the preservation of the life of the whole system.
9. In emergencies it may, but does not always, take control of the system itself or have a helper personality take over. It may not always be aware that it can do this and should be instructed to do so by the therapist, as PwDID sometimes commit suicide or at least attempt it.

Similarly, Comstock (1987a) identifies four primary responsibilities of the Center, her name for the ISH:

1. To protect the life;
2. To ensure the healing from the past for each personality;
3. To integrate the alternate personalities (APs) when their work is completed and they believe there is no longer any purpose for them here; and
4. To strengthen and empower the birth personality to live the life alone.

Comstock (1987b) states that Centers, in contrast to APs, may or may not have an appearance. The APs may find it disconcerting to have a voice (that of the Center) come from "nowhere," and so the Center assumes an appearance. In one case mentioned, the Center first appeared to one of the personalities as a shadowy translucent figure and then developed a more solid appearance.

In relating to the concept of a sense of being in characteristic #3, above, Adams (1989) mentions Roberto Assagioli's (1888–1974) insight presented in the concept he named *psychosynthesis* in his book of the same title. He proposed the following:

> "the existence of a spiritual self and of a superconsciousness which are as basic as the instinctive energies described by Freud" (p. 193 in Assagioli [1984]). He distinguished between the "Self" and the "personal self" or ego which is the result of life experiences and development. The "Self" is central, ongoing, and "unaffected by the flow of the mind stream or by bodily conditions and the personal conscious self should be considered merely as its projection in the field of the personality." This image is that, perhaps, of an initial nucleus of Self, which given life experiences, develops an ego or personal self. The therapeutic focus of Psychosynthesis is ultimately to facilitate a re-identification and uniting of the personal self with the contents of the "Higher," more knowledgeable Self. (Adams, 1989, 138)

Allison (1980) states that the ISH attempts to guide the patient toward sound mental health and that after the ISH is fused with the main personality, there is no further splitting into APs. Allison considers the ISH an entity rather than a true personality. It has no desire to lead a separate life. He has found as many as six different entities within one individual, each with a clearly defined rank. He has also found an inner-self personality in treating some patients. It is a rescuer personality often created by the ISH and is the strongest and most active protector of the main personality.

I believe that Comstock (1987b) best explains the confusion over the true ISH and secondary helpers. She says that a Center, when first called upon by the therapist, may desire to respond, but being unwilling to communicate itself, it will send along a helper personality to pose as the Center. She further states that the true Center is compassionate, with a gentle, noncompetitive attitude rather than an adversarial air, and that this one quality—compassion—can help the therapist identify the true Center.

In some of the popular books about a PwDID, the patient's life was recounted by the ISH, and the ISH revealed which AP was in charge when various incidents occurred. This is the memory trace referenced above. Although the ISH's statement of which AP was in charge at any given time cannot be proven, there have been many confirmations of medical records for the PwDID. Since the ISH information and the medical records agree on location, this adds credence to the remainder of the information. Of course, the medical records do not state which AP is in control during the stay.

2. History

Dr. Ralph Allison is given credit for the modern discovery of the ISH. (*Modern* here refers to the resurgence in cases of DID in the early 1970s.) Since the time of Allison's publication of his findings in 1980, researchers have found that a similar phenomenon was known and written about when DID was frequently discussed in the late 19th century and the early part of the 20th century. However, DID was so rare then that no therapist encountered the phenomenon more than once and thus could not make comparisons. Allison thought that the first time he encountered the phenomenon it was an anomaly and therefore not that important. It was only after finding the same characteristics in several patients that he gave it the name *ISH*. The first patient's name was Janette, with an ISH named Karen. Allison tested the various personalities, and Karen's "test results indicated that she was perfect—absolutely without faults" (p. 56). Karen was also described as the source of love, appreciation, truthfulness, coping ability, and artistic talent within Janette.

Dr. Cornelia Wilbur, Sybil's therapist, encountered a similar entity she called the *memory trace* (Schreiber, 1973). Wilbur, however, identified only one of the primary abilities of the ISH: memory of all personalities. Similarly, Fraser (1987) investigated the DID literature and found that Pierre Janet, the French psychiatrist prominent a century ago, described one personality in a person with DID as having a memory of all the other personalities. Fraser also reports that Morton Prince, one of the earliest American writers on dissociative phenomena, in discussing a particular DID patient, referred to one personality with characteristics similar to the ISH as "Alpha and Omega."

Rogo (1987) recounts the case of Doris Fischer, a patient with DID who was treated by Rev. W. Franklin Prince beginning in 1909. One personality he found was named Sleeping Margaret; Prince held almost nightly discourses with her while Doris was asleep. He consulted with Sleeping Margaret about the best way to handle Doris's problems and was impressed by her maturity, psychological wisdom, and compassion for Doris. Prince was able to continue communicating with this personality (still while Doris slept) after all other personalities were fully integrated.

3. Therapy Functions

The ISH would probably not prove as interesting if it did not prove so therapeutically useful. In fact, some therapists warn other therapists not to get too involved with the phenomena of the ISH and thereby forget that their purpose is to heal their patient. Adams found that about 90% of the therapists who responded to her survey had direct contact with numerous ISHs (690 clients) and frequently or occasionally sought advice from the ISH, as they found the advice helpful, sometimes essential. Over 95% of the information reported by the ISH is accurate all or most of the time. Fraser (1987) believes that a therapist will be more effective after knowing that the ISH exists, even if the therapist does not use the abilities of the ISH. If the ISH is used, it can advise on which traumas the therapist should cover next and give advice if the therapist feels stalemated during the therapy process. Adams found that about 50% of the therapists who have used the ISH believe that each person with DID has an ISH and that 57.5% believe all unitary persons (nonmultiples) have an ISH.

Allison states that the ISH is revealed in a number of ways, including through visions, automatic writing, speech, and the presence of an inner voice. The respondents to Adams's survey reported that the ISH may emerge spontaneously (67%), may be hypnotically or nonhypnotically requested, or may send a messenger through the host or an AP. Some examples of first communication between a patient and his or her ISH, as reported by Comstock (1987b), are given in a later section.

One way the ISH can be useful to the therapist is by simply describing the patient's problem. Allison (1980) states that the ISH expects to be a working partner with the therapist. For example, Allison was treating a patient named Babs. Her ISH, named Tammy, described eight problem areas that Allison needed to help Babs handle. Allison found the advice very useful, and Babs's final fusion involved her ISH. Allison told her to lie down, put herself in a trance, and join Tammy. She was to ask Tammy to bring God's healing power into her, to be ready to accept it, and to ask that all good be fused together and all evil cast out. The next morning the true birth, or main, personality, five years old, manifested itself when Babs awoke. This frequently happens in DID therapy; that is, the final personality is one that has not been met before. If this final personality is a child, it can be hypnotically progressed to match its physical age.

Caul (1984) reports on a group therapy and videotape technique he used with one patient, during which further ISH characteristics were revealed. The "group" consisted of the various APs in one patient. Each AP was given a chance to speak and to help select a group leader. The therapist only observed. In this case, the patient had a well-defined ISH. The APs decided that the ISH would be the group leader for that session. During the session, the ISH told the host personality that the latter had acted inappropriately the previous night. The ISH spoke in a very controlled and well-modulated voice. A hostile AP came out and said the therapist was playing favorites toward one of the APs (not the ISH). The therapist realized the hostile AP was correct in that view. The APs wanted a different personality to act as the group leader in the next session. Another AP terminated the session. Caul concluded that the ISH rarely assumes an executive role, tends to get tired during prolonged activity, and retreats once fatigued. Other therapists have found that 20 minutes is about the longest the ISH can remain in control.

Caul recounts another group session in which three patients were involved. Hostile APs emerged from each patient, and the session became too chaotic and could not continue in that manner. Caul asked all three clients to allow their ISHs to emerge. The ISHs greeted Caul and introduced themselves to each other. The ISHs of two young people who had been fighting just moments before communicated with each other.

"One stated to the other, 'I see you have quite a problem.' The other replied, 'Indeed I do. Do you have any suggestions'"

Comstock (1985) states that it is more important for the client to communicate with her Center than for the therapist to communicate with the Center. Allison also emphasizes the importance of the patient's knowing her ISH and not just the therapist. Comstock contends that communicating with the Center is the most valuable asset a person with DID has and that this skill must be developed. Comstock (1987a), who believes that a therapist can offer her energy to a Center, describes her method for doing so.

According to Comstock (1987b), a Center does not usually intervene in the daily activities of the various personalities but may use its power to prevent a suicide. It will not always be successful; the suicide may be connected more to past events than to present circumstances. Thus, therapists should not think they have failed if a patient commits suicide. Comstock further states that Centers are very involved in abreactive and flashback experiences. The Center can work with the therapist in getting the most benefit from these experiences. A Center can also decide when a particular personality is ready for integration.

Comstock (1987a) maintains that the true Center is not interested in specific situational outcomes and does not give unsolicited personal advice about the therapist or other people, except with specific intent for the PwDID's growth. The Center cares for all personalities equally and pays attention to the inside personalities even while consulting with the therapist. An AP may be able to cross amnestic barriers and believe that he or she is the Center. As treatment progresses, the Center may appear more sophisticated and competent. The Center can always develop greater strengths and abilities. The Center is primarily a consultant; it does not direct therapy and will not just obediently follow the therapist's directives.

Centers have numerous abilities. Centers can accelerate healing, but they are not always attuned to the physical body and its condition. Centers can adjust the perceived passage of time, alter sensations, and slow personalities down to sleep. They have knowledge of each AP's past and can change their ages. A child personality can be made to grow up to better understand a situation, or an adult personality can be regressed to learn a childhood lesson and leave adult complexities behind. Centers can also intensify feelings. They can blend personalities for strength, for learning opportunities, or for integration. The Center may speak freely with the therapist, but it rarely converses with the therapist after integration. This is in contrast to the case of Sleeping Margaret, described above.

Comstock (1987b) reports that Centers can also make changes in internal architecture, so it can be assumed they designed the original arrangement of the APs. Arrangements are visible to the APs. Descriptions given by the APs include closets, large and small rooms, barrels with overflow vessels, and elevators of various sizes leading to a basement and sub-basements, stairs and landings, and separate apartments. Billy Milligan's personalities were described as living in cells (rooms) and as being "on the spot" when in control of the body. The therapist may suggest changes in these internal structures to place personalities closer or farther away.

Centers have their limits, according to Comstock (1987a). They cannot stifle abreactions unendingly, always control personality behavior, or keep personalities asleep or young forever. Since they are often focused on one system (the original personality and its associated APs), they do not fully understand relationships or transference with the therapist. The Center is also unaffected by trance. Some people with DID have reported their Center "gone" for periods of time, from a few minutes to fourteen days. When asked later to explain, the Center may state that it was deep inside, or "off" somewhere. The Centers do not have a clear memory of where they were, but they do understand concepts that they did not understand before. I maintain that this occurs because an ISH contacts spiritual levels above itself, such as higher helpers, which will be discussed shortly.

4. Psychological Nature of the ISH

Earlier, I provided some general statements about the nature of the ISH. I will now give more specific details.

One of the most commonly reported characteristics of the ISH is its seeming lack of emotion. One of the best descriptions of this and other properties comes from Allison:

The ISH is that part of an individual's consciousness that is free from emotion. It is not neurotic. It is pure thought and uses good judgment. ... It does not necessarily respond to cultural demands. As one multiple personality's ISH told me: "I have many functions. I am the conscience. I am the punisher if need be. I am the teacher, the answerer of questions. I am what she will be, although never completely, for she has her emotional outlets, which I do not need. But she will have my reasoning ability and my ability to look at things objectively. I will always be here and always be separate, but the kind of separateness which is yours, a oneness with a very fine line of distinction. An emergency backup, perhaps. If I am gone, she is just a body. She can send part of me off and leave a small portion. But if all is taken, she is just a shell. I am kept busy sorting out the different messes and problems created between the alter personalities. (1980, pp. 56–57)

Allison further comments that although not emotional, Karen (the ISH of a patient named Janette) was also the source of love, appreciation, truthfulness, coping ability, and artistic talent. The ISH is characterized by qualities of love, knowledge, and strength and is incapable of emotions such as anger, fear, and guilt. Allison informed Bechtel (1989), the author of a book about a multiple named Kit Castle, that an ISH speaks in an emotionless, somewhat stilted fashion, similar to a computer-generated voice.

Beahrs (1983) states that the ISH is similar to the hidden observer in hypnosis research or to the observing ego of psychoanalysis. John Watkins, developer of the concept of ego states, told Beahrs that the hidden observer (i.e., the ISH) cannot have significant power for action or else there would be no further problems. Nagy (1986) had patients use a daily log or journal as part of their treatment. He identified as the ISH one AP that he describes as calm, objective, and insightful about most other APs and competent in all situations.

Bliss (1986) believes that personalities are created by self-hypnosis. Despite this reductionist viewpoint, he describes properties of what he calls hidden observers that are "remarkably omniscient," that are "insightful psychiatrists without recourse to texts," and whose "advice was a model of clarity" (p. 141). One particular hidden observer named

Doneata knew about the other APs but had a specific age (older than the patient); she was not ageless like some ISHs. In another patient, Bliss reports that the hidden observer, nameless and not very cooperative, was referred to by the patient as *the voice* (p. 142).

As discussed earlier, Fraser (1987) maintains that the ISH usually has the same gender as the birth personality. However, Allison describes the ISH as having no gender. Andorfer (1985) reports that the ISH of a patient he was treating was asexual. Comstock (1987a) contends that an ISH may be a male or female inside a male or female body.

Andorfer describes Esther (a woman with DID), her APs, and her ISH called Athena (the Greek goddess of wisdom). Athena had complete access to the memories of all the other personalities, could search for a particular item, and could monitor consciousness, but she rarely did so. Although Esther had never finished school, Athena apparently was of superior intelligence and had a quick grasp of concepts such as personality and cognition. "Her thinking was logical, methodical, and introspective, and she alone had a psychological grasp of time" (1985, p.). Although asexual and all but emotionless, Athena expressed strong nurturing feelings for Esther (the core or host personality) and one AP. She exhibited composure, poise, and maturity, in addition to having a general memory of each of the other APs. "She was able to attenuate or completely eliminate the visceral experience of an emotion that accompanied the perception or recollection of an event by one personality, by reassigning all or part of the visceral emotion to another personality" (p.). In addition, she could "write" and "produce" customized nocturnal dreams for Esther, as well as alter details of recurring dreams. All of these abilities were employed at one time or another during treatment. Comstock (1987a) reports similar dream phenomena with other ISHs.

Ludwig et al. (1972) discuss several APs in one individual in their report on physiological and psychophysiological differences among the APs. The first "alternate" personality to appear in one particular patient seemed to have the characteristics of an ISH. (Normally the ISH is not considered an AP and does not appear first.) This entity served as a memory trace, a role usually performed by the ISH. Called Sammy and sometimes referred to as the lawyer or the mediator, he described himself as purely intellectual, rational, and legalistic. He was interested in accumulating knowledge for knowledge's sake, represented pure reason, and displayed no emotion. Ludwig et al.'s interpretation of an "Adjective Check List" (ACL) showed Sammy with the highest number of favorable items compared to other APs. Sammy is described by the ACL as obliging, mannerly, tactful, optimistic, friendly, outgoing, reflective, serious, nonaggressive, self-controlled, and heterosexual.

Ross does not discuss much about ISHs, but he makes the following comment:

> Concerning the "superior" intelligence of the dissociated ego in DID patients, I want to say a couple of things. Some skilled therapists feel that the patient's inner observer embodies a superior spiritual knowledge (Comstock, 1987). It is my experience that Inner Self helpers can be excellent cotherapists, but they do not have transcendental abilities: In Myers's terms, the subliminal self may be equal to the supraliminal in IQ, but it is not necessarily more intelligent. (Ross, 1997, 33)

I speculate that these characteristics closely resemble the spiritual aspect of humans that I call Spirit. In victims of abuse, they function more as rescuer rather than creative inspirer, such as of scientific insight or the impetus to produce a luminous score of music.

5. Parapsychological and Religious Phenomena

I assert that parapsychological and religious phenomena are related to contact with the Spirit aspect of humans, similar to an encounter that a near-death experiencer (NDEr) has with the transcendental realm of an NDE and the consequent transformation of the NDEr's life. Allison's description of the ISH includes statements such as the following:

> I have had conversations with the ISH aspect of my patients, and I've discovered that they regard themselves as agents of God, with the power to help the main personality. ... Some of the higher-ranking ISHs never seem truly to fuse; they continue to exist as spiritual teachers of the main personality. ... The final step before total recovery is positive spiritual fusion. This occurs between the final resulting personality and the ISH. It can happen so quietly that the patient remains unaware of

the fusion, or the patient may experience either a vision or a strong sense of spirituality. Many patients have said that it occurs with a conscious determination to follow God as they understand Him. (pp. 109–10)

Allison adds that in addition to knowing the patient's history, the ISH can predict the future with great accuracy, but he gives no examples. Although this is not necessarily related to the ISH aspect of his DID therapy, Allison states that during therapy he has witnessed parapsychological phenomena for which he has no explanation. Metaphysical descriptions of the ISH given to Adams in her survey include a unifying element, hyperintellectual and inhuman, an invincible part of the human spirit, one's own spirit or soul, the guardian of the spirit, aspects of the Spirit of God, an old soul from built-up lifetimes, and/or a part of the patient's unconscious that is in touch with even higher helpers.

In a patient named Jonah and his ISH named Sammy, Ludwig et al. (1972) state that Sammy told them during one interview that another personality was brewing inside Jonah. This new personality was described as "scattered but gathering" and would be an amalgamation and condensation of many thoughts, actions, motives, and attitudes. This new personality would be very belligerent and angry. However, this personality never emerged during therapy. Was Sammy an ISH, was the ISH wrong, or, as I believe, did intervention and treatment prevent the complete formation of this additional personality? Although the therapists who report that ISHs could predict the future did not give examples, the predictions were most likely of this nature, that is, of new personalities or events concerning the patient.

Comstock (1985) states that Centers have the ability to directly communicate with other Centers verbally and nonverbally or "in seeming inexplicable ways." For instance, "A therapist may experience replication of the physical feelings of the PwDID before an abreaction. The therapist may have a visual image from the scene, may make a remark or take out-of-character action based upon a 'hunch' or may have a sudden insight about the person or the past which defies 'reasonable' explanation". Although Comstock does not use these words, she implies that the client's Center is communicating with the therapist's Center telepathically.

Comstock (1987b) cites some examples of Center-to-Center communication between therapist and patient, as mentioned above, but the examples are difficult to summarize. Instead of calling it telepathy, she gives the communication several possible identifications, such as empathic trance, intuition, projective identification, indwelling attention, or serendipity. Its use is more important than its mystery. Perhaps C. G. Jung's concept of synchronicity would be another relevant term.

6. One Specific ISH

One particular biography of a PwDID discusses her ISH in detail, including her final integration. The PwDID is "Kit" Castle. Her original name was Elizabeth Katherine Castle, and Kit is a nickname, short for, *Katherine, It's Time*, the title of her book. The book, written by Stefan Bechtel, is based on 40 hours of interviews with Kit a year and a half after her integration, which Kit refers to as her birth. She feels that she did not exist prior to then but was seven different personalities, named Kitty Rosetti, Penny Lavender, Jess, Liz, Me-Liz, Little Andrea, and Little Elizabeth. As mentioned earlier, it is not completely unheard of for the final personality to be an identity other than the birth or host personality.

Castle had an ISH named Michael (the name means "one who is like God"), whom Bechtel discusses in a preface section called "Note to the Reader." The bulk of the book describes numerous adventures of Castle's seven alter personalities. According to Bechtel, Allison believes the ISH is not an AP because none of the ISHs he had encountered had a date of birth. In contrast, most of the APs recall being "born" as a result of a traumatic incident in the life of the PwDID.

Kit's therapist was the psychiatrist Dr. Ralph G. Walton. In the foreword to her book, he describes himself as a mainstream psychiatrist. However, as he writes, working with Kit challenged much of his conventional training:

> The experience of therapy with Kit raised questions for me not only about human identity, but forced me to confront fundamental metaphysical issues of reality. Events that transpired during our hours of therapy quite literally sent shivers down my spine, raised goosebumps on my skin, and more often started me thinking about developments in modern physics than psychiatry. For example, I believe that

the confluence of spin, energy, and identity, as outlined in Kit's description of the "final farandola"[1]—the high-velocity spin that she maintains completed her transformation into a whole, unified personality—to an outstanding degree mirror some of the recent developments in quantum mechanics and theoretical physics, which indicate that the ultimate nature or identity of the universe is very much related to the concept of spin. (Castle and Bechtel, 1989, viii)

The knowledge of the farandola was presented to Kit by Michael, also described as a *guide*, a term frequently used by NDErs. He was visible only to Kit and her various APs. Michael would appear wearing a dark coat and a dark hat. He said he was her lifelong friend and protector, and she thought of him as a guardian angel. An unnamed DID therapist with whom Bechtel consulted explained that perhaps Michael, Kit's ISH, created the farandola as a method to visualize a process that she would not otherwise understand.

The following is a description of Michael in the main text of the book. Kit was in a difficult situation, caused by one of her APs, and she had not been in contact with Michael for a decade. The reason she had not in contact with Michael was that she had thrown him out, without good cause. Michael had informed the AP named Liz that he could only appear if she allowed it. She had to let him return. A decade later, she (not necessarily Liz) called his name and he replied.

"My child," he said gently. "My child."

He took her in his arms and held her and comforted her he didn't say anything more. He just held her and rocked her for a long, long time, like mother would rock a badly frightened child.

---

[1] The definition of *farandole* from *the Second College Edition of the American Heritage Dictionary* (1982) is "a spirited circle dance of Provençal derivation, or the music for such a dance." The word *farandola* did not appear in that dictionary, but I assume it is a variation of *farandole*.

She wept.

Michael had been so dear to her once. Over the terrible, gray years of her childhood, before she gave up hope completely and threw him out of her life, he had come to her a thousand times. He had been her guide and protector, her teacher, her beloved friend. She didn't know exactly where he came from. She just knew that he was there when she needed him the most. Michael told her she had a porch light inside her heart, and that when there was a danger and she cried out for help, he could see the light go on. He would come down out of the sky to help when he saw that porch light in her heart. "There will be times when you're afraid, and times you'll feel alone, but you must never forget that your real father watches over you always," Michael told her. "And that he'll send me to help you when there is danger."

It was true: whenever she feared for her life and cried out in her heart, he would appear, smiling gently, always wearing that same dark coat and dark hat. Sometimes her tears made spots on that coat. ... His manner was always stiff and formal, ... he had saved her so many times! More than once, she thought, she would have died without him. (Castle and Bechtel, 1989, 98–99)

Bechtel was curious about who Michael was, so he gave Kit a series of questions that she was to ask Michael and then type out his replies. Bechtel listed three replies that do not seem to explain anything, a sort of jabberwocky. The answers raise more questions than they provide meaningful answers. Asked to describe who and what you are, the response was, "I am Michael. I am created by my creator, who is your creator. I am created by the same force that created all that you can see and all that you cannot see. I am a healer. Some will see me as an enabler, although this is a misconception." To the question of whether he was a part of Kit, or Kit was a part of him, the response was, "I am both one with Kit, and yet not one with Kit. She is both one with me, and yet not one with me. The explanation is that I reside not only in this plane, but in many, many parallel dimensions that exist." To the question of what was his purpose, the response was, "I am created specifically as guardian and healer of this child. I cannot tell you if I have been gifted with all knowledge. I can tell you that when a question arises, the answer is provided, for me as well as for her. She is her own creator and therefore self-knowing, but is also of this world, so is also self-denying. My function is to create balance" (Castle and Bechtel, xiv).

One day Michael informed the AP named Me-Liz that her mitochondria were out of whack and that she would have to use a farandola to fix them. This message from Michael came at a point in her life when a new medical problem was occurring about every three weeks. Me-Liz was a personality with strong spiritual interest; she would sometimes see other "*beings of light.*" I would classify her as a helper personality. She most closely functioned with Liz. Liz was a "bad" girl (i.e., she engaged in activities that society or religion does not condone), and Me-Liz was good (she always thought of herself as a virgin). When Liz was in pain, Me-Liz took it away. If Liz felt guilt and shame, Me-Liz would remove those feelings. When Kit talked to her doctor about what Michael had told her, her doctor said the mitochondria are a kind of powerhouse, or energy center of the cell, and that he had no idea what a farandola is. Me-Liz discussed the farandola with Michael, and he explained it:

> Calmly and gently, with an unfathomable smile, he'd doff his black hat and demonstrate a slow, stately, slightly comical spin. Arms uplifted, hat doffed in one hand, that enigmatic smile would come around again and again. It was the spin of the farandola, he said. This was not a dance that was to take place in the visible dimension. It was to take place inside her cells. It was a dance that would create so much heat she would be transformed.
>
> It would kill her, he said.
>
> And it would make her whole. (Castle and Bechtel, 1989, 169)

Shortly after Kit began therapy with Dr. Walton, something unusual happened. All of the APs could hear the questions that Dr. Walton asked. No longer was one AP "in" and the others "out." Michael explained that this was part of accelerated collective therapy, the first great slow spin of the farandola.

There were a number of preliminary farandola spins before the final one. In each, Kit would get somewhat better, psychologically and physically. For instance, one time she was admitted to the hospital for what was thought to be tuberculosis, detectable by x-ray. After a spin, the doctor could no longer detect the tuberculosis. The description of the final farandola was mostly about the trepidation that each of the APs felt when they realized the life they had been living for so many years would be gone. I will not describe the individual details. Bechtel states that Kit believes she could not have been integrated without her faith in the farandola, but of course many other people have been integrated without such a device.

> Kit did feel that she was born the day of her final farandola and had to learn many simple activities, including simple arithmetic and how to tie her shoes. Michael explained what happened to the other APs to her, as follows:
>
> "Little Elizabeth was diffused," he said. "Little Andrea was diffused. Jess is now with a medical student in Hamilton, Ontario, Canada. He is to this student what I am to you. Penny Lavender resides in a level where a form of communication is tonal in nature. Me-Liz resides with her 'real father.' Liz resides with her 'real father.' Kitty resides in the area of color that surrounds you. She is not our view, but remains near. It will be necessary for her to make a reappearance for a very short period of time. There is unfinished business." (Castle and Bechtel, 1989, 302)

Does the statement about Jess imply that an AP can become an ISH?

Kit discussed with Michael what she could do to end the cycle of abuse in society. She told Michael that she was only one person and didn't have the ability to change the world. His reply was, "We all have the ability to change the world, if we only take responsibility for changing ourselves" (p. 303).

Bechtel reveals that as part of Kit's research on DID after her integration, she spoke to an unidentified leading authority on DID. A few days after she spoke with the authority, Michael informed her that he would like to speak to the therapist. While she was on the phone,

Michael spoke through her, and she lost time and had no recollection of the conversation. Afterward, in speaking to the therapist, Kit obtained the following information. Michael reported that there were others and that they were in desperate need. A whole new layer of APs emerged, three years after supposed integration. Dr. Richard Kluft reported that he has previously encountered that phenomenon. Dr. Kluft believes that Kit's integration was incomplete since Michael survived, but I believe that an ISH is part of our spiritual nature and not an AP. Kit reentered therapy as her book was being written, but I could not find any additional information about her.

It should be noted that Bechtel encountered a juvenile fiction book by Madeleine L'Engle (1918–2007) titled *A Wind in the Door*, which mentions mitochondria in connection with a farandolae. Bechtel inquired if Kit had read the book, and she denied it, though it is possible that one of her personalities did read it. *A Wind in the Door* is part of a trilogy about one family. The first book in the series, *A Wrinkle in Time*, won the Newbery Medal in 1963. L'Engle's books are often at the confluence of religion/spirituality and modern science.

7. Alternative Explanations

Without discussing unconventional reasons, I will provide several explanations for the existence of the ISH. Most are based on theories for creation of the APs, only that in this case the ISH, the personality, has more advanced abilities. These theories are as follows:

1. Creation by evolution of helper personalities
2. Creation by circumstances or situation
3. Creation by example, imitation, or remembrance
4. Creation by an ego state
5. Creation by the therapist

All DID therapists have encountered helper personalities—those that help solve messes created by hostile or persecutor personalities. For instance, a helper personality may drive to a hospital after one of the APs makes a suicide attempt. Thus, many therapists believe these helper personalities simply develop greater competence and appear much different from the other APs. A behaviorist may say that rewarding the reliable behavior of a helper personality encourages more of that behavior. Therapists who strongly believe that the ISH is a difference of kind, not a difference of degree, hold that helper personalities were created by the ISH, not vice versa.

Many APs are believed to be created by situations or circumstances that the host personality does not have the psychological or physical resources to handle, at least not at the time of creation of the AP. For instance, a child abused by his parent may be unable to express his anger for fear of reprisal, so he creates an AP to express his anger. Likewise, a person with DID who has low self-esteem and feels weak-minded and hypersensitive may create an AP that is superintelligent and nonemotional. Actually, it is not just another AP, it is the ISH—and it has been there all along.

Some APs can be created from examples of behavior encountered earlier in life. For instance, a person with DID who remembers a favorite teacher may create an AP with behavior similar to that teacher. An ISH often acts as a therapist, so presumably the patient admires her therapist and creates an AP with similar characteristics. Fraser characterized the ISH as psychologically minded. It should be pointed out that in two cases previously described, the personality I identified as an ISH made its appearance prior to therapy. One case was that of the ISH called Guardian Angel. The other case involved a patient named Jonah and his ISH, Sammy. Jonah's parents (mother and stepfather) had a violent altercation when Jonah was about six years old. The stepfather was hospitalized and the mother briefly incarcerated. When the two "got together at home again, Sammy emerged and calmly informed them that they had behaved irresponsibly and that it was unwise for them to fight in front of their children" Andorfer (1985). Appearance prior to therapy is the exception, but I argue that the ISH has been constantly present and its activity only becomes apparent after therapy begins.

John and Helen Watkins's theory is that each AP represents a different ego state. Whereas a normal individual can differentiate between which set of behavior patterns to use for each situation, a person with DID compartmentalizes his behavior according to one or two predominant emotions or traits. The ISH simply represents an intelligent, emotionless ego state.

A possible factor in each of the above explanations is iatrogenesis (doctor-caused phenomena). In most cases the ISH does not appear until therapy has begun. Of course, some writers who are skeptical of DID in general believe that all APs are created within the patient—therapist relationship, but the ISH concept is especially prone to this explanation. In Adams's survey (1989, 140), respondents were allowed to make unstructured comments. One respondent commented that the ISH is "the only type of personality the incidence of which seems to correlate with the therapist's belief system." On the other hand, one stated, "If this is iatrogenic, I'll eat my license to practice psychology." Another stated that labeling the ISHs as iatrogenic is "a function of the ego of some professionals who need to feel that they can really create something." Obviously, I maintain that the ISH is not iatrogenic; it is an aspect of human spirituality.

8. Beyond the ISH

Allison (1985) describes some details about the higher helpers (HHs), who are above the ISH. This information came from unpublished material he provided to me, so even though I employ quotations, no page numbers are listed. Some additional information about the ISH itself is also provided. The ISH identifies itself as "the best within the patient's mind," but "higher helpers identify themselves as spirits, not parts of the patient's mental mechanism." These HHs generally appear only in patients with more than five APs and thus are more severely dissociated. The ISH, despite its abilities, which have previously been described, becomes worn out and must call upon HHs for advice. Allison generally has to insist upon meeting the HHs, as they do not spontaneously present themselves. When Allison asks to meet an HH, the patient appears to enter a mediumistic trance state, and then Allison is introduced to the first member of the HHs. Each of the HHs has a specialized function, but they all work together as a board of directors of sorts. This board would regularly seek Allison's advice, as he was considered an expert advisor. They would try Allison's suggestions internally to see if any would help. Even when the suggestion did not help, this did not discourage the HHs from asking for more recommendations.

A lower-level HH may be the deceased spirit of someone who died several hundred years ago and has been assigned by God to help a patient. These HHs' stories of their lives on earth cannot be proven or disproven. Beyond that, an HH may be a spirit who has never been incarnate. Because of this, the HH cannot appreciate the difficulties humans have in carrying out its ideas. Hence, an HH may work with another HH that was incarnate and only with specific APs.

Beyond the second HH may be a third HH who was incarnated many thousands of years ago, perhaps in a highly religious role. This third HH may train other helper spirits. These student helper spirits may spend two hundred years being educated prior to becoming independent HHs.

Allison learned that if he doubted an HH's honesty, he could not successfully treat that patient. Once he accused an HH of lying and the HH did not function for several weeks until Allison determined that the HH was correct and apologized. The HH indicated that if Allison did not trust it, then the patient would not trust it either, which would make the HH powerless.

One manner in which HHs can assist the therapist is by relaying "what is really the patient's concern of the moment." The HH may also make suggestions to the therapist for rehabilitating the patient. Comstock (1987a), in discussing ISHs, states that they do not give orders. Allison explains that although HHs will not instruct a therapist on how to do a particular function, they have told him "what needs to be done, in what order, and by what deadline." He felt he knew what to do when the time arrived to accomplish the goals set by the HH. HHs can also discern the internal effects (beneficial or not) of previously prescribed medications.

There are several precautions to take when employing the HHs. A therapist is not to overuse them; otherwise, the patient may become jealous and ignore the HHs' advice inside his or her head. After exposure to a therapist, the HHs are less effective upon returning inside, with no reason given for this. Also, when talking to an outsider, an HH cannot control the disorder inside the patient's mind. The recommended maximum conversation time with an ISH is 20 minutes per day. Allison prefers to have the patient ask the HH his questions and then give him the HHs' answers. This leads the patient to recognize and trust the HH when Allison is not around.

Although most discussions with the HHs are in regard to a patient's therapy, Allison has had brief philosophical/religious discussions with them. "All higher helpers consider themselves under the guidance of a Supreme Being." The beliefs of the HHs appear independent of the religious upbringing, if any, of the patient. The HHs can distinguish "between alter personalities, helper spirits, and evil spirits by the way they look inside the mind, as well as by their behavior."

To remove evil spirits, HHs recommend an exorcism only after the "anger energy," which attracted the evil spirit in the first place, has been neutralized by psychotherapy. After the "emotional electromagnet" that attracted the evil spirit has been discharged, "any worthy individual may call upon a higher power to send the evil spirit out of the patient, back to where it belongs."

After fusion of the APs, the HHs remain available to the patient. All of the HHs responsible for a certain number of APs also seem to integrate into one, "so that the entire guidance function is located in the higher helper who has always had the assignment of helping the primary personality."

This concept of HHs corresponds well with Max Freedom Long's contention that the High Self has access to resources beyond itself. The individual human does not have to concern herself with those higher levels; the High Self knows when it requires further assistance and automatically seeks it.

9. ISH Summary

Therapists of people with DID, if they have not encountered the ISH phenomenon themselves, may discount the importance of using the ISH in their therapy. This summary of findings on the ISH should acquaint the reader with the phenomenon and the fact that some therapists consider use of the ISH essential. DID therapy time is usually very long, and interaction with the ISH may decrease it. Therapists with suicidal patients should be especially interested in this information, because the ISH is known to have intervened to prevent suicide. When compared to the abilities of an AP, the abilities of the ISH are a difference of kind and not of degree. Although most ISHs show similar characteristics, they have some individuality as well.

Some of the previous, nonspiritual explanations of the ISH phenomenon may be given by a therapist, but my theory is that the ISH is the "Spirit" aspect and that each human being "has" an ISH. In the physical world, we operate with our personality (a spiritual component of ourselves separate from the ISH) and physical body. Although we normally have only one personality with which the ISH functions, our ISH cannot simply eliminate intruding personalities, especially if they have legitimate functions. One of the reasons that the ISH may not directly have "all the answers" to healing a patient is that it is more spiritual and less connected to the physical and psychological nature of humans. In chapter 11, I discuss how there is a hierarchy of spirits in each person and how each is less connected to the physical body.

F. Findings about and Phenomena of DID

1. A Healthy Disease?

DID is sometimes referred to as a healthy disease, meaning that the creation of an AP (called splitting) may prevent further mental breakdown or physical destruction of the core individual. One form of breakdown is to retreat into an autistic or similar state, totally shutting oneself off from the outside world. A second possibility is to become psychotic, to more or less lose control. The third possibility is to somatize the problem, that is, to turn what is a mental illness into a physical problem. The last possibility is to attempt suicide and, if successful, to completely destroy the vehicle for the personality. There is often one AP that seeks suicide, but there are also helper or rescuer personalities that work at nothing but prevention of harm, such as committing suicide. These helper personalities rarely appear to perform a function for the outside world, but they may assume control of the body if one destructive personality attempts suicide. For instance, the helper personality could call a doctor after the person ingests an overdose of pills or take control of an automobile after a destructive personality drives toward a cliff.

In addition to the above forms of breakdown, Ross (1997) states that a fundamental conundrum for many PwDID is the problem of "attachment to the perpetrator." In the case of childhood abuse, the victim of the abuse needs the perpetrator in order to survive. A five-year-old girl being sexually abused by her father cannot simply get up and leave the situation, so she imagines that the abuse is happening to someone else. "She may float up to the ceiling and watch the abuse [i.e., have an OBE] in a detached fashion" (p. 64). The problem often becomes that the victim may then feel responsible for the abuse. Ross informs the patient that even though she may have derived some pleasure during the abuse, such does not demonstrate that she wanted it emotionally. This guilt over responsibility for the abuse may result in adult women who were abused as children seeking out men who are abusers and defending the abusive action instead of leaving the person who perpetrates it.

I have no quarrel with therapists who argue that creation of APs may be healthier than other options. The argument remains the same: DID is a departure of the original personality. The problem is that the original spiritual body may not know "who" (i.e., what type of AP) will enter when it departs. If the original personality were bent on suicide, then any option would be better in the long term. If the AP commits suicide, then the splitting option was not "healthier;" however, when dealing with spiritual decisions, it is not a reliable measure to judge healthiness.

2. Gender Differences

Early statistics showed a ratio of almost nine females to one male among those who developed DID. The responses in the two survey studies previously discussed (Putnam et al. [1986] and Ross et al. [1989]) were 81% and 92% female. The ratio is now listed by the *DSM-III-R* as three to nine times more frequent among females. I agree with researchers who believe the ratio is more nearly equal (two or three to one), but men with the disorder are usually processed through the criminal justice system and women through the mental-health system. Putnam found that males with DID are readily found in mental-health facilities, but they are commonly misdiagnosed with personality disorders or as substance abusers. Bliss (1984) states that male patients tend to be more sociopathic with a higher incidence of alcoholism, whereas females are more hysterical with anxiety-related symptoms. Carlisle (1986) provides a report on 15 PwDID he found in a state prison. The total number of inmates screened for DID was not provided. Carlisle states that in many cases, an AP committed the crime and the host personality and APs were unable to prevent it. "In one case the crime was committed to put the host in an institutional setting." I believe most mass murderers, serial murderers, or "publicity" murderers either are PwDID or have an intruding spirit. Some examples will be discussed in chapter 10, on spirit intrusion and release.

However, there are some indications that schizophrenia is more common in men. Since I believe that schizophrenia is partial dissociation, there may be a factor in the spiritual body–physical body relationship that makes it easier for a woman to completely dissociate and for a man to partially dissociate. The higher ratio of women with DID may also simply reflect the fact that girls are more likely to be sexually molested than boys and that most PwDID have been victims of such abuse.

3. Frequency

Until 1970, DID was thought to be very rare; only several hundred cases had been discovered nationwide. Researchers are now finding that DID is much more common. The fact that the *DSM-III* gave more prominence to DID resulted in more correct diagnosis of the problem. These newer figures should not be compared to the old ones to show a rate of increase, because the baseline for comparison is incorrect. However, based on social inputs into the cause of the problem (which is discussed in "Etiology" and again in "Conclusions"), I believe there will be a major increase in the incidence of DID within the next few years, possibly a million cases or more. Putnam (1986) states that 1972 is the year the number of cases began to accelerate. The significance of 1972 will be discussed later, in chapter 12 of this book.

In *People Magazine* (1979), Dr. Cornelia Wilbur, Sybil's analyst and a well-known writer in the field of DID, estimated that there are possibly 5,000 PwDID in the United States. A current estimate by the National Alliance for the Mentally III is that 0.01% to 0.1% of the population has DID. Schizophrenia will be discussed in another chapter; however, some information is given here to shed light on the commonality of DID. Bliss et al. (1983) report that 27 of 45 patients (60%) admitted to a single inpatient psychiatric service unit with auditory hallucinations (often considered a symptom of schizophrenia) were discovered to have personalities responsible for the voices. Each year there are about 300,000 new cases of schizophrenia reported (Ubell 1986). If the above figure, 60%, is correct, then that is 180,000 new cases of DID each year. Sixty percent appears high because the base of 45 patients consisted of those who were both willing to cooperate and able to enter a trance state. Even if the figure is 10%, that is a very significant number of new cases. Similarly, Ross reports that in one study, 23% of foster children who were difficult to manage met the criteria for DID.

In Sangamon County, Illinois, where I reside, the reported cases of child abuse grew from 66 in 1975 to over 4,000 in 1985. There may have been some underreporting in the earlier year, but in any case the increase is astounding. Since child abuse is a major factor in DID, a proportionate increase in DID could be expected.

4. Family Patterns

I believe that the tendency to get DID may not be, and probably is not, inherited, but it may run in families because an AP in an adult may be the abuser. The *DSM-III-R* states that DID is more frequent in first-degree biological relatives of people with the disorder. The tendency to get DID may not be inherited, but the tendency to dissociate may well be inherited. Spiritual causes and inherited tendencies are not antithetical. The factor of child abuse will be discussed more in the section titled "Etiology."

In a DID parent who abuses his or her child, the host or original personality of the adult may not be aware of the abuse and may strongly deny that it has occurred if a therapist questions the perpetrator about it. When there are two adults in the family, one would think that one of those adults would be mentally healthy enough to be aware of the abuse, but that second adult may passively approve of the abuse. For instance, if the father (often under the influence of alcohol) is abusing the child, the mother may live in fear of her husband.

5. Amnesia

Amnesia is defined as total loss of memory or gaps within memory. Here, the word *amnesia* implies no recollection whatever. A person would not say she had amnesia if she remembered a face but not a name. Some causes of amnesia, other than dissociating, include Alzheimer's disease, injuries to the head, and substance abuse.

In the section titled "Description and Diagnosis," signs used by therapists that suggest DID are listed (p. 220). Amnesia is not mentioned directly, but it is considered a prime requirement for a definitive diagnosis of DID. Time distortion (sign 6), disremembered behavior (sign 7), and possession of unrecognizable objects (sign 9) are indicators that help determine if the patient has amnesia. A therapist cannot simply ask a patient if he has amnesia, because the patient would most likely answer "no."

When one personality departs the body and another arrives, several possibilities arise, depending on the circumstances of the APs. One possibility is that the personality or personalities not in control are in a sleeplike state. When a particular personality regains control of the body, it is similar to waking up. The awakened personality does not stop to inquire what was happening, because he or she believes he or she was sleeping. A PwDID is often defensive because she is often accused of doing things she knows she did not do (see item 7 under "characteristic signs"). Inquiries to the family are often important since it may be easier to ask them if they saw the subject do something that she says she did not do.

Professionals who treat DID often speak of one- and two-way amnesia. Normally the host personality is not directly aware of personalities that follow, but later personalities are often aware of those that precede them. If the host personality, A, is not aware of personality B, nor B of A, then this is two-way amnesia. If B is aware of A but A is not aware of B, this is one-way amnesia. Not only can there be awareness, but also there can be communication. As related in the section on diagnosis, Allison (1984) was not surprised by dialogue between the host and an AP, but amnesia of the dialogue was unusual.

Although professional journals are often the best sources of information, they can be limited in that they discuss generalities from information presented by a therapist who has treated many DID patients. To review some useful information, it is often necessary to present specific case histories and detailed descriptions. This discussion is, to a great extent, based on cases reported in popular books. How valid several individual cases are is not certain. Perhaps an individual case is a quirk and 99% of all cases are much different. Regardless. the alternates' descriptions of themselves as reported in the book *The Minds of Billy*

Milligan, by Daniel Keyes (1981), are very interesting. The alternates report themselves by being "on the spot" when in control of the body. By *spot*, they mean in a bright spotlight. When they were not on the spot, they were asleep in "cells" surrounding the spot. Allison (1980) mentions a person with 35 APs, where the situation was like a boardinghouse in which each personality had a separate room.

The awareness of an inactive, or "sleeping," AP often seems to be an emotional awareness rather than event awareness. The AP is not able to indicate where the personality in control was at any given time, though it may know who (not necessarily by name) the control personality was at the time. This is consistent with the concept that the inactive alternates remain attached to the body and can pick up some nervous system impressions. When discussing memory of behavior, it should be noted, as Kluft (1985) observes, that true memory involves actual participation in the event discussed. If the original personality, or Alternate A, "wakes up" in a body and is told or speaks of what "he" or "she" did (i.e., an action performed bodily when another alternate, such as B, was in control), then Kluft refers to this as knowledge of an event and not true memory. The AP not in control may refer to the original personality as being a weakling for not standing up for herself.

Similar to learning about an activity but not remembering it is figuring out that "someone else" must be using the same body. Arthur, the very intelligent AP in Billy Milligan (Keyes, 1981), was able to figure out what was happening and eventually became aware of many of the other APs. Mesulam (1981) reports a case where two personalities (the host and one AP) communicated by way of written notes (this was apparently before therapy began). Nagy (1985) had the various APs keep a journal so they could become aware of each other and what the others were thinking. Kluft (1984) describes two sisters he was treating concurrently. He had the sisters agree not to discuss their therapies. Each sister had a personality that described seeing her sister being abused, but each sister was amnestic for abuses done to the other personalities in her own body.

The above discussion describes reasons for not remembering behavior, as in sign 7. Sign 6 (time lapses or time distortion) is similar, but instead of being told of unremembered behavior, the patient may wonder where time disappeared to. An AP may experience days or weeks between periods of having bodily control. When coming into control, an alternate may wonder where the time went. It certainly must be disconcerting to appear on occasion in an unknown location, not knowing the time, wondering where the time went, dressed in strange clothes, and not knowing anyone. Therapists say that PwDID are survivors and learn to adapt to these situations. It seems as though it is usually not chance that leads a certain personality to take control of the body. When the original personality or one of the less physical APs is threatened, a violent personality will often take control and handle the situation. Perhaps the violent personality's appearance is triggered by adrenalin in the bloodstream or some other, unknown bodily cause.

Finally, another way of considering if a person has amnesia is to ask if unrecognized objects or handwriting have been found. Frequently these objects will include clothes, because if the original personality is staid, almost certainly there will be an AP that is flamboyant and wears wild clothes. Handwriting will be discussed under the topic of psychophysiology.

6. Typical Alternate Personalities, and Their Names and Numbers

Prior to 1979, DID was referred to as *dual personality*. Much has been learned about the main types of alternates from the two surveys described earlier. Putnam et al. (1986) express many figures regarding AP type. In some cases, the figures seem inconsistent. For instance, in the text, 85% of the subjects had a child personality (the AP is younger than 12 years of age), but the chart showed only 75%. The patients were all adults. Putnam et al. also note that the high number of infant, child, and adolescent personalities may explain why regressed behavior is sometimes noted in PwDID. In 30% of the cases, an AP reported his or her age as being older than the patient's.

An AP of the opposite gender was reported in 53% of the cases. There were only eight males in the entire group, but six had a female AP, though the sample was too small to be conclusive. In 68%of the cases, the personality seeking treatment was unaware of the existence of other personalities, and in 72% of the cases one or more of the APs were unaware of other personalities. There was a depressed personality in 70% of the cases. Suicide attempts were made by 61% of the patients (one of these attempts was successful). In 53% of the patients, there were incidents of an internal homicide, wherein one AP attempted to kill another AP. Gale (1986) states that frequently one AP may punish a more vulnerable child AP, believing that the child misbehaved. It may even go so far as attempting to kill the child.

In 34% of the cases, there was self-mutilation inflicted by one personality on another as punishment. Assaultive or destructive behavior directed outward was reported in 70% of the cases. Homicidal behavior was attributed to one specific AP in 29% of the cases, and six of the patients allegedly committed a homicide. In this survey, the patient was more likely to be a victim of sexual assault (or rape) than a perpetrator. Remember that 92% of the subjects were female, and females are more likely to be victims in the general population. In the survey, 48% were victims and 20% sexually assaulted another. The researchers did not address the question of whether the assaults by females were actually committed by a male AP. Sexual promiscuity was engaged in by 51% of the cases. Other characteristics included an obsessive-compulsive personality and a personality analgesic to pain (both 45 percent). A substance-abuser personality, which occurred in 52% of the cases, will be discussed in section 12 of this chapter.

In their survey of 236 cases, Ross et al. (1989) report the following percentages of various personalities: child personality, 86%; personality of a different age, 84.5%; protector personality and persecutor personality, 84% each; personality of the opposite sex, 62.6%; personality identified as a demon, 28.6%; personality identified as another living person, 28.1% personality of a different race, 21.1% and personality identified as a dead relative, 20.6%

If the spiritual concept is considered, it is very easy to comprehend why there can be so many APs. Once the original spirit body of the patient departs the physical body, any number of roaming spirit bodies can take advantage of the unoccupied body.

TABLE 6.1. Functions of Personalities

Patient's Problem	Personality's Task
Emotional Experiences	
Fear	Be afraid
Unhappiness	Be happy

Sadness and depression	Be depressed
Fear of crying	Cry for her
Sense of shame	Be ashamed
Loneliness	Be lonely
Bitterness	Be bitter
Guilty feelings	Be guilty
Suicidal thoughts and feelings	Have courage to commit suicide
Anger and rage	Experience anger
Homicidal thoughts	Kill for her
Loss of trust	Love and trust
Loneliness	A playmate, a brother, a sister, a friend who died
Unloving mother	A good, kind mother
Feel ugly	Be beautiful

Skills

Feels stupid, incompetent,	Be an intellectual, a singer, an artist,
and untalented	or a writer
Shy and afraid of people	Be friendly, gregarious, and unafraid of people; be assertive
Unloved by mother	Be like mother, or like a sister who is preferred by the mother
Mistreated	Be unafraid to retaliate for abuses
Feel physically weak	Be strong and pugnacious, and fight like a boy
Unpopular and shy	Be a comedian, or be able to party, dance, and get drunk
Want to escape, but afraid to	Run away

Sexuality

Inability to cope with	Handle sexuality to the point of

heterosexuality, rape, sexual abuse	promiscuity and prostitution
Homosexual impulses	Be a lesbian

Motivation	
Sense of inadequacy, inability, futility	Push to achieve and excel

Source: Bliss (1980)

Just as one AP may face pain and humiliation by fighting back, another AP is frequently a child that simply absorbs the pain. For instance, in Billy Milligan, one of the primary APs was David, age eight (Billy was 26 at the time). David was referred to as the "keeper of the pain" or as "empath." (A summary of all the personalities in Billy Milligan is given in the "Case Histories" section.) Allison (1980) states that Debra, a childlike personality in a patient named Carrie, protected Carrie from hurt. The Putnam et al. (1986) and Ross et al. (1989) surveys both mention the high frequency of child personalities, but neither survey discusses their function.

At times the APs will have last names; at others, just first names. Quite frequently the names imply a function or disposition. For instance, "Melody" may be the name of an AP interested in music; "Banana Split Girl" may be the name of an AP that likes banana splits. One of Billy Milligan's APs was named Ragen and was referred to as "keeper of the rage." Some APs are created to perform minor roles. Allison (1980) reports that one patient named Carla had an AP for the exclusive purpose of watching reruns of a children's TV program. This could be called a personality fragment given its singular function.

Some of the characteristics of the APs seem unrelated to their purpose or function. For instance, in the "Psychophysiology" section it will be shown that an AP brings with itself all the characteristics of a different person. That section cites mostly laboratory studies, not individual cases. The "Case Histories" section will note atypical observations reported by therapists. The following paragraphs discuss typical characteristics.

Therapists treating PwDID have long noted an unusual range of characteristics of the personalities that control the physical body at various times. One characteristic is age range. Most of the people appearing for therapy are between the ages 20 and 40, although more children are now being treated. Within these young-adult bodies, therapists may find APs ranging from infants to senior citizens. Some are even too young to talk.

Another typical feature is that there can be alternates of either gender in a host physical body. Alternates are more commonly the same gender as the host personality, however. If there are more than five alternates, there is almost always one of the opposite sex. It can sometimes be very troublesome for an AP to be in an opposite-sex body. Allison (1980) reports one case where a male AP was in control of a female body. "He" had an urge to go to the restroom while in a store. "He" went into the men's room (it apparently was not busy) and became alarmed when "he" found something missing. Opposite gender personalities may also explain some mutilations. Although many mutilations may be done by persecutor personalities for unexplained reasons, in other cases the motivation may be the result of occupation by an AP of the opposite gender. The simplest example is a male AP trying (and sometimes even succeeding) to cut off the breasts of the host female. In reading about DID, I have not encountered a case of a female AP cutting off the penis of the male host personality. However, in a later chapter I will discuss a case in which a dominant female spirit intruder in a male body, not necessarily a full personality, chose to undergo sexual reassignment surgery and the male host personality could observe and anguish over the surgical removal of his penis from a position above the surgeon, similar to an autoscopic NDEr observing the resuscitation of his body.

In addition, the handwriting of each personality is usually different. This can be confirmed by graphoanalysis. If there are more than three or four personalities who can write, then one will probably write with the opposite hand when compared to the others. Putnam et al. (1986) found an AP writing with the opposite hand in 37% of surveyed cases. Many of the personalities have identifiable accents, either regional or foreign-language based. Usually the original personality has not been exposed to that foreign language or has not been to the respective region of the country.

Sometimes one of the APs will have a major physical impediment such as blindness or deafness. This phenomenon must have been confirmed by tests that can tell if there is faking (i.e., a sudden loud noise behind a "deaf" AP to which the AP responds), but no therapist actually describes a test. If the original personality is able to see and hear, then there obviously is no organic tissue damage to explain sensory loss. The traditional explanation is that a sense loss is an hysterical conversion reaction. Therapists who treat disorders other than DID have long known about "hysterical blindness."

My explanation is that the invading spirit body remembers characteristics from its "former" body. Quite frequently APs will describe hair or eye color not present in the physical body they are occupying. Again, they are simply remembering their "former" bodies and consider hair and eye color as an important part of "self." In addition to major impediments such as blindness, there are often minor and little-known physical problems in only one of the many APs. For instance, one of the personalities in Billy Milligan, named Adalana, had nystagmus, a rare eye ailment in which the eyes dart back and forth.

Persecutor personalities enjoy bringing pain or discomfort to the host personality. Brassfield (1983) reports a case with an AP named the Slasher, who stated that his purpose was to make the host personality pay for wrong actions and feelings. The Slasher did this by means of razor cuts. Shelley (1981) describes a case where an AP was a belligerent macho-type Marine sergeant who punished the host personality (a woman) by frequently rubbing poison ivy on her inflamed left hand and forearm. The AP used a glove so there was nothing on the right hand. When the woman was placed in a hospital, the Marine had no access to poison ivy, so on two occasions he smashed her hand against a metal chair. PwDID with incidents such as these may be misdiagnosed as masochistic or as having a self-defeating personality.

Some of the APs may be homosexual, independent of the original personality. Inside a male body with a heterosexual original personality there may be a male homosexual AP or a female lesbian AP. If the AP is a heterosexual female and attempts sex with a male, the host personality may be referred to as homosexual.

Jorn (1982) reports a case in which one of the personalities had anorexia nervosa. This personality apparently prevailed by suppressing appetite in all the personalities, as the 29-year-old woman patient was extremely underweight. She checked into a hospital weighing ninety-three pounds, and at one time her weight fell to 75 pounds. Anorexia nervosa is being seen much more frequently and is addressed in journal articles or during workshops at conferences on DID. Perhaps many people with eating disorders have DID and that fact is just being recognized. Since anorexia nervosa is so easy to recognize by the sufferer's visible emaciation, past treatment for it was undertaken without considering that it may be a symptom of DID.

7. The Birth Personality

Comstock (1987b) provides some information on the birth personality. She states that the identity of the birth personality is determined from the moment of conception and is not a choice to be made. The birth personality is frequently sheltered and therefore may be quite young when identified. The 32 birth personalities Comstock identifies range in age from five months prebirth to five years old. She does not explain if this means that the birth personality only ages when it is in control of the body or whether it is the birth personality's age when last in control. After reading many cases, I conclude that the therapist usually identifies the birth personality as the one who came in for therapy (also referred to as the presenting personality). Comstock, however, states that the earliest she has ever found the birth personality was eight months after therapy began. The birth personality remains young and weakened until some healing has been accomplished and some integration has occurred. It can then age.

I first discovered a young birth personality in Allison's book (1980) and a book by one of his patients (Hawksworth, 1977). In the latter case, Allison was attempting to fuse some APs into what he thought was the primary personality, a man named Dana. Later, the three-year-old birth personality appeared.

During therapy for one patient, Comstock could not seem to find the birth personality of a DID patient named Linda. The APs said she was dead. Comstock regressed them to Linda's last appearance. The APs reported that a mist appeared before them. This condensed to a cloud, darkened to a spongy substance, and hardened into a wall, after which time a mirrorlike surface appeared on the wall so the APs only saw a reflection. Comstock had the APs look behind the wall, and there they found little Linda, "furious that she had been found and disturbed from what she had believed was her peaceful death." Systems (birth and all alternate personalities) do not usually argue over the identity of the birth personality. After integration, the birth personality is the only remaining personality and is of the proper age.

Comstock (1987b) states that the birth personality has special capacities that enable the person to live life more easily than the APs do. These capacities include the following:

1. She does not tire as quickly;
2. Her feelings flow more naturally and have a greater range of affect;
3. She has an easier time making decisions;
4. She has greater depth; and
5. Optimism and resiliency are more natural for her.

8. Other Illnesses

One of the signs mentioned in the "Description and Diagnosis" section that should direct a therapist to suspect DID is headaches. This is certainly not surprising if a spirit body's primary control mechanism of the body is the brain. One possible reason may be that each spirit body uses the parts of the brain in different ways. Each personality may activate different brain regions, reflecting the differing thought patterns and personality traits native to that AP. This could have significant ramifications for sudden blood flow and neural behavior changes within the brain. Based on this explanation, it would be expected that less frequent switching would result in fewer headaches, because after a period of time the alternate spirit body can redirect the flow of blood to the required sites. However, this may take days or weeks, and by then another personality (i.e., spirit body) may have entered the body—and the difficulty commences again.

9. Lowered Sensory Awareness

Allison (1980) reports the phenomenon of lower sensory awareness, a state confirmed by other researchers. The physical world appears dulled to a PwDID. This applies to all senses and includes colors that do not appear bright, poor contrast between colors, or colors appearing as though filtered. In addition, full, rich sounds are not heard; tactile feelings are diminished; and aromas are undetected except at high concentrations. Food often tastes bland even if well seasoned. These factors may not apply to every original AP or to all APs.

Mesulam (1981) provides two representative examples of what may be called *lowered sensory awareness*. He describes 12 cases of people with an abnormal temporal lobe EEG and describes their DID conditions or the "illusion" of possession. In Case 4, the patient states that when she is in her "first personality, colors all appear brown or more brownish in hue" (p.). In Case 6, the patient "describes sudden distortions of color (objects appear yellow-orange) that precede a temper outburst" (p.). In an article about DID in children, Fagan and McMahon (1984) state that after fusion, the child may report colors being brighter.

10. ESP Experiences

In a previous section, on the ISH, I discussed parapsychological phenomena. Ross (1997) recognizes a strong connection between ESP and dissociation that may or may not be separate from the ISH. I consider parapsychology/paranormality and ESP to be functional equivalents. Paranormality is the broadest category and ESP the most restricted (since it relates to human perception). Since this book is about human abilities, I aver that the two are equivalent. Ross comments,

> The exclusion of ESP from serious mainstream psychiatry is antiscientific. This is true whether or not ESP is real. If ESP is real, then its exclusion from mainstream scientific study is based on prejudice, not a scientific attitude. On the other hand, if ESP is illusory, it should be studied just like any other set of symptoms, delusions, or hallucinations. ... ESP is closely linked to dissociation. ... If ESP actually happens, it means that the relationship between mind and body is

different from that postulated by contemporary reductionist science. If ESP actually happens, the physics of the universe, and the interaction of mind and matter, are far from fully accounted for; the same is true of the psyche. If telekinesis is real, mind is a physical force in the universe, as real as electricity, magnetism, or gravity. Psychiatry then becomes the physics of the mind. If DID is real, a model of the mind must change, independently of the reality of ESP, therefore the ESP-dissociation linkage is a double threat to reductionist dualism. ... The difficulty is that they [ESP experiences] aren't obviously delusional. (219–20)

Ross's remarks are very relevant to my thesis that the realm of the paranormal, which would include ESP, is closely related to our spiritual nature. Ross notes that DID will provide a counter to biomedical reductionist psychiatry, since parapsychological phenomena indicate thought or action at a distance, without an intervening physical medium.

Although Ross states that he does not do past-life work, he has had patients report past-life intrusions into their paranormal experiences. He also reports that he has "watched a non-DID patient age regressed to the intrauterine state and complain about an unsuccessful legal abortion, but I did not believe that this was a real memory of an event that occurred at two months gestation. Such memory is impossible. ... Another patient described listening to an argument between her parents while a fetus, understanding the words, and reacting to their meaning" (p. 354).

In the chapter on NDEs, I presented information showing that there have been intrauterine NDEs and awareness of the outside world, so I disagree with Ross's contention that such memory is impossible. Allison (1980) reports that one patient of his, named Babs, was conceived out of wedlock and that her father had wanted to abort her. Babs had her first sense of being unwanted while still in the womb. (This information was reported by Babs's ISH named Tammy.) Other patients have also reported to Allison on prebirth feelings.

Allison (1980) comments that in his treatment of patients he has observed parapsychological phenomena for which he has no explanation. This is certainly not surprising, because parapsychological phenomena are related to spirituality. (This chapter provides evidence that DID is related to the spiritual realm.) Perhaps Allison did not want to discuss details of these phenomena because he thought his book might not be taken seriously.

Two examples of parapsychological phenomena are described in *The Minds of Billy Milligan* (Keyes 1981). When Billy was at the Athens Mental Health Center, a female patient left in a state of panic or hysteria. Danny and David were two of Billy's personalities with strong empathy for other emotional people, and one or the other could, and did, clairvoyantly locate the missing woman. On another occasion David visualized a female patient about to fall. Another AP, Ragen, realized that what David was seeing was probably going to happen, so Ragen rushed to the location and caught a girl who was ready to go over a railing. This is an example of precognition.

11. Demographics

The early cases I reviewed usually involved lower-middle-class individuals. Of course, ones like Eve and Billy Milligan usually have more severe problems than the average PwDID in order to make the news and have films produced about their lives. Recent research, though, shows that PwDID often have above-average intelligence, have college degrees, have engaged in postgraduate studies, and hold professional-level jobs.

Perhaps a professional job is a minor source of stress, at least of the kind of stress that tends to produce switching. If an engineer had an AP that was not an engineer, any attempt to perform an engineering function would prove difficult. Usually the proper personality shows up for a task, and the engineer personality (perhaps the host personality) could take control if engineering work had to be done. For instance, in Billy Milligan there were three personalities that liked to paint or draw. Each preferred a different subject for painting, such as landscapes, still lifes, or portraits. When Billy was confined and sent to art class, one of the artist personalities would take control of Billy's body.

12. Substance Abuse

A high percentage of PwDID are substance abusers. They may use legal or illegal drugs or alcohol. One researcher comments that sometimes the original personality may drink alcohol so she can state that she had had a blackout when she fails to remember something that an AP did.

In some PwDID, only one of the APs may be the culprit in the substance abuse. But unfortunately, when the original personality returns to his body, the drugs may still be in the blood and he still feels the effects. Substance abuse can greatly reduce the prognosis for effective treatment. Ross notes that all of his integrated patients lost their addiction to various substances.

13. Fusion

Therapists generally consider their goal to be one of integrating all of the APs of the individual into one functioning personality. They call this process *fusion* or *integration*. I have no disagreement with a therapist's basic goal of seeking to have one individual personality that can handle all ranges of the emotional spectrum without switching into APs (or splitting to create new ones). Later in the book, I will present a spiritual explanation of what occurs during fusion.

14. Childhood DID

The "Etiology" section will describe how DID is almost always caused by abuse, usually sexual, during childhood. Most cases of DID, however, are not diagnosed and treated until the person reaches adulthood. Kluft (1984) states that he could find no cases of childhood DID in the literature between 1840 and 1979. Perhaps one reason for this is that some of the signs of DID are considered normal childhood behavior. This is especially true when it is considered that the parents of the child may also have DID or other dissociative disorders.

Kluft (1984) compares the symptoms of five childhood DID patients to two lists of childhood predictors of DID prepared earlier by him and Dr. Frank Putnam. There was less involvement with imaginary companions than expected. One patient said his APs were different from his imaginary friends. Other therapists have speculated that the imaginary friends that many children have may become APs in abused children. Kluft (1984) found that three DID-identified boys resumed normal growth and development after two to four months of treatment. This is a much shorter time than for adults, revealing that the process of forming APs is in development and can be arrested in children. For treatment to be effective, the abuse must obviously stop.

15. Splitting and Switching

Splitting is creating a new personality, whereas switching is changing among existing personalities. Splitting may continue in adulthood, provided that the first split occurred in early childhood. During therapy a patient may resplit after an apparent fusion.

In their survey, Putnam et al. (1986) found that 87% of the patients made spontaneous switches from one AP to another or to the host personality. In 92% of patients, this switch occurred in seconds or took up to five minutes. Putnam (1985) studied the actual process of switching. Putnam states the switches usually occur rapidly and may be signaled by an eye roll or eyelid fluttering, facial twitching or grimacing, and bodily twitches, tremors, or shudders. There may also be facial flushing or cold perspiration. Other instrument-measured changes are discussed in the "Psychophysiology" section, below.

G. Psychophysiology

1. Introduction

This section presents some very important information to support the overall hypothesis that DID is spiritually based. As mentioned in chapter 1, people representing religion or any spiritual viewpoint have too easily been willing to separate the spiritual aspects of humankind from the physical body. This separation cannot be made. Human physical bodies and emotions are controlled by the spiritual element in the body. However, this does not imply that every time something goes wrong with a person's physical body he has committed an "evil" act and is being punished for it. It is especially not true that a divine spiritual being punishes the physical body for evil done by the spiritual aspect of a human being.

In this section, I will demonstrate that the apparent physical changes occurring when a switch in personality is made are the result of a new spirit body controlling these aspects. Even more significant changes may be discovered in the future, as this field of study is less than 40 years old. I refer to these as physical aspects, but this includes items such as dominant-hand functioning. Physiological changes to be discussed include neurophysiology and any psychological state that can be measured by a test, handedness, vision, and others. Some measures are more subjective than others, and changes may occur without a change in personality, as they can in any individual.

The hypothesis of change coming from outside the organism is consistent with the observed facts. The prevailing notion that the organism internally creates the psychological factors to handle demanding situations would not explain the associated physiological changes. The section called "Typical Personalities" lists problems cited by Bliss (Table 6.1) regarding the original personality and the type of personality "created" (i.e., tasks it will accomplish). An angry AP, if coming from within, would not need the following things just to express anger: a different eyeglass prescription, writing with a different hand, responding differently to drugs, a different voice pattern, and a different sexual preference. There may be some physiological factors that relate to the AP's function. For instance, an AP that expresses anger may have an unusually rapid adrenal response. These changes and the others to be discussed here are most rationally explained by physiology as regulated by the spirit body.

Invasion by wandering spirits is not completely random. The first time a person dissociates, a spirit body with the required characteristics to handle a task will most likely appear in order to take control. I have no quarrel with psychiatrists who argue that APs handle functions that the original personality cannot handle because of psychological trauma. Since it is not totally random, there could be restrictions on which spirit body can take control of the body.

Other factors besides altered bodily functions, attitudes, and responses are the abilities that come with the changes. IQ changes will be discussed later in this section. Under "Case Histories," some unusual abilities of APs will be discussed. For instance, Tommy, one of the APs in Billy Milligan, was an escape artist. He could quickly escape from a straitjacket. The most reasonable explanation for his quickly developed skill is that he brought the skill with him when he arrived as another spirit.

Foreign-language abilities were discussed under the subhead "Typical Personalities." The other explanation for foreign-language ability (apart from arriving with a spirit body) derives from a particular AP studying a language. For instance, Arthur, the rational, very intelligent AP in Billy Milligan, was one of the APs that occupied the body a high percentage of the time. He would go to a library and study. He taught himself Arabic.

Thus, some skills can be learned, but it took the high intelligence of the Arthur personality arriving from outside to effectively exhibit this skill.

2. Research Involving Instrument Measures

An early study performed by Ludwig et al. (1972) included many types of tests for psychological profiles, as well as psychophysiological and neurological measures of the various personalities of a DID patient. These researchers were able to verify that there was no transfer of memory between personalities. In a test for galvanic skin response (GSR) to emotionally laden words, they found that the various personalities did not share affectual experiences. In the comparison of EEGs, they found alpha blocking in the original personality and in the ISH personality, Sammy. Alpha blocking was not present in the other two personalities. They believe the differences in EEG were not explainable on the basis of differences in alertness. A fairly hostile alter named Usoffa Abdulla was found to be insensitive to pain. The overall conclusion of Ludwig et al. is that in no way could the results, taken as a whole, have been produced solely through the mechanisms of deception or intense role-playing, especially by this unsophisticated patient of average IQ.

Pitbaldo and Densen-Gerber (1986) studied the visually evoked response (VER) among three personalities in a 30-year-old woman. The investigators explain that VER is determined by the involuntary nervous system and thus is not subject to deliberate control by the patient. Two of the three personalities required glasses to view the pattern, but all three were tested with and without glasses. The researchers reported significant differences among personalities, and one personality reflected a 64% change between wearing and not wearing glasses. There was no difference for the other two, with or without glasses.

Brende (1984) studied an electrodermal response in three different personalities. He requested each AP to either attempt to control emotion or express emotion. He found differences among the personalities in the extent to which they could control or express emotions. He also found that there were lateralization differences among the various personalities; that is, each side of the brain seemed to operate differently in each personality.

Larmore et al. (1977) performed measurements on the four personalities for a person with DID, including one personality that I believe to be the ISH. The tests included heart rate, blood pressure, EEG, GSR, electromyogram (EMG, which measures muscle activity), and average evoked visual response (AEVR). The researchers concluded that there were not significant differences among the personalities for most measurements except that the AEVR responses appeared as if four different people had been measured.

Differences in electroencephalogram (EEG) pattern are discussed as one change that occurs when a person switches personalities. An EEG measures electrical potential in the brain. Psychophysiologists generally consider there to be four different wave patterns. Waves in a normally functioning person are called beta waves and have a frequency of approximately 21 hertz (cycles per second). In deep sleep, the frequency of the waves is about four hertz. In between are alpha and theta waves. Alpha waves occur when a person is dreaming, but they can also occur when the person is awake and relaxed. Even when comparing two waking states, there can be some changes. As was mentioned in another section, some people with temporal lobe epilepsy have DID symptoms, though most people with DID do not have temporal lobe epilepsy. Temporal lobe epilepsy is measured as a "spike" in the EEG chart. Psychophysiologists can normally distinguish one patient's chart from another. Difficulties with EEG measurements have also been mentioned, as different researchers have reached different conclusions about what the differences demonstrate. The previous discussion is meant to show that there is some subjective interpretation to this type of measurement, so all researchers do not agree.

Coons et al. (1982) conducted some EEG studies with two DID patients and a control. They found that the control showed more significant changes than the DID patients, and they concluded that intensity of concentration, mood, and degree of muscle relaxation, which reflect changes in emotional state, are more likely to cause EEG differences than a change to a different personality. They did notice differences in eye movement and muscle activity among the various personalities, but these were subjective impressions.

3. Visual Changes and Response to Medication

One major part of anatomy that seems affected when personalities change is the eyes. At times there may not seem to be a change in visual acuity when the switch occurs, but that may be because both personalities have 20/20 vision. Some of the personalities are even blind, but the traditional explanation is probably hysterical blindness.

Dr. K. R. Shepard, an eye doctor, and Dr. B. Braun, a well-known therapist and researcher in the field of DID, report (1985) on a wide variety of vision-related factors as personalities change. They measured such factors as refractive status, visual acuity, ocular tension, keratometry, color vision, fundus, visual fields, and extraocular vision in a number of patients and found substantial changes as the personalities changed.

Morgan et al. (1986) performed several measures of vision on various personalities in ten DID patients. For controls, they asked ten volunteers to react (act) in a similar manner to changes that would occur in the DID patients (an aggressive AP would be compared to a control acting aggressively). Condon et al. (1969) conducted a frame-by-frame analysis of a film about the real person who came to be known as "Eve." The authors of *The Three Faces of Eve* prepared a private film of four of Eve's personalities: Eve White, Eve Black, Jane I, and Jane II. Condon et al. were able to identify a visual anomaly called *strabismus* in one of the personalities, a condition where the eyes may move divergently. Since this was only occurring in these personalities for fractions of a second, it is referred to as *microstrabismus*. This condition could not be observed at normal projection speed, but only by doing a frame-by-frame analysis. The frequency of strabismus was 56 in Eve Black, eleven in Eve White, six in Jane I, and zero in Jane II.

The Putnam et al. (1986) study of a hundred patients revealed 46% of various APs responding differently to the same medication. AP-specific responses within a patient were also commonly observed with regard to alcohol (35%), food (39%), and allergies (26%).

4. Psychological and Other Test Differences

There are also significant psychological differences between various personalities. For instance, Fine et al. (1985a) found major interpersonality differences in levels of depression among personalities in the four patients that they measured. Depression was measured according to the Beck Depression Inventory. The tests were completed by the various personalities, who sometimes held the pencils different hands to complete the inventory. In a separate report, these same researchers (1985b) noted differences in communication style among the various personalities. They classified the communication styles in the categories of cognitive (rational arguments and logic), affiliative (personal/emotional), and coercive (threats and manipulation).

5. Handedness and Other Differences

When a switch in personality occurs, one of the most common differences easily noted is a change from functioning with the right hand to the left hand or vice versa. It is difficult to quantify this type of research, but it has been verified in many studies. In their survey, Putnam et al. (1986) found changes in dominant handedness in 37% of their cases.

Restak (1984) states that speech pathologist Christy Ludlow has found differing voice patterns in each AP of a PwDID. Ross (1997) has observed dramatic differences in penmanship from one AP to another. Other differences noted by Ross in one AP of a patient, but not in the original personality, include deafness, muteness, homosexuality, and the frequently incurred gender change. Some of these differences are discussed under "Typical Personalities" or "Case Histories."

H. Etiology

Etiology is one area where most researchers are in agreement. All evidence points to child abuse as the major cause of DID. Wilbur states that 97/100 PwDID have a background of being abused as children. Other researchers almost always give figures in the 90-plus percent range.

Child abuse, especially sexual abuse, generally refers to an incestuous relationship or acts performed by a family member or other trusted adult. Normally, abuse is thought to occur in the home by the parents, with neighbors and friends not suspecting it. Braun and Sachs (1985) state that the abuse must be frequent, unpredictable, and inconsistent.

For instance, a child might be told he is loved and then be abused. Thus, an otherwise normal child who is sexually molested once by a stranger is not likely to develop DID. Occasional sexual abuse by a family member who only infrequently visits may also have occurred in PwDID. Many case histories mention abuse by a relative other than the parents.

As previously mentioned, DID, to some extent, may enable a person to remain more functional than if he or she employed alternative responses to abuse. For instance, Braun and Sachs (1985) report that abused children who do not develop DID are likely to be frigid, impotent, and unable to express joy and pleasure. Thus, there may be some individual characteristics that cause some people to dissociate and develop DID while others develop different psychiatric problems.

Child abuse can cover a broad spectrum. According to some researchers, in about 70% of cases involving DID, the abuse was sexual. Torem et al. (1986) found a correlation only between sexual abuse and dissociation. The other two types of abuse with which they attempted to develop a correlation were neglect and emotional abuse. Another type of abuse might be physical, such as beating, cutting, and burning. In the category of abuse, Wilbur (1984) includes chronic exposure to sexual acts and sexual displays. An example includes insisting that a child sleep in the parental bedroom until the age of eight or nine years.

A major factor in abuse resulting in DID is the age at which the abuse occurred. In most cases of DID, the initial abuse appears to have occurred prior to the age of six or seven. Stern (1984) studied eight cases to develop a hypothesis of backgrounds and causes of DID and concluded that the first episode of splitting occurred in all subjects between the ages of six months and seven years. In some isolated cases, abuse up to age ten or twelve may result in DID. The critical factor is when the abuse first resulted in the formation of an AP. At the age of six or seven years, change seems to occur in childhood development (relationship of spirit body to physical body), because that is traditionally when a child starts school. Rather than a specific age for this developmental change, the factor may be teething, which from the loss of the first tooth to the appearance of the last permanent tooth may be several years. If the abuse occurs after the age of seven or the abuse is not sufficiently traumatic, the child may have major psychiatric problems, but the problems most likely will not include DID. Abuse after the age of seven, or less traumatic abuse, is likely to result in partial dissociation and intrusion, which will be discussed in chapter 10.

Riley and Mead (1988) report an unusual case in which they evaluated a girl before her first split occurred. At the age of 14 months, the girl exhibited normal behavior when living with her guardian parents. Shortly thereafter, arrangements were made for a transition to the biological mother. The subject was abused by her brothers and biological mother. By her third birthday, she had developed an AP. Another child of the biological mother had died from sudden infant death syndrome. Riley and Mead believe that the concept presented by Stern (cited earlier) of a split occurring by the age of six months is virtually impossible, but I disagree with them and believe that it is possible, as the spirit bodies are already occupying the physical body.

Gross (1986) reports a very tragic case of profound abuse. The amount of abuse is almost beyond belief. It consisted of rape, sodomy, fellatio, and other physical abuse. In addition, the abuse victim, a PwDID, witnessed her uncle committing suicide with a gun and her mother having an abortion and seeing the aborted fetus. This individual had been conceived as a twin, but her father kicked her mother, which caused the twin to die in utero. Her ISH said her first split occurred while she was still a fetus, when she felt a jerk. Whether this could have been the same kick that killed her sister is unknown. She felt trapped and wanted to get out, and then an AP took over.

Rather than using the term *parental abuse* and possibly implying involvement of both parents, Allison (1980) reports that there is often a "good" and a "bad" parent. DID may not occur until the "good" parent abandons the child. A more common situation is the abuse of a daughter by her father. DID may not occur until the wife divorces the father and leaves the child with him. In some cases, the "good" parent simply died, but the child may think of that as abandonment. This probably represents Allison's view based on his patients and not on a survey of a large number of cases. Some researchers classify the nonabusive parent as a disinterested, fearful, or passive onlooker.

Since DID has only recently come under close scrutiny, many correlations between DID and abuse cannot be made yet. For instance, it is known that about 95% of PwDID were abused, but researchers do not know what percent of people who were abused become PwDID.

Braun and Sachs (1985) state that for DID to develop there must be predisposing, precipitating, and perpetuating factors. Determining a psychological profile afterward is called a retrospective study, which is not considered as scientific as a prospective study (in which the study group is profiled beforehand).

The predisposing factor to developing DID is a tendency to dissociate. Though there are some tests that measure tendency to dissociate (see the "Description and Diagnosis" section), those tests measure the current tendency to dissociate. This tendency may arise from any past abuse (determined retrospectively) and does not identify factors prior to any abuse that will result in dissociation if abuse does occur. It would be very difficult to develop any such test (a prospective study), as it would have to be given to a person at the age of two or three and then be correlated with abuse that results in actual dissociation.

Allison (1980) identifies several psychological traits in PwDID. One is that PwDID do not learn from experience the way normal people do; they do not understand cause-and-effect relationships. This was discovered after the patients developed DID (retrospectively) and does not necessarily prove that the trait existed prior to the onset of DID.

Child abuse is sometimes viewed as part of a broader spectrum. The wider category is trauma. DID can be viewed as a symptom of posttraumatic stress disorder. A trauma may be the death of a loved one, or the death of a person not necessarily loved but with unusual circumstances, such as a violent murder. Another example of trauma may be alcoholism in the family. Voien and Schafer (1986) state that in 30% of the cases where child abuse/neglect occurs, there is alcoholism in the family. Even if there is no overt abuse, DID is more likely to occur in an alcoholic family. Even after integration, a patient can relapse if there is further trauma, even if the trauma is unrelated to the additional abuse. Examples of trauma include hearing about a death, illnesses, accidents, assaults, and natural disasters (Ross, 1997).

It is often found that there is a family pattern to DID because much child abuse is performed by a parent's AP. Thus, the cycle is perpetuated. The fact that an AP often is the abuser is reason the child sees this love–abuse dichotomy. The original personality of the mother or father may show affection for the child, but when the child acts like a child it may bring out a hostile AP in the parent, who then abuses the child. Braun

(1985) studied the families of eighteen DID patients, and in 94% of the cases found another family member with DID or other major symptoms of dissociation. Family members included aunts and uncles, not just parents, siblings, or children. Braun concludes that the data support the hypothesis that DID is a transgenerational problem. A transgenerational problem does not necessarily imply that it is genetic. A parent does not abuse his or her child due to a genetic predisposition, but rather because abuse is learned from observing/being a victim.

This section is primarily oriented toward the time of the first dissociation. Most of the information concerning the first dissociation and the appearance of an AP is derived from an interview with either the AP that appeared or the Inner Self-helper (ISH), which has a complete memory of which personality is in control at any given time. The ISH may be used if a particular AP can only stay in control for a few minutes, is mute or feeble-minded, or is difficult to summon. Some APs simply have difficulty remembering when they first assumed control. Regression to when the AP was not present may also be used to determine when an AP first appeared. The information supplied by the ISH has often been verified by others based on recalled events and behavior. Some people may question the acceptability of the ISH as a source of information. If the ISH says that personality Q was in control at 3:00 p.m. on May 14, 1979, confirmation is difficult. If personality Q is violent, it might be possible to verify from an event, such as a police investigation, that the PwDID was acting violently at that time. According to Braun (1984), gathering the histories of some APs may involve collating information from several personalities.

Once the first dissociation has occurred, additional APs can occur at any time or age. Often, these additional APs are also associated with traumatic events such as rape. As discussed earlier, APs are sometimes associated with the inability to express a full range of emotions, and each time a shortage of emotion appears, an additional AP may appear to fill the void. Another factor often associated with creation of APs is having imaginary playmates as a child. In some cases, these imaginary playmates simply help the child cope with loneliness, but at other times they become secondary personalities.

Though conventional psychiatric explanations may seem adequate for some people, a spiritual rationale for the observed phenomenon of

274

developing DID after experiencing child abuse is more valid. Once the original spirit body is traumatized when in its own body, it finds it easy to depart the body. One or any number of discarnate spirit bodies are willing to invade and take control of the physical body for their own purposes, which in most cases are not friendly. In the previous chapter, on NDEs, there is a section called "A Unique Journey." When the NDEr was in his spirit body at a bar, he noticed that when a man fell over drunk, an "aura" around the drunk opened up and allowed spirits of deceased alcoholics to enter his physical body. I maintain that something similar happens to a traumatized child; the trauma opens the child's protective aura, through which undesirable spirits may enter.

I. Treatment

Personality is a reflection of the occupying spirit body. The standard interpretation is that the individual creates a new personality from within. The goal of therapy should be to create a stable original personality that will not depart when threatened, and a spiritual interpretation will create additional methods for achieving that goal. From a spiritual perspective, APs are actually eliminated rather than integrated during therapy. Therapists generally describe their goal in treating a PwDID as one of fusion, integration, or unification of the APs into the original personality. Kluft (1985) defines fusion as the patient's achieving three stable months of the following:

1. Continuity of contemporary memory;
2. Absence of overt behavioral signs of multiplicity;
3. Subjective sense of unity;
4. (If hypnosis was used,) the absence of APs using hypnotic reexploration;
5. Modification of transference phenomena consistent with the bringing together of personalities; and
6. Clinical evidence that the unified patient's self-representation includes acknowledgement of attitudes and awareness, which were previously segregated in separate personalities.

There is no conflict between this basic goal of therapy and the spiritual interpretation of the "cause" of the problem presented in this book.

Ross believes the fact that the APs can be age-progressed proves that they are not people, but I disagree. Infant APs are easier to communicate with after age-progressing them. In one minute, an AP can be age-progressed by ten years. Elsewhere, though, Ross states, "Different alters claim to have different origins. Persecutors sometimes state that they were discarnate entities floating in the ether prior to entering the patient's body. In such cases, the persecutor will usually acknowledge that the body is the host body, and she will claim to have an unaffected astral body which is not harmed by the cigarette burns or wrist slashes" (Ross, 1997, 340).

ISSTD publishes a booklet titled *Guidelines for Treating Dissociative Identity Disorder in Adults*. These guidelines also address treatment for dissociation less severe than DID. A DID therapist does not have to be a medical doctor unless it is necessary to prescribe medication for some symptoms, though the therapy process is challenging for a therapist.

Kluft reviews the various types of treatment that have been used on PwDID. These include psychoanalytical psychotherapy (with or without hypnosis), behavioral treatments, family intervention, group treatment, videotape interviews, hypnotherapeutic intervention, and reparenting. Some may help in the short term but will not help to achieve integration. For instance, Kluft says that behavioral approaches can make dramatic changes in manifest pathology. Thus, this approach may cut down on some violent activities by one of the APs. Family intervention is more of a necessary adjunct, rather than a principal means, of therapy. If a child is involved, the family that is abusing the child must be made to realize past mistakes. The switching process must be explained. For instance, it may be necessary to explain that criticism does not change the patient's behavior but instead causes him or her to switch personalities. Ross (1997) states that treatment more closely resembles dynamic psychotherapy and classical analysis than it does the correcting of neurotransmitter imbalances.

If the patient is an adult in a new family environment, the new family must be made aware of the situation. It may be necessary to explain the DID to a husband and to mention why social workers are involved in a therapy team (to aid in the new family dynamics). A divorce may be necessary if the marriage partner will not cooperate. If there are children in the new family, it is necessary to explain the situation to them as well. For instance, if the children are old enough to walk and understand, they may be told to get out of their mother's way if she starts acting in a certain manner.

Group work is sometimes better for project-oriented therapy such as occupational, art, and music therapy. Kluft (1985) prefers psychoanalytical psychotherapy and states that the therapist must establish a quality relationship with the various APs, uniting them in a common interest. The therapist must not become too involved with fascinating phenomena and differences. Kluft lists twelve steps to be taken, which he took from several writings by Braun. These steps are as follows:

1. Developing trust;
2. Sharing the diagnosis with each AP and making the patient realize the situation;
3. Establishing communication with the accessible APs;
4. Having the APs sign a contract agreeing not to harm themselves, others, or the body they share;
5. Gathering the history of each AP including its origins, functions, problems, and relationship to other APs;
6. Solving the APs' problems, including setting limits;
7. Mapping and understanding the structure of the personality system;
8. Enhancing interpersonality communication;
9. Achieving resolution toward unity and facilitating blending rather than power struggles;
10. Helping patients develop new intrapsychic defenses and coping mechanisms, and learn adaptive ways of dealing interpersonally;
11. Working through problems and supporting the solidification of gains; and
12. Following up.

Although all steps are equally important, a person not familiar with DID may not realize the importance of step 2, which concerns the patient's desire to get well. Some patients may not realize how serious their situation is.

Ross states that he often forms treatment alliances among the APs, including hostile and persecutorial types, and can sometimes integrate them as a group. The hostile ones must be treated evenhandedly. In some patients, the anger in a persecutorial AP can serve as an antidepressant. The therapist may find it necessary to explain to the APs that in integrating them they are not being sent away but that a part of them will be a constituent of the integrated whole person.

Hypnotism is frequently used to reach APs. According to Ross, patients can usually be taught to switch to a different AP by simple request. The patient will usually nod his or her head and close his or her eyes, at which time a different AP emerges. Hostile APs may be more difficult to convince to go back inside. After he gets to know some of the APs, Ross may ask to speak to an AP he has not met before. Some APs can only be contacted by indirect conversation, with a known AP acting as an intermediary. If an AP says it cannot discuss a certain subject, it is often because a controlling, persecutorial AP is in the background preventing the discussion.

Earlier, I mentioned false memory syndrome. Ross says he tries to be aware of information coming from memory only. Providing a lot of details does not prove that a memory is true. Without outside confirmation, a memory cannot be known to be true or false. However, the content of the memories is symbolic of inner conflicts, regardless of whether the memories are true. Auditory hallucinations may also contain important information. Encouraging a schizophrenic to listen to the voices he or she is hearing is not recommended, but Ross states that for DID therapy, "voices are a form of interpersonality communication that is encouraged and cultivated. ... DID therapy is the only form of psychiatric treatment in which auditory hallucinations are deliberately amplified" (Ross, 1997, 320).

APs often have difficulty with time. An adult PwDID may not have been abused for years, but some of the APs may believe the abuse recently happened. Ross also sometimes has to explain to the patient (or a specific AP) that there is a difference between inside reality and outside reality. In the inside world, each AP has its own body, but in the outside world they all share one body.

Treatment of a PwDID is not a short-term process. Curing the patient, not palliating his or her symptoms, is the goal. A treatment period of five to seven years is fairly common. With visits to the therapist twice per week, those with fewer personalities may achieve integration in less than three years. While most therapists believe that the therapist must not make moral judgments about sexual matters, Ross informs his patients that he does not approve of continued involvement with prostitution. One or more of the APs is probably participating in prostitution and is more reluctant to integrate if its desires are being met. I imagine that this could be compared to an alcoholic being allowed to continue to drink during addiction therapy. Ross also advises against trying to be the patient's friend or assuming the role of a rescuer.

Treatment may be very expensive. However, the expense to society may be even greater if one of the APs is a criminal. Ross estimated that there were over 500 therapists who have treated DID at the time of his writing. Follow-up is essential. There may be relapses after some of the early fusions or after final integration is believed to have taken place. Ross has observed that being integrated can be difficult for a patient, as he or she can no longer "check out" and allow an AP to handle a demanding situation.

J. Case Histories

Case histories are interesting because they concern human beings. Each case of a PwDID has its own story, circumstances, and struggles. Statistics are sterile and reveal only part of the story. Reading what actually happens to these patients is very different. This book is written with the hope that by identifying the spiritual source of DID, solutions can be found. However, it is up to society to address the child-abuse issue. Some detail on early cases will be given for historical perspective. Although some very old cases are mentioned below, for more recent cases information is given that makes the subject more interesting and contributes to the hypothesis that DID is best explained spiritually.

The first reported case of PwDID by modern medicine was the case of Mary Reynolds. Most of the information to follow was reported by Kenny (1985) and Carlson (1984). Mary was born in Birmingham, England, in 1785; her parents were Baptists. In 1791, there were religious riots in Birmingham. Though these riots were not directed at the Baptists, the Reynolds family decided to leave for America. The parents arrived in 1794. Mary and her brother, after staying with their maternal grandparents, followed in 1795. The family eventually settled in Cherry Tree, Pennsylvania, a small farming community in the western Alleghenies. Since there were no Baptist churches, the Reynolds joined the Presbyterian Church. Mary had only one AP and diagnosis, as DID was only speculated from readings about her condition years later.

A significant case of early dual personality described by Kenny was that of Ansel J. Bourne. Ansel, born in 1826, was a carpenter in Rhode Island. In 1857, he had what would be considered a religious experience. After ignoring a suggestion in his mind to go to a chapel, he was struck blind, deaf, and speechless. While contemplating his relationship to God in this state, he found that his sight was first restored. He wrote a request for forgiveness from people he had injured and began going to the chapel where his mind earlier suggested he go. Several weeks later his speech and hearing were restored. After hearing a voice say he should go to work for the Lord, he became an itinerant preacher.

In 1881, his wife died, and he soon married a widow and resumed his carpenter trade. On January 17, 1887, he withdrew his money from a bank account and disappeared. About February 1, 1887, he rented a store in Norristown, Pennsylvania. He used the name of Albert John Brown (note the same initials) and said he was from Newton, New Hampshire. He lived peaceably. In March, he rapped on his landlord's door and asked where he was. Addressed as Mr. Brown, he said he was not Mr. Brown but Ansel Bourne. He returned to Rhode Island and never became Mr. Brown again.

In 1890, Ansel Bourne was hypnotized to see if his life as Mr. Brown could be recovered. The facts about his travel to Norristown seemed plausible, but the day he said he was born in New Hampshire was exactly the same day that Ansel Bourne was born in New York City. The personality of A. J. Brown was not very different from that of Ansel J. Bourne, but Mr. Bourne said he knew nothing about how to be a shopkeeper. Today, this episode would be called a fugue, a dissociative disorder less severe than DID.

Keyes's (1981) book about Billy Milligan was written when there were thought to be few cases of PwDID. Now that there are thousands of known cases and cures, each individual case loses its uniqueness. Well-known cases run the gamut from the innocent woman with personalities such as Banana Split Girl to the criminal/rapist type in Billy Milligan.

Billy, or at least the body referred to as Billy Milligan, was arrested as the "campus rapist" in Columbus, Ohio, in 1977. One of the women he attacked was an optometry student who was able to recognize the eye ailment known as nystagmus in her attacker. A review of Billy's life was later given by "the Teacher," who indicated which personality was in charge at any given time. Adalana, the lesbian, actually "raped" the student. Ragen had been trying to rob the woman, but Adalana took control temporarily and wanted to be held, caressed, and loved by another woman. Arthur got mad at Ragen for the incident and said that if Ragen had not been drinking and lost control, Adalana could not have taken over.

It is difficult to summarize the personalities in a case as complex as Billy Milligan (Keyes, 1981). Undesirable personalities were discovered after the original ten and were generally kept from taking control until doctors unfamiliar with DID interfered with Billy's therapy program. The differences in APs are amazing but are not that unusual for a PwDID. IQs of the APs range from David and Danny's, < 70, to Ragen's, 114. Arthur thought it beneath his dignity to take an IQ test. The APs generally tried to keep Billy, the original personality, from assuming control because he frequently attempted suicide. Each personality described himself or herself with different physical attributes, such as hair and eye color, as well as exhibited manifest differences, like accent and ability. The APs were twenty-three in total.

TABLE 6.2. The Personalities in Billy Milligan

Personality	Eye Color	Hair Color	Age	Other Unique Features
Billy	Blue	Brown	26	High school dropout
Arthur	-	-	22	Englishman, rational, emotionless, smokes pipe, very intelligent, reads and writes fluent Arabic, atheist, wears glasses, capitalist

Ragen	-	Black	23	Writes and speaks Serbo-Croatian, Slavic accent, communist, atheist, protector personality, mustache, color-blind, extraordinary strength, expert in weapons, munitions, and karate
Allen	-	-	18	Manipulator personality, only cigarette smoker, only one right-handed, plays drums, escape artist, paints portraits
Tommy	Amber	Muddy blond brown	16	Antisocial, electronics specialist, plays saxophone, paints landscapes
Danny	Blue	Shoulder-length blond	14	Frightened and afraid, paints only still lifes
David	Blue	Dark reddish brown	8	Keeper of pain, absorbs hurt and suffering, confused
Christene	Blue	Shoulder-length blond	3	Little English girl, reads and prints but has dyslexia
Christopher	-	Brownish blond	13	Christene's brother, British accent, plays harmonica

Adalana	Brown	Stringy black	19	Lesbian, shy, lonely, introverted, keeps house, eyes drift from side to side (nystagmus)

The Undesirable Personalities (According to Arthur)

Philip	Hazel	Curly brown	20	Thug, Brooklyn accent
Kevin	Green	Blond	20	Small-time criminal
Walter	-	-	22	Australian, big game hunter, eccentric, mustache
April	Brown	Black	19	The bitch, Boston accent
Samuel	Brown	Curly black	18	Orthodox Jew, only one who believes in God, sculptor and wood carver
Mark	-	-	16	Zombie, stares at wall
Steve	-	-	21	Impostor
Lee	Hazel	Dark brown	20	Comedian and prankster
Jason	Brown	Brown	13	Vents built-up pressure
Robert (Bobby)	-	-	17	Daydreamer
Shawn	-	-	4	Deaf

Martin	Gray	Blond	19	Snobby New Yorker
Timothy (Timmy)	-	-	15	Lives in own world
The Teacher	26		Fused Billy	Brilliant, sensitive, fine sense of humor, complete memory of personalities

Of all, the AP called the Teacher sounds most like an Inner Self-helper (ISH). Arthur came close to being an ISH because of his rationality and lack of emotion, but his atheism would be very unusual for an ISH. The intelligent Arthur deduced that there were other personalities using the same body. Arthur and Ragen reached an agreement that Arthur would generally have control when Billy was out of prison and unthreatened, but Ragen would have control in prison. When the functions of the undesirables were not necessary, Arthur temporarily kept them from being "on the spot." Later, Arthur lost his dominance and was unable to control the other APs. Banishing them gave him less control over their actions when they did assume control. A later incident, described in chapter 10, occurred when some medical personnel administered Thorazine and in so doing, as predicted by Arthur, brought out the undesirables. When asked why the undesirables were around when their functions were no longer necessary, Ragen replied, "What should we do? Murder them" (p. 122)? Arthur declared Samuel, the Orthodox Jew, as undesirable because Samuel argued with Arthur about the existence of God.

Arthur eventually reached the point where he could sometimes tell what Billy was thinking. He could definitely tell when Billy sensed fear. Arthur told the psychiatrist that he was trying to teach Billy to think logically and that Ragen was teaching him to express anger. Once they had taught him everything, they would disappear. Billy was released from prison in 1988, and his current location is unknown. Although treated, he is not believed to have been cured of DID. However, he does not appear to have been imprisoned since his release in Ohio in 1988, so perhaps, if he is still alive, the criminal APs are not active.

Janette, the original personality in one of Allison's cases, was quiet and timid. Lydia, the first AP to make her presence known, complained about being trapped in a piss-ass body and said that Janette did not want to have any fun. Lydia talked about getting control of the body, as she realized she was sharing the same body with another person. When she did gain control, she was interested in drinking, dancing, and having sex.

A view of how irrational spirit intruders can become is portrayed in the case of Wanda, an AP in one of Allison's patients. Wanda thought she could kill the original personality (Carrie) and all the other APs and then have the physical body to herself. Wanda could not understand that the death of the body would make it impossible for her to occupy that body.

K. Other Theories

The professionals who are treating DID consider DID to be a result of creations from *within* the mind itself. In contrast, this book claims that DID is the result of almost complete intrusion from *outside* by another spirit body after the original spirit body has departed on account of experiencing trauma. There are two other concepts of DID that I will present here. One alternate theory is by Michael Kenny, PhD, a social anthropologist and professor at Simon Fraser University. The second is Ralph Allison. He has been mentioned numerous times, but his theory is slightly different from the normal model of DID therapists.

1. The Sociological Model

Many believe that DID is socially caused, because it is an acceptable method for individuals to vent frustrations or seek recognition. Scholar Michael G. Kenny does not believe DID exists as a true mental illness; he believes DID is created by either the people who exhibit it or their therapists. He interprets the fact that in the past it has taken an average of 6.8 years to diagnose a patient with DID. During that time the patients have been to many therapists, meaning that the patients "shop" until they get the desired diagnosis.

Kenny also states that past publicity has helped the situation get out of hand. Many of the people who turned up with DID in the 1970s had read the book or had seen the movie *The Three Faces of Eve*. Kenny believes that the true home of the mind is in society and that dissociation or psychic fragmentation is culturally conditioned. His analysis can be summarized as follows: "There is a concept, an increasingly normative ideology, and a socially interlinked troupe—made up of patients, therapists, and theorists—which together function to both generate and propagate this particular idiom of distress for a public well ready to subscribe to it and demonstrate its truth." Kenny does not believe that hypnosis is a special or altered state but that it is a cultural delusion. He believes that the hypnotized person goes into a state where new rules apply, but that is because the subject wants it that way or because clues are sent to him by the therapist. Therapists are criticized for trying to compete for honors in particular areas, such as who can find the most APs in one person (the figure is now over four hundred).

2. A Therapist's Alternate Model

Ralph Allison has developed a new DID theory (available on Allison's website, dissociation.com) since his original book, published in 1980. It still differs from the standard psychiatric theory of dissociation. He uses Plato's and Aristotle's concept that each human has an "irrational soul" and a "rational soul." Later these become mind and soul. Allison refers to the rational soul, or spirit, as Essence. I call this Spirit. Allison equates the terms *mind* and *personality*. What he formerly called Higher Helpers are now called Celestial Intelligent Energy.

Allison believes that MPD and DID are different disorders, although they have some similarities. For instance, in MPD resulting from trauma, the first AP appears before age six; eventually there are many APs; and there is no resident original personality. In some cases, only one of the children in the family is the victim of abuse. Allison lists the illness as DID when there is only one AP, it appears after age six, and there is a resident original personality. Allison does agree with most therapists that the APs are a survival mechanism.

In the MPD situation, "the first dissociation is the separation of the Essence from the Personality at the time of the life threatening trauma. This causes the Essence to take on the job of ISH, which is equivalent to Disaster Control Officer. The ISH immediately sends the Original

Personality off to somewhere safe" (p. 2). The ISH programs the first AP to be a false front that will not anger the abuser. The ISH then selects another AP, often a persecutor AP, to handle anger. When this AP makes a mess of a situation, a helper AP is created to clean up. Other APs are created as necessary for specific situations. My concept could be in agreement with this, except on the point that the ISH selects a spirit of a deceased person for specific characteristics that are helpful. Some of the later APs could be random, without a specific purpose and not chosen by the ISH. After treatment and integration of the APs, the ISH/essence integrates into the original personality, a process referred to by Allison as *spiritual integration*.

Allison also discusses other variations involving imagination. Some therapists speculate that dissociation is the result of an active imagination, but Allison disagrees. He divides imagination into two types: inspirational and emotional. "Inspirational Imagination is used by the Essence and the Personality to create great works of art and valuable inventions. It is the most powerful ability of a human mind" (p. 2). This closely resembles my idea of one of the functions of the Spirit.

Emotional imagination can be a two-edged sword. A desirable example is an imaginary playmate to keep a child company. However, Allison mentions an undesirable case in which a boy at age four was locked in a closet while his sisters were being abused by their boyfriend. Years later, the grown-up boy killed an innocent person and claimed that his "other" did it. This other was not a true AP but an internalized imaginary companion (IIC). An IIC is created by the original personality to handle unmanageable emotions, whereas an AP is created by the ISH. An IIC has no conscience or social judgment. However, an IIC can be eliminated by an act of the will of the patient. A person with DID may also have a number of IICs. The ISH can identify if certain behavior is due to an AP or an IIC.

L. Addressing the Skeptics

Ross (1997) lists twenty-five errors of logic made by skeptics who believe that DID is not a real mental illness. Many are self-explanatory, but I may provide an additional detail in parenthesis. The errors are as follows:

1. Arguments are applied only to DID that could just as well be used against all other psychiatric disorders.
2. Skeptics overgeneralize from biased samples (the assumption that one or two are factitious cases means that all cases are factitious).
3. DID is not valid because its treatment has not been proven effective.
4. DID is not a disease because it is influenced by culture (an artifact of biomedical reductionism).
5. The absence of cases outside North America proves that DID is a North American artifact. (Note that earlier Ross commented that the ICD called it a conversion disorder, but the symptoms were similar.)
6. The increase in diagnosis of DID in the 1980s is evidence of its artifactual nature.
7. DID was rarely diagnosed in the 19th century.
8. Skeptics make appeals to authority. (It is a political process.)
9. Validity can be inferred from anecdotal short-term treatment outcome. (Diagnostic validity does not depend upon treatment outcome.)
10. Bad therapeutic practices call the validity of DID into question.
11. Diagnostic criteria for DID are vague; therefore, DID is not valid.
12. Unproven etiology invalidates DID. (Schizophrenia also has no proven etiology.)
13. Lack of proven physiological differences between alters invalidates DID. (I maintain that physiological differences have been validated.)
14. The validity of DID can be disproven by accumulating examples of false-positive diagnoses.
15. If repression is not proven, DID is not real.
16. The diagnosis of DID encourages irresponsible behavior.
17. Multiples are really just borderlines.
18. DID is an artifact of suggestibility in highly hypnotizable individuals.
19. It is impossible to have more than one personality in the same body (irrelevant to a valid diagnosis).

20. A few clinicians are making all the diagnoses. (These "few" actually number in the hundreds.)

21. Incorrect references are indicative of careless research in skeptical literature (citing substandard work by skeptics as authoritative).

22. DID has been created experimentally, which proves it is not valid. (If someone created it experimentally, that person could be sued for unethical conduct.)

23. DID must be completely unconscious to be genuine.

24. If satanic ritual abuse and alien abductions are not real, neither is DID. (The accuracy of DID memories is irrelevant to its validity.)

25. The extreme case escalation tactic creates a perception of extremism.

After explaining why the skeptics who believe that DID is not a "real" disorder, Ross admits that to some extent he agrees with them with the following statement:

> It is true that iatrogenic cases of DID are a serious problem; it is true that memory is reconstructive, error-prone, and highly influenced by social-psychological variables; it is true that DID is socially constructed (how else could it be?); it is true that DID patients can construct elaborate and detailed false memories; it is true that DID can be used for secondary gain; it is true that incompetent therapists are practicing in the field (I have acted as expert witness against them); and so on. (p. 244)

Since these are errors of logic, the correct logical conclusion is that DID is a real disorder and that it can be treated to complete remission through therapy. I especially endorse Ross's conclusion that DID is a hierarchically superior disorder that, when corrected, results in the disappearance of other, incorrect diagnoses, such as bipolar disorder, substance-abuse disorder, homosexuality, and even schizophrenia.

M. Conclusions

In this chapter, I have endeavored to provide evidence that there are two distinct behavioral aspects following severe trauma to a child. One aspect is showing behavior characteristics of a completely separate person, and the second is the beneficial aspect of the ISH, which is the Spirit of traumatized people assisting with correcting the situation. This is the overall hypothesis of my entire book, consistent with the ancient Greek philosophers and the Bible, that humans have at least two distinct spiritual aspects referred to as soul (*psyche* in Greek; *nephesh* in Hebrew) and Spirit (*pneuma* in Greek; *ruah* in Hebrew). In chapters 8 and 9, I will demonstrate that shamans and Eastern concepts of human spirituality agree with this concept of multiple spiritual aspects of humans.

In the next chapter I will present considerable information on end-of-life experiences. These includes predeath visions and other phenomena that occur when a person is close to dying or has very recently died. I will also review some after-death communication, which can take place immediately or any number of years after death.

Chapter 7

AFTER-DEATH COMMUNICATION AND END-OF-LIFE EXPERIENCES

A. Introduction

In chapter 5, I provided evidence that a human spirit form can survive outside the physical body and may communicate with deceased people, usually relatives. In this chapter, I will present information further supporting such a claim by offering documentation that unusual phenomena also occur when a person is approaching true death and/or that communication between a living person and a deceased person can occur, even many years after death. I will only provide situations where the deceased has initiated the communication. I will not be discussing mediumship or channeling, in which a living person seeks to initiate the communication through a medium. The first part of this chapter addresses after-death communication (ADC), while the second part discusses end-of-life experiences (ELEs). ELEs may include some ADC, but the section on ADC involves primarily an exchange of information to a person who is healthy. Having an ADC is sometimes referred to as *piercing the veil*, the semitransparent or diaphanous barrier between the living and the dead.

B. After-Death Communication

Unless otherwise noted, my primary reference for the first part of this chapter on ADC is the book *Hello from Heaven!* (1995), written by Bill Guggenheim and Judy Guggenheim. Bill has spoken at several International Association for Near Death Studies (IANDS) conferences on ADC. He describes his younger self as a business-oriented stockbroker with a nonspiritual viewpoint on life until he attended some Elisabeth Kübler-Ross workshops in the mid-1970s. That sparked an interest in possible survival after death, and in 1988 he heard a voice telling him, "Do your own research and write your own book. This is your spiritual work to do" (p. 13). He realized he had heard that voice once before, in 1980. He had been at home with his wife and three children when the voice distinctly said, "Go outside and check the swimming pool" (p. 14). Although he felt no urgency, he went to the pool and found his youngest son, less than two years old, underwater in the pool. Bill rescued the boy, who recovered without medical attention. His son would likely have died if Bill had not listened to the "voice from nowhere."

Bill and Judy (hereafter referred to as "the authors" or "the Guggenheims") comment that psychologists, psychiatrists, bereavement counselors, and even members of the clergy have historically classified these ADCs as hallucinations, delusions, or fantasies caused by wish fulfillment, imagination, or magical thinking resulting from grief. The authors state that as many as 20% of the normal population have had an ADC. I have heard a university medical professional state that as many as 75% of widows and widowers have reported an ADC. While I believe that overall the cases presented by the Guggenheims are rather convincing, any individual case could be classified as an alleged ADC.

The authors began collecting stories using flyers at numerous locations. When the subject of ADCs gained more attention, newspapers began publicizing their efforts. Then the Guggenheims began speaking to various organizations, from whose members they would obtain more stories. They define an ADC as "a spiritual experience that occurs when someone is contacted directly and spontaneously by a deceased family member or friend" (p. 16). They define communication broadly, for instance, as just sensing the presence of a deceased person without any sensory input. They did not include information gained through a séance or a Ouija board. In addition to case studies, the Guggenheims mention some very famous fictional accounts of ADCs, such as when Hamlet's deceased father speaks to him and, from Charles Dickens's *A Christmas Carol*, when Ebenezer Scrooge's deceased business partner, Marley, appears and speaks to Scrooge.

Also interspersed among the Guggenheim cases will be a few narratives collected by Janis Amatuzio, MD. Several of her accounts of NDEs appeared in chapter 5, but I did not explain her background. She is the founder of Midwest Forensic Pathology, which does pathological work (generally meaning autopsies as part of a death investigation) for several smaller counties in Minnesota. She is referred to as "the

Compassionate Coroner," mostly because of her willingness to speak and listen to bereaved families. She also speaks to many organizations about her work. When she mentions ADCs in her speech, someone often approaches her afterward and adds his or her own account of messages from the dead or of ELEs, often beginning with a phrase like, "You won't believe this." These cases are, of course, anecdotal, as are most of the reports in this chapter. However, this does not necessarily make them any less reliable or real. Amatuzio conveys these narratives to the public in two books she authored: *Forever Ours: Real Stories of Immortality and Living from a Forensic Pathologist* (2002) and *Beyond Knowing: Mysteries and Messages of Death and Life from a Forensic Pathologist* (2006).

Parts of her books are about her own venture into medicine, with more emphasis on her personal life in the second book. Her father was a doctor, and she entered medical school over 35 years ago, when fewer women did so. She relates two of her own mystical-like experiences, the first one at age four and the other as an adult. I believe these incidents affected her openness to the idea that spiritual episodes are not fantasies. When she was growing up she had two imaginary friends, Rara and Gerry.

Later in this chapter I will discuss the findings of researchers Peter and Elizabeth Fenwick, who coined the term *end-of-life experience* (ELE). Their research did include some ADCs, but I will aggregate all of their research in one section of this chapter. However, I will include some ADCs from other sources in this early section of this chapter.

C. The Guggenheim Study

1. Types of After-Death Communication

The Guggenheims divided the responses to their inquiry about ADCs into the following categories (one chapter of their book for each category; the chapter titles are listed below). There had to be at least three responses to create a particular category.

Sensing a Presence: Sentient ADCs
Hearing a Voice: Auditory ADCs
Feeling a Touch: Tactile ADCs

Smelling a Fragrance: Olfactory ADCs

Partial Appearances: Visual ADCs

Full Appearances: Visual ADCs

A Glimpse Beyond: ADC Visions

Encounters at Alpha: Twilight ADCs

More Than a Dream: Sleep State ADCs

Homeward Bound: Out-of-Body ADCs

Person-to-Person: Telephone ADCs

Material Matters: ADCs of Physical Phenomena

Butterflies and Rainbows: Symbolic ADCs

Exception to the Rule: "Fearful" and Other ADCs

Timing Is Everything: Before the News

Expect the Unexpected: ADCs Years Later

Validation: Evidential ADCs

Special Delivery: ADCs for Protection

Saving Grace: ADCs for Suicide Prevention

Confirmation: ADCs with a Witness

The Best of the Best

The last chapter's cases could fit into any the preceding categories.

2. Most-Convincing Types of ADCs

I believe the cases that most convincingly illustrate that ADCs are not grief-induced hallucinations are incidents in which a life was saved; the incident occurred well beyond the normal grief period; there was some physical validation of the ADC; or there was a witness. A majority of the authors' cases that I summarize are from these categories.

The incidents in which an ADC saved a life are important, because people frequently die in accidents. Why is it that not everyone receives a forewarning of an impending accident so it can be prevented? Could it be that there is a spiritual purpose for one person remaining alive and a spiritual purpose served in having another person die? NDErs are often told they must return to fulfill a life purpose. Could those who did not receive a forewarning have already accomplished their purpose? The answers to these questions may be difficult to understand if the accident victim is a child. Still, rational minds often have difficulty understanding spiritual purposes. Also interesting are the ADC instances in which a message was received by a third party to be passed onto another person for whom the message was intended. This type demonstrates that the intended recipient may not be able to tune into the communication methodology of the deceased but that another person is attuned.

In the chapter on NDEs, I described how some NDErs could have their spirit body travel to any place, or any person, simply by a desire to be there. Some of the Guggenheims' ADC cases that I summarize also illustrate this phenomenon, as the location of the person receiving the message oftentimes is unknown to the person who recently died. Of course, we cannot know the intent of the deceased person. I will frequently mention that these ADCs confirm many concepts about deceased relatives that were conveyed in Chapter 5 on NDEs.

To follow are examples from 353 accounts listed in *Hello from Heaven!* and also from Amatuzio and some from authors of books on NDEs. I believe these illustrate that most ADCs are unlikely to be hallucinations resulting from bereavement, wish fulfillment, or magical thinking. In some cases the message does not make sense until the context is known later. In all of the following cases, the important information was received. However, most noteworthy are two things: a deceased relative cared enough to contact these people, and these cases offer confirmation of a life after death.

The authors changed the names of the people mentioned, so I will use the Guggenheims' assigned names. I categorize the specific cases with one or two main characteristics, but there may be an additional feature in the incident.

3. Specific Cases

a. Years Later, Unknown Information

One episode that Amatuzio reports involved a twenty-two-year-old man named Greg appearing to two people after his death from an automobile accident. The events were related to Amatuzio by Greg's mother. Greg appeared to a woman named Sheila who lived in California but had been Greg's (and his brother's) favorite babysitter at least ten years earlier. The first "visit" to her was on the night of his death, but three days later he again appeared to Sheila, this time with his grandmother, who had died from cancer two years before Greg was born. On the night of his second appearance, he also appeared to his girlfriend, Trish, and said he was fine and not alone.

One of Amatuzio's narratives came from a sheriff's deputy who did not have much of a belief in Amatuzio's unusual stories. However, one day the deputy came to relate an incident to the coroner. About ten years earlier a man killed his wife and then committed suicide. The man's father, George, refused to believe that his son could do that and asked the deputy to have two other crime bureaus, including the FBI, investigate. The two bureaus concurred that it was a murder—suicide. However, one day George came to the deputy and said that his son had appeared to him in a dream, stated that he had made a mistake, mentioned that he was "okay now," and asked his father to let the matter go. A few days later George died in his sleep. (There is a section of this chapter titled "Letting Go," to which this case could also apply.)

b. Unexpected Death

Claire woke up early one morning by being pinched and saw the image of a close work colleague named Hugh, who seemed sad. He told her that he "didn't make it" and then said "good-bye." Claire turned on the radio and found out that Hugh's seaplane had gone down in a river and that he had tried to swim ashore but had drowned.

In most predeath visions, a person is ill and knows that he or she will die shortly. Morse (1990) does note one case with a strange twist in which the person had had an NDE earlier in her life. June had a cardiac arrest at the age of five and thereafter had a pacemaker inserted. During that surgery, she had an OBE and noticed that one doctor was right-handed and the other was left-handed. She then went through a long tunnel into a warm *light* she called "the light of God." She said she had no fear of death. She had had some difficulties in her life, as her parents had died when she was young and her sister had died of a drug overdose. June eventually married and had a child. Morse did not say at what age these two events happened. One day June was having a cup of coffee at her kitchen table when her deceased sister appeared and informed June that it was her time to go. The sister drank a cup of coffee. June related this incident to her aunt and uncle, who had raised her and her two brothers, but not to her husband. She did thank her husband for the wonderful life they had together and for her child. That night her pacemaker failed and she died in her sleep. The Guggenheims would classify this as a full-body appearance.

c. Confirmed Time of Death

An interesting ADC case was reported to Amatuzio by a chaplain. The chaplain heard the information from the young wife of a man (they were recently married) who had died from blunt-force head injuries in a car accident. His spirit was standing next to her on the bed and informed her of his accident at 4:20 a.m. (he had been working late). She called 9-1-1 and said her husband's car was in a ravine where it could not be seen from the road, but she was not very specific as to location. The emergency services found the car 20 minutes later. The dead man's organs were donated.

d. Appearing Much Younger and Healthier

In the chapter on NDEs, I mentioned that when an NDEr sees a deceased person, that person is always healthy and usually in the prime of life, even if he or she had had a number of infirmities at death. For instance, the blind can see, the lame can walk, and people who had missing limbs have had those limbs restored. This last type of situation occurred in an ADC when a woman named Becky dreamed of a young person whom she had befriended and who had had one leg amputated as a result of bone cancer (the eventual cause of death). The deceased girl said to Becky, "Look, I've got my leg back!"

Cynthia, whose son was profoundly retarded and died at the age of eight, having never spoken, spoke to Cynthia one day. (Note that NDErs always specify when "speaking" with spirits that the communication is telepathic and always clearly understood.) During an NDE, the NDEr is in spirit form and has no physical body. When a person receives an ADC, even if he or she can observe a solid body, the communication is telepathic, I am quite certain, even though the person who heard the message has a physical body and the deceased has manifested a physical body. In another case, a clear message was received from a person who had suffered from Alzheimer's disease prior to death.

e. Resolving Animosity; Delays in Appearance

Some of the information on NDEs, and other sources to be discussed in chapter 10, indicate that a deceased spirit, especially a person with a troubled life, does not necessarily proceed immediately into the *light*. A case that illustrates this phenomenon is Adeline, who saw her uncle Ned at the foot of her bed one evening just before falling asleep. Ned, an alcoholic, had died nine years earlier. Ned said to Adeline that she should inform Millie and Belle (Adeline's mother and her sister, the latter being Adeline's aunt) that "I am all right *now*" (emphasis added) and "to stop worrying." Adeline was reluctant to tell Millie and Belle of the ADC because of their rigid religious views; however, it turned out that Belle had received the same message without a vision, and Millie had told her it was a dream. Adeline convinced them it was not a dream. The Guggenheims state that there are healing centers in spiritual realms for people with illnesses such as alcoholism. Perhaps the *now* emphasized above indicates completion of a substance-abuse course in the spiritual realm. A woman named Marla did not have her alcoholic and abusive husband appear to her until 21 years after his death. He said he was "fine now." Afterward, Marla felt an incredible sense of peace.

f. Protection Cases

Glendalee was driving her truck on a highway one day when she was startled to hear someone say, "Stop the truck!" At first she did not stop, but then her name was called. She recognized the voice as that of her father, who had died 15 years earlier. Finally, he said, "Baby! Stop!" and she slammed on the brakes. A rapidly moving car came from a side street on the left and missed her truck by several inches. Glendalee believes she would have died if she had not heeded her father's voice.

In the chapter on NDEs, I argued that meeting deceased relatives is an indication of their survival in some form after death. This is reasonably common. However, in protection cases, I posit that the voice could be coming from the protected person's own Spirit, emulating the voice of a trusted person in his or her life.

Florence had two incidents in which her deceased father spoke to her. The incidents occurred eight and 16 years after he died. In many of the previous cases, the words were specific on what might happen, what to do, and/or what not to do. In both of Florence's cases the message simply slowed her down to avoid accidents. In the first incident, her father had her slow her car so he could view the countryside, but he knew that an improperly tightened wheel was ready to fall off the car, which would be dangerous at a high rate of speed. In the second incident, he had her stop walking in order to view a building. If she had not stopped, a hammer that fell from a roof would have hit her and/or the two children behind her, whom she unintentionally blocked when she stopped.

Another question that arises following posthumous forewarnings is this: how did the decedents know that these incidents would occur? Assuming that a deceased, disembodied spiritual body in an afterlife can observe the physical world, it is simple for that entity to observe two vehicles on a collision course. But how does a deceased spirit know that a tire will disintegrate, as has been reported? The concept of a High Self knowing the future of an individual is one level of knowledge, but the future of a tire is another level. Of course, their futures are intertwined. In another case, a woman received a warning from her deceased son not to take a flight months later. Everyone on that flight died. How does a spirit know that far in advance that a plane will crash?

Another example of protection and evidence is the case of Marsha. After waiting a few minutes at a railroad crossing and not seeing an oncoming train, she drove around the gate at a train track. She heard the voice of a friend, Josh, who had died in a vehicle hit by a train five years earlier. Josh shouted, "Drive this car!" She did not respond, but then she felt a foot stomp over hers on the gas pedal. The vehicle shot forward and barely missed the train. The next morning, Marsha had a big bruise on the top of her right foot, indicating that a seemingly physical but invisible force had pushed on her foot. This and a previous case illustrate how a person who died in a particular type of accident may help people in similar situations.

In chapter 5, on NDEs, I discuss a finding referred to (from a book with the same title) as the *Third Man factor*, the Third Man being an entity that assists a person who is near death (Geiger, 2009). In that chapter, I mentioned that instances of the Third Man factor would be discussed in this chapter. Here are those cases. By the nature of the Third Man factor, these are generally protection cases, but they may involve simple comforting to the living individual.

Stephanie Schwabe, a geomicrobiologist, was collecting sediment samples from an underwater cave on Grand Bahama Island, specifically a place called the Blue Hole, part of the Mermaid's Lair. She had previously explored there with her late husband, Rob Palmer, who had died earlier that year while diving at another location. Since it is dark in an underground cave, and perhaps since the only place where a diver may exit the cave is from the point where she entered, a diver always establishes a guideline to follow back to where she entered the water. Normally, Stephanie relied on her husband to keep track of where the guideline was. On this occasion, after collecting her samples, she was ready to return but could not find the guideline. She began to panic, as she did not have much air left in her tank. Then she felt a presence she believed/knew was her dead husband, providing her advice and encouragement in a manner he often adopted. This calmed her down, and shortly thereafter she spotted the guideline and returned to safety with only minutes to spare.

In 1998, Peter Hillary, son of Sir Edmund Hillary of Mount Everest fame, was attempting to complete Robert Scott's final journey to the South Pole (Scott died in the attempt) with two other men. On the 18th day, he became aware of a presence that he recognized as his mother, who had died in 1975. She made several other appearances. On the 36th day, he sensed other presences in his tent that he recognized as two dead former climbing partners. On the 39th day of his expedition, he saw his mother again and noticed that clouds passed through her.

Kenneth Cooke was a merchant seaman who was on a freighter that was torpedoed by a German U-boat in 1943. The ship sank in several minutes, and only 14 of the 57 crew members made it to life rafts, 750 miles from land, with few provisions. People were dying of starvation and thirst. On the 25th day, a man named John Arnold died after telling Cooke that he had talked with God and was told that Cooke and some other crew members would be saved. On day 36, Cooke saw John Arnold and heard him say again that he would be saved. On day 43, when Cooke was ready to commit suicide, he heard John Arnold's voice again. He forestalled the suicide, and later that day he was spotted by an airplane. He was rescued shortly thereafter.

g. Validation Cases

Validation cases often involve finding things that were hidden away by the deceased and could not be found until the deceased communicated with the living. I am familiar with one story, about Emmanuel Swedenborg (1688–1772), who was a famous scientist in his day but who later turned to spiritual studies. Some of his views on the spiritual world will be discussed in a later chapter. He reportedly could speak with deceased people, not necessarily his own relatives.

In one case demonstrating Swedenborg's abilities, a man had a project performed for him and died shortly thereafter. Another man, who had done the work, was hounding the deceased man's widow for payment. The woman thought her late husband had told her he had paid for it, but she could not find the receipt. She asked Swedenborg if he could be of assistance, probably knowing of his reputation. He allegedly visited the deceased and asked the man where he had put the receipt. The receipt was found at the hiding place indicated by Swedenborg.

Lydia received a message from her brother-in-law (her sister's deceased husband) saying that the two women should remove the drawers in his desk and look carefully. Lydia told her sister of this, who then found $3,000 hidden in the desk. Lydia was an intermediary, as normally it would be expected for the message to go to the decedent's widow.

h. Identity Confirmed Later

In all of the previous cases, the deceased person who appeared was known. The following illustrates an example in which the deceased person was unknown, but his identity was determined later. Lucille had a man appear at the foot of her bed one night. He called her Mary and said that her mother was looking for her and she should look for her mother. The man did not identify himself but said that Lucille would learn his identity when she found her birth mother, as Mary was her birth name and Lucille her adopted name. She went to a club for adoptees and found her birth mother after making one phone call. The man who had appeared at the foot of her bed was her grandfather, who, when he was dying, had asked his daughter to find her daughter (i.e., Mary/Lucille). The two women met. In the photograph the mother brought with her, the grandfather had on the same suit worn by the person Lucille had observed at the foot of her bed.

i. Visits to a Child

It is not unusual for small children, age six or younger, to be able to discern spirit entities that adults cannot. These may be angels, spirits of the deceased, or "imaginary friends," which I maintain are friendly spirits.

Dr. Allan Hamilton (2008) personally encountered an interesting case of ADC. He reveals the story of a boy named Thomas who had been seriously electrocuted and was in the burn unit at the Shiners' Burn Institute in Boston. The boy had burns on over 90% of his body.

His father died of a heart attack from stress soon after. The doctors decided to use the skin of the deceased father for skin grafts, as the genetic connections would result in less rejection of the new skin than if cadaver grafts were used. The boy had been unable to communicate for a period of time prior to surgery, as he was in a coma. However, shortly after the graft, the boy awoke and inquired about his father. Hamilton lied and said the father was fine, but then the boy reported that he saw his father standing silently at the foot of his bed. He called out, "Hi, Dad." Hamilton then admitted to the boy that his father had died. The boy said that what he was seeing must be his father's ghost. The boy survived and benefited from improved treatment later in life.

An example of evidence of the idea that children can be spontaneous, see spirits, and get information of which they were previously unaware is the case of the dying grandmother (no names given). This involves a vision, but not one by a person near death. The woman's grandchild went to her mother and said there were two grannies in the bedroom. The second granny was "a *lighted* body named Beth," and she spoke to the grandchild and the granny. The mother and grandchild went back to the bedroom to find that the grandmother had died. The name of the grandchild's great-grandmother was Beth, a fact the child had not known beforehand (Morse, 1990).

j. Witnesses

The Guggenheims describe a number of cases they refer to as "ADCs with a witness." In most of these cases two people saw the same spirit, but in some situations the unusual behavior of animals provided indications of the presence of a spirit. In one case, the animal seemed joyous to see the spirit, but in several other instances the animals seemed disturbed even though they had known the deceased person whose presence they sensed.

The cases that the Guggenheims referred to as "the best of the best" often involved children and family. While emotionally satisfying, those cases did not have as much corroborating evidence as the above cases. Therefore, I will not forge into great detail here, except to highlight a special few cases.

k. Letting Go

Some cases of these "best of the best" involve letting go of a deceased person. In one situation, Neil lost his 19-year-old son Ken, who had died in his sleep from heart arrhythmia. A year and a half later, Neil was at the cemetery, where Ken spoke to him, saying,

> Dad, it's me. I wish you would turn me loose so that I could enjoy where I am. You and Mom always taught me and brought me up to be with God. Now you're keeping me from Him and from enjoying heaven.
>
> I cannot reach the fulfillment that God wants for me because you're holding me back. I would appreciate it if you would just turn me loose and let me enjoy it here. He [Ken] told me [Neil] that he was perfect in God's sight. And he described how beautiful and how peaceful it was there. (p. 349)

Neil realized his son was correct. When he turned Ken loose, the pain of the loss left him. He felt peace in his heart and also felt closer to God than he had ever felt before.

The following incident reported to Morse (1990) by another physician illustrates the principle of letting go or asking for permission to die, but

303

the person sending the message was critically ill, not deceased. A five-year-old boy was in a coma as a result of a brain tumor. The family was constantly praying for his recovery. The family's pastor came to the hospital and informed the parents that in a dream the boy appeared to the pastor and asked the family to quit praying for him, because he was supposed to go. The family accepted that the dream was genuine. When they next prayed, they gave the boy permission to die. The boy temporarily regained consciousness, thanked them for letting him go, and died the next day. Morse also reports that Elisabeth Kübler-Ross told him of a similar case in which a seven-year-old boy with leukemia asked his mother to turn off the oxygen, as it was his time. He had had a predeath vision revealing that his grandfather would be waiting for him once he died.

I. Messages for a Third Person

Earlier, I discussed the notion of intermediaries. Valerie lost her son, John, to cystic fibrosis. She visited the cemetery several times but usually spoke to no one while there. During one visit, she heard her son say she needed to be there to help someone else. She went over to a man who was planting flowers on his son's grave. Still sensing John's guidance, she spoke to the man. The man told her that his son, Troy, had been murdered. Valerie heard John say the following, which she passed on to Troy's father:

> That's why you're here, Mom! You've got to tell him that when those men were strangling his son, when they were in the act of killing him, Troy left his body. There was no suffering. The pain was gone.

> Mom, the only ones who are suffering are the people down there who are alive. You are the sufferers! Troy is with us now and he's okay. And he feels sorry for those who killed him. (p. 351)

Troy's father was overjoyed to receive this information.

m. Murder Victims

A similar incident happened to Arlene, whose 21-year-old son Russ was murdered. Arlene was a member of Parents of Murdered Children and often wondered why good, decent people are murdered. One night she dreamed she went to heaven. She spoke to her son, who was so radiant and happy that she forgot to ask, "Why are good, decent people murdered?" Afterward, she did not think the question important.

n. Assistance in Healing

Occasionally during an NDE, there is an encounter with spirits (not necessarily former humans) who know that the NDEr needs to remain alive, but the spirits are unsure of what to do to repair the illness. Of course, since the NDEr lived, it is assumed that the problem was corrected, thus demonstrating that spirits can assist in physical recovery or at least possess knowledge of it.

Kathryn was worried about her daughter Krista, who, in her early twenties, had metastatic ovarian cancer. Kathryn perceived the presence of her father-in-law 12 years after his death from cancer. He said Krista was going to be all right, as "We've been able to do a great deal here" (p. 363). Krista's recovery went smoothly.

Another healing situation involved Meredith and her former sweetheart, Vic, who had died seven years earlier. Meredith tripped and fractured her ankle. She was given crutches and was instructed to stay off her feet for six to eight weeks. The next night she dreamed she was in a peaceful place with Vic. After asking to look at her foot, he moved it back and forth until she heard a click. When she awoke, she found that her ankle was healed. Recall the kahuna in chapter 2 who healed a broken ankle instantaneously. In chapter 10, another case of instantaneous bone healing will be discussed.

o. Physical Phenomena

I am not including any information from the Guggenheims' book about physical phenomena, such as clocks stopping at the instant a person dies, but I did find one case of an ADC from an unusual source. A self-described skeptic named Michael Shermer (editor of *Skeptical Inquirer* and author of books attempting to debunk the paranormal) had an incident involving electronics occur to him that caused him to question his own skepticism. His article was published in *Scientific American* in October 2014. He was preparing to be married to a woman from Germany. She held beliefs similar to his. Some items had been shipped to her new location in America, including a radio that had belonged to her deceased grandfather, who had raised her. She missed him and wished he could be with her on her wedding day.

When the radio arrived before the wedding, Shermer had tried unsuccessfully to get it to operate, even installing new batteries. He most likely turned it to off mode and hadn't tuned it to any station since it was totally inoperable. On the day of their wedding, he and his bride heard romantic music coming from a room. They traced the sound and found that it was coming from the previously nonworking radio in a closed drawer. They realized it must be a greeting from her grandfather on her special day (Shermer, 2014).

4. Reports from Outside Sources

A majority of the findings I proffer originate from literature specifically regarding NDEs and ADCs. However, I treasure finding similar concepts from outside those specific fields. In the book *Hasidic Tales of the Holocaust* (1982), by Yaffa Eliach, I found the following incidents of ADCs or assistance from the beyond. This type is only a fraction of the total tales in the book, but the others did not involve ADCs. I believe the author used real names. At the end of each tale, Eliach states how she obtained the information. In some cases, the person involved was still living (that was about 35 years ago), but in others the information had been passed on to family and friends.

a. Dreams for Safety or Recovery

Abram Grinberg joined the Red Army in Poland before the Germans occupied his town. His army unit was split into two groups, one going to Siberia and the other to a combat unit. He first indicated he wanted to go with the combat unit, but his mother appeared to him in a dream and said he must go to Siberia. He changed his plans and later found out that entire combat unit was killed.

b. Dancing for the Dead

Most of these ADCs were dreams and the message was from a relative. Moshe, age 14, was a devout follower of the deceased Grand Rabbi of Bobov. Moshe enjoyed singing the rabbi's melodies. At the Mauthausen camp in Austria, it was bitterly cold. One day the prisoners had to go from the shower to the square for a head count. Many fell, and Moshe was nearly frozen when he heard the rabbi speak to him. After much effort, Moshe began to dance to one of the rabbi's melodies; he was one of the few survivors that day.

c. Medical Advice

Esther and her six-year-old daughter, Ann, were hiding out in a pit with a number of other people, who were not always friendly. Conditions were horrible and food scarce. If something happened to Esther, there would be no one to take care of Ann. Esther developed an abscess in one of her teeth. The pain was terrible, and she could hardly see, hear, or move. Then Esther distinctly heard her deceased mother state that if she followed her instructions, she would recover. Esther did so, and in a few days the swelling receded, sparing her life.

d. Asking Favors from God

Gina was only eleven years old but had to perform slave labor at Auschwitz in order to survive. Gina developed a high fever and was on the verge of death. One night Gina's mother dreamed of her father, who said, "My child, I stood before the Almighty God and beseeched Him to save this one grandchild of mine, your daughter." The next day Gina asked for something to eat, and that day the Russian soldiers liberated the camp.

e. Years Later

In many of Eliach's cases, the time of death of the person appearing in the dream was not specified, but in most cases the time was short. In the Guggenheims' cases, the period of time was not more than 35 years.

Eliach related one tale that took place over an unbelievable number of years.

A Hungarian officer was paid well to bring back to Hungary two prominent "generals" captured on the eastern front. The two "generals" were actually the Grand Rabbi of Belz and his brother, both of whom had escaped from a ghetto. The officer had all the papers and the various license plates he needed to pass through various checkpoints. At one point the officer was so confident that the situation was proceeding well that he stopped at a bar to have a drink. When he returned, he could not find the car. It turned out that it was where he had parked it, but it was shrouded in a mist "to conceal it from eyes that were not supposed to see it" (p. 40).

When the officer and two passengers arrived at the first checkpoint in Hungary, the border guard and his superior would not let the vehicle through, as they did not have any orders about the "generals." The Hungarian officer was worried. While he was considering an alternative plan, three Hungarian generals on beautiful horses rode up and ordered the border guards to let the vehicle through. The generals on the horses saluted the "generals" in the vehicle. The Hungarian officer commented that he knew all top-ranking Hungarian generals but said that he did not recognize the three on horses. The rabbis in the car stated that they recognized the men as their father, who had died in 1927, their grandfather, who had died in 1894, and their great-grandfather, who had died in 1855. All were rabbis. Eliach concludes that they were top-ranking generals in God's almighty army.

D. End-of-Life Experiences

For End-of-Life Experiences (ELEs), I rely on the following as my primary sources: *At the Hour of Death* (1977) by Karlis Osis and Erlendur Haraldsson; *The Art of Dying* (2008) by Peter Fenwick and Elizabeth Fenwick; and *Into the Light* (2007) and *Learning from the Light* (2009), both by John Lerma. Supplemental sources will also be included.

1. The Osis and Haraldsson Study

Osis and Haraldsson's book is interesting because it is a cross-cultural study of people near death in hospitals in the United States and India. The authors believe their findings support the hypothesis of postmortem survival. The authors defined the term *hallucination* as "imagery coupled with a misapplied sense of realness." They discovered three main types of hallucinations: rambling and confused, coherent and preoccupied with themes of this life (mainly reliving enjoyable times in the past), and coherent and indicative of a transfer to a postmortem existence. Examples of the third type, some of which are similar to NDEs, include claiming to see living or deceased people, religious or mythological figures, or otherworldly environmental scenes.

Osis and Haraldsson questioned their respondents about medications, types of illnesses, and fever. They concluded that 80% of the people who had seen apparitions were unaffected by medication. They also considered that high temperature might be a possible cause of hallucinations. However, 58% of the dying people had a normal temperature. In 34%, the fever was less than 103° Fahrenheit, and in only 6% were the fevers over 103° Fahrenheit. In the United States, about two-thirds of the patients had cancer or heart disease. In India, there were more infectious diseases. Fewer than 13% of the respondents in both countries were being treated for stroke, brain injury, or uremic diseases, all illnesses that may cause hallucinations. Osis and Haraldsson conclude that hallucinogenic-type diseases tended to reduce the possibility of seeing apparitions rather than to increase it.

With few exceptions, most of the findings for these ELEs were the same regardless of age, sex, education, religion, or socioeconomic status of the respondent. The fact that educated people had the same type of experience downplays the explanation that such phenomena are a result of the superstitions of uneducated people. Osis and Haraldsson concluded that the core phenomenon of the dying experience is not much affected by individual, national, or cultural factors.

a. Visions of Deceased People versus Religious Figures

In Osis and Haraldsson's study, of the 70% of those who went on to die, about 70% saw apparitions of deceased people. About 83% of those people were relatives, and of those about 90% were close relatives, such as grandparents, parents, siblings, or offspring. The study reports that Americans tend to see relatives more frequently than do people in India; Indians saw more religious figures. Religious figures that Americans observed included angels, Jesus, and Mary. Americans were also more likely to see deceased females (61% did). American males saw females more frequently—71% of males saw females, compared to 51% of females seeing females. In addition, religious Americans were more likely to see females. In India, females were not seen as often (only by 23%), especially by Indian males (13%). People in either culture who were not near death but who hallucinated other people were much more likely to have hallucinated a living person. In some cases, the apparition, although a biologically close relative, was not well-known by the dying person, such as a mother who died in childbirth appearing to her child. Osis and Haraldsson contend that mental patients and people with drug-induced hallucinations rarely see deceased close relatives, indicating that drugs are more likely to interfere with an ADC than to cause them.

b. Takeaway Purposes

The apparitions are often described by the person near death as being there for "takeaway" purposes or as "guides," i.e., to take the living person to the afterlife world or another mode of existence. In Osis and Haraldsson's study, for patients who died within ten minutes of discerning the apparition, 76% of the apparitions were for takeaway purposes (82% in the United States and 71% in India). Following seeing an apparition, 27% died within an hour, 20% in one to six hours, and 62% within a day. People who had rambling-type hallucinations tended to live longer. The apparitions had the semblance of being external instead of being a mere projection of wishful thoughts by the patient or of medical prognosis by the doctor. Some people did not observe the person they expected to see. In many cases, the person did not expect to die until he or she saw the apparition. For instance, one Hindu man definitely expected to live, but he died with ten minutes of saying,

"Somebody is calling me." More than half of the apparitions lasted less than five minutes; 17% lasted over one hour.

c. Willing versus Called

All Americans but one were willing to accompany the apparitions. Many people in India would see *yamdoots*, messengers of the god of death, Yama, and thereafter not desire to proceed with the messengers. The yamdoots usually made authoritative calls and even employed force, whereas the persons seen by Americans appeared to beckon the dying person to join them. Yamdoots can be viewed positively, but more frequently they are viewed negatively. When the Indians had positive feelings, it was usually from seeing other gods. About one-third of Indians resisted the takeaway gestures. One factor for this may have been age. The average age of the Americans in the study was early sixties, while the Indians' average age was midforties, so the latter may have been more reluctant to leave life. Age may also have been a factor determining which generation the dying person observed. The following table illustrates this information:

TABLE 7.1. Generations Observed by a Person Near Death

Respondents who:	United States	India
Observed previous generation	41%	66%
Observed present generation	44%	29%
Observed next generation	15%	5%

d. View of the Afterlife

The majority of apparitions occurred in the natural surroundings of the room. In India, 94% occurred in the room; in the United States, 62% did. More Americans observed the apparitions in a heavenly environment. Visions of the environment were only one-fifth as common as visions of people. One-third of the visions were of this world, but the two-thirds of another world were similar to those seen by people having an NDE. Gardens with grass and flowers were common, but most respondents just described a heaven. Seventeen mentioned *lights* or colors, but many others inferred a heavenly scene. Six heard beautiful music. More people reported seeing gates than most NDErs do, and one recognized St. Peter, who told him to go back. In a case similar to many NDErs' experience, a man asked why he was sent back when what he saw was so beautiful. One man discerned his deceased wife standing on the other side of a river, waiting for him to cross. This is reminiscent of a border in NDEs. One American had a glimpse of his sister in this otherworld environment. She had died the day before, without his knowledge. Earlier it was stated that few Americans perceived apparitions as threatening, but many Indians did. However, Americans did observe more threatening environments than did Indians; however, no one reported seeing a hell.

e. Mood Changes

One phenomenon Osis and Haraldsson observed was a sudden change in mood following an encounter with an apparition. They were careful to specify changes, as some people could be in a positive mood all of the time. The figures are not overwhelming (41% positive, 30% no change, 29% negative) because many people simply do not show their positive mood as much as other people do. Women were not any more likely to exhibit emotions than were men. The negative emotions were felt by those who did not realize they were going to die, or by Indians who observed unfriendly yamdoots. The words most often used to describe positive mood changes were *peace*, *joy*, and *serenity*. Of some apparitions, it was said that "they light up"; one was described as looking "radiant." People who have visions of living persons rarely show these positive emotions. The positive emotions were more likely to occur if death came in a short time. Closely associated with this positive mood change was that some people appeared to lose their pain from illness just before death. This could be the beginning of detachment of the spiritual body from the physical one and is similar to what happens in NDEs. One man who had been blind for five years seemed able to see just before he died. Osis and Haraldsson state that Elisabeth Kübler-Ross informed them that she observed one schizophrenic become completely lucid before she died.

f. Wrong Person

The cases in India did add one twist that did not occur in the United States sample. In approximately half a dozen of the Indian cases, the dying person reported that he found himself in an otherworldly environment, only to have a "spiritual accountant" inform the messengers that they had brought the wrong person. When one man recovered, another man with the same name at the hospital died within minutes. One Indian male said God sent him back, but he died within two minutes. Another Indian male reported a physical pain that he did not previously have; he was forcibly returned.

g. Omens and Other Unusual Incidents

In one case in India, a man reported that a Yamdoot was coming to take him away, but he did not want to leave. At the moment the sick man said, "There he [the Yamdoot] is." A flock of crows on the tree outside his window flew away, and then the man died. One Indian, who was in his midtwenties and ready to be discharged from the hospital, reported that he observed someone dressed in white clothes, but he would not go with him. The man died within ten minutes. In India, nurses are often Christian, so the nurses may use the word *angel* to describe these beings even if the dying patient does not. One man who was ready to die said he saw angels coming down the stairs, and when everyone looked at the staircase, a glass on one step simply shattered into many pieces without falling first. One American atheist saw a vision of Jesus.

h. Family Knowledge

Some individual cases from Osis and Haraldsson's study are interesting. From general readings on NDEs, it may appear as if those on the other side know what is happening here on earth. For example, one deceased sister knew the children of the person near death, although the children were born after the sister's death. However, that may not always be the case. One woman held a conversation with her husband, who had died 17 years earlier. She disclosed to him family events since the time of his death.

i. Near Death but Recovered

Osis and Haraldsson also collected information on people who recovered fully (120 cases). Their cases were different from normal NDEs in that the apparitions or visions occurred while they were conscious. Out-of-body experiences were rarely reported. One exception was an Indian man who said he visited several Indian holy places such as the Taj Mahal. One woman commented that she saw nothing but space. In most recovery cases, the patient observed an apparition of a deceased relative or of God, who informed her that the spirit world was not ready for her. Osis and Haraldsson expected more apparitions of living people among those who recovered, but they conclude that afterlife-related apparitions were as common among patients who came back as among those who died. One young boy recognized his deceased uncle, who had been a doctor. The uncle informed the boy that he should take his medicine. The boy rapidly recovered. One woman observed her deceased mother and then said she was going with her mother, but instead she recovered.

j. Conclusions of the Osis and Haraldsson Study

Although there are some major cultural differences between the two countries, both appear to indicate a living person making a transition to a postmortem world. The study's findings are consistent with reports of other research covered in this chapter.

2. The Fenwicks' Study

Dr. Peter Fenwick is a neuropsychiatrist in Britain and the former president of the British branch of IANDS. Elizabeth, his wife, has written a number of books, and the couple collaborated on a previous book on NDEs, *The Truth Is the Light* (1997), prior to writing *The Art of Dying* (Fenwick and Fenwick, 2008), the focus of my discussion in this chapter. The Fenwicks' study in Britain is a contemporary version of Osis and Haraldsson's, adding a third country with similar evidence of postmortem survival. The Fenwicks' study includes some accounts with types of information not presented in other studies, including healthy people observing a spirit of a deceased person leaving the body and oddities at the time of death, such as clocks stopping.

The Fenwicks' ELEs include ADCs, but I will only use the term *ELEs* when describing their findings. Although most frequently employing the term *ELEs*, they also refer to the phenomena as *approaching-death experiences*. The Fenwicks also surmise that NDEs are actually Temporary-Death

Experiences (TDEs), i.e., that the person actually died and encountered what would happen if he or she actually died. The Fenwicks note that a person near death often speaks of a preparation for a journey, not an ending or the beginning of a journey, not the end of a life. They also add, "It's about letting go of this physical world and preparing for what's going to happen next" (p. 18).

a. Sources of Information

The Fenwicks use the term *carers* for the people they interviewed in their survey, i.e., the persons caring for patients in a hospice. Reports they collected on ELEs also include information conveyed to the carers by patients' visitors. In addition to reviewing medical records, the Fenwicks asked the carers what medications the dying patients were taking and informed the carers which ones often cause hallucinations, asking them if they thought the dying patient appeared lucid at the time of their ELE. The Fenwicks initially asked these carers about past experiences with the terminally ill; that is, this was a retrospective study. Next, they asked the carers to record future incidents and their frequency. These incidents provided the Fenwicks with material for a prospective study, which could be further analyzed.

Similar to the Guggenheims, the Fenwicks sometimes spoke to groups about ELEs and gathered new accounts from the attendees. At times, they were impressed by the sincerity of the people relating their accounts. One man disclosed an incident in which, many years earlier, he went with his father to visit his father's friend John in a hospital. The hospital staff informed them that John had died and asked them to drive to John's sister Kate and inform her. This was in 1950; Kate did not have a phone. When they arrived, Kate said she knew her brother had died and related the specific time, as her brother had verbally communicated with her the minute he died.

Common explanations for these ELEs are drugs, expectations or wishful thinking, dying brain pathology, or a need for comfort. Other factors include cultural and religious beliefs or mental illness. However, the Fenwicks ascertained that postsurgery patients who are given the same drugs as the dying virtually never have visions of the departed. Carers "were all very clear that there is a real difference between deathbed visions and drug-induced hallucinations" (p. 80). Drug-induced hallucinations often include visions of insects or dragons, or frightening scenes. These patients exhibit anxiety or fear, whereas ELEs are a positive experience. Some patients can exhibit both symptoms just minutes apart. For instance, one man saw insects and thought the nurses were going to poison him, but then he knew things were better when he saw his deceased mother sitting on the next bed. In another incident, Valerie was caring for her ailing father when he reported seeing his deceased wife and son (Valerie's brother). She assumed it was the medications she was giving him. After he died, she found all of the pills she thought he had taken. The Fenwicks comment that hallucinations resulting from organ failure have many of the same characteristics as drug-induced hallucinations, but the patient is usually confused.

b. Spirit Visitors

The Fenwicks state that only 2% of spirit visitors in their study were religious figures and that 70% were deceased relatives and friends. The remaining 28% were gestures of recognition that could not be identified, such as the patients' focusing their eyes on a place in the room other than on the physical visitors, or waving or pointing at something the healthy visitors could not see. Instead of spirit visitors, some dying people observed beautiful places. Most dying people did not intimate any fear of the visitors, and the visions seemed to resolve their fear of death. People who have ELEs, especially ones in which the visitors tell them "All is well!" or "I'm fine!" also lose their fear of death. However, when people say they lose their fear of death, they imply a fear of where their spirit may end up. The Fenwicks comment that while death itself may be nothing to fear, the actual experience of dying is not always pleasant.

Frequently the patient will not realize that living visitors in the room cannot discern the spirits in the room. For example, one woman asked her daughters to wave at their father, who had died a few weeks earlier, and they complied although they could not observe him. A patient can be comatose or unconscious and then be lucid for a very brief period of time to greet a spiritual visitor. One woman was in extreme pain and barely aware of her surroundings when, three days before she died, she became happy and lucid, speaking in the language of her birth that she normally only used when speaking with her parents. After that incident, the pain seemed to be gone until she died. In the Fenwicks' nursing home study, they were informed a number of times about people with advanced Alzheimer's disease (who could not recognize members of their family) becoming lucid and alert shortly before death and recognizing their family (terminal lucidity). Just before death a patient may become peaceful and serene, or cheerful and elated. Other ELE patients may express surprise, delight, and acceptance.

Confirming other studies that demonstrated that deceased people appear in their prime of life when appearing to a living person is the case of Keith Scrivener. His father-in-law was dying from stomach cancer and was emaciated. Keith had an infant son. One night he awoke to see his father-in-law bending over the child. The father-in-law appeared younger, happy, healthy, and of normal weight. When the father-in-law's death during the night was confirmed, the time was the same time that Keith had awakened in the night. It might seem unusual that the father-in-law would contact his son-in-law when his daughter was right there. The Fenwicks believe that only some people are sensitive to this type of communication.

c. Empathic and Shared Experiences

A person may occasionally mirror the same pain or emotions of a dying person she knows. Sometimes she may know who the dying person is, but other times she may not find out until later the identity of the person who died. One man, Raymond Hunt, had visited his hospitalized father who was dying of lung cancer. Later, Mr. Hunt was asleep at home when he awoke with great chest pain and difficulty breathing. He then experienced great love and peace. I would classify the latter as an empathic experience, as described in the chapter on NDEs. Since his father actually died, it would not be an empathic NDE but an empathic death experience. After this incident, Mr. Hunt no longer feared death. An argument could be made that this incident, and the case in chapter 5, in which the mother felt the pain of her daughter as she was killed in an automobile accident, contradicts the ADC case (Valerie in the Guggenheims' study) in which the parents were told that their son had felt no pain as he was being murdered, because he had "left his body."

An example of a shared experience was Carole, who woke up incredibly happy at 4:00 a.m. At 6:00 a.m. her father called and said that he learned Carole's mother was dead when he had tried to wake her. The mother had an appointment at the hospital that day but was not considered seriously ill. When Carole spoke with her daughter later that day, and without relating her own experience, the daughter reported that she also awoke at 4:00 a.m. and was incredibly happy.

Empathic experiences may involve senses rather than feelings. Among these phenomena are having visions of *light* or hearing beautiful music. Carers and others sitting with the dying may also see the *light*. They may also hear beautiful music.

d. Ghosts

During World War II, Irene and her sister were walking. They both saw a man on a bridge in a military airman's uniform. They thought the man was Irene's boyfriend, Harold, as Harold was in the military. Before they reached the bridge, Harold disappeared. The next day, the sisters were informed that Harold's aircraft had been shot down and he had died the previous day, at about the same time as they had observed him. I consider two people observing the same spirit of a deceased person to indicate that it was not a hallucination. However, detractors might consider it to be a folie à deux.

e. Dream Encounters

The Fenwicks also had cases in which the messages of death came in dreams. To one man in the navy, the dream came to him when he was in a submarine two hundred feet underwater. This would indicate that communication from a deceased person to a living person does not utilize the electromagnetic spectrum, as messages in that form cannot penetrate that much water.

The Fenwicks interpret such dream encounters as being driven by the dying person. However, in one case a woman delivered a child who had to be put into an intensive care unit. At 3:00 a.m., the mother correctly sensed that her child had died. Could a two-day-old child have driven that experience? The mother believed that a bonding had occurred while in the womb.

In some Guggenheim ADC cases there were indications that some alcoholics could not communicate immediately after death, as they may have needed some reeducation in the afterworld. In some NDE accounts there were indications that people who commit suicide may have difficulties in the afterlife. However, the Fenwicks mention the case of Jean Cheesman's estranged husband, who was bipolar and committed suicide. He appeared to her at the end of her bed in a dream and told her not to cry, as he was finally at peace. The time of his death matched the time of her dream.

Another example of the end-of-life phenomenon comes from the writings of NDE researcher Melvin Morse. Morse (1992) presents a case of a boy named Cory, who was dying of leukemia and had a number of visions. The time span before death was not specified, but it appears to be on the order of months before his actual death, not hours or days as in the study of the Fenwicks or Osis and Haraldsson. The visions were dreams that occurred during sleep, but I surmise they were views of a world similar to that of an NDEr or a person just before dying. Of Cory's first vision, he reported that he "traveled up a beam of light to heaven, where he crossed a moat on a rainbow bridge and visited the crystal castle" (p. 53), where he spoke with God. In a later vision of the crystal castle, he met an old boyfriend of his mother, a man who was crippled. His mother had never mentioned him to Cory. Cory said the man could now walk. The mother was able to determine that the man had died on the day of Cory's vision. Cory described God as an old man with a beard and a halo, which was contrary to what his parents had taught him. I am not asserting that God has this appearance, but rather that Cory was not just reiterating what he had been taught. At one point, Cory was informed in a vision that he would die at a certain time, regardless of whether he continued his chemotherapy. Cory, after deciding to discontinue treatment, died within a few days of his predicted death. Morse depicts several other examples of predeath visions by children that are similar to NDEs and to predeath visions reported by the Fenwicks or Osis and Haraldsson.

f. Belief in the Afterlife

In today's society, many people do not have a belief in an afterlife, perhaps more so in Europe than in the United States. Although the Fenwicks do not mention this, the type of afterlife is also relevant. Many fundamentalist Christians believe in an afterlife, but only one in which a believer is with Jesus or God. Most fundamentalists do not believe in communication from deceased relatives. I am not sure what their basis for that belief is. There is the story of Lazarus in one synoptic Gospel (Luke 16:19–31), in which a deceased rich man, who did not share his bounty with people when he was alive, is told that he cannot contact his relatives to warn them of the consequences of avarice. However, he was in a place of torment, and the supposition that there cannot be contact from there does not necessarily apply to the heavenly side of the afterlife.

Quite frequently, I surmise that strict interpreters of the Bible confuse the gist of a passage with the details. In 1 Samuel 28, for example, King Saul was afraid of an upcoming battle and decided to consult with the recently deceased prophet Samuel. When Samuel was alive, Saul disobeyed him and did not kill all of the Amalekites, as commanded by God through Samuel. Because of this, Samuel asserted that the Lord had reneged Saul's kingship, and Samuel anointed David as Saul's successor. Saul did not leave without a fight. Saul also expelled the mediums and spiritists from the land (v. 3b). He desired to speak to Samuel through a medium. Someone informed Saul that there was a medium in Endor. Saul went to her disguised, asking to speak to Samuel. She reported that Samuel's spirit came out of the ground. She realized that the disguised man was Saul and that she was afraid she would be killed. Saul said he would not do that, and then he asked for Samuel's advice. Samuel replied that the Lord had not changed His displeasure with Saul for not killing the Amalekites. Samuel predicted that Saul and his sons would die the next day. Saul did die, and David became king.

My interpretation of this passage is that Samuel was actually contacted but had the same attitude toward Saul that Samuel had had when living. I have no problem with people who believe it is not a wholesome practice to consult with mediums, but that is different from reasoning that there cannot be contact with the dead. Death does not make a person a sage, but in this case Samuel's prediction came to be. In the cases I report in this chapter, the contact was initiated by the deceased, not the living. Note also that Samuel said that Saul would be with him. The normal expectation would be that Samuel would be in heaven while Saul would be elsewhere. Of course, the materialist would consider this entire passage to be a myth or legend, and that no such incident occurred.

On occasion, ADCs and ELEs can change people's minds about the afterlife. For example, one man, Brian, commented that he had a belief in an afterlife, but his elderly aunt had a deep conviction that death was the end of everything. As she lay dying, she asked to speak to Brian. Once he was there with her, she told him, "You were right after all" (Fenwick and Fenwick, 2008, 27).

John Burgess described himself as an atheist but questioned his own disbelief as a result of two episodes. The first was when he was with his grandmother the night she died. She informed him that his deceased grandfather had visited her the night before. On the day she died he was in the bathroom washing his face and became very faint. He glanced at his watch and later determined that it showed the exact time that his grandmother had died.

g. Premonitions in the Seemingly Healthy

At times the visits by deceased relatives can be a premonition of impending death. In one case disclosed by the Fenwicks, a woman was visiting her mother, who was elderly but not unhealthy. The mother reported that she clearly observed her mother, who had been deceased for over thirty years, standing in the doorway. The mother had a massive stroke the next day and passed on a few days later.

One report involved two visits from the beyond. The information was relayed by Sheena. Her mother, who was very sick in 1968, observed her recently deceased father at the foot of her bed. The mother desired to go with her father, but he asserted that it was not her time yet and that her family needed her. He said he would be there with her when her time on earth was completed. In 1978, she was seriously ill again but not considered in danger of death. One day she revealed to Sheena that she was going to die. She had been visited by deceased members of her family, who informed her that it was time to go. Sheena had so many skeptics among family and friends that she even began to wonder if her mother dreamed those ELEs and consequently gave up fighting her illness. How sad that nonbelievers can turn a moment of joy about joining deceased members of their family into a fear that a person was hallucinating.

h. Sensitivities

The Fenwicks refer to some people's ability to receive messages from the deceased as *sensitivity*. Gill Scrivener reported to the Fenwicks that he knew of a five-year-old who was taken to see his dying grandmother. The child could not understand why everyone was crying when his grandparents were so happy together (he could see his deceased grandfather with his grandmother). In another case, a five-year-old child told her mother that the room was "packed with people," most of them dressed in old-fashioned clothes. To the child, those people looked as real as living visitors. Many children lose these abilities as they age, but a few others retain the ability.

i. Synchronicities

Carl G. Jung coined the term *synchronicity*, more or less meaning "an unusual coincidence." There is a famous story of a woman reporting a dream to Jung about a gold scarab beetle. Jung heard a noise at a window, which he opened, and found a common beetle with a golden sheen.

Another subject area discussed by the Fenwicks is unusual mechanical incidents that occur near to the time of someone's death. It would strike most people, especially those with a mechanistic viewpoint, that physical objects would not respond to someone's death. These include occasions when clocks stop, pictures fall off walls, or televisions turn off. Animals may also act strangely. There is almost always a connection between the object and the person who died. If man A dies, and in spirit visits his brother B, a dog or cat may sense man A, even if man B does not sense the presence of his brother and the animal did not know man A very well.

Dr. Sue Brown, who described herself as nonreligious, experienced the room in which she was sleeping light up at 4:00 a.m. A few minutes later the hospital that was treating her mother called to inform her that her mother had just died. A man named Neil Handley also experienced his bedroom being lit up. In addition, he heard a cord snapping. This could be the silver cord referenced in Ecclesiastes 12:6–7 (LT) as "the silver cord is cut off. ... Then ... the spirit shall return to God who gave it." Within a minute the hospital called to inform Neil that his father had died. It is interesting that about a month earlier Neil had a dream in which his father, who was healthy at age 76, said he would be leaving at the end of the month. The father was hospitalized with a stroke on the last day of that month.

j. Childhood ELE

Like children's NDEs, childhood ELEs are interesting in that a child will simply say what he or she is experiencing without offering analysis. Amatuzio first heard about this incident after speaking with the deceased child's mother. The 15-year-old boy who died, James, had progressive muscular dystrophy. Despite this, he was surprisingly cheerful. James made two interesting comments just before he died. The first was that he needed more gravity, as he was going up. I would interpret this as meaning that his spirit body was rising from his physical body. Shortly thereafter, with his eyes closed, he asked about the playground he saw with all the kids playing. A few minutes later he died.

k. A Historical Case

The Fenwicks reiterate an ELE that piqued the interest of Sir William Barrett to write a book titled *Deathbed Visions* (1926). He was mentioned in chapter 4 as a former president of the Society for Psychical Research (SPR). The incident happened to his wife, Lady Barrett, an obstetrician. She was called to an operating room where a woman named Doris was dying from a hemorrhage after delivering a healthy child. While dying, Doris had a radiant smile and commented on the lovely brightness and wonderful beings. After exclaiming that her deceased father was coming, she looked puzzled, as Vida was with him. Vida was Doris's sister and had died three weeks earlier, but Doris had not been informed of this because of her health condition. Doris could not understand why her sister, whom she thought was living, was with her deceased father.

I. Conclusions of the Fenwick Study

The Fenwicks' position is similar to the concepts presented in chapter 4; they believe that that the mind is not identical to the brain. The Fenwicks conclude that if these findings are confirmed, then it appears that the mind has the capacity to travel and to interact with the minds to which it is closely linked.

3. The Lerma Study

Another book with very interesting information is *Into the Light*, by John Lerma, MD. The subtitle is *Real Life Stories about Angelic Visits, Visions of the Afterlife, and Other Pre-Death Experiences*. The last term will be abbreviated as *PDEs*. Lerma was the medical director of a hospice in Houston and obtained his information from patients shortly before they died. He now works as a consultant in the hospice field.

Some of the information Lerma acquired is similar to the Fenwicks' ELEs, but then he introduces something unique: a life review not within the context of an NDE. The message in the life reviews has a strong resemblance to those that occur in NDEs. The Fenwicks did not report life reviews in any of their ELEs. The life reviews mentioned in Lerma's book were not carried out in the typical NDE sense, but rather they were discussions with angels and scenes of mistreatment of others or of poor decisions. The best comparison I can recall is when Ebenezer Scrooge in Charles Dickens's *A Christmas Carol* reviews his life's consequences.

In one Fenwick case, a dying man petitioned an angel for a short extension of his life so he could meet his yet unborn son. Other than that, patients did not report many religious visits. In contrast, Lerma maintains that a few days before death there are often a half dozen angels in the room, and within the last few hours 30 or more angels assist the dying person. Lerma's information came from speaking directly to dying people. Lerma also claims that a patient may carry on a dual conversation, that is, with an angel and with Lerma, without appearing to have a change in consciousness. The conversation with the angel is telepathic. The angels or deceased humans with whom the dying person was speaking were often in the corner of the room. The angels normally had the classical wings employed by artists. By comparison, the angels that NDErs observe often do not have wings.

Lerma states that he has interviewed more than 2,000 terminally ill patients and recorded more than 500 PDEs. Some of the information he obtained from his patients confirms or explains some aspects of NDEs. For instance, Lerma asserts that there are many variations of what heaven is because angels know what makes the person feel most comfortable. This corroborates the reports from NDErs that heaven or paradise may appear different to each person.

Lerma presents his information as a series of individual cases. He says that some quotations of the patient were from notes and some from memory, so they may be a paraphrase. Some items I put in quotation marks are the major point Lerma learned from a particular case and not a quotation of the patient. The names were all assigned by Lerma. I will emphasize an unusual feature, a finding that supports a previous finding, confirmation of situations that were found in NDEs, or a valuable life lesson.

a. Matthew

Matthew was a nine-year-old boy who was blind from retinal blastoma. However, in his dreams he could ride on dolphins. He also had names for some of his angels. Matthew felt that he was undergoing his illness in order to bring his family closer to God. Lerma comments that as a doctor, he found this to be a challenge, but he came "to believe and understand the concept that suffering serves a real purpose in the world" (p. 40). This theme will be reinforced in other cases. Matthew said, "Those people who hurt and kill people are very sick and need not be judged but helped, especially through prayer" (p. 42).

b. Susan

Susan was raised a Christian but then became a Buddhist. She was in a vegetative state for three years after having sustained an injury caused by her husband, William. William had power of attorney, and although he knew that Susan would not desire to extend her life artificially, he was reluctant to let her go on account of his own guilt. William then had several incredible encounters with angels who explained that Susan was suffering and that he needed to let her go and forgive himself. Lerma and Susan's sister also had unusual spiritual incidents that confirmed that removing her feeding tube was the correct action to take.

c. Leon

Leon was a 78-year-old Baptist minister with colon cancer. His family did not visit very frequently. He was prejudiced and very judgmental, thought NDEs were hallucinations, and believed that angels do not appear to people today. It took a while for him to be convinced that he was conversing with angels.

An angel told him how important Mother Mary is. (It should be noted that Lerma is a Catholic, and Catholics often speak of the importance of Mary. However, many of Lerma's findings are not standard Catholic doctrine. Lerma is very tolerant of anyone's religious beliefs or lack thereof.) Leon treated his wife as subservient and married her out of obligation, not because he loved her. What is really unusual is that he was shown what his life would have been like if he had married the woman he really loved and that he was made to understand that his life would have been filled with more joy had he married that woman. In my reading of life reviews during NDEs, I do not recall any cases of life with an alternative choice. Leon's lack of love for his wife was why she did not visit him often. He had raised his children with discipline rather than affection, and thus had an estranged relationship with them.

As a minister, he often spoke out against gays but was informed that God does not make mistakes and that in a gay relationship there is still a male and a female. I would interpret this as a female spirit intruder, a topic to be discussed in chapter 10. After his PDE, Leon said, "The key is being spiritual and not solely religious" (p. 56). Leon also reported that there are generational blessings and generational sin, and he was given a few extra days to apologize to his wife and children. He commented that his new desire to learn about God's love would bring a generational blessing to his family. Generational effects are another theme of Lerma's study.

d. Katarina

Katarina, 42, was the mother of two teenagers. She had cervical cancer and a history of drug abuse. She had seemingly changed her life, turning to God when she became ill. This made her angry at God, as she felt abandoned. An angel informed her that "it was fine to act that way and to feel what she was feeling, as this showed God that she loved and acknowledged Him; all God really wants is for us to acknowledge and have a relationship with Him. The angel commented that God fully understands our pain, suffering, and despair as well as the difficulty of their purpose, because He lives within us and experiences it with us" (p. 78).

Although she would die soon, Katarina had a flash-forward in which she observed her daughter growing up and helping other people. One day, while speaking with an angel, she was able to grab a white, fluffy angel feather about six inches long. (There were no feather pillows at the facility.) She gave the feather to Lerma. The feather kept getting smaller. By the time Katarina died, the feather, stored inside a plastic bag, had disappeared.

e. William

William had lung cancer and had come from Argentina. He was transferred to hospice. He spoke German. Early in his life, he had been in charge of a concentration camp gas chamber. While speaking with Lerma, "He recalled one night when a beautiful Jewish woman stopped before entering the showers and looked him straight in the eyes. There was no fear in her face, and the look of true compassion burned into his soul. This vision haunted him the rest of his life" (p. 90).

For several days he was comatose, and when he awoke he asked how long he had been unconscious. Lerma said about two days, and William commented that he felt like he had been in hell for hundreds of years. When he was there, he was with many Nazi and Roman soldiers who were involved in mass killings. He said he could hear their thoughts and feel their anguish, and it mirrored his own. William noticed that there was a bright light in the distance. After what he thought was years, he cried out for help. One of the *light beings* was the Jewish woman at the concentration camp. She radiated love, said she had forgiven him even before he killed her, and said she would escort him from his guilt. William was informed that he had to experience the suffering he inflicted on others, and he simultaneously entered the minds and bodies of all the people he killed, sensing their pain and fear. When he was ready to forgive himself, his victims also forgave him, and he was bathed in unconditional love. "William realized that they were all one and what he did to others he did to himself" (pp. 96–97). William concluded that darkness is the result of free will and that we need God within us, as we cannot defeat darkness by ourselves.

f. Mildred

Mildred was an 82-year-old woman who had ovarian cancer. At one point she observed her parents, who appeared to be in their early thirties and healthy. Her parents informed her that an angel would be coming later to assist her to cross over to them. According to Lerma, one angel came as predicted and told her, "I've always been with you. I've always been here" (p. 104).

g. Father Mike

Father Mike was a 78-year-old retired priest who had once been president of a Catholic university. He had head and neck cancer and was in great pain, but he refused medication as he believed his suffering would help souls around the world. He said he needed angels to protect him, as deep pain makes a person vulnerable to darkness. At one point Father Mike commented on the color of Lerma's aura. (Not many priests speak of auras.) Father Mike also spoke about hell as being a separation from God and something we create. He also commented that technology has made things worse in the short term, but if technology is integrated with spirituality, then together they will eliminate war, famine, and disease. He also had a rather interesting supposition (the following is from Lerma, quoting Father Mike):

> Like a caterpillar, we have these dormant cells within us, called imaginal cells, which, once activated, will undergo metamorphosis and create a mind, body, and spirit change, just as the butterfly is the changed caterpillar. We, like the

monarch, will become free to experience and become one with the universe. At this point, we become co-creators with Christ, who lives within each one of us. He is the "imaginal self" within us. (p. 126)

To some extent, this is what I am saying is possible when we live in harmony with our own Spirit and higher spirit beings.

h. Joanna

Joanna was a 28-year-old mother of three children, suffering from advanced breast cancer. Her mother had died from breast cancer when Joanna was one year old. Joanna had had a good relationship with her father. He had thrown a celebration for her at age sixteen. On the way home, her father was shot to death, and Joanna "decided then never to let anyone into my heart. ... I knew this was the only way I could survive this life and keep from hurting myself and others" (p. 134). During her life review she came to understand that the reasons for her choices stemmed from this inability to love others. She reiterated what other people with PDEs have said about the importance of free will. Two of her comments were very striking insights into spirituality: "Everyone is given an infinite number of chances to seek the *light*, which is connected by faith to God, the infinite supplier of all answers" (p. 140). "God said all of our choices have consequences" (p. 141).

In chapter 10, I will demonstrate the consequences of some poor choices.

i. George

George was a 53-year-old prisoner convicted of an incident in which he, as part of a drug deal, killed four people. He felt much guilt. The spirits of the four he killed appeared to him and forgave him, but he could not forgive himself. There was a discussion with angels concerning poor choices and how George was partially influenced by a dark entity that first entered his great-grandfather and then continued influencing his family through "generational sins." This dark energy altered his family's genes and made chemicals that enabled him to react to a situation in a violent manner. Later, George said that to some extent we all have this dark side. "We should not hate it, but embrace it, understand it, and move forward" (p. 164).

George reported that his mother was there to take him to the afterlife, but Lerma reminded him that his mother was still alive in New Orleans. George said no, that she had died in the aftermath of Hurricane Katrina, and this proved correct. George had a son Jerome, who was also in prison. Jerome was released from prison a week early and was able to visit his father before he died. George shared with Jerome what he learned from his life review. Jerome had a turnaround in his life, gave up drugs, and began counseling drug addicts.

j. Dr. Johnson

Dr. Johnson was a 68-year-old doctor, lawyer, and judge, dying of lymphoma. He was orphaned at eight when his parents were killed in a car accident. He was raised a Lutheran, but while practicing as a physician in an emergency department he observed so much brutality, especially child abuse, that he became an atheist. He felt God would not allow such atrocities. He was involved with Mothers Against Drunk Driving (MADD) and Teens Against Drunk Driving (TADD), trying to make a difference helping others. In the hospice, he began experiencing things outside his atheist belief system.

After Dr. Johnson reported a vision to Lerma, Lerma explained to him that angels come for everyone, regardless of their beliefs or actions, including murderers and child molesters. One day Dr. Johnson saw his deceased parents with another person, whom they introduced as the drunk who had killed them. His parents said it "worked out the way it was supposed to" (p. 190).

Dr. Johnson also commented that the angels were able to show him events from the past, present, and future, all intermingled. This would appear to confirm the time distortion that may occur within the context of an NDE. Some of the concepts that Dr. Johnson affirmed were rather interesting when considering that common spirituality often views behavior as either benevolent or opprobrious. Here are two of the important concepts he learned:

- "However, during the review process, we never ask ourselves what we did to have fun. God asks us what we did to make ourselves happy on earth, because it's through true joy, fueled by truth and love that we can make more changes than through anything else. ... Joy is at the core of everything. ... You can change things through joy and happiness" (pp. 191–92).
- "Don't be concerned about other people's suffering so much that you take away their opportunity for growth. ... You have to be very careful who you take pain from. Suffering teaches you when to trust other people as they share their lessons. It develops your discernment" (pp. 192–93).

Lerma maintains that the angels had the same message whether it came through Buddhists, Christians, Hindus, or even this atheist. However, I am sure that Dr. Johnson, when he died, was a believer in a spirit world.

k. Rachel

Rachel was a 48-year-old Jewish woman from Argentina with Huntington's disease. She had been on a ventilator and had an endotracheal tube, unable to speak. When those devices were removed, she said she had messages from Jesus for Lerma and a nurse in the room. Lerma had never discussed his personal life with Rachel, but the night before he had been praying for his son who was in a potentially abusive situation (Lerma was divorced). Rachel commented that Jesus had heard his prayer and that everything would be okay. She also encouraged Lerma to continue his hospice work and share what he was learning. Rachel then told the nurse that her son who had died after being molested was with Jesus at the foot of the bed. She also explained that Jesus had died for political, not spiritual, reasons.

Concerning her own illness, Rachel explained that she accepted her challenging disease for a reason and would do it again. Here are several of her explanations:

- "All my pain and suffering is to raise the level of humanity. All my sacrifices go toward making God's creation a better place for our children and grandchildren and all the generations to come" (p. 203).

- "Suffering in its true form is to be separated from God" (p. 205).
- "People ... want to heal their body when they need to heal their relationship with God" (p. 205).
- "Most people who get this level of understanding [i.e., Rachel's] actually decide they don't want to be healed. They want to help people. It's an act of unconditional love" (p. 205).

These statements support the lessons learned or taught by Matthew, Father Mike, and Dr. Johnson. I presented a similar case in the NDE chapter in which a man named DeLynn explains why he chose before birth to come into a body with cystic fibrosis.

Later on, Rachel said that the biggest lesson of the twentieth century is to forgive Adolf Hitler. She said his biological father was a Jewish man who repeatedly raped Adolf's mother. I am not sure this agrees with historical information. She also said that the rift with Muslims and Jews is partly the result of generational sin from the time of Abraham. When Lerma and her rabbi were discussing Rachel, they both agreed that she was a highly evolved spirit.

I. Jean Pierre

Dr. Jean Pierre was a 67-year-old anthropological pathologist diagnosed with multiple myeloma, which results in excruciating pain. Although classifying himself as an agnostic, he "was filled with inner joy as he conveyed his spiritual insights [to Lerma]" (p. 213). His cosmic assistant in traversing the universe via a "wormhole" was named Michael (not the archangel). Some of the insights he received from Michael are as follows:

- "The key to a joyful and less-convoluted life review is to examine one's actions on a daily basis, and ask God for complete guidance to create the necessary changes that ultimately lead to peace and love. This will allow one to see death as a symbol for a more peaceful and beautiful life" (p. 214).
- If spirituality and science worked together, it would result "in both interstellar and intergalactic travel through matter, and even

wormholes. He gave details of meeting other peaceful souls not only in our galaxy, but in the far reaches of the universe" (p. 215). Later, Lerma paraphrased Jean's saying that travel would involve teleportation using gravity machines to distort space and time.

- According to Jean, Michael allowed him to view the big bang, or what is considered to be the creation of the physical universe.

- "Despite the millions of people belonging to faith-based churches, only a few are truly praying and carrying out unconditional acts of love and kindness to balance the opposite forces" (p. 216).

- Jean was able to view various mass extinctions during the life of the earth and "was told that man could possibly pass, as those before us did, into oblivion, into the sixth extinction that he, as a scientist, knew was already in progress. ... When God engineered the planet, He secured its existence through self-protective mechanisms, including tsunamis, hurricanes, volcanoes, and climate changes" (p. 218).

- "He [Jean] understood for the first time that science without God was virtually limited, and that science with God was unlimited. 'The S factor,' as Dr. Jean Pierre phrased it, is the missing link and de rigueur to our soul's survival" (p. 219).

- "As far as total peace on earth, that will occur when man learns to unconditionally love his entire psyche, including his darkest part. Only then will man be able to make a quantum leap toward our heavenly realm here on earth" (p. 220).

- "God did not promise to remove the consequences to our actions; He just promised to forgive us. These consequences act as lessons to make us stronger and more resilient beings" (p. 221).

- Confirming what several other cases in this section stated, Jean discerned "that hell is definitely a self-separation from God, as God never separates Himself from us. Guilt is the darkest, deepest, and most potent emotion" (p. 222).

4. Lerma Sequel

Lerma has a sequel book entitled *Learning from the Light: Pre-Death Experiences, Prophecies, and Angelic Messages of Hope* (2009), in which he sometimes employs the terms *higher self* and *divine self*. In one appendix of the book, Lerma compares how various characteristics are exhibited by our *ego* and *higher awareness*. He defines *ego* as "an exaggerated sense of one's own importance and a feeling of superiority to other people" (p. 243). He defines *higher awareness* as "part of our non-ego-based identity, which is empowered by the values that connect us to God" (p. 243). I prefer to have two classifications of ego: true or virtuous ego, and false or baneful ego. An individual ego is what separates humans from animals.

a. Lerma's Father

One of Lerma's accounts is the death of his own father. As he lay dying, the father reported that he saw his deceased parents and a deceased brother, all youthful. He also reported that he observed a five-year-old girl in the room, whom a nurse could not see. It occurred to him later that it may have been a child of his that was miscarried, but he was not able to confirm that speculation.

Later on in the book, Lerma states that his father reported that more humans are becoming aware of their sixth sense, which includes telepathy, clairvoyance, precognition, and intuition. I suggest that special senses may also develop as a consequence of further integration of Spirit into the physical body, but this could be several generations away.

b. Mary

Lerma called Mary on the evening after the funeral of her husband, Bill. She said that as she was sobbing on her bed, a white *light* came to the edge of her bed and then defined itself as Bill. He gave her a glimpse of heaven, and she said it was much grander than typically described. Bill said he would ask God to heal Mary of her severe arthritis and advancing glaucoma. On her next visit to an ophthalmologist, her glaucoma was gone. No mention was made of any changes in her arthritis.

c. Sarah

Sarah was born blind due to an atrophied optic nerve. At the age of 29 she was dying of breast cancer. Both of her parents had died of cancer. Several weeks before she died, Sarah reported that mother, Mary, had appeared to her and said she would be able to see before she died. This did happen during the last ten days before Sarah's death. Lerma had given her some crayons to draw with, and she drew with the right colors. Sarah also observed her deceased parents, who appeared to be about her age. Lerma performed some EEG and PET scans on Sarah's brain while she was able to see. The optic region in the occipital cortex was functioning similar to that of a person with sight although the optic nerve was not repaired.

d. John Masters

Lerma reported that a number of people whom he judged to be mentally competent had visits over the years from what they described as dark angels, during which the room they were in became very cold. For example, one room had an 18-year-old schizophrenic woman in it, and the nurses claimed it often had a cold draft. Lerma commented that the girl's mother said her deceased father had dabbled in black magic.

John L. Masters was a 47-year-old schizophrenic man (also diagnosed with DID) in a locked-down psychiatric ward at an oncology hospital. He had been a member of a motorcycle gang, and his middle initial, *L*, stood for his nickname, "Legion," the name used for the evil spirits in a madman whom Jesus healed. John's brother said that John had also dabbled in the occult. John felt he was possessed by demons and asked for a priest.

The priest, Fr. Doherty, spoke to John, who reported that some evil spirits did not want him to go with God's angels, as they felt they would be judged. The room was very cold. Fr. Doherty came back the next day and performed an exorcism that I will not describe. Some other exorcisms are described in detail in chapter 10. Lerma also reviewed some videotapes of John's room when no one was present. In these tapes, John appeared to be levitating two feet in the air.

e. Synchronicity

While the previously mentioned Sarah was near the end of her life, Lerma went out to lunch. He saw an accident (caused by a drunken driver) and proceeded to help an injured man named Daniel, who was pinned under a vehicle. Daniel said he noticed a little girl next to Lerma holding onto his coat. He asked Daniel the girl's name, and Daniel said her name was Sarah. Daniel was removed from the vehicle but then died. Lerma then received a phone call from the hospital stating that Sarah had died a few minutes earlier.

A few days later a woman and her daughter came to Lerma at his clinic. The daughter mentioned that a friend of hers, JR, had been drunk a few days prior and had killed someone. This was the same accident at which Lerma had assisted. JR was remorseful about the accident he caused, served two years in prison for manslaughter, and then attended college. He now works with people who have alcohol and drug problems. He has had visions of Daniel, the man he killed, and Sarah, the girl Lerma attended.

f. Dying Children

Dying children would often mention animals to Lerma. A seven-year-old boy named Jimmy informed Lerma that a little boy named Matthew, whom Lerma had helped two years earlier, said he would be taking Jimmy for a ride on the dolphins. Lerma said there was no way Jimmy could have known about Matthew and the dolphins. When Lerma looked into Jimmy's eyes, he could see Matthew riding a dolphin.

g. Misty

Misty was a former athlete dying of bone cancer. At one point, as he listened to her heart for several minutes with a stethoscope, Lerma thought Misty had died. He pronounced her dead before he left the room. Fifteen minutes later he went back. He found that Misty's mother, Mary, was shaking Misty, asking her to come back. Misty came back to life, stating that she was drawn back by her mother's sorrow and pain. Lerma said that Misty was the fifth patient of his for whom this type of thing had happened.

The remainder of the information is from questions that Lerma posed to Misty after her return. To the question of whether there was life on other planets, she answered yes. To another question, Misty replied that a "soul, when it leaves its body, may choose to stay on the earthly plane of existence or to move forward" (p. 168). Many of the people, she said, who choose to stay have died suddenly, in accidents or by being murdered, and did not have a chance to say good-bye. These people are filled with the dark side of their essence and live off another's energy. They are ghosts or evil spirits lurking on the earth. However, Misty maintained that God "will never cease from helping his lost sheep find their way back home" (p. 169). (The topic of spirits remaining on the earth will be discussed further in chapter 10. Note, though, that earlier in this chapter I discussed some victims of murder or accidents who had moved on after forgiving their murderer or the person who had caused the accident.) Several days later Misty died, and her mother, who had first called her back, saw a bright flash of *light* come from the foot of the bed as her daughter died.

h. Maggie

Maggie was dying of bone cancer. An angel appeared in her room. It permeated Maggie's body, and Maggie was informed she would be able to heal other people but not herself. Nothing happened for several weeks, but then this occurred:

> Visitors and medical staff began to notice that merely walking into her room would result in the alleviation and often permanent removal of their chronic pains and emotional distress. Word spread around the hospital of Maggie's abilities to abolish one's pain, and soon workers were visiting and being healed through Maggie's loving touch, and other patients were wheeled from other rooms, at her request, and were healed from several types of pain. My [Lerma's] own migraines would spontaneously remit after Maggie touched my forehead. I had heard of cancer patients who were able to reduce their doses of morphine and methadone by 90% and remained almost pain free for weeks through means of meditation, but to heal others and not thyself was beyond comprehension. Maggie was meditating, and what pain was relieved was not for herself, but for everyone else in her presence (pp. 181-82).

Another of the healings was of two young children who had been deliberately burned by their stepfather, using gasoline set ablaze. Their nurse was named Stacey, and she was healed by Maggie first from a ten-year battle with anxiety and depression after the death of her daughter.

Lerma said he had never seen a person's depression change so rapidly. To heal the burned children, Maggie had to be wheeled in on a gurney to their isolation room. The children had been crying, but they followed Maggie's commands and appeared to be in a trance, involved in a silent conversation, presumably with Maggie and several angels. The children stopped crying. Maggie made several other visits to the children before she died, emphasizing forgiveness for their stepfather. After these visits, the children's pain could be controlled with Tylenol. Three months later they were still undergoing rehabilitation but did not need skin grafts and had no scars.

i. Grace

A woman named Grace spoke with her spiritual visitor, whom she believed to be Mary Magdalene. Mary Magdalene revealed to Grace that Jesus's "Second Coming was not to be viewed as an apocalyptic event, but a personal revelation. He was to be sought within our souls and not in the clouds" (p. 151). Her visions reinforce Luke 17:21, in which Jesus says, "For behold, the kingdom of heaven is within you."(LT) Grace also stated that if a critical mass of people understood this concept, the world would rapidly change for the better.

j. Lerma's Conclusions

Lerma's conclusions mainly reinforce some of the previous comments made by individuals who were about to die. As he writes,

> Whether my patients were from different races and cultures, perceived or identified themselves as being pious or non-pious, life-givers or life-takers, atheist or agnostic, new-age thinkers or old-age thinkers, believers or non-believers, homosexuals or heterosexuals, lovers or fighters, the one constant observation that I discovered was the similarities in their visual, emotional, and spiritual experiences as they were about to leave this world. Their final visions and messages all came from a loving, spiritual world, which has existed around and in us since the beginning of time. The message of love, forgiveness, non-condemnation, and non-judgment mentioned

day in and day out is constant, no matter what one does or thinks (pp. 223–24).

k. My Conclusions of the Lerma Studies

Since Lerma's findings of visits by numerous angels prior to death are much different from some other studies and a majority of personal experiences near a dying person, I surmise that further research is required for verification. However, many of Lerma's findings are consistent with NDE, ELE, and ADC studies. Concepts like generational sin will be discussed in chapter 10. Forgiving ourselves, realizing the consequences of our actions, and accepting the dark part of our nature are also important concepts of my book. In several cases, a dying person indicated that his or her suffering would be beneficial for all of humanity.

5. *Trudy Harris's Hospice Findings*

Whereas Lerma's books are extremely interesting and thought-provoking, other books by people who work in hospice care rarely find as many life reviews or angels as Lerma encountered. Trudy Harris, RN, is a former hospice nurse and the author of *Glimpses of Heaven: True Stories of Hope and Peace at the End of Life's Journey* (2008). She found other phenomena at the end of life, such as sweet smells and beautiful music.

During her work, Harris felt that each person received what he or she needed in order to die peacefully. The patients were often open to sharing their experiences if the people nearby were open to hearing them. One patient commented to Harris just moments before he died, "Trudy, there is no such thing as time. Dying is like walking from the living room into the dining room, there are no beginnings or endings" (p. 20).

Brian, a three-year-old boy, died of leukemia. Harris described him in words Lerma often used to describe dying children, saying that they had an understanding of life beyond their years. Brian's mother had no belief in an afterlife. However, on the first anniversary of his death, she had a dream that prompted her to comment that she now knew that her boy was safe and loved. The mother was Jewish, and the dream was that her boy was in a tent. In Jewish folklore, a tent represents the house of God.

Although most people in Harris's narratives were believers in God before they arrived at hospice, one amusing incident happened to a man who was a nonbeliever. Johnny said he did not believe in God and disparagingly referred to Harris's visits to him as being from "the God person." One day when Harris was there, Johnny was smoking in a screened-in porch. He inquired about a picture of Jesus on the wall in which Jesus is knocking on a door. Harris explained that the door is a person's heart. She asked Johnny what part of the picture seemed unusual. He said the door did not have a doorknob. She explained that it had to be opened from the inside and that Jesus had to be invited in. She said to Johnny that when he was alone he should ask Jesus if Christ really exists. Johnny died that night. When Harris stopped by to pick up his things, she did not see the picture on the wall. The nurse at the hospice said there was never a picture of Jesus on that wall—and that porch was the only one at the facility.

One case epitomizes the concept of synchronicity. In the chapter on NDEs, I mentioned one NDEr who saw his life as similar to a jigsaw puzzle; the parts of his life all seemed to fit together. A patient named Jackie informed Harris about a life review that he referred to as the tapestry of his life. He said "that God had been showing him and explained carefully what the different colored threads meant and where they had taken him. He said he understood now the choices he had been given and the options he had chosen, and like so many other patients [Harris] cared for, both before and after Jack, he seemed not at all saddened by what he saw, only enlightened and comforted" (p. 64). But Jack did have a few questions. A few days after hearing this, Harris attended a spiritual retreat in which a last-minute substitute spoke on the topic "The Tapestry of Our Lives." Harris took copious notes at the retreat. When she discussed the notes with Jack, they answered almost all of his questions.

E. Chapter Conclusions

I believe that many of the cases presented in this chapter indicate that we are never too old to learn, that we can even learn on our deathbed. The lessons these cases teach are appropriate for all humans, but each individual case is especially pertinent to the person to whom it happened. They all indicate a postmortem existence.

In the next chapter, I review a theory of human spiritual nature from ancient India but as researched by a naturalized American doctor originally from the Middle East. Her primary research subject was another naturalized American, who could observe the human aura and convert those observations into medical conditions.

Chapter 8

EASTERN CONCEPTS OF HUMAN SPIRITUALITY

A. Introduction

In chapter 1, I commented that I would discuss concepts of human spirituality from Eastern religions and philosophy centered upon the nature and function of the spirit bodies that reside in the human being's physical body. I also mentioned that I would involve ideas from the occult. The word *occult* means "hidden or secret." Since occult is often thought of as sinister, another term perhaps less frightening is *esoteric*, which has secondary meanings of "undisclosed, confidential, concealed, or cloaked." In chapter 11, I will be discussing mysticism, and when that term is used in a Western religious framework, it is often referred to as *esoteric Christianity*. These two sources of information will be used together, the original information being from ancient Hindu and Buddhist traditions, but first conveyed to the West through an organization called the Theosophical Society, which is often classified as an occult organization. *Theosophy* means "divine wisdom." The Theosophical Society's founding members chose the name based on their interpretation of these Eastern concepts.

The Theosophical Society, founded in 1875, was first dominated by Europeans, but shortly thereafter some Americans became involved. The world headquarters of the society is in India; the American branch is located in Wheaton, Illinois, a suburb of Chicago. The most prominent founder of the organization was the author Helena Petrovna Blavatsky (1831–1891), often known as Madame Blavatsky. She is considered brilliant by her promoters and a rogue by her detractors. I will not be discussing the controversies in her life (e.g., as a medium) or some other questionable early affiliates of the organization. Blavatsky's two most well-known books are titled *The Secret Doctrine* and *Isis Unveiled*.

The books were allegedly dictated (a recent New Age term would be *channeled*) to her by "masters" or "ascended masters" of the spirit world. Originally from Russia, with a German father, she became a US citizen in 1878, but shortly thereafter she left America for India, never to return.

Anyone familiar with New Age writings is sure to come across terms such as *etheric body, subtle body, astral body,* and *chakras.* These were terms first presented to the West by Mme. Blavatsky and the Theosophists. My principal sources of information for this chapter are the writings of Dr. Shafica Karagulla (1914–1986), a Turkish-American psychiatrist who studied the new terminology. She studied psychiatry in Scotland and went to Canada, where she worked with world-famous Dr. Wilder Penfield (1891–1976) at the Montreal Neurological Institute in the early 1950s. Penfield, the author of *The Mystery of the Mind: A Critical Study of Consciousness and the Human Brain*, believed that the mind was separate from the brain. Karagulla came to the United States in 1956 and became an American citizen. Her interest in unusual abilities was aroused after someone suggested that she read a book about Edgar Cayce (1877–1945), sometimes referred to as "the Sleeping Prophet." While in a self-induced unconscious trance, among other abilities, Cayce allegedly could discern medical conditions in people miles away and suggest cures.

Dr. Karagulla's first book was titled *Breakthrough to Creativity: Your Higher Sense Perception* (1967). In this book, Karagulla describes her findings while working with those who possessed higher-sense perception (HSP). For example, a person, "Diane," was able to view a human aura and determine medical conditions about the person being observed. Another person, "Kay," with whom Karagulla worked, was "sensitive" to the health conditions of other people.

Karagulla's second book, *The Chakras and the Human Energy Fields*, is coauthored with Dora van Gelder Kunz (1904–1999). Kunz was the anonymous "Diane" in the first book. The latter book was published in 1989, three years after Karagulla's death. It is a Quest Book, published by the Theosophical Publishing House. Kunz was president of the Theosophical Society in America from 1975 to 1987 and was editor of its journal. While working with Karagulla in the early 1960s, Kunz was also president of a corporation and had a family. Although Dolores Krieger is the author of the book *Therapeutic Touch*, Kunz worked with Krieger in developing the concept, probably by explaining how to transfer vital energy into the energy field of the person seeking assistance.

Kunz had had the ability to observe energy fields ever since she was a child. She was born on Java to Dutch parents who managed a sugar plantation. Her parents taught her to meditate at a young age. Her mother and grandmother also had psychic abilities. Her son does not, so the ability apparently follows a matriarchal line in this family. Kunz authored a book of her own, *The Personal Aura*, published in 1991. It is also a Quest Book. She also wrote another book, titled *The Real World of Fairies*. Fairies are allegedly pure spirits; that is, they do not have physical bodies and are often classified as nature spirits. Renee Weber, a university professor, wrote a foreword to *The Personal Aura* and made the following comment about Kunz: "She never uses her clairvoyance in pursuit of the trivial, the frivolous, the sensational, for the sake of the curious, for personal gain, for power or control, or for any unethical reason" (Kunz, 1991). I consider Karagulla and Dora van Gelder Kunz to be very responsible people of high integrity. I maintain that the findings presented in their books have a great potential for helping us to understand our spiritual nature and the causes of many health conditions.

As will be described later, human energy fields are indicators of health problems in the physical body and also of psychological health. Changes or abnormalities in these energy fields normally predate changes to the physical body (i.e., incipient conditions) by a considerable period of time, and thus understanding them could result in much better preventative health measures. Of course, the patient would have to desire to change from a mental viewpoint and then comply with any recommendations on how a lifestyle change could eliminate or alleviate some future health conditions. In addition to its having a great potential for medical diagnosis and treatment, I consider the concept and detection of human energy fields to be readily testable under a double-blind protocol.

I have often referenced Max Freedom Long's concepts of the three spiritual selves of human anatomy as derived from the kahunas. The descriptions in Karagulla's and Kunz's books, to some extent, are not in agreement with Long's concepts. Since Long's concepts are simple and valuable explanations, I often employ them. But where the concepts in Karagulla's and Kunz's books provide a more detailed explanation, I prefer them. For the first part of this chapter, I will be using information from *Breakthrough to Creativity, The Chakras and the Human Energy Fields,* and *The Personal Aura.*

In all of the descriptions of etheric and astral bodies to follow, except where the information is stated to be from another person, the evidence presented is assumed to come from Dora van Gelder Kunz, or "Diane," in *Breakthrough to Creativity,* as explained to Karagulla. When she was young, Dora Kunz studied under another controversial Theosophist, C. W. Leadbeater (1854–1934). Although most of Kunz's statements were from her personal observations, some of her comments may have come from information given to her by her mentor.

B. Human Spiritual Nature and Energy Fields

As outlined by Kunz, there are three main energy fields that she could observe around a human body. The first of these energy bodies she called the *etheric body* or *vital field.* It extends roughly three to five inches beyond the periphery of the physical body and then gradually fades away. Kunz could observe it in three dimensions; that is, it was not just extending out from the sides, but one could look through it to see the physical body. The etheric body is closely connected to the physical body and simply dissipates (into a universal etheric field) over several days once the physical body dies. It may also be called the *subtle body.* It is extensively involved in regulation of the physical body and may actually be composed of a physical-like substance. The etheric body revitalizes the physical body, but the exact mechanism by which this is accomplished is not known.

The second energy field is the astral body. The word *astral* means "starry." Kunz refers to this energy field as the *personal aura* in the book of the same title. The astral body is also referred to as the *emotional body* or *emotional field,* as it is mostly involved with human emotions. The astral body is thinner and of a finer nature than the etheric body. It extends outward, twelve to eighteen inches from the physical body. The etheric body and the astral body are not independent. They interact with, and cannot function totally independent of, each other. By looking at the astral body, Kunz could distinguish between temporary emotions (e.g., anger arising from a single incident) and long-term hostility. Temporary states pass out of the aura. Forgiveness can increase the rate of release.

The third energy field is the *mental body*. As the third energy field, the mental body is finer than the other two and also interacts with the other two (i.e., they are interdependent). It extends about two feet or more from the physical body. Much less evidence is presented about this field. As Kunz describes, "When an individual comes into the presence of a well beloved person all three of his energy fields are intensely bright. ... A purely physical sex emotion appears to 'muddy' the emotional field and all the mental field" (Karagulla, 1967, 159). Although general sizes were specified, these fields may expand. The mental body does not begin at the end of the astral body, and the astral body does not begin where the etheric body ends. They coexist in the same space. Each body is different but not separate.

The fourth and final spirit body Kunz calls the *self*, and she presents very little observational information about it in these books other than mentioning its existence and stating that the etheric, astral, and mental fields combine to form the personality, whereas the self "is reserved for the deepest and most enduring essence of that which each of us really is—our true being" (Karagulla and Kunz, 1989, 25). People need to be able to determine the difference between the personality and the self. Some of Kunz's information on this concept of human nature likely may have come from Theosophical teachings on the subject.

The other concept that Kunz discusses are chakras. These are seven major spinning wheels (the meaning of the word *chakra*), vortices, or spiral cones of energy roughly parallel to the spine, moving from the base of the spine to the skull. Two are part of the head. These chakras generally correspond to various organs or glands in the physical body. Various properties of these wheels are often indicators of the health of the body. These chakras are generally associated with the etheric body, but Kunz maintains that they are still active at the astral level, albeit less so than the etheric body. In drawings or paintings of the chakras, they have to be rendered in two dimensions, but Kunz could see them in three dimensions. Each of them has a number of inner spokes or petals and outer spokes or petals. They are sometimes described as flower-like. For instance, the crown chakra has 12 inner spokes and 80 outer ones radiating out from each of the inner ones, for a total of 960 outer spokes.

The crown chakra is the dominant seat of consciousness. These fields are always in a continuous process of change. "The important factor in such change is whether it is taking us in the direction of negativity, ill health, and disease, and whether this pattern can be altered in the direction of self-integration, health, and wholeness" (Karagulla and Kunz, 1989, 27).

C. Other Unusual Abilities

In addition to Dora Kunz and "Kay" (Frances Farrelly), Karagulla references some pseudonymous doctors with unusual diagnostic or healing abilities. For example, Dr. Dan reported that he could see patients' energy fields, but he always used standard medical examination procedures and laboratory tests to verify his energy-field diagnosis. Dr. Philip maintained that he could see any organ inside a patient's body. He reported the ability to give a patient his or her lifetime medical history and current diagnosis within a few minutes of meeting the person, but like Dr. Dan, he confirmed the current diagnosis with laboratory tests. Although Dr. Philip was born with some special natural abilities, he stated that he improved his accuracy by attending "classes" while he slept (i.e., while he was in a dream state). These classes trained him to see into the bodies of patients and observe their condition.

Dr. Norris could diagnose people from a sensitivity in his hands. His hands could also heal people. He could also tune into a patient from a distance. On one occasion, one of his patients was out of the country and phoned him about a severe problem that some doctors in the other country could not diagnose. The patient was considering exploratory surgery. After a few questions and a period of silence, Dr. Norris diagnosed an obscure allergy that a simple treatment was able to cure.

Dr. Gloria could sense the flow of energy to determine problem areas of the body or sense the movement of brain fluids, which can be a factor in some illnesses. Regarding Dr. Gloria and several other doctors, Karagulla describes them as having "magnetic" healing in their hands. Dr. George could foresee the results of his surgery before performing it. On several occasions, he successfully performed a surgery that others felt the patient could not survive. On another occasion, he discerned that an alternate incision point needed to be used. An out-of-place artery would have been severed if the ordinary incision point had been chosen. Another doctor seemed to know when one of his patients was seriously ill and needed to contact him. One day, after having been out of the office for a few days, he was in a minor traffic accident. While waiting for his car to be towed, he felt that a patient needed to contact him. When he had access to a phone (this was before cell phones), he called the patient directly. The patient was seriously ill and had been attempting to contact him.

Some of the people Karagulla investigated were not in the medical field. One man named Paul managed to get a job at an engineering firm doing technical writing although he had no degree. On several instances, he contributed greatly to technical discussions. One day he found himself talking about an off-site location in great detail, although he had never been there. "He found that if he put his mind on a problem for several days, studying it intensively from all angles available to him, he reached a point where suddenly the solution and the plan flashed into his mind complete in every detail" (Karagulla, 1967, 87). This appears similar to the tout ensemble phenomena for musical composers or to Nikola Tesla, discussed in chapter 3. On one occasion Paul was given a project that was expected to take six to eight months to complete, and he had the complete solution in one week. He also explained that if a complicated piece of the machinery broke down, he could tune into it and immediately know what was wrong.

Karagulla also discusses a man named Reverend Stanley, who had an excellent dowsing ability. The dowsing rod would bend when he walked over water. Karagulla informed him that she had been experimenting with a material that seemed to inhibit certain types of HSP. After she wrapped the material around his hands, the rod worked as effectively. However, he said he felt an energy coming through his feet. When she wrapped the material around his feet, the dowsing rod did not work.

Karagulla narrates several other HSP abilities such as psychometry and predicting or altering which side of a flipped coin will come up. She mentions a businessman who seemed to know what problems were occurring in various offices of his company without physically visiting them. Another man who had made some interesting scientific discoveries said he had no particular HSP. However, when asked how he made his discoveries, he reported that he watched himself do it, sort of like watching himself on TV. This appears similar to an NDEr watching himself or herself in a panoramic life review. Karagulla comments that people who effectively use their HSP do not need statistics to prove that their ability exists. Since our materialistic society disparages such abilities, those with them do not often publicly proclaim them. Negative attitudes can inhibit the ability of a sensitive.

In the East, such paranormal sensitivities are accepted as complementary to the practice of yoga. In the West, these abilities are acknowledged in the religious realm, provided that the person who has them holds fairly orthodox religious views. Otherwise, they may be considered witchcraft and consequently be condemned. In chapter 12, on mysticism, I will be discussing some other paranormal phenomena that occur around mystics, including Catholic saints. Although the number of mystics among saints is much higher than those in the general population, many mystics were not saints and many saints were not mystics; they were people who simply led exemplary lives.

D. Experimental Methodology

Although some of the people whom Karagulla had Kunz observe were friends who came to visit, frequently these people would go to a medical clinic where Kunz would describe their energy field. Kunz sat about 20 feet away from the patient and assessed the chakras and the general etheric field. Karagulla would then obtain the medical records and compare Kunz's observations to the condition of the patient. Kunz never spoke to the people she was observing. There was usually an excellent correlation to the actual medical diagnosis of the patient. Karagulla commented that Kunz was as accurate as an x-ray machine. Since Kunz had no training in physiology, she had to describe what was happening on a physical level in layperson's terms. Weber reported that an experienced psychiatrist whom Kunz knew, a man skeptical of clairvoyance, once consulted with Kunz. He informed Weber, "In all my life I have never felt so profoundly understood by anyone. ... I felt as if she could see right to the bottom of me. The nuances of her perception are without equal in my experience" (Kunz, 1991, xiii). Karagulla would also, on occasion, have two sensitives view the same subject to verify that what they were observing, sensing, or diagnosing was comparable.

Karagulla was not involved in Kunz's book *The Personal Aura*, which involved less rigorous methodology. The aura is the astral or emotional body. Kunz would observe the aura of a person and then describe it to an artist named Juanita Donahoo nearby, who converted Kunz's verbal description into a full-color illustration. However, any painted color is much duller than actual astral colors. These sittings usually took two to three hours. There were about 18 people in all, ranging from a pregnant woman to several children (from less than one year old to adolescence), and including an adult over age 90. These illustrations were mostly done back in the 1930s. Kunz did not write the book until the 1980s, and in it she compares some of her descriptions/illustrations from 50 years earlier to the patient's actual conditions in the intervening years. It is more difficult to directly associate with a physical condition any emotions observed in an aura.

E. Sensitives and Their Abilities

I will now discuss some other of Karagulla's individual test subjects and general comments. I usually use the term *sensitive*, whether the person was making an observation (visually sensing a normally invisible field) or feeling the medical problem of a patient. Later, I will discuss a more recent term that some people use to describe themselves: *medical intuitive*.

Karagulla classifies many of these abilities as clairvoyance and defines *clairvoyance* as "an ability to consistently see phenomena beyond the range of normal physical sight" (Karagulla, 1967, 232). This would include observing internal organs. Several of the sensitives could magnify an organ to ten or more times its normal size in order to see minute details. Kunz can look at the etheric level and observe an "etheric" color, but then look at the physical level (even at internal organs) and find that the organ is its normal physical color. Some sensitives see only the etheric field, whereas others see only the emotional field. Some may see the etheric field but not the chakras. Kunz could see all of the energy fields.

Karagulla comments that sensitives can turn their abilities on and off. Using these abilities takes intensive work, normally limited to about one to three hours per day. After that duration of time, the sensitive's accuracy may be reduced. Thus, the sensitives do not routinely walk around viewing the energy fields of random people. A number of other factors may also affect a sensitive's accuracy and abilities, including his or her own physical health and fluorescent lights (especially noted for Frances Farrelly). Antihistamines could affect Kunz's ability. If Kunz were using a medication, a smaller dosage could normally be prescribed for her than for a normal patient. Sensitives are not in a trance state when performing their observations for diagnosis; they are aware of their surroundings. Their pulse rate, blood pressure, and respiration rate are normal.

Karagulla also noticed that there seems to be pupil dilation in the eyes of sensitives when the eyes are actively working, even in bright light. The gaze appears intent and slightly rigid. One sensitive would refer to it as using her "inner eyes," but the physical eyes are evidently involved in the process of observing the energy fields. Karagulla speculates that the sensitives may be forerunners of an evolutionary change in humanity.

The previously named people in the section on unusual abilities were people that Dr. Karagulla encountered in her studies, but the following people were active subjects whose abilities she used and observed. Some details of their lives are presented to demonstrate that they are intelligent, responsible people. Many of these people had had their abilities since childhood.

"Kay," or Frances Farrelly, was born in 1911. Although not able to observe auras, she was clairvoyant, was clairsentient, and had precognitive abilities. As an example of the third ability, on several occasions she either exited early or never even boarded a train that was about to have an accident. When she needed answers to problems that could be stated with a question, she would use the "stick" method. She asked a question that could be answered with a "yes" or a "no." She would rub her finger on a polished surface. If the answer was no, her finger would continue to move, but if the answer was yes, her finger would stick to the surface. The "stick" method was known as the Digital Excitation Response at SRI International, where much research was performed on topics such as remote viewing. The sponsor of the research for many years was the Department of Defense. Kay was also aware of nature spirits. People with her clairsentient ability to sense pain could have that ability interfere with their own lives if they randomly picked up the pain of a nearby person.

"Mike" is an artist and sculptor who often sees a mental image of a completed artwork before he begins it. Able to place himself into a historical context, he even hears foreign languages at the scene of the historical location. In addition, Mike has an unusual form of synesthesia in that he "tastes" various colors. Some of the other sensitives in this study associate color with sound or smell. As discussed in chapter 5, on NDEs, a number of NDErs develop synesthesia after their NDE.

One of "Ben"'s unusual abilities is to see waves of motion emanating from the forehead of a person who is speaking. He can interpret these waves to determine if the thinking of the speaker is quick, slow, clear, or divergent. When asked how he does this, he reports that he brings his consciousness inward to the center of his brain. A number of other sensitives recounted a similar withdrawal inward. However, other sensitives so matter-of-factly entered their heightened state of awareness that they never thought about the method by which they did it.

"Laura" is another sensitive who can see energy fields, but she has more interest in the emotional and mental state of individuals. She has noticed that for depressed individuals, there is a leaking of energy in the vital field, and the emotional field has a great deal of gray color. Although colors are a part of these energy fields, the location of a specific color may alter the interpretation of its meaning. Karagulla commented that she would like to study the energy fields of the mentally disturbed to determine if she could gain insight into correcting the problem of mental illness.

F. Oceans of Energy, and Negative Aspects

All living things, and even inanimate matter, have an etheric component ("etheric double"), and Kunz could observe how various etheric bodies of living and inanimate matter would interact. As Kunz explained, "We live and move in a vast and complicated ocean of energies" (Karagulla, 1967, 161). These fields are called the "universal" or "general" fields. During interesting intellectual conversation, for instance, the mental field first receives an inflow of energy, which then spreads to the emotional and vital bodies. During a performance, an actor's emotional field may extend outward to include the entire audience. Sensitives like Kunz can observe these increases in energy flow but cannot answer why some people are open to the flow and others are not. Grief can result in diminishment of these energies.

With regard to inanimate matter, crystals have a stronger etheric component than amorphous matter does. Kunz could identify types of jewels by the energy pattern around them. She was able to discern a synthetic topaz from a natural one by its level of energy rather than its pattern. She further noticed that music changes the brightness of the energy field in a crystal. She could also distinguish between the north and south poles of a magnet and between a radioactive and nonradioactive substance (two iodine solutions). Earlier I mentioned psychometry but did not explain what it is. A psychometrist is a sensitive who is "for the moment participating in the physical, mental and emotional environment that has been connected with an object" (Karagulla, 1967, 241). Metals and crystals have naturally stronger etheric fields and therefore make better objects to attempt to "read," especially if the jewelry is associated with some strong emotional attachment. Karagulla discusses a professor who had several sensitives report nearly identical readings of the same piece of jewelry. Paper letters can also "hold" the impressions of the writer.

Some people exploit the energy fields of other people. After having it described to her a number of times (first by Francis Farrelly), Karagulla developed a term, *sappers*. These psychological parasites are people who are usually self-centered with closed energy fields. Instead of picking up energy from the ocean of energy, they pull energy from other people around them. Karagulla does not explicate in great detail, but she asserts that self-centeredness is not the same as being selfish. In fact, sappers often vocalize about altruism and speak kindly of their victims. In some cases, the pulling of energy may be from anyone in the vicinity, but in other cases the extracting may be from one specific person. Some parasites who are compulsive talkers can wrest energy from victims simply by speaking, whereas others may pull the energy by looking at a person with a steady, unbroken focus. Still, others need to be in close proximity to entice the energy away. The victim of the energy theft becomes exhausted and irritable. While the victims are drained of energy, the parasite often feels exhilarated.

In chapter 1, I briefly mentioned vital energy and commented that I would not spend much time discussing it. I also wrote about the mana of the kahunas in chapter 2. In the East, this energy is called *prana*. I believe I need to comment on life, or vital, energy, as it relates closely to the material in this chapter. Kunz referred to energy fields that would appear to her as visible light, and since the normal light everyone sees is energy, the light she sees would be an energy. However, I do not know that the normal laws of physical energy apply to this type of energy, but it does follow some laws and is not totally random.

First of all, I am not sure if the conservation of energy, from physical energy to vital energy and vice versa, applies. We currently do not have methods for measuring a quantity of vital energy, so how could there be a balance or conservation of something that is immeasurable? Within its own realm there does appear to be a conservation of energy, seeing as when a sapper pulls energy from another person, the sapper is invigorated. However, Karagulla notes that some people mutually discharge each other's energy field and that both become exhausted as a result.

With regard to detecting normal physical bodily parameters that are not in the normal human sense range, standard science has developed various methods to measure them. For instance, there are thermographic images of the body that measure infrared light emitted, and ultrasound can be employed for diagnosis of ailments using a sound frequency outside the normal range of human hearing. Some animals can hear in the ultrasonic range. Standard science also has techniques such as magnetic resonance imaging (MRI) and positron emission tomography (PET) scans of the body, but these measure known physical parameters, which are not the same as the energy fields observed by sensitives with HSP.

Kunz describes an ocean of energy. It would be difficult to measure how much energy is being removed from an infinite source. According to Kunz, crystals have an etheric field that can interact with people, but can a crystal's etheric energy be reduced? This is just one of many complicated questions that would necessitate much research in the future.

G. The Etheric Body and the Chakras

Most of the information in this section is from *The Chakras and the Human Energy Fields*. In this book, Karagulla and Kunz posit that a comparison may be made between what Kunz observed and how physicists probe at quantum levels of the atom. Since the etheric body is the basic pattern upon which the physical body is built, they speculate that it would be interesting to explore the relationship between the genetic code and the etheric pattern. They describe the etheric body as follows:

> To the clairvoyant, the etheric body looks like a luminous web of fine bright lines of force which, in a healthy person, stand out at right angles to the surface of the skin. Its texture may be fine-grained or coarse, a characteristic which repeats itself in the physical body type. Each organ of the body has its etheric counterpart, through which the etheric energy circulates constantly.

> The color of the etheric body is a pale blue-grey or violet-gray, slightly luminous and shimmering, like heat waves above the Earth on hot days. ... There is an etheric web of the finest texture that acts as a natural barrier between the etheric and astral fields, and protects the individual from opening communication between these two levels prematurely. (Karagulla and Kunz, 1989, 30–31)

According to Kunz, substance abuse may tear the web separating the two bodies. I speculate that various types of trauma, such as abuse, may act similarly.

The seven characteristics of the etheric body that Kunz deems important to evaluate are as follows: color, brightness, motion, form, angle, elasticity, and texture. Some of these are similar to the chakras, but others are different. In a healthy person these characteristics would be as follows: the color is the standard color; the brightness is uniform throughout; the motion is rhythmic; size, shape, and symmetry are important for the form; the etheric body should be at right angles to the physical body; the elastic property should be able to stretch and expand; and the texture should be firm and fine. In a calm and healthy person, the energy flows evenly and smoothly. "Positive emotions are more economical for the whole system" (p. 32). Kunz also reports that the energy seemed to flow in a figure eight pattern, with the crossing done at the heart.

On the other hand, energy flow may be too slow or too rapid. Sunlight in small amounts is beneficial, but prolonged exposure may reduce a person's etheric energy. Tension (i.e., stress) may also deplete energy reserves, which, in turn, may affect any organ of the body. When a person is ill, the outline of the etheric body becomes uneven and energy flow to the chakras is diminished. Kunz comments that ulcers result from emotional tension, but this also depends on the individual, as an affected person may have a weakness in the solar plexus (i.e., loss of energy flow). I comment on this because recent findings since the book was published indicate that ulcers are often caused by an infection that can be treated with antibiotics. Is Kunz's assessment incorrect, or are there different types of ulcers, some caused by tension rather than infection? Or could the decrease in energy flow on account of tension result in the body's inability to fight the infection? I comment on this because some of my readings about infection-based illnesses, not related to this subject matter, indicate that a large number of people may carry the infecting agent in their bloodstream or in another part of their body, but only a small percentage of these people actually develop the infection. Thus, it is possible that this energy flow observed by Kunz is the major factor in determining in whom the infection spreads and becomes dangerous to health, and not whether someone carries the infecting agent. "When the energy pattern is closely knit, it is very resistant to invasion from the outside world, but when loose and porous it can be penetrated more easily, and therefore the subject is apt to take in whatever may be in the surrounding environment" (Karagulla and Kunz, 1989, 92–93).

The chakras are the mechanism for transmitting and transforming energy from one field to another. The chakras are described as follows:

> In both form and mode of motion they resemble a wheel, with the central core acting as a hub, around which petal-like structures revolve. Through this core the energies of the different fields focus and circulate, and around it the energies whirl centrifugally and pulsate rhythmically, so that the whole looks like a flower whose petals are in constant harmonic motion, somewhat like the effects achieved in time-lapse photography. In fact, in Indian literature the chakras have been referred to as lotuses because of their flower-like form, and because they have a central root or stem which connects

them energetically to the spine and nervous system. The cores
or hearts of the centers are points of interaction where energy
flows from one field or level into another. They are also
associated with specific abilities or powers of consciousness
related to one or another of the other fields, such as the
emotional or mental. (Karagulla and Kunz, 1989, 33–34)

For instance, the chakras can step up or down or change speed
from one field to another (typically, the emotional field is faster than the
etheric). These spinning wheels draw energy at their core and disperse
it along the periphery. They are always spinning. The colors vary from
chakra to chakra. The Tantric traditions, expressed in both Hindu and
Buddhist writings, describe the chakras. The Hindu system emphasizes the
static side, whereas the Buddhist system emphasizes the chakras' dynamic
functions. Kunz's observations are closer to the latter.

There are a number of properties of the chakras that Kunz observed
in determining their condition. These are color, luminosity, movement,
size, elasticity, and texture. As Karagulla and Kunz maintain, observing
chakras can explain more than just physical conditions:

The chakras also reveal a person's quality of consciousness
and degree of personal development and abilities, through
the variations in the etheric centers and their interconnections
with those at other levels. In a simple, rather undeveloped
person, the chakras will be small in size, slow in movement, dull
in color and course in texture. In a more intelligent, responsive
and sensitive person they will be brighter, a finer texture and
with a more rapid movement, and in and awakened individual
who makes full use of his powers, they become coruscating
whirlpools of color and light. (Karagulla and Kunz, 1989, 36)

The chakras roughly correspond to endocrine glands, but special
characteristics often affect more than one chakra. For instance, a person
who identifies with his or her feelings would have more active solar plexus
and heart chakras. The following descriptions provide some specific
information about each chakra after a mention of the endocrine gland
most often associated with that chakra (where relevant) and the chakra's
location.

Crown chakra: Pineal gland; top of head. Reveals the spiritual quality, and the state of consciousness of the individual in connection with the inmost self. Shines more brilliantly in people who meditate. People exit through this chakra when they sleep. The halo painted around the head of Christ and the heads of various saints by early and medieval artists may represent some artists' ability to view this chakra, which is perhaps especially visible and brighter due to the holiness of the individual subject. Later artists may simply have painted the same effect without actually discerning the chakra. This chakra merges into the realm of cosmic consciousness. As previously mentioned, the crown chakra has 12 golden central petals and 960 secondary petals.

Brow chakra: Pituitary gland; between the eyes. Divided into two sides, one side rose and yellow and the other blue and purple. Total of 96 petals. Associated with the mind and may be directed upward toward higher thoughts or downward to the mundane world. Strongly connected to creativity and new ways of doing things.

Throat chakra: Thyroid and parathyroid glands; neck area. Silvery blue in color. Has 16 petals and is about six centimeters in diameter. May be larger for people who are singers or accomplished in public speaking, or those engaged in creative work of any kind.

Heart chakra: Thymus gland; upper chest. Twelve petals. Glows golden yellow in color. Linked with the higher dimensions of consciousness and with one's sense of being, and thus has a close relationship with the crown chakra. Point of integration in the whole chakra system and a primary factor in spiritual transformation. Obviously related to the physical heart (especially the valves) and the thymus gland; also affects the immune system.

Solar plexus chakra: Adrenal glands; the pancreas. Also affects the liver and stomach. Has ten petals. Multicolored, with light red and green predominating. Strongly connected to the emotional field, as astral energy enters the etheric field here. Active in people with strong desires. Disturbances here affect the digestive system.

Spleen chakra: Frequently not considered a major chakra but does have an important role in the overall system. Displays a spectrum of colors with yellow and rose-red paramount. Absorbs vitality from the general field and distributes it to the other centers. The spleen chakra provides one of the three most important points of entry into the body for etheric energy, the other two being the lungs and the skin. The appearance of this spleen chakra does not seem to be affected after the spleen is surgically removed.

Sacral chakra: Closely related to sexuality. Color is red (but white in Tibetan Tantrism). Not as related to medical interest, and therefore Kunz did not spend much time with this chakra. This is the only chakra that rotates in a different direction in men and women. It is also a slightly different color in each gender, rotating clockwise in males and counterclockwise in females.

Root chakra: Base of spine. Associated with life energy and with the aspect of the self called the will or the fundamental intentionality of the person. The color is clear to orange-red and is very vitalized in spiritually developed people. Kundalini energy, which arises from this chakra, will be discussed in a later chapter.

Subsidiary chakras: There are said to be 21 others involved in energy distribution, but Kunz thought the most important of these were those in the palm of each hand and those in the soles of the feet, as these are significant in the practice of healing or therapeutic touch.

If a gland associated with a particular chakra is surgically removed, the abnormality in the chakra does not disappear. The chakra is still visible, although it is altered. A disease may be in a nearby area to the chakra that reveals the problem. For instance, if the throat chakra is not normal, the disease may appear in the thyroid gland, the chest, or the breast.

H. The Astral or Emotional Body

The astral body (so named by Paracelsus [1493–1541]) is embedded in a universal astral field and "is a fluid world of fast-moving energies, shimmering with color and full of symbols and images that move us with their beauty or fill us with fear and anxiety, since it can be responsive to false and negative ideas as well as to those which are noble and uplifting" (Karagulla and Kunz, 1989, 48). It is dynamic and reflects potentialities realized, possibilities unfulfilled, success, disappointment, love, and hate. People often first think of negative emotions such as envy, resentment, and hatred, but there are virtuous emotions such as caring, empathy, compassion, and harmony related to this body. Weber (1991) also comments that Kunz mentioned to her that there are two insidious emotions, but these are rarely mentioned in the normal list of emotions. These are self-pity and claiming a "victim syndrome." If a person is very emotional, he or she may also respond to the emotional field of nearby people by means of the general astral field.

As Karagulla and Kunz (1989) explain,

> When the feelings are not under the control or guidance of the self, or responsive to ethical principles, they can be wild and chaotic. In such cases, the person who identifies himself primarily with his emotions can be at the mercy of all its storms and stresses, swinging between extremes of love and hate, joy and sorrow, happiness and pain. ... The material of the astral world is very impressionable, and responds quickly to the thought forms or images which we imbue with our feelings. (p. 51)

Each individual also affects the general astral field. Every person has the ability to reject negative feelings that originate from outside of us (i.e., from the general field). There are a number of cone-shaped vortices placed symmetrically around the edge of the aura that act as valves or energy-exchange mechanisms with the general field. These may act as protection mechanisms, but Kunz does not explain the specifics of activating the "valves." There is another protective device that shields a child in utero from the emotional shocks that the mother may encounter, but some negative effects may penetrate through (Kunz, 1991). Health and healing depend upon the natural, harmonic, and unimpeded flow of vital energy from the universal field. An individual can control or inhibit this flow and can also enhance it.

The energy level of the emotional field moves more rapidly than the etheric field and is perceived as a higher frequency of both color and sound. The astral chakra normally rotates at twice the speed of the etheric chakras, and a differing rate of rotation (i.e., not 2/1 [referred to as dissonance]) indicates a likely problem. An even more prominent indicator of a current or future health problem is when the direction of rotation changes from clockwise to counterclockwise. Kunz explains that the core part of the chakra could also have a conflicting dual movement, that is, turning both clockwise and counterclockwise. In this case the patient is likely to develop a cancer growth. The astral chakras are petal-like structures similar to the etheric field chakras, but the astral ones are always brighter. However, the astral chakras are interacting with a universal astral field while the etheric chakras are interacting with the universal etheric field. An individual absorbs those energies available from the universal field with which the individual is already synchronized.

Whereas the etheric field is about the same distance from every part of the physical body, the emotional field is more an ovoid bubble of various colors. The emotional field is self-luminous; that is, the light is not reflected light from without. From use of her skills, Kunz learned the significance of these colors and their various shades. Colors near the edge of the aura indicate that they are being used freely, whereas those closer to the physical body indicate inhibition. Observations and interpretation of the human energy field must be accompanied by empathy in order to glean meaning from them, as this is not a mechanical function of the brain (Kunz, 1991).

The levels above the diaphragm are often lighter in color and indicate a person's potentialities. The region below the diaphragm is usually darker and coarser and indicates active experiences. Cravings and appetites are heavier and are also located in the lower part of the aura. In a number of Kunz's illustrations of the aura, there was a dark, ruddy area near the bottom. Kunz indicates that it seemed to imply selfishness or self-centeredness, but this trait was not necessarily deplorable, as it can simply represent a desire to be assertive or to express oneself. The colors around the head are indicators of intellectual and spiritual qualities. Red colors in the aura usually imply anger; grief appears gray; and anxiety is a gray-blue color. Between the upper and lower regions there is a green band. More recent emotional scars are closer to the green band. If there is symmetry between the upper and lower segments, it indicates the person is more fully utilizing his or her emotional resources. In general, emotions have real physical consequences (Kunz, 1991).

The flow of energies between the astral and etheric fields may be harmonious and rhythmic or disharmonious, dissonant, and disturbed— the latter likely to lead to illness. Although located similarly to the etheric chakras, the astral chakras are not associated with physical glands or organs. Disturbances in the astral crown chakra are likely indicators of mental distress. The most active astral chakra is located at the solar plexus. From there, astral energy is dispersed throughout the body.

I am not going to discuss all of the individual explanations of the 18 people for whom chakra illustrations were prepared. Here are some comments that could have wider implications. The father of a four-year-old child had been killed in an accident a year before her illustration. Her aura had a pronounced drooping at the edges. I would assume it was a result of her grief. I do not know if Kunz knew that the father had died or whether she added the explanation of the droop after she had heard that the father had died. Kunz did not comment on whether this was a typical time for the effects to remain so pronounced.

I. The Mental Body

Just as the astral body is of a finer material or operates at a higher frequency than the etheric body, the mental body operates at an even higher frequency, is finer grained, and is faster moving than the astral body. It is ovoid in shape, like the astral body, but is much larger, extending to about three feet from the physical body. It is responsible for intuition and insight.

> The conceptual or abstract mind cognizes meaning of a higher order; the ideas which give events their significance; the unities which underlie life's variables; the structure, proportion, balance, harmony, order and lawfulness of nature; the relationship between human life and the earth, as well as between the individual and mankind. This dimension of the mind is a universal attribute, even though it may not be developed to the same degree in all of us. (Karagulla and Kunz, 1989, 59)

The mental body can affect the disease process, but it can also "be a powerful force for health, growth and change" (Karagulla and Kunz, 1989, 59). The astral and mental bodies disintegrate after death, but not as rapidly as the etheric body.

The mental body is constantly interacting with the astral and etheric bodies, even if the person is not involved in a mental pursuit. Through the mental body's connection to the astral body, thinking and emotion can never be completely separated. Well-balanced emotions are necessary to complete actions generated by the mental body. Each spirit body is a necessary part of human nature. Just as the astral chakras normally rotate at twice the speed of the etheric chakras, the mental chakras normally rotate at twice the speed of the astral chakras, which is four times the speed of the etheric chakras.

The universal mental field is constantly interacting with an individual's mental chakra system, and its brightness and rhythm are indicators of mental-body development. Meaning and interpretation of experience are also derived from a deeper level of the self. "Ideas which are charged with mental power strongly influence other individuals" (Karagulla and Kunz, 1989, 61). This applies to negative thinking as well as to positive convictions.

Ideas and thoughts, whether written or spoken, become part of

> a common vision or world view based upon a strong mental image. Such a mental image has come to be known as a thought-form. The spread of ideas is achieved through the mind's ability to construct a powerful and well-defined image within the mental body, and then direct it toward its object with clarity and intensity. This ability to project one's thoughts clearly is an important factor in successful teaching, as well as in political life. But the ability to create strong thought-forms can also react upon us negatively, for if they become too rigid they can surround and imprison us within a wall of our own thinking, thus preventing the inrush of new ideas and fresh mental energy. We then become ideologues, or fanatics who reject all but their own interpretations of truth. (Karagulla and Kunz, 1989, 61)

National purpose or national character also depend on the thought patterns of an entire nation.

Karagulla and Kunz (1989) discuss the case of a man whose thoughts of wish fulfillment led him to become a paranoid schizophrenic. A clairvoyant who informed the man of this problem before his breakdown was asked how she was able to distinguish between "the patient's thought-form from an actual astral entity" (Karagulla and Kunz, 1989, 62). The clairvoyant's answer to the question was as follows:

> How would you differentiate between a living person and a statue? Isn't one obviously alive, while the other is not? The same holds true on the astral and mental planes. An actual person, even though dead, has a quality of vitality about him, so that he moves, changes in response to what is going on. In contrast, a thought-form is lifeless and static, and its energy comes from the astral and mental fields of the individual who harbors it. (Karagulla and Kunz, 1989, 62)

Regarding thought forms, Karagulla and Kunz explain as follows:

> The great advantage of being able to see thought-forms is that we can become aware of what we are generating, and thus change them to more constructive images. But even if we cannot see them clairvoyantly, when we realized that our thoughts have the ability to affect others directly and that we energize them with our emotions, we begin to feel a degree of responsibility for our thoughts that was previously reserved only for our actions, and indeed come to a knowledge that thoughts *are* action of a kind, in that they affect behavior. (Karagulla and Kunz, 1989, 62)

J. The Self or Causal Body

The fundamental reality in every human being is the self. Karagulla and Kunz refer to this in Western writings as the soul or spirit, but I am convinced it corresponds to my use of the latter term. It is also termed the "causal body" because "it carries the Self's fundamental intentionality to *be*, and this is the ultimate cause of our existence" (Karagulla and Kunz, 1989, 65). This dimension "persists through all the changes and vicissitudes of our life" and "is the source of all that is best in us, and can exert a powerful influence for growth and self-transformation" (p. 65). As Kunz writes, "Self-identity is the one constant in a world of change" (Kunz, 1991, 27). I opine that the causal body is not the ego in the sense of egotism, but it could be thought of as our true ego.

The causal body is even finer or more ethereal than the etheric, astral, or mental bodies. "The Self is not constrained by the usual limits of time and space and causality, but is able to experience the universality of life and to perceive meanings and interrelationships which are often hidden from us during physical existence" (Karagulla and Kunz, 1986, 66). While Kunz claims that there is some truth in Descartes's famous line "I think, therefore I am," she believes a better expression would be, "I am, therefore I think and feel, and what I think and feel reveals what I am" (Kunz, 1991, 42).

Reincarnation is one of the major beliefs of Theosophy, and this self is what reincarnates. As Karagulla and Kunz (1989) explain,

> Those fruits of experience which we have transformed into enduring qualities mark the growth or evolution of the individual self. These are retained from life to life within the causal body which becomes a composite of the highest qualities of the Self: insight, intuition or direct knowing, creativity, intentionality, aspiration to God or the Good, and the purest forms of love and compassion. It can be called the true vehicle of self-awareness, if by that we mean universal consciousness focused in the individual self. (p. 66)

Although reincarnation would imply the long term, Kunz (1991) comments that she would not claim that the self is eternal. She also notes that there is a karmic relationship between the mother and child. She reflects on this when discussing the aura of a pregnant woman. Reincarnation merely extends the effect of past experiences to those from a previous life. Karma is sometimes defined as "the consequences of previous thoughts and actions." The seeds of changes we make in ourselves become the seeds of what we shall be. Karmic indicators are not specific prescriptions for future or predetermined events but, rather, are the kinds of situations that we will encounter during life. How we respond to a particular situation is up to us. "Being born with a handicap, for instance, is from the immediate point of view bad karma, but long term it can represent an opportunity for inner growth" (Kunz, 1991, 70).

K. Illnesses Related to the Brain

Much of the earlier part of this book is a discussion of mental disorders and how they may be related to spiritual influences and corrected by employing spiritually related techniques. Kunz discusses some of those mental disorders and how they appear to a clairvoyant. She never discusses spiritual entities being attached to a person.

In several dyslexics, Kunz observes that "there is a slight local dislodgment of the etheric field from the brain material in certain segments of the visual pathways" (Karagulla and Kunz, 1989, 125). For correcting the problem, Kunz surmises that melodious sounds may assist in synchronizing the pattern and overcoming the dyslexics' difficulty with visual interpretation. In a person with Down syndrome, Kunz reports that there were striking disturbances in the etheric regions of the pituitary, thyroid, and thymus glands and also in the cerebellum. In a child with autism, two major circuits of the brain that are normally synchronized were not synchronized. The most striking was a dysrhythmia between the etheric, astral, and mental fields. There was no disease in this particular child, but rather a time lag in registering impressions from the outside world, which in normal people is done almost instantaneously. Kunz generally concludes "that autism appears to be a condition of malfunction in the nerve impulses between the gray matter of the brain and other centers. The displacement of the etheric from the brain substance is very severe. There is both a lack of synchronization and integration among the etheric, astral and mental levels, and in addition there is a gap in the interconnection at the etheric field" (Karagulla and Kunz, 1989, 132). In this case, and others in which only one person is observed, the analysis or suggestions for corrections may only apply to that specific person and not be universal for everyone with that disorder.

Other than the idea that music may be helpful to a person with dyslexia, Kunz does not propose any remedies for the above brain disorders. People with these disorders would most likely consult with a neurologist. The following are clairvoyant descriptions of mental disorders for which assistance from a psychiatrist is likely to be sought.

A 13-year-old patient with obsessive-compulsive disorder (OCD) ritualistically washed his hands, often after hearing voice commands to do so, but he was not hearing voices when Kunz observed him. The patient also commented that melodious music seemed to soothe and dampen his compulsive thoughts. He was taking an unspecified medication for his OCD; therefore, some of the clairvoyant perceptions may have been induced by the medication. Kunz reports that the dysrhythmia in the etheric (particularly the solar plexus chakra), astral, and mental bodies was greater than she had ever seen before, especially the inability to control the emotional body. Kuhn suggested that giving the patient a small task to perform and then having him carry the task to completion might help him. He needed to find satisfaction in small achievements. In a patient diagnosed as schizophrenic, Kunz maintains that there was a split in all of the chakras.

Kunz also observed a number of people being treated for addiction to illegal drugs, but she did not necessarily specify which drug a patient was taking when she made her observation. Thus, it is difficult to summarize. A general statement is that although as a physical substance the drug affects the etheric body, in treatment it is important to address emotions or astral-body influences. Kunz notes that opiates can even affect the direction of rotation of a chakra.

L. Healers and Healing

In the book *The Chakras and the Human Energy Fields*, Kunz notes that Karagulla's main interest in this collaborative effort was the accuracy of medical diagnosis using clairvoyant vision. She points out that her own primary emphasis was the healing process (e.g., the previously mentioned therapeutic touch).

Kunz maintains that the three requirements for a healer include a genuine feeling of compassion, a desire to assist the person who is sick or in pain (i.e., a sensitivity), and a willingness to give consistent effort. According to Kunz, rootedness and detachment are two qualities that are important in the healing process. Detachment is freedom from attachment to the results of our own actions. The healer must scrupulously avoid any trace of vested interest in the outcome. "When we are able to detach ourselves from personal interest, we can reach out to people in a much more enduring way" (Kunz, 1991, 189).

I previously mentioned the secondary chakras on the palms of the hands. During a healing session involving use of the hands, energy flows from these into the etheric field and chakras of the patient. It is also important that the patient not have negative self-images. These negative images are often mental, but there may also be harmful emotional patterns. Proper visualization by the patient can make it easier to accept the healing energies. The healer needs to practice centering in order to open himself to higher energies. Stillness is another state that is important, as is living in the present. Although not necessarily related to healing, two or three times a day it is good for each person to center himself and send out thoughts of peace.

Many practitioners who use therapeutic touch feel a sensation of heat or tingling in their hands. The patient may have a similar perception. The healer may be attracted to the source of the problem, which may not be where the symptom is perceived.

Although not necessarily typical, it was not unusual for disturbances on the etheric, astral, or mental fields to take years before manifesting in a physical illness. It requires perturbations at all three levels to result in a disease, but it can originate at one specific level, e.g., begin as an emotional problem, spread to the etheric and mental fields, and then spread to the physical body.

Healing power exists everywhere in nature. Medical procedures do not cure the patient; they merely remove the impediments to healing. Kunz reports that there are sites over the earth where the universal field is extra strong. One example that she has observed is a half-mile stretch along the Ganges River ("double-decker etheric energy") where many pilgrims enter the river.

Kunz also offers some advice for everyone from her analysis of people and their spiritual components. For instance, it is okay to acknowledge that you feel angry, but it is fruitful to add "at this moment" so that you recognize that it is not a permanent condition. When depressed, it is often helpful to become involved in physical movement. Kunz recommends folk dancing because, in addition to movement, the music is harmonizing and the companionship of others is helpful in relieving the depression.

M. An Unusual Healer

Karagulla and Kunz (1989) twice attended healing services (1970 and 1974) conducted by a well-known Christian healer from the 1950s to the mid-1970s named Kathryn Kuhlman (1907–1976). Kuhlman wrote a book, *I Believe in Miracles*, and had a television program of the same name. On the program, patients who were healed would appear along with doctors who confirmed the healing.

Kuhlman was considered by some to be the successor to Aimee Semple McPherson, a controversial healer who worked earlier in the twentieth century. A medical doctor named William Nolen wrote a book arguing that a number of people who claimed they had been healed had simply felt inspired at Kuhlman's meetings. A few days later there was no change in their medical condition. However, I read several books in the 1970s that confirmed many actual healings. Kuhlman began her ministry in Pittsburgh, Pennsylvania, in the late 1940s and was still performing services in a church there in the 1970s. She also traveled to other locations in the United States and around the world where thousands of people would attend.

The services were spontaneous and dramatic and would last about four hours; Karagulla and Kunz went early to observe the situation. There was organ music and a choir, and Kunz felt that this built up a thought form that enveloped the auditorium. Before the formal healing service, Kuhlman joined the choir, and Kunz noted that her astral and etheric fields were very bright and could expand to fill a large area. Kuhlman's chakras were bright and fast moving, and the astral and mental levels were harmonious, synchronized, and well integrated.

The organ continued to play during the actual healing service, and Kunz reported that a rainbow-hued pattern of color enveloped the entire auditorium but centered where Kuhlman stood. The energies she developed were both etheric and astral and attracted an even higher force Kuhlman called the Holy Spirit. Kuhlman said she was not the healer but was an instrument of the Holy Spirit.

Kuhlman did not know who would be healed and could not choose the candidates. However, when there was a healing she could point to a place in the auditorium and identify a body part of someone in that area that was healed, for instance, a heart, back, or stomach. Usually she did not name a specific disease but occasionally said, "Cancer." I say that her form of healing should not be classified as faith healing, as skeptics and nonbelievers in the crowd were often healed.

The patients who were healed would often feel a tremendous surge of energy, either heat or a bolt of lightning, pass through them, and the force of this may have even been felt by a person sitting beside them. Kunz describes this energy as "coming from a deep spiritual level right through the emotional and etheric fields. The solar plexus and crown chakras were the two most affected. The 'bolt of lightning' sensation came when these two and then all the other chakras were speeded up" (Karagulla and Kunz, 1989, 177). The proper balance of the sick person's chakras came instantaneously and persisted. This speeding up of the chakras system stopped the disease process. The book mentions that crutches and braces would be thrown away; that is, the physical aspect of the healing was instantaneous. I can understand how properly aligning the chakras and the three fields would affect an organ or soft tissue, but I am not sure how a chakra would affect bones. However, I will mention later how meditation corrected rheumatoid arthritis, so it is possible that the crutches and braces thrown away were for arthritic problems and not bones. Most likely arthritis is an astral- or etheric-field problem that is correctable.

After a healing, a patient might go up to the platform with Kathryn Kuhlman. When she touched the healed person on the forehead, he or she would fall over backward. The book called this "slain with the power," but I have more frequently heard this referred to as "slain in the Spirit," that is, the Holy Spirit, the Third Person of what Christians call the Trinity. Kunz at first wondered if the healings would have a long-term effect.

> She [Kunz] had an opportunity to observe a patient with rheumatoid arthritis who had been healed by Kuhlman the year before, and noticed that a tiny link had been made between the person's higher or spiritual level and the emotions. It was as though the healing energy had penetrated the astral body, and this had effected a real and enduring change in the person.
>
> It is spiritual energy that produces a transformation of the emotional patterns, and this can create a lasting change in the astral body. For the patients, the experience was one of complete joy, and in consequence many of them became

warmer and more open in their relationships with others. (Karagulla and Kunz, 1989, 178–79)

Karagulla and Kunz conclude, "Kathryn Kuhlman was undoubtedly a unique healer, with the ability to tap spiritual energies of great power" (p. 178).

N. Accuracy of Kunz's Medical Observations

Although none of Kunz's HSP abilities were tested in a strictly scientific double-blind manner, the following instances provide examples of her medical diagnoses that, according to Karagulla, were correct. While observing another sensitive (the previously mentioned "Vicky"), Kunz noted which etheric centers and corresponding endocrine glands might give Vicky future physical problems. Twenty years later Vicki did develop the symptoms predicted by Kunz.

In another case, Kunz was looking at the abdomen and the internal organs of a patient and described a blockage there. The patient had not had any gastrointestinal symptoms but had not been medically evaluated. Kunz recommended that she consult her physician and undergo an x-ray examination. Results of these tests showed a blockage of the colon exactly at the point Kunz had indicated. Three days later, cancer of the descending colon was diagnosed and surgically removed.

O. Spiritual Techniques

Kunz also discusses meditation but does not explain any recommended method. Although meditation is a withdrawal away from immediate physical and emotional distractions, it is not just a withdrawal into an inward passive state.

> It is a dynamic experience of the identity of the Inner Self with the whole of things—whose compass is so great as to be, in fact, limitless. ... Identifying with this timeless self gives us the power of control over our feelings and our actions. It is a source of intuition, of creativity, and of the strength to take the direction of our lives into our own hands (Kunz, 1991, 183). ... [Intuition is] the kind of immediate understanding

which reaches beyond the usual processes of the mind and gives direct insight. ... It is the intuition which tells us without words what we should do. (Kunz, 1991, 191).

When we meditate and send peace and love outward into the world, our aura expands, and this breaks up the scars of traumatic events. Utilizing meditation results in "achieving a sense of unity with the inner, timeless self, [with which] we develop the will and the motivation to break old, restrictive patterns and rebuild ourselves" (Kunz 1991, 194). The ultimate goal is the integration of the timeless with the personal self.

However, meditation is not simply something that involves the self or mental field. Through this unity with the timeless self, the rhythm of the chakras is altered (in a positive direction); new energy flows in; and destructive habit patterns can be broken. Meditation is physically and emotionally therapeutic. One example of this is a young woman who had little self-confidence and a severe case of rheumatoid arthritis, which typically has more severe symptoms than osteoarthritis. A few years after meditating, she became self-confident and her arthritic symptoms disappeared (Karagulla and Kunz, 1989).

Another skill besides meditation that can be developed is visualization, which affects the brow chakra. It should be obvious that joyous and peaceful visualization can have a peaceful and tranquilizing effect. A recommended symbol to visualize is a tree, because it needs to be rooted in the earth, needs to get sustenance from the sun, and endures the winds and weather.

P. My Suggestions for Confirming if Spiritual Body Diagnosis Is Medically Accurate

Earlier, I commented that I thought these concepts about HSP would be testable under standard Western scientific standards. The Theosophical Society or other organizations familiar with these concepts could supply a list of five candidates to observe and diagnose a human energy field. However, since this is a new field and there is no standard for proving that people have this ability, I would prefer that the medical intuitives provide some evidence of their ability and undergo preliminary testing.

The difficult part may be finding five medical doctors who would be willing to attempt a diagnosis of some patients by simply looking at them in order to compare them to the sensitives' diagnosis. But assuming five doctors could be found, I would then have these two groups of five people each observe ten selected patients. I would recommend that the patients have only one or two major conditions and that those conditions be fairly pronounced. A variety of illnesses and conditions is recommended. The symptoms should not be easily noticeable, such as a person with emphysema constantly coughing or an alcoholic who is drunk.

The five doctors and the five sensitives would observe the patients and submit their diagnosis of each in writing. The diagnosis could be very specific, such as of a heart or lung problem, or more general, such as of a problem in the chest area. The diagnosis would be evaluated by a separate group of doctors to compare with the patients' actual medical conditions. The sensitives group may have to be taught not to use terms like *abnormal throat chakra*, as it would be obvious to which group they belonged. The sensitives group would also have to be told to only specify current conditions in the patients and not where they think future problems may arise. However, a physical examination may have to be performed afterward to verify that a sensitive did not detect an undiagnosed, but an actual, problem. If the abilities actually described in this chapter exist, there should be a major difference in the accuracy of the diagnoses between the two groups.

Q. Conclusions

Although Kunz's description of the spiritual makeup of humans is slightly different from Max Freedom Long's interpretation of the kahunas, Kunz and Long do agree that each human has multiple spirits residing in the physical body. These spirit bodies affect our health, and unusual patterns in the spirit body can be a predictor of future physical body problems.

In the next chapter, I go into more detail of some shamanic concepts beyond those of the kahunas, as described in chapter 2. Some of these concepts relate to NDEs and introduce the topic of some health issues being related to soul loss, which I now refer to as soul fragmentation.

Chapter 9

SHAMANISM

A. Introduction

In chapter 2, I discussed the spiritual concepts of the kahunas, the shamans of the native Hawaiians. In this chapter, I will discuss two topics: Native Americans and a scholarly study of worldwide shamanism.

Although there were different types of kahunas, they lived in close geographic proximity, and their beliefs were probably similar from island to island, perhaps akin to other Polynesians in the South Pacific. Max Freedom Long, however, claimed that isolation in the Hawaiian Islands prevented contamination of their ideas. In this chapter, I will include the writings of a healer, an anthropologist who studied among shamans and then developed a course to teach the underlying principles of shamanism. I will also include a scholarly worldwide review of shamanism.

Each Native American tribe may have similar ideas but perform their work in a different manner, depending on the resources available. For instance, healing herbs used among the Native Americans in forested New England would be much different from those used in the desert regions of the Southwest United States. The US Pharmacopeia recognizes hundreds of herbs used by Native Americans. Of course, the Native healers administer them in a different form than is currently used by other Americans. For instance, Native Americans use willow bark to reduce pain. Willow bark contains a form of acetylsalicylic acid, the active ingredient in aspirin.

To demonstrate that I am not using only sources based on the same viewpoint, I am including the following account from the book *The Discovery of the Unconscious: The History and Evolution of Dynamic Psychiatry* (1970) by the late Henri F. Ellenberger (1905–1993). The examples he provided of "dynamic psychiatrists" are Pierre Janet (1859–1947), Sigmund Freud (1856–1939), Alfred Adler (1870–1937), and Carl Jung (1875–1961). Ellenberger's book is about talk therapy. He believed that the healing methods of shamans are based on their rapport with their clients and are early forms of dynamic psychiatry. He would probably not agree that they are based on a spiritual understanding of humans. Ellenberger summarizes an account of a Western doctor in South America:

> We are indebted to Dr. Federico Sal y Rosas for a detailed study on the soul loss disease among that population [Quechua Indians of Peru]. From 1935 to 1957, Sal y Rosas noted 176 cases of *Susto* (the Spanish word for "fright"). ... The Quechua word *Jani* designates the disease as well as the soul and the healing cure.
>
> The Quechua Indians believe that the soul (or perhaps part of it) can leave the body, either spontaneously or through being forced. The *Susto* disease can occur in two ways, either through fright caused, for instance, by thunder, the sight of a bull, a snake, and so on, or because of malevolent influences, not following upon fright (the latter being called "*Susto* without *Susto*"). Among the malevolent forces that can produce the abduction of the soul, the influence of the earth is considered supreme. The Quechuas show a great fear of certain slopes and caves, and especially of the old Incan ruins. Whether the *Susto* occurs following a fright or not, in both cases the power to be propitiated is the earth.
>
> How can a disease be designated as *Susto* when it was not preceded by a fright? It may be diagnosed as such when an individual loses weight and energy and becomes irritable, has disturbed sleep in nightmares, and especially when he falls into a state of physical and mental depression called *Michko*. The matter is then clarified by a *curandera*. ...
>
> Sal y Rosas compiled statistics on 176 patients, mostly children or adolescents afflicted with *Susto*, but who underwent a medical examination. It was found that these patients belong to two distinct groups. The first consisted of 64 emotionally disturbed individuals suffering from anxiety, depression, hysterical symptoms, and the like. The second group included 112 patients afflicted with physical diseases such as tuberculosis, malaria, postdysentery colitis, malnutrition,

anemia, and so on, all further complicated by emotional disturbances.

> A remarkable fact is the frequently successful outcome of the healing procedure. With praiseworthy honesty, Sal y Rosas writes: "I have personally observed many cases of typical or even atypical *Susto* abruptly improve or recover completely after one or two sessions of *Jani*. ... Such a success achieved by a humble rural *curioso* or by a peasant woman, with their primitive and savage psychotherapy, contrasts with the failure of graduated physicians—among them the author of this article—in the cure of *Susto*." (pp. 7–9)

Thus, we have a Western-oriented physician verifying shamanic healings and also examples of taboos and the consequence of breaching one of those taboos.

This is my own speculation since reading about this concept of soul loss, but later I will explain that mental problems resembling posttraumatic stress disorder (PTSD) or traumatic brain injury might be the result of soul loss. PTSD has been in the news quite frequently due to its frequent diagnosis among soldiers. It is considered chronic and may require several years of expensive therapy to treat. Sal y Rosas states that the *Susto* illness was corrected in one or two sessions with the shamanic-type healer. Although PTSD is not mentioned in the next section, I intend to demonstrate that other mental disorders treated with reductionist-oriented therapy have had severe consequences, and therefore that shamanic methods should be considered as an alternative method.

Another example of the ability of a shaman comes from the book *The Scalpel and the Soul: Encounters with Surgery, the Supernatural, and the Healing Power of Hope* (2008). Its author, Dr. Allan Hamilton, conveys an incident that happened when a child patient died of cancer. Hamilton, very emotionally involved with the boy, canceled his family vacation when the boy died. A few days later he had a terrible stabbing pain in his back and was incapacitated. A Navajo graduate student who was working with Hamilton dropped by his house. When he saw Hamilton's condition, he left and soon came back with his grandfather, a medicine man. The shaman deduced that Hamilton was emotionally preventing a child who had died from being able to join his ancestors in the afterlife. Close relationships with deceased ancestors is a common theme among indigenous societies. For example, although the Day of the Dead in Mexico is observed on Catholics' All Soul's Day, similar ancestral-honoring practices were held in pre-Columbian times. The back pain came from the child's kicking to release himself. Hamilton, of course, realized it was the child who died of cancer. When he agreed to release the child, the pain left. The Navajo medicine man gave him some herbs to drink as a tea for several days. Hamilton noted that a doctor needs to have empathy for his patients but warned against being too emotionally involved with them.

Native Americans' spiritual concepts fall within the general category of animism, the notion that all of life has a spiritual component and that certain locations or places have a stronger spiritual character. A person can go to these places for special ceremonies or simply stay there for a period of time to be rejuvenated. In chapter 1, I noted Sherwin Nuland's disparagement of the concept of life energy. For followers of animism, the concept of life energy is not a speculation but an accepted fact, such as the concept of mana among the kahunas. Other views closely related to animism include totemism (an animal or natural figure representing a tribe) and pantheism (a belief in multiple gods). Another concept that many indigenous peoples have is something that Medicine Grizzlybear (Bobby) Lake refers to as the "Law of Cosmic Duality, that is everything has two sides: day and night, physical and spiritual, matter and energy, life and death" (p. 70).

B. Native Healer

In previous chapters, I have used the term *shaman* as a common designation employed by anthropologists. In North America, the terms *medicine man* (or *medicine woman*) and *Indian doctor* are commonly used. However, Lake, a prominent medicine man, titled his book *Native Healer: Initiation into an Ancient Art* (1991) because he perceives that shamans are too often associated with sorcery and not necessarily healing, his own specialty. However, he asserts that the position of the Native healer is "comparable to that of a physician, psychologist, priest, teacher, and mystic, all rolled up into one" (p. xvi). Therefore, I will use the phrase *Native healer* in describing his work and methods.

As part of their belief in animism, Native healers consider vital life energy to be a source of spiritual power that can manifest through animals or places. These include the following: "Raven, Hawk, Eagle, Bear, Wolf, Coyote, Deer, Salmon, a Bug, a two-headed Snake, or the sweat lodge, a waterfall, wind, lightning and thunder, a star, the Moon or Sun" (p. 3). Lake's primary source of power is a grizzly bear, hence his name. These animals or places are considered to be helpers of the Great Spirit or Great Creator. They can be used for self-protection, self-guidance, and self-development. Parts of various animals are often used in healing, such as feathers or hides. "All human beings have the universal right to communicate with creation and the Great Creator. Unfortunately, they seldom make the sacrifice needed to use this right" (p. 76).

1. A Calling and the Training

While medical doctors in Western countries must be intellectually bright and usually have empathy for people, being a Native healer is thought of as a true calling, perhaps even a destiny. A call to healing may involve a dream, a mystical experience of enlightenment, an illness, an accident, or an NDE. It also often involves a vision quest. Children often followed their parents or grandparents into this vocation. In some cases, tribal elders may know from a child's date of birth that he or she has healing abilities. An accomplished Native healer can often recognize other people with the potential to be healers even among a large crowd. There may be an inherited tendency to enter a trance, which is often employed in analysis of a problem and eventual healing. It is an "art" rather than a science. A person with the calling and who refuses to honor that calling may have many difficulties in his or her life.

As part of his journey to becoming a Native healer, Lake describes three NDEs that he encountered. The first occurred during a fever when he was four years old. He was playing with some imaginary playmates and followed them. He ended up lost for four days but was then taken home. He awoke with a burning fever to observe a deceased ancestor performing a healing ceremony over him, during which he saw a horrible black thing leave his body. He screamed, and his parents came into the room. They were glad that he was alive, as he had earlier been pronounced dead.

Lake had another NDE, this one when he nearly drowned at age nine. Again, he saw some Indian elders and was informed that he would be a healer. In this episode, he was also pronounced dead but woke up several days later. Lake makes a comment that many NDErs might agree with: "Death itself is nothing to fear; it is the circumstances which leads to the climax of death that is terrifying" (p. 74). All of Lake's NDEs helped influence him as a healer. Lake's third NDE occurred when he was a teenager and was involved in a major automobile accident during which he sustained multiple fractures and internal hemorrhaging. During his NDE, he was told by a clan mother that he had to return to the living. After four days in intensive care and six days in a coma, he had an important dream. He realized that dreams are the door between the physical world and the spiritual world. As part of his training to become a Native healer, he had to learn to discern the difference between ordinary dreams and spiritually significant dreams. In the latter, a person may call upon supernatural aid.

Lake received most of his training in Northern California, but he is originally from a tribe in upstate New York. His wife, Tela Starhawk Lake, is also a Native healer. The training is quite rigorous, and there are not many Native healers remaining. Training involves a long apprenticeship under another Native healer and much personal sacrifice of time and a comfortable life. In addition, healers are not financially well compensated and must be employed in a standard occupation and carry on their healing as an avocation. Fasting and sweating in a sweat lodge are often involved in a healing ceremony, which may take several days. There may be suffering involved. In addition, a healer must lead a "clean" life, for instance, minimizing alcohol intake and especially not using alcohol when performing a healing. In appendix D, I have placed Lake's list of spiritual violations. Most of the violations that cause sickness are laws against nature or the Creator's laws. For example, it is acceptable to hunt and fish if proper prayers are offered but it goes against the laws of nature to hunt or fish without offering prayers beforehand. Lake also comments that "stealing within the tribal system was not tolerated, while stealing from enemy tribes was considered honorable" (p. 125).

While Lake contends that various violations he lists are true spiritual offenses, perhaps they are simply taboos. Although the word *taboo* is specifically Tongan (Polynesian) and is used by other Polynesians, in general the term implies social customs that are forbidden. It also infers a moral and often religious judgment.

An apprentice healer must learn his or her mentor's philosophy, expertise, methods, and approaches to healing. The apprentice must also learn myths and legends. Lake, in particular, learned additional techniques including the use of herbs; transmitting healing with his hands; seeing clairvoyantly into the past, present, and future for diagnosis; reading omens; soul traveling for distance healing; retrieving lost or captured souls; changing the weather; and properly conducting rituals and ceremonies to achieve the desired results.

Although there may be a standard healing herb used for each specific illness, Lake asserts that he prefers to consult with his inner guide on the use of herbs for each patient. In general, he prefers to gather the herb at the time of intended use, saying a prayer while gathering it, rather than using off-the-shelf herbs. He does not explain what he does if the herb is not in season. One herb he particularly likes is wormwood. Some herbs may be administered externally rather than internally. Tobacco is also important for a healer. As Lake explains, when Native healers use tobacco, they generally prefer it to be a wild Native variety and not commercially produced. "Smoking and praying with tobacco is the main ingredient for almost all Native ceremonies; it is probably the most ancient ritual we have, and it is still being used today. The tobacco is offered to the spirits as payment in exchange for their assistance. Smoke from tobacco offered to the Great Spirit of the Universe, our Creator, carries our prayers to him from the physical world into the spirit world" (p. 37).

Each Native healer may have a special technique or may specialize in a specific illness. For instance, there can be trance healers, sucking doctors (those who suck pain or poison, which Lake does), and spiritual doctors (those who treat mental illnesses). A female healer often specializes in childbirth and problems related specifically to women. Lake includes an entire chapter on female healers and important things in a woman's life. For instance, when a woman is having her menstrual period, she is being purged by nature. During this time, women "can abstain from sex, quit eating meat, fast on soups high in potassium, drink lots of herbal teas and fruit juices; they can also lie in the moonlight at night and pray for themselves and bathe in cold water for strength instead of hot water" (p. 97).

Lake spends a considerable time in his book describing the use and construction of a sacred sweat lodge. For him, it is a "tool for self-discovery, apprenticeship, healing, and transpersonal development" (p. 155). He would then use the lodge "for doctoring, healing, spiritual development, vision seeking, therapy, and holistic health" (p. 159).

2. Dreams and Visions

In learning to interpret or utilize dreams as a healer, Lake explains that the unconscious right side of the brain is involved in imagination, instinct, intuition, and "the seat of powers of clairvoyance, ESP, telekinesis, clairaudience, precognition, soul travel, dreams, and visions" (p. 29). He claims that in dreams, he saw his children before they were born. The medicine people who trained him "even taught [him] how to change dreams to prevent an accident or injury, or to communicate long distance with others in a dream. They taught [him] how to acquire a dream ally and how to learn from the animals, birds, ghosts, spirits who taught [him] secrets of herbs, medicine making, and healing in dreams" (p. 32). He was also taught to recognize omens; for instance, he is very wary if he sees or hears an owl, as owls can be considered as protectors because they warn of potential difficulties ahead. If these symbols repeatedly appear in dreams, then that is as ominous as a physical appearance. Native healers learn to speak to what is seen in nightmares or recurring dreams.

Beyond dreaming, there are also vision quests and power quests. Dreams can be vague and confusing, but visions are clear and longer lasting. Power quests are used to acquire an ability to accomplish a specific task. Both quests generally require purification in the sweat lodge and are usually from four to thirty days long, although a week may be more common.

3. Healings

Lake reports that he has "doctored people for cataracts on their eyes, or blindness, people who had chronic arthritis, broken bones, torn ligaments; [he has] doctored people who had cancer, Hodgkin's disease, and leukemia: men with prostate gland disorders, women with female organ problems and cysts on their ovaries, children with diseases, elders whose vital organs such as the gall bladder, kidneys and heart were weakening" (p. 116). Less difficult cases he has treated include "bug bites, colds, flu, bronchial infections, asthma, food cause poisoning, cuts, bruises, mental breakdowns, anxiety, nightmares, panic attacks, skin rashes, allergies, and infections" (p. 116). He has also dealt with possession and with people affected by sorcery. Lake asserts that most of them were healed temporarily, partially, or completely. Lake states that he would often pray to the Creator to ask if he should attempt a healing. Some cases he could not handle.

His general classification of illnesses includes four categories: mental, physical, emotional, and spiritual. Lake claims that "the patient's sickness can be directly traced to committing a violation against the natural and spiritual laws, or they may have inherited the violation. Not knowing the law is no excuse for violating it" (p. 117). Among the violations to which Lake has attributed sickness are "killing rattlesnakes without just cause, digging up burying grounds, gathering herbs and roots without a proper prayer and agreement, polluting sacred waters, having sex upon ceremonial grounds, making bad prayers and wishes against others, abusing spiritual knowledge and powers, stealing, tormenting and experimenting on frogs and animals, playing with power or witchcraft, attending funerals while unclean in body and soul and not purifying oneself afterwards" (p. 118).

I affirm that Native healers base their healing on spiritual principles. I am attempting to explain that some mental and physical illnesses are related to spiritual principles. However, there are some major differences between indigeneous and Western concepts. For instance, Lake states that he assisted in healing one non-Indian man who had severe osteoarthritis. Lake reports that the cause was that the man "shot and killed large animals such as the bear, buffalo, elk, deer, and those without proper ritual and agreement. His wife had handled, cooked, served, and eaten while she was on her moontime (menses)" (p. 118). Although I would agree that there is a fair amount of arthritis in this country, I would think that if everyone who killed and ate a deer, or that any woman who prepared meat during her menstrual period, developed arthritis, there would be a much higher percentage of our population with arthritis. Of course, I speculate that in the etiology of illnesses according to Native American concepts, the same cause or violation of a spiritual principle may result in different illnesses.

In spite of some conceptual differences, many of Lake's healings relate to those I have described throughout my book. One example is relevant to healings of mental illnesses that I will discuss in chapter 10. Several days before the patient came to him, Lake was having tormented dreams about being drunk and running over an elderly woman. He was also hearing disruptive voices during the day. The patient who came to him was an American Indian who was afflicted with dreams about dead people. His white psychiatrist concluded that he was paranoid (I assume schizophrenia) and gave him medication, which was not helping him.

Lake's wife assisted him in the healing ceremony. They could "see" that while drunk one night, the patient had driven over an elderly woman and killed her. He spent time in prison but still felt guilty and was tormented by his victim's ghost and her dead relatives. The Lakes asked the patient to beg forgiveness from the woman's ghost and also have the Great Creator forgive the patient. They made an offering of tobacco and food to the deceased. They used the power of wolves and ravens to remove the deceased person's ghost from the earth plane. They also gave the patient some natural herbs to purge the narcotic medication in his system. Lake reports that a week later the patient was normal and happy.

Another healing Lake describes in some detail was of a Vietnamese grandmother living in the United States. Following gallbladder surgery, she fell into a coma and had to be placed on life support. The family requested assistance. Lake and his wife had to adjust the ceremony performed in the hospital, as they could not burn tobacco around the oxygen apparatus. Their spirits told them that since the woman did not like living in this country, her soul had returned to her home country. The Lakes used soul travel during meditation to bring her wandering soul back to her body. By the time they came back from their meditation trance, the patient was awake. Lake had also seen a snake in spirit form on the patient. Later, she admitted that she had killed a snake after it bit her. Lake commented that her killing of the snake was responsible for her original illness.

In the above instances, the procedures may have taken only several hours. However, some of the ceremonies, especially if they involve a sweat lodge, may entail two hours to four days. Native American doctors do not schedule appointments every 15 to 30 minutes.

Although the previous two healings involve spiritual factors, Lake delves into this spiritual—physical relationship even further with a discussion about omens, psychic phenomena, sorcery, and sickness. Lake reports that he personally researched 20 cases of Native patients dying at a hospital, often the result of a surgical procedure. He claims that in 17 of them there were omens prior to the death. These omens were generally "the sudden and strange appearance of certain animals, birds, snakes, toads, or bugs, either in or near a patient's room prior to surgery" (p. 128). A psychiatrist admitted to Lake that omens would sometimes appear during psychoanalysis of Native patients.

Lake's book was written 25 years ago, but he mentions a case of autism. This illness has been receiving much more publicity recently than it did 25 years ago. In the case reviewed, the child was an eight-year-old Indian girl. Her home life featured verbal, mental, and physical abuse, as well as substance abuse, poverty, parental fighting, and neglect. The treatment was performed by Tela Starhawk Lake. Her analysis was that the child was under the protective custody of "the Little People." These are imaginary playmates on a spiritual level with whom the child was communicating to protect herself from her actual physical situation. Tela Lake was able to determine this by clairaudiently listening to the conversation between the girl and her imaginary playmates. "Tela claimed that the Little People were not projections from the child's unconscious mind, but were in fact real psychic entities, who became constant companions of the child, especially during periods of torment, abuse, and neglect" (p. 140). She had to convince them to relinquish control and then convince the child to communicate with her mother. The mother confessed her neglect and agreed to seek psychotherapy and participate in Native activities. Three years later the child was healthy and doing well in school. Lake speculates that the same spiritual factors may be occurring in some cases of juvenile schizophrenia and mental retardation.

4. Conclusions on Lake

Lake does not dwell much on the details of human spiritual nature. He occasionally states that we have a body, mind, and soul, and that we all have spiritual guardians of some kind. Some of his healings may approximate those among indigenous peoples described by Oesterreich in chapter 10.

C. A Different Perspective

Lake's views inform us of the internal perspective of a Native American healer, but how do his views compare to those of others who have studied shamanism around the world? One such study is the classic work by Michael Harner, *The Way of a Shaman* (1990, 3rd ed.). Harner is an anthropologist who studied shamans among various cultures and had several shamans train him to become a shaman. Thus, he has an academic outsider's perspective, but he also internally understands what a shaman experiences. Most of Harner's findings and concepts confirm those of Lake, but some appear contradictory. His findings also support other concepts in this book not related to shamanism.

According to Harner, the word *shaman* comes from the language of the Tungus people of Siberia. The following is Harner's definition of a shaman: "A shaman is a man or woman who enters and altered state of consciousness—at will—to contact and utilize an ordinarily hidden reality in order to acquire knowledge, power, and to help other persons" (p. 20). Harner states that archaeological and ethnological evidence suggests that shamanic methods are 20,000 to 30,000 years old and have not changed much over time because the methods are effective. Shamanic knowledge was probably acquired through trial and error over hundreds of human generations and is similar across wide areas of the world. Among the areas mentioned by Harner are aboriginal Australia, native North and South America, Siberia and central Asia, eastern and northernmost Europe, southern Africa, Indonesia, Japan, and China. Earlier, I included an entire chapter on the kahunas of Hawaii, who originally came from Polynesia.

Becoming a shaman requires dedication and self-discipline. Lake seems to emphasize that people are born with a penchant for shamanism, but Harner appears to believe that anyone can acquire the skills for elementary work in the field. Harner distinguishes between family shamans, who were generally less advanced and worked among close relatives, and professional shamans, who were more powerful and worked within an entire community. Many people can become a shaman, but only a few are outstanding in their abilities—and that may take many years of practice. "A true master shaman never challenges the validity of anybody else's experience" (p. 45) or tells a person that what he or she experienced was a fantasy. Shamanic knowledge can only be acquired through experience, not from a book or from a verbal description. It is not necessary to understand how shamanism works in order to employ its methods effectively. Harner has developed workshops to train Westerners in shamanic methods and now has those he originally trained conduct those workshops through the Foundation for Shamanic Studies.

1. States of Consciousness

Harner explains shamanism in terms of various states of consciousness. Typically, people operate in an ordinary state of consciousness (OSC). When performing shamanic work, a shaman operates in a shamanic state of consciousness (SSC). The latter is within a broader area called *altered states of consciousness* (ASC). Harner then states that things considered mythical (or fantasy) in an OSC may be real in an SSC and vice versa. Things experienced or viewed in an SSC are also referred to as *nonordinary reality*. They are not hallucinations. Both states are valid within their own context. He further contends that people most prejudiced against the concept of nonordinary reality are those who have never experienced it. However, dreams are an ASC, and everyone has experienced those. A shaman has conscious control over the direction of his travels but does not know what he will discover. Harner also comments that some shamans can see future events in an SSC.

A shaman generally works in the dark or with her eyes closed to prevent distraction from ordinary reality. When in an SSC, a shaman may appear to be in trance, but she is usually aware of ordinary reality and does not have amnesia for what occurred in the SSC. A shaman can exit an SSC to return to an OSC at any time. A shaman operates in nonordinary reality only a small portion of the time. Otherwise, a shaman is an active participant in community life. Harner's main emphasis is on healing and maintaining health. "Nonordinary reality is entered not for play but for serious purposes" (p. 21). Healing is generally accomplished by restoring beneficial power or extracting harmful power.

Harner recommends that an SSC be entered through the rhythmic beat of a drum or possibly rattling, singing, or dancing. While in an SSC, a shaman may also recite a "power" song. Harner entered his first shamanic journey under the influence of ayahuasca, a hallucinogenic drug, while performing anthropological studies in the Ecuadorian Andes in the late 1950s. During this incident, he heard beautiful singing from beings that had the bodies of humans but the heads the birds. He reports that he was given information that was only to be revealed to people who are dying. After describing what he encountered to a shaman, the shaman told Harner that he had never met anyone who had encountered and learned so much on a first ayahuasca journey.

2. Guardian Spirits and Power Animals

In order for a shaman to perform his work, it is necessary for him to employ a *guardian spirit* and other helping spirits. Other names for the guardian spirit include tutelary spirit, familiar spirit, or just friend or companion. According to Harner, this is the fundamental source of power for the shaman. Without a guardian spirit, it is virtually impossible to be a shaman, especially for healing. He comments that all people probably have a guardian spirit, at least in childhood, but that a shaman knows how to actively participate with it.

Shamanic work often includes a shamanic journey to the Lower World. What is interesting is that the entrance to the Lower World exists in ordinary, as well as nonordinary, reality. In ordinary reality a shaman may picture a cave or a hole of a burrowing animal as the entry point. Harner's description of entering this world is as follows:

> Entrances into the Lowerworld commonly lead down into a tunnel or tube that conveys the shaman to an exit, which opens out upon bright and marvelous landscapes. From there the shaman travels wherever he desires for minutes or even hours, finally returning back up through the tube (henceforth

called the Tunnel) to emerge at the surface, where he entered.
(p. 25)

Closely related to the guardian spirit is the *power animal*, which represents the guardian spirit in an SSC. If a person has not lost her guardian spirit, then her Power Animal will often appear to her when entering an SSC. It may take human form later. When shamans speak about a Power Animal, they are not speaking about a coyote or a bear but about the species of coyote or bear. Harner describes how to find your guardian spirit / Power Animal and how to have a shaman recover it for you, but I will not describe these procedures. They involve entering the Upper World.

When a shaman recovers a wandering guardian spirit, the shaman generally blows it back into the person's chest area, the main part of the physical body in which it resides, although the power flows throughout the body. If a person has lost and regained her guardian spirit, it is important to perform a dance that that type of animal might do in order to make it feel at home. The Power Animal exists in nonordinary reality, and one's dancing enables it to experience ordinary reality. This dance should be performed at least weekly. The dance should include making the sounds of that animal. It is best not to do this in public, at least among people who do not understand what you are doing.

Power Animals are never domesticated animals and are not lower species of animals, such as insects. A Power Animal can be a mythical animal. Some shamans believe they can metamorphose into their Power Animal. A guardian spirit / Power Animal is always beneficial no matter how fierce an animal it is and should not be feared. Before Harner became experienced in shamanism, a shaman could observe Harner's own Power Animal. When a Westerner finds his or her Power Animal, it is not unusual for that person to realize that he or she has felt a close kinship to that animal during his or her life. When a shaman desires to assist another person, the assistance should go to the person's Power Animal and not directly to the person.

Many shamans believe that a guardian spirit / Power Animal can make a person resistant to illness. Shamans call illnesses power *intrusions*, and serious illness is usually only possible when a person is "dis-spirited" and has lost his guardian spirit. Symptoms of this loss include depression, infectious disease, pain, and poor decision making. When you feel powerful, your Power Animal is more active—and that is a good time to make important decisions. A person can ask his Power Animal questions by journeying down the tunnel. Consulting with your Power Animal is sometimes called *divination*.

In addition to a person's being dis-spirited after losing the personal guardian spirit, a person can also lose his or her "soul." Harner does not define the term *soul loss*, but losing one's soul in a shamanic framework is definitely not the same as a religious interpretation of what happens, such as a person's possibly being damned after dying as a result of leading a dissolute life. Harner reports that soul retrieval (i.e., recovery of the last soul parts) is complex, but he does not describe it.

In addition to using the guardian spirit, shamans can use *spirit helpers* in their endeavors. While there is only one guardian spirit, there can be many spirit helpers. In general, by spirit helpers, Harner means plants. Similar to Power Animals, wild (the undomesticated species of) plants have more power than domesticated plants.

NDE researcher Rommer (2000) considers the following to be an NDE, but it appears to me to be a rescue possibly by a Power Animal, although the person it happened to, Ron, a Native American, thought of it as assistance from the Holy Spirit. While sledding when he was a young child, Ron fell through a frozen creek on an Indian reservation in upstate New York. The water underneath the ice was flowing and out of control, carrying him downstream. Ron believes the Holy Spirit touched him four times, doing the following things:

- Stopped him from traveling further downstream with the current
- Put him upright although he was still under the ice
- Pushed him back upstream toward the hole in the ice
- Helped push him out of the water onto the ice (there was a small girl on the thin ice pulling on him, but she was not strong enough to do it alone)

Ron says he now has healing abilities, but they are not described. He reports that he had his healing ability since he was a boy, but he did not specify whether or not it began just after the above episode.

3. *Healing*

Harner also discusses illness caused by power intrusions. Emotional disequilibrium, such as anger, can harm other people, but shamanic principles can protect a person from these outside influences. Intrusion can sometimes affect one particular area of a person's body. Shamans can often sense this area when they pass their hands over the person's body. The sensations they feel are usually heat, energy, or a vibration. Experienced practitioners of Therapeutic Touch and Reiki report a similar phenomenon.

Harner cautions that only experienced shamans should attempt to remove these intrusions, as the intruding influence can affect the shaman if it is not disposed of correctly. Harner never mentions these intrusions as resulting from the spirit of a deceased person. Harner reports that in nonordinary reality the intruder might have the appearance of a spider or some other undesirable creature. The shaman would have a small piece of a plant inside his mouth in which a spider might customarily make its home. When he sucks out the intruder, it will be attracted to the plant material, which can then be disposed of. Another alternative method of dealing with intrusions includes inducing an intrusive spirit into a packet of tobacco and then disposing of the tobacco at a remote location. A third alternative is for the shaman to become like the patient. This resembles psychoanalysis and employs the principle of countertransference.

Shamans also use power objects to deal with power intrusions. The main object discussed by Harner is a quartz crystal. After purchase, a quartz crystal may need to be cleansed, as its past history is not known. The complex procedure for cleaning it will not be described. Karagulla wrote about how information with strong attachments is stored in crystals and how sensitive people can "read" this information.

D. A Scholarly Survey of Shamanism

A third view of this subject can be found in the writings of the late Mircea Eliade (1907–1986). Eliade was a scholar of the history of religions, or comparative religious studies. His major book on shamanism is titled *Shamanism: Archaic Techniques of Ecstasy* (1994, 4th ed.). Eliade reviewed thousands of international scholarly publications in the fields of anthropology and ethnology. He sometimes coins his own terms, like *hierophany*, a variation of the word *theophany*, for "a divine manifestation." He felt that *theophany* was too religious; *hierophany* means "a manifestation of something sacred." His term for ordinary states of consciousness, in contrast to the sacred, is *the profane world*. The word *profane* has as its original meaning "outside the temple." His use of the word *ecstasy* is also different from the usual religious sense. Eliade utilizes the word to indicate visions, significant dreams, or trance states.

Another term that Eliade utilizes numerous times, but which I had to search for in an unabridged dictionary, is *psychopomp*. The word indicates someone who escorts the dead to the underworld (the realm of shades). The word in Greek means "guide of souls." In Western mythology, that was the function of Hermes. Perhaps much of Western mythology was derived from shamanism. For instance, Eliade describes a widely spread Native American myth (one that also occurs in several other indigenous peoples' mythology on other continents) that is similar to the Greek mythological story of Orpheus and Eurydice. Orpheus traveled to the underworld (Hades) to bring back his wife, Eurydice, but he failed to reach his objective when he disobeyed the order not to look back at her until both had reached the upper world. When he reached the upper world, he looked back, but she was still in the underworld and had to remain there. These myths are sometimes called epics.

Eliade's book emphasizes studies in Siberia and central Asia. Eliade's shamans were all men, so I will use the word *he* when referring to them. Some of the sources he reviewed considered shamans to be madmen or charlatans, and those with a religious viewpoint considered them to be demonic. Eliade disagreed with those views. Shamans do not represent an aberrant and sinister mysticism.

Eliade notes that the shaman has a major social function in society, in addition to his shamanic practices. He may also be a storyteller and/or poet, and in hunter-gatherer societies be expected to locate wild game for hunting or to bring good. In general, "the shaman specializes in a trance during which his soul is believed to leave his body and ascend to the sky or descend to the underworld" (p. 5). Eliade believes that basic shamanic elements are archaic but that there can be cultural influences in each particular society. For instance, he notes that current north Asian shamanism has in some ways been influenced by Buddhism.

Eliade maintains that a shaman may or may not be a religious leader. For instance, the shaman may not be involved in sacrificial ceremonies. "A large part of religious life takes place without him" (p. 8). Some of the concepts of the indigenous peoples mentioned by Eliade are actually close to the modern term *deism*. Eliade's term for *deism* is *deus otiosus*, or *idle god*, that is, when a creator god is no longer involved in its daily operations. One group described it as follows:

> Benevolent as the gods and spirits "above" may be, they are unfortunately passive and hence of almost no help in the drama of human existence. They inhabit "the upper spheres of the sky, scarcely mingle in human affairs, and have relatively less influence on the course of life than the spirits of the 'this below,' who are vindictive, closer to the earth." (p. 186)

However, celestial gods may have messengers or servants who assist humans. The word *angel* is derived from the Greek word for "messenger."

Eliade uses the word *spirit* to refer to the soul of a dead person, a nature spirit (e.g., gnome, nymph, or fairy), or a mythical animal, among other possibilities. Although a shaman may seemingly be possessed, the shaman controls his spirits rather than being influenced or controlled by them. In some cases, the shaman may appear to be possessed, but it is a temporary condition. After ending his trance state, he generally exhibits no harmful aftereffects.

Eliade mentions the infrequent use of narcotics (hallucinogenic drugs usually obtained from mushrooms or plants) for reaching these other worlds. Harner used ayahuasca for his first visit to the underworld, and frequently encountered its use in South America, but does not recommend drug use. He believes that sonic-driven means, like drums and rattles, are as effective in reaching these other worlds. Various narcotics that Eliade does mention are hemp, jimsonweed, tobacco, mushrooms, and hashish.

In chapter 5, on near-death experiences, I mentioned the story of Er, as recounted in Plato's *The Republic* and cited by Raymond Moody, as including something similar to an NDE. Eliade comments on this episode and believes it was influenced from both Eastern philosophy and shamanic concepts. He had these comments on the experience of Er:

We see to what an extent an archaic myth or symbol can be reinterpreted: in Er's vision, the Cosmic Axis becomes the "spindle of necessity" and astrological destiny takes the place of the "heavenly book." Yet we may note that the "situation of man" remains constant; it is still by an ecstatic journey, exactly as among the shamans and mystics of rudimentary civilizations, that Er the Pamphylian receives the revelation of the laws that govern the cosmos and life; it is by an ecstatic vision that he is brought to understand the mystery of destiny and of existence after death. The enormous gap that separates a shaman's ecstasy from Plato's contemplation, all the difference deepened by history and culture, changes nothing in this gaining consciousness of ultimate reality; it is through ecstasy that man realizes his situation in the world and his final destiny. We could almost speak of an archetype of "gaining existential consciousness," present both in the ecstasy of a shaman or a primitive mystic and in the experience of Er the Pamphylian and of all the other visionaries of the ancient world, who, even here below, learned the fate of man beyond the grave. (pp. 393–94)

1. The Calling to Be a Shaman

Eliade states that shamans develop their profession by several means. Some inherit a tendency, whereas others receive a spontaneous call or election (by the gods or ancestral spirits, often in a significant dream). Others may be selected by the clan or by an elderly shaman who first questions his own spiritual helpers to see if his choice is correct. An individual may simply choose to become a shaman; these shamans are often felt by the clan to be less powerful than those who inherit the ability or receive a call. As Eliade notes, "It is not the point of departure for obtaining these powers (heredity, bestowal by the spirits, voluntary quest) that is important, but the techniques and its underlying theory, transmitted through initiation" (p. 14). For example, being struck by lightning is an indication of being chosen by a sky god.

A preliminary indicator of who may make a good shaman is often what modern society calls a *psychopathic condition*, such as spontaneously entering a state similar to an epileptic seizure. Potential shamans may love solitude or have prophetic visions. In some societies, they are described as physically weaker than the average person. Having a father who is a shaman is not a guarantee of a shamanic call by the spirits, although it is common. A father may select only one of his children to become a shaman, or the ability may skip a generation and a grandfather will select a grandchild. In some societies, the ability seems more hereditary than in others. There can be an initial selection, but the clan may follow the progress of the individual and later not accept his calling as true. An individual may think himself a shaman, but if no one asks his advice, then his own appellation is meaningless. However, some groups consider a calling by the spirits, such as in a premonitory dream, to be obligatory, and this calling cannot be refused or else illness or death may result. Lake also emphasized this.

Being cured of a serious illness, similar to having an NDE, may also be an indicator of the potential to be a shaman. Some individuals are cured of an illness after becoming a shaman. If the shaman did not start his training early enough, perhaps the illness was a warning that he was ignoring his calling—and being cured may bespeak that he is on his destined path. A person's life being saved by a supernatural apparition may also denote that that person should become a shaman. Unlike the Third Man factor discussed in chapter 5, in which modern ordinary people are assisted by a seemingly human companion, among indigenous people the rescuer is often an animal.

2. Training and Initiation

Regardless of which method originally guides the person who is choosing to be a shaman, he needs to undergo training or apprenticeship in shamanic techniques, functions of the spirits, specialized vocabulary, the symbols of spiritual power, and mythology. A member of a tribe may have a single ecstatic experience, but that does not make him a shaman unless he undergoes further training. The techniques may come from older shamans and tribal elders or from visions, dreams, or trance states, which often include messages or songs from deceased ancestral shamans. These are classified as an initiation. Eliade comments that shamans often seem to have a strong ability to concentrate. Although sometimes described as physically weaker in some societies, the shaman, when participating in shamanic activities, may have a large amount of energy or stamina.

Many tribes also have a ritual initiation for males to become official members of the tribe, during which they acquire their guardian spirit. Thus, every member of the tribe could be considered to be in the early stage of becoming a shaman. Shamanic initiation to become an advanced practitioner with multiple guardian and tutelary spirits and the ability to enter an ecstatic state is a separate ritual or ceremony, and there may be a separate ceremony for each stage of initiation. Many of the ceremonies and procedures may take a long time, such as a vision quest or a sweat lodge, and the public is not invited. A final ceremony is only for public confirmation. Any additional abilities do not arise as a result of the ceremony.

Three features often included in ecstatic initiation include the mythological dismemberment or other torture of the physical body followed by a renewal of internal organs (symbolic resurrection), a descent to the underworld, and an ascent to the sky (celestial ascent) to dialogue with gods and spirits. Harner only discusses the first. The dismemberment may be by a mythical animal in the underworld while the shaman is in a self-induced comatose state and may even seem to be dead. This ritual death may last for several days. The shaman's soul may be transformed into an animal. In another culture, the torture is described as being performed by the souls of the shaman's ancestors. Eliade does mention that the torturing animal may become the shaman's helping spirit or the equivalent of Harner's Power Animal.

In another clan, the older shaman symbolically does the following: washes the neophyte's brain to give him a clear mind, inserts gold dust into his eyes to give him clear vision to see wandering souls, and pierces his heart so that he may have sympathy for the sick and suffering. Elsewhere, Eliade mentions that dismemberment is a reduction to a skeleton, which "indicates a passing beyond the profane human condition and, hence, a deliverance from it" (p. 63).

In describing the initiation and training of an Iglulik Eskimo, Eliade made several interesting comments:

> [The master instructing shaman] extracts the disciple's "soul"
> from his eyes, brain, and intestines, so that the spirits may

know what is best in him. After this "extraction of the soul" the future shaman himself becomes able to draw his soul from his body and undertake long mystical journeys through space and the depths of the sea. ...

[The master obtains the disciple's enlightenment, which consists] of a mysterious light which the shaman suddenly feels in his body, inside his head, within the brain, an inexplicable searchlight, a luminous fire, which enables him to see in the dark, both literally and metaphorically speaking, so he can now, even with closed eyes, see through darkness and perceive things and coming events which are hidden from others; thus they look into the future and into the secrets of others.

The candidate obtains this mystical light after long hours of waiting, sitting on a bench in his hut and invoking the spirits. ... "Nothing is hidden from him any longer; not only can he see things far, far away, but he can also discover souls, stolen souls, which are either kept concealed in far, strange lands or have been taken up or down to the Land of the Dead."

For the moment let us observe that the experience of inner light that determines the career of the Iglulik shaman is familiar to a number of higher mysticisms. ... Such mystical experiences were in some manner accessible to archaic humanity from the most distant ages. (pp. 60–62)

3. Various Spirits

The shaman must learn to utilize the spirits of the deceased. He may also call upon "familiar" or "helping" spirits. These familiar and helping spirits often present themselves in animal form. In addition, the shaman can call upon greater "tutelary" spirits and, above them, divine or semidivine beings. A tutelary spirit is usually the soul of a deceased shaman or a celestial spirit. A person can have more than one guardian spirit; powerful shamans always have more than one. Eliade states that plants may be helping spirits, which is in agreement with Harner. These various spirits often provide protection during descent to the underworld.

In addition to animals, shamans may consider other things or various conditions to be guardian spirits. These include the following: "night, mist, blue sky, east, west, woman, adolescent girls, men's hands and feet, the sexual organs of men and women, the bat, the land of souls, ghosts, graves, the bones, hair and teeth of the dead, and so on" (p. 106).

According to Eliade, a shaman turns himself into an animal, rather than an animal taking control of the shaman. When acting as an animal, the shaman often wears a mask or the skins of a dead animal while performing a dance. "Each time a shaman succeeds in sharing in the animal mode of being, he in a manner reestablishes the situation that existed in illo tempore, in mythical times, when the divorce between man and the animal world had not yet occurred" (p. 94).

Although it is not directly related to shamanism, Eliade mentions the Ghost Dance religion of North America, which developed around 1890. It is a form of collective dancing and singing in a circle that can induce a mystical-like experience among some of the participants. Some partakers feel that they communicate with the dead during the dance. Of course, dancing in conjunction with a religious movement is not unusual. The Whirling Dervishes in the Middle East are such a group, as were the Shakers.

Each shaman has his own particular song, and each speaks in a secret language when communicating with his various spirits. This language is similar to the noises the shaman's Power Animal makes. Some groups believe that when a shaman is in a trance he can understand the languages of all of nature, not only that of his own Power Animal. According to Eliade, guardian animals do not have their power as animals but as intermediaries from higher spirits.

Eliade did confirm one additional view of Harner. This view is that when a person "has obtained a guardian spirit he is bullet and arrow proof. If an arrow or a bullet should strike him he does not bleed from the wound, but the blood flows into his stomach. He spits it out, and is well again" (p. 100). Although this seeming invincibility is a phenomenon that occurs among shamans worldwide, I am not sure if the following falls into the purview of spirit protection. Numerous times Eliade mentions that when shamans are in a trance state, they apparently can cut themselves with knives and the wounds seem to instantly heal, or they can hold red-hot coals in their hands without being burned. This is sometimes referred to as "mastery over fire" or "insensibility to heat." In chapter 2, I mentioned how the kahunas of Hawaii could walk on lava without burning themselves.

In contrast to protectiveness, Eliade describes a guardian spirit called a *damagomi* in the Achomawi Native American tribe that shaman refer to as a *pain*; that is, this guardian spirit can cause illness as well as be a source of protective power. One the activities of a shaman utilizing a damagomi is similar to a death prayer that some kahunas could perform, as described in chapter 2. A shaman can send a damagomi away to enter another person, make that person sick, and eventually cause him or her to die. The kahuna death prayer could kill someone within a few days.

4. Mythology

Being able to communicate with animals is seen in some Western religious traditions. Some indigenous societies believe that at one time all of humanity lived in peace with animals and could communicate with them. There was a "primordial catastrophe," after which people became "mortal, sexed, obliged to work to feed [themselves], and at enmity with the animals" (p. 99). This is, of course, similar to the fall of humanity in the Bible. During ecstasy, some shamans are able to restore this paradisal condition. Eliade gives further explanation of this: "Following some acts of pride or revolt by the first shamans, God forbade them direct access to spiritual realities; they can no longer see spirits with their bodily eyes, and ascent to heaven can be accomplished only in ecstasy" (p. 130). Confirming Harner's importance of dreams, Eliade states the following:

> It is always in dreams that historical time is abolished and the mythical time regained—which allows the future shaman to witness the beginnings of the world enhanced to become contemporary not only with the cosmogony but also with the primordial mystical revelations. ... It is always in dreams that the candidate receives initiatory regulations (regime, taboos, etc.) and learns what objects he will need in shamanic cures. (pp. 103–4)

Other beliefs about what life in ancient times was like are that every person had the capabilities of a shaman. Many shamans also believe that in the past the shamanic divine right was received directly from celestial spirits. As a result, many shamans claim that even modern shamans are not as adept as their ancestors were many generations ago. As a result of this spiritual deterioration, some shamans do not attempt the dangerous journey to the underworld. The use of narcotics necessary for humans to enter into communication with various spirits is an example of the decadence of formerly natural abilities to achieve ecstasy. Several north Asian peoples believe that everything in the underworld is an inverted image of the earth. When it is night here, it is daytime there; summer here is winter there; rivers run backward there; and what is broken on earth is whole there.

Some Western mythologies have a resemblance to shamanism, but the two may be much different deep down. For example, while the concept of *hell* is derived from Norse mythology, which is often similar to shamanism, has multiple levels, as does the underworld described in Dante's *Inferno*. Some societies may appear to have shamanic elements incorporated into their beliefs, but the society does not have a shamanic structure. For instance, even in Western society, the temptations and mental tortures some Christian saints undergo may appear similar to those that happen in shamanic initiation, as previously discussed.

5. Common Themes

There are a number of commonalities that Eliade found in most shamanic systems. Among these are the "Cosmic Tree" or "Axis of the World." The sky, earth, and underworld are connected by a cosmic or central axis. This axis passes through an opening. Although all people can make sacrifices to the celestial gods, only a shaman can communicate on all three levels. Similarly, the North Star or Pole Star is thought by some groups to be the "Pillar of the World."

Other common themes include a bridge, a rope, a ladder, stairs, magical flight to the various heavens (usually seven, but there can be more), or reaching heaven by way of magical flight. Note that in 2 Corinthians 12:2, St. Paul reported that he knew a man who was "caught up to the third heaven." Not many modern Christian scholars discuss multiple heavens. The Cosmic Tree has seven branches (note that the number seven was very important in the Mithraic mysteries [Mithras was a city in ancient Greece]). A rainbow, which of course has seven colors, is thought of as a bridge between the sky and the earth. In one indigenous group, the same word is used for rainbow and bridge. In maritime cultures, the journey to other worlds may often use a boat. The symbolism of the ladder also appears in Genesis 28:12–15. Jacob dreamed of a ladder between earth and heaven, with angels ascending and descending on the ladder.

Eliade gives further details on the concept of a bridge or ladder. During *illo tempore*, the paradisal time of humanity, all people could cross over to heaven without obstacle. Later, people could only cross after death or in ecstasy. Now, the crossing is strewn with difficulties for most people, but shamans can easily cross because they have undergone ritual death and resurrection. The people who succeed in making the safe passage are those who have transcended the human condition; the passage "can be accomplished only by one who is 'spirit'" (p. 486). Ecstasy restores the condition that existed *in illo tempore*. Eliade also cites Matthew 7:14: "O how narrow is the door and how difficult is the road which leads to life, and few are those who are found on it."

In addition, Eliade mentions that there are black shamans and white shamans, but it is not always clear how the two differ—and some shaman can be both. Some are thought to have relations with evil spirits, but in some descriptions it is ambiguous as to what those are. When discussed by shamans, the underworld does not imply evil. "Sometimes the bipartition of gods into celestial and chthonic-infernal is only a convenient classification without any pejorative implication for the latter" (p. 186). In a discussion about Eskimos, Eliade mentions that evil spirits are nature spirits that have been angered by people's violations of taboos, or they may be the souls of some of the dead who have become cruel and vicious. Sorcery often implies using these various magical powers for harm, but Western religious sojourners may have classified all shamans as sorcerers.

Shamans and sorcerers around the world "are credited with power to fly, to cover immense distances in a twinkling, and to become invisible" (p. 140). Eliade states that his sources are incomplete on explaining travel, but I suspect that it is an out-of-body experience by the shaman and not the physical body moving. North American shamans claim to have power over the atmosphere, to bring or stop rain and to melt icy rivers. In addition, they know future events and can discover thieves.

Eliade also comments on an observation by Harner of what I called *psychic surgery* in the previous section. In one of several such instances described by Eliade, a shamaness performed "surgery" on her son, and the observer saw blood and gaping flesh. A few minutes later the wound had closed. During the surgery, the shamaness felt as if she were on fire, so she constantly drank water. Elsewhere, Eliade further describes some features of this "inner heat." It "forms an integral part of the technique of 'primitive' magicians and shamans" everywhere in the world (p. 412). It is sometimes referred to as "mastery over fire" and seems to abrogate physical laws. In chapter 11, I will describe this phenomenon in relationship to mysticism (*incendium amoris*). Also, note that shamans can have a paradoxical relationship to heat. In the description just given, the shaman is generating heat, but previously I mentioned that a shaman (similar to mystics in this regard) can have an insensibility to heat, that is, not be burned by heat that would burn people in a normal state of consciousness.

Similar to Karagulla and Harner, Eliade mentions rock crystals, especially quartz, and their relationship with a shaman and light. Shamans feel that there is "a relation between the condition of a supernatural being and a superabundance of light" (p. 138). Some shamans use a quartz crystal for *scrying* (my term, meaning use of a crystal ball to focus attention) by asking a spirit in the crystal for the cause of the illness.

6. Healing Function of the Shaman

The primary function of the shaman is as a doctor and healer. Illnesses in shamanic societies was generally attributed to loss of soul. Various shamanic-culture people believe the soul departs from a specific part of the physical body, but groups differ on the location of the departure. Thus, the shaman "announces a diagnosis, goes in search of the patient's fugitive soul, captures it, and makes it return to animate the body that it has left. It is always the shaman who conducts the dead person's soul to the underworld, for he is the psychopomp par excellence" (p. 182).

Although Eliade includes the following description in a chapter on shamanism in central and north Asia, I believe it is applicable to many other shamanic and indigenous peoples' beliefs:

> Several conceptions of the cause of illness are found in the area, but that of the "rape of the soul" is by far the most widespread. Disease is attributed to the souls having strayed away or been stolen, and treatment is in principle reduced to finding it, capturing it, and obliging it to resume its place in the patient's body. In some parts of Asia the cause of illness can be the intrusion of a magical object into the patient's body or his "possession" by evil spirits; in this case, cure consists in extracting the harmful object or expelling the demons. Sometimes disease has a twofold cause—theft of the soul aggravated by "possession" by evil spirits—and the shamanic cure includes both searching for the soul and expelling the demons. (p. 215)

Eliade further states that many indigenous peoples believe that humans "can have as many as three or even seven souls. At death one of them remains in the grave, another descends to the realm of shades, and a third ascends to the sky" (pp. 215–16). The realm of shades is sometimes called the kingdom of shadows, and the soul there is the one about which the shaman is most concerned. One of these souls causes illness by its flight during earthly life. Only a shaman is able to determine that the soul has fled and is able to return it. Physical health depends upon a balance of spiritual forces. It is not always necessary for the shaman to go to the underworld to return the soul. The shaman may simply go to another place on the earth to find the soul. In other instances, he may ascend to the sky to find the wandering soul.

A séance (healing procedure) in Eliade's parlance is not the same as a séance traditionally thought of as conducted by a Spiritualist, which would involve a darkened room and the participants quietly sitting around waiting a message from a deceased ancestor. "Séances [by a shaman] that include a descent to the world below may be undertaken for the following reasons: (1) sacrifices to be conveyed to ancestors and the dead in the nether regions; (2) search for the soul of the patient and its return; (3) escorting the dead who are unwilling to leave this world and settling them in the land of shades" (p. 238). A séance among the Tungus people in Asia, for example, may involve drums and chanting, dancing, a fire, the shaman dressed in a costume, and the sacrifice of an animal. There may be unusual phenomena, like the levitation of objects or a shaking similar to that found during the early days of a Spiritualist séance. When the shaman reaches the underworld, a spirit enters him. That spirit supplies the answers.

In some cases, in order to extract an evil spirit from a patient, the shaman must take it into his own body, and this may result in more suffering by the shaman than the patient. Although trances/séances are the most common procedure for healing, a shaman may perform an animal sacrifice. A shaman may also invoke the Supreme God as one of his methods, but this practice is not common.

This complex relationship of ecstatic journey, illness, and use of spirit helpers is further explained by Eliade, as follows:

> The shaman's ecstatic journey is generally indispensable, even if the illness is not due to the theft of the soul by demons or ghost. The shamanic trance forms part of the cure; whatever interpretation the shaman puts on it, it is always by his ecstasy that he finds the exact cause of the illness and learns the best treatment. The trance sometimes ends in the shaman's "possession" by his familiar spirits. ... We have already seen that, for the shaman, "possession" often consists in entering into possession of all his "mystical organs," which in some sort constitute his true and complete spiritual personality. In most cases "possession" merely puts the shaman's own helping spirits at his disposal, realizing their *effective presence,* through all perceptible means; and this presence, invoked by the shaman, and not in trance but in a dialogue between the shaman and is helping spirits. (p. 328)

As an example of how this concept of soul loss even appears in the Bible, here is a passage from 1 Kings 17:17–24 (LT):

> And it came to pass after these things that the son of the woman [this is the woman who used the last part of her flour to prepare a meal for Elijah], the mistress of the house, fell

sick; and his sickness was so sore that there was no breath left in him. And she said to Elijah, What have I done to you, O prophet of God? Are you to come to me to call my trespasses to remembrance and to slay my son? And Elijah said to her, Give me your son. And he took him from her bosom, and carried him up into the upper chamber where he abode, and laid him upon his own bed. And he cried to the Lord and said, O Lord God, why hast thou also brought misfortune upon this widow with whom I sojourn by slaying her son? Then he stretched himself upon the boy three times and cried to the Lord and said, O Lord my God, that this boy's soul return to him again. And the Lord heard the voice of the Elijah; and the soul of the boy he returned into him again, and he revived. And Elijah took the boy and brought him down from the upper chamber into the house, and delivered him to his mother; and Elijah said to her, See, your son lives. And the woman said to Elijah, Now I know that you are a prophet of God and that the word of the Lord in your mouth is truth.

Perhaps many of the Hebrew patriarchs and prophets were people with advanced shamanic powers. Another example may be when Moses outperformed the Egyptian priests.

According to Eliade, when discussing shamanism in the Americas, a shaman removes an injurious object (often sent by a sorcerer) by suction. Harner discusses this issue thoroughly. The magical objects inserted by a sorcerer/magician may be "pebbles, small animals, insects; the magician does not introduce them *in concreto*, but creates them by the power of his thought" (p. 301). Eliade also discusses various purifications, rituals, and prohibitions in which a shaman may be involved before performing a séance. These include avoiding a pregnant or menstruating woman and avoiding impurities and certain foods.

7. Relationships to the Dead

Some peoples of central and north Asia have a rather ambivalent attitude toward deceased family members. The long-term dead are often thought of as tutelary spirits who act as protectors. However, the recently dead are often feared because, as we learned in chapter 5 (on near-death experiences) and in chapter 10 (on spirit intrusion), the dead may not realize they are dead. They may return to their family and create difficulty for the family, even attempting to take the living family members with them. To prevent this, a shaman may hold a purification of the house or may escort the soul to the underworld. Sometimes, the shaman performs the psychopomp procedure only if the deceased is believed to be haunting the living. During the psychopomp ceremony, the voice of the shaman may sound similar to that of the recently departed person. When the shaman arrives in the underworld with the soul he is escorting, he usually endeavors to find a close relative to whom he can entrust the recently departed. The shaman usually returns home by another road.

8. Trips to the Underworld

The Altaic people of north Asia describe a trip to the underworld that is unlike any previously described. Although earlier the underworld was described as not evil, danger seems to prevail in this description. In the underworld, there are seven levels, just as most groups speak of seven heavens. When the shaman goes to the underworld, he is accompanied by his ancestors and helping spirits. Eliade's description varies from Harner's in that in Eliade's version, the shaman travels a distance on the surface of the earth before finding a hole through which to enter the earth. Upon entering the hole, he finds a bridge, "the breadth of a hair," crossing a sea. "At the bottom of the bridge he sees the bones of countless shaman who have fallen into it, for a sinner could not cross the bridge" (p. 202). He sees other sinners tormented by the vices they had while living, for instance, a glutton surrounded by gourmet food that he cannot reach. According to Eliade, "the bridge symbolizes passage to the beyond, but not necessarily to the underworld" (pp. 203–4). A bridge can also signify "passing from one mode of being to another—uninitiate to initiate, or from 'living' to 'dead'" (p. 204).

Another description of the underworld, this one from the Yukaghir people of Asia, is interesting. While a shaman, accompanied by his helping spirits, was on a journey to find a lost soul in the underworld, he came to a stream. On the other side of the stream, he saw tents and people. There was a boat nearby, and he used it to cross the stream. He met the souls of his patient's deceased relatives and the soul for which he was searching. The deceased relatives did not want to give the shaman the soul for which he was searching, and so he snatched it by force. My point in listing this is that in an NDE the stream would be a border that an NDEr felt that if he or she crossed, he or she would not return. The shaman, however, was able to cross the border and then to return.

E. Conclusions on Shamanism

The aforementioned writers on shamanism do not necessarily discuss names for the spirit bodies in humans, but their concepts are obviously spiritual. The concept that soul loss is a major factor in mental illness is one of the prime topics of this book. Later, I will refer to this as *soul fragmentation*. Harner refers to an Upper World and a Lower World, and the Upper World may be thought of as related to Spirit or High Self, while the Lower World is related to a soul or astral level.

In the next chapter, I review numerous methods for removing spirit intruders, a condition that arises when a fragmented soul has not completely transitioned to the world of *light* and seemingly enters the soul field of another fragmented soul here on earth.

Chapter 10

SPIRIT INTRUSION AND RELEASE

The refusal of modern "enlightenment" to treat "possession" as a hypothesis to be spoken of as even possible, in spite of the massive human tradition based on concrete experience in its favor, has always seemed to me a curious example of the power of fashion in things scientific. That the demon theory will have its inning again is to my mind absolutely certain. One has to be "scientific" indeed to be blind and ignorant enough to suspect no such possibility.

—William James (Baldwin, 2003, xxi, no reference to William James)

A. Spiritual Influences on Behavior

1. Introduction

In chapter 6, on dissociative identity disorder (DID), I surmised that an alternate personality is a different spirit body assuming control of another person's physical body. In almost all DID cases, frequent trauma, usually sexual or physical abuse, occurs to the patient prior to age seven. This is before the birth personality's spirit body bonds strongly to the physical body. Consequently, the original spirit body can depart temporarily and a second spirit body can take up occupancy. The spirit of the original personality remains in the vicinity of its physical body and can return.

In this chapter, I demonstrate that at any age, and even if the original spirit body is bonded to its physical body, a second spirit body may invade, penetrate, cohabit, attach to, or intrude upon the original spirit body and influence behavior. The intruding spirit bodies are primarily human spirit bodies that have not been prepared for departure from the earthly plane. However, indications will be given that there probably are evil spirits or demons other than earthbound human spirits. Earthbound spirits try to remain in areas familiar to them from their physical lives. Therefore, the people most at risk of spirit intrusion are family members, people who are naturally sensitive to these spirits, and people who have addictions similar to the addiction the earthbound spirit had while in its own body.

2. Completing the Death Experience

For several therapists, the primary treatment for a person with an intruding spirit is to have the invading spirit "complete its death experience." In a typical NDE experience, the human spirit body eventually returns to its physical body. The therapy methods to be discussed are based on the possibility that the discarnate spirit cannot return to its deceased physical body, but also that it cannot or will not enter the transcendental realm. In this case, the discarnate spirit may choose to cohabit the physical body of a living person. The therapeutic methods described in this chapter appear able to remove these intrusive spirits by convincing the spirits to enter the transcendental stage that the spirits missed, thus freeing the patient from a variety of unexplained symptoms. Terms employed for removal of these spirits are *release*, *depossession*, and *deliverance*. One therapist (McAll) who worked mostly with spirits that remained in the family used the phrase "freeing from ancestral control."

During Ritchie's OBE journey in his NDE (see "A Unique Journey," chapter 5), he allegedly observed spirits of deceased alcoholics enter into the body of a drunken man who had collapsed as a result of his drinking. Upon his collapse, an opening appeared in his spirit body, and the spirits of the deceased alcoholics entered him through that opening. I think it is possible that a similar situation occurs when the various vulnerabilities to spirit intrusion are discussed in the sections of this chapter dealing with therapy. This opening of the spirit body (or "psychic opening") may explain why some people are vulnerable to intrusion, often the result of trauma, while others seem impervious.

3. An Analogy for Spirit Bodies Sharing a Physical Body

I have developed my own analogy from the physical world for what may be occurring when a spirit body intrudes. Chemists refer to molecules as having two possibilities for making bonds between atoms. For many inorganic chemicals, the bonds are called *ionic*, as an electron from one atom is transferred to another atom. The simplest example is table salt, sodium chloride. Normally, an outer orbit of electrons is filled if it has eight electrons. The inner orbits are irrelevant in bonding. A sodium atom has one electron beyond eight. Chlorine has seven electrons. When these bond, the single electron of a sodium atom is transferred to the chlorine atom. Thus, they both now have filled orbits. For sodium, the inner orbit has eight and the new orbit has zero. However, the negative charge of the electrons now does not match the positive charge of the nucleus, and thus the atoms are ions, or unbalanced-charge atoms. Similarly, carbon atoms, as in organic molecules, have four electrons in the outer orbit. When one carbon atom bonds to another carbon atom, the two share the eight electrons and, thus, seem to have filled orbits.

My analogy is that in DID a spirit of a deceased person has almost completely moved into the space of the normal spirit that should occupy that body, as in an ionic bond or complete transfer of an electron. In cases of intrusion, the spirit has simply attached itself to the normal spirit and brings its own desires but does not completely control the original body. It is, instead, a sharing arrangement, but not necessarily equal. The intruding spirit may only be 10% of the total or, in some cases, 90% Thus, the degree of control by a spirit of its victim may be minimal or may approach that of an AP.

When thinking about the actions of electrons, one must remember that although electrons are particles and have mass, in a small particle like an atom, the electron is more like a cloud of charge distributed over a wide area. Physicists often use a planetary model of an atom, describing it as a positively charged nucleus surrounded by negatively charged electrons in orbit around the nucleus. For the simplest atom, hydrogen, there is one electron orbiting around a single proton (the nucleus). However, that single electron is not in a single plane similar to the planets in orbit around the sun. Instead, the charge of that single electron is distributed around the nucleus in all directions. The electron is thus often compared to a "cloud" of charge rather than described as a single point in space at a given time. Thus, when I reasoned above that an electron is transferred from one atom to another or shared, it should be thought of as a cloud of charge moving from one area of space to another. A spirit body is more like a cloud or energy field that can move from one area to another, and two of these energy bodies can penetrate the same physical body. The spirit of a deceased person is an energy field that is no longer attached to its own physical body.

These earthbound, discarnate, or bewildered spirits often do not understand their predicament, either immediately after their own "death" (of the physical body) or when they intrude upon or (partially) possess the spirit body of another living person. Frequently, the earthbound spirits are those of people who have died as a result of violence or an accident, had their own psychological problems, did not have a committal service, or were addicted to some substance. In the case of an accidental death, the earthbound spirit may be confused. If the deceased person had an addiction, its spirit is seeking to fulfill its addiction. Even if they had been well-mannered and admirable people in life, these earthbound intruding spirits can cause confusion and destructive tendencies in the bodies they cohabit with the spirit body of another living person. These earthbound spirits are, of course, the same ones that totally control a body in a person with DID. Note that in the Ross et al. (1989) survey, over 20% of people with DID stated that one of their alters was a deceased relative.

Although more of the evidence to be presented here is based on intrusion by the earthbound spirit of a deceased person, there is no reason a living person cannot have his or her spirit body partially leave the body (especially if that person has some dissociative characteristics) and intrude upon another living person. The above-mentioned Ross et al. survey found that almost 30% of people with DID have one alter that is that of another living person. In these latter cases, if the main part of the spirit body is still with the living person, then the influence it has should be smaller. The life of an intruding living person is also affected by intrusion into another person, that is, it is not leading its own independent life. The findings of Max Freedom Long (1948) about low and middle selves moving around and entering or influencing the living are also appropriate explanations of control by another living person, as well as by the dead.

In chapter 9, on shamanism, the people the shamans healed are referred to as incurring soul loss. Later in this chapter, I will discuss therapists who classify clients seeking their assistance as experiencing soul fragmentation. I maintain that this is a better term than *soul loss*.

A client who needs therapy may have a fragment of his or her spirit body missing, and this provides an access point for a discarnate spirit to intrude into the spirit body or aura of the client. It is also possible that the intruding spirit is only a fragment of a complete spirit body. The main spirit body could enter the *light*, but a portion or fragment could be held back to attach to a living person.

4. Mental Disorders

Invading spirits can create many problems. The psychiatric symptoms of intrusion include schizophrenia, delusions, thought disorder, panic attacks, depression and mood swings, eating disorders, obsessive-compulsive disorder, phobias, substance abuse, gender identity problems (most likely if the intruding spirit is the opposite gender of the person intruded upon), and suicidality, to name but a few. Some patients actually describe themselves as being possessed, feeling like two people, or having weights on their back. Some symptoms may be relieved in one session, whereas others may take multiple sessions to eliminate.

While these are primarily mental or psychosomatic symptoms, a number of therapists report healings of physical illnesses, such as alleviation of headaches, unexplained pain, gastrointestinal disturbances, nausea and vomiting, palpitations, paresthesias and analgesias, involuntary movements, paralysis, and seizure-like episodes including epilepsy. These healings do not suggest that everyone with those physical illnesses has spirit intruders. When a spirit intruder attaches itself, the fragmented spirit body of the host will not have sufficient energy to function normally. The decrease in energy may be from one particular section of the physical body, the location of the physical illness to come. The spirit intruder may also be a drain on overall energy, leading to depression or an infectious agent that affects the entire body, in addition to causing other symptoms.

Just as DID is usually the result of severe trauma, other types of trauma are most likely responsible for a person's vulnerability to intrusion. The types of trauma are rather diverse and not limited to those listed here. A familiar example is posttraumatic stress disorder (PTSD). Another example may be the aftereffects of anesthesia. Just as sleep is a normal temporary departure of the spirit body from the physical body, anesthesia forces the spirit body out—and it may not fully return following the effects of anesthesia. Emotional states as common as grief and compassion may also leave people vulnerable.

Addictions are another primary reason that can make someone susceptible to intrusion. However, addiction itself may also be the result of an intrusion. In this area of study, distinguishing cause from effect can be difficult. Many therapists maintain that people who already have a spirit intruder are more likely to attract others. Therapy for multiple spirits is complex. It is difficult to surmise how pervasive spirit intrusion is within any one population. Therapists often believe the percentage to be high in general, but only people with extreme difficulties usually seek out a psychotherapist.

5. Chapter Outline

This chapter will be a presentation and discussion of various therapists and their theories, methods, and results. The success of this wide array of therapies is based on the respective therapists' approach to handling the invasive spirit. I answer the following questions:

1. Why are some spirits earthbound?
2. What individual characteristics or circumstances cause a person to be intruded upon?
3. How can the problem be treated after it occurs?
4. How can the problem be prevented?

6. Therapy for Disorders Arising from Spirit Intrusion

Although in this chapter I will generally use terms like *spirit intrusion*, this behavior has historically been called *possession*. In the *DSM-IV*, *possession* is defined as "a conviction that the individual has been taken over by a spirit, power, deity, or other person." A therapist named Adam Crabtree (1993) discusses possession and its implications. Crabtree proposes a working definition for it: "possession is the experience of being taken over by some outside intelligent entity" (Crabtree, 1993, 254). The term *experience* is used because the event is subjective. Likewise, *outside* implies invasion by an external being. *Entity* is employed because the intruder appears to have a self-contained existence. The entity appears intelligent because it seems to have a purpose, plan, or thought.

The term *possession* is phenomenological and subjective and does not typically represent an objective explanation. The client's mind feels invaded by foreign thoughts, desires, and impulses. Crabtree considers hearing voices to be a symptom of possession, but he distinguishes these from the thought disorders and voices of schizophrenia. He also notes that the World Health Organization (WHO) has included possession in its International Classification of Diseases (ICD-10). The WHO seems more open than the American Psychiatric Association to concepts outside of mainstream Western medical tradition. Another distinction that must be made is between pathological and culturally supported possession. An example of the latter is that a shaman may enter an altered state of consciousness and appear temporarily "taken over," but he or she easily returns to normal consciousness with no aftereffects. Also, there needs to be a contrast between spirit possession and demon possession.

Crabtree alludes to the concern that if possession is recognized as a formal diagnosis in the *DSM*, this may give credence to would-be exorcists among people who are not trained in psychotherapy. These attempts have often failed miserably and have caused extensive harm to patients. While agreeing that harm can be done, Crabtree does "not believe that clinicians are in a position to make a final judgment about the existence of spirits or their ability to possess individuals, and I do not think such a judgment has a place at this stage of the discussion of the data" (Crabtree, 1993, 257). Crabtree has never used exorcisms, but he concedes that an exorcism may be appropriate by a trained therapist who is familiar with dissociative states.

Crabtree holds that a therapist "can diagnose and successfully treat possession without taking a stand on the ontological status of possession" (p. 257). The concept of possession provides a workable basis for therapy even if the therapist does not believe that independent entities are affecting the client. If an outside force seems real to the client, it should be treated as such by the therapist. These therapists represent a wide variety of backgrounds and beliefs. Some consciously lead the intruding entities to the *light*, but others unconsciously do the same. The therapist may simply consider a demon to be a dissociated ego state. My book contributes to an understanding of the intrinsic nature of possession, how it can be prevented, and how to treat it.

In chapter 2, on the kahunas, I introduced the concept of thought forms. Long's alternative name for these is *eating companions*. The Magus, mentioned soon, called thought forms *elementals*. It is possible that the mental problems discussed in these therapy sections may be under the control of thought forms rather than intruding spirits, although they may function together.

Before my analysis of therapy, I will review the concepts of a modern healer. One of his identifications is as the Magus of Strovolos (a suburb of Nicosia on Cyprus). *Magus* is the word from which *magician* is derived, but it does not connote stage magic. The plural of *magus* is *magi*, as some translators employ for the three visitors to the Christ child in the Gospel of Matthew. Other translators use *astrologers*, since the three visitors observed a star. And even other translators use *three kings*, with very little basis for that translation. In the Acts of the Apostles (8:9–25), there was a man named Simon Magus (or Simon the Sorcerer) who wanted to purchase the ability of the apostles to lay hands on people so that they might receive the Holy Spirit. He was castigated by Peter for having his heart in the wrong place.

A university professor from the United States, Kyriacos C. Markides, investigated and presented the spiritual concepts of this magus in a series of books. While his concepts do not always agree with Long's concepts of kahuna lore, the Magus of Strovolos does seem to be able to produce interesting results employing his concepts. To reiterate an earlier point, the kahunas' concepts serve as a springboard for discussion, not as a fixed conviction.

B. The Magus

1. Introduction

Two primary questions arose during my investigations into spirit possession: (1) Are most symptoms of mental illness the result of invasion by deceased human spirits only? (2) Are the frequently encountered voices of animal invasions carried out by the spirits of animals? In the studies discussed here, I will provide much insight into these topics and into the nature of spirit helpers.

2. The Magus's Spiritual Concepts

I learned about the Magus of Strovolos at a conference on near-death experiences, where a psychologist reported that she had traveled to study under him. The following is a summary of the findings about the Magus and his explanation of human spiritual nature. Although the Magus developed his own terminology, many of his findings support Long's concepts of multiple spirits that the latter learned from the kahunas.

While most writers on spirit possession that follow this section were discoursing about their own findings, Markides (1987, 1990,[2] 1991) was writing his observations of the Magus's healings. Markides is a professor of sociology at the University of Maine. He was born on Cyprus and came to the United States in 1960. During a visit to Cyprus in 1978, Markides heard the name "the Magus of Strovolos." He recalled hearing the term as a youth and being told to avoid the man with satanic powers whose home was crowded with spirits. He met the Magus of Strovolos that year and proceeded to study his techniques. Markides spent many summers on Cyprus to observe the Magus. He also took a semester-long leave of absence from his professorship to be there. Spyros Sathi was the pseudonym for the Magus referenced in the book, but his actual name is Stylianos Atteshlis (1912–1995). Atteshlis reportedly severed his relationship with Markides before the former's death.

Markides does not claim to understand what the Magus of Strovolos is doing on a spiritual level. His books contain a glossary of terms, as many nonstandard terms are used to describe human spirituality. Markides's description is that of an observer, but it is obvious that he admires Atteshlis. The term he uses for Atteshlis is *Daskalos*, meaning "teacher" or "master."

Atteshlis taught that humans consist of a gross material body; a psychic body; a noetic body; and the Inner Self, pneuma, or Spirit. Each body has an etheric double. The psychic body is the body of our

---

[2] The 1990 book was actually published first in 1985. It was then reissued by a different publisher in 1990. I reference the 1990 edition, as it contains the most basic information.

feelings, sentiments, and desires, and is centered around the heart. The noetic body is the body of our thoughts and is centered on the head. These divisions closely correspond to Long's description of the low and middle selves. Atteshlis explains that the psychic and noetic bodies could function together; he often referred to them as "the psychonoetic body." The psychonoetic body perfectly matches the shape of the gross material body (1991). Unfortunately, Markides did not obtain more information from Atteshlis on the nature of the other spiritual component in humans, which he calls the Inner Self, pneuma, or Spirit, and which I have called High Self, Inner Self-helper, or Spirit.

3. Using the Concepts Only Beneficially

Atteshlis founded an organization among a circle of friends to whom he taught techniques on employing spiritual powers. Atteshlis claimed he had unusual abilities as a child, such as receiving advice from spirit guides, but that he improved upon those abilities through much practice. Atteshlis asserted that it takes extreme concentration to peer into the spirit world, saying that few are prepared to go through the rigorous training. This ability to concentrate is beneficial not only for understanding the spiritual world. Atteshlis avowed that "the key to understanding matter is in concentration" (1990, 191). Students must learn to become masters of their own emotions and thoughts. Atteshlis "claimed that one of the preconditions for mastering healing is the ability to truly love your fellow man" (1990, 199). Among the duties he taught are the following: fighting black magic, performing exorcisms, healing, fighting injustice, and fighting evil *elementals* by dissolving them and replacing them with benign ones.

Atteshlis only desired that these spiritual abilities be used for helpful purposes, as he maintained that spiritual knowledge can be dangerous if the person employing it has not ridded himself of egotism. Atteshlis also observed his students' outward behavior, as the powers he reportedly developed could be used for evil. Atteshlis did not claim to do the actual healing himself; rather, he saw himself as an instrument of the Holy Spirit, of whom he asked permission to heal. In some cases he did not attempt healings, as he knew the attempt would not be successful, usually for karmic reasons. He also claimed to use other spirit helpers in his work.

His alleged principal advisor was Yohannan, the evangelist John who wrote the fourth Gospel and the book of Revelation. Markides referred to Atteshlis as a Christian mystic. Markides was not among the inner circle of students-in-training, but he did sit in on informational meetings with the students.

Although Atteshlis was Greek and lived on an island where Greeks and Turks often fight, the Turks thought of him as one of their own. Despite his constant problems with local Greek Orthodox Church leaders, he was a good friend of the late Archbishop Makarios (1913–1977), a political and spiritual leader of the Greek Cypriots.

4. The First Healing Observed

The first healing I describe concerns the removal of two human spirits that inhabited a 26-year-old woman. Markides (1990) observed this entire procedure and had met the woman before Atteshlis met her. This case has many unusual features providing insight into the spirit-intrusion process. Although multiple-spirit intrusion has been discussed before, in the chapter on DID, this case is rather unusual in that the two intruding spirits were connected to each other in life, as husband and wife. According to Atteshlis, they died together during the Allied bombing of Hamburg, thirty-three years prior. The possessed woman was Jewish, having arrived on Cyprus from Israel with her mother and aunt. The two spirits were Nazi followers who had participated in the Holocaust. The spirits specifically chose to torment Jewish people because of the hatred they had developed as Nazis. Atteshlis said the spirits had previously driven several other Jewish people mad. The spirits frequently urged the woman to commit suicide. The two Nazis knew that they were tormenting the woman, but she did not know she had spirit invaders, let alone ones who were Nazis. The woman and her family were obviously horrified. Atteshlis asked the woman beforehand if she believed in God, and she replied yes. He said that was good, because he could not have helped her if she had said no. The woman had been normal until she dreamed of demons tormenting her. Medical doctors and several psychologists, had not been able to help her. As Markides writes, "She felt that they [i.e., the spirits] took her soul away and that her body was dead" (1990, 13).

417

Atteshlis was familiar with many mystical traditions around the world. In helping this woman, he used an exorcism in accordance with the Jewish Kabbalah. The entire procedure will not be described, but one point is very important in that it provides evidence of a spiritual—physical interaction. Atteshlis worked with a lighted candle about two feet away from him. Whenever he concentrated on the flame, it changed shape. Whenever he stopped working with the flame, it became very still. The complete procedure took 20 minutes. Afterward, he told the woman and her mother that the spirits could no longer harm the woman or anyone else, that they had been sent "to a place where they can rest in peace until they come to their senses" (1990, 17). He said that if they tried to affect her telepathically, she should recite a little prayer that they had quoted during the procedure and concentrate on the flame of a white candle. He also commented that it was amazing how people carry their hatreds beyond the grave.

A week later Markides visited the woman, and she said she had not heard voices since the meeting with Atteshlis. Markides asked her for elaboration, and she said the spirit intrusion had begun four years earlier. Two incidents had occurred. First, something seemed to enter her head. Then, something seemed to enter her whole body, beginning at her feet. Both incidents occurred after she'd had a disagreement with a boyfriend. One of the first things the spirits told her was that they were going to marry her to their world and that she would be unable to marry in this world.

Markides later asked Atteshlis for more details. Atteshlis stated that the spirits' relentless hatred resulted in a failure to make a complete transition to the psychic world. The spirits were oscillating between the gross material world and the psychic world. Such spirits can touch the material world "by taking possession of a human being who lives here on Earth and has certain phobias or is in a psychological state that permits these spirits to enter the person" (1990, 21). Possession can take place only "when the individual vibrates analogously with whoever or whatever tries to enter him. In other words the person must himself have the predisposition to hurt" (1990, 21). Atteshlis said he never judged anyone; he simply corrected the problem. The two other types of possession, by elementals and by demons, will be discussed shortly, but the root cause is similar.

Atteshlis also explained the importance of the candle flame. He stated that he was trying to pass the spirits through the element of fire in order to isolate them and then thrust them into a psychonoetic abyss. Atteshlis created angelic elementals to escort the spirits to the abyss. He explained that by removing the spirit intruders in this way, he helped not only the woman but also the two Nazis. In the psychonoetic abyss, the spirits will be calmed down so that they become conscious of their evil nature, although the specific details will not be remembered. Markides asked Atteshlis if it was a sort of purgatory, and Atteshlis replied yes, but one which the Nazi spirits themselves created. Similarly, once when he was trying to help a living patient with suicidal tendencies, Atteshlis told Markides that people who actually commit suicide "may be trapped in the ethers of the gross material world, unable to move to the higher psychic planes" (1990, 160).

After confirmation of the healing a week later, Markides informed Atteshlis of the success. When he learned this, Atteshlis said that he already knew it and did not act surprised. Markides states that Atteshlis was sure of his craft. When he told the woman she was cured, it was not simply to give her confidence that everything would be okay. He knew he had cured her.

5. Other Healings

Atteshlis outlined several past cases of human possession. One case involved a man who died during a long courtship, during which he had not engaged in sexual relations with his fiancée. His overwhelming desire for her kept him floating in the etheric world. At night he would enter a bat and come into his former fiancée's room to draw blood and etheric energy from her. This occurred when Atteshlis was much younger and was not sure what to do. He requested assistance from a spirit helper named Father Dominico. Father Dominico told Atteshlis to be present in the room at night with the young woman. After the bat entered, he was to close the window, kill the bat, and burn it. The young woman, who had been slowly going mad, groaned and screamed while the bat was dying, but she was calm afterward. Atteshlis advised the family to have a priest bless the house. Atteshlis did some further work on his own to disentangle the spirit from the etheric world.

6. Elementals

Atteshlis stated that possession by humans who reside in the etheric world is fairly rare, and that much more frequently he encountered possession by elementals. Elementals also influence people who vibrate at the same frequency as the elemental (Markides, 1991). Elementals are defined in Markides's books as "Thought forms. Any feeling or any thought that an individual projects is an elemental. They have shape and a life of their own independent of the one who projected them"(p. 220). In Markides (1991), Atteshlis explains that the form of the elemental cannot be eliminated. The energy the elemental needs must be depleted, thus rendering it unable to function. Atteshlis says that the spirits of humans can be the most difficult to remove because they cannot be destroyed or dissolved. Although his terms are different, Long (1948) similarly states that the kahunas were strong believers in the independent existence of thought forms.

There are two kinds of elementals: those produced subconsciously and those produced consciously. Elementals produced subconsciously are more emotional. Those produced consciously are made of noetic substance, enabling the person who created them to develop the power of visual imagery. They enable the person to accomplish a specific task. Long would describe them as, respectively, those produced by the low self and those by the middle self.

Elementals can take many forms. For instance, a person can create an image in his or her mind of friendliness with a species of animal. Whenever that person encounters an animal of that species, the elemental that has been created will enter the creature and control its behavior to make the animal friendly. The biblical story of Daniel in the lions' den illustrates this ability. The forms that elementals usually display to the person who created them can be dependent on the society in which they were created. For instance, Atteshlis maintained, "Elementals of hate and jealousy look like snakes because in our culture we have this association" (1990, 39).

According to Atteshlis, "The power and form of elementals will not be dissolved until they have accomplished the task for which they have been built" (1990, 39). Sooner or later, elementals return to the person who created them. Once they have been created, it is best not to directly fight them but to ignore them or appear indifferent to them. Running away from them is not the same as ignoring them. People often fall prey to the elementals they themselves create. These elementals return to the person who created them and absorb energy from that person. They often return when least desired. Elementals are frequently responsible for habits and obsessions such as smoking, gambling, and drinking. An elemental can become so strong in a person that it leads him to become mentally unstable. Elementals bring about problems arising from egotism, such as anger, ostentation, hatred, victimization, and pride.

Atteshlis also describes the case of a demon, invoked by a black sorcerer, affecting people. The sorcerer made a mannequin of a demon and placed it in a bottle. A demon-elemental was induced into the mannequin bottle and was then placed near the people the sorcerer had been paid to injure. The victims began bleeding, but Atteshlis said he cut the connection between the demon and the victims. He characterizes these demons as emanations of Lucifer. The complete details of Atteshlis's explanation of the function of demons will not be recounted, but he did say that they acquire the shape of human beings because they adapt themselves to whatever they see.

7. Mental Illnesses

In his second book, Markides (1987) further examines Atteshlis's explanation of mental illness and some of his cures. The most frequently mentioned illnesses are those in the schizophrenia spectrum, and the most-mentioned symptoms are delusions and hearing voices. The undesired voices and optical illusions result from the psychic and noetic worlds directly affecting the acoustic or optical nerve. Markides notes that most of Atteshlis's work involved mental symptoms and that his cure rate would be the envy of many psychiatrists.

Atteshlis attributes most mental and psychological problems to the elementals that the victim herself creates. Victims experience periods of lucidity, as the elementals are not always present. As Markides writes, "Madness is the inability of the material brain and the solar plexus to express the inner condition of the psychonoetic body" (1987, 25). When he uses the term *solar plexus*, this probably means that the chakra in that area is a major factor in mental illnesses.

Markides asked Atteshlis about the two kinds of voices heard by schizophrenics—the evil kind and the benign/therapeutic type. Atteshlis states that the evil voices are the elementals whereas the benign voices are angelic elementals/entities. He further maintains that mystics, through meditation, can enter the angelic elemental realm and be in full control of their own thoughts and actions.

One method Atteshlis used to cure schizophrenia was to create contrary elementals. For instance, one soldier had observed much bloodshed and was probably suffering from PTSD. Atteshlis said he created elementals of love, peace, and understanding for the soldier. One reason his trainees must improve their concentration is that it takes strong powers of visual imagery to project these benevolent elementals into the victims. For some cures, Atteshlis took an insane person out of the body and performed therapy on the psychic plane. He said he had many techniques and that each situation had to be evaluated for the best therapy method. In many cases, after seeing the patient once, he continued therapy at a distance.

Atteshlis essentially attributes all behavior to that of elementals, stating, "There is nothing within the experience of human beings without the existence of an analogous elemental" (1987, 31). However, he comments that insanity can result from a biological defect or injury (i.e., trauma) to the brain. Nevertheless, the majority of cases of schizophrenia are the result of evil elementals, with demons and departed humans as secondary causes. He reiterates that a person cannot be under the influence of a wicked spirit unless the person vibrates on the same plane. Also among his ideas is that various types of possession can occur in conjunction.

Atteshlis explains that a personality, and actions taken by any person, are based on the elementals present. In one case, a young man had many difficult-to-handle elementals. Although Atteshlis warned his parents that simply removing (dissolving) the elementals could cause problems, the parents insisted that he do it. The young man afterward had no ambition to do even the simplest tasks. The symptoms sounded similar to those in cases in which a frontal lobotomy done on criminals resulted in the complete loss of willpower. Atteshlis also warned that psychoanalysis in which memories are only brought to the surface could be destructive unless those memories were replaced with positive elementals.

8. Physical Healings

Atteshlis also performed physical healings, one of which I will describe here. It involves a woman with paralysis due to moving vertebrae in her back. Atteshlis said that to cure her, he would have to make the bones soft and malleable in order to reset them. After performing the softening procedure, he asked two other women present to feel the bone. They said it felt like a sponge. The bones were hardened after he reset them. The procedure took about 20 minutes. Afterward, the patient got out of bed, bent over, and felt no pain. Atteshlis told her to avoid some particular foods and to take a vitamin supplement. It happened that she had an appointment with her doctor later that day. The radiologist commented that there was a marked difference in her x-rays from those taken a week before. Markides has the x-rays. He also asked the woman what the treatment felt like. She said it felt like an electric current was running through her back when Atteshlis was working on her.

9. Other Spiritual Abilities

In addition to healing, Atteshlis displayed a variety of other spiritual abilities. Based on his discussions with Markides, these include out-of-body travel, dematerialization and rematerialization of objects, transmutation of metals, knowledge of the material in a book by "feeling" it, bilocation, being consciously in seven places at the same time, and controlling weather. He could also induce in himself a state of superconscious self-awareness. In a later chapter, I will discuss mystical experiences and how the above abilities are often typical of mystics.

Atteshlis was opposed to fortune-telling. He felt that those who told the future could see accurately only three days in advance. The arrangement of elementals determines the future, according to Atteshlis, and thus human thought could change the arrangement of elementals over periods longer than three days. Relatedly, Long (1948) believed that kahunas could rearrange the future. Perhaps they were dissolving old elementals and replacing them with new ones.

Atteshlis had a successor named Kostas, whom Atteshlis considered as qualified as himself to teach his concepts. Kostas provides some advice on spiritual development in Markides's third book (1991). For instance,

Kostas contends that a person doing out of body travel ("exomatosis") must leave elementals behind to protect the physical body. If not, a mental breakdown may result. A person using exomatosis must never do it out of curiosity or for personal reasons, but only to be of service to others.

Markides (1991) states that he and others felt a torrent of energy flood them when Kostas touched their heads. If Atteshlis had worked on healing for a while and seemed drained of energy, Kostas would breathe deeply and flood Atteshlis with etheric energy (i.e., mana). A meditation with a breathing technique for increasing energy is also described in Markides's book. In addition, Kostas claims that he lived for about a year with almost no food, as he could energize his etheric double directly from *light*. However, he gave up the practice of not eating when he realized he was having difficulty staying in his body (i.e., experiencing involuntary exomatosis).

Atteshlis and Kostas could also heal at a distance by viewing a photo of the person to be healed. They could determine if, perhaps, the person was already deceased. While looking at one photo, Markides noticed that Kostas breathed deeply in order to create elementals. These elementals assist in the healing, and remain with the person in future photos. Atteshlis once knew he had already assisted in healing (in person) a man when he saw a photo of the man 25 years later. Only Atteshlis or Kostas, or others with their abilities, can see these elementals. In addition, one of Atteshlis's hobbies was creating paintings into which he claimed he could imbed elementals.

From his conversations with Atteshlis and observations of his technique, Markides learned that the key to self-healing is undistracted and focused concentration combined with a powerful desire for healing. Many of Atteshlis's recommendations for healing include the use of herbs or other, unusual foods. His explanation for using them is that everything consists of vibrations and that disease is a vibration that can often be corrected by a countervibration.

10. Relating These Concepts to Other Therapists

Many of the cases that I will now present appear to be based on intrusion by the spirits of deceased humans. While confirming that this can happen, Atteshlis attributes more of these symptoms to elementals than to deceased human spirits. In the next section, I will review the work of a university professor who studied the concept of possession throughout history. Both Atteshlis's and this professor's concepts are based on a spiritual concept of humans, certainly much different from the materialistic concept that behavior is genetically or chemically based. It could be a combination of elementals and spirits. For instance, a person who consumes too much alcohol may have elementals first influence his or her behavior but then have a spirit enter when it is attracted to the vibrations of the elementals present in that person.

C. The Possession Historian

1. Introduction

The best collection of possession cases prior to 1921 was assembled into a book by German professor T. K. Oesterreich (1880–1949). Because his wife was Jewish, he was forced from his professorship when the Nazis took control. He scoured extensive literature on the phenomenon of possession, ranging from comments by his contemporaries to history books and reports by anthropologists. Oesterreich's book, *Possession: Demoniacal and Other* (1966, English translation), is considered a classic in the field. In this section, I use Oesterreich's term *possession*. In most other parts to follow, I have used the term *spirit intrusion*. Although extensive, the incidents I review from the book are only a small fraction of the total collection he presents.

2. Classification System

Oesterreich developed a classification system to organize his book. His two major categories of possession are *somnambulistic* and *lucid*. Somnambulistic possession infers that the possessed person does not have a recollection of the events during the possession period, whereas a person lucidly possessed can remember what occurred. In lucid possession, the patient does not lose consciousness. Roughly, somnambulistic possession may correspond to dissociative multiple personalities, whereas lucid possession corresponds to intrusion. Ross (1997) holds that lucid possession is similar to DID without amnesia and that somnambulistic possession is similar to DID with amnesia between alters.

Other divisions by Oesterreich include artificial and voluntary possession. An example of voluntary possession is a shaman in a trance state during a ceremony. He also grouped cases by those occurring in more technically advanced civilizations and those occurring among indigenous societies. In addition, he distinguished between cases in which the possessor exhibited the characteristics of another human, a demon, an animal, or a "god" with certain powers, such as insight into the future.

3. Early Christian Era

Oesterreich's text begins with several biblical quotes referencing possession. He establishes the historical continuity of the possession phenomenon by noting similarities in phenomena between his findings and other writers of the biblical period. Some of these writers were not Christian. For instance, Oesterreich quotes a second-century writer named Lucian. Lucian discussed a contemporary "famous Syrian from Palestine" who freed people from infirmities such as foaming at the mouth. The Syrian charged high fees for his services.

Another case, this one from the third century, involves a woman who visited some wise men (sages) because her 16-year-old son could not work or learn because he was possessed by a demon. As the mother described, "The eyes with which he looks forth are not his eyes" (p. 6). The mother further stated that the demon revealed "that he is the spirit of a man killed in war who died loving his wife" (p. 6). When the wife of the dead man remarried three days later, it angered him. He expressed his anger through the behavior of the 16-year-old child. One sage gave the woman a letter containing threats that she was to read to the demon. No results were reported.

Oesterreich also includes a Christian writer of the fourth century, Zeno of Verona (300–ca. 371), who states, "For the impure spirits of both sexes which prowl hither and thither, make their way by deceitful flatteries or by violence into the bodies of living men and make their habitation there: they seek refuge there while holding them in a bondage of corruption" (p. 7).

Zeno proceeds to claim that to exorcise a spirit of this type could bring physical distortion to the face and body of the victim. During the exorcism, the spirit reported when it first entered the victim and gave his or her name when living, also providing other verifiable facts about its own life. However, there is no indication that Zeno attempted to verify these "facts." Justin Martyr (100–165), a writer and saint of the second century, specifically comments that people allegedly possessed by demons are actually possessed by "the souls of the dead." Martyr relates these to the term *demon* when he writes about "those who are seized and cast about by the spirits of the dead, whom all call demoniacs or madmen" (p. 330).

Gregory the Great (540–604) reported on multiple possessions in a girl who initially went to witches and sorcerers to remove a spirit. The original devil departed, but many others entered her. She was subject to fits, so her parents took her to a bishop who, after days of prayer, healed her.

Some of the early church recommendations may, on the surface, seem to contradict the findings of the soon-to-be-discussed Christian psychiatrist Kenneth McAll, whose healing method is described later in this chapter. For instance, an early church father stated that the Host (Eucharist) should not be given to a possessed person. However, another early Christian recommended Communion every day. Based on extensive familiarity with the subject, I would recommend that the Eucharist not be given to a victim when the possessing spirit is actively in control and the victim is acting irrationally.

Origen (ca. 185–ca. 254), a well-known early church father, thought that exorcists were generally uneducated people. He also stated that demons should not be questioned or spoken to. Instead, "The force of exorcism lies in the name of Jesus" (p. 167). However, even many early Christians believed that the power from the name of Jesus resulted from the name itself and not from the man named Jesus. Origen also commented that when incantations are used, they may only be effective in their "proper" language. When translated into another tongue, they are often not effective.

4. Oesterreich's Interpretation

Oesterreich's interpretation of the cause of possession is unclear. Perhaps he only intended to collect information, not to explain it. He refers to the concept of spirits as "an old theory," seeming to reject it. However, he does not attempt to explain possession by discussing behavioral psychology, mentioning chemical theories of the brain, or deeming possession to be total fraud. In some cases he suspects fraud, though he suggests it may not have been deliberate. For instance, Oesterreich states that the life history reported by the purported possessing spirit is "a matter of pure imagination or reminiscences" (p. 31). He notes that a first personality is seemingly replaced by a second, but this second personality is simply a complex state of the original personality. The second personality is merely a deceptive appearance. If the original personality treats the alleged demon as a real living person, the demon will behave accordingly. Later, however, Oesterreich maintains, "Such a conception of fraud on the part of the possessed must be regarded as an absurd hypothesis when the cases are considered as a whole and it is observed how the patients suffer from their state. ... No one will ever pretend, however, that this latter [fit] is simulated, for the bodily strength displayed by the possessed during the fits is so great" (p. 64). Oesterreich also comments that in educated civilizations, cases of possession disappear or retreat into the shadows. I suspect that possession does not so much disappear but that it is given new nomenclature, namely *mental illness*.

Possession and spirits are interrelated. Oesterreich maintains that when belief in spirits is not taken seriously, the necessary autosuggestion is lacking. In other words, a person acts possessed when he convinces himself he is possessed. Similarly, he cures himself when told he is cured. From my knowledge of DID as discussed in chapter 6, the concept of iatrogenic, or the result of therapist suggestion, causes must also be considered.

Oesterreich routinely employs the term *soul* to indicate something occupying the physical body. He further comments that the present-day standard that says that humans consist solely of a material form and that there are no souls or spirits that penetrate the physical body is completely new by the standards of history. My objective is to refute that materialistic concept.

5. Features of a Possessed Person

When a purported possessing spirit takes active control, a new physiognomy is observed. In one case, a woman who was purportedly possessed by a man she had known did not desire to be seen by people who had known the man because they would recognize his features in the possessed woman. Such changes may include a deep male voice from a woman or young girl. The victim may have hideous outbursts of laughter, make sounds like a savage animal, use vulgar language, display violent behavior, or frequently mock religious practices or symbols. The spirit may speak of the person it has invaded in the third person and make its opinion the exact opposite of the victim's. In one case, a woman was compelled by an alleged demon to beat her beloved child. A possessed man may beat his wife or children. Some physical motions can be involuntary when the spirit appears to control the body directly. This control can defy normal physical concepts, such as two grown men being unable to control a young girl. However, Oesterreich notes that violent activity is less likely "when the patient believes himself possessed not by a demon but by the soul of a deceased person" (p. 25). In advanced cases, the patient's will is powerless to prevent extreme distortions of the body. In this sense, possession is often viewed as a contest of two wills.

In describing somnambulistic possession, in which the victim has lost consciousness and is amnesic for the period of possession, Oesterreich cites alleged multiple possession, such as a case in which a young woman could speak as either two men or an old woman. This case could easily be one of DID. Oesterreich observes that in somnambulistic possession the transition is rather abrupt, not gradual. There is usually a physical signal of transition, such as closing the eyes. This is similar to switching to an alter in DID. Upon regaining normal consciousness and being informed of what happened, the person often regrets the words or action.

The factor of substance abuse appears in some of Oesterreich's examples. Oesterreich also relates a case from the early nineteenth century in which two alleged demons in a peasant woman barked like dogs or meowed like cats.

6. Occult Practices, and Possession by the Living

Oesterreich also describes the writings of Ludwig Staudenmaier (published in 1912) in which Staudenmaier discusses experiments with his own automatic writing. As a result of these experiments, he developed a number of obsessive personalities. Eventually these personalities spoke, rather than wrote, to Staudenmaier. The voices were evil in character and would often fabricate information or claim to be a famous person. The exception to this was one personality that appeared to be that of a child whom Staudenmaier claimed had helped him to develop a better understanding of artistic values.

Oesterreich reports that while some people believe in possession by the living, he was able to find only two such cases. In both cases the possessed person was a woman who knew the man who allegedly possessed her. In one case the description was too brief to determine the nature of the relationship, but in the other the relationship was different from those reported by Adam Crabtree (1985) or Kenneth McAll (1982), to be discussed shortly. In those cases the alleged possessing person appeared to "force" itself into the lives of the victim. In the case reported by Oesterreich, a woman had an affair with a man who was rather passive about it and ended the acquaintance. She, however, held conversations with his spirit, claimed to observe his actions, knew his thoughts, and wrote messages received from him; she used automatic writing to write the messages received.

7. Spirit Carryover and in Between

Oesterreich frequently references an 1836 book titled *Nachricht von dem Vorkommendes des Besessenseins* by Justinus Kerner (1786-1862). Oesterreich quotes Kerner, who wrote, "A spirit may dwell within a spirit" (p. 47). In my opinion, that may not be completely correct. Two spirits may occupy (cohabit) the same physical body, but one does not dwell within the other. However, it is possible that if spirit A is possessing person B, and B dies, his spirit may intrude upon person C and bring spirit A along. Some therapists' work that I review later in this chapter refers to this as *nesting*. Oesterreich quotes one writer who discusses a related case in the seventeenth century in Loudun. In this situation, mass possession occurred among nuns at a convent: "The two spirits fight in one and the same field which is the body, and the soul is as if divided" (p. 51). Aldous Huxley (1894–1963) had an interest in spiritual matters and wrote a book about this possession case entitled *The Devils of Loudun*.

One thesis of my book is that spirits of the deceased can enter a living person. The spirit of a person may vacillate between entering another person and entering the underworld. In one case cited by Oesterreich, the demon, speaking through its victim, stated that when he died he was attracted to Satan because he had not resisted Satan when living. Another spirit stated that he was not damned for any crime but that he chose the underworld. In addition, this spirit stated that he had many dwellings, and in fact he would leave one victim temporarily to torment others. This spirit claimed to enter through the host's feet.

Oesterreich reports that during his research, he found a number of instances where several spirits described the world they "lived" in when not cohabiting another person. For example,

> He gave with a shudder of fear particulars of the place in hell where he had been. "Everything which is here esteemed beautiful, lovable, and agreeable, becomes down there hateful, nauseating, and shapeless. The devil forces one to continual copulation with the women with whom one has had one's way on earth. There is a stench, filth, and loathsomeness which can hardly be borne." (p. 62)

This is similar to some distressing NDEs and to descriptions a therapist discussed later encountered.

8. Possession/Obsession in Modern Times

To Oesterreich, the term *possession* implies that the person feels divided. The term *obsession* implies states in which the person has incorrect beliefs or compulsions. The contemporary mental disorder names for some of these obsessions, with Oesterreich's example in parentheses, are as follows: schizophrenia (delusions), somatization disorder (hypochondria), obsessive-compulsive disorder (feeling contaminated), and tic disorder (using blasphemy). According to Oesterreich, obsessions are frequently encountered in the lives of saints, mystics, and the deeply religious. The obsessive phenomena are usually encountered early in life, and these people become holy by resisting the evil inclinations of the possessing spirit. Oesterreich recognizes the connection between possession and obsession when he contends, "Possession does not denote a lesser but rather a deeper disturbance of the mind than does obsession" (p. 83).

Oesterreich also reviews some of the causes of possession and methods for elimination of invading spirits. He notes that simply being around possessed people makes possession more likely to occur. For example, priests who conduct exorcisms often fall victim to the phenomenon themselves.

9. Spirit Entrance

Oesterreich cites two occasions when entrance of a spirit occurs. The first is, of course, the first time the spirit enters. In one example, this first entrance occurred in a child after a bout of typhus. Other therapists have found that an illness may weaken the natural barriers to these spirits. The second type is reentrance, in which the spirit may temporarily depart the body or simply remain attached without any influence. When it reenters, the victim may or may not realize it. In one case, a "black spirit or black monk" who tormented a girl could be seen and even conversed with her when outside her body. But then, approaching from her left side, and feeling like a cold hand, he seized the back of the girl's neck and entered her body. The victim then lost consciousness.

10. Exorcisms and the Placebo Effect

Whereas Malachi Martin (1976) states that exorcisms often take place in the home, Oesterreich maintains that they should occur in a church or some other place consecrated to God. Oesterreich does agree with Martin in that the exorcist must always address the possessing spirit, not the person possessed. Martin will be discussed later in this chapter.

Oesterreich recounts some exorcisms done by non-Christians. In Japan, a spirit claiming to be a fox could not be enticed to leave a girl by threats or inducements. However, it consented to depart if a feast was prepared for it at a certain hour and was placed in a temple sacred to foxes. The exorcist prepared a meal of the favorite foods of magic foxes, including mice. At the specified hour, the possessed girl claimed that the fox had left. In another case in Japan the spirit departed when threatened.

11. Gender Issues

Oesterreich comments that he finds possession much more common in women than in men, and almost all cases he reviewed occurred among less educated people of lower socioeconomic status. Oesterreich never attributes child abuse, especially of a sexual nature, as a cause of possession, but this may explain why the balance is skewed toward women, as girls are more likely to be abused. Oesterreich quotes an Italian writer who described a condition he observed among a group of people in northern Russia. The condition occurs almost exclusively in married women, often beginning on their wedding day, and continuing for many years. Symptoms include fits, convulsions, contortions, a feeling of oppression or rats running over the body, and the use of abusive language or obscene expressions. "Sometimes the woman falls into an ecstasy or begins to predict the future, speaking the name of the demon who has taken possession of her" (p. 204).

12. Indigenous Societies

Oesterreich believed that indigenous people are more suggestible than modern, civilized people and that the possessed state is often caused by a physical malady. Common phenomena during spontaneous possession are "fits" and uncontrollable shaking. In this state, the voice changes and the victim does not recognize former friends. In one case cited, the victim seemed frightened of a missionary, a friend he normally trusted.

One method of exorcism described by an ethnologist, Leo Frobenius (1873–1938), includes the following: a man possessed by "a black spirit" was taken to a priest and priestess (of a native religion), who worked in conjunction with a guitar or violin player. The musician played notes that reproduced the names of the black spirit. In this case, the music continued day and night for a week. The victim was rubbed with medicine, and the spirit eventually departed. Frobenius thought the victim had been in an epileptic state, but Oesterreich disagrees and believes the state was brought about by way of suggestion. Following the departure of the black spirit, a joyous ceremony was held. During a dance of joy as part of this ceremony, possession by desirable "white spirits" frequently occurs. These white spirits are described as prophetic.

During an exorcism in Africa, which involved singing and dancing, an interview with an alleged spirit yielded some interesting information. One spirit reportedly was a bard who had wandered through the territory several decades prior to the time of the exorcism. At that time, the possessed woman was a young girl and had known the bard. The date of the bard's death was not specified, but this information apparently demonstrates that a person's spirit may travel a considerable distance after death.

Oesterreich includes a report from central Africa concerning a man who murdered several people. The murderer felt he had been changed into a lion. The murder was committed when he leapt from the tall grass beside a road onto his victim. Some early Christian writers commented on alleged possession by animals, as displayed by their characteristic sounds; animals noted were wolves, dogs, lions, serpents, and bulls.

Oesterreich also discusses voluntary possession among indigenous peoples. To many indigenous people, the possessed person is an intermediary between the physical and spirit worlds. Oesterreich concurs with the observation others have made that the psyche of indigenous people seems less firmly seated than the psyche of Westerners. Therefore, indigenous people may be more subject to autosuggestion. For example, a young tribal chief in the Tongan islands first felt inspired and then low-spirited. He went to a shaman, who said a woman who had died two years earlier wanted the chief to join her. He died two days later as a result of the suggestion that he was wanted in the world of the deceased. Another example appears similar to the death prayer of the kahunas discussed in chapter 2; this example is from the Australian aborigines: "If a savage believes himself struck from afar, he lies down and slowly dies in consequence of the psychic affection. There is only one remedy, that is, the counteracting of the influence by another wizard of the same kind" (p. 239). Later, the same author states, "Not only the living but also the spirits of the dead may exert influence to cause death from a distance" (p. 239). In chapter 9, I discussed taboos. Indigenous people often are fearful if they believe they have violated a taboo. The fear may induce illness or even death.

In central Africa, in the religion of the Bori, voluntary possession is generally induced with a musical instrument. During the ceremony, the spirit may enter any member of the community. The one chosen often begins to prophesy. The spirit evoked, called Alledjenu, is not identified as that of a deceased person. However, a similar ceremony by a different tribe and described by a different writer does not discuss prophesying but relates the following phenomena in the possessed person: hysteria, grunts or squeals, convulsive movements, and catatonia. The Bori concepts were forbidden by Islamic rulers at the time, but they persisted nevertheless.

The Melanesians distinguish between diseases of the mind, such as delirium and possession. In many aboriginal societies, all disturbed mental states are believed to be the result of spirits. Knowledge of the future is brought from a spirit. When this spirit takes control, the whole body may convulse. Oesterreich quotes one writer who states that madness from possession is not distinguished from prophecy. In one group of Melanesian islands, people distinguish between possession with a particular purpose and the mischief of wandering ghosts. Melanesians wait five days after a person's death before attempting to call upon the deceased's spirit.

In New Guinea, people consult the dead for answers about various cures. The family member chosen as medium is placed in a trance, usually with incense fumes. An image of the deceased person is placed near the medium on the presumption that the soul of the deceased can then pass from the image to the medium. If the results are disappointing, the image is discarded, because it is assumed the soul did not attach itself to the image.

Oesterreich also reviews various phenomena from north Asiatic peoples, including some Scandinavians. Their practices are similar to other indigenous societies. Early Western travelers to these places seemed determined to expose all shamans as impostors; however, many later investigators found a "psychological genuineness" about shamanistic states. Still, some charlatanism may be a natural aspect of the phenomenon. The shaman himself believes in the phenomenon and is not trying to trick anyone. The more archaic the tribe, the less theatrical the shaman appears. One example of a shaman's sincerity is that he may state that he has not received an answer from the spirits to their question when it would be easy to fabricate one.

13. Earlier Civilizations

In ancient Babylon, most exorcisms involved people with ordinary sicknesses, not mental symptoms. In ancient Egypt, possession was sometimes by a "god"; the possession state commenced during a dream and resulted in ecstasy, during which the person might prophesy. This book will demonstrate that possession by a god is actually communication with the Spirit aspect of that same human.

Oesterreich also delves into artificial and voluntary possession in earlier civilizations. Two time periods are discussed: the Greco-Roman period and Oesterreich's own period, the 1920s. Grecian beliefs in possession by so-called higher spirits have been briefly discussed. Oesterreich reviews information on various mystery schools such as Delphi and the Pythoness, noting that Homer did not mention prophetic abilities. Oesterreich deduced that the concept must have been introduced later.

In the Pythoness school, the prophetic priestess had to remain a virgin. The Pythoness drank from a certain spring, sat above a cleft in a rock, and breathed the vapors rising from the water. This threw her into an ecstasy. Priestesses in other rites were known to have drunk ecstasy-inducing spring water. The inspired priestess could foretell the future or give counsel. Often interpreters would frame a question based on discussions with an inquirer and then interpret the reply from the priestess. The early Greeks believed that a god, usually Apollo, entered the priestess's body or soul. When the priestess said "I," she was speaking for Apollo. Later, Greeks were skeptical of that explanation. Modern researchers have found no cleft in the earth at the temple of Apollo or any ecstasy-inducing springs. Oesterreich reasoned that her state may simply have been autosuggestion. Oracles such as these priestesses were held in high regard by Plato.

Although their influence waned, the Greek oracles remained until the fourth century, existing nearly a millennium in total. Christians often believed the oracles to be inspired by demons. Origen commented, "It is not the part of a divine spirit to drive the prophetess into such a state of ecstasy and madness that she loses control of herself" (p. 329). However, Christians did not perform exorcisms on these inspired people.

The Greeks interpreted the term *possession* in wider terms than did others. To the Greeks, possession included inspiration, especially of the poetic type. Once Plato had Socrates state that inspired people are "possessed by a spirit not their own;" he also said they compose "from the impulse of the divinity within them" (p. 347).

With regard to ancient Greek civilization, Oesterreich states the following:

> The historically obscure centuries between the Homeric and classical periods seem to have been filled to an extraordinary degree with belief in the invasion of the real, and even of the human soul, by the transcendental. ... Belief in the immanence of the divine occupied a far more prominent place than the corresponding belief in the diabolic. In the mysteries, oracles, and also the Dionysiac cult it was everywhere the divine, and not the diabolic which broke the outer husk of this world and streamed into the soul of man. Any attempt to characterize the religious spirit of Hellenism must needs represent this divine inspiration as one of its lofty and specific aspects. (p. 156)

I also discuss this concept of the divine within in a review of the word *genius* in chapter 12, showing how this term has changed over the centuries, beginning with the ancient Greeks.

14. Middle Ages

Demons and possession cases, or *energumens*, were common during the Middle Ages. At that time, the ability to remove evil spirits was frequently mentioned in the lives of the saints. In one case, the evil spirit stated she was the spirit of a woman who had led an evil life and had died twenty years earlier. Oesterreich comments that in the Middle Ages the spirit was more commonly a demon or devil, but in more modern times the victim is usually possessed by the spirits of the dead.

The Jewish medieval Kabbalah tradition provides an example in which the spirit stated he was the soul of a drunken Jew who had died impenitent. The soul wandered for a long time before entering a woman while she was in the act of blasphemy. The woman was symptomatic of epilepsy/hysteria. The Jewish exorcist reprimanded the spirit and commanded it to leave, which it did, protesting. Oesterreich also provides the following case from a Jewish ghetto in Poland. The victim was named Esther, but the spirit (dybbuk) was a great Talmudic scholar who had become a heretic. The rabbi, who was known for miraculous cures, commanded the dybbuk to answer his questions. The voice coming from Esther was male. According to Oesterreich, the dybbuk related the following:

> After death he had been cast out of hell with insults and opprobrium. He wandered for a long time, but could no longer remain without habitation and finally entered a pig. (After the pig was slaughtered he lived in a draft horse.) ... At length he decided to try man. The occasion was propitious. He knew that Esther had illicit relations with a young man, and watched the moment when she abandoned herself to his embraces; at that instant he was permitted to enter into her. He ended his narrative by begging not to be driven out; in life and after death he had suffered so greatly that they should have pity on him and grant him a rest. This prayer appeared to make no impression on the rabbi. (p. 209)

During the exorcism Esther struck the rabbi, who struck back. A sound was heard at a nearby window. There was a hole in the window the size of a pea, apparently through which the dybbuk escaped. Dybbuks are discussed later in this chapter.

According to Oesterreich, Martin Luther regarded all mental illness as the result of possession, and suicide as the common consequence of possession. Luther relied more on prayer than on ceremonial exorcism.

15. Modern Church Views (to 1920)

Oesterreich describes three spheres of thought in which belief in possession still existed in 1920—many Catholics, conservative Protestants, and Spiritualists. Generally, convictions about demons and spirits of the dead are declining. My book may reverse that decline.

Even today, the Catholic Church conducts exorcisms. The church believes in consecrating various objects, such as a crucifix. Oesterreich cites writer Aug. Stohr, who stated that people who claim to be possessed may react with rage at the sight of a crucifix. In his opinion, in a case of actual possession, a person would only react to a consecrated crucifix. Stohr also claims that demons should be able to detect a hidden object. Martin (1976) cites the case of a possessed woman who reacted to a crucifix placed under her bed without her knowledge. However, the crucifix was placed under the bed by the possessed woman's brother. The brother had been concealing the crucifix while speaking to her. She did not detect it at that time.

The second sphere where the belief in possession persists is conservative Protestantism, though Oesterreich does not discuss it. Today, Don Basham, whose work on Christian deliverance will be reviewed shortly, would probably be considered a member of this group. The third sphere where this belief persists is spiritualism. Some fields of parapsychology and the New Age would be considered successors to spiritualist concepts.

16. The Middle East and Asia

Several cases from Syria and Palestine cast light on the part of the body through which the spirit departs. Don Basham states that the throat is usually the avenue of departure. In one case cited by Oesterreich, a spirit in a young girl subject to epileptic fits was commanded by a holy man to depart. The spirit suggested that it would leave by the head or eye, but the holy man forbade it. The spirit then suggested leaving by her toe, and the holy man accepted. However, when the holy man struck the girl on the shoulder and left a wound, the spirit departed through the wound.

In India, there are many classes of demons and "gods of madness." The type of intruder is determined by appearances, the behavior of the possessed person, including appearances, desires, and memory of the possessed person. There are legends of possessed people who were healed by the Buddha's mother while she was pregnant with him.

In Ceylon (now Sri Lanka), spirits respond to threats. If a verbal threat by the *capua* (exorcist) is not effective, the capua may strike the victim many times with a bamboo pole, after which the spirit typically departs. In Thailand (formerly Siam, in Southeast Asia), ordinary doctors may perform exorcisms, striking the body with a rod. Symptoms of a person who has spirit intruders may include giddiness, vomiting, sobbing, groaning, and muteness.

In China, people often believe in concepts similar to spiritualism. Although possession may occur, Chinese people often believe they can contact deceased relatives or "gods" through a medium. At times, their beliefs amount to ancestor worship. Cases reported by Oesterreich often come from missionaries. In one case, a man felt influenced by a spirit that claimed to be divine and demanded to be adored. The victim's symptoms were epileptic attacks, mania, and homicidal impulses.

Oesterreich comments that there is so much information available on the possession phenomenon in Japan that it is difficult to collect it. There is even a religious sect that specializes in exorcism. In one case Oesterreich did describe possession by a *tengu* spirit. The person possessed "becomes preternaturally learned or solemn, reading, writing, or fencing with a skill that would not be expected from him" (p. 228). Oesterreich compares this to a Greek claiming to be inspired by Apollo or a Muse. Although China, Japan, and Korea have always had more dense populations than Western countries, rarely do those countries experience epidemics of possession. Oesterreich also notes that ecstasy, as part of Eastern religions, is practically nonexistent in China, Japan, and Korea.

17. Conclusions of Oesterreich's Study

Overall, Oesterreich's results are inconclusive. He agrees that the denial of the soul is very new and that the possession phenomenon is not fraud, but the fact that it seems to die out in modern civilizations indicates to Oesterreich that the alleged cases do not consist of real possession by a rogue spirit. While he thought the concept of possession was dying out, in my opinion it was rather that in his time people who exhibited signs of possession were institutionalized, away from observation.

Although Atteshlis did perform some therapy, I presented him mainly for his overall theories of the spiritual nature of humans. Oesterreich was presented for historical background. In the next section, I begin with a therapist who developed a method for removing spirit intruders by conversing with the spirit and persuading it to depart. She also has some major input into how clients become vulnerable to earthbound spirit intruders and why the spirits became earthbound instead to entering the *light* to which NDErs proceed.

D. New Age Healer

1. Introduction

In this section, I discuss the therapy method of Edith Fiore, PhD, author of *The Unquiet Dead* (1987). I titled this section "New Age Healer" because Fiore's practice is in California and her other writings and prevention methods for spirit possession appear similar to New Age techniques. Her training is in conventional behavioral psychology. Fiore believes that most people in mental institutions are possessed by earthbound spirits and that the personalities in DID patients are also earthbound spirits.

2. The Reason Why Spirits Remain Earthbound

Fiore describes her patients as possessed by deceased entities called *earthbound spirits*. Fiore believes there are five basic reasons for spirits to remain earthbound or to fail to complete the transition to the afterlife. The reasons are as follows:

- Ignorance, confusion, or fear (especially of going to hell)
- Obsessive attachment to living people or places
- Addiction to drugs, alcohol, smoking, food, or sex
- A sense of unfinished business
- A desire for revenge

These reasons are exacerbated if the person dies suddenly. For instance, people who commit suicide remain earthbound more than others. The spirit of the person who commits suicide is just as depressed as before death and can carry this emotional state into its victim. According to Fiore, after death, discarnate spirits "have all their previous attitudes, prejudices, addictions, skills, interests, fears and hang-ups" (p. 37), and these become manifest in the person to whom the spirit becomes attached.

3. Reasons Why People Are Susceptible to Intrusion

Entry by a spirit can occur as the result of an accident, a blow to the head, or any condition that results in unconsciousness, leaving the aura vulnerable to entry. Children are more susceptible to intrusion than adults because their spirit body is more loosely connected to their physical body. Fiore's list of reasons why spirits remain earthbound and her reasons for why people are susceptible to spirit intrusion are supported by many of the therapy methods that will be discussed henceforth.

It is important to understand the time and circumstances that were present when the earthbound spirits enter a person. Though Fiore did not quantify her study, I suspect the most serious factor leaving one open to spirit intrusion is substance abuse. Some of the circumstances that cause intrusion may be unavoidable, but before intrusion every person can choose to partake of some substances and completely avoid others. Fiore said she has had clients who picked up the earthbound spirit of a deceased alcoholic after drinking as few as two glasses of wine or on the first time they became drunk. That statement reminded me of William Wilson, a cofounder of Alcoholics Anonymous. He came from a nondrinking family but claimed that he became an alcoholic the first time he took a drink as an adult. Perhaps a spirit had entered him previously under other circumstances. Usually, though, a substance-seeking entity will only enter a person who already consumes that substance. It is possible that almost any addiction (even to legitimate drugs) is caused by an intruding entity. Some fortunate individuals may get drunk many times before picking up an earthbound spirit, but cocaine and some hallucinogenic drugs probably invite an intruding entity the first time the substance is used, because the substance fragments the person's spirit body to a greater extent. After a person has been cohabited by an intruding entity that desires a particular substance, the host person gradually loses his freedom of choice. Substance-abuse entities are often reluctant to leave. Fiore once treated a woman who had eighteen alcoholic spirits in her, even though she had not drunk alcohol for four years. These entities often take more sessions with the therapist than do more benign entities.

Other sources for spirit entry include the Ouija board, automatic writing, tarot cards, and attending séances. Fiore classifies some of these as willing possession because when using a Ouija board, the user asks a spirit to give him an answer.

4. Therapy Method and Symptoms of Intrusion

Fiore's primary therapy method involves various steps. First, she and the patient discuss the patient's symptoms to determine if the cause is actually intrusion. She states that about 70% of the people who come to her are possessed, but this high number may be due to referrals of difficult cases by other psychologists. She has treated over five hundred people with her method and has also trained other therapists. Initially, Fiore engaged in long discussions with patients to assess the likelihood of intrusion, but she has since developed a set of questions she asks her patients. The following are indications of intrusion:

1. Persistent lowered energy level
2. Changes in personality or rapid mood swings, especially after substance abuse
3. Inner conversations or thoughts, especially if commands are used in a berating tone
4. Substance abuse, including overuse of recreational drugs and an inability to give them up despite strong effort
5. Extreme impulsiveness
6. Breaks in consciousness
7. Inability to concentrate; being "in a fog"
8. Anxiety or depression for no apparent reason
9. Sudden onset of physical problems without an obvious cause
10. Emotional or physical symptoms while reading Fiore's book, including heart pounding, sweating, difficulty breathing, trembling, or tingling. These symptoms are caused by the intruding spirit.

Fiore encourages her patients to see a doctor for their physical symptoms. In many cases, patients may have come from a doctor who told them their problems were psychosomatic. Fiore employs hypnosis and ideomotor signals, a common technique used by hypnotists to get a yes or no answer to questions. One finger is designated as the yes and another finger as the no answer to a question. When asked if there are any other entities occupying the same body, the answer may be yes, or both fingers (yes and no).

After determining that there is an intruding entity, Fiore attempts to converse with the entity, usually through hypnosis. At this point, she considers the intruding entity to be her true patient. If she can persuade the spirit to leave, and assuming there is only one, the client (or host person) who came in the door will return to normal. In conversing with the entity, Fiore attempts to discover something about its history and the time of entrance into her client. The likes and dislikes of the entity may be explored to determine if they correlate with the problems or activities of the client. Except in cases of substance abuse, the client, in a later discussion with Fiore, will often recognize either the possessing spirit or the circumstances of its initial entry. Some clients have had as many as 50 entities invade them. None of these are referred to by Fiore as demons.

The depossession technique used by Fiore is based on events similar to those that occur in an NDE. Fiore usually induces the entity to depart by having it survey its surroundings, searching for a deceased relative or the *light*. Normally, the patients report seeing deceased relatives or friends and agree to leave with them and go into the *light*. These close relatives are already in the realm of *light* and are not other earthbound spirits. If the entity sees the *light* only, Fiore tells the entity to go into it. If the person is a substance abuser, Fiore tells the patient he will get what is needed in the spirit world. She believes that spirit healers help taper off desire for these substances. Some spirits have returned to their host because they did not have a firm enough connection to the loved one leading them to the *light*. This can usually be corrected in another therapy session. If the relatives or the *light* technique above do not seem effective, Fiore receives help from specialists in the upper spirit world, similar to Atteshlis allegedly receiving advice from a spirit helper named Fr. Dominico or a DID therapist receiving advice from the therapist's own ISH.

5. Specific and General Cases

Fiore provides numerous examples and case studies in her book. In one case, a woman was not getting along with an employee at work. The problem had begun four years earlier after the woman sustained a serious injury. A male spirit entered her at that time. The conflict with the employee was actually between the intruding entity and the employee.

Within seconds of addressing any spirits that may have been with her, I [Fiore] noticed a distinct shift from a blissful expression to one of total agitation—a "violent" reaction. There was my evidence! Her crying was so strong that I almost discontinued the recording. However, I invited in the spirit's loved ones, as I routinely do, and witnessed the entity calming down. I continued and shortly observed the tension in her body abruptly release. I ended the depossession and brought her out of trance.

He didn't want to go, she reported, starting to cry softly. "I don't know why, but I feel sad."

"What else are you aware of?"

"I can feel a fluttering here." She pointed to her chest. "When he doesn't feel threatened, everything calms down."

"Could you tell me who it is?"

"A man. For some reason, I feel sure it's a man. I don't know who, though."

Since he probably had not left, I asked her to close her eyes again, and to monitor the reactions she felt as I talked specifically to that spirit. Tears streamed down her face as I pointed out how hard it was for a man to be trapped in a female body. Then I invited him to go with his loved one, perhaps his mother, to the spirit world where he would be in his own strong, healthy, male body. (pp. 58–59)

If clients report that only some of their problems are eliminated after a depossession session, Fiore may probe for additional entities. Quite frequently there is more than one intruder, especially if substance abuse is involved. The first intrusion weakens the aura and creates further vulnerability. A child who becomes possessed is likely to be multipossessed by the time of adulthood. Some entities just follow others. One client was cohabited by two sisters, the one following and trying to control the other. When the first spirit left, the second followed.

Fiore has found that every homosexual patient she has treated was conditioned to become homosexual by a domineering spirit of the opposite gender. Other problems corrected include paraphilias such as transsexualism and transvestism, diminished sex drive, PMS, memory and emotional problems, phobias, and all types of substance abuse. Several persons were relieved of obesity following depossession, but there are many other possible causes of obesity. Fiore says a rapid weight gain following surgery or a death in the family could be a sign of spirit influence. In one case a woman began to have a problem with her weight immediately after her hysterectomy. Again, depossession is no substitute for sound medical advice.

In one case, the intruding entity considered himself to be a friend, but the possessed person, who was overweight, returned to normal weight after the depossession. The spirit's motive of trying to be helpful does not prevent problems for the inhabited person. In another case, a compassionate surgeon, after "dying" in an accident, returned in spirit to his hospital and entered an infant who was still in the womb but about to be born prematurely.

Though some people do not object to a benevolent spirit's remaining, it is a mistake to keep a spirit earthbound and unable to advance to higher spiritual realms. It is important to lead a spirit to higher realms and not just command it to depart. If forced to depart, the spirit would still be earthbound and look for another person to enter and influence. Most spirits remain ten years or fewer before advancing to a higher realm or cohabiting another individual. However, one spirit is reported to have wandered about for 40 years.

6. Preventing Intrusion

The best way to prevent intrusion is to avoid the circumstances that have caused it to happen to others. Preventative measures include not using drugs or alcohol (to excess) and avoiding use of Ouija boards or automatic writing. It may be difficult to prevent illness and other means of entry, but Fiore describes a White-light technique she uses to help prevent attempted entries by earthbound spirits.

> Using your creative imagination, imagine that you have a miniature sun, just like the sun in our solar system, deep in your solar plexus. This sun is radiating through every atom and cell of your being. It fills you with light to the tips of your fingers, the top of your head, and the soles of your feet. It shines through you and beyond you an arm's length in every direction—above your head, below your feet, out to the sides, creating an aura—a brilliant, dazzling, radiant White Light that completely surrounds and protects you from any negativity or harm. (p. 141)

Although Fiore does not state it, she obviously does not intend the White-light technique to be used as an excuse for continuing actions that cause intrusion, for instance, using it prior to getting drunk. If the White-light technique sounds too unusual, Fiore says that reciting the Lord's Prayer and the Twenty-Third Psalm also provides good protection. Having a positive mental attitude toward life is also very helpful. At funerals she suggests that mourners mentally instruct the deceased to look for loved ones or to go to the *light*.

E. Spiritualism

1. Introduction

When most people think of spiritualism, they think of contact with the dead in a séance or through a medium. However, there is also a healing aspect to spiritualism, the premier early explanation of which is a book by Carl Wickland (1861–1945), MD, *Thirty Years Among the Dead* (1924). Wickland's cases fall into the category of unwilling possession by the dead. The reader has every right to be skeptical of Wickland's information. It is only because of its consistency with other therapists' theories that his information is included. Wickland himself warns against certain occult practices, of which spiritualism would be considered an example by some therapists.

Wickland's concept is very simple. When a person "dies," his spirit body leaves the physical body behind. Wickland uses the term *transition* because only the physical body dies. If the person knows the spiritual "facts of life" before death, he knows what to expect at the transition, when his spirit body advances to the higher spiritual world. If the person is unprepared, or does not look for his deceased relatives to guide him, then his spirit body becomes earthbound. The spirit body often does not realize it has lost its physical body and tries to go about life as normal.

2. Healing Method

Wickland's wife was allegedly a psychic sensitive, and her body could be taken over by spirits. If a person with an illness that Wickland suspected was caused by an earthbound spirit came to him for healing, he would administer an electric charge. The electric charge would dislodge the obsessing spirit, which would then enter Mrs. Wickland, who was in a trance state. Wickland would then converse with this obsessing spirit and try to convince it of the true nature of the spiritual world. He would also discuss how it could escape its earthbound situation. His primary term for a person inhabited by an earthbound spirit is *obsessed*.

If Wickland was successful, the spirit could advance, usually by following a deceased relative. If the obsessing spirit was too firmly grounded in its views from having lived on earth, it could not be convinced to advance on its own. Instead, it would be taken away (from Mrs. Wickland) by advanced spirits, to a place where it would be given a long education. If these obsessing spirits are not removed, they will remain until their destructive desires are outgrown or until advanced spirits intervene. If the host person dies, then the obsessing spirit is free to obsess another person.

Wickland worked for over 30 years before he wrote his book. He said that his wife was protected by a group of intelligent spirits known as the Mercy Band. One member was Silver Star, a deceased American Indian. Wickland says American Indians rarely become earthbound. Some members of the Mercy Band were formerly obsessing spirits that Wickland had freed earlier.

3. Reasons for Remaining Earthbound

Although some spirit persons Wickland encountered died a natural death, it is important to note that many obsessing spirits were of people who had died accidentally in the prime of their lives. They expected to be accomplishing something; after death, they simply continued to try to accomplish their former goals. Goals are part of the spirit body, and the spirit body does not realize the physical body is missing—it is still trying to accomplish the goals it had when it inhabited a physical body. When a person dies of illness or old age, he or she may have received a summons by a deceased relative prior to actual death (see the discussion of Osis and Haraldsson in chapter 7, on ELEs). In this case, the person is prepared for death and is welcomed to the higher spirit world with his or her relatives. In addition, an elderly person near death probably has fewer life goals. A majority of people feel joy at seeing their deceased parents, but this is not always true. If people believe they have not led good lives, they may be ashamed to see their parents and avoid going toward them. Some spirits are more concerned with remaining at a favorite location rather than achieving a goal.

4. NDE Phenomena in Wickland's Therapy

There is a strong similarity between Wickland's and Fiore's healing methods, though on the surface they may appear different. They both seek to complete the death experience for the obsessing spirit. Fiore uses hypnosis to contact the obsessing spirit and then has the obsessing spirit look around for a *light* or a loved one. Wickland employs only the deceased-loved-one aspect of the transcendental NDE. After Wickland suggested the patient look for a deceased relative, the patient frequently responded, "I see my mother" (or other people). One woman who had committed suicide looked around and saw a girl holding a baby. She had been pregnant when she committed suicide, and Wickland explained to her that the spirit of her baby was also liberated at the time of her death. The baby was being returned to her.

In several cases, the obsessing spirit could not move toward the recognized person. In many cases, the spirits had wandered for years, so the person who was seen or answered may have died after the now earthbound spirit has made its transition. Wickland would then tell the spirit to will itself to join the recognized person, and it would. It is interesting that the person seen by the earthbound spirit often appeared in a beautiful landscape with magnificent colors. These description sharply parallels accounts of transcendental NDEs. In Chapter 5 on NDEs, it was noted that researcher Kenneth Ring found that seeing the *light* and encountering deceased relatives are almost mutually exclusive; one or the other may occur but rarely both during the same NDE. Seeing the *light*, beautiful scenery, or encountering deceased loved ones are equally valid methods of completing the death experience, and if one aspect is not successful in removing the spirit, another may be tried.

5. Reasons Why People Are Susceptible to Intrusion

Wickland lists multiple possibilities for why some people attract earthbound spirits. Other conditions permitting impingement include a natural predisposition; a depleted nervous system, such as a nervous breakdown resulting from trauma; psychic experimentation, including automatic writing and use of a Ouija board; and sudden shocks. A formerly wandering spirit is attracted to people with the above conditions (or in the above situations). The attached spirit brings with it beliefs (including disbelief in an afterlife), dogmas and faulty teachings, physical ailments and habits, desires, and/or addictions it had when it was in its own physical body. It attempts to live the way it formerly did. For example, when a person dies, he takes with him in his spirit body any desire for addictive physical substances. As one spirit told Wickland, "The desire for anything belongs to the soul, not the body." When a person is earthbound, she has these desires, but the desire cannot be satisfied without a physical body. When the earthbound spirit obsesses another person, the desire can be satisfied only by inducing the host to consume the addictive substance, whether it be alcohol, a different psychoactive drug, or tobacco. Attitudes such as selfishness, pride, vanity, greed, ambition, miserliness, and religious orthodoxy are also carried into the obsessed person. These earthbound spirits often remain in the environment of the earth where they formerly lived, so the family is at risk. One patient of Wickland had 13 different spirits dislodged. Seven were recognized by the patient's mother as relatives or friends the patient had known while the former were alive.

Wickland maintained that the phenomenon of obsession cannot possibly be fraudulent. He had many confirmations of the information given to him by an obsessing spirit. For instance, a spirit may have given its name and address, and later Wickland confirmed that the person once existed and had had the physical disability, habit, or addiction the patient was relieved of, such as drinking, arthritis, or backache. He noted that some spirits spoke in foreign languages that his wife did not know. Mrs. Wickland had no recall of the conversation between her husband and the obsessing spirit because she was in trance. Wickland claims that the thousands of personalities his wife has taken on cannot be explained by a subconscious theory of suppressed memories from childhood.

6. Confusion in a Different Body

The early part of the conversation to remove an obsessing entity consists of trying to convince the earthbound spirit that it has lost its own body and is controlling another. Learning the name of the individual is sometimes difficult because the spirit may not have used its own name for many years. (Critics would say that too many suggestions are given and that the subconscious of the patient assumes a suggested identity.) Since spirits do not think they are dead, it is often meaningless to ask them the year they died. The remainder of the conversation relates to reasons the spirit is earthbound. Preliminary judgments can sometimes be made from the condition of the person being treated. Sometimes during the conversation, the spirit may reexperience death.

In the section about the work of Fiore, I mentioned how beliefs, actions, and addictions can cause a person's spirit to become earthbound. In many cases the cause may be a combination of these circumstances. Wickland had his own prejudices of spiritualism, implying that anyone who did not agree with him would have problems with being earthbound after bodily death. In his book, he attacks two views of life after death. One, of course, is held by people who do not believe in life after death. Since they do not believe in a spiritual world, the cannot imagine themselves as dead when their spirit bodies leave their physical bodies, since they believe that all thought ends at death but see that they are still thinking clearly. When they begin talking with Wickland through the body of Mrs. Wickland, they cannot understand how they can be dead and simultaneously be talking to someone. Though people raised with religious beliefs may believe in a soul and in life after death, if their views are too narrowly religious, they may be even harder to convince than nonbelievers. Dogmatic religious people expect to find themselves in heaven with Jesus or in hell after they die, and when they do not find either, they simply cannot believe they have actually died.

Although earthbound spirits do bring their physical ailments with them, they do not cause only physical problems. Even a physically and psychologically normal person in life can, when his or her spirit becomes earthbound, cause problems for the person whose magnetic aura is entered. However, most earthbound spirits had been disturbed when living. Some problems that Wickland was able to correct using his method include mental symptoms such as dementia, hysteria, melancholia, auditory hallucinations, suicidal tendencies, marriage disturbances, and criminal tendencies of all types. One spirit bluntly stated that the majority of crime is committed under the influence of spirits. Wickland warns that the fate of suicides is especially miserable. They are likely to remain earthbound until their physical life would naturally end. In some cases they, instead of obsessing others, simply watch the misery they have caused their families.

7. Protecting Oneself from Obsession

How can a person be protected from earthbound spirits, and how can a person eliminate them after they have entered without going to a session like Wickland's? One advanced spirit told Wickland that a person could repeat the phrases "I am master over my own body and I shall be" and "I am master and nobody can interfere." The obsessing spirit should not be dwelt upon, but a kind thought can be sent to it.

Needless to say, after removal of the obsessing spirit, the ill person is healed. Wickland had a medical degree (psychiatric) and presumably could correctly recognize a cure. It would be better if independent verification was available, but it is not. The patient was not necessarily healed after one treatment. There was often some improvement after the first session, but not a total cure. Wickland did not report any failures. He never claims he healed everyone he treated; he simply gives examples of cures.

8. A Word of Caution

I leave the following note, not directly related to Wickland's book. *Channeling* is a popular word today to indicate communication with the dead. This book does not present evidence on whether communication with any deceased person can occur. If communication does occur, Wickland warns that dying does not make a person a sage, though he does rely on much information from spirits. Unlike many channelers, his information never concerns future events. Those who believe in channeling often believe that the dead with whom they communicate are omniscient. Although some NDErs felt they learned the secrets of the universe during their NDE, that feeling is exceptional. The information was erased prior to their return. If they had actually died, they would probably be unable to communicate that information back to the living. Some people who describe themselves as channelers claim that they are receiving messages from upper-level spirits and not from deceased human spirits. I would not make any important decision in life based on alleged communication with the dead, but I would heed any message of impending danger.

F. The Hypnosis Expert

1. Introduction

I have referenced Adam Crabtree (1985) in several chapters of this book. He is a therapist working in Toronto and has narrated programs on Canadian Broadcasting about science and the paranormal. A former Catholic priest, he eventually married and had children. In this section, I discuss select portions of his book about intrusion by human spirits, both living and dead. Crabtree relates that he treated about 50 clients with apparent intrusion over a seven-year period. The symptoms he has treated include mild to severe disturbances; his results, as he documents, have ranged from minimal change to radical improvement.

Crabtree's clients have told him that they felt possessed by alien entities that subtly communicated with them. Crabtree finds it best to treat a client as if the situation is just as described—whether it is actually true or not is unimportant. The client did not have to believe in the objective reality of possession for the condition to be relieved or for the symptoms to disappear. Crabtree finds he has to therapeutically treat the intruding entity as well as the client.

In assisting patients, Crabtree uses two treatment approaches. In one approach, he is concerned only with his client, or the victim of intrusion.

In other cases, he is concerned about the intruding entity and believes it is necessary for the victim and intruder to reach an understanding of the reasons their relationship occurred. Crabtree's therapy method can involve completion of the death experience, similar to other therapeutic methods discussed. At other times, he uses reason to persuade the entity to leave.

2. Intrusion by Discarnate Family Members

Other therapists send Crabtree many cases. Sarah Worthington was one such referral. She was depressed and could hear an interior conversation. Crabtree had her relax and close her eyes. He was then able to elicit a conversation that Sarah did not remember when the session ended. The voice identified herself as Sarah Jackson, the client's grandmother, who had died 15 years earlier. Sarah J. had bequeathed her piano to her granddaughter and had entered her while she was playing the piano. The grandmother felt she had mistreated her own daughter, which resulted in the daughter's mistreating the granddaughter, Sarah W. Sarah J. thought she could help her granddaughter, but instead she added confusion. The grandmother, through Crabtree, was eventually able to restore communication between the daughter and granddaughter. She eventually departed from Sarah W. Crabtree says he has never attempted to formally verify information that the intruding entity knew but that his client did not.

In another referral, a client named Jean did not have any particular symptoms other than feeling an alien mass inside her body. She had an older, mentally disabled sister named Amy, who died at the age of 20. After Crabtree helped Jean to relax, Amy began to speak through Jean and revealed that when Jean was five years old and looking at Amy in her crib, Amy found that by using Jean's body she could go places and learn things that were impossible for her to go or to learn on her own. Amy's existence, as far as the outside world was concerned, was completely ignored by the rest of the family. She was never taken outdoors and was not included in family photos. However, Amy did require much attention, so Jean was frequently ignored. Crabtree believes that Jean's jealousy of Amy's attention made her open to intrusion. During the session, Crabtree asked Amy to look around. First, she saw two friendly presences. Next, she saw an elderly man who said to her, "Come now. I'll show you the possibilities. The world is bigger than you think." Although Amy felt secure with this elderly man, she refused to leave with him. Crabtree had a heated argument with her, and she finally left. Jean's alien mass disappeared, but several years later Jean felt her sister was still "around," but not as an interfering influence. These next two cases illustrate that intrusion by a deceased family member may actually begin prior to death.

3. Intrusion by Living Family Members

All of Crabtree's intrusion cases with a living family member involve a parent. In one case, the client was a professor named Art who was divorced from his first wife and was considering a second marriage. He constantly heard derisive remarks from an inner voice. This voice was really responsible for his divorce, created problems with his colleagues, and was about to break up his impending marriage. He could identify the voice as his mother's, who lived in Detroit, but he thought of it as just an aspect of his own personality. It turned out that even in his teen years, his mother would stroke and tease him in order to sexually excite him. In my opinion, this is probably when she was able to intrude into his psyche, as perverted sexuality is definitely an avenue for intrusion.

Crabtree was able to talk to the mother, Veronica, through Art. She felt her relationship to her son was appropriate. However, when asked how it could be good for her or her son, she admitted she had not considered the question. Her attitude began to change. She realized she could not be living her normal life in Detroit when she was "with" her son. Her son also realized that he had allowed the relationship to continue. During Art's therapy, his mother had cancer surgery, and she realized that in being with her son, she had robbed her physical body in Detroit of essential vitality. (This information came through conversation with the entity in Art and not by direct contact.) The departure of the entity was gradual, but the inner voice eventually stopped. Art related to people better afterward, and Veronica had a new lease on life.

G. Christian Deliverance

While many of the therapeutic concepts discussed in this chapter seem rather New Age, a number of Christian therapeutic methods support my contention that the spirit of a deceased person can remain earthbound and affect living people. Most Christians generally maintain that at death, a person is judged and sent to heaven or hell, although Catholics have a third option called purgatory. One of the methods discussed involves demons that are allegedly not human.

1. A Christian Psychiatrist

a. Introduction

In his 1982 book, *Healing the Family Tree*, the late Dr. Kenneth McAll (1910–2001), an English psychiatrist and professed Christian, discusses spiritual methods to cure some of the ailments mentioned in this chapter. McAll believed that many "incurable" patients could be victims of ancestral control, particularly by deceased relatives. By drawing a family tree, he helped the patient identify any ancestor who may be causing harm. McAll asked Jesus Christ to cut the bond between ancestor and patient. McAll's prayer for ancestors originated from experiences in China, his birthplace. During his time in China, he witnessed some unusual cures by untrained Chinese Bible women. One example was the cure of a "devil mad" man, who was not helped by an herbalist or a witch doctor. The man was ready to be stoned to death when a small Christian woman, who also believed in the Chinese superstition of good and evil spirits, approached the battered and bleeding man and began to pray a simple prayer of exorcism in the name of Jesus Christ. The man slumped over unconscious but was cured.

There is a note of precaution for this and for things described in sections to follow. For these sorts of symptoms, medical attention should always be sought and followed. Spiritual intervention is not a substitute for medicine, but rather an addendum to it. The spiritual aspect of humans is greatly connected to the functioning of the physical body; therefore, when spiritual problems are corrected, almost any physical healing may occur.

<u>b. Intrusion by the Living</u>

Although many of McAll's patients were influenced by deceased relatives, some were bothered by a living relation. A woman named Ruth, age 60, came to McAll's office and said she was having heart trouble. She talked about her son incessantly. McAll told her he thought there was a problem in her relationship with her son. She stormed out of the office and even called back to say she was going to file a complaint against him. McAll did nothing. Ruth came back to his office a few days later. She reported that after the call she had walked around and stopped in a church to rest. Then she heard a voice say clearly, "You have never cut the umbilical cord of your youngest son." Ruth thought that McAll had followed her into the church, but she did not see him. She heard the voice again and answered, "If this is true, Lord, I will do it now." She then had the strange feeling of a pair of scissors cutting the umbilical cord. Ruth's heart problem did not recur.

Ruth was not the only one healed that day. Her youngest son was a schizophrenic, confined to a mental hospital 450 miles away, and his wife was suffering from tuberculosis. Since the death of his father when the boy way eight years old, Ruth had directed much of his life. She even chose his wife. She was still directing his life, even though he was now 35 years old. On the day his mother cut the umbilical cord, he felt a sudden release and requested the hospital to allow him to visit his brother—and his request was honored. His schizophrenia was gone, and his wife felt unusually well that day. After several tests, she was eventually discharged from the TB sanitarium. The case is interesting in that there were healings of a psychosomatic illness (undiagnosable heart trouble), a mental illness (schizophrenia), and a physical, germ-related illness (tuberculosis). (By the way, the nontechnical name for a parent interfering in the life of an adult child is *hovering*.)

<u>c. Bondage and Healing Methodology</u>

Although the above cases concerned interference by a living person, most cases involve people influenced by the spirit of a deceased relative. McAll, who refers to this as bondage of the living to the dead, identifies five main categories of spirits that bind themselves to living people:

1. Ancestors
2. Unrelated persons
3. Stillborn, aborted, or miscarried babies
4. Inhabitants of a particular place
5. Those under occult control

McAll practiced in England. He centered his healing on what he called a "Eucharist of deliverance." Prior to this service, McAll drew a family tree and identified those for whom he and others were going to pray during the service. Persons specified included alcoholics, those with a mental illness, those who had committed suicide, those with unacceptable behavior, and those not given a proper burial service. In cases of stillborn, miscarried, or aborted babies, he found it helpful to give the baby a name so that the prayer could be more personal.

There were usually only a few people present at McAll's services. The living person for whom the service was being held was not always present, and the service may have been performed without that individual's consent or knowledge. If possible, McAll recommended that subjects be present so that they could accept Jesus Christ's love for them and their ancestors and can continue to pray for their ancestors. To receive the benefits of the service, the subjects did not need to be Christian. If voluntarily the subject of prayer, however, they must have had an open mind about experiencing the power of Jesus. Prior to beginning the service, the group prayed informally to ask that the Father gather the dead for whom they were praying, that the living and dead receive forgiveness, that Satan leave, and that the Holy Spirit compensate for the group's shortcomings. The actual service began with the Lord's Prayer.

In his book, McAll contends that there are four distinct stages during the service. In the first stage, the "Deliver us from evil" in the Lord's Prayer asks that God free the living and dead from bondage to the Evil One. Through the blood of Jesus Christ, sacramentally present as the Communion wine, the prayer asks that the bloodline of the living and dead be cleansed, that any hereditary seals and curses be broken, and that evil spirits be cast out.

The second stage concerns forgiveness for both the living and dead. If the living subject of the prayer has difficulty with forgiveness, then his or her cultivating the desire to forgive is the first step. However,

McAll writes that the cases in which the Eucharist did not bring expected changes failed on account of a lack of forgiveness. If a sinful habit seems to pass from one generation to the next, forgiveness for all generations is requested. Recipients of the prayers not only are asked to forgive the dead, but they also ask the dead to forgive them.

The third stage involves the actual consecration and receiving of the Eucharist. The symbolic family tree is placed on the altar. Ancestors who showed maladjusted behavior are named and prayed for. If voices are heard, they are preferably identified and prayed for. If the service is being held for several specifically known deceased persons, McAll preferred to have one or several people receive Communion on those decedents' behalf, say the name of the deceased persons, and pray for the Lord to come to the persons named.

In the fourth stage, McAll shifted the focus from the needs of the dead to the needs of the living. The group used laying on of hands for the prayer recipient and made the sign of the cross on the recipient's forehead. Sometimes Eucharist services were held several days in a row, but McAll stressed that one service conducted with love is more important than many routine ones.

In his writings, McAll surmises that the Eucharist service he used employs all the traditional means to drive out evil: scripture, prayer in Jesus Christ's name, confession of sin and subsequent absolution, profession of faith, the Lord's Prayer, fellowship in worshipping, praise, Communion, laying on of hands, and blessing.

d. Examples of Reported Healings

The illnesses, as well as the recipients of prayer for healing, are quite varied. From many cases, I have first separated out four types of major problems, namely, schizophrenia, phobias, anorexia nervosa, and homosexuality, and one group of related causes, namely, abortion, miscarriage, and stillbirth. McAll said he had seen over six hundred healings related to the latter group of causes and over fourteen hundred healings in all during his practice. The most interesting cases involved a person being healed when that person was not even aware that a service was being held. Some cases involved two of the above, such as hearing voices in conjunction with having anorexia or after experiencing a miscarriage.

i. Hearing Voices

Gil was a good student and athlete until the age of 14, when his father died. He then began conversing with his deceased father, imitating his father's mannerisms for the next twelve years. Gil's mother had not liked her husband and could not remember attending his burial service. McAll held a committal service for his father on a Saturday afternoon. Gil, who was in a mental hospital and unaware of the service, suddenly thought it was selfish for him to demand his father's return to life. Even though he did not believe in God, he found himself praying that God would look after his father. Gil then appeared completely normal, from that time to the time of McAll's writing.

Although religious people often refer to one of McAll's abilities as a gift of discernment, a more secular term for this ability is *clairvoyance*. During one Eucharistic service in England for an American woman whose son was a schizophrenic, McAll "saw" at the side of the church a dark hunchback figure. As the prayers ended, the hunchback seemed to float upward to join a number of gowned figures who were grouped around the Lord, saying, "We will look after you [i.e., the dark figure]." McAll later explained his vision to the other people, and the American woman stated that the hunchback was her father, who had committed suicide. She had not previously informed McAll about him. Subsequently, her son's schizophrenia disappeared.

Another case of schizophrenia is discussed in a chapter about ghosts. A woman named Maggie had conversations with an invisible friend named Peter who frequented a certain riverbank. She described him as unkempt, and he was even referred to as Peter the Tramp by local people who saw him at the riverbank. Often he would vanish. Three clergymen held a Eucharist service on the riverbank, and during the service Maggie saw Peter, this time dressed in white, rise from the riverbank and thank those praying for his release. Maggie never saw or heard from Peter again.

The two previous case shows a relationship to NDE phenomena and best illustrates the completion of the death experience. The gowned figures who came to look after the hunchback, and observing someone dressed in white (Peter), are both typical of NDE reports. This assistance from beyond is what is most likely occurring in most cases reported, but there are rarely visions to confirm the other cases.

McAll considered his most dramatic case to be a 50-year-old woman named Claudine who was hospitalized after 12 years of chronic schizophrenia. An operation was performed and, as a result, she lost her sight and speech, became overweight, and lost her hair. McAll said a simple prayer for her. By the next morning, her hair had grown a quarter of an inch, the other problems were gone, and she returned to society.

ii. Anorexia Nervosa

McAll also had good results treating anorexia nervosa. Perhaps some improvements in counseling techniques and earlier diagnosis have increased the survival rate from the illness, but McAll stated that 30 to 50% of anorexia victims die as a result of the disease. McAll claimed that he had cured (using the phrase "are now quite well") 51 of 66 people he had treated for anorexia nervosa. For example, an 18-year-old young woman named Judy had been seriously injured at the age of eleven in an automobile accident away from home in which her father died. In their concern over Judy's condition, the family had the father's body shipped home for cremation. When Judy recovered and heard of her father's death, she became depressed, developed schizophrenia, and then developed anorexia nervosa. She tried to commit suicide in order to join her father. She was her father's favorite child. The family held a Eucharistic service for the father, and the next morning Judy began eating normally.

iii. Phobias and Homosexuality

McAll also reported successful treatments for eliminating phobias by his method. For example, one woman had developed a paralyzing fear of water. It was discovered that her uncle had drowned in the *Titanic* wreck. A committal service was held for him, and the woman became completely free from her phobia. Similarly, a teenage girl suffering from agoraphobia (a fear of going out in public) saw her dead grandfather and had "conversations" with him through automatic writing. A priest celebrated a Eucharistic service but did not specifically say a prayer for the grandfather or the girl. However, the grandfather stopped appearing, the "conversations" ceased, and the agoraphobia was overcome.

Another case involving a phobia and a second symptom involved a patient named Cliff. Cliff was in his thirties, was homosexual, and feared chaplains. McAll discussed the boy's early life with his mother. She reported that as a nurse and pregnant with Cliff, she had had sexual intercourse with a patient who was an army chaplain. McAll had the mother seek repentance and also asked Cliff to forgive his mother. Cliff's homosexuality disappeared along with his fear of chaplains.

Some bonds with the dead are willingly continued by those who suffer from a mental disorder. One woman named Georgina, who had been labeled schizophrenic, had blackouts lasting from three to 14 days. During her blackouts she was amnesiac; thus she may also have suffered from dissociative identity disorder. Georgina stated that she had previously entered into a lesbian relationship with a nurse, who later died. Georgina would "daydream" herself into contact with her dead friend and hold conversations with her. McAll and Georgina went to a priest and, while kneeling before an altar, formally cut the bond with the dead friend by commanding the intruding spirit to go "in the name of Jesus Christ to her appointed place." Georgina screamed and afterward described feeling as if there were a hole in her head that now was clean. The blackouts ceased, and she is now married. In another case, McAll attempted to help a woman in a lesbian relationship, but he stopped when she continued with her lifestyle. My opinion is that the spirit causing the tendency toward homosexuality is unlikely to leave if its relationship is being satisfied. Or, as McAll says, the possession void must be transferred to Jesus Christ.

iv. The Unborn

McAll cites many examples of engaging in healing prayer for an aborted, miscarried, or stillborn baby. One family was affected by all three types of interrupted pregnancies: the eldest child, Elizabeth, was born after an abortion and became a drug addict; a grossly overweight daughter named Evelyn was the next child born after a miscarriage; and the youngest, a boy named Charles, adopted to replace a stillborn child, became a compulsive thief at the age of seven. A Eucharistic service was held for the deceased infants, and as a result Elizabeth, Evelyn, and Charles were healed.

In another family, a nine-year-old child who was acting irrationally threatened her brother with a knife. She was diagnosed as epileptic. The behavior had been occurring for four years. McAll could not find anything in the family tree, but he asked the child how many siblings she had. She replied, "Three brothers and three sisters." The mother had said the child had three brothers and two sisters. The child told McAll that her mother had flushed her sister Melissa down the toilet. Actually, the doctor handling the mother-to-be had caused an accidental abortion, and even the husband had not been informed of this fact. The mother had planned to name the child Melissa.

A woman named Mildred had stomach pains for two years; no medical cause could be found. She reported she had undergone an abortion while still a teenager. A committal service for the aborted infant was held, and the pains stopped by the end of the service. The pains had begun at the time the woman became a Christian. A psychiatrist may explain the pains on the basis of a guilt complex, but McAll believes it was only when the child had spiritual access to her mother as a result of her conversion that the child could cause the pains.

Even major physical symptoms can be eliminated by a Eucharistic service for a miscarried or aborted baby. At a prayer service for her two miscarried children, one woman reported that her spinal osteoporosis disappeared. A second woman found that her chronic colitis was cured four days after a service.

v. Ghosts and Occult Practices

McAll also discerns that there are ghosts who remain around certain areas. He asserts that it is possible to release such places haunted by "the unquiet dead." One man whom McAll knew prayed at sites where an unusual number of automobile accidents had occurred. On one stretch of road, there had been 17 accidents within a period of six months. After prayer, there were no accidents on the road in the next six months. McAll also eliminated an unnamed ghost in a schoolhouse. (A Eucharistic service is capable of releasing a spirit even if its name is not known.) McAll's opinion was that hauntings often occur in places where there was an accident or where occult practices took place. This is probably because the spirit of the original person involved remains in the physical area.

McAll also maintains that disturbances can occur in people as a result of occult practices, such as astrology, Ouija boards, automatic writing, fortune-telling, divination, séances, tarot cards, witchcraft, and transcendental meditation. For example, one woman began having visions of devils and heard voices telling her to destroy herself as a result of seeing one film about the Devil. A simple prayer with McAll eliminated the problem.

e. Conclusions

In his writings, McAll compares the release from control by a spirit to release from control by alcohol. In the next two sections his reasoning will be shown to be correct. McAll says psychiatric disorders do not exclude demonic control; there can be mental illness exclusively, mental illness with demonic control, or solely demonic control. He does not provide a definition for demonic control.

I believe that McAll's anecdotes support the concept of intrusive spirits. McAll is very evangelistic in the presentation of his healings, but he may be in the same position as Dr. Raymond Moody, who coined the term NDE and whom McAll quoted concerning the "realm of bewildered spirits." Psychiatrists will most likely say that McAll's ideas are too religious and therefore not scientific. Conservative religious groups will say he is not following the Bible closely enough regarding events after death. McAll, for instance, interprets Hebrews 9:27 ("Just as a man is destined to die once, and after to face judgment" [NIV]) as not specifying when after death that judgment occurs. In 1 Peter 3:19–20 ("He [Christ] went and preached to the spirits in prison who disobeyed long ago" [NIV]), Christ is said to be preaching to spirits in prison, and in 1 Peter 4:6 ("For this is the reason the gospel was preached even to those who are now dead, so that they might be judged according to men in regard to the body, but live according to God in regard to the spirit [NIV]), the Gospel is being preached to those who are dead. McAll highlights the fact that the early church fathers taught the importance of loving and forgiving the dead through prayer. Several hundred years later in church history, Eucharistic services were held for a number of days after a death.

Although it is not a biblical basis for what transpires after death, I was taken aback that McAll did not use the Old Testament biblical phrase, "Visiting the iniquity of the fathers upon the children, and upon the children's children, to the third and fourth generation" (Exodus 34:7, Numbers 14:18, Deuteronomy 5:9 [slight variations], LT). It certainly indicates that parental behavior affects a child.

I believe that McAll had powerful spiritual gifts that may have enabled him to achieve these healings. Christian healers usually state that God or Jesus does the healing, but the fact remains that some individuals have a charism (gift of the Holy Spirit) for calling upon God's healing power.

McAll does not really explain the theory behind his work. His results certainly imply that the spiritual element of a deceased person may exert control on a living person. Prayers and other Christian actions may induce the spiritual element to leave or force it out. Frequently, the spirit is that of a person who died an early death, a person who was not given a proper Christian burial, or a person who was influenced by a person from a previous generation who also had a disturbed personality. When medical professionals state that a mental illness is genetically caused, I opine that the difficulties in a later generation are caused by a spiritual connection between generations and are not genetic. In the next section, I discuss a controversial priest in a foreign country, so a cross-cultural factor is introduced.

2. Out of Africa

a. Introduction

The Rev. Emmanuel Milingo (1930–), former Catholic archbishop of Lusaka, Zambia, and author of the book *The World in Between* (1984), has developed a method that he alleges removes evil spirits from affected individuals. As a result of this activity, he was removed from his position as archbishop and was sent to Rome. Nevertheless, he carried his controversy with him—in early 1989, pontifical authorities began investigating the "faith healing" Masses he was conducting in Rome, attended by thousands. Later on he was in trouble with the church hierarchy when he married outside the church and invalidly ordained some other married men. For these violations of church policy, he was excommunicated from the church in 2006.

Milingo is a native African, and his detractors have mostly been white missionaries and a few African priests. In his book, Milingo discusses the world of spirits of which most native Africans seem to be aware. He claims to be able to speak to the dead through another person.

b. Group and Individual Healing Sessions

Frequently, Milingo held group healing sessions. These were not exclusively for people with spirit intrusion disorders; they were also for the physically sick. Beginning with prayers of praise, thanksgiving, and adoration, Milingo then called upon angels and saints and began "calling the diseases" through the Holy Spirit. This aspect is often traumatic, as the sick experience their symptoms more severely at this time. Tumors may become very painful, and epileptics may fall into convulsions. "The possessed cry, shake, speak strange languages, and twist themselves and roll on the ground. Those who are subject to phobias, anxieties and worries sometimes just weep, their tears coming down their cheeks without control" (p. 29). Some feel a burning fire. These activities indicate that the Holy Spirit is at work. The group then calls on Jesus Christ to show his powers and authority over Satan, sin, and death. Evil spirits may again make patients roll on the floor, screaming and crying. Specific illnesses may be named, or Jesus may be asked to heal them all. Holy water is sprinkled on the patients; the crucifix is raised; and Jesus is asked to seal his work with his precious Blood. Prayers of thanksgiving to the Holy Trinity end the ceremony.

Milingo also conducts individual expulsions of spirits with a method that sounds similar to Basham's. He cautions against disturbing an evil spirit and then failing to send it away. To identify the enemy by name, Milingo asks a series of questions: Who are you? How many are you? How long have you been with the person? Where is your habitation in him (or her)? What diseases have you caused in him (or her)? If the information is not volunteered, he orders the spirits to name themselves. These devils do not always have names, but they may be named after a vice or an ailment. The editor of Milingo's book states that Milingo is uncertain whether evil spirits incorporate human vices or are persons in their own right.

The exorcist must not get angry with the evil spirit, but he may use the authority of Jesus, remaining inwardly calm and confident. In one case, evil spirits attempted to deflect the act of exorcism by afflicting the possessed person with epileptic fits. There are different ranks of evil spirits, which Milingo sometimes refers to as "parasites." These evil spirits have told Milingo, "We have no other aim than destroying a person's life" (p. 31).

c. Communicating with the Deceased

In the following passage, Milingo relates a case of spirit intrusion to illustrate a deceased relative's communicating through her living sister.

> Is it really the dead who come and speak to the living? For me this is beyond discussion, because I have dealt with many of them. Let me just give one example. One day a woman came to my office and called me to follow her to the hospital where her sister was very sick. We went together to the hospital, and when we arrived we found that the sister was dead. I went into the room and took hold of her hand. I was able to ascertain what had killed her, but the cries of people were such that I could scarcely utter an audible word of prayer. Realizing that there was nothing more I could do for her, I was able to give her absolution because she was still warm.
>
> Then came the day for the funeral Mass. During the Mass, at the time of consecration, I felt a sudden force pulling me towards the corpse. I placed myself straight in front of it and went on praying intensely for the departed spirit. After the funeral one of her sisters could not overcome her sorrow, and they brought her to me. I took her into my private chapel and we began to talk. It was not long before I found myself talking with her dead sister who had just been buried. She smiled and said to me: "Thank you for arriving in time at my bedside and for giving me absolution. I was going to be condemned and now that you have offered Mass for me, I am happy with God." I excused myself for having arrived late at her bedside

in the hospital, and said that I could not do more than just give her absolution. She answered: "It was decided that I should die. But you know what happened." ... Then she explained the cause of her death. She was speaking through this sister of hers, because she loved her especially and she knew that she was the one who would suffer most from her death. Even now, if we want to have messages from her, we can use the sister as a medium. The dead sister has often come to her. (pp. 88–89)

Milingo does not seem to indicate that this is an unhealthy occurrence. In contrast, Western therapists normally find mental problems in an individual who is carrying the spirit of a deceased person.

d. Dark Spirits and Multiple Spirits

In the Zambian region where Milingo practiced, the people call earthbound spirits *Ngozi*, the spirits of the witches. These are the hard-hearted sinners who ask God to close paradise to them. They obtained all they wanted from this earth and enjoyed the superiority they had over many simple people. They cannot stand seeing their offspring and relatives happy, and that is why they go on taking revenge, causing sickness and deaths in the family. As Milingo reports:

One day we were delivering a young girl in her teens, and found afterwards that she was possessed by a relative who had died twenty-eight years before, and whose name, according to family custom, this girl had been given. The living relatives gave her the name in good faith, in order to remember the dead aunt. For many days we failed to speak to the evil spirit. However, the powers of the Lord were always pinching the spirit whenever we prayed for the girl till one day the spirit gave way and confessed: "I am ___. This girl bears my name. Unfortunately I am here in a place of darkness, and as long as she bears this name she will have to suffer with me." We immediately asked the evil spirit to leave her, and we told the spirit that from that time on we had changed the girl's name. We were moved to hear that the aunt's spirit was in a place of darkness, and we asked her, "Can we help you with our prayers?" She answered: "No need of your prayers." We were shocked, and personally I am still shocked, to have heard such a definite "No."

Milingo has also encountered multiple spirits. One 16-year-old girl who was thought to be suffering from heart failure was delivered from 25 devils. The process lasted two years. Among the devils was her long-deceased grandmother, although Milingo says it could have been an evil spirit taking the grandmother's name. Since Africans pay great respect to their ancestors, an evil spirit may take the name of a deceased but respected family member. Milingo also discusses guardian or protecting spirits. In one person he found 30 spirits, ten of whom were guardian spirits. Perhaps this is similar to helpful personalities in a person with DID. Another example is of one woman who had five spirits: a Portuguese, a Canadian, a Bemba, a Nsenga-Luzi, and a snake. She knew the languages of the humans perfectly and changed languages with such ease that in my opinion it would seem unlikely that she had DID. Use of a separate language by each spirit is fairly common. Animal spirits are less frequently encountered by Western therapists.

e. Difficulties with Missionaries

Milingo believes that one reason missionaries have such difficulty converting natives is the formers' failure to understand the latters' relationship with their ancestors. Milingo has never met a missionary who accepted what he wrote about speaking with the dead and with evil spirits. Native Africans believe that the God of Westerners is not concerned with their daily problems. Africans have been communicating with their ancestors for millennia. Their traditional medicine men recognize the individual need for a continuing relationship with ancestors. The shamans speak with their ancestors, and in return the ancestors express their concern for the living people's everyday problems. In contrast to missionaries, Milingo tries to convince the natives that Jesus "has the mysterious power to be present at the ancestral worship ceremonies if called up in any way to intercede for the needs of the clan, the tribe and the whole community" (p. 93).

f. Conclusions

This section is an example of assimilating the Bible into indigenous cultures. Although the conversations Milingo had with spirits are much different from previously discussed or soon-to-be-discussed therapies, these findings support the concept of communication with the dead as well as the idea of spirit intrusion.

3. *Charismatic Deliverance*

a. Introduction

This section will deal almost exclusively with a book by Don Basham (1926–1989), *Deliver Us from Evil* (1972). It details how Basham progressed from being a minister of a traditional congregation to having a ministry centered on delivering people from demons. Basham did not use the term *exorcism*, though I believe there are a number of similarities between the symptoms and causes of the alleged demons that Basham encountered and those previously described. However, the method of removing a demon's influence is quite different from previously discussed methods.

b. Piquing His Interest

Prior to becoming interested in deliverance ministry, Basham developed an interest in the charismatic renewal. A charism is a gift of the Holy Spirit. The charismatic part of his congregation was a separate weekday prayer group, not a part of his Sunday teaching. The charismatic renewal opened Basham to miraculous healings. His book describes how he progressed to perform deliverance healings. For example, one man was cured of an eye problem, but his wife, Irene, received no healing for her epilepsy. She would often have her seizures during church services. One day during the midweek prayer service, the group prayed for her. Suddenly, animal-like sounds began to pour from her lips. Basham saw an angry glare in her eyes much like that of a caged animal. (He would frequently see that glare later, when he developed his deliverance ministry.) Then Irene asked those around her where she was. When her husband informed her, she did not know who he was. When he answered, she said she did not have a husband or a home. Basham left that church and moved to another, but later he heard that Irene had died. Doctors suspect Irene had a seizure at the top of the basement stairs and struck her head on the basement floor after falling. I surmise that an intruding spirit induced her to commit suicide.

Another case that piqued Basham's interest in the subject was Mrs. Stern. One day Mrs. Stern told him that she knew the voice of God when God spoke to her. Later, she told Basham that something evil was keeping her from obeying God. Still later she said that the voice she had thought was God's had begun to make lewd suggestions, to curse, and to tell her that great harm would come to her if she did not obey. When Basham attempted to assist her, she ran to a neighbor's yard and trotted back and forth like a wild animal in a cage. Basham was unable to help her.

Basham began to read about evil spirits in the Bible. One day he was a guest speaker at a small-town church and was told that the congregation would pray for a man possessed by demons. The afflicted man, named Sam, could not remember anything. Basham recalled that evil spirits have names, so he said, "By the authority of Jesus Christ, I command you to tell me who you are" (p. 62)! The reply was, "Forgetfulness." The man began to tremble, and when Basham commanded the spirit of Forgetfulness to leave, the man began to tremble even more. Then, "an invisible mask seemed to slip from Sam's face and some lurking—did I dare say 'presence'—behind his eyes seemed to melt away" (p. 63). Sam looked different and began to quote scripture. He said that for years he had heard a strange voice, and prior to coming to the meeting that night the voice told him that if he went to the meeting he would die.

Basham had been writing about his experiences with charismatic healings. When his first book was published, he gave up his full-time congregational ministry. While a guest speaker one day at a church, the minister of the church told him, "The Lord shows me that you will be greatly used in a ministry of deliverance, discerning and casting out evil spirits" (p. 73).

After these early experiences, Basham went to Derek Prince (1915–2003), an English scholar who was familiar with deliverance. Prince told him that *possession* is too strong a word for translation of the original Greek. *Afflicted* by a demon is probably a closer translation. Prince also reported that a Christian can just as easily be afflicted by a demon as a non-Christian can. Prince described how he rid himself of a demon with a "filthy temper." He felt something leave through his mouth. Afterward, he did not experience the irrational anger he had felt prior to the removal.

c. Symptoms of Release

One sign that Basham frequently observed during deliverances was a gag reflex. According to him, most evil spirits leave through the mouth. Early in his ministry, Basham did not know what to expect. One victim complained about confusion. When Basham gave his command for the spirit to leave the man in the name of Jesus, the man lunged across the altar rail and began gagging. After the second command, the man was healed. An observing minister commented that their group had just been praying and that what was needed instead was authority.

According to Basham, physical symptoms that frequently occur during deliverance include "screams, shaking, convulsions, weeping, hysterical laughter, writhing, fainting, sighing, groaning, choking, gagging, retching, and actual vomiting" (pp. 137–38). However, Basham states, "Many, perhaps most, deliverances are quiet and unfrightening" (p. 200). The few noisy ones get noticed. For many, the sign of deliverance is simply a relaxation of inner tension.

A woman named Sister Sadie had observed the healing of the confused man. She told Basham that he should bind the evil spirit before casting it out; otherwise, it might enter another person in the room. She also said that Basham should both fast and command the spirit to return to the pit. Basham studied the scripture and could not find a basis for those objections. Binding is mentioned, but not in regard to evil spirits. In Luke 8:31, the spirits asked not to be sent back to the abyss. In one case, Jesus told his apostles that "this kind" of evil spirit can only be cast out by prayer and fasting, implying that fasting does not apply to all cases. Later in Basham's book, we learn that Sister Sadie was delivered from a spirit of false prophecy.

Basham describes several methods to protect oneself from demonic influence. Two should be obvious from the aforementioned discussions: not overindulging in carnal appetites and avoiding occult practices. A third is specifically Christian. Basham refers to it as "Pleading the Blood," which entails claiming one's right as a Christian to be protected from the Evil One.

Basham describes a method to determine if the cause of a problem may be a demon or simply a carnal desire. He lists various Christian practices to try, stating that if the desire does not depart, a demon could be the cause. Being compelled to perform destructive acts can also be a reason to suspect demons. Another reason is the previously described reaction to the idea of deliverance. Basham describes how a carnal desire can result in entrance of a demon when the desire is indulged to excess. In an example, a woman felt a compulsive desire to throw herself sexually at men. Upon leaving, the demon named itself as "wantonness." The victim reported that the feelings had begun while she was viewing a pornographic film.

d. Types of Malevolent Spirits

I now turn to a discussion of the types of spirits removed by Basham and observations of others. Basham's healings can be divided into several types. These classifications of symptoms relieved are my own summary, not that of Basham.

1. Physical symptoms such as deafness, epilepsy, or asthma
2. Addictions such as to food (i.e., gluttony), tobacco, alcohol, or other drugs (illegal or legal)
3. Vices such as pride, vanity, hate, jealousy, resentment, foulmouthedness, and temper
4. Phobias and negative emotions such as general fear, frustration, and worry, or specific fears (perhaps resulting from trauma) such as hydrophobia
5. Results of occult practices, such as astrology, necromancy, fortune-telling, palm reading, consulting a medium, and witchcraft
6. Combinations and unclassifiable, such as the previously mentioned cases of confusion, forgetfulness, and depression

Parapsychological phenomena observed when the subject was under the influence of a demon are described in a tape-recorded case cited by Basham. The minister who recorded the tape reported that while he was talking with the inner Judy, when the patient Judy was hypnotized, a harsh voice interrupted and said he wanted to kill Judy. When asked who he was, the voice replied, "Some call 'us' Satan, some call us demons." The minister disclosed that he did not believe what he had heard until the voice told him intimate details of his private life that only he (the minister) knew. Inner Judy said she knew there was another uncanny power inside her but was told that the powers would kill her if she revealed their existence. Basham states that hypnosis "can lead to demonic activity" (p. 138), although in this particular case he does not infer that the minister caused it.

e. Reasons for Failure to Achieve Release

Basham speculates about why deliverance achieves spectacular results in some cases but is a miserable failure in others. To be delivered, the victim must admit he has a demon from which he desires deliverance. Some people may refuse to surrender their addiction (i.e., their demon). For example, one man did not want to completely give up alcohol. He preferred to imbibe within reason. In another case, an evil spirit identified itself as nicotine. The victim, declaring that nicotine could not be an evil spirit, refused to renounce it.

Other failures might be attributed to the minister. The minister must take authority in the name of Jesus. It also helps in removal to induce the demon to name itself, as naming the demon weakens its hold. The demons are often willing to use stronger terms than are used in today's society. For instance, instead of reporting its vice as eating too much, a demon will identify itself as gluttony. In addition, the victims must renounce the demon, preferably in the name of Jesus. However, Basham states that a Christian does not have to understand what is occurring in order for him to be effective in removing demons, as it is a Christian's right to be free from them. And finally, the victims must be willing to forgive anyone who has harmed them.

To prevent reentrance, victims must fill their lives with positive attitudes. Basham's recommendations were obviously religious, such as reading scripture and praising God. Discipline and healthy personal relationships are also important. The latter can be more easily understood in terms of addiction. If a person has an alcohol demon removed, he cannot congregate with former drinking friends. One biblical passage that can be difficult to fathom is Matthew 12:45, in which an evil spirit departs a man but returns to find the house (i.e., the person it had left) "unoccupied, swept clean and put in order" (NIV). The evil spirit brought with it seven other spirits. Basham says the victim failed to fill his life with positive Christian attitudes and thus was reentered by the original spirit and seven new spirits.

f. Self-Deliverance

Basham contends that a person can minister her own deliverance. The previously mentioned case of how Derek Prince released himself from his filthy temper was a self-performed deliverance. Basham, too, discharged two evil spirits from himself. Upon realization of how involvement in occult practices can invite demons, he recalled that he had once attended some Spiritualist séances, and asked God for deliverance. Another time, he became very fearful on an airplane and realized there were several other times in his life when he was engulfed by similar feelings. He believes he identified when the fear emotion began, as he recalled that when he was eight or nine years old, his older brother took him to a horror movie and he became terrified. My book proposes trauma as a possible cause of soul fragmentation and spirit entry. While a simple scare is not trauma, a child's being terrified can result in soul fragmentation. Recall that earlier I stated that a child's spirit body is less fully bonded to her physical body than in an adult. Basham was delivered from these manifestations as he thought about his own fears:

> First, I felt something like roots tear loose from the lower part of my back, right in those vertebrae where the throb and ache were located. Then the thing moved into my midriff, rolling and churning and convulsing. I felt it rising up through my chest and into my throat, choking me. I doubled over the side of the bed and began to retch in an ugly gasping convulsion.
>
> Yet somehow, even then, I could feel the presence of God. It was as if I were some kind of sponge filled with dirty water being twisted and wrung by a pair of giant loving hands. I retched one more time and a stream of hot bile came out my nose and mouth, and I could sense I was in physical contact

with the true nature of the filthy spirit which had lodged within me.

Then as suddenly as they had begun, the gagging and the convulsion ceased.

Cautiously I raised up, and—Oh! I cannot describe what I felt like. It was as if I had experienced some kind of inner bath or shower. I felt shining clean and at peace—a peace such as I had never known. (p. 183)

After this self-deliverance from fear, Basham found he had developed two gifts: word of knowledge and discernment of spirits. Basham also divulges his method for group deliverance, in which he commanded all spirits in a group to come out. For example, one time, prior to the command, the group of people said a prayer in which forgiveness was granted to people who had harmed them; psychic practices were renounced; and faith in Jesus Christ was reaffirmed. After the command, nothing occurred for half a minute. Then there were moans, sighs, and a volley of coughs.

g. Conclusions

The reader should be able to see the similarities in symptoms and causes between healings by Basham and healings by the previously discussed healers. However, I believe that many people's gagging or coughing may just be a group reaction and not an indication of something spiritual happening. It is my interpretation that spirit removal by this method carries the spirit to a realm where it can be educated, as reported by Fiore and Wickland. The spirit can no longer intrude upon another person. The name the spirit gives itself could simply be the reason it chose to remain earthbound. Of course, it is always possible that Basham is dealing with a different type of spirit, not those of deceased persons or thought forms. Basham did not define demons until the appendix of his book, in which he quotes first-century Jewish historian Josephus: "The spirits of the wicked dead that enter into men that are alive" (p. 219). The translation of Josephus's work that I reviewed used the following words: "for the so-called demons—in other words, the spirits of wicked men which enter the living and kill them unless aid is forthcoming" (Josephus, 1843). While Basham contends that the scriptures do not support Josephus's view, he does speculate on ideas that have poor scriptural basis. For instance, he reports that "some biblical scholars believe that demons are the disembodied spirits of a pre-Adamic race of beings, inhabitants of earth before God created Adam and Eve" (p. 219). Since they once had bodies, they seek to be embodied again. Basham maintains that other scholars propose that demons are the spirits of fallen angels and earth women. He also noted that there is apparently a rank within the demonic realm, as both the Greek words *daimon* and *daimonion* (the latter being a diminutive form) are translated as "demon." This topic will be addressed later. In the next section, I describe some Catholic exorcisms that potentially involve spirits that may be demons from another spiritual realm rather than simply human spirits that have not properly transitioned to the *light*.

4. Catholic Exorcisms

a. Introduction

The Roman Catholic Church has an official ritual to be used for exorcisms. It includes certain prayers, scriptural readings, and procedures. Each exorcism necessarily also involves many spontaneous decisions by the priest, as he is led by Jesus Christ and the Holy Spirit. The ritual may last many hours or several days, even a week. The late Malachi Martin (1921–1999) was an ordained Jesuit priest in the Catholic Church, but he was not an active priest at the time he wrote the book *Hostage to the Devil* (1976). He considered himself to be in the traditionalist branch of the church, and his views on exorcism and other church topics are considered controversial.

The book *People of the Lie* (1983) is by psychiatrist and popular author M. Scott Peck. Peck relates that he has participated in several exorcisms. Other than stating that a team of Christians was involved, he does not describe any of the exorcisms. However, he does comment that most of his observations agree with those described in Martin's *Hostage to the Devil*. Peck himself is a convert to the Episcopalian Church. Most of the exorcisms Martin recorded were conducted by Catholic priests and were assisted by a second priest and a team of Christian laypeople.

b. General Description of an Exorcism

General descriptions by Martin will be followed by an individual case he presented in detail. These alleged possessions by the Devil may be the extreme consequence of control by the spirit of a deceased person, or they may be by demons that are agents of Satan. In Martin's book, the symptoms are not very different from those exhibited by a very antagonistic personality in DID, except that the victim seems to progressively deteriorate. This deterioration often begins in adolescence and not usually prior to age seven, which is a critical age for people who have DID. However, the full symptoms of DID do not necessarily show up in children, and Martin may not have had enough evidence about the early characteristics of people who ended up "possessed by the Devil." The possibility that the spirit described by Martin as being demonic, that is, suprahuman, is left open for further examination. The possessing entities described by Martin have probably more deeply penetrated the physical body than happened in those cases, previously described, of Don Basham.

Prior to the actual exorcism, family and friends of the afflicted person often report parapsychological phenomena occurring in the person's presence. As Martin commented:

> [O]bjects fly around the room; wallpaper peels off the walls; furniture cracks; crockery breaks; there are strong rumblings, hisses, and other noises with no apparent source. Often the temperature in the room where the possessed happens to be will drop dramatically. Even more often an acrid and distinctive stench accompanies the person. (p. 10)
>
> ...
>
> Violent physical transformations seem sometimes to make the lives of the possessed a kind of hell on earth. Their normal processes of secretion and elimination are saturated with inexplicable wrackings and exaggeration. Their consciousness

seems completely colored by the violent sepia of revulsion. Reflexes sometimes become sporadic or abnormal, sometimes disappear for a time. Breathing can cease for extended periods. Heartbeats are hard to detect. The face is strangely distorted, sometimes also abnormally tight and smooth without the slightest line or furrow. (pp. 10–11)

The one feature that all cases, without exception, appear to have in common is a "peculiar revulsion to symbols and truths of religion" (p. 13).

Similar and other types of parapsychological phenomena also occur during the exorcism, such as the following:

inexplicable stench; freezing temperature; telepathic powers about purely religious and moral matters; a peculiarly unlined or completely smooth or stretched skin, or unusual distortion of the face, or other physical and behavioral transformations; "possessed gravity" [the possessed person becomes practically immovable, or those around the possessed are weighted down with a suffocating pressure]; levitation; violent smashing of furniture, constant opening and slamming of doors, tearing of fabric in the vicinity of the possessed, without a hand laid on them; and so on. (p. 13)

Martin stated that the 15 priests he has known who served as exorcists had many years of experience as parish priests, exhibited good moral judgment, had sound religious beliefs, and were usually pragmatic rather than intellectual. He also noted that it is preferable for the priest to have assisted at an exorcism prior to being the priest in charge of one.

The exorcisms described by Martin usually took place in a location with which the victim was familiar, such as a bedroom. Since objects may fly across the room, everything except the bed and a table for necessary supplies (such as crucifix, candles, holy water, and prayer book) were removed to prevent those assisting from being injured. The windows were boarded up because sometimes members of the team seemed to be propelled toward a window. In recent years, sessions have been tape-recorded. A restraining device, such as a straitjacket, leather straps, or rope, was also typically kept nearby.

There were normally four laymen who assisted, frequently one of whom was a doctor. These assistants must not only be physically strong but also ready to take personal insults, to have their darkest secrets revealed, and to follow the exorcist's orders. They were not to take any initiative except on command and were instructed never to speak to the possessed person.

Martin identified six events or stages of the exorcism:

- Presence
- Pretense
- Breakpoint
- Voice
- Clash
- Expulsion

The Presence is an atmosphere that everyone in the room can feel; it has no location and is described by Martin as "intent on hate for hate's sake" (p. 18). Pretense is the ability of the evil spirit to hide behind the personality of the victim to whose memory it has access. As the Pretense begins to break down, the victim usually becomes violent and repulsive. At the Breakpoint, members of the team may experience confusion and even think they are going insane. Sensory input is befuddled: the eyes hear, the ears smell, or the nose tastes sounds. At this point, the victim may utter nonhuman sounds. The spirit also begins to distinguish itself from the victim. During the Voice stage, a confusing babble is emitted from the victim; it may include echoes, screaming, sneering, or groaning. This voice must be silenced by the authority of Jesus Christ's name for the exorcism to proceed. The Clash stage is a contest of wills between the exorcist and the possessing spirit. At this point the exorcist seeks to gather as much information as he can to identify the alien spirit, because this will make the final expulsion easier and simpler. Identifying itself is a submissive act of the spirit's will to that of the exorcist. When the Expulsion is complete, a receding voice or some other noise may be heard, but sometimes there is only dead silence. However, the team knows the exorcism is complete when the Presence is totally and suddenly absent. Sometimes the victim remembers everything that occurred; other times, nothing at all.

c. Zio's Friend and the Smiler

In a case called "Zio's Friend and the Smiler," the exorcist was a priest named Fr. Peter, and the victim was a girl named Marianne, nicknamed the Smiler by people who knew her. "Smiler" was also the identity the spirit gave itself during the exorcism. Fr. Peter died a year after the exorcism due to a coronary thrombosis. The priest who had assisted in the exorcism believed that the date of Fr. Peter's death was accelerated as a result of the exorcism.

Martin did not provide any family history of Marianne, although information on her parents and one brother is supplied. They appeared normal. The characteristics that may have led to Marianne's invasion were her arrogance and intellectual pride. For example, as a college student in a philosophy class, Marianne would constantly throw doubt on any statement made by her professor, a nun at a Catholic college. As Martin states, "There didn't seem to be any desire on her part to find out something true or deepen her knowledge, only a disturbing viciousness, a stony-faced cunning with words and arguments alternating with a sardonic silence and smirking satisfaction, all leading to confusion and curiously better derision" (p. 43). However, it is impossible to determine if her attitude had its origin in the entry of a spirit for some unknown reason or if the spirit entered because of her pride.

Marianne transferred to a different college. One day while studying, she met someone she simply identified as "the Man," who informed her about a kingdom. It is impossible to determine from Martin's information if this man was real. More likely he was a hallucination. In the final stages of Marianne's descent into despair, the Man informed her that she had married nothingness and had thus become a member of the kingdom. Martin notes that each case illustrates attitudes that are popular in our society but that are pushed to the extreme in the possessed person. This particular case emphasizes the notion that there is no significant difference between good and evil and being and nonbeing; all values are subject to personal preference.

Symptoms of Marianne's illness show that she suffered a progressive deterioration. While still in college, she avoided visiting her parents except on rare occasions; gradually she became more fearful, reticent, and shy. Eventually she dropped out of graduate school, stopped attending church, began living with a series of men, and no longer cared about her personal appearance. Her language became filled with obscenities, and her weight dropped from 130 to 95 pounds.

One incident Marianne reported to Martin was very intriguing. As she explains,

> Another day, I picked up a young man on Third Avenue. We went to his apartment and had intercourse. He was gentle; but when I was finished with him, he was a very frightened being. I guess I showed him a side of his character he never guessed existed. And I could see by his face that he was scared. I insisted he make coffee. Drinking it while still naked, I told him how much I hated him and how much he hated me really, and that the more he loved me and I, him, the more we hated each other. I can still see the blood draining from his face and the fear in the whites of his eyes. He was obviously afraid of some trouble. (p. 49)

One day Marianne was accosted by a mugger from behind. She turned around, smiled at him, and said, "Yes, my brother?" Looking scared, he backed away and then ran. Another day, after hearing thuds and crashes coming from Marianne's apartment for hours, neighbors called the police. It was a hot summer day. When the police entered, the apartment was freezing and the smell stomach-curdling. The freezing temperature was also noted during Marianne's exorcism.

Marianne always emitted a terrible odor and rarely displayed emotion except at the sight or sound of religious objects. One day her brother, who had not seen her in eight years, came to visit her. She was not the same person he had known, although she still exhibited some similar mannerisms. She seemed to be "repeating what somebody else was telling her" (p. 51). Waves of fear would sometimes come over him during the visit. His mother had suggested he leave a crucifix hidden in Marianne's room. When she went to the bathroom, he

> placed the small crucifix under her mattress. No sooner had Marianne returned and sat on the edge of the bed than she turned white as chalk and fell rigidly to the floor, where she lay jerking her pelvis back and forth as though in great pain.

> In seconds the expression on her face had changed from dreamy to almost animal; she foamed at the mouth and bared her teeth in a grimace of pain and anger. (p. 58)

After this incident, Marianne was taken to her parents' apartment. Psychic phenomena became frequent there, and her extreme reaction to religious objects made her family suspect the cause was more than physical or mental illness (they knew she was not a substance abuser). The eventual exorcism followed the pattern described in the general description. Martin reported that when the voice phase was reached, the spirit conveyed a message of utter and undiluted superiority. As Martin commented, this superiority "was neither sweetened by compassion nor softened by an ounce of love nor eased by a grain of condescension nor restrained by one whit of benignity toward one of less stature" (p. 74). Marianne recovered. Martin did not describe anything about her life afterward.

d. Other Cases

I will only briefly summarize the other cases reported by Martin. In "Father Bones and Mister Natch," the person exorcised was a Catholic priest (Fr. Yves) who had been relieved of his priestly duties and even formed his own church. His mother was subject to seizures. His case clearly resembles one of the features of schizophrenia, namely, thought insertion, or words that came to him unbidden, including when he was conducting Mass. At another time he became catatonic. He did not become violent during the short exorcism, but the room was cold and at one point there was an acrid odor. The exorcist tried to use reason rather than being in control, and he began receiving the same thoughts Fr. Yves had been receiving. When the exorcist did assume control, the exorcism proceeded rapidly.

In the case titled "The Virgin and the Girl-Fixer," the person exorcised was a transsexual, originally Richard but later called Rita after the transsexual operation and when the exorcism began. Rita had participated in a Black Mass and had had intercourse with the male "priest." After that incident, she felt she had a shadow. "It was like a twin spirit or soul of his own soul or spirit. And it possessed his own thoughts, memories, imagination, desires, words" (p. 215). She developed an odor and would have peculiar fits or lose her self-awareness. At the mention of the name of Jesus, Richard/Rita became "a writhing mass of hate, fear, and disgust" (p. 224).

During the exorcism there was fear in the room. Wallpaper peeled off the wall. The exorcist (Fr. Gerald) was injured during a violent episode and had to postpone the exorcism for a month. At one point, Fr. Gerald also experienced "derealization." When Richard/Rita was asked one question, one of his eyes "appeared luminous, slitted, evilly joyous" (p. 236). At another point, all those present began to hear a mob of voices shouting, screaming, and murmuring mercilessly in agony. When Fr. Gerald gave the command for the spirits to leave, they first gave an earsplitting scream before they became fainter and fainter. Rita now asked to be called Richard.

In the case "Uncle Ponto and the Mushroom Souper," several new concepts are introduced that will come up later in other therapeutic modalities. The person exorcised was named Jamsie. His parents had been either prostitutes or pimps and were also involved with drug trafficking. Jamsie could observe and converse with a spirit friend named Uncle Ponto. Martin referred to it as a "familiar spirit." The exorcist (Fr. Mark) had witness another instance of a prostitute's having a familiar spirit. Appearing more humanoid than human, Ponto always had physical distortions, although Jamsie never saw him from head to foot all at once. Ponto was about four feet six inches tall. One of his knees was higher than the other, and he had other bodily and facial distortions. Ponto only began to bother Jamsie after the latter's parents had turned to underworld activities. At first, Ponto's visits were occasional, but eventually they became almost constant; his thoughts were present even when Jamsie did not see him. Whenever Ponto appeared, there was a strange lingering odor. The first time Ponto became visible, he told Jamsie that he had been with him for many years. Jamsie's decision to undergo the exorcism finally came only after Ponto had urged him to commit suicide.

Although it is speculation and not important to Jamsie's recovery, Jamsie's manager Jay at one radio station was identified as a perfectly possessed person. Even Ponto, as a sign of deference to Jay's spirit, did not want to be near Jay. Jamsie experienced turmoil, even panic, when in the presence of Jay and his evil spirit.

During the exorcism, Fr. Mark could not initially converse directly with the true evil spirit but had to use Ponto as an intermediary to carry messages. Eventually Fr. Mark could speak with the true evil spirit, which identified itself as one of many parts of a kingdom. Fr. Mark and his assistants could hear a deafening sound, but after a while they realized the sounds were of confusion and defeat. Ponto became distorted and disconnected, and Jamsie announced that he was "free." The concept of a hierarchy of spirits above the one present in the possessed person will be met with later in several therapeutic methods.

The case of "The Rooster and the Tortoise" illustrates the dangers of occult activities performed under the guise of parapsychology. It also shows the dangers of experimenting with the powers of the mind. Carl, the man who was exorcised, was a natural psychic as a youth and was very brilliant academically. He became involved in activities such as out-of-body travel, telepathy, trance states, reincarnation, and attempts to find "the true and original Christianity." Fr. Hearty, the priest who exorcised him, was from Wales. Martin claimed that many Welsh Celtic people are more naturally psychic than people of other ethnic groups. Fr. Hearty met Carl while in one of Carl's parapsychology courses. Carl could often read people's minds, or at least their state of mind or mood, but he could not read Fr. Hearty's (his was "opaque"), and this always puzzled Carl. Fr. Hearty asked Carl if he presumed that all spirits were beneficial.

As a result of his psychic training, Carl was able to see auras around objects. He also learned how to do astral travel. Sometimes during the exorcism he would leave his body and the exorcism had to be stopped. This particular exorcism took place in a library. At one point, all of the books fell to the floor, one shelf at a time. To one of Fr. Hearty's questions, the spirit responded, "The living are surrounded by their dead. Those of the dead who belong to us, they do our bidding. Everyone in the Kingdom does our bidding" (p. 386). In several later sections of this same chapter, some earthbound spirits appear to be under the control of demons. However, the therapists in that section do not recommend exorcisms. Fr. Hearty then told Carl that he must renounce all his psychic powers. He demanded that Carl look at a chair, and Carl realized that the chair no longer had an aura. He saw it as everyone else saw it. Fr. Hearty then knew that the Tortoise (the nickname of the evil spirit) had departed.

e. Conclusions

In this section I have pointed out some similarities between spirit possession to mental illness, such as hearing disparaging voices. However, there are just as many contrasts. Martin did not mention the manner in which these individuals were treated by mental-health professionals before undergoing an exorcism. Normally, the Catholic Church requires a mental-health analysis before allowing an exorcism to be performed.

In the next section, I discuss a secular English psychiatrist who explores this realm of possession, but his distinctive terminology makes it difficult to make direct comparisons with the work of other therapists.

H. The Possession Psychiatrist

1. Introduction

Arthur Guirdham (1905–1992), a British psychiatrist, attributed much abnormal behavior to possession or other psychic causes in *The Psychic Dimensions of Mental Health* (1982). By the time of the book's publication, Guirdham had been practicing psychiatry for over 50 years. Guirdham states that he had frequent encounters with parapsychological phenomena over the years, both in patients and among his friends. He has his own terms for mapping human spiritual components that sometimes seem consistent with those previously presented. I will discuss those terms throughout this section. Many illnesses that are common today were not mentioned when he first began practicing. Others that were prominent then are no longer diagnosed today (e.g., neurasthenia). Other disorders have simply been given new names.

Although the term *psychic* can have different meanings today, Guirdham uses the term for anything related to the psyche or the soul. When he says a person is psychic, he usually means that the individual has precognitive, clairvoyant, or telepathic abilities. The natural psychic faculties should not be repressed; Guirdham feels that he was most effective as a psychiatrist when he made psychic contact with patients.

However, he considers current (when he was writing) morbid interest in psychic phenomena to be symptomatic of a civilization's end. Use of Ouija boards, among other practices, is an open invitation to be attacked by discarnate entities. In his opinion, a discarnate entity is the psyche of a deceased person in a place between this world and the next, called Hades. Guirdham maintains that the number of discarnate entities is on the increase.

2. Spiritual Terms

Guirdham considers the psyche to be an immortal component of human nature. The psyche is not our personality or our ego; instead, it separates from the personality and the physical body at death. He also believes humans have individualized spirits that can communicate with the Holy Spirit. According to Guirdham, "the psyche exists out of time" (p. 10) and thus can see into the future and past. The personality is activated by "lusts, ambitions, fear and regrets" (p. 10) and is riveted in time, concerned with the past or future. The psyche, however, can directly perceive without sensory input. Guirdham explains that there is no such thing as multiple personality but says that there may be several psyches, that is, the original and several other discarnate entities. His term *psyche* seems similar to my use of the term *Spirit*, but I believe each individual has only one Spirit. Guirdham claims that the psyche enters a human body at the moment of conception. He once commented that some of his female patients with psychic abilities were able to determine during intercourse that their child was conceived, by detecting the entry of the child's psyche.

3. Benign and Malign Possession

An example of benign possession that Guirdham encountered arose during a telephone conversation. A friendly psyche of a deceased person took over the voice of the caller and gave some important information to Guirdham. Guirdham had known the deceased person and clearly recognized the voice during the short message. In several cases, the message was almost always correct and helpful, either for Guirdham's personal life or for the life of one of his patients. When the voice of the original caller returned, Guirdham asked the caller about the message.

The person did not know what he was talking about. This indicated a brief, but complete, takeover of the caller's body, with no long-term consequences. In one case, Guirdham's wife heard the interrupting voice, corroborating his claim.

In malign possession cases, if the patient is aware of the struggle, the phenomenon is called obsessional. If the patient is totally unaware of what she is saying, it is a case of possession. Adults who are possessed were often obsessional as children. Although not as severe as possession, obsessional states are also related to the psyche and discarnate entities. People who are obsessional often have similar backgrounds. They often had a difficult birth and experienced night terrors as children. Children with night terrors often later display obsessional tics and twitches, which Guirdham believes are "a protective reflex designed to throw off an invading entity" (p. 63). I would regard the difficult birth as the source of trauma, a common factor in obsessional and possessive states. Guirdham, who had experienced night terrors himself as a youngster, does not believe these are hallucinations. Instead, he sees them as true materializations of discarnate (and evil) entities.

In addition, hallucinogenic drugs are often a pathway for entry by discarnate entities, by creation of a "psychic void" between the psyche and the personality. Painkilling drugs are less likely to induce possession than are the hallucinogenic type, for example, LSD. Alcohol rarely induces possession, except for chronic alcoholism. Violence while under the influence of alcohol can be a sign of possession.

4. Various Illnesses

Although he uses the term *mental health* in his title, some of the illnesses Guirdham discusses are not considered related to mental health. For some of these illnesses, a person may see a completely unrelated medical practitioner, such as an internist or a neurologist. Among the mental illnesses, behavior patterns, and physical illnesses Guirdham believes to be determined by the psyche are somnambulism (sleepwalking), hyperactivity, epilepsy, asthma, dyspepsia and colonic spasms, manic depression, migraine headaches, Meniere's disease, hysteria, anxiety, schizophrenia, and psychopathology. Guirdham believes that hyperkinetic children act the way they do in order to escape discarnate entities. He thinks most of these children do escape and end up quite normal.

Another illness indicative of possession is epilepsy. Unlike hyperactivity, it rarely abates in adulthood. Throughout history, people with epilepsy have been known to have psychic abilities. The illness is sometimes called *the Sacred Disease*. The discarnate entities present in epilepsy are generally malignant, and the epileptic acts as a dissipater of the evil in the vicinity. Epilepsy's convulsions are an attempt to repel the invaders. Some attempts to repel are not successful. Sometimes the epileptic becomes so chronically possessed that he cannot function in society. According to Guirdham, some patients actually see a discarnate entity prior to having an epileptic fit. The Russian writer Dostoevsky had a near mystical experience before his attacks, having feelings of joy, bliss, and oneness.

5. Evil

Guirdham speculates that people with migraine headaches are often psychic, especially having precognitive abilities (usually manifested in dreams). These migraine attacks often coincide with difficulties in the lives of the sufferer's friends and relatives. People who suffer from migraine frequently report having had childhood night terrors. The headaches may be especially severe if the person has had an encounter with "a human transmitter of evil." These transmitters may be possessed themselves but are not necessarily so. They also may or may not be in active control, or even aware, of their state and may use various psychic powers to gain control over others, even if they claim good intentions.

Guirdham says that evil is a force in itself, not just the absence of good. Some pillars of society, though seemingly very respectable, can radiate evil. The less we believe in evil, the more vulnerable we are to it. The terms describing evil have also often evolved. Actions that were originally described, centuries ago, as good and evil are now described in the milder terms, *right* and *wrong*. When psychiatry began describing these realities, these terms became *stable* and *unstable*, and finally *adjusted* and *unadjusted*. Disease can be a manifestation of the force of evil. Guirdham feels that particularly good people with psychic gifts often act as magnets for evil or for evil people. Guirdham maintains that evil is detected by the psyche, although the personality may react to what the psyche has detected. Evil is not just an abstract impression; it is actually a vibratory pattern that can be detected. Physical symptoms that the psyche produces in the body as a reaction to the evil include vomiting and various skin reactions.

6. Mental Illnesses

Guirdham believes that there has been a major recent increase in adolescent mental illness. For instance, anorexia nervosa is a covert rejection of materialism and of life itself by seeking to overcome the limitations of matter. However, it may result in possession when the body becomes exhausted. Guirdham opined that electroconvulsive therapy (ECT) may be an effective treatment in advanced stages of the illness.

Schizophrenia represents a level beyond other mental illnesses. The number of people suffering from it increased dramatically in the decades before he began writing. Schizophrenics seem withdrawn from reality and often lack feeling. In paranoid schizophrenia, the person is more withdrawn from people than from reality. Many schizophrenics can be considered failed mystics. They know there is a reality beyond the physical, but they choose the wrong path to reach it. The illness is a classic case of multiple possessions by discarnate entities, most evident in catatonic schizophrenia. "The fragmentary nature of schizophrenic thought and behavior is due to the individual being inhabited by an unharmonized collection of discarnate entities" (p. 242). Guirdham says that ECT is effective in some cases, though the effects may not last. He states that ECT literally blasts the possessing entity away.

Paranoid schizophrenics are more likely to have only one entity or to be under a general force of evil. Paranoids can be great leaders of cults and anarchist organizations and are often involved in witchcraft and black magic. David Koresh of the Branch Davidians cult in Waco, Texas, who shot federal agents, certainly had many characteristics of a person with paranoid schizophrenia. Guirdham does not believe that the great cold-blooded mass murderers of a political type, such as Joseph Stalin, are possessed by discarnate entities; rather, they are transmitters of evil. Their psyche is essentially dead.

In school, Guirdham also learned about people called "moral imbeciles"—people who simply had no concept of right and wrong. He was told there were very few of them. Today, these people are called psychopaths, and their number has increased dramatically. Guirdham says many of them are physically and socially attractive; they interview well but behave badly. Alcohol and drugs may also be factor in psychopathic behavior, but not necessarily. Guirdham believes that for psychopaths, the psyche of the person chosen for possession was already functioning in darkness, not in the world open to us by the individualized spirit. There is also a connection between psychopathic behavior and the decay of civilization, as indicated by corruption and anarchy. "At the end of civilization the darker discarnate entities gather like vultures at the fringe of human consciousness" (p. 251).

Guirdham certainly had some interesting theories, and his long-term experience as a therapist is definitely impressive. However, his examples are not of cures he performed on his patients, as most of the other books include in their discussions. Rather, the examples focus on his impressions from a lifetime of treating patients. He definitely agrees that discarnate entities are factors in human behavior. He believes there is a spiritual basis for evil.

The next few therapists highlighted contribute to an understanding of that concept, with an emphasis on "dark-force entities" as well as on discarnate human entities. These therapists allege that conditions in former lives must be processed during the therapeutic process. They also found nonhuman entities that are called demons or dark forces. The first one, a doctor now living in Australia, uses much of the terminology I developed in chapter 8 to explain the process of spirit intrusion and release.

I. Therapists Dealing with Additional Factors

1. Introduction

The previously mentioned therapy methods for spirit intrusion generally incorporate the idea that a person who died with unresolved issues is not able to transition and move into the *light*. Several recent therapists have found earthbound entities, but they also have found that some behavioral issues are related to past lives. These therapists maintain that they never specifically inquired about previous lives, but they may have asked a client to go to the source of his problem during hypnosis. It is then that the client began describing a life many years before his birth.

The five main books dealing with these therapeutic methods are as follows:

- *Entity Possession: Freeing the Energy Body of Negative Influences* (1997) by Samuel Sagan, MD
- *Remarkable Healings: A Psychiatrist Discovers Unsuspected Roots of Mental and Physical Illness* (1996) by Shakuntala Modi, MD
- *Healing Lost Souls: Releasing Unwanted Spirits from Your Energy Body* (2003) by William J. Baldwin, PhD
- *Freeing the Captives: The Emerging Therapy of Treating Spirit Attachment* (1999) by Louise Ireland-Frey, MD
- *Rapid Entity Attachment Release: A Breakthrough in the World of Spirit Possession and Releasement* (2011) by Athanasios N. Komianos

Three of the other therapists previously discussed (Atteshlis, Fiore, and Guirdham) also mention reincarnation, but they do not necessarily relate past lives to spirit intrusion as do the therapists discussed in this section.

2. Reincarnation

The idea of reincarnation has been around for centuries. A number of early Christian writers including Origen were proponents of reincarnation. Some people believe this view was disposed of to gain more control over people's lives by implying that a person has to "get it right" in this life. However, many people who discuss the topic of reincarnation fail to mention the concept of karma, or consequences for actions in a past life. Some people only associate karma with punishment for past actions, but acting kindly toward others can result in desirable consequences. Desirable consequences do not imply wealth or power in a later life, but they do imply a rewarding and satisfying present life. In fact, easily obtained wealth and power can be obstacles to spiritual growth. Between lives, a person will plan certain circumstances for his or her next life in order to resolve problems from previous lives. Karma is always taking place, and most consequences often occur during a current life.

Modi mentions one patient who allegedly had severe injuries to his neck in numerous past lives. She had to relive and release each incident in a past life in order to correct the current problem. If there are consequences associated with each incident, I would imagine that the karma associated with them many lives ago would have already been satisfied. If the karmic debt from the original incident was satisfied, then the patient should not need to relive the incident. I would also tend to associate karma with actions done to possibly harm others; that is, they were performed by a perpetrator. Being a victim should not create karma. However, I have read the work of some researchers who allegedly found scars or other physical indicators on people who were victims of crimes or accidents in an immediate past life, for example, a scar where a man was shot or stabbed to death in his recent past life (a life that can be verified, although it cannot be proven that the man was that person). Of course, a person could have difficulties related to a past life that do not involve karma. There are numerous other books that discuss investigation of past lives using hypnotherapy, but many of those therapists do not find demons and do not employ angels for removing the demons. An example of one such book is *Many Lives, Many Masters* (1988) by psychiatrist Brian L. Weiss. He claims to have progressed more than four thousand patients to past lives. Trauma, either in earlier childhood or in a past life, is recalled, relived, released, and resolved, as is done in psychoanalysis for current life trauma.

Some therapists claim that their clients can remember entering the *light* after death in a former life and then, after a period of time, entering an unborn child to become a new life. One patient did say that the entire soul did not enter the embryo at conception but that some fragment of the soul does enter at conception (the remainder of the soul enters prior to or during birth). In between lives, a person usually plans the circumstances for his next life and determines if he has any special purpose in that life.

There are two dilemmas I see in the concept of reincarnation. One is that there has been such a rapid increase in human population in the last two centuries, a six- to sevenfold increase, that if everyone alive today were regressed to two centuries ago, all of them could not have been alive then. One way to accommodate this irony is assume that the number of years between incarnations has been greatly reduced. That is, a person living centuries ago was reincarnating once every five hundred to a thousand years but is now doing it once or twice each century. However, many people reportedly come back to close relatives, which would be meaningless 500 hundred years later. Some scholars on the subject may be able to explain this dilemma if reincarnation is a reality. It is also possible that numerous people at this time are simply experiencing their first incarnation.

I did an Internet search to discover the total cumulative population of the earth since the dawn of humanity. An answer calculated by the Population Reference Bureau estimated it at 100 billion to 110 billion. This would allow for each current person to have incarnated about 15 times. However, many therapists who say they deal with past lives claim each person has had over a hundred past lives.

As I explain it, mental theories at some point must correspond to physical reality. A physicist can develop an equation that seemingly explains the physical world, but if the prediction of that equation of what will happen under certain circumstances is incorrect, then the equations/theory must be discarded. A therapist can claim to have found hundreds of past lives in numerous people, but if that does not correspond to the actual population of the earth, the concept must be incorrect or not properly understood.

The second dilemma regarding reincarnation is related to the types of former lives. While Modi and the previously cited Brian Weiss claim that most lives were ordinary and very few were famous people, it seems to me that very few recalls involve a death in infancy or early childhood, which was quite common centuries ago, as many people did not live to adulthood. Of course, it is possible that lives involving a death before age seven are simply not remembered. From my brief reading on the subject, children between the ages of three and six are the most likely to recall an alleged past life. Modi states that we reincarnate into many races, cultures, and religions, and that these reincarnated identities may be male or female, rich or poor, or victims or perpetrators of crimes, and have many occupations and types of death experiences. This is in contrast to those who hold that we often return to the same family.

When I read about situations in some past lives that created difficulties in Modi's patient's current life, it appears that many were able to read and write. The vast majority of humans have only been able to read and write in the last two hundred years, indicating at most two or three incarnations. Some patients are unable to access past lives. According to Modi, memory of those lives can be blocked by demons or can be inaccessible for other various reasons. Modi always tries to determine if the information on past lives is a result of false memory syndrome (discussed in chapter 6, on DID).

While these two dilemmas would tend to make me skeptical of reincarnation, the concept of past lives does greatly explain one idea I have presented, and will further explore in a later chapter. This is the concept that humans are developing a closer relationship with their Spirit as time goes on and as human history amasses. If reincarnation occurs, then it elucidates for us that this is a gradual process that increases with each life. Without reincarnation, are we modern humans simply more fortunate than our ancestors to have greater access to our Spirit? The reality of past lives, earthbound spirits, demons, or other spiritual influences (to be discussed later) attached to the patient is irrelevant if the patient is relieved of symptoms or is suffering as a result of these therapeutic modalities. That is, a patient could be simply creating a sensory symbol of a demon or a past life to resolve an internal conflict. Three therapists previously discussed, namely, Atteshlis, Fiore, and Guirdham, also believed in reincarnation, although they did not involve it in their therapy.

J. The Therapy Method of Sagan

1. Entities and Therapy Method

Samuel Sagan, MD, often writes about soul fragmentation, a process resulting from trauma. Soul fragmentation is very similar to soul loss, previously discussed. Sagan speaks of the human body using terms similar to those employed in chapter 8, on Eastern concepts of human spirituality.

He practices in Australia, where he founded the Clairvision School to teach his method of accessing information, such as emotional blockages, from patients. He does not describe the method in detail, but he refers to the techniques as ISIS, the acronym for Inner Space Interactive Sourcing. He claims that this technique does not involve hypnosis, suggestion, creative visualization, guided imagination, or positive affirmations. It does entail an expansion of perception in which the client becomes aware of movements and energies within herself. The therapist is referred to as a "connector." The client must declare the presence of an entity, never the connector. According to Sagan, a client may refer to the presence she detects as attached to her. However, this presence is distinct and foreign, with an autonomous consciousness that has its "own desires, emotions, and thoughts" (p. 6). Sagan claims that entities are not "unresolved complexes, subpersonalities, or parts of the clients 'shadow'" (p. 29). Rather, entities are usually simple, with predictable behavioral patterns. The presence creates cravings in the client for specific behaviors, activities, and food or drug substances. After becoming aware of a presence, a client can distinguish natural cravings from those generated by the presence. After the presence is cleared, cravings significantly subside.

An entity may also desire activities that involve emotional intensity. It may enjoy casual sex with multiple partners but may be reluctant if caring for a partner is involved. These entities always want something, as described in the following (a direct quotation):

- It can be a particular desire or an addiction, such as drinking, sex, or drugs.
- They can be focused on a particular emotion, such as pain, melancholy, suffering, punishment, guilt, violence, and so forth.
- They may want to be looked after, taken care of and nurtured.
- Some just want to be left alone to hide inside, slumbering in a warm and snug environment.
  (p. 15)

These entities may induce a desire to procrastinate, act irresponsibly, or instill fear and doubt. "Anything that decreases mental acuity and favors inner blurriness seems to be welcomed and favored by entities" (p. 18). Thus, mental acuity may increase after the entity departs.

While an entity has an overall adverse effect, the client may derive benefit from an entity. The sensual enjoyment that is taken to excess by the entity is still pleasurable to the client. If an entity has been around a while, the client may relish the familiarity. According to Sagan, only a few entities speak to the client. However, they may provide internal disparaging self-perception, even if not a voice similar to what a schizophrenic may encounter. The entity may have a greater influence when the client is alone.

Entities can also cause physical illnesses, which go away after removal. However, even if an entity caused an illness that has become chronic, removal of the entity may not restore normal function. Some psychological problems may remain but are easier to resolve once the entity departs.

There are three stages for clearing an entity. The first stage is discovery, or becoming aware of the entity. In the second stage, consisting of observation, Sagan often has the client observe the entity for several weeks before clearing it. Observing the entity does not give it more power. The therapist often asks, "What does it want?" During the observation stage, the client explores the benefits of the entity, as the client may decide not to have it removed. However, keeping it can exacerbate the symptoms for which the entity was responsible. The client also seeks to understand when and how the entity became attached, as the client may be able to prevent future occurrences. The same entity never returns if properly cleared, but a new entity may be seeking the same pathway for entry.

The final stage is clearing. The client usually observes the entity departing, or the client may feel immediate relief. The entity is taken into the Great Light, after which it can no longer become attached to another person. If an astral fragment, it becomes undifferentiated astral light that is then recycled. As Sagan writes, the connector

> must be in touch with a particular frequency of spiritual light in which the entity will be processed. This implies the collaboration of certain spiritual beings. The clearer must therefore be linked to nonphysical guides or angels that will assist in the process. This cannot be improvised, and requires that one has received approval from these beings to carry out the work, like a "clearing license." Of course these beings must be real guides or angels, not entities trying to impress

you by making lots of vibration and letting bogus light rain onto your head. (p. 176)

A connector or clearer must be emotionally stable, healthy, and unreactive to threats. The technique requires in-person training by a qualified clearer. Entities can detect weaknesses in the connector. The use of standard psychotherapy is rarely successful for removing entities.

2. Human Spiritual Components

Sagan describes his theory in terms of an etheric body, an astral body, and a self. Entities consist of etheric and astral substance. He also says there are "perverse" energies that consist only of etheric substance. Sagan further delineates that the astral body and ego are part of an upper complex. For a person to find his or her self, he or she "must disentangle it from the astral body" (p. 42). Mystics are able to achieve this disentanglement, usually as a result of training and practice. People with DID have likewise become somewhat disentangled as a result of trauma and can have a relationship with their Inner Self-helper (ISH).

The lower complex consists of etheric and physical bodies. During sleep, the ego and astral body lose interest in the lower complex and direct their activity to the astral world. At death there is a final dissociation between the two complexes. When a person dies, the astral body can no longer have the desires fulfilled that it previously could get from the etheric/physical world. Suppressing a desire while living is not the same as eliminating the desire. Sagan does not mention thought forms, but he does comment that thoughts are a tangible form of astral matter.

Sagan's portrait of the higher self or Spirit closely parallels what I have been trying to project in previous chapters.

> The Spirit is the immortal flame, the part in which metaphysical freedom already shines. One does not become enlightened by enlightening one's Spirit, but by unveiling it. For the Spirit is already fully enlightened and connected with the Divine. To one who knows the Spirit, or Self, the idea that it could be trapped in the material world after death sounds more than fanciful, for if there is one part in human beings that can never be lost, it is precisely the Spirit. (p. 111)

3. Death

The astral body consists of a multitude of desires. "On an astral level, you are not a person, you are a mob" (p. 48). These bits do not necessarily communicate with each other. The higher ego can harmonize and unify these bits and transform them into "accomplishing the works of the Higher Self" (p. 49). If the astral bits have not been penetrated by the light of the ego, they fragment upon bodily death. These fragments will persist in desires and addictions. The fragments endure even if they were suppressed during life. Thus, Sagan concludes the following:

1. "A small fraction of the astral body remains attached to the Ego, which departs for the journey into the intermediary worlds;
2. A big part crumbles into undifferentiated astral dust;
3. Various bits break off and drift away in space as fragments." (pp. 51–52)

When a person reincarnates, only a few memories that were in the small fraction that were attached to the ego can be remembered. For its new life, the ego gathers fresh astral material to form a new astral body. This new material does not have any memories.

These astral fragments wander about in astral space looking for something to satisfy their desires. In the astral world, like attracts like, so an astral fragment that seeks alcohol will gather around people who drink or at locations where alcohol is served. Sagan notes that this is natural and has little to do with moral concepts. A fragment is not evil and usually has a singular personality characteristic, and the behavior it induces may not resemble the behavior of the person in whom the fragment originated. The fragment is not seeking to harm anyone, but it may do so while satisfying a craving. In addition to fulfilling desires for physical substances or emotional attractions, astral fragments seek familiar places. Thus, close relatives of the deceased person have the highest risk of attracting a fragment of the deceased. With a few exceptions, entities are not full spirits of a deceased person. Instead, they are merely etheric and astral fragments or energies.

Sagan also explains that an astral fragment, especially a more structured one, can sometimes have an etheric layer attached to it.

This makes the fragment denser. The etheric layer then acts like a glue to attach itself to the etheric body of other humans. The etheric layer also requires some of the vital energy of a client. This may explain why many people with entity attachments are also depressed, as the entity consumes much of the host's energy.

Sagan also discusses cremation. He reports that fire can destroy the etheric body, which would make it more difficult to form an etheric layer on the astral body. Thus, the astral fragment is less likely to attach to a living person. However, Sagan also claims that cremation needs to occur after the deceased has undergone his or her life review. If it occurs earlier, the astral body does not quite detach and the trauma of the burning can cause it to enter lower astral planes. Holy yogis are not cremated, as their practices in life are believed to prevent fragmentation at the time of death.

Sagan reports that at funerals in India, people wear white because it reflects astral fragments. Black attracts these fragments. Family members are considered impure for a number of days after the death, and certain foods are avoided. In India, as well as in a number of other countries, food is offered to discarnate entities. Interestingly, Sagan claims that people with Alzheimer's disease or schizophrenia appear to begin the process of astral fragmentation before death.

Sagan provides an example in which a woman had an astral fragment of a man who had committed suicide and had seemingly attached to his stepdaughter, whom he had abused. My study also indicates that suicide is more likely to result in an earthbound entity, what Sagan would call an astral fragment of the deceased person. In a later chapter, I will discuss how when an abuser dies, he is more likely to attach to a person he had abused.

I would also add that I consider alternate personalities (APs) in a person with DID to be much greater than a fragment. Therapists who treat patients with DID often speak of "personality fragments" that have only one minor function in a person with DID, and not a multidimensional personality. Thus, a DID fragment may correspond to Sagan's concept of an astral fragment, but a complete AP more closely resembles a full or almost complete astral body. That is, it did not divide into numerous fragments upon death of the physical body.

While Sagan only uses the term *astral fragments*, according to the Eastern concept presented in chapter 8, there is also a mental body. Some writers in this field may opine that a full astral body may have mental and emotional components rather than two separate bodies (mental and emotional). The high intelligence of some APs, for instance the AP named Arthur in Billy Milligan, would indicate that Arthur is the complete or nearly complete mental body of a deceased person. Knowing a foreign language is certainly more complex than the simple desire of an astral fragment.

Sagan says that animals also have astral bodies. However, the astral body of an animal probably does not fragment upon death because animals do not have the complex desires of a human being.

4. Pregnancy

Sagan defines the soul as a combination of the astral body and the higher self. He says that according to the Hindu tradition, the soul arrives in the fourth month of pregnancy, but he admits that other esoteric traditions have different beliefs about when the soul arrives. Later, he reports that astral fragments may remain in the womb after a miscarriage or an abortion, but he does not specify at which time this occurs. These fragments remaining in the womb may be why McAll found behavioral difficulties in children born after an abortion, stillbirth, or miscarriage. Even though it may arrive at a certain time, "the incarnation of the astral and the Ego into the physical and etheric is a very gradual process" (p. 71). Some argue that the process is not complete until about age twenty-eight, but in mature and responsible people it can occur much earlier.

Sagan reports that he could fill a book with case studies of postabortion entities. He recommends that any woman who has had an abortion or miscarriage be checked by someone who can clear entities. Later, though, Sagan claims that if a pregnant woman has dark or perverse energies in her astral body, it is possible that during a miscarriage these energies may be transferred to the embryo and thus expelled during miscarriage.

5. Catching an Entity

Sagan reports that our bodies have numerous natural defense systems to prevent entities from entering. It is when these defense systems break down that entry can occur. One breakdown that can occur over which a person has little control is being unwanted by a mother during pregnancy. A mother's use of alcohol or other drugs, or being physically abused during pregnancy, can have similar results. An entity can go directly to the embryo in these situations. The fact that an entity came so early in life does not make it any more difficult to clear, but there may be more psychological work that needs to be done to resolve emotional problems after a lengthy association. If a woman at one point has two embryos, and if one of them dies, the astral fragment of the deceased twin may attach to the remaining embryo. Sagan speculates that this may happen more frequently than is currently believed to happen.

Sagan also comments on entity entry as a result of drug use or surgery. As he writes, "Among the most common factors is the consumption of certain drugs, either for intoxication or for medicinal purposes. Alcohol, sleeping pills, pain killers, anesthetics, and a whole range of narcotic drugs from marijuana to heroin all create a disorganization of the defense system and can cause breaches" (p. 93).

He notes that one glass of wine or one marijuana cigarette does not pose a problem. He explains that surgical general anesthesia leaves a person vulnerable to penetration by an entity but that local anesthesia is not as dangerous. In addition to the anesthesia, a scalpel making an incision opens the etheric body's defense system. Chronic illnesses in which the sufferer is very weak also create openings.

Any time a person undergoes physical or emotional trauma, the etheric astral system of defense can temporarily collapse. If a child is lonely or afraid, he or she may ask for, and thus attract, a nurturing fragment. Natural disasters and wars can make an observer (or someone injured) lose some defense. If numerous people die at the location, there may be more fragments in the vicinity. Sagan also cautions that when people hear about entities, they "suspect them everywhere and develop a kind of phobia that is completely unjustified" (p. 62). Furthermore, entities should not be used as scapegoats for other difficulties.

In addition, Sagan mentions ghosts, maintaining that a ghost appears to be an "extremely crystallized astral fragment, possibly coated with an etheric layer" (p. 103). This etheric energy enables a ghost to affect matter and create sounds or to act like a poltergeist.

6. Past Lives

How do entities relate to past lives? Some therapists whose practices involve past lives simply treat incidents in those past lives as they would an incident earlier in a client's current life. Sagan discusses several cases. In one of these, an angry and vengeful fragment waited in "astral space" for the person it had left at death until the same person reincarnated, at which point the fragment attached itself to the new physical body. In another case, a fragment of a person seeking revenge in one life waited in astral space until the person against whom it sought revenge had reincarnated, at which time the fragment attached itself. In a third case, the entity was a fragment of a woman who remained in astral space after her death in a previous life and then entered herself in a later incarnation. An entity that is not a fragment of a particular person may also follow that person from one life to the next; however, entities actually search for a vibration frequency. The same frequency could be present in a different person from the person to whom the fragment was previously attached. Sagan describes this vibration as "similar astral features and psychological dispositions" (p. 125).

7. Cords and Bits

Sagan maintains that just as there is a physical umbilical cord during pregnancy, this cord has an etheric component that is not necessarily severed at birth. For this cord to remain a few years after birth is acceptable, but it can become a twisted relationship if it lasts too long and prevents the child from reaching maturity. Psychotherapy will not be successful if the cord is not severed. The cord is a link to another person's consciousness. Some patients with cords may have benefits (mentioned earlier) that make it difficult for them to act upon a desire to sever the cord. "A cord is a kind of etheric-astral pipe through which energies and emotions circulate more or less constantly" (p. 133). Although mother—child is the most common type of cord, cords can be formed between two people in a sexual relationship. A cord can continue in the form of a fragment after one party's death.

While entities are astral fragments or bits from outside a person's normal astral field, Sagan has also found that bits from a person's normal astral field can separate into astral space. These are connected to the body by cords, similar to those previously discussed. Since the astral field is the link between the ego and the etheric and physical bodies, the second and third cannot fully function without a full astral field. Symptoms include a lack of energy, stamina, motivation, drive, purpose, self-confidence, courage, and joy. These lacks can be accompanied by psychological and physical disorders. It usually takes more therapy time to recover these lost bits than to remove an entity that should not be there. When these bits are restored, some people finally believe that they are fully alive.

8. Beyond Fragments to Extraordinary Fragments

Sagan maintains that about 99% of entities are astral fragments from dead people, but some entities can be worse. In one case, a woman had an entity that had been sent to her by a sorcerer. The woman had not participated in any occult activity. Although Sagan feels that this type of entity can lead to further mental deterioration and is even less amenable to conventional therapy than regular entities, it is just as easy to clear.

Sagan says that clients with entities have a high rate of canceling appointments and provide unusual reasons for being late for appointments (the real reason is the influence of the entity). In one case, a woman said her "spirit-guide" was giving her advice about what to do with her life. Sagan summarizes what she reported: "You have a spirit-guide that pushes you to eat chocolate and that watches you when you have sex. He doesn't want you to be with your husband because he is jealous, and he wants you to masturbate while thinking of him. Moreover, he takes his energy from your heart. Isn't that a bit suspect, altogether" (p. 154)?

Sagan concluded that the spirit guide was just another entity, which he believes happens frequently. The client never returned to see him. Another female client realized that what she believed to be a spirit guide (often appearing as a nun) was actually an entity. She had it cleared, and subsequently gave up a fifteen-year smoking habit within ten days.

In the next section, I discuss a psychiatrist who originally came from India but whose terminology more closely resembles Western perspectives.

K. East Meets West: The Therapy Method of Modi

1. Introduction

Psychiatrist Shakuntala Modi has interesting therapeutic methods that support many of the previously mentioned therapies. Her book is titled *Remarkable Healings: A Psychiatrist Discovers Unsuspected Roots of Mental and Physical Illness* (1996).

Modi hypnotizes her patients, but she claims she never asks leading questions or gives suggestions during this time. Modi asks hypnotized patients to go to the source of their problems. Many of them go to early childhood or prenatal occurrences. In some cases they proceed to a traumatic event in a past life. She uses other standard psychotherapeutic techniques without involving spiritual entities before using her unusual spiritual method.

She states that her theories were derived entirely from her psychiatric findings and not from her personal beliefs. Her book's foreword was written by a patient who had helped her greatly, a professed Christian. She also reports that her patients identified some of their problems to be the result of "demons," a typically Western religious concept. In addition to demons, she refers to the spiritual forces that assist her during therapy as God and angels, *beings of light*, or guides. She also discusses leading spirit intruders into the *light*.

Through her work, she determined that many of her patients had experienced trauma, possibly as far back as prebirth, and that this trauma often allowed the entrance of spiritual entities. Her book uses the terms *spirit*, *entity*, and *soul* (which she defines as the immortal part of the human) interchangeably. My research indicates that Spirit is a different spiritual components of humans, separate from soul, but I do use the word *spirit* to refer to an earthbound entity. She also uses *heaven*, *light*, and *the presence of God* synonymously, as well as *energy field* and *aura*. She refers to entering the *light* at the time of death as the same thing as classically entering heaven.

2. Causes of Mental Disorders

Based on findings from her hypnotized patients, Modi attributes mental illness to the following:

- Current life traumas including prenatal and birth traumas
- Past-life traumas
- Possession or attachment by earthbound spirits
- Possession or attachment by demon spirits
- Soul fragmentation and soul loss
  (p. 43)

Modi sometimes refers to the collection of the above situations as "baggage." While some of the problems associated with prenatal and birth trauma may cause lifelong conditions, some in her list appear to begin later in life, such as a current-life event that activates the pain of a past-life event or birth trauma. For instance, a person may have been hanged in a previous life, and it is only a new neck injury that activates the memory of the past-life hanging. The person now has major neck pain or a fear of choking that far exceeds the seriousness of the recent injury.

A similarity to this phenomenon has been discovered recently in the field of genetics. A gene may carry a propensity for an illness or disorder, but geneticists have found an "epigenome," a simple molecule or fragment of a molecule that can activate the gene. The epigenome is not actually part of the gene itself. A physical substance or a traumatic event in a person's life may activate the epigenome, which in turn activates the gene.

When spiritual intervention is requested, hypnotized patients often describe "seeing a brilliant white Light and beings of the Light in it" (p. 340). Patients usually describe the beings as entities from their own religious context. Patients may also recognize one or more guardian angels and guides they may have known in a past life. If deceased relatives or loved ones are seen, they appear young and healthy, even if they were old and sick when they died.

3. Prenatal, Birth, and Past-Life Traumas

Modi states that unborn children record the emotions, thoughts, and pain experienced by their mother during the pregnancy as if these were their own personal perceptions. Even a mother's previous desire to have an abortion may cause the child to feel rejected and worthless. Such feelings can last a lifetime. Modi states that some patients can recall numerous births, including when they were originally "cast out from God." According to one theory of reincarnation, all people's souls were once connected to God, but they had to depart on numerous physical journeys, which they must complete before they return to God. Modi speculates that sudden infant death syndrome (SIDS) may be the result of a child's realization that he or she has chosen the wrong body to achieve his or her purpose, and thus the child's spirit departs. Since his or her life was so brief, that child's spirit can probably reincarnate rather quickly.

A single symptom or multiple symptoms in a patient may be the result of trauma in one past life or in multiple past lives. The symptoms may be psychological, such as phobias, panic attacks, eating disorders, addictions, personality disorders, and sexual or relationship problems. Some symptoms, such as indecisiveness, may simply be a personality trait rather than a mental disorder. Thus, symptoms may be part of Axis I or Axis II (personality disorders) of the *DSM*. Patients who are suicidal often allegedly committed suicide in a previous life, but they may have been influenced by an earthbound entity or demon just before they committed suicide. The burden of having committed suicide has devastating effects on the soul. The soul carries the responsibility not only for taking its own life but also for bringing about downstream effects on family members or others affected by the suicide. A patient who has committed murder in a previous life purportedly encounters in a later life the person he or she murdered in order to atone for the previous action by assisting the former victim to form a respectful relationship with him or her. If the patient was the victim of a murder, he or she may need to forgive the perpetrator. Phobias may exist as a result of traumas in a previous life, but not all traumas involve another person. Trauma may arise from an accident or a natural disaster. The trauma still requires resolving. Modi calculates that 30% of primary symptoms and 70% of secondary symptoms come from past lives. A primary symptom is the reason that the patient first comes in for therapy. Secondary symptoms are elicited during the therapy process.

In discussing birth feelings, Modi cites the work of Thomas Verny, MD, with John Kelly, titled *The Secret Life of the Unborn Child* (1981). Verny states that a mother's persistent thoughts are much more important to her unborn child than her fleeting thoughts are. The thoughts of the father about the mother and child are also extremely important. This suggests that a child in utero is a sentient being, which is easier to understand with a spiritual model.

4. Earthbound Entities

Modi describes her discovery of earthbound human entities during a therapy session. In that session, the voice she began interviewing through a hypnotized patient described living in a different body in a year that occurred after the patient's birth. She knew it could not be the patient's previous life. After many more findings, Modi drew certain conclusions. The patient may experience some physical pain or emotional problems, such as phobias, related to what caused the intruding spirit to die, but this pain will present in an altered form, for example, abdominal pain in place of a deceased father's stomach cancer. Thus, a spirit can transfer problems from a previous life to the person it has joined. As a result, there is no limit to the types of psychosomatic problems that can result from an intruding earthbound entity. Modi states that the disruptions in the patients' lives often have no measurable physical correlates. For instance, back pains do not show any abnormality in an x-ray, but the pains are eliminated by Modi's spiritual therapeutic method.

The difficulties caused by earthbound entities may be intentional or unintentional. An example of unintentional intrusion is shown in several incidents in Modi's book. In one of these, the patient who was intruded upon by a discarnate entity was simply grieving a deceased person in his life. The spirit of the deceased person may simply have been trying to console the grieving patient, but it became attached. Thus, the spirit and the patient may each bear some responsibility for the situation. Whereas Modi mentions grief numerous times as being an opening for entities, psychologists believe that grieving is necessary and that its absence can eventually result in psychic harm. My explanation would be that it is acceptable to miss the deceased person, but a grieving person should wish the deceased a good spiritual journey into the *light* and not hope that his or her spirit remains on earth. If a person with a demon inside him- or herself dies and remains earthbound, that demon may travel with that person's spirit when it attaches to a living person. An example of intentional intrusion is a spirit seeking revenge.

When hypnotized, patients can often see spirit forms that cannot be seen in normal vision. Some earthbound spirits (that is, of deceased humans) appear to overlap the whole body of the patient, but at other times they are located at specific parts of the body, such as the head, chest, or leg, usually the part of the body in which the patient is experiencing pain. Several entities (even over a hundred) may overlap each other, similar to the layers of an onion. These earthbound spirits may also be compressed into a demon spirit. Modi's therapy generally addresses removal of the demons prior to the earthbound entities, as the entities may be interconnected with the demon and may depart with the demon. Such entities may appear angry, confused, or evil. When there are numerous levels of them, the patient may become tired from the process of removing each one. It is possible to have angels assist in removing numerous layers of demons in one hypnotherapy session by guiding the demons to the *light* without Modi's identifying and guiding each one.

Earthbound entities may attach themselves at any age, even to a fetus in the womb. For example, one entity Modi cites had been a miscarried child; it first attached itself to its mother, but then when the mother became pregnant again, the entity attached itself to the baby in the womb. Some entities may intrude into the same person in different lifetimes. Although time has little meaning in the spiritual realm, the discarded entity must "know" it can "wait" for a later incarnation.

The majority of earthbound entities are deceased family members, acquaintances, or aborted or miscarried fetuses, but to have entities that are strangers is not uncommon. In one of Modi's cases, the spirit of a young woman's aborted child was first trapped inside a demon before joining the grieving mother. One demon reported that many demons remain around abortion clinics, as grieving makes a person more vulnerable to spirit intrusion. Some earthbound entities claimed to be imaginary playmates of a child when the child was young. My interpretation of such a scenario is that a living child could play with the earthbound entity of a deceased child while the latter remained external and unattached. If the living child has an occasion for his or her aura to become vulnerable, then the earthbound entity (imaginary playmate) enters or attaches itself. Many imaginary playmates are not earthbound entities but are friendly nonhuman spirits.

While most of the earthbound entities simply have their former human desires, several to which Modi spoke during hypnosis reported that they were working for Satan. According to Modi, there are active training schools in hell where methods are taught for how to enter a person's aura. The entities are told to look for negative feelings in people, as those feelings lower a person's vibrations, thus opening the energy field and making it easier to aurally intrude upon. If not influenced by a demon, most earthbound entities are not seeking to harm the patient, but they do indirectly interfere in patients' lives.

Modi provides a list of conditions (below; a direct quotation) that open up people for intrusion by earthbound entities and demons. Many of these are similar to the ones presented by other therapists discussed in this chapter.

- Physical conditions, such as sickness, anesthesia, surgery, accidents, unconsciousness, etc.
- Emotional conditions, such as anger, fear, hate, depression, compassion, grief, etc.
- Drug and alcohol use
- Rock 'n' roll music
- Video games
- Entities on board
- Occupations
- People with soft, fuzzy, and porous boundaries of their energy field
- Missing soul parts and their connecting cords
- Entities coming in from another dimension
- Voluntary possession or invitational possession, such as using a Ouija board, automatic writing, sitting in the séance, channeling, playing with conjuring games such as Dungeons and Dragons,

and Demons, and inviting a spirit to come on board voluntarily out of love

(pp. 215–17)

Modi expands her explanation of these conditions; for example, it may not be the rock 'n' roll music itself but the volume at which it is played in conjunction with lights at a live performance that may create disharmony in the person's nervous system and open the energy field. Intense auditory and visual stimuli (sensory overload) are also created by video games, which affect children, whose auras are more permeable, more so than adults'. "Entities on board" means that people who already have some entities have a weaker energy field. People in the healing professions may be more vulnerable, possibly because they are more likely to be around people who have recently died. Various true psychics, clairvoyants, and channelers often have those abilities because they have more porous boundaries to the spiritual world. However, Modi states that less spiritually developed people also have softer shields. Elsewhere, Modi comments that swearing and being angry attracts entities and demons and also weakens the aura. Pornography can open a person's shield for possible intrusion and also cause the viewer to consider his or her partner as an object rather than a person. According to Modi, the people who produce pornographic films are under the control of demons. She does not elaborate on the phrase "from another dimension," but she does say that this kind of demon can enter even if a person has an intact energy shield. However, this type of intrusion is infrequent.

With these multiple conditions making a person vulnerable to spirit intrusion, including feelings people normally have (such as compassion), nearly every person possibly has these entities, but some may be less likely to present symptoms that would lead them to consider consulting with a psychiatrist. This is contradictory to Sagan, who thought it an infrequent occurrence that entities attached to a living human. Modi does report that some people with distinctive purposes in their lives have a special shield or bubble around them making them able to more easily be devoted to their purpose, unhindered by an entity.

Similar to other therapists (especially Fiore), Modi provides a list of reasons why spirits may remain earthbound after they have shed their physical body:

- Ignorance and confusion
- Strong emotions—anger, hate, love, fear, jealousy, and the desire for revenge
- Addiction to drugs, alcohol, cigarettes, food, gambling, or sex
- Obsessive attachment to a person, a place, or an object
- Past-life connections
- Unfinished business
- Demon possession and influence
- Interference by Satan, his demons, and earthbound entities who work for him
- Influence through missing soul parts
  (p. 229)

Modi discourses further about this list. For example, committing suicide does not automatically imply that a person cannot go to the *light*. However, many of the spirits recently released from their body (whether by suicide or another type of death) believe they do not deserve to go to heaven, so they avoid the *light*. They may be even more confused if a demon was a persuading factor in their decision to commit suicide. Other people avoid the *light* because they do not feel dead. Since they can still think, perceive, and feel emotions when disembodied, they fear that if they do go to the *light* they will be dead. A spirit can even be drawn toward a person it hated in life, for the purpose of revenge. Being drawn to a grieving person has already been discussed.

If the spirit of a recently deceased person is under the influence of a demon at death, the demon will try to influence the spirit not to go to the *light*. Prayers by the living can assist a departed spirit to go to the *light*. The spirit itself can recite prayers or Bible verses to drive away demons. One angel informed Modi that turning your mind to God and the *light* is one way to protect yourself from entities and demons. We should pray to God to "cleanse, heal, shield, protect, illuminate, guide, enlighten, balance, transform, and bless [us]" (p. 51). Modi provides a prayer of protection that can be recited to ward off entities and demons. Thus, it appears that confusion about the *light* may be a factor in why spirits remain earthbound.

One addiction implies that seemingly different predeath situations can cause the same symptom in a host. An obese person could have either the spirit of a starving person or the spirit of a person who was also obese before she died. This makes sense when viewed as the attitudes of both spirits seeking to fulfill their craving for food.

If an entity has been with a patient a long time, the patient is more likely to accept her unusual behavior as a part of who she is. If the entity recently attached itself, the patient may comment that a particular behavior is very unlike her normal self. Behavioral problems of all types, such as hyperactivity and violent outbursts, may be more noticeable in children, as they have not yet learned to control mechanisms that an adult may use if a certain situation arises.

Similar to the previous therapist (Fiore), Modi comments that if the patient reacts emotionally when reading her book, it may be a spirit that is causing the stress. Modi also agrees with Fiore that homosexuality is caused by a spirit of the opposite gender. That is, a female spirit inside a male host will desire to have relations with another male. If the influence is only mild, the patient could be bisexual, sometimes following the host's natural tendency and sometimes that of the spirit. I agree with Modi that this occurs when the spirit first attaches itself prior to puberty. If a spirit enters after puberty, the spirit is unlikely to change the sexual orientation of the host. Modi does not comment if she was able to end homosexuality in any patient.

Modi does present some statistics on the percentage of her clients who had earthbound entities. These are people who came to her with psychiatric problems, and thus the percentages do not relate to the general population.

- Ninety-two percent had an earthbound spirit.
- Eighty-two percent had multiple earthbound spirits.
- Fifty percent had spirits of relatives.
- Seventy-seven percent had spirits of strangers.
- Sixteen percent had spirits of miscarried or aborted fetuses. (pp. 278–79)

Modi reports that she removes spirits from the patient prior to past-life therapy, as the spirit may be reporting its own past life rather than the patient's past life. However, in other parts of her book, she implies she is aware of whether she is conversing with a spirit or the client.

5. Demons

When searching for the source of the problem, the patients may describe an area of darkness or a "black blob" inside them that they identify as a demon without having Modi suggest its presence. The demons can be different colors, shapes, and forms. If the demons have eyes, the eyes are sinister-looking. Demons also have ranks (a hierarchy); some demons are more powerful and knowledgeable than others. They are trained to bring illnesses and problems to humans. As mentioned earlier, the same demon may possess the same person in multiple lifetimes. Some demons claim to work on other planets.

According to some Christian traditions, demons may once have been *light* beings in heaven who subsequently made a choice to follow Satan rather than God. Thus, the demons encountered by Modi were able to see that at their core they had a spark of *light* and that they could turn away from Satan with Modi's persuasion and angelic assistance. That is, they were not exorcised and forced to depart. Similar to Sagan, Modi does not believe demons or entities should be exorcised, as they can attach to another person. They should be treated as confused and as deserving of compassion. The demons or entities are released into the *light* rather than sent back to Satan.

Modi does not provide a time line of when she first found entities or demons. Apparently later in her therapy, she also discovered that demons can install spiritual devices in patients for a variety of purposes, notably to assist the demons in their work. These devices can be seen by the patients when hypnotized. The devices are in many shapes and sizes and have many purposes, including causing pain, interfering with normal body processes, assisting the demons in communicating negative thoughts or focusing negative thoughts on the patient, or preventing a person from receiving spiritual strength from the *light*. Angels are usually employed to explain the functions of the devices and then to remove the devices, as the devices cannot be engaged in a conversation.

According to Modi, God/*light* and the angels are much more powerful than Satan and the demons but will only interfere to assist humans if requested to do so. Demons only have as much power as humans give them. Humans should not deal directly with demons; instead, they should let God and the angels remove them. A person will be rescued by God or angels if their assistance is simply solicited.

In addition to relief from emotional and mental symptoms (e.g., depressive thoughts), Modi states that a number of physical healings have resulted from her method of removing spirits or demons. A psychiatrist without spiritual understanding might contend that the patient imagined or fantasized the earthbound spirits or demons and that the improvement was the result of the placebo effect. Modi claims that her method could be successful in relieving suffering even if the therapist does not believe in the reality of past lives or various types of spirits. A nonspiritual therapist can simply conceive of demons and entities as figments of the imagination or as representative of the internal struggle in the patient's psyche but still address them as if they were real.

Although Modi presents statistics on the various types of entities or spiritual sources that cause difficulties, she offers no hard figures on the percentage of patients who were cured. She reports that occasionally there will be a complete cure of both physical and emotional problems in one hypnotherapy session, but most patients took multiple sessions—and only a few experienced a significant reduction in adverse symptoms. However, she notes, as do some of the previously discussed therapists, that curing of a physical illness by way of her spiritual therapy method does not necessarily imply that everyone with that physical illness has the same or any spiritual or psychological basis for the cause of the illness. The cause could be physical or mental, for example, a headache caused by an injury or stress, or cancer resulting from environmental factors.

6. Soul Fragmentation / Soul Loss

In the circumstances leading to soul fragmentation, a trauma may be physical, emotional, sexual, or spiritual. Modi describes the symptoms of fragmentation as follows: "Patients suffering from soul fragmentation and soul loss feel an emotional loss even without looking at and examining their souls under hypnosis. The patient's intuition allows them to recognize the unnatural condition of their souls. They feel spacey, in a fog, and disconnected from life" (p. 393).

Specific words and phrases employed to describe this condition may be *not whole*; *empty or void inside*; *spaced out*; or *disconnected*. A hypnotized patient can observe holes or spaces in the soul indicating that parts of the soul are missing. Having fragments can interfere with life physically, mentally, and emotionally and can affect a person's spiritual growth. Modi classifies the immortal human aspect as the soul, as well as the spiritual part that can fragment. For therapeutic purposes, it may not matter what title the fragmented part is given, that is, whether it is seen as a fragment of an immortal soul or as an astral fragment. In my context, the immortal aspect is called Spirit.

Modi maintains that soul fragments may leave the physical body while the person is still alive, but another fragment may stay isolated inside the patient and not progress in age as the main part of the soul progresses. According to Modi, this latter fragment, when contacted, may appear to be of the age when the soul originally fragmented, often when the person was a child. The patient (while hypnotized) can observe this child part as it physically appeared at the time of the fragmentation. Psychiatrists sometimes refer to this as an inner-child issue. I compare fragmentation to what a shaman speaks of as *soul loss*, which a shaman can correct by retrieving the soul.

The more severe the trauma, the greater the extent of fragmentation. Fragmenting and dissociation may occur anytime, from in the womb, through birth, to just before death and by various mechanisms. One rather unusual mechanism of causing a soul to fragment is casting spells or curses on others. From chapter 6, it is known that dissociation can begin in the womb. Also, there may be missing soul parts (fragments) from a past life that continue to cause problems in a current life. When Modi recovers fragments, they are cleansed, healed, and integrated with the patient.

Portions of the fragmented soul that are not in the physical body may be in the possession of relatives or even of a person who abused the person in question. This spiritual accounting is a bona fide explanation for the psychiatric term *identification with the perpetrator*. This term, discussed in chapter 6 (on DID), describes why abuse victims often speak admirably of their abusers. Likewise, the inverse of this is also possible: the patient is in possession of the fragment of another person's soul fragment. My interpretation is that some of the soul fragments of other people in Modi's patients are not much different from an earthbound entity. For the patient to heal, these fragments need to be either returned to the patient (if originally part of the patient) or removed from the patient (if an outside astral fragment). A fragmented soul creates holes and weaknesses in one's being that can continue into future lives. Modi's therapy involves removal of earthbound entities, demons, and the soul fragments of other living people. When Modi has a person in the *light* between lives, she asks the soul, with angelic assistance, to retrieve any soul fragments that are in the possession of others or demons.

There are multiple places to which a soul fragment can proceed.

- "Soul fragments going to another living human being;
- Soul fragments leaving the body during a trauma and returning later;
- Soul parts in possession of a living person on the earth while the main body of the soul has gone to heaven after the death of the body;
- Soul parts going to heaven with the deceased person who had possession of them, although the patient is still living on the earth;
- Soul parts remaining at the location of the trauma that caused the soul to fragment;
- Soul parts in possession of Satan and his demons; and
- Soul parts stored in a warehouse in hell by Satan."
(p. 378)

I will not go into further detail on these.

7. Summary of This Section

In reading Modi's explanations of each individual case, I assert that they appear logical. Overall, though, her complex interplay of factors such as entities, demons, devices, influences, past lives, and connecting cords seems much more complicated and, thus, less believable than the therapeutic methods discussed earlier in this chapter. I interpret what Modi calls *the soul* as something more closely resembling the astral body as presented by Sagan in this chapter and in chapter 8, the latter on Eastern concepts of human spirituality.

The next therapist I review arrived in this field from a totally unrelated occupation but coined and copyrighted a term that describes removal of several classes of spirits. He has a method other than exorcism for removing dark forces. However, it cannot be known if these entities are the same type as the ones in the exorcisms described by Martin (1976).

L. A Dentist-cum-Spiritual Therapist: William Baldwin

1. Introduction

William J. Baldwin (1939–2004) graduated from dental school in 1970. As part of his practice, he engaged in hypnodontics, the use of hypnosis for suppressing pain in dentistry. He then became interested in using hypnosis for past-life therapy. He developed this technique into what he titled Spirit Releasement Therapy (SRT). He left the dental field in 1982 and obtained his PhD in psychology in 1988. His doctoral thesis is titled *Diagnosis and Treatment of Spirit Possession Syndrome*. In place of standard hypnosis, the methodology he developed has clients focus their awareness on sensations in their bodies and then translate those sensations into words. Baldwin then directed questions to the sensation, uncovering events in the clients' past that may have been responsible for the sensations. He concentrated on the emotional state of the client, not on intellectual analysis. As the patient discoursed, a common nonloading question might have been, "What happens next" (p. 2)? His book I review here is titled *Healing Lost Souls: Releasing Unwanted Spirits from Your Energy Body* (2003).

Baldwin has found several main types of influences that affect behavior. One is simply past-life events and employing therapy without involvement of spirits. The other therapeutic methods he discusses in his book involve intrusive entities that usually are the result of physical or emotional trauma. The first involves earthbound deceased humans, terminated pregnancies, or mind fragments (variously termed *spirits*, *entities*, and *discarnate entities*). The second type focuses on dark-force entities (DFEs), similar to the demons discussed in relation to Modi. The third type regards entities not previously encountered, mainly extraterrestrials. He classifies these entities as a group as "parasites." Perhaps the alleged entities he removes are just manifestations of the client's reifying of his internal struggles, but if that is all that is needed to achieve a fuller life, then propitious results are all that a therapist can expect. Baldwin reports that he has conducted over six thousand therapeutic sessions.

Baldwin maintains that his model is "a working hypothesis without scientific proof" (p. xiii). His method cannot prove reincarnation, survival of death, or possession by discarnate entities, but "therapy sessions often bring immediate and permanent relief from symptoms and conditions that have plagued people for years" (p. xxii). However, he also states that his findings are not "a panacea for all the ills of humanity" (p. xxii). These statements could apply to all of the therapeutic methods discussed in this chapter.

When William James was making the statement about possession and demons presented on the first page of this chapter, he probably had only minor knowledge of shamanism and its long tradition of voluntary and pathological possession. Baldwin also emphasizes this failing of science when he writes, "A large part of human experience lies outside the parameters of the scientific method" (p. xxiii). This is similar to LeShan's contention, presented in chapter 1, that Type B events, which lie in the Realm of Consciousness and Meaningful Behavior, cannot be compared to events in the Realm of Sensory Experience. Only the latter can be studied by the scientific method.

Perhaps James's reference to science's being in fashion can be compared to the nineteenth-century French phrase *fin de siècle*. The phrase means "turn of the century," referring to the artistic climate of effete sophistication in that period of time (the late nineteenth century). Modern science claims to be beyond reproach or effete sophistication. The general attitude is that if science contends that something is true, then it is a fact. Materialism is an assumed fact built into today's science, and thus science deviates from its original meaning of "to know." The mechanistic/medical model is more properly a working hypothesis, one that, after evaluating the information in my book, should be discarded.

2. Discarnate Entities and Soul Fragments

Baldwin agrees that most spirits are simply confused and do not desire to harm the client. Many of them do not believe they have died. An entity's influence can be benevolent, self-serving, malevolent, or neutral. The spirit may bring the abilities and medical problems that it had when in its own body. Like Modi, Baldwin reports these conditions are usually psychosomatic, with no or very minor physically measurable basis for the perceived malady.

If a recently deceased person with an entity attaches itself to a living person, the original entity becomes "nested," or appears as an entity within an entity. One of Baldwin's examples may be similar to this, but it also seems a contrast. He found the spirit of a deceased victim of child abuse attached to a child currently being abused. It is a contrast because an abuse victim did not choose that role in this life, whereas substance abusers often initially choose to use one or more substances. Baldwin reports that there are often many entities, not all nested, and that these entities tap into and deplete the energy of the host. Chronic fatigue is a frequent indicator of the presence of discarnate entities.

Baldwin also discusses the energy body, a term also used by Sagan. He reports that spirits generally attach to one of the chakras or to the surface of the body. A soul fragment may follow an organ removed from a deceased person, and thus be transferred to the recipient. He even cites a fragment that arrived in a blood transfusion. Baldwin believes that an earthbound soul maintains its personality structure. These traits are carried into the unwitting host to which it attaches.

Modi attributes a person's having reduced protection from these entities to a softening of the natural shield of protection. Baldwin refers to this as a "loosening of ego boundaries." As a former dentist, he has found that one "codeine tablet taken for relief of pain from a dental extraction can alter the consciousness sufficiently to allow entry" (p. 17). He agrees that addiction is a common reason for spirits to remain earthbound, as drugs and alcohol loosen the ego boundaries. However, he states that a spirit of a deceased drug abuser or alcoholic may attach to someone who was not a drug or alcohol user, and slowly begin to bring about substance abuse in the host. Most previous therapists who addressed this topic felt that spirits only attached to living people who already had a penchant for substance abuse, sometimes a specific substance. According to Baldwin, ego boundaries can be maintained by strengthening the "spiritual immune system."

Baldwin discusses relationships between two people and possible influences of past lives and attached entities. He believes it is important to discover if relationships in past lives could be affecting the current relationship. Attached entities in a current life, especially if the attachment occurred recently, may affect partners' attitudes. One client claimed he seemed to bond quickly with a woman he had just met. However, when the man had his entities led away, the woman broke off the relationship. Baldwin concluded that her true relationship was with one of his entities. Entities that enter after a good relationship has formed may cause difficulties in the relationship. Other entities may be present for karmic reasons, that is, unfinished business between the two.

Baldwin also discusses planning for a new life during the period between two lives. He refers to the main plan or road map as a *lifescript*. During the playing out of this script, there may be several checkout points, or possible times of death. "An attached entity can hasten death or prolong life, thus interfering with any potential checkout point and the intended learning" (p. 21). The lifescript does not usually include any planned spirit intrusions, but there may be some exceptions.

Similar to many other therapists mentioned herein, Baldwin maintains that homosexuality and gender dysphoria occur after an entity of the opposite gender attaches itself to a host. I have mentioned, and Baldwin agrees, that to affect gender orientation, the attachment must come at an early age, at least before puberty, but possibly earlier. I have not discussed this issue in regard to other therapists, but I am persuaded that an entity that affects the sexual behavior of a person in whose life it has intruded probably had difficulties in that area of its life when living in its own body. If the spirit of a grandmother, without sexual difficulties in her life, attaches to her grandson to console him, her discarnate earthbound soul is unlikely to affect his sexual orientation. A probable example of a nested entity and its ability to affect behavior would be a client of Baldwin who sensed in himself homosexual tendencies after his gay uncle died. Since the uncle was a man, the sexual influence was coming from the female nested entity that had made the uncle a homosexual. Baldwin claims he had several male clients who were preparing for transsexual surgery. After releasing a dominant female entity, the clients no longer desired to be gender reassigned. Another man was able to eliminate his transvestite (cross-dressing) tendencies. An older architect with gender dysphoria was reluctant to remove a woman's spirit because he felt she was possibly responsible for his artistic ability. Baldwin respected his client's wishes not to proceed with release of the spirit.

After discovering the entities by asking the questions about sensations previously discussed, Baldwin began a dialogue with the entity. An indicator of probable entities is use of words like *we*. Another indicator is that the client has deep internal struggles over his or her behavior. During dialogue with the entity, Baldwin was frequently able to obtain the name the entity had had when in its own body. In addition, the entity may have supplied a date of when it was alive. In some cases, the entity lived hundreds of years ago. As part of the dialogue, Baldwin may have also asked the entity if it had known the host in a previous lifetime. He assumed the entity provided truthful answers.

The entity is released by having it focus upward. Usually, it will see a brilliant *light* and family or friends, who encourage the entity to join them in the *light*. When the entity does so, there is a joyful reunion, as the entity is now home. Baldwin then has the client proceed through a sealing-light meditation to fill the void of the departing entity and establish a protective bubble to ward off other entities. The client then proceeds to more standard therapy so that she can determine why she was vulnerable and determine how not revert to the ingrained behavior she may have taken for granted for many years. Baldwin mentions multiple entities in some clients, but he does not discuss if they are handled differently or if each one has to be led individually to the *light*. Recall that Modi could request the assistance of angels to remove numerous spirits all at once instead of one at a time.

Baldwin states that in most terminated pregnancies (abortion, miscarriage, stillbirth), the soul of the child goes to the *light*, but those that do not often stay with the mother, possibly to attach to a later fetus. "It is not unusual for a new baby to be born with an attached spirit of a would-have-been sibling" (p. 39). This finding would agree with McAll (1982), who believes that children born after a terminated pregnancy often have intruding spirits. A lifescript usually includes a possible prebirth termination. When Baldwin attempted a dialogue and the entity did not appear to have a name or remembrance of a body but was not hostile as a dark-force entity would be, he suspected a preterm child. Similar to Modi, Baldwin believes that the spirit of an aborted fetus carries with itself the trauma of the abortion if it attaches itself to a host. If twins were conceived but one fetus dies, the spirit of the deceased one is likely to attach itself to its living twin. However, my opinion would be that if a fetus chooses to terminate its life because it has abnormalities, this would be a spiritual choice, one not resulting in an earthbound entity.

Sagan maintains that fragmentation occurs at death. Baldwin's concept of fragmentation more closely resembles that of Modi in that it occurs while alive and in that the mind fragments formed can attach to living hosts. These fragments do not recall dying, because they have not died. The cases presented by Baldwin more closely resemble those of Modi in that fragments are caused by various severe traumas, especially to children. While not usually portrayed as trauma, Baldwin claims the following:

> The practice of witchcraft and black magic, and the casting of spells, hexes, and curses, for example, can cause fragmentation of the practitioner, witch, or sorcerer. It is significant that the fragment of consciousness gives energy to the curse. This fragment remains with the victim of the magic spell or curse. There are always dark-force entities involved in this sort of intrusive activity (p. 68).

These practices are classified as occult activities, which a number of therapists have identified as an opening for spirits.

A person with missing soul fragments is more vulnerable to spirit intrusion, probably because the ego boundaries are not a strong. Soul fragments can also attach to another living person. Baldwin's therapy for soul fragmentation involved the client's scanning her body to find voids or empty places. The client was instructed to follow threads from those empty spaces, which usually led to a trauma in this or another lifetime. After the traumatic event was processed to peaceful resolution, the soul fragment was welcomed back and the client felt more whole.

3. Dark-Force Entities

The Western/Christian concept of fallen angels also exists in other religions and mythical traditions. Baldwin does not desire to understand any connection to diverse religions, but he does say the following:

> For the purpose of counseling, the Devil or Satan (defined as Adversary) or Lucifer (defined as Light Bearer, the archangel

cast from heaven for leading the revolt of the angels) is not categorized as a metaphor nor an actual being but is one aspect of the spiritual or nonphysical reality, a cultural construct that is meaningful in the therapeutic work with the client who describes these images. This is not a statement of belief or disbelief.

Whether it is imagination, archetype, collective hallucinations, mass hypnosis, a projection of the beliefs of the therapist, or something else again, dark forces seem to exist in some form and are capable of intruding on individual lives in this reality. (p. 74)

Dark-force entities (DFEs) are usually arrogant, hostile, defiant, and disruptive. Baldwin does not believe that the DFEs are the same as a person's shadow personality. Most abuse perpetrators have an attached DFE. When the perpetrator dies and becomes a discarnate entity, the DFE will usually accompany the entity as it attaches itself to the person he or she was victimizing, since connections or threads have already been established.

The people who attract DFEs often have feelings of intense anger, hatred, rage, or desire for power. It appears to me that the cause and resulting behavior are difficult to distinguish. Does rage invite DFEs, or is it caused by them? DFEs may sometimes search for positions of power rather than for a specific person. That is, when a person in power retires, the DFE may leave that person and go to a successor. DFEs also seem to tend to target the very young or people involved in aberrant sexual experiences.

In addition, "DFEs understand only the energy of the lower three chakras: survival, fear, threat, lust, greed, power, antagonism, competition, control, [and] bullying. This resembles the human ego at its worst. They can work alone, in small bands, or as part of larger dark networks" (p. 75).

A dialogue can be held with these entities, in which they will describe their relationship in a hierarchy with other DFEs. Their leaders may threaten them "with pain, punishment, and annihilation if they disobey their commanders or fail in an assignment. They believe without question and blindly obey the commands of their superiors" (p. 76).

Clients' descriptions of DFEs are similar to Modi's, such as black blobs and also as vicious or scary animals or monsters. They may have red eyes and sharp teeth, and may growl or hiss. The DFEs are told that they have no *light* in themselves and that the *light* is harmful. Their only reward is being allowed to continue to exist. Even being discovered constitutes failure and inevitable punishment. Since they were never in a physical body, they do not bring illnesses from existence in a former body, but their presence may result in various illnesses in the hosts.

Baldwin's method for removing DFEs closely parallels Modi's. "The process of spirit releasement of a DFE utilizes imagination, visual imagery, and invocation of spiritual beings of Light" (p. 86). While his process leads the DFEs to the *light*, this is not the same "place" to which earthbound souls are led. *Place* may not be a proper term, as where the DFEs are taken is not a physical location.

Like Modi, Baldwin had the DFEs look at the core of their being. When they did so, they observed a *light* that expanded, eventually enfolding them. Various *beings of light* may assist Baldwin in this process. The DFEs, after realizing that they had been lied to by their superiors, declared that they choose the *light*. Of course, Baldwin had no way of knowing if there was one less DFE in the universe to infiltrate humans, but he did report that many clients had major improvements in their lives after the DFEs were removed, although these clients were not necessarily completely cured.

4. Extraterrestrials

Everything in Baldwin's book may be controversial, but this topic may be most of all. About half of Baldwin's clients reported that extraterrestrials (ETs) influenced their behavior. I again remind the reader that clients are people who go to a therapist and that they do not necessarily reflect the general population. One possibility for explaining the ETs may be that being from another planet and solar system is a modern form of mythology. Another manner to portray these alleged influences is to compare them to a shamanic journey. The beings a shaman encounters during a spiritual journey are "real" within their context, but they are not physical beings. Baldwin wrote a book on the topic, titled *CE-VI: Close Encounters of the Possession Kind*.

Although having entities from another planet is different from abduction by ETs, both of these things may affect behavior. In one of researcher Ken Ring's books on NDEs, he claimed that the psychological profile of people who had an NDE was similar to that of people who claimed to be abducted by ETs. Some people claim to have been abducted, when their physical body is known to have never left a room.

Baldwin's ETs are naturally nonphysical and are not spirits of deceased extraterrestrials. Similar to some discarnate entities, some of the ETs "have been adrift and wandering for a long time and don't know how to get back 'home'" (p. 103). However, in another place Baldwin states that the ETs claim to be reporting to a nearby spacecraft. They are not aggressive or hostile, but like DFEs they are secretive and do not like to be disturbed. They are often condescending and claim they are something else other than a discarnate entity or a dark force. Baldwin reports that their auditory and visual senses may not be in the same ranges as humans', but apparently he is able to converse with them.

Similar to Modi's devices placed by demons, Baldwin has found devices planted by ETs. For one client, it was a mechanical clamp on her ears. When Baldwin had the ETs remove the clamps, the woman's hearing improved a bit but did not return to normal. The ETs claimed the clamps were part of an experiment on humans. Proponents of ET visits to Earth often claim that ETs are conducting experiments on humans, allegedly to improve human beings. Baldwin does not consider their presence beneficial to humans. Sometimes the ETs apologized for an intrusion they had made into the client's life or for inserting the devices. ETs also have a command or hierarchical structure, similar to DFEs.

During conversation, Baldwin explained to the ETs why they were unwanted and they agreed to depart. Sometimes, the ETs can be under the influence of DFEs, which, to Baldwin, indicated that the realm of Lucifer/Satan extends beyond Earth. Baldwin employed the services of the rescue *spirits of light* used in DFE therapy to remove the ETs.

5. Other Concepts of Baldwin

Baldwin also claims that he can do spirit releasement therapy for a person who is not physically present. A client acts as a surrogate for the distant person. For instance, one female client was sexually abused as a child by her father. Baldwin had her regress so she could look at her father's eyes during the abuse. The red color in his eyes indicated he was under the influence of a DFE at the time of the assault. Baldwin was able to perform a remote spirit releasement therapy on the woman's father, as well as therapy for her in his presence, which included past-life encounters between them.

M. Late Start: The Therapy Method of Louise Ireland-Frey, MD

1. Introduction

Louise Ireland-Frey (1912–2014), MD, received a standard medical education at Tulane University. Having retired from medical practice in 1943 for health reasons, she began employing hypnotherapy when she was in her late sixties. She took a course from William Baldwin on SRT in 1985, and he wrote the foreword to her book *Freeing the Captives: The Emerging Therapy of Treating Spirit Attachment* (1999). Ireland-Frey prefers the term *psyche* to describe the aspect of person that survives death. She may speak directly to the intruding entities she finds in her hypnotized clients, but initially she may use a "finger method" for determining if there is an entity present. Rather than asked to provide a verbal response, the client is told to designate movement of one finger as a yes reply and another finger as a no reply to questions about the presence of entities. She often refers to her therapy as rescue work.

2. Types of Intrusion

Ireland-Frey states that at death most people go to the *light*, but those with negative attitudes are often drawn to a dark place, the lower astral level, appropriate to their nature at the time of their death. However, in another place in her book she refers to earthbound entities on the lower astral plane. In between are people whose psyches begin to wander before moving into the aura of a living person. Ireland-Frey employs several terms to describe the extent to which these wandering spirits can affect a living person. These are presented below.

Terms	Degree of Affect
Influencing, shadowing	Mild (e.g., mood swings)
Oppression, harassing	More noticeable and frequent
Obsession	More effect on the body, sudden changes in behavior, unnatural traits
Possession	Nearly complete control, possibly DID or alcohol idiosyncratic intoxication

Note that *possession* in this context refers to the degree of control. In some incidents in this chapter, *possession* may imply that the entity is a demonic being. This range of control may correspond to various parts of a spectrum found in many disorders.

Ireland-Frey agrees with many other therapists in this field who state that wandering spirits are attracted to people with similar desires (e.g., addictions) or with kindred health conditions, people residing within the vicinity of where the entity had lived while in a body, or people with a caring attitude that makes the entity feel comfortable. These entities may rob their hosts of their energy and also confuse them. The spirit is unable to progress on its own spiritual path while entangled in the aura of the host. The intruding entity may be another living person. The reasons Ireland-Frey gives as to why these entities remain earthbound are similar to other therapists', such as addictions or unfinished business. While Modi and Baldwin always seem to lead entities to the *light*, Ireland-Frey may lead the entity to a *place* of *light* that is not *in the light*.

Ireland-Frey also cautions that when a client claims that she was abused as a child, some type of validating evidence should be found to corroborate the claim. A client could contain an entity of a child who was previously abused and is now making the claim. The client may not have been abused but may have had the intruding spirit of an abuse victim attach itself for another reason.

Whereas Modi refers to spiritual beings that are helpful in removing entities as *angels*, Ireland-Frey refers to them collectively as *bright beings* because they are rather diverse in their nature. Ireland-Frey also claims to have a special spiritual advisor named Master Ching whom she can ask for advice during the therapy process with a particular client whose therapy is unusually tedious. Atteshlis also claimed to have a spiritual advisor to assist him. Ireland-Frey reports that Ching is always with her, but his presence is more felt when his advice is requested to actually assist her. Of course, these assisting beings may be simply an aspect of the therapist's own Spirit.

In addition, Ireland-Frey speaks of using compassion when conversing with entities and not exorcising them. However, most of her clients had symptoms less severe than those of the clients described by Martin (1976). She also comments that the more malicious the client or entity initially appears, the more the client is distressed and in need of therapy.

3. Employing Higher Levels of Spirits

Ireland-Frey also does remote releasement of entities, but she cautions about on whom this method can be performed. She does not want to interfere with an individual's free will. The mind of a hypnotized surrogate is allegedly able to access the mind of the remote client. For remote work on a child, the parent's approval is sufficient, but Ireland-Frey claims that the higher mind / higher self of a remotely located adult can be asked through the surrogate if it will be acceptable to perform the releasement. The answer is usually yes, but permission can be denied. While results of any spirit releasement are subjective, remote cases are more so because the remote client may never return to the therapist and report the consequences.

In addition to encountering earthbound entities, during therapy Ireland-Frey has encountered thought forms, elementals, extraterrestrials, oaths, vows, curses, spiritual viruses, and minor and major demonic forces. She also has found nested entities; she usually treats the nested entity first. In the next section, I discuss a therapist whose removal technique closely parallels the work of Carl Wickland a century ago, but the update makes it much easier to employ in therapy.

N. Another Modern Greek Therapist

The last hypnotherapist I will discuss is Athanasios N. Komianos. His book is titled *Rapid Entity Attachment Release: A Breakthrough in the World of Spirit Possession and Releasement* (2011). He cites Plato's *Charmides*, quoting Socrates: "The great error of our day [24 centuries ago] in the treatment of the human body, that physicians separate the soul from the body" (p. 9).

Komianos found that spirits can't tolerate even a small amount of electricity. He engages in dialogue with attached spirits in a hypnotized client, but if spirits are reluctant to depart, he shocks the client with electrodes attached to acupuncture points. Komianos traces the history of electricity in therapy, dating back to the time of the ancient Egyptians and Greeks, who shocked patients with electric fish. Hippocrates used electric fish to treat headaches and arthritis. Many doctors employed electricty to treat war-related neuroses and shell shock in veterans of World War I. Modern medicine does recognize the use of electricity for mental-health conditions, although medicine does not connect its use to removing spirits. In any event, the results vary considerably. Electroconvulsive therapy (ECT) has been known for a number of years. The more recent similar method is called cranial electrotherapy stimulation (CES), which uses a much lower strength of charge than ECT. Other recent methods include transcranial magnetic stimulation (TMS) and transcranial direct-current stimulation (tDCS). The electric attachment points for these therapies are usually on the skull, whereas Komianos may use acupuncture points on other parts of the body.

Komianos's electroacupuncture method is different from similar methods in that the electricity can be administered without needles. Thus, the person operating the device does not have to be a certified acupuncturist. He also determined that the therapist's intentions are important to the process and that the therapist must have a rapport with the patient to be successful. Komianos also ascertained that neurotransmitter levels are affected by this method. He agrees that his concept does not "prove" the existence of entities, but effective therapy is some evidence for their existence.

Komianos delves into some history of his term *attachment*. Apollonius of Tyana (ca. 15—ca. 100 CE) demanded that spirits confirm their departure with some specific unusual physical manifestation, such as an unnatural sound. The *Rituale Romanum*, the document of ancient Roman exorcisms, categorizes demons by four activities: infestation, oppression/harassment, obsession, and possession. The latter most closely resembles the work done by Martin (1976), previously discussed. This stage includes incidents rarely encountered by previous therapists, such as superhuman strength, secret knowledge of the exorcist's private life, and an aversion to sacred objects. Komianos also mentions an unorthodox exorcist named Fr. Johann Joseph Gassner (1727–1779). When he became popular, he was reviled by both the medical community and many church leaders. Gassner was mentioned by Ellenberger (1970), whom I have previously referenced. Ellenberger has an interesting comment in reference to Gassner that is very germane in the present day, as many modern religious leaders ignore spiritual healing: "Curing the sick is not enough; one must cure them with methods accepted by the community" (Ellenberger, 1970, 57). The same may be said about all of the therapists I have been discussing.

Komianos provides a list of some common psychiatric disorders that may be related to spiritual entities, although the same symptoms can have physical causes: amnesia, epilepsy, migraines, narcolepsy, night terrors, gender dysphoria, and alien hand syndrome. Komianos has found several clients who had not been able to become pregnant for many years but who in turn became pregnant shortly after the release of a spirit intruder. In discussing gender dysphoria and homosexuality, Komianos includes the concept of an intruding spirit of the opposite gender. Although the following is not the same as changing a homosexual, he does mention a case of a woman he had known earlier in life as a beautiful young woman. When she came for therapy, she was very overweight, she had facial hair, and a doctor had told her she had a hormonal imbalance with excess testosterone. Komianos discovered a malevolent male spirit who did not believe he was dead. When asked to look at this male spirit's body, the spirit realized it was a female body. The male left after receiving an electric shock. A month after release of the spirit, the client had lost forty pounds and had no facial hair, and her hormone levels were normal. This case demonstrates that a spirit of the opposite gender can have major physical effects on the person carrying the intruder. Baldwin mentions difficulties with hexes and curses. Komianos has an excellent comment on the consequences of proclaiming them. He states, "When you curse someone, it is precisely what you attract for yourself, or your family" (p. 54).

I have previously mentioned organ transplants and changes in behavior that resemble the behavior of the organ donor. Komianos cites an incident from his extended family. The man receiving a liver transplant apparently had an out-of-body experience (OBE) during surgery and could see the surgeons removing his liver and then inserting the transplant. During this OBE, another man approached him and asked for his liver back, and the two had a discussion. When the recipient recovered, he had enough influence to find the name of the deceased donor. He reported that the donor's description fit the person encountered during the OBE who wanted his liver back.

Komianos calls the removal process *hypnoscopesis* Although it may not be much different from hypnosis, he claims that the client during hypnoscopesis is actively involved in finding the root of the problem. He says his process is not much different (other than the fact that it uses electricity) from the method of the sleeplike trance used in ancient Greek mystery schools, such as at the Temple of Asklepios. The rod of Asklepios (with a single snake), often confused with the caduceus (which has two snakes), is named after the Greek god of medicine and healing.

Similar to many other therapists, Komianos provides a list of symptoms that may be indicators of spirit attachment:

- Low vitality and/or extensive fatigue
- Character shifts or mood swings
- Hearing voices
- Abuse of drugs, including alcohol
- Excessive compulsive behavior
- Vacant eyes
- Memory problems or inability to concentrate efficiently
- Sudden onset of anxiety or depression
- Behavior out of character
- Unusual sexual behavior and/or infertility problems
- Sudden onset of physiological problems with no apparent medical cause
- Sudden onset of panic attacks, phobias, or nightmares
- Depression or suicidal tendencies
- Self-destructiveness
- A tendency to be clumsy
- Surgery in which full chemical anesthesia was used
- Being a victim of sexual or physical abuse
- Existence of phenomena that some would classify as paranormal (pp. 98–99)

Also, like other previously cited therapists, he finds that some clients who come late to or otherwise miss sessions will develop pains all over their body during the session. His opinion is that "a client should not be looked upon as a victim, but as the causative agent of his own trouble" (p. 169).

Like other therapists, Komianos has found fragments of a personality attached to a client. In one case, it was a fragment of a rapist attached to the woman he had raped. Although he could converse with the entity, Komianos determined it was a fragment, since the man was apparently still living. In Komianos's clients, earthbound spirits are the most common, but he has also encountered dark entities. Komianos describes a multisession treatment of a client who apparently had a demon or dark entity attached to her for many years, including periods when she had participated in occult activities. While many clients feel much better after release of entities, release of long-term dark beings often results in physical symptoms, such as convulsions and vomiting. Postrelease therapy may be extensive. For this, Komianos provides some possible spiritual practices to use, such as lighting candles or having a pet, that expedite the therapy process. When dealing with purely physical illnesses, one may speak of a cure. In psychology, a therapist is more interested in healing, improvement in behavior, a personal understanding of and ability to improve coping skills for dealing with life situations or behavioral challenges, and the implications of healing in the client's life. Therapists are rarely miracle workers, although some cases in this chapter approach a miraculous level of transformation.

In the next section, I discuss the Jewish concept of spirit attachment. No specific therapist is reviewed.

O. A Jewish Concept of Spirit Attachment

A term that directly relates to spirit attachment is *dybbuk*, which is derived from a Hebrew word meaning "attachment" or "to adhere" (*Encyclopedia of Religion* [ER]). Jewish sources dating back to the time of King Saul discuss spirit possession, but cases were not regularly reported until the sixteenth century. Josephus (1843), first-century Jewish historian and chronicler of the destruction of the Jewish temple in 70 CE, specifies that evil spirits are the souls of the deceased. Between the seventeenth and twentieth centuries, there were about eighty narrative tales of dybbuks (*ER*).

The *ER* explains the reason for the souls of the deceased entering the living, as follows:

> Classical Jewish sources generally regarded the afterlife as entailing a stay of up to a year in Gehenna, a purgatory that was thought to refine and purify the soul in preparation for its entrance into the Edenic heavens. According to sixteenth-century conceptions, however, particularly evil individuals lacked sufficient merit to gain admission to Gehenna. They would thus linger in a tortuous limbo of unspecified duration. Respite for such a soul could only be obtained through its taking refuge in the body of a living person; possession also allows the soul to negotiate the terms of its admission to Gehenna through the intervention of a rabbinic exorcist. (p. 2533)

The 16th-century tales of attachment by dybbuks originated around the Galilean town of Safed and eventually spread into eastern European writings. As these stories explain, "Many victims were thought to have been possessed as a punishment for a previous sin of omission or commission" (p. 2534). Physical signs of dybbuk possession include epileptic collapse ("falling sickness"), unnatural strength, and swellings under the skin. These signs were sometimes confirmed when the person who was allegedly possessed spoke in an unknown language or exposed the sins of other people present. The exorcism procedure includes obtaining the name of the spirit. It may also include thunderous blasts of a ram's horn, as such was believed "to discombobulate demonic forces" (p. 2534). The dispossessed spirit could then enter Gehenna.

Belanger (2003) writes about the dybbuk phenomenon after discussing it with Rabbi Gershon Winkler of the Walking Stick Foundation in rural New Mexico. The foundation combines studies of Judaism and shamanism, primarily Native American shamanism. Winkler uses the term *demon* when discussing dybbuk phenomena, but not necessarily pejoratively. He contends that demons can be good or bad and that they were created after human beings; they are not of this world and not of the other world, but are of a little bit of both. Winkler reports that the dybbuk is attracted to someone whose soul and body are not fully connected. Such a person may have melancholy or a psychosis, and the person's inclinations will attract a dybbuk spirit that has similar inclinations. Winkler confirms that a person possessed by a dybbuk often has knowledge that he would not normally have.

Winkler reports that there is a second type of "good" possession. In this case, the possessing dybbuk comes to a person who has a difficult problem. The dybbuk had previously struggled with that problem and overcome it, and thus is able to offer assistance and encouragement. Winkler refers to this type of dybbuk as a spirit guide. When the person with the problem solves it, the dybbuk departs. "The Jewish concept of dybbuk recognizes that our physical world and the spiritual world can intertwine for both positive and negative reasons" (Belanger, p. 2).

Winkler has conducted exorcisms using techniques described by the teachings of kabbalism. He confirms the use of a ram's horn. There is also a method of exorcism described in the Old Testament. David played a harp to quell an evil spirit in King Saul (but the playing could not make it permanently depart), though the nature or origin of that spirit, other than evil, is not described in 1 Samuel 16. Josephus spoke about demons as being the spirits of wicked men. One method he described for removing these spirits included use of the root of an herb whose leaves can emit *light*, but a *light* that is only visible in the evening. Of course, the use of herbs would be in accord with shamanic methods. The involvement of *light* would concur with removal of such spirits by leading them to the *light*. The alleged spirits in the removal incidents of previous therapists were not determined to be wicked; instead, they had addictions or were just confused. The spirits may appear more wicked if they have demons or dark beings attached to them. These exorcisms do not seek to drive the spirit away but to heal both the person who has the dybbuk and the dybbuk itself.

The next section offers some insights into the concept of beneficial and inimical forces operating in the same person, similar to an ISH aiding a person with DID.

P. Confirmation of a Meditator

1. Introduction

In chapter 6, I discussed the Inner Self-helper (ISH) aspect as an aid in therapy of people with DID. I believe this is the same as the High Self, so I have used the word *Spirit* to identify it. This section will present the findings of psychologist Wilson Van Dusen (1923–2005), PhD, from his book *The Presence of Other Worlds* (1974). Some of his findings on higher-order spirits make them appear to be related to the Spirit, but he also discovered much about lower-order spirits in hallucinating patients. The description here will concentrate on what Van Dusen reported from his patients. However, it must be noted that the information appears in a book that attempts to demonstrate that Van Dusen's own findings are similar to descriptions provided by Emanuel Swedenborg. Swedenborg was an eminent natural scientist in his day (1688–1772); in his midfifties, he began to study religious matters. His father was a bishop. Swedenborg claimed to be able to see into the spirit world during his meditations and to have visited heaven and hell. Some followers of Swedenborg consider that the findings of NDE research confirm much of Swedenborg's description of the hereafter. Van Dusen states that his study of hallucinations was not conducted to verify Swedenborg; it was not until three years after he conducted his study that he discovered the correlation with Swedenborg. In one of his later books, Van Dusen (1999) identifies himself as a mystic. He grew up in a home without any religion.

2. Method for Obtaining Information

Van Dusen, a licensed clinical psychologist at a state mental hospital, set out to describe his mental patients' hallucinations. The patients were either chronic schizophrenic, alcoholic, brain-damaged, or senile. He found his patients' hallucinations similar despite their different diagnoses. Some of his patients returned home after a few months; some had been in the hospital many years. It was not easy for Van Dusen to encourage the patients to discuss their hallucinations since they knew other people were not experiencing them. Van Dusen writes that some patients became so involved in their inner processes that they shut themselves off from the outside world.

Van Dusen asked his patients to describe the hallucinations, and he offered no reward. Many did not want to reveal the obscene nature of the voices they heard. Van Dusen asked for a word-by-word account and would actually converse with the hallucinated voice that was using the patient as an intermediary. Occasionally, the voices would speak directly to Van Dusen using the vocal cords of the patient. Van Dusen treated the hallucinations as reality because they were real to the patient.

Van Dusen determined that the patients encountered two orders of experiences. The undesirable or lower-order hallucinations were mostly voices, but there were some visions among these. The desirable or higher-order ones included voices but also included abstract, symbolic, and creative visions that the patient did not always understand. I believe there are similarities between these higher-order hallucinations and the ISH/Spirit in that they both attempt to assist the patient.

3. Higher-Order Hallucinations or Spirits

In Van Dusen's research, the higher-order hallucinations composed about one-fifth of the total experiences. One man's higher order appeared as a *light* or radiant like the sun. The higher order respected the man's freedom and would withdraw if it frightened him. "The higher order is much more likely to be symbolic, religious, supportive, and genuinely instructive; it can communicate directly with the inner feelings of the patient" (p. 123). Van Dusen encouraged his patients to approach the higher order because it had great power to broaden the individual's values and "appeared strangely gifted, sensitive, wise and religious" (p. 125). One patient encountered a Christlike figure who communicated mind-to-mind. Another man had a female vision that demonstrated knowledge of religion and myth far beyond the patient's comprehension.

According to Van Dusen, the higher order thinks in universal ideas, is very powerful emotionally, and has a ring of truth. When a woman of the higher order described herself as an emanation of the feminine aspect of the Divinity and Van Dusen implied she was divine, she was offended and reiterated that she was only an emanation of the divine. This idea sounds similar to Long's concept that the High Self is able to contact spiritual beings higher than itself. One patient had, in one hour, the higher order show him hundreds of universal symbols that he found entertaining but could not understand. "One patient described a higher order spirit who appeared all in white, radiant, very powerful in his presence and communicated directly with the spirit of the patient to guide him out of his hell [i.e., lower-order influences]" (p. 134).

Not all patients experience the higher order. The higher order claims power over the lower order (including demonstrations not described by Van Dusen) but "has indicated that the usefulness of the lower order is to illustrate and make conscious the patient's weaknesses and faults" (p. 124). The lower order knows of the presence of the higher order but cannot see it. Van Dusen encouraged one patient to become more acquainted with the higher order; when he did so, the "evil plotters" disappeared. Van Dusen did not state that the patient became completely well; most likely only some of the lower-order spirits departed. Van Dusen reported one higher order that knew a language other than the patient's; no lower order knew a different language.

4. Lower-Order Hallucinations

The lower-order spirits described by Van Dusen are very similar to the spirit intruders previously considered. However, Van Dusen would probably not agree that they are the spirits of deceased humans, although most of his patients "thought these were other living persons." Van Dusen states that the lower order never has a personal identity; it accepts any name or identity given. The lower-order spirits that Van Dusen encountered had no awareness or personal memories that enabled Van Dusen to trace them as individuals or that gave any evidence of higher-level thinking or experiencing. However, Van Dusen claimed that "when identified as some friend known to the patient they can assume this voice perfectly" and that "the personal memory was taken off at their death leaving more interior aspects" (p. 131). Van Dusen was impressed by the similarity of these lower-order hallucinations to accounts of possession described in the Bible.

In Van Dusen's research, the voices of the lower order would often appear suddenly. The patients described them as normal human voices. Although voices are more common, one man had a vision (one that he called "the other order") so real that he attempted to hit it and, in so doing, injured his hand on a wall. The lower order voices use obscene language; suggest lewd acts; and tease, torment, and scold their victims. They prey upon guilt, steal memories, threaten death or disaster, encourage suicide, suggest foolish acts, make promises they do not keep, and give helpful-sounding advice that proves incorrect. Many patients continue to believe these lower-order voices even though the former are constantly deceived by the latter.

The lower order can control a particular part of the victim's body, but it takes a period of time to accomplish this. One man grew deafer as the lower order worked on his ear, whereas another man's eye went out of alignment. Other parts controlled include the tongue and genitals. One woman reported she had pleasurable sexual relations with her male spirit, but another patient reported that "tiny devils" tormented her genital region.

The lower-order voices are irreligious or antireligious, have interfered with Van Dusen's patients' religious practices, and have even referred to themselves as demons from hell. One claimed to be Jesus Christ, but his attitude confirmed that he was of the lower order. One lower order claimed he could read Van Dusen's mind, but he actually could not. Another claimed it could see objects or hear words remote from the patient's senses, but Van Dusen could find no evidence to support the claim. The lower-order beings' memory was limited to occurrences since its intrusion into the victim. Although there can be many lower-order spirits, there is a kind of hierarchy, and only the lowest members are known to the patient or Van Dusen. According to Van Dusen, Swedenborg reported that our lives may be the little free space at the confluence of giant higher and lower spiritual hierarchies. Although this chapter may concentrate on lower-order harmful spirits, receiving assistance from *light beings* occurs quite frequently in therapy. Van Dusen's conclusions are consistent with previous findings that each person has a Spirit that is always available to aid in therapy. Some of the assistance may come from the Spirit aspect calling upon spiritual levels above itself.

5. Confirmation by Another Therapist

Ross (1997), author of the previously mentioned book on DID, mentions a Native man (no further description) who had schizophrenia with one good voice and one bad voice. The bad one wanted to assault people, acted in an unpleasant manner, and claimed to be the Devil. The good voice tried to soothe the patient by advising socially acceptable behavior. This confirms Van Dusen's findings about higher- and lower-order influences on human behavior.

In the next section, I discuss some cases I originally found while investigating DID, but these appear to me to have more features in common with spirit intrusion rather than being complete personalities in conjunction with amnesia.

Q. Intrusion Cases from DID Literature

1. Introduction

In this section I present behavioral cases that I found in literature (primarily journal articles) about Dissociative Identity Disorder (DID) but which lack the requirements to be full secondary personalities. I conjecture that these cases demonstrate that DID is simply the farthest end of a dissociation spectrum or the complete takeover of a body. A person with DID normally has amnesia regarding the alternate personalities. While in most of these cases there was no amnesia, all the other indicators of an entity that affects behavior are present. I use the term *multiple personality* in these cases, as most of the articles were written before the change from Multiple Personality Disorder (MPD) to DID.

2. Intrusion by Deceased Family Members

Scialli (1982) reports on a case of DID, but I am not sure if the symptoms indicate a full personality. The male patient was the fifth of six children, and his younger brother died in infancy when the patient was two years old. He idealized his father but it could be an incidence of identification with the perpetrator. The patient felt he could communicate with his father telepathically. When the boy was sixteen, his father developed a respiratory infection. The patient felt his telepathic communication sustained his father through one more year of life. The patient overdosed on aspirin prior to his father's death, and began hallucinating discs, spots, spiders, and bugs that attacked him. After his father's death, he had hallucinatory experiences, including hearing his father tell him he had made his mother's heart condition worse and that he was responsible for his younger brother's death. This case illustrates undesirable family voices, both before and after death.

3. Occult Practices as a Factor

Galvin and Ludwig (1961) discuss a case of witchcraft among people of Spanish-American heritage living in Colorado. The views of these people are a synthesis of ideas from medieval Spain, American Indians, Anglo folk medicine, and standard medicine. Bewitchment (*embrujo*) is conducted by an evil witch (*bruja*) but can be overcome by a friendly bruja or *curandera*. A seventeen-year-old patient named Mary came to Drs. Galvin and Ludwig a few days after being visited by her aunt G., whom she feared and hated. Aunt G. was a bruja and an ugly middle-aged woman who reportedly was the mother of fourteen children, most of whom she gave to agencies because of her incompetence and neglect. Mary began going into trances after her aunt's visits. Galvin and Ludwig believe that Mary was simply blaming her unwanted sexual feelings on her aunt, but I suspect it is more likely there was spiritual intrusion by the living aunt, who had trained in evil magic (occult practices). Generally, it is the occult practitioner who is subject to intrusion, but in this case it was the intruder. In addition to her occult practices, the aunt had her own spirit intruders along with multiple indicators of soul fragmentation.

4. Abuse as a Cause

Crisp (1983) discusses a case in which Diana, unlike her siblings, was the member of a family who was not beaten by her father. The father was seductive and sexual in his behavior toward her, but Crisp did not state the extent of the sexual relationship. When she was the age of thirteen, her father died. During adolescence, she had a number of homosexual and heterosexual experiences. At the age of eighteen, she began to hear the voice of a woman named Julie, who indicated she had come into existence just before Diana's father died. I interpret this as indicating that trauma caused by observing others being abused, and not just experiencing abuse oneself, may also result in spirit intrusion. Soldiers in battle can develop PTSD from observing injuries to their fellow soldiers.

Although all cases of child abuse sound horrid, a case described by Bowman, Blix, and Coons (1985) is especially so. The father is now serving a life sentence for incest, sodomy, and rape. The victims were Debra and her sister Kim. Debra was diagnosed with DID, but she is discussed here because one of her personalities, discovered after fusion of several other personalities, was masculine, had no name, and insisted that her incest was enjoyable and that her father had a right to do it. Sometimes the patient heard this personality's voice accompanied by other voices, one of which was her father's voice condemning her for sending him to prison. This case illustrates that voices are sometimes living family members.

5. Epilepsy or Abnormal Temporal Lobe EEG

Mesulam (1981) describes a patient who experienced hallucinations and déjà vu as well as rage, panic, and depersonalization; had anorexia nervosa; and was suicidal. She felt she was possessed by the Devil and that Satan had taken over her body. A voice inside her would tell her to do horrible things. She had undergone a rite of exorcism by a priest, but she was unable to describe the procedure because she lost consciousness early in the rite. She was apparently still having problems after the exorcism. Several drugs reduced the frequency of some of her symptoms. This case illustrates that a person with severe dissociative symptoms may feel possessed by the Devil, but the feeling is probably related to a discarnate human spirit with a dark being attached to it.

Schenk and Bear (1981) also discuss temporal lobe epilepsy and multiple personality. Interestingly, their patients were from the same hospital where Mesulam (1981) was practicing, and the article was written about the same time as Mesulam's piece. While some cases appear to be the same in the two works, most were different.

Under the topic of related dissociative phenomena, Schenk and Bear discuss the case of a woman who was exorcised by a priest. This was undoubtedly the same case as that discussed by Mesulam. While Mesulam did not comment on the effects of the exorcism, Schenk and Bear state that the patient felt that the exorcism was somewhat successful. I speculate that in cases similar to this, the patients have multiple intruders and the exorcism may eliminate some, but not all, of the intruding spirits.

These studies by Mesulam, and Schenk and Bear, demonstrate that epilepsy may be a strong indicator that some form of spirit intrusion has taken place. However, these patients were in a hospital setting, whereas many patients with epilepsy in outpatient clinics may not have any, or at least have less severe, indicators of spirit intrusion.

6. Posttraumatic Stress Disorder

Young (1985) recounts the case of a secondary personality in a person who had posttraumatic stress disorder (PTSD). The trauma was a war experience, and the alter was a dead comrade of the patient. The dissociation developed as a result of guilt, denial, and identification with the lost comrade. This case illustrates intrusion by a deceased friend. The reason why many intrusions are by family members is that family members stay around areas with which they are familiar—and when a psychic opening happens, they are in the vicinity to take advantage of it. In this case, the spirit of the deceased friend remained in the vicinity of the living friend. Guilt and identification with someone can also result in psychic openings.

7. Transgendered

Schwartz (1988) reveals a case of concurrent DID and transsexualism. A more common term today is *transgendered*, but I will use the original author's designation. At the time DID treatment began, the male patient had already undergone sex reassignment surgery. As a boy, he had been sexually abused by both his mother and father. The mother had tried to raise him as a girl; she had him do all the household chores and other traditional female tasks. Alters began to appear when he was three or four years old. He was also sexually abused by a junior high school counselor. After this patient's sex reassignment surgery, so many therapists had sex with "her" that she thought she had a sign on her back reading, "Have sex with me." Schwartz discovered that the patient had DID. She conversed with some of the male alters. One male alter complained bitterly about being in a female body. He told about his apprehension during the proposed surgery and related the following about the surgery itself.

He described what it felt like to be on an operating table, watching, and feeling his penis being cut off while he was unable to stop the surgeons. He said he had experienced all the pain, since he was the alter created to endure the father's beatings. The anesthetic had no effect on him. He said there were times, especially the time of the year that the surgery was done, when he couldn't control his screaming and rage (p. 50).

The description is reminiscent of an NDEr describing a surgery or resuscitation, except that NDErs usually do not feel pain. Another male alter in this case said, "He [the patient] can no longer just fear castration or have castration anxiety; he has been castrated" (p. 50). This alter held jealous hatred toward other males. Schwartz concludes that because the surgery is irreversible, other people considering sex reassignment surgery should be analyzed for DID; in this case, "A powerful alliance of all the female alters had presented themselves for the reassignment surgery. The few male alters were not strong enough to intercede" (p. 50). I maintain that all alters are spirit intruders and that DID represents a much higher degree of control exerted by such intruders. If this person had had his DID successfully treated to the integration stage, he would have been the original personality (a male) with the anatomy of a woman.

Barlow, Abels, and Blanchard (1977) describe a male patient considering sex reassignment surgery. The authors note that other researchers were beginning to find that many patients were dissatisfied with the surgery, which is essentially irreversible. They quote another source as stating that mistaken gender identity is considered fixed and irreversible by the age of three. The case they report concerns a man named "John" who was in his early twenties. He was the youngest of three children, rather frail, and as a young child had helped his mother with many household chores. He began cross-dressing as early as age four and slept in the same bed as his mother. His father, previously seldom home, permanently left the home when John was eight.

At the age of fifteen, John began reading about transsexualism and found a physician who prescribed some estrogen for him. This eliminated his unwanted erections and eventually resulted in breast enlargement. He came to the authors' office and was diagnosed as a transsexual. He was a good worker at a fried-chicken restaurant, but his mother insisted he "make a man of himself." He joined the navy, but he was promptly discharged. Though a test revealed that he had a normal male chromosomal pattern, he began preparing for sex reassignment surgery. By various measurements (motor behavior and card sort tests), he was found to act more frequently like a female. He assumed the name Judy and could even wear a bikini. Judy was referred to a medical center in a nearby state for sex reassignment surgery. The authors did not hear from Judy, but one day a research assistant came back from the fried-chicken stand and said that "Judy" was "John" again. John came to their office, acting in a very masculine manner, and told his story.

The owner of the fast-food restaurant, who liked John as a worker, suggested that John see a physician in another city on his way to the gender identity clinic. The restaurant owner and the physician were both members of the same fundamental Protestant religion, which was quite different from the Baptist faith of John, who was not religious. The physician told John that his real problem was possession by evil spirits. A healing session lasting two to three hours was held. It involved exhortations, prayers, and the physician's laying on of hands on the head and shoulders of John. John appeared to faint several times, but the result was the exorcism of twenty-two evil spirits, which the physician called by name as they left. John felt waves of God's love coming over him during the session. The physician wrote a letter to the authors explaining that the spirit of the woman in John had disappeared. Generally, society thinks of fundamentalists who conduct deliverance activities to be uneducated, but in this case he was a physician.

John immediately began acting like a man, but he still had large breasts. After returning home and living with his mother, he began to have some feminine feelings again. His restaurant employer took him to a well-known faith healer, who told him he had sexual problems. The faith healer laid his hands on John, and during the ten- to fifteen-minute session, John appeared to faint. When he stood up, his breasts were gone.

The authors of the case followed John's progress for two and a half years. There was almost a complete reversal from feminine to masculine reactions on the tests involving motor behavior and card sorting. John reported that he was sexually aroused by men for several months after the healing, but that eventually went away. In their conclusion, Barlow et al. note that suggestion, persuasion, and any other psychotherapeutic procedure have been ineffective for transsexuals. It is especially amazing that the changes could occur in a few hours. They did not observe the laying on of hands and tended to doubt the rapid disappearance of the breasts. Overall, though, they do not doubt that John was a transsexual who assumed his biological masculine gender identity after an exorcism.

John's case has some items that were not mentioned in the section about Basham's deliverances. The faith healer (really a misnomer) was undoubtedly a charismatic, rather than a fundamentalist, healer. Calling the spirits by name as they leave seems to add to effectiveness. (In item 3, "Charismatic Deliverance" [beneath section G, "Christian Deliverance"], which is about healings by Basham, the spirits named themselves during the exorcism. Catholic exorcisms also involve the spirits naming themselves.) What the authors described as John's fainting was not actually fainting. What happened to him is known as being "slain in the Spirit [the Holy Spirit]," a common thing at charismatic healing services. "Fainting" can happen to people at a service without a healing occurring. Barlow et al. believe that the healer knew that John had a sexual problem because of his breasts, but the healer could have also known it from what is labeled *discernment* (information received from the Holy Spirit). Another example is what occurs when a charismatic healer calls out a healing in the audience. The nearly instantaneous disappearance of the breasts would not be considered unusual at a charismatic healing service. However, some unscrupulous people with no true healing abilities are able to employ a semblance of this charismatic gift for the purpose of financial gain. In a later section, exorcism in the Bible will be discussed.

Although this section recounts primarily cases that support previous research on spirit intrusion, the above article really introduces a new method of eliminating psychosexual disorders—exorcism, but much different from the Catholic exorcisms discussed earlier or Basham's deliverance. Basically, I consider exorcism another way to remove intruding spirits. While Fiore cautioned against just throwing the spirits out, since they could then invade another person, I maintain that a correctly performed Christian exorcism properly handles the spirits and relieves them of their earthbound status, although it does not necessarily send them into the realm of *light*. Recall that Atteshlis, Fiore, and Wickland reported that they could send intruding spirits of deceased humans to a spiritual reeducation center if they were still unprepared to enter the *light*.

8. Other Cases

Gruenewald (1978), in an article on analogues of multiple personality, reports on one patient who received "messages from within" and conversed with the entities who sent them, beginning with one or two and ending with nine. At times, the patient seemed separate from the entities and could listen to several of them conversing without being involved in the conversation. I suspect that two partially invading spirits can converse among themselves, with the host personality being simply a listener. In schizophrenics, the patients believe that the voices they hear are directed at them.

One day, Berman (1981), a social worker at a hospital, had an elderly woman named Mrs. Roth come to say she was trying to find the mother of a 17-year-old runaway. It turned out that the runaway, Pram Lamentis, was living inside Mrs. Roth. *Pram* is a British word for a baby carriage, and *lament* refers to sorrow. Mrs. Roth was co-conscious with Pram. Berman asked Mrs. Roth the circumstances of Pram's arrival. The last of Mrs. Roth's seven sisters had died a month before. She said she was feeling lonely, and perhaps that was why she allowed Pram to stay. Mrs. Roth wanted to go on a trip to Bermuda with her daughter, but Pram was afraid of the water. With a psychiatrist's assistance, Berman was eventually able to get Mrs. Roth to leave Pram at the hospital, but Mrs. Roth became irate when billed because she thought Pram should pay for the service. Her case illustrates several effects: (1) loneliness may bring about an intrusion; (2) sympathy may not always be a good quality; (3) weakly connected spirits may leave if emotional stability is regained; and (4) phobias may be due to intruding entities, probably an earthbound spirit. Intruding spirits do not always remember their name and may use names assigned by their host or a therapist.

9. Preventing Intrusion

Finally, I remind the reader of the case described by Ludwig et al. (1972) in section E, "The Inner Self-helper," of chapter 6, on DID. The ISH said another personality was "scattered but gathering." This may represent how a spiritual entity arrives. The spirit body is like a cloud, and it may take a period of time of staying around a person to gather its strength in order to be able to enter if the opportunity arises. The roaming spirit cannot penetrate unless a weakness is found. Fiore provides one of the best discussions of weaknesses.

10. Reclassification of Some Mental Illnesses

Ross (1995) suggests the reclassification of several diagnostic entities as dissociative disorders. Among the disorders he suggests are conversion disorder, which is now classified as a somatoform disorder, along with hypochondriasis and dysmorphophobia, and intermittent explosive disorder, which is classified as a disorder of impulse control. Other possibilities for reclassification include unipolar depression, borderline personality disorder, and psychosexual dysfunctions. He also suggests that it might be possible to talk to the psychic fragments responsible for schizophrenic voices in DID patients. I suspect that he is correct in all of his suggestions.

In the next section, I explain how some of the behavioral issues I have discussed in this book may arise from a materialistic society that does not understand the basis for the behavior (spirit intrusion) and, thus, improperly treats trauma or condones other behaviors that lead to soul fragmentation and resulting spirit intrusion.

R. Modern Society: Specific Cases

1. Introduction

In this section, I present some cases of people who have appeared in the media in the last forty years that indicate probable spiritual intrusion. In some situations it is impossible to substantiate specific dates or to confirm evidence. The section on notable people discloses that spirit intrusion does not just happen in people of lower socioeconomic status. The section on criminal behavior demonstrates that spirit intrusion is a major contributor to crime and, thus, to the public-borne costs of our criminal justice system.

2. Notable People

One morning on a television interview program, playwright Arthur Miller was interviewed after he had written his biography. He had been married to actress Marilyn Monroe for several years. He said she had been abused as a child, and I believe others have confirmed that information. He then commented that he had never seen her unhappy in a crowd. Yet she committed suicide over fifty years ago, so she must have been depressed. Intruding spirits very often occur among abused children, and major mood swings, such as proceeding from an exuberant mood in some circumstances to depression in other circumstances, is a good indicator of spirit intrusion.

Five years after television news journalist Jessica Savitch's death in 1983, two books were written about her life. Both books use the word *golden* in the title. *Time Magazine* included some important information in its press section. Jessica was anorexic and would throw tantrums over the slightest inconvenience. At times, her drug abuse (she used cocaine, among other substances) was so debilitating that she could barely function. She did have a remarkable gift for talking to a TV camera, however. One author recounted "that Savitch once told a colleague that her trick was to focus on a spot in the middle of her head and project it through her eyes to the other side of the lens. 'She would send this energy force out like a laser,' he recalled. 'You'd step back and say, "Christ! What was that"!

Although some people develop a similar phenomenon without understanding it, others develop it through improper "occult" training. Jessica's first marriage lasted ten months. Five months into her second marriage, her husband committed suicide. Three weeks later, she (at the age of thirty-six) and her date drowned in an automobile "accident." In my investigations of the phenomenon of intrusion, it appears that accidents happen much more frequently to people who have spirit intruders. These people seem to carry a black cloud around with them that constantly brings misfortune, although in many cases it does not interfere with material success.

These abnormal distributions of problems can also affect families. In other words, no individual in the family has more than one unusual occurrence, but the family as a whole seems to experience many tragedies.

McAll (1982) and Crabtree (1985) write about spirit intrusions that remain in families. One example of this type of familial spirit intrusion may be a famous political family. One son in this family died under unusual circumstances during World War II; one daughter had mental problems (possible schizophrenia) that were not corrected by a frontal lobotomy; two other sons were assassinated with guns (both were described as charismatic, and one reportedly had an insatiable sexual appetite); and a fourth son had a passenger in an automobile he was driving die under some unusual circumstances. Two other daughters seemed unaffected. The following generation of this family has had incidents of cancer at a very early age. Another member died as a result of drug abuse.

Some writers may sensationalize the biographies they write and give a biased view of their subject, but the book *The Lives of John Lennon* (Goldman, 1988) lists a significant number of intrusive disorder symptoms. John Lennon was a heavy drug user. (Substance abuse often induces multiple spirit intrusions.) Among his symptoms, in addition to drug abuse, were a violent temper (despite his preaching peace), anorexia nervosa (much less common in males), and having indiscriminate sex (perhaps even engaging in homosexual activity). Rock music is dissociative, and the more years spent playing it or listening to it, the more dissociation one experiences. Elvis Presley became a drug addict (most of the drugs he used were legal), as do many rock musicians.

Some justification for the claim that rock music can induce dissociation should be given. The phrase *induce dissociation* is used because it is possible for a person to partially dissociate (undergo soul fragmentation) and be open to intrusion when no spirits are around to take advantage of the situation. Schrekenberg and Bird (1987) performed an experiment that did not use rock music but rather an arrhythmic drumbeat. The subjects were mice, and three sets were used. One group listened to classical music; a second group heard nothing; and the third heard an arrhythmic drumbeat. After two months, the classical group and the quiet group performed similarly in a maze, but the arrhythmic drumbeat group had trouble finding their way around the maze, stood still or wandered aimlessly, and were hyperactive and aggressive. Although some groups of people attack rock music for its lyrics, I conjecture that it is the loudness and melody that are more damaging to the relationship between the physical body and the spirit body. Satanists often prefer heavy metal music, which is at one end of the spectrum that moves from light rock to heavy rock to acid rock to heavy metal. I opine that the more extreme the music becomes and the louder it is played, the more soul fragmentation the music induces in its listeners.

Another source of information for this claim comes from the book *The Secret Life of the Unborn Child*. The author, Dr. Thomas Verny (1981), claims that a fetus who is kicking can be calmed down by her mother's listening to certain classical music (Vivaldi and Mozart), but rock music (and some classical music) can drive the fetus to distraction. Fetal heart rate and fetal kicking were used as the barometers of distraction.

3. Criminal Behavior

In an article in *Psychology Today* concerning aging prisoners, Chaneles (1987) reports that his "research suggests that among those who will be at least sixty to seventy before they are released [Author's Note: twenty to forty at the time of crime], 80% have led an actively abusive life involving drugs, alcohol, and hallucinogens. Many have been intensely promiscuous bisexuals. Most place high value on physical strength, aggressiveness, violence, and predatory behavior expressed through gang membership" (p. 49). The substance abuse and sexual behavior are indications of spirit intrusion, and the consequent behaviors are likely the result of spirit intrusion.

Methvin (1989) chronicles the abduction and murder of two girls in South Carolina. The local investigators called upon the expertise of crime analyst John Douglas of the FBI Academy's National Center for the Analysis of Violent Crime. Douglas and a team of authorities drew up a probable profile of the murderer. The psychopath would most likely be twenty-eight to thirty-five years old and have had an unsuccessful marriage, a prior criminal record for obscene phone calls and assaults on women, an obsessive-compulsive personality, and a weight loss after the first kidnap–murder. He may also have collected erotic literature featuring women in bondage. After the second murder, the police arrested and convicted a man who fit the description on all accounts. While being interviewed, the accused man gave this response to a question: "The Larry Gene Bell sitting here could not have done such a thing, but there's a bad Larry Gene Bell that could have." Assailants frequently know that they carry an influencing personality within themselves, but no one else, including criminal psychologists, seems to fathom the simple and long-believed explanation of spirit intrusions. Bell was executed in 1996.

Authorities at least know that pornography is a factor in many psychopathic murders. Executed serial killer Ted Bundy (alleged to have committed over a hundred murders) divulged to psychologist Dr. James Dobson that hard-core pornography was the fuel for his fantasies and that alcohol reduced his inhibitions. All of his victims had long dark hair, indicating an obsession. Bundy also said that other serial killers to whom he had spoken all had a significant interest in pornography, usually beginning at an early age. Although all spirit intruders cause a perpetrator to become desensitized to the suffering he or she is causing in others, I hold that this is especially true of spirits that arise from viewing pornography.

Whenever reading about or seeing multiple murders in the media, I attempt to follow up on the descriptions of the person accused. For instance, Gene Simmons in Russellville, Arkansas, killed sixteen members of his family in one rampage. He was known to have abused his wife and was once accused of incest. There is ample evidence that the victims of abuse have spiritual intruders, whether by DID or by a less extreme variety of mental illness, and it is likely that the perpetrator of the abuse is also acting under the influence of an intruding spirit and/or nested demon. In Philadelphia, Gary Heidnik was convicted of torturing, murdering, and even cannibalizing several women. He said he heard voices instructing him to kill his victims. A person who murdered five schoolchildren in California was a chronic alcoholic. Receiving the death penalty or a sentence of life in prison does not mean much to these killers, as they are under a strong influence of an intruding spirit, and prison is irrelevant to an intruding spirit.

4. Parental and Caretaker Difficulties

Another problem that is occurring much more frequently these days is that some mothers kill their children, usually while the children are still infants. Toufexis (1988) reports that the mothers said they were very depressed after giving birth. The illness is sometimes referred to as postpartum depression ("baby blues"). DSM-III does not list postpartum problems separately. For some women, the depression lasts only a few weeks, but for others it can last for months. Toufexis claims that these women also have mood swings, loss of appetite, and insomnia. Some hear voices telling them to kill their children. One woman said she felt completely beside herself. Toufexis then quotes psychiatrist Ricard Fernandez as stating that the women have thoughts of suicide or killing their babies, and "These are *invasive* [emphasis added], terrifying ideas that can drive them crazy." These symptoms are each an indication of intrusion by an obsessing spirit. It is possible for the trauma of birthing to physically weaken any woman, which can result in temporary intrusion, but mothers who actually kill their children often have a family history of mental illness, indicating family tree spirit influence rather than the catchall category of genetics.

A person can find examples of spirit intrusion and its tragic results almost anywhere. The *Wall Street Journal* included an article by Trost (1988) that reported the following about day care personnel. A ten-month-old child named Ashley Snead died while being cared for by a sitter named Martha Guba, who was a grandmother in her late fifties. The child died from ingesting prescription antidepressant drugs administered by Mrs. Guba. A neighbor reported that Mrs. Guba liked babies who took naps. Mrs. Guba was sentenced to prison for ten years for child neglect.

What the parents did not know when they hired Mrs. Guba was that she was convicted in 1968 of neglecting her own children, had been hospitalized for mental problems, was a heavy user of prescription drugs, and had an alcoholic as a former husband. Although neglecting children, mental problems, and drug use are typical symptoms of spirit intrusion, possibly the best indication came from what a police interviewer reported about Mrs. Guba. This police investigator testified that he had never interviewed anyone quite like Mrs. Guba. "She had mood changes right in front of me," he said. "She would go from happy to sad to happy to sad." Mood swings are often indicative of spirit intrusion or DID.

5. Hidden Child

At a 1987 conference about multiple personality and dissociation, Dr. Roland Summit discussed the phenomenon of the hidden child. Many victims of abuse feel that they have a child personality inside. Billy Milligan had several child personalities that could accept pain rather than react with anger, as some personalities do. Summit mentioned that Christina Crawford, the daughter of actress Joan Crawford, wrote about her mother's abusive behavior and reported a hidden child inside herself.

In *Psychology Today* there was an article about runaway children and what happens to them. Large numbers of these individuals, even the boys, end up working as prostitutes. It is interesting to read articles by authors who do not understand the concept of intrusion or the hidden-child syndrome. The author of the article was absolutely amazed at the response when a prostitute, age eighteen, who had been on the streets for six years was asked what she would most like to have. She replied, "A doll." A psychiatrist may conclude she was reverting to a period of happiness. The reply does not seem unusual, because many prostitutes were abused as children. Many have had abortions and carry many intruding entities in and around themselves. One or more of these entities is likely to be a child, possibly even the prostitute's own aborted child. It is this hidden child that wants to play with a doll. Since there are many spirits around or in a prostitute, it is very simple for one of these spirits to transfer from the prostitute to the other person during sexual relations between the two. This transfer concept applies to any type of sexual relations with a person who has intruding entities, whether the type is male–female, male–male, female–female, or adult–child, and whether it involves payment for services or is voluntary. The phrase *consenting adult* does not mean anything to a spirit.

6. Other Cases

The book *The Life of a Real Girl* (1986) is Johanna Garfield's own story about regaining mental health. Garfield grew up in a wealthy suburb of New York with many comforts and privileges. Her father was successful, and her mother was very talented. Johanna began to show signs of emotional disturbance by the time of her adolescence. She had anorexia before the term was widely known, and on occasion she would also compulsively overeat. She developed a drug dependency (Dexedrine) and began to feel there were two Johannas. One was witty, charming, and popular. "The Other Me" was a terrified young woman who felt that her charm was due to the drugs she took, that she inhabited a secretly ugly body, that she was afraid of sex, and that she was terribly, terribly sick. The terrified child was most likely the intruder. Johanna spent some time in a mental institution but is now well, has a husband and three children, and is a freelance writer. Her book was republished in 2000. Although not mentioned, I believe that Johanna experienced some type of trauma early in her life. Trauma can just as easily happen in families with outwardly favorable circumstances.

In the next section, I discuss one Bible quotation that employs phrases such as *evil spirit*, *unclean spirits*, and *demon-possessed people*, showing how these support my concept of spirit intrusion and removal of those spirits. The remaining quotations from the Bible appear in appendix E.

S. A Discussion of Applicable Bible Quotations

In this section, I will list one Bible quotation relating to evil spirits, unclean spirits, or demons. In appendix E, I will list the remaining passages. The purpose of this section and of appendix E is to demonstrate that *evil spirits*, *unclean spirits*, and *devils* and *demons* may be used interchangeably and that removal of these entities often results in physical and mental healing. Here, and in appendix E, I will present this information in titled sections, followed by a short explanation. Of twenty-eight Gospel passages quoted, five were written by three evangelists, four were written by two evangelists, and five were reported by only one evangelist. It is interesting that the Gospel of John never mentions healing of people with evil spirits. The only use of similar terms in the book of John is after Judas accepted a piece of bread from Jesus at the Last Supper; John reports that Satan entered, or took possession of, Judas (13:27). Luke confirms Satan's entry but states that the entry occurred when Judas went to the chief priests about the betrayal and not at the Last Supper (Luke 22:3). After the betrayal, Judas committed suicide. Later, I will explain why John rarely speaks of possession. Other than in the Gospels, there are only three passages that mention possession by spirits: one in the standard Old Testament, one in the Apocrypha, and one in the book Acts of the Apostles.

The quotations are taken from the New International Version (NIV) of the Bible. Terms like *evil spirits* and *demons* that are employed in several other translations, such as the New King James Version (NKJV), the Lamsa translation, the Revised Standard Version (RSV), and the New American Bible (NAB), are also listed. I used my own judgment to determine when the passages were describing the same situation.

I have organized the terms to describe evil spirits in the table below. The abbreviations are as follows: *ES* for "evil spirits," *US* for "unclean spirits," and *DP* for "demon-possessed." *Poss.* is short for "possessed." I consider the terms to be functionally identical. The one passage I have chosen to list here could have been placed in chapter 6, as the behavior described in the Bible is similar to a behavioral pattern of a person with DID. I waited to list it here because terms such as *demons* were not used in chapter 6, but they appear frequently in this chapter.

The legion of evil spirits who attacked the swine:

	NIV	NKJV/RSV	Lamsa	NAB
Matthew 8:28–34	DP	Demoniacs/DP	Lunatics	Demoniacs
Mark 5:1–20	DP/ES	US/Satan	US	US
Luke 8:26–39	Demons	Demons/US	Demons/US	Demons/US/DP

Matthew

When he arrived at the other side in the region of the Gadarenes, two demon-possessed men coming from the tombs met him. They were so violent that no one could pass that way. "What do you want with us, Son of God?" they shouted. "Have you come here to torture us before the appointed time?" Some distance from them a large herd of pigs was feeding. The demons begged Jesus, "If you drive us out, send us into the herd of pigs." He said to them, "Go!" So they came out and went into the pigs, and the whole herd rushed down the steep bank into the lake and died in the water. Those tending the pigs ran off, went into the town and reported all this, including what had happened to the demon-possessed men. Then the whole town went out to meet Jesus. And when they saw him, they pleaded with him to leave the region.

Mark

They went across the lake to the region of the Gerasenes. When Jesus got out of the boat, a man with an evil spirit came from the tombs to meet him. This man lived in the tombs, and no one could bind him any more, not even with a chain. For he had often been chained hand and foot, but he tore the chains apart and broke the irons on his feet. No one was strong enough to subdue him. Night and day among the tombs and in the hills he would cry out and cut himself with stones. When he saw Jesus from a distance, he ran and fell on his knees in front of him. He shouted at the top of his voice, "What do you want with me, Jesus, Son of the Most High God? Swear to God that you won't torture me!" For Jesus had said to him, "Come out of this man, you evil spirit!" Then Jesus asked him, "What is your name?" "My name is Legion, " he replied, "for we are many." And he begged Jesus again and again not to send them out of the area. A large herd of pigs was feeding on the nearby hillside. The demons begged Jesus, "Send us among the pigs; allow us to go into them." He gave them permission, and the evil spirits came out and went into the pigs. The herd, about two thousand in number, rushed down the steep bank into the lake and were drowned. Those tending the pigs ran off and reported this in the town and countryside, and the people went out to see what had happened. When they came to Jesus, they saw the man who had been possessed by the legion of demons, sitting there dressed and in his right mind; and they were afraid. Those who had seen it told the people what had happened to the demon-possessed man—and told about the pigs as well. Then the people began to plead with Jesus to leave their region. As Jesus was getting into the boat, the man who had been demon-possessed begged to go with him. Jesus did not let him, but said, "Go home to your family and tell them how much the Lord has done for you, and how he has had mercy on you." So the man went away and began to tell in the Decapolis how much Jesus had done for him. And all the people were amazed.

<u>Luke</u>

They sailed to the region of the Gerasenes, which is across the lake from Galilee. When Jesus stepped ashore, he was met by a demon-possessed man from the town. For a long time this man had not worn clothes or lived in a house, but he had lived in the tombs. When he saw Jesus, he cried out and fell at his feet, shouting at the top of his voice, "What do you want with me Jesus, Son of the Most High God? I beg you, don't torture me!" For Jesus had commanded the evil spirit to come out of the man. Many times it had seized him, and though he was chained hand and foot and kept under guard, he had broken his chains and had been driven by the demon into solitary places. Jesus asked him, "What is your name?" "Legion," he replied, because many demons had gone into him. And they begged him repeatedly not to order them to go into the Abyss. A large herd of pigs was feeding on the hillside. The demons begged Jesus to let them go into them, and he gave them permission. When the demons came out of the man, they went into the pigs, and the herd rushed down the steep bank into the lake and was drowned. When those tending the pigs saw what had happened, they ran off and reported this in the town and countryside, and the people went out to see what had happened. When they came to Jesus, they found the man from whom the demons had gone out, sitting at Jesus' feet, dressed and in his right mind; and they were afraid. Those who had seen it told the people how the demon-possessed man had been cured. Then all the people of the region of the Gerasenes asked Jesus to leave them, because they were overcome with fear. So he got into the boat and left. The man from whom the demons had gone out begged to go with him, but Jesus sent him away, saying, "Return home and tell how much God has done for you." So the man went away and told all over town how much Jesus had done for him.

It is hard to explain why the demons or evil spirits desired to enter the swine, seeing as they would have to leave when the swine died. Perhaps they did not know the swine would run into the lake and drown. Although the man had to be troubled in order to live among the tombs, according to Fiore, living there may have exacerbated his problem. Matthew's account differs from those of the other two evangelists in that there were two men. Plus, Matthew named the people Gaderenes, whereas the others used "Gerasenes" and "one man."

There is much evidence in these passages for multiple intrusions or DID, as the alters can be aware of each other and one can refer to all of them as a legion. The following description is from Keyes (1981) when Billy Milligan was administered Thorazine.

> Three guards, holding a mattress in front of them, rushed Ragen [a protector alter], pinning him to the wall. Three others pushed him, face down, on the bed, holding his arms and legs. Arthur [an extremely intelligent alter] stopped Ragen. Nurse Pat Perry heard Danny scream, "Don't rape me!"
>
> Arthur saw another nurse with a hypo and heard her say, "A shot of Thorazine will stop him."
>
> "Not Thorazine!" Arthur shouted, but it was too late. He had heard Dr. Wilbur say that antipsychotic drugs were bad for multiple personalities and caused worse splitting. He tried to slow the flow of blood to keep the Thorazine from going to his brain. Then he felt himself being lifted by six pairs of hands and dragged out of his room, down into the elevator, out onto the second floor and Ward 5. He saw curious faces peering into his. Someone stuck out his tongue. Someone talked to a wall. Someone urinated on the floor. The smell of vomit and feces was overwhelming.
>
> They threw him into a small bare room with a plastic covered mattress, and locked the door. When Ragen heard the door slam, he got up to break it down, but Arthur froze him. [The remainder of names are of various APs.] Samuel took the spot, dropping to his knees, "Oy veh! God, why have you forsaken me?" Philip cursed and threw himself to the floor; David felt the pain. Lying on the mattress, Christene wept; Adalana felt her face wet in the pool of tears. Christopher sat up and played with his shoes. Tommy started to check the door to see if he could unlock it, but Arthur yanked him off

the spot. Allen started calling for his lawyer. April, filled with desire for revenge, saw the place burning. Kevin cursed. Steve mocked him. Lee laughed. Bobby fantasized that he could fly out the window. Jason threw a tantrum. Mark, Walter, Martin and Timothy raved wildly in the locked room. Shawn made a buzzing sound. Arthur no longer controlled the undesireables.

Through the observation window, the young Ward 5 attendants watched Milligan bang into the walls, spin around, babble in different voices and accents, laugh, cry, fall to the ground and get up again. They agreed that they were witnessing a raving lunatic. (pp. 321–22)

This behavior pattern is similar to that of the man described in the above Bible verses as "possessed by Legion." Breaking chains may appear to be an incredible feat of strength, but Arthur trained Ragen how to control the flow of adrenalin in order to perform unusual feats of strength. Once, Ragen even pulled a toilet from its foundation.

In the next section, I present information showing why trauma that induces soul fragmentation is a better model than the medical/neurochemical model of behavioral abnormalities. In chapter 12, I will show how the medical model may actually be harmful.

T. The Nonsolutions of Materialistic Psychiatry

1. Introduction

In chapter 4, I presented a significant amount of information from the book *The Irreducible Mind*, by Emily Kelly. She discusses the findings of two early writers in the field of psychical research, F. W. H. Myers and William James. From their writings and other recent research, she demonstrates that the mind must be considered separate from the brain, although they usually function together.

Now that I have discussed various indications that abnormal behavior may be corrected by employing a spiritual concept of human nature, I will review another book that is critical of biological reductionist concepts for explaining abnormal behavior. The authors of the book do not view the solution to the problem as a spiritual explanation, but I believe their concept is compatible with my hypothesis. However, they do assert that biological reductionism is based on a "mechanistic" worldview. In fact, one of the authors states that the current medical model is only one possible model and that it "could be characterized as atheistic, male chauvinist, or mechanistic-reductionist" (p. 106). My view is that this medical model may be responsible for an attitude of "just give me a pill and don't ask me to change my lifestyle" that many patients present to their doctors. The book is titled *Pseudoscience in Biological Psychiatry: Blaming the Body* (1995) (hereafter abbreviated *PBP*), and the principal authors are psychiatrist Colin Ross, MD, and Alvin Pam, a psychology PhD. *PBP* was briefly referenced in chapter 6.

2. Trauma, Not Neurotransmitters

The book primarily criticizes the concept that if a person is mentally ill (psychopathology), as diagnosed by the criteria in the *DSM-IV*, the illness must be due to brain chemicals (generally neurotransmitters) that are not functioning properly or are present in an incorrect quantity (i.e., a biochemical imbalance or neurotransmitter dysregulation). Therefore, it is the duty of the psychiatrist to find a medication that will correct the problem. The two most common neurotransmitters mentioned are related to dopamine or serotonin function. The medications are not necessarily for those specific neurotransmitters, but they do affect how they perform. For instance, many antidepressants on the market today are classified as Selective Serotonin Reuptake Inhibitors (SSRIs). The authors quote two catchy phrases used by biological reductionist researchers, "no twisted thought without a twisted molecule" and "strange people, strange substances" (p. 8), as if catchy phrases imply reputable science.

Before I delve further into the biological basis of psychiatry, and Ross and Pam's refutation of it, I will attempt to explain the model of abnormal behavior in their book. The *DSM-IV* is primarily driven by descriptions of the symptoms of the disorders. Ross and Pam believe that the etiology of the illness needs to be addressed. Their conviction is that the most frequent cause of many disorders is trauma, primarily childhood sexual or physical abuse, violent crimes, rape, war, and other trauma. As they explain, "Serious chronic childhood trauma is the overwhelming major driver of psychopathology in Western civilization. ... Psychopathology represents the normal human response to chronic childhood trauma" (p. 122). Therefore, the psychiatrist must get to the root cause of the illness and address it psychotherapeutically, not with pharmaceuticals. However, the authors do not deny that medications may be temporarily necessary during the therapy process, for instance, if the patient is suicidal. Dr. Ross says that he has prescribed SSRIs during treatment of DID but not as a cure for the patient. The authors also employ the concept that neurotransmitters or other molecules can "mediate" an illness. For instance, a person who has been traumatized in a past incident may generate molecules in response to a triggering incident that will create a mental-illness symptom, but the improper molecules did not cause the illness.

3. Genetics

The authors are harshly critical of the idea that mental illness is caused by genetics. They believe that the environment of the home is the more likely culprit. The bioreductionists ignore the home environment, stating that "if it [a mental illness] runs in families, it must be genetic," although they often phrase it as a "genetic predisposition" or "genetic loading." The authors of *PBP* believe that family violence is passed on when children observe their parents abuse them or their siblings. These children are traumatized by the abuse and later, when they are adults, behave in the same manner toward their own children.

Ross and Pam reviewed a number of studies in which the children were allegedly reared apart from their birth parents, but that "apart" time may be after the early formative years when they were with the birth parents or with one birth parent and a stepparent. For instance, a state social service agency may not take a child away from the abusive birth parents until age eight. However, when that child is determined to have mental disorders at age seventeen, he or she would be classified as raised in an adequate home setting (i.e., the adoption or foster home), and therefore background is not a factor in causing the disorder. Many family studies also do not take into consideration poverty. Poverty may result in children being raised amid inferior and more violent street surroundings, even if the parents exhibit normal behavior. In some cases, the adoptive or foster parents may not have been screened properly by a social agency. In other cases, the guardian parent may seem satisfactory, but the abuse is by a stepbrother or stepsister. These are more frequent in modern society's blended households. One statistic reported is that 16% of girls state that they were victims of sexual abuse, and 38% of women had experienced sexual abuse before the age of eighteen. Some biological psychiatrists may be aware of sexual abuse in the family of a patient, but rather than conclude that the trauma was the cause of the psychopathology in the patient, the psychiatrist assumes it indicates genetic problems in the family.

Among the specific disorders that bioreductionists conclude are related to genetics are alcoholism, schizophrenia, anxiety disorders, and depression. Pam reviewed the scientific literature for how the genetic conclusions were reached and found that the logic was not sound. I will not delve into all the details here; however, I will mention that some of the discredited studies were employing research methods utilized in infamous eugenics studies a century ago. In almost none of them was the home environment considered as a potential cause; in fact, it was often dismissed as irrelevant. The authors of *PBP* believe that the bioreductionist concepts have become an ideology, but the bioreductionists believe that these concepts are necessary if psychiatry is to be a science.

4. Compatibility with Spirit Intrusion

I consider the trauma concept to be compatible with my spiritual hypothesis based on the observations of NDEr Ritchie that I reported in the section called "A Unique Journey" in chapter 5, on NDEs. He noticed that living people were surrounded by a faint luminous glow, "like a second skin made out of pale, scarcely visible light." He also refers to this as a cocoon. Recall that when the drunken man went unconscious from the effects of the alcohol, the cocoon of *light* opened up and spirits of deceased alcoholics were able to enter him. I maintain that this cocoon of *light* is a protection mechanism. When a person is traumatized, this cocoon opens up, which allows various spirits to enter. I also suggest that spirits or elementals (thought forms) may alter the internal chemistry of the human body so as to produce mental illnesses. Although stress is not a mental illness, spirits or elementals can induce stress in an individual, and this stress can induce somatic (body) changes. Other therapists' name for this cocoon include "a natural shield of protection" and "ego boundaries."

5. Reductionist Fallacies

Pam contends that there are two major logical errors that can be made concerning pharmacological response to medications. One error is to assume that because a biochemical molecule can induce a condition, the condition therefore is always caused by a biochemical response. For example, he notes that administering a dose of sodium lactate can induce a panic disorder but that most people with panic disorders have normal levels of sodium lactate in the bloodstream. The second error is to assume that if a psychiatric problem is corrected by a medication, the biochemical imbalance that the medication supposedly corrected was the cause of the problem. The error is that this form of thinking is proceeding from an effect to a cause.

Many mental illnesses have multiple symptoms, and while the medication may relieve one of the major symptoms, it is not a cure. In fact, "no psychiatric disorder has ever been 'cured' by medication" (p. 41). Many psychiatric medications are known to be drugs that patients stop taking because they dislike the side effects. He adds that "a harsh assessment would be that no substantive results have been tendered for the pathogenesis of any major psychiatric disorder" (p. 42). In chapter 1, I mentioned the term *promissory materialism* to describe the concept that eventually a physical brain basis for all mind functions will be found. I would classify the unending search for a molecular basis of mental illness as promissory psychiatry. The authors of *PBP* classify these searches for malfunctioning genes or molecules as "fishing expeditions" that often consume a significant amount of resources.

Pam notes that aspirin can relieve headaches, but that does not imply that headaches are precipitated by an aspirin deficiency. Ross states that simply because a mental illness responds to medication does not imply that it has a biological cause, especially if the medication only relieves symptoms and does not completely cure the illness. Ross also comments that biological reductionists assume that if two mental illnesses respond to the same medication, then the two are variants of the same disorder. He notes that bulimia often responds to medication used for depression, but bulimia has long been considered a completely different disorder, not a variant of depression. New medications to stop smoking are variants of depression medications.

Ross also disagrees with the biological psychiatry contention that if a genetic or biological basis for mental illness is found, it will reduce the stigma of mental illness. He notes that for cardiovascular disease, genetics is only considered to be a predisposing factor and there are other lifestyle choices that contribute to the disease. Other diseases, like cancer, also have environmental variables, but somehow biological psychiatrists infer that mental illness may be purely genetically based. With regard to a gene for alcoholism, Ross surmises that prior to human use of alcohol such a gene could not have evolved. With regard to depression, Ross considers that the positive response to medications that supposedly correct the biochemical imbalance is not much higher than the response of those given a placebo (50% to 30% for one class of medications), especially when deleterious side effects are considered.

Ross criticizes the categories in which some mental disorders are placed in the *DSM-IV*. He notes that some are based on historical artifacts, some on residual effects of Freudian theory, and many on political turf wars among *DSM* subcommittees. For instance, a new item called *brief reactive dissociative disorder* that is known to be trauma induced was proposed for the *DSM-IV*. However, in final published edition, that disorder was classified as an acute distress disorder. Thus, its suggested name had to be changed, as it could not have *dissociative disorder* in its name and still be a distress disorder. However, if the condition persists for over one month, it is called posttraumatic stress disorder (PTSD) and is in the category of an anxiety disorder. I am not sure how it was placed in that category in the *DSM*, as it is a frequent problem among people serving in military war zones. I agree with Ross that both acute distress disorder and PTSD should be classified as dissociative disorders. Ross also notes that all DID patients meet the criteria for schizophrenia. He states, "DID is a test case demonstrating that bioreductionist psychiatrists cannot differentiate a disorder they consider to be hysterical and artifactual from a disorder (schizophrenia) they consider to be a biomedical brain disease" (p. 125).

Ross undertook a monumental effort to review every article published in the *American Journal of Psychiatry* from 1990 to 1993, totaling about

7,000 pages. He looked for errors of logic that he had previously identified in those articles. In all of those articles, he only found one article that stated that its conclusions were based on reductionism in its approach. In the list below of errors of logic, I will not cite the article itself he was reviewing. However, if a quotation from the original article was used and I repeat it, I will specify "original" after the page number, indicating it was not Ross's interpretation of the information.

- "Erroneous conclusions in one paper are used to support erroneous conclusions in others" (p. 131).
- One article admitted, "A focus on genetic markers for manic-depressive illness gets much more attention that stories about the less fashionable report of successful psychotherapy" (p. 132, original).
- "Even when an overwhelming environmental factor [Author's Note: in this case, abuse and self-injurious behavior] is identified, however, the reductionist can invert it into evidence of primary etiology lying in the genetic domain" (p. 133). Another example of this was that in another study, the authors stated that although four (of five) patients in their study had no family history of schizophrenia, they concluded that the illness is genetic.
- "The ideological bias that extrasensory experiences are a symptom of mental illness is enshrined in the DSM-IV criteria for schizotypal personality disorder, and this false assumption confounds all studies of schizophrenia spectrum disorders. The idea that hallucinations are always pathological, and presumably due to organic brain dysfunction, also pervades psychiatry and confounds research" (pp. 136–37). The original authors of the paper state, "It is notable, therefore, that more than one-half of the subjects in this study reported that their hallucinations served adaptive functions, and a sizable minority wished to continue experiencing the hallucinations" (p. 137). This would seemingly confirm the findings of Van Dusen reported earlier that 20% of voices are friendly.
- The inference that there is a gene for child abuse never occurs in child abuse literature because it is not driven by a reductionist

ideology but rather is suggested by bioreductionist psychiatry. This concept was mentioned several times in the book.

- There were numerous reports with negative conclusions (what Ross disparagingly calls "fishing expeditions") to find chemical imbalances in the bloodstream or differences in MRI or PET scans between mental patients and controls, but none of the studies found a correlation. Ross notes that in rare cases there may be a molecule for one specific symptom of a mental illness but never for the multiple symptoms required to define the illness as a psychiatric disorder.
- In numerous studies, questions about childhood physical or sexual abuse were never part of the investigation procedure unless it was the immediate precipitant of the patient's recent abnormal episode.
- Two studies were performed using PET scans for two different mental illnesses. In one study, asymmetry was classified as abnormal. In the other study, symmetry was classified as abnormal.

6. Why Reductionism Survives

Ellen Borges (1995), a sociologist, is the author of one chapter in *PBP*. She notes that the use of medications, the principal therapy of bioreductionist psychiatrists, can be less expensive than psychotherapy. Although most people think in terms of an individual office visit to a doctor, institutionalized patients and those who benefit from other government-subsidized programs may have only five or ten minutes per week or per month with a psychiatrist. Pills can be relatively inexpensive and easy to dispense in that short time period. The difference is that use of medications will probably never end, whereas psychotherapy treatments may eventually end and perhaps prevent recidivism for some prisoners.

Susan S. Kemker (1995) is an author of part of another chapter in *PBP*, on the education of psychiatrists. She discusses the problems with her education and how the current bioreductionist psychiatrists are improperly training future psychiatrists by perpetuating their own beliefs. She reports that her learning was based on the following assumptions:

- If it is being taught, it is true and important;
- If it reaches print in a major journal, it is scientific;
- If it is scientific, it is both worthwhile and objective, free of cultural bias;
- The conclusions are more important than the methodology.
  (p. 243, direct quotations)

She states that when she was a resident, she hoped to develop into a strong clinician with skills in multiple areas such as individual, group, and family therapy, working with multidisciplinary teams, and prescribing medications. She does not feel excited about neurotransmitters and was not taught to learn about the patient as a person. She also senses that when patients are told they have a chemical imbalance, "personal efforts and responsibility have no part to play in getting better" (p. 247, quoting from another source).

7. Trauma-Related Syndromes

In another chapter of *PBP*, authors David Sakheim and Susan E. Devine propose a new type of illness: trauma-related syndrome. These authors are also aware of the problem of veracity of trauma-recovered memories. This was discussed in the chapter on DID as false memory syndrome. They state that besides providing information about actual traumatic experiences, a recovered memory of trauma could also involve malingering for secondary gain, delusional material, metaphoric communication, incorporated material, exaggeration, symbolic meanings, confusion, misperception, and distortion (p. 260). Due to the veracity issue, it may be simplistic to view trauma as the root of all problems but should be considered for many disorders.

Sakheim and Devine speculate that the following disorders are likely to be trauma-related: "borderline personality disorder, post traumatic stress disorder, the dissociative disorders, brief psychotic reactions, adjustment disorders, and even some anxiety disorders, psychotic disorders, affective disorders, eating disorders, substance abuse disorders, and paraphilias" (p. 266). Later, they appear to include all personality disorders. Thus, trauma-related disorders would appear to cut across a number of categories in the current diagnostic system.

"At present, no current diagnostic grouping sufficiently acknowledges traumatic etiology or the wide variety of diagnostic categories in which trauma can have an impact" (p. 266).

Sakheim and Devine note that if therapists were more aware of trauma-related syndromes, they may view the patient differently. For instance, it would be easier to understand how a patient "pathologically flees from closeness" if the therapist were aware of trauma inflicted by a parent or that the patient is "manipulative," if such was the only attitude the patient could have employed to survive the abuse. Finally, they maintain, "Any diagnostic system can only be a guide to the clinician, and can never replace the patient's own understanding of his or her life" (p. 269).

8. Implications of the Trauma Model

In the concluding chapter of the book, Ross lists a number of empirically testable predictions that follow from the trauma model. I will not cover them here. Following those, he lists three implications for health care. These are as follows:

- Primary prevention of major mental illness through prevention of severe child abuse is possible. This can be shown by intervention studies.
- Long-term sequelae of severe child abuse are generating over $100 billion [Author's Note: this was over 20 years ago; the cost has probably at least quadrupled] in psychiatric and medical health care cost per year in North America. The vast majority of these costs are unrecognized and misattributed. [Author's Speculation: incarcerating victims of child abuse or victims of other trauma who then become criminals themselves means that the costs to our criminal justice and prison system double again (probably).]
- Trauma-specific psychotherapy is the most financially cost-effective intervention in psychiatry.

While many of the problems I attribute to spirit intrusions are much less severe than the traumas discussed in *PBP*, I consider them to be related. As I mentioned in the introduction of this chapter, there are many degrees of spirit intrusion, and those in *PBP* represent a higher percent of influence on the original personality. Ross uses the term "schizophrenia spectrum disorders." The word *spectrum* is becoming more in vogue to describe behavioral issues, e.g., autism spectrum disorders. Perhaps I should use the term *spirit intrusion spectrum illnesses.*

My paraphrase of Cassius speaking in Shakespeare's *Julius Caesar*, act 1, scene 2, is this: The fault, dear reductionist, is not in the genes or neurochemicals of the mentally ill, but in the trauma they have undergone, that resulted in a fragmented soul.

While the authors of this book probably do not support the concept of soul fragmentation and spirit intrusion as factors in mental illness, they do recognize that trauma is the primary cause of mental illness, and resolving the trauma will promote the body to correct any neurochemical imbalance. My concept places the soul fragmentation as the consequence of the trauma, and the mental illness results from spirit intruders that may enter a soul that has been fragmented. In some cases, leading the spirit intruders from the client is sufficient, but in others the initial trauma may need to be processed. Biological psychiatry addresses neither of these issues.

This chapter presented numerous therapeutic methods employed to treat soul fragmentation and spirit intrusion. Clients therefore have many options to seek treatment and to choose a method that agrees with their own views of the nature of humanity. Whereas many people who undergo NDEs or spiritually transformative experiences (STEs) have a transformation of their view of life, a client with a mental illness does not necessarily need as severe a modification. But if the client is a confirmed materialist, any therapy discussed in this chapter would involve a radical change in that individual's philosophy.

Another nonchemical type of therapy alluded to is the biblical story of David palying a harp to calm an intruding spirit in Saul. Perhaps, with today's better analysis of music and its effects, a cure for some types of mental illness may be found in music therapy.

In the next chapter, I discuss mystical, peak, and kundalini experiences; how these relate to my concept of a higher self; and the unusual physical phenomena that may occur around a person who is fully engaged with his or her higher self. I maintain that the ISH or higher-world beings are therapeutic aspects of this higher self, but they have many other functions and affect behavior in many ways.

Chapter 11

MYSTICAL EXPERIENCES

Alice: There's no use trying. One can't believe impossible things.

The Queen replied: I daresay you haven't had much practice. When I was younger,
I always did it for half an hour a day. Why, sometimes I've believed as many as six impossible things before breakfast.

—Lewis Carroll (pseudonym for Charles L. Dodgson [1832–1898]), *Alice in Wonderland*, 1865

A. Introduction

I have chosen the title "Mystical Experiences," as this is the phrase used within Western cultural and religious traditions to describe the event of uniting with a higher power. Other names for the phenomenon include *spiritually transformative experience, peak experience, exceptional human experience, transcendent* (or *transcendental*) *experience, numinous experience, cosmic consciousness,* and *unitive consciousness,* among many others. A mystical experience may be referred to as an ecstatic state or a mystical state of consciousness, within the broad category of altered states of consciousness (ASCs). Ecstatic states are similar to trancelike experiences, although the two are not necessarily synonymous.

The term *ineffable* is frequently used by mystics and near-death experiencers (NDErs) to explain the indescribable quality of their experiences. Mystics have often employed symbolic language or metaphors to portray their experience. I will try to explain the several stages through which a person must pass to reach a full mystical state. Whereas an NDE (near-death experience) may appear suddenly, most mystics have had lower-level experiences before reaching a full ecstatic state. Although my general explanation for a mystical experience is that the person is simply in contact with his own Spirit, it is difficult to use mystical states to demonstrate the separate aspects of human spirituality. Therefore, I will try to demonstrate that when a person enters this ASC called mysticism that paranormal events events frequently occur. These changes may occur during the experience or may come on gradually, possibly similarly to the aftereffects of an NDE. For some mystics, the paranormal is normal (although not constant). Some mystics may speak of their "oneness" with nature and all of creation, while others believe the experience to entail an overpowering sense of the divine rather than nature. I make no judgment as to whether one kind of experience is a "higher" variety than another.

B. Psychiatry and Mysticism

Modern therapeutic psychiatry is reductionist; that is, it posits that states of consciousness and behavior are dependent upon the neurochemicals operating in the brain. However, there are some psychiatrists who hold that an ASC may contain important information for a person's life. Therefore, some psychiatrists do attempt to study the area of spirituality in relation to psychiatry. In 1976, a group called the Committee on Psychiatry and Religion (CPR) formulated a publication called *Mysticism: Spiritual Quest or Psychic Disorder?* (CPR, 1976). This publication is volume IX of a series of publications by the Group for the Advancement of Psychiatry. In the book, the committee emphasizes mysticism in the Jewish, Christian, and Hindu religions, briefly acknowledging Islam and indigenous cultures. Although the book is short, I consider the authors to have presented a reasonable discussion, one devoid of the reductionist bias.

Some psychiatrists are interested in mysticism because a mystic "attributes a greater reality to this inner world, or to a belief in a transcendental or supernatural world" (p. 715). This impression is similar to schizophrenic detachment. Mystical detachment (withdrawal) from the real world to a higher reality is sought, but for schizophrenics it happens unwillingly, and is likely not a higher reality.

Psychedelic/hallucinogenic drugs may be used to achieve transcendent and ecstatic states that are similar to mystical states, though they may produce undesirable features. When not in a mystical state, a mystic usually leads a dependable life, unlike schizophrenics, who often have difficulty functioning. Many mystics are high-functioning people in ordinary life, When in a trance, a mystic may become cataleptic, a condition that also comes over some schizophrenics. Some mystics never enter a trance state. The CPR admits that it is a formidable task to distinguish between a mystical state and a psychopathological one (i.e., a mental illness).

CPR notes that the goal of most mystics is to achieve "Union" with a supernatural power that is considered to be ultimate reality. A number of Roman Catholic saints have been mystics. Information about their unusual powers will be discussed. Keep in mind, however, that being a Catholic mystic is no guarantee of sainthood. In fact, some mystics may hold unorthodox, even heretical, beliefs that are definitely disliked by churches or denominations that depend upon either the authority of clerical hierarchy or their own strict interpretation of the Bible. Thus, many mystics may be alienated from established religious authorities. For instance, some mystics, or even those who are not mystics but who are familiar with the basic structure of mysticism, may surmise that Jesus was simply an ordinary human on a mystic path, not the Son of God as taught by most Christians. Many mystics hold that they experienced God directly and therefore do not need any "divinely based" authority. In contrast, one Catholic saint and mystic who was very orthodox was St. John Vianney (1786–1859; referred to as the Cure of Ars [France]). He was most well-known as a confessor, spending many hours a day in the confessional. People from all over France came to him. He ate very little food and encountered various disturbances that some people associated with the Devil. His mystical gift was that if people in the confessional were not informing him of some significant sin in their life, he would either tell them what it was or tell them to review their life and figure out what it was.

Although many mystics are affiliated with a church or religious denomination, there are a number of "secular" mystics. For instance, a Canadian named Richard Maurice Bucke wrote a book over a century ago called *Cosmic Consciousness*, and he was not particularly religious. His experience happened spontaneously on one occasion, and he was not on a program to attempt to reach that state. His book lists historical people whom he believes attained cosmic consciousness.

CPR mentions two terms that are often used by many religions and mystics: *transcendental* and *immanent*. *Transcendental* may be thought of as being in the presence of an awesome force or power; *immanent* implies a close and personal relationship with that force or power.

1. The Mystic Way

While a number of people may have a mystic experience once or twice in their lives, a number of people seek these experiences through various practices, usually involving prayer and asceticism. One established methodology, not a guarantee of results, is called the Mystic Way. CPR employs the stages of the Mystic Way from the writings of Evelyn Underhill, who will be discussed in detail later. The fifth and final stage is Union, in which mystics believe they are in a spiritual marriage between God and their soul. However, Jewish mystics refrain from claiming Union with God. Some mystics of the East maintain that there is another stage involving total annihilation of the self and absorption into the Infinite. Buddhists refer to this as nirvana; Hindus, as samadhi.

According to CPR, in the Western Christian tradition there have been several major periods of strong mystical activity, that is, more people involved in the mystic quest than in other periods. These were the Classical era (third century, the period of the Desert Fathers), the medieval era (fourteenth century), and the Renaissance (seventeenth century).

At least three founders of Christian religious orders are considered mystics, but members of their congregations do not necessarily require all members to be on a mystic path. These were St. Benedict of Nursia (ca. 480–547), considered the founder of Western monasticism; St. Francis of Assisi (1181–1226), believed to be the first person to undergo stigmata, and founder of the Order of Friars Minor, commonly called Franciscans; and St. Ignatius of Loyola (1491–1556), founder of the Society of Jesus, commonly called Jesuits. St. Ignatius's *Spiritual Exercises* also has similarities to mystical training.

My opinion is that many religious movements begin as a small group of people oriented to a mystical path. When these people attempt to draw in many others, they inevitably decrease the strict routine required to achieve mystical states. Sometimes religious groups with a mystical leaning are started by a person with a strong magnetic personality, but the group falls apart when that individual is gone or when he or she becomes enamored with abilities and attention rather than the mystic path. An example of a religious movement founded by a mystic is Quakerism (formal name, Religious Society of Friends), founded by George Fox (1624–1691). Fox emphasized a person's finding his or her own "inner *light*." The Quakers have no formal clergy.

While most common mystic paths are mentally/prayer oriented, "movement" of various types can induce at least the lower stages of the mystic path. The Whirling Dervishes are an example of this from the Middle East, while the United Society of Believers, popularly known as the Shakers, is an example in the Western Christian tradition.

The word *yoga* means Union. the practice was originally intended as a mystic path. However, nowadays yoga is often more a form of body training referred to as postural yoga. There are specific branches of yoga, one of them being the previously mentioned kundalini. There are numerous other branches of yoga, each with its own emphasis, such as on breathing techniques.

Sometimes a mystic is not even involved in a religion that promotes the mystic views of the spiritual world that the religion espouses. Emanuel Swedenborg (1688–1772) was a renowned scientist who later in life turned to spiritual understanding through his many visions. His writings on the spiritual world were the foundation of a much later religion called the New Church, as well as the foundation of other, unaffiliated Swedenborgian churches. A mystical poet and artist named William Blake (1757–1827) was influenced by Swedenborg. One of Blake's famous poems, "Auguries of Innocence," begins with the following stanza, which may be considered to impart a classic mystical perspective:

> To see the world in a grain of sand,
> And heaven in a wild flower,
> Hold infinity in the palm of your hand,
> And eternity in an hour.

I have already mentioned that hallucinogenic drugs may bring on experiences similar to a mystic state, including trances, but they often bring on unwanted side effects. This use of a drug is sometimes referred to as psychedelic mysticism, and it may cheapen the experience and keep its adherents at lower stages of the Mystic Way. One advocate of the use of psychedelic drugs was Aldous Huxley (1894–1963), of the famous British family. The title of his book on the subject of resorting to drugs to achieve a spiritual goal is *The Doors of Perception* (1954). His other major book on spirituality/mysticism is titled *The Perennial Philosophy* (1945), but his most famous book is probably his novel *Brave New World* (1932).

Earlier, I mentioned the trance state that mystics sometimes enter. Being in this trance state does not necessarily imply being completely unaware of the physical environment, but the sensations are different. Some may be muted (fuzzy images), and others may be magnified. For instance, some can hear the blood throbbing in their blood vessels. Some may experience synesthesia, a sensation discussed in the chapter about NDEs.

CPR states that hallucinations in mystics may be unformed or formed. Unformed hallucinations feature unclear pictures or inaudible sounds. The formed hallucinations are mostly visual and can be "unnatural" (not conforming to physical reality), but they often conform to the religious background of the individual. I may compare this to mythological observations by shamans on their otherworld journeys. The mystic may describe what she sees as "more real" than the physical world, a phrase often used by NDErs.

Schizophrenics also have hallucinations but those are delusions with little meaning, CPR lists three contrasts between the hallucinations of mystics and schizophrenics:

> First, his [the mystic's] retreat is facultative rather than obligatory; second it is partial rather than complete, as compared to the schizophrenic's retreat; third, he finds it possible, frequently desirable, to associate with others who share his view of the world—that is, he participates in mystical fraternities, while the schizophrenic rarely is able to form or maintain similar affectionate ties with others. (p. 784)

The CPR does see similarities between schizophrenics and mystics, but I do not agree that these similarities exist. I believe that the CPR's views represent the old psychoanalytical viewpoint. They comment that schizophrenics and mystics are both withdrawing from social reality to a form of primary or infantile narcissism. CPR provides the following statements about the mystic:

1. He or she is an individual who finds living within his society stressful.
2. He or she retreats from his or her society and the reality which it sponsors by withdrawing his or her interest from both and by then reinvesting that interest in impressions that arise from within.
3. He or she takes advantage of his or her ability to retreat to the psychic position that existed during his or her infancy, when the only reality which had access to his or her consciousness was the reality of inner sensation.
4. He or she reinforces his or her retreat and overcomes the loneliness that it would create by joining with others to form an elite, democratic, and abstemious mystical fraternity.
5. He or she claims authority for his or her departure from, or rebellion against, the religious establishment by asserting that he or she has been granted immediate experience of the divine, which supersedes traditional authority.

CPR provides other interpretations closely allied to psychoanalytical language that will not be summarized. Psychoanalysts often consider mysticism to be a deficiency in normal functioning, whereas I consider it to be an advancement of human spiritual functioning.

CPR is cognizant of the connection between mysticism and creativity, even using a well-known quote of Albert Einstein: "The most beautiful, the most profound emotion we can experience is the sensation of the mystical. It is the fundamental emotion that stands at the cradle of true art and science" (p. 788). I remember once reading that when Einstein was a child, he imagined what it would be like to travel on a beam of light. CPR also notes that an often utilized word to describe creativity is *inspiration*, which derives from "in spirit." Many other scientific advances, such as those by Tesla discussed in chapter 3, were made by those who held reverence for nature or mystical mystical views instead of by rationalists.

In addition to the scientific forefront, charismatic leaders in other areas of human advancement base their views on a transcendent power. Rationalists, on the other hand, were often rigid in their views. CPR discusses three people who had a major impact on society and whose views the CPR deciphers as very mystical:

- The basic theme of Vincent van Gogh's art is to unite with a divine heavenly being.
- Albert Einstein had a sense of oneness with the universe and its marvelous order.
- Abraham Lincoln's concept of saving the Union had similarities to a mystical concept of Union.

CPR draws a comparison between a mystic's having a desire for intimacy with the divine, and creative people's desire to understand natural laws, whether they be artistic, scientific, or philosophical. Just as mystics have alternate periods of depression and joy, many creative people have periods of depression. The creative phase may be considered analogous to the manic phase in bipolar disorder. CPR comments that one significant scientist warned against scientists being excessively trusting in pure logic, as they need to combine that with imagination. The latter brings subjective truth into the process of scientific knowledge. Logical and linear thought accesses, controls, modifies, evaluates, and synthesizes these creative elements into a meaningful quintessence.

CPR contends that mysticism in the past has been a significant social force for rebellion. This rebellion may take three forms:

- The mystic may secede from larger society and wait for change.
- The mystic may encourage changes in popular standards (this is what the biblical prophets did).
- The mystic may become a messianic leader and threaten institutions of society, religion, or politics.

However, those who have successful revolutions often replace an established authority, but then the revolutionary ardor dies out and the new form often has the same faults as the old order.

CPR maintains that within our culture some people are choosing a mystical path because of various factors. These include the following:

- Discouragement in the face of the potential for nuclear holocaust
- The breakdown of social and ethical norms in our culture
- The breakdown in acceptance of religious authority
- Material comforts, which provide more time for nonmaterial satisfaction
- The success of science, which has led more people to seek something beyond the rational

C. A Study of Human Spiritual Nature

The previous section of this chapter briefly mentioned the Mystic Way— various methods or programs, depending on the religious background of the individual, for achieving a seeming unity with the divine or with nature. Before delving into these methods, I am going to describe a formal study of spontaneous experiences, that is, single or infrequent mystical-like experiences beginning with ones from Sir Alister Hardy. I introduced him in the section of the NDE chapter on shared experiences. Hardy was a marine biologist and a Fellow of the Royal Society. He did not begin writing about spirituality/religion until he retired from his biological studies. I maintain that many of his insights in his 1979 book *The Spiritual Nature of Man: A Study of Contemporary Religious Experience* are definitely in agreement with the case for human spiritual nature that I am presenting in this book. He relates this following childhood experience of his (which took place at an unspecified age):

> One day as I was walking along Marylebone Road, I was suddenly seized with an extraordinary sense of great joy and exaltation, as though a marvelous beam of spiritual power had shot through me linking me in a rapture with the world, the Universe, Life with a capital L, and all the beings around me. All delight and power, all things living, all time fused in a brief second. (p. 1)

Furthermore, Hardy states that he agrees with Sir Charles Sherrington, Sir John Eccles, and Lord Brain in "that mental events may belong to a different order which somehow, in a way we do not *yet* understand, is linked with a physical system. The mystery of the mind-body relationship is still unsolved; no doubt in time the two elements will be united in a single philosophy" (p. 8). In my book, I am attempting to shed light on this unsolved mind—body relationship.

Hardy describes himself as a convinced Darwinian. He believes in natural selection but also thinks that selection is not always by chance. He regards the difference between humankind and our animal ancestors to be greater than that separating animals from plants. I maintain that these differences are due to spiritual differences. He states that even a convinced atheist like Richard Dawkins regards the evolution of subjective consciousness as the most profound mystery facing modern biology.

Hardy's fame as a scientist was helpful in providing some free publicity for his proposed study, and readers were invited to send in any personal experiential encounters they felt were appropriate. Hardy did not ask for mystical experiences, and many of those provided were not. His group, the Religious Experiences Research Unit (RERU), also sent out pamphlets describing their goals and requesting responses. There were some responses in which the person writing was obviously mentally ill, and others in which the person was self-important, but a vast majority of the responses demonstrated a deep sincerity. He also did not find the elements of superstition, wishful thinking, or contradictory theological theories, maintaining that very few of the responses were hoaxes. RERU also asked for the responder's current age, age when the experience happened, and gender (about two-thirds were female). In a number of cases, the experience occurred many years before. The fact that it was remembered indicates that a change had happened to the person involved. Recall that many NDErs described their experience almost identically to the original description provided many years earlier. Hardy notes that these experiences also transpire in atheists, agnostics, and children, not just to people who hold spiritual beliefs. However, the experience may lead to an interest in religion.

In analyzing the responses, RERU employed a number of various categories and subcategories, and most of the experiences fit into multiple categories. For instance, the category may be the type of sense(s) involved, that is, visual, auditory, or tactile, or even extrasensory. The respondents may categorize the experiences by the behavioral changes the experience precipitated, by cognitive and affective elements, and by the pattern of the experience. The individual's circumstances at the time (the trigger) of the experience were duly noted, the most frequently reported of which was being out in nature. For others, it may have been visiting sacred places, reading poetry, or listening to music. Some may have felt like they were in a period of despair or were enduring a personal crisis that suddenly became joyful. Some felt that the experience had happened while they were physically active, including enduring a difficult childbirth, but for others it was when they were relaxed. In total, there were over ninety-two categories and subcategories in which to group the experiences. Joy or happiness was the most common category, but reverence or wonder was also common. The length of the responses varied from a simple postcard to twenty typed pages. When categorizing and analyzing some of the experiences, Hardy excluded ones that were purely parapsychological and not spiritual. Overall, about three thousand incidents were categorized.

When NDErs have an autoscopic experience, they often see their lifeless body below while their spirit body above is carrying out the thinking. In two of Hardy's cases, the people were watching their physical body perform an act that required thinking. In one case, a preacher watched himself giving a sermon from the pulpit. A woman observed herself doing multiple tasks over many hours, including interacting with other people. These could be classified as doppelgänger experiences.

A common way (over 20 percent) to describe the situation in which the person felt himself to be in was in the company of a Power or a Presence but not of another human. One person described the situation as follows as she watched Halley's comet in 1910:

> It knew something about the Universe which I didn't know. I connected "It," as I called it, with other inexpressible feelings, and decided that there was a power behind the visibly inner universe with which one could come in contact if one knew how. ... "It" was beneficent ... could bring me to a state of bliss. ... "It" could also be stern when approached in the wrong way. (p. 56)

This Power or Presence in respondents' lives served to sustain, encourage, strengthen, guide, or compel them. One person felt it gave him (or her) infinite resources, and another reported that it was there during sorrow or difficulties. In a follow-up questionnaire to respondents who mentioned a Power or Presence, over three-fourths reported that they thought it was unequivocally personal. Only a few thought it impersonal. One respondent who had a difficult time with the concept of a personal God nevertheless had a very real sense of gratitude. During a World War II battle, one young man's fear was taken away by a Presence. He was later injured, but he lived for many years afterward, never forgetting the original encounter. For one woman, this Presence made it easier for her to love people with whom she was having a difficult time.

With regard to changes in their lives, some people felt a Power beyond themselves all their lives; others felt a gradual development of this Power throughout their lives; and some felt a radical change in their lives. Finally, some individuals felt that the experience did not result in long-lasting changes. With regard to the consequences of the experience, Hardy made the following comment:

> It is not always easy to distinguish between an actual experience and the consequences. Where it has been of a sudden or dramatic kind it may be easy to note certain obvious differences it has made, to see definite changes in the attitude of behaviour of the person concerned. In other cases such developments may be felt to be part of the experience itself, consisting as it does in a gradual awareness of new potentiality for growth and understanding. Because almost every spiritual experience worthy of consideration must have some affects, it might be thought to be superfluous to have a special division for them. (pp. 98–99)

Over 10% of respondents felt that the experience indicated that they had a sense of purpose, but these people did not claim preferential treatment or feel that it made them arrogant or more important than others. One person described the sense they had as their being maneuvered to carry out some divine purpose. This person felt he undertook some things he did not feel he was qualified to undertake. Another person described it as a benevolent Providence in charge of his life. Another person used the phrase *divine guidance*, which even applied to smaller events in this person's life. The pattern of this person's life became a mosaic in which even seeming disasters eventually turned advantageous. Someone else held that coincidences are a part of a plan. While not using the word *purpose*, one person felt that love and service to humankind was the will of God for everyone.

In a number of cases, *light* was an important aspect. For one man out in nature, it appeared that a bright *light* was turned on and colors were more vivid. However, another person felt it overwhelmed by a "Dazzling Darkness" (p. 67). For many, these overall experiences may have been very brief, but one woman, when she was ill, felt a "tangible warmth, light and useful peace" that lasted for hours (p. 92). Earlier, she had asked some people to pray for her. She believes that the experience was the answer to their prayers. One man was told by a doctor that he possibly had cancer and that he should see a specialist. While he was taking a walk, colors seemed very brilliant, everyone smiled at him, and his worries disappeared. When he went to the specialist a few days later, he learned that there was nothing seriously wrong with him. Another woman feared for her child's life as he was being operated on, but while she was praying, the burden was lifted. She knew her child would be all right, and the child was.

One woman's description supports my contention that these experiences are an encounter with an individual's own Spirit, but Spirit may then connect to spiritual realms beyond itself or be connected to the Spirit aspect of select or all humans. This woman woman described her experience as follows:

> At first appearing mainly as 'my' higher Self, progressively it was found to be collective in a supra-personal way—the higher one went in awareness, the more one realized that this Self was one with that of others, also with created things— with all. This is the nearest to an experience of God" (p. 77).

While most experiences of this type are moments of quiet reflection, one person provided the following description: "The ecstasy deepened and intensified. I began shouting. I knew that all was well, that the basis of everything was goodness, that all religions and sciences were paths to this ultimate reality" (p. 78).

Throughout this book, I have frequently mentioned parapsychological/paranormal phenomena. One form of the paranormal or ESP is telepathy, or transfer of information from one person to another without the aid of the senses. On this topic, Hardy comments as follows:

> If experimental scientific evidence for the existence of telepathy could be established, I believe that it would help people to accept a spiritual philosophy which is greatly needed in our modern materialistic society; it would show that there was a mental extension of the individual's psyche beyond the physicochemical structure of the brain and so would lend plausibility to the concept of there being a spiritual dimension outside that of the strictly physical, material world. (p. 44)

Other types of ESP discussed by Hardy include precognition, clairvoyance, supposed contact with the dead, and apparitions (over 3% of respondents).

One example of the paranormal involves precognition by a woman who had a vision of her child lying on a road. She altered her normal routine and arrived just as her son fell as he stepped off his school bus; he looked just like he had in her earlier vision. For these types of events, Hardy prefers the term *paraphysical* to *supernatural*.

In chapter 10, I discussed problems with mental illnesses and how these may be related to spirit intrusions. Although this case of a woman does not demonstrate spirit intrusion, it does indicate a rapid and permanent healing from a psychosis and suicidal behavior as a result of a spiritual encounter involving forgiveness. She had a desire to be forgiven and had visited a psychiatrist and a chaplain. "Then quite dramatically the whole picture changed overnight. The weight of guilt had been lifted and I was myself again, quite rational and ready to go home again. ... I believe that God had forgiven me" (p. 60). Neither the psychiatrist nor clergyman could explain what had happened. Forgiveness was important in about 4% of the RERU cases.

Many scientists disparage religion, which they contend is based on faith, while they maintain that they gain knowledge by way of reason and experimentation. In contrast, several RERU responders obtained knowledge in the following ways. Although in one case the knowledge was religiously oriented, this is not how most religious people typically view knowledge. The people who reported the third and fourth examples below had no connection to organized religion.

- One man said, "I KNOW" (p. 56), referring to the contention that he did not have to think, believe, or reason. This knowing was in regard to questions or problems, not religious beliefs.
- "[While meditating during a time of emotional stress] I had for how long I do not know—an intense feeling of having slipped out of time and of *knowing* in a quite different way from intellectual knowledge. Knowing with all my being what is meant by the concept God is Love. I felt that I had experienced divine love in its reality and immediacy" (p. 109).
- One person said to himself, "So that is what it is all about!" But he cannot say what it was he saw (p. 110).
- "A great inward light seemed to illuminate my thoughts, I experienced the magnificent sensation of arrival. I was filled with joy as though I had just discovered the secret of world peace. I suddenly *knew*. The odd thing was that I did not know what I knew. From then on I set out to define it" (p. 110).
- One Jewish NDEr I have met felt that during her NDE she had insight and knew the reason for the Holocaust, but could not remember the reason, and does not feel it is now necessary to understand it.

Some other unusual descriptions of these mystical experiences include the following:

- One person felt it as a joy sweeping over her, moving from one side of her to the other.
- One woman interpreted the feeling as not being united with God but being aware of the Universal Self, the Absolute.
- While these experiences often make people feel they are part of something greater, one woman felt she had to stand on her own. NDErs often receive messages appropriate to their circumstances.

I can envision that woman's message as being probably pertinent to her situation.

- One man who did not believe in supernatural beings one day heard the message, "All men are brothers" (p. 113)! That filled him with joy and happiness, and that became his religion.
- Rather than trying to interpret these experiences, one person who wrote about these types of experiences said that it is best just to say, "It just Was" (p. 105).

Opinions of the respondents can vary as to how or why these experiences happen. One person felt that the experience came from outside and was not asked for; another person (probably of a religious viewpoint) held that God never intrudes on us and we must approach Him; and a third view is that the initiative must come from within the people themselves.

In addition, Hardy has a discussion about illegal drugs causing mystical or religious experiences, but he is mostly quoting other studies and not his own research. He discusses one book, *Mysticism: Sacred and Profane*, by R. C. Zaehner, who claims that drug-induced experiences and "nature mysticism" are the profane variety and not the same as religious mystical experiences, which are caused by the grace of God. However, Hardy then discusses another book, *Inglorious Wordsworth* by Michael Paffard, who argues that Zaehner is incorrect because the various ascetic practices and mortifications of the flesh, such as sensory deprivation (some on the Mystic Way spend periods of time in dark caves) or fasting among acknowledged religious mystics, may affect the chemistry of the body to produce mystical effects. Another experimental scientist, Walter Pahnke, MD, also a graduate of Harvard Divinity School, in a chapter titled "LSD and Mystical Experiences" in the book *LSD, Man and Society*, has "shown that altered states of consciousness (ASC) may be produced by chemical means; the chemicals themselves do *not* produce the divine ecstasy, but affect the brain in such a way that a rarely accessible region of the sub-conscious mind becomes available to those who already have, perhaps unknown to them, a mystical streak within them" (p. 97).

In another scientific paper, Pahnke maintains that Hindu yogis often use breath control to achieve ASC. This breath control could affect carbon dioxide levels in the blood and induce an ASC. My own opinion is that drug-induced ASCs are often similar to mystical experiences but are fraught with dangers, as the individual may enter undesirable realms of an ASC.

At the end of his book, Hardy defines spirituality as such:

> So I have decided to end this book with a statement of what I conceive to be some of the essential features of man's spiritual nature—particularly in regard to his religious feelings. ... It seems to me that the main characteristics of man's religious and spiritual experiences are shown in his feelings for a transcendental reality which frequently manifest themselves in early childhood; a feeling that "Something Other" than the self can actually be sensed; a desire to personalize this presence into a deity and to have a private I-Thou relationship with it, communicating through prayer. (p. 131)

While Hardy maintains that this feeling of transcendental reality is more important than the other two types of religious experience, the *numinous* (awareness of the holy) and the *mystical* (the feeling of the merging of the self with divine reality), I tend to more closely associate transcendental reality with the mystical.

D. The Physical Phenomena of Mysticism

1. Introduction

The intertwining of spirituality and the paranormal has been emphasized throughout this book. The paranormal frequently occurs in near-death experiences (NDEs) and among people with dissociative identity disorder (DID), especially during encounters with the Inner Self-helper ISH). I would like to delve into the connection between the paranormal and mysticism. Namely, I will be discussing the book *The Physical Phenomena of Mysticism* by Herbert Thurston, SJ (a Jesuit priest). He lived in England[3] between 1919 and 1938, where he explored the subject that became the book, publishing some papers and also giving lectures. After Thurston's

---

[3] Thurston wrote with British spellings, but I have converted these to American English except when appearing in a quotation.

death in 1939, another Jesuit collected the papers and lectures into the above book, published in 1952 (Thurston, 1952).

I will supplement Thurston's findings with information from the book *The Sanctified Body* (1989) by Patricia Treece. She concentrates on saints who lived in the last two hundred years and on some non-Catholics and non-Christians, since, as she says, she "can point to Sufi saints, Hasidic saints, Pentecostal saints, Tibetan lama saints, American Indian saints, yogic saints, Methodist saints, and on through the whole great macrocosm of sanctity in the human family" (p. 18). Her well referenced book is not about religion or saints, but about how the physical body is affected by holiness. Treece has degrees in journalism, anthropology, and French; she was a convert to Catholicism. She can speak and/or read several languages and thus was able to review original writings on numerous saints.

The database for Thurston's book is primarily from the lives of Catholic saints, many, but not all, of whom were considered mystics. There is no official definition to use for determining that a saint or holy person is a mystic. In some cases, I may mention that the person entered a state of ecstasy or a trance, so those holy people were probably mystics. If more than one of these paranormal phenomena happened to one person, then that person was most likely a mystic. However, that could be a circular definition; that is, if a person levitates and has a sweet fragrance around her, the person is a mystic; if a person is a mystic, he may levitate and have a sweet fragrance around him.

Biographies of a saint were often written shortly after the saint's death, or information was gathered from investigations that were done for the sainthood process. Thurston notes that many Catholic mystics did not become saints, and the phenomenon he investigated was not sufficient to have them declared a saint. Reasons for a person to be considered as a saint include scholarly writings, especially about religion; service to the poor or sick; leadership qualities such as those necessary for serving as an abbot or abbess of a famous monastery or founding a religious order; or an alleged miracle performed before or after death. In the early church, martyrs were often declared saints without formal investigations. People would frequently come to pray at the graves of reported holy people, and often there would be numerous purported miraculous cures among the visitors. The various phenomena to be discussed, such as levitation, are not considered miracles as is a healing attributed to prayers offered to a deceased prospective saint, asking him or her to intercede with God to effect the healing. The individual considered for sainthood had to have led an especially holy or virtuous life. The evidence discussed here for the paranormal can be considered corroboration of the contention that the person led a virtuous life or was favored by God. However, Thurston does include in his database some mystics who were not sainted, as he was primarily relating the phenomena to mysticism or holiness, not to sainthood.

Since Thurston was writing over seventy years ago, some of the individuals who were considered venerable or blessed (i.e., in the early stages of sainthood) may now have been canonized as saints. The writing about a life of a saint is called hagiography, *hagio* being a prefix meaning "saintly" or "holy." Literature dealing with lives of the saints is called hagiology. It should be noted that the same word or phrase, originally in Latin, may have several translations from romantic languages to English. For instance, *Santa Barbara*, from the Spanish, becomes *St. Barbara*, whereas *Santa Cruz* becomes *Holy Cross*. In French, *Holy Cross* is *St. Croix*.[4] In an earlier section of this chapter, I mentioned that some mystics may have unorthodox views, but to become a saint in the church a person has to have orthodox religious views (although his or her lifestyle may be unorthodox).

To me, Thurston seems like a thorough investigator. Although he may mention biographical information, he does point out that some witnesses may have been unreliable; that the investigations began long after the person's death and thus were hearsay and not first-person accounts; or that the person being interviewed was fairly old at the time of the interview. Thurston may also specify why the testimony was considered reliable. While some myths or fables about various saints arose after they died, sainthood investigations by the Congregation of Rites are very meticulous. These investigations include a person referred to as "the Devil's Advocate," who argues that the mystical gifts and possibly other incidents in the proposed saint's life disqualify him or her for sainthood.

---

[4] I may use the words *saint, saintly,* and *holy* (or *holiness*) interchangeably as adjectives, or *saint* may be used for a holy person not canonized by the Catholic Church.

Thurston's examples are primarily from the thirteenth century, but they go as far as one German nun who was still living when he was writing. Most of the saints lived in Europe, but some were Spanish-speaking people from Mexico or South America. Some of the saints are well-known, such as St. Francis of Assisi and St. Ignatius Loyola, but many of them are rather obscure. Thurston sometimes employs the term *seraph* in relation to some of the saints. However, at no point does he define that term. Two specific people for which he uses this term are St. Francis of Assisi (1182–1226) and Saint Catherine of Genoa (1447–1510), the latter being one of the few women he studied who was not a nun. Generally, a seraph (plural: *seraphim*) belongs to one of the orders (usually the highest and closest to God) of celestial beings.

Most of the phenomena I will be discussing in this section do not necessarily directly fit into my hypothesis that humans have two spiritual components. Some of the phenomena have to do with the physical body of the people after their death, whereas my studies primarily concern the relationship between a spiritual component and behavior while living. Although Thurston's book is primarily about physical phenomena, such as levitation, he does briefly mention other phenomena, such as foreknowledge of events, that might be considered mental phenomena. Another phenomenon often associated with mystics, but only fleetingly mentioned by Thurston, that might be considered a hybrid of the physical and mental types is bilocation, or being seen at a location away from the place where the physical body is located. Treece thoroughly discusses bilocation.

Thurston's studies do show that the paranormal is a valid phenomenon that should not be discarded by science. It needs to be explained, not dismissed. Thurston does not necessarily make a conclusion on why these paranormal events occur. He is not trying "to propound any theory regarding the origin for supernatural character of the manifestations" (p. 70). He is not attempting to interpret the data but is simply presenting paranormal phenomena with valid evidence, or as he says, "to state and classify facts" (p. 233). Thurston notes that these mystics often have knowledge of distant or future events, but he recognizes that nonreligious individuals also have the ability of foreknowledge. Thus, any of these abilities or other mystical gifts are not proof of sanctity.

Thurston does seem to be well acquainted with literature on what at the time was called "psychical research." He alludes to F. W. H. Myers's book *Human Personality*, which I have previously mentioned. He also discusses the investigations of the Society for Psychical Research and the religion called Spiritualism, including one particular practitioner named Daniel Dunglas Home (1833–1886). In addition, he is familiar with psychiatric/psychological terms such as *dissociation*, but some of the terms he utilizes are no longer in use, such as *neurosis*. He notes that mystics sometimes exhibit behavior that was classified as hysterical neurosis, but a classification like that is not a scientific explanation for paranormal phenomena; it simply shows that something seemingly physical can be connected to a mental state. Thurston believes there is convincing evidence that Spiritualists can levitate heavy objects like tables. His contention is that if that can be done, then people should be able to levitate. Of course, skeptics would argue that these people do not levitate tables, saying that the people who are allegedly doing it are simply good illusionists.

Centuries ago, many people thought that if something unusual happened and it was not from God, then it was a result of diabolical magic. Some of Thurston's research dates back to the time of the Inquisition. Although it was a horrific institution and a blemish on the church, he notes that if a person admitted (falsely) that he used trickery to induce the paranormal and then sought forgiveness, the Inquisition often punished the person but let him survive. If the person did not admit trickery, he might be executed. Thus, confessions of trickery may be invalid. In addition, at least in Spain, the Inquisition was a state institution, and in some cases stigmatics were brought before the Inquisition to intimidate them for political purposes rather than for religious purposes.

What are some of the physical phenomena that Thurston investigated? Although he has separate chapters for the below-mentioned topics, he often states that one individual may have a number of these occur. In fact, exhibiting only one of these gifts would be unusual. The gifts are sometimes referred to as mystical, or the Greek-derived word *charismata* may be used. Thurston's list of physical phenomena is as follows:

- Levitation
- Stigmata (the wounds of Christ)

- Tokens of espousal
- Telekinesis
- Luminous phenomena
- Immunity to fire/heat
- *Incendium amoris* (fire of love)
- Bodily elongation
- Odor of sanctity
- Incorruption of the physical body after death
- Absence of rigor mortis (cadaveric rigidity)
- Blood prodigies
- Inedia (survival without food and/or water)
- Multiplication of food

Two items above that I will not be discussing, other than to note them here, are telekinesis (movement of objects without a known force) and bodily elongation. Thurston only discusses telekinesis in relationship to people receiving Communion (a consecrated Host) by its purportedly flying from the priest's hand to the recipient's mouth. This is a rather limited area of telekinesis. Thurston thinks that some of the people who allegedly did this were using trickery and an unconsecrated Host. Thurston only listed a few questionable cases of bodily elongation, which seems more difficult to relate to holiness.

2. Treece's Study

Treece's book discusses the failure of materialism to address human psychological behavior. She notes the importance of the physical body to human spirituality:

> The one thing every spiritual tradition I know has in common
> is that in all authentic mystics from the Sioux Black Elk to the
> lotus-postured monk, in the thrust toward God the body is a
> seriously trained as the mind or soul. ... [The body] becomes
> as sanctified as mind and soul. (p. 8)

She mentions some areas of modern scientific research, such as biofeedback, that would be in agreement with religious ascetics as early as the second century. Treece would agree with Thurston that the following phenomena are not the touchstones of sanctity but rather aspects of a virtuous life. As she writes,

> Those virtues will generally include (remember, *in heroic proportion*) such things as large-mindedness, optimism, a realism that sees beyond the narrow concerns and illusions of contemporaries, inner joy that is not dependent on things "going well," courageous adherence to moral values even in immoral societies, a steady good-naturedness, spiritual wisdom (which may resemble foolishness to non-mystics), simplicity, almost always a strong sense of humor, and always great humility, a trait that has nothing to do with a lack of healthy self-esteem.

> But more than any of these qualities and more than any physical manifestation, passionate love is the infallible sign of holiness—love for God and love for the entire human family down to its least lovable member. (pp. 11–12)

I consider Treece's material to be a significant update to Thurston. She demonstrates that these research findings are consistent with modern research, which often refutes the mechanistic/reductionist paradigm.

3. Levitation

Although some of the phenomena that Thurston reports transpire after death, what happened while the saint was living often occurred in a state of ecstatic trance or rapture and were thus rare. This is especially true for levitation, as these mystics were not repeatedly lifted above the ground during normal conversation.

Most mystics are not trying to attract attention to what is happening to them. In some cases, though, the religious community in which they lived was embarrassed by feats of levitation. For instance, St. Joseph of Cupertino (1603–1663), the patron saint of air travelers, aviators, and astronauts, was forbidden from saying Mass in public because he would frequently levitate and was once observed doing so by the pope. He would sometimes levitate to kiss a statue of Jesus or Mary. Sister Mary of Jesus Crucified (1846–1878) soared to the top of the tree, but she came hastily down when commanded to do so by her Mother Superior. The next day, one of her sandals was found at the top of the tree. When asked to explain how she flew, she replied that "the Lamb" had carried her. I cite this example to demonstrate that the people involved cannot explain what is happening to them. Thurston found about 200 incidents of levitation in hagiography and maintains that at least one-third of them had respectable evidence and the other two-thirds did not have adequate testimony but were probably not myths. Some mystics who knew that levitation and related phenomena were happening during prayer time might limit their prayer activity to a private room.

Other signs and wonders are similarly conspicuous, such as luminosity. An example of a combination of the two topics of levitation and luminosity is an observation of St. Bernadino Realino, SJ (1530–1616). The story is told by a gentleman of rank and high character. The gentleman was waiting outside of Realino's room when he saw a bright *light* in the room through a crack in the door and thought there might be a fire. The gentleman pushed the door open a little farther and saw Realino in ecstasy and levitating two feet above the ground. The bright *light* was well beyond that of a normally lit room. (This will be described further under "Luminous Phenomena.") In some cases the radiance seems to come from the holy person himself (as in Realino's case) or from a holy object, such as a cross emitting *light* onto the person. Treece comments that some witnesses are not sure if holy people are emitting the *light* or are bathed in *light* from another, unnatural source.

Objects other than the person can be affected. Once, a number of people were having difficulty trying to raise a large cross (thirty-six feet high) and place it into the ground. St. Joseph of Cupertino flew to the cross and easily lifted and placed it. This incident was not documented until many years after it allegedly occurred, but only shortly after his death.

A sort of variation of levitation, which is often considered to be moving straight up, is moving horizontally without seemingly touching the ground. This is sometimes classified as agility. A St. John Joseph (1654–1739) was getting older and had to use a walking stick. One day while he was in a cathedral, his stick was knocked from his hand, but when he asked for help from his patron saint, he was able to move through the crowd without touching the ground. Although most cases of horizontal levitation are only for short distances, one time this same saint, while in ecstasy, traveled a distance of two miles while half a foot above the ground. Treece also mentions a variation of this, in which a person does "fast traveling" or travels a great distance in a brief time.

Treece mentions a Sufi named al-Hallaj (858–922) who levitated. He was killed by other Muslims who considered him to be a heretic. One of the most well-known Sufi mystics, a poet, is popularly known in the West by the name of Rumi (1207–1273). Some others whom Treece mentions as levitators include St. Gaspar del Bufalo, St. Magdalena di Canossa (1774–1835; canonized in 1988), Fr. Francis Xavier Seelos (1819–1867; born in Bavaria and died in New Orleans), St. John Bosco (1815–1888), Francis Luyckx (1824–1896), Gemma Galgani (1878–1903), and St. Joquina Vedruna de Mas (1783–1854; canonized in 1959). This final woman was a mother of eight, but after her husband died she founded a congregation of nuns.

4. Stigmata

Stigmata (meaning "marks") is the appearance of the wounds of Christ on a person's body. The most common and visible ones are in the palms, on the back of the hands, and on the feet.[5] There may be a wound in the side as a result of the stab wound to Christ (John 19:34), and there are variations in the site and the form of the stab wound (chest, abdomen, left side, right side, including variations in size and shape). Some other stigmatic wounds are as follows:

- Puncture wounds on the forehead representing the crown of thorns (often a first sign of future wounds)
- Lash marks on the back representing Christ's being scourged with whips
- Dislocation, a depression, or black and blue marks on the shoulder representing the carrying of a cross

---

[5] It should be noted that in actual crucifixions, the nails are driven through the wrist because only the wrist bones can support the weight of the body. There is only muscle and skin tissue between the palm and the fingers. A nail would easily rip through the muscle–skin tissue.

Simply having marks on their bodies is not all that happens to these mystics. An abbess observed that during the ecstasy of Elizabeth of Herkenrode, around 1275, she reenacted Christ's Passion from arrest to entombment for an entire day. The abbess could see blood spurting from the stigmatic wounds; they were not just abrasions on the surface of the skin. Elizabeth also made loud sounds and struck herself as soldiers struck Christ. These reenactments were more likely to occur on Fridays (or Thursday evenings if arrest is included) and during Lent, and the wounds would often rapidly disappear after Elizabeth came out of the ecstatic state.

After St. Francis's death, his corpse appeared to have actual black nails, formed out of flesh, in his hands. When the head of a nail was pushed in, it appeared to come farther out on the other side. Accounts of this phenomenon were written 20 years after his death, by someone who was alive during Francis's lifetime. The "nails" in the feet protruded from the bottom of his feet and would have been very difficult to walk on. These nails would be difficult to generate by autosuggestion or a pathological condition. In contrast, for one nun, Gemma Galgani, the arrangement of the wounds in the feet made it appear that one nail was used for both feet. Stigmata may affect normal functioning. For example, a priest named Padre Pio (now Saint Pio [Pius] of Pietrelcina, 1887–1968), had difficulty walking when the wounds were visible. Some of these details make it unlikely that the stigmatic was faking, self-inflicting the wounds, or seeking publicity. Thurston reports that most of them had an intense unwillingness to court notoriety.

Although Thurston discusses the possibility that stigmata may have occurred prior to St. Francis of Assisi, he is commonly believed to be the first person on whom these wounds appeared. They reportedly appeared on him in 1224. Thurston finds it interesting that this phenomenon never occurred prior to Francis but that as soon as it was publicized it happened numerous times, although it is still exceedingly rare. Thurston notes that even the apostle Paul, in Galatians 6:17, states that he has the marks of Christ "in my body." However, I would be inclined to refer to the wounds of Christ as being "on" a body, not "in" it. Most biblical commentaries do not espouse that St. Paul had the visible wounds of Christ. What seems interesting is that between St. Francis's death in 1226 and the late Padre Pio a great majority of the other stigmatics were women, virtually all of them nuns in convents who also had ecstatic visions and frequently exhibited other mystical gifts. Padre Pio was still living when Thurston wrote about him. He was canonized a saint in 2002.

Thurston discusses the possibility that in some cases stigmatic wounds could be self-inflicted, but certainly not in all cases. He does not reach a conclusion as to whether those that are not self-inflicted are miraculous or supernatural in origin or have pathological causes. For example, simply meditating on the Crucifixion could naturally induce bodily symptoms without those bodily symptoms being supernatural through what Thurston calls a "Crucifixion complex." Thurston admits, "The ecstasy of a mystic and the trance of a hysterical patient are very closely allied and cannot always be readily distinguished" (p. 40).

With regard to the suffering that stigmatics seem to undergo from the wounds and by reenacting the Passion—and this may apply to other illnesses, with which a number of them are afflicted—Thurston has some valuable insight:

> The impression left upon me has been that the subjects who were so favoured or afflicted were all suffering from pronounced and often extravagant hysterical neuroses. Many of them were intensely devout (of course it is only in the case of people whose thoughts were concentrated on religious motives that one would expect to find this type of manifestation) but in others piety was combined with eccentricities and with apparent dissociations of personality which were very strange and not exactly edifying. I find it difficult to believe that God could have worked miracles to accredit such people as His chosen friends and representatives. (p. 205)

5. Tokens of Espousal

Tokens of espousal are a rather unusual phenomenon. Only women receive them. The person has a ring marking, usually on the right hand, indicating the individual is espoused to Christ. In an earlier description of the Mystic Way, it was mentioned that many mystics thought of their soul as being in a marriage with God. In the nineteenth century, witnesses described the ring of a nun named Celestine Fenouil as vivid red with tiny crosses at intervals. It was brighter on Sundays. Her ring came after stigmata, whereas for St. Catherine of Siena (1347–1380) the ring appeared prior to her stigmata. For another holy nun, the ring was only visible to others when she was in rapture.

6. Luminous Phenomena

Luminous phenomena are one of the most interesting topics of mysticism, since *light* was encountered numerous times in connection with near-death experiences. This is one of the most common phenomenon. Throughout his book, Thurston makes reference to a "Treatise on the Beatification and Canonization of Saints," written by Prosper Lambertini, later Pope Benedict XIV (1675–1758; pope from 1740 to 1758). In the treatise, he attributed luminosity to natural, and not miraculous, causes, holding that it was often the clothes of the person that radiated.

Among the well-known saints who exhibited luminosity were Saint Philip Neri (1515–1595; referred to as the Apostle of Rome), St. Charles Borromeo (1538–1584), St. Ignatius of Loyola (1491–1556), St. Francis de Sales (1567–1622), Saint Catherine de Ricci (1522–1590), St. Alphonsus Liguori (1696–1787), and St. Louis Bertrand (1526–1581). They may have become luminous when saying Mass or preaching. On one occasion, the *light* around Bernadino Realino, previously mentioned as levitating, was so bright that it hurt the observer's eyes, who could barely see Realino's body. Another person described him as lighting up an entire room. St. Lidwina of Schiedam (1380–1433) was sensitive to natural light and thus stayed in a dark room, but to visitors that room was completely shining with "divine light" that did not bother Lidwina. Her room was also redolent; odors of sanctity will be discussed later.

Treece considers luminosity to be one of the most common phenomenon in saintly people. She lists numerous individuals who exhibited it: St. Peter Eymard (1811–1868), St. Jeanne Thouret (1765–1826), Fr. Francis Paul Liebermann (1802–1852), St. Gaspar del Bufalo (1786–1837; also levitated and bilocated), Vincent Morelli (d. 1812), Leopold of Gaiche (d. 1815), Mary Maddalena Bentivoglio (1834–1902), St. Giuseppe Sarto (Pope Pius X) (1835–1914), St. Andre Bessette (1845–1937), Francis Luyckx, St. Julie Billiart (1751–1816), St. John Vianney (1786–1859), St. John Bosco (1815–1888), Fr. Jean Edouard Lamy (1853–1931), Fr. Francis

Xavier Seelos (1819–1867), and Fr. Aloysius Ellacuria (1905–1981; born in Spain and died in Los Angeles; also levitated and bilocated).

Although not born in America, St. Frances Cabrini (1850–1917), an Italian immigrant known as Mother Cabrini who eventually became a US citizen, was sharing a room with another nun. This other nun awoke during the night and found the lampless room flooded with *light* due to Cabrini's presence. She then requested a private room. Treece also mentions that Protestant healer-mystic Agnes Sanford (1897–1982) reported occasions when *light* would appear around Cabrini. One of Sanford's books is titled *The Healing Light.*

Treece notes that Christian paintings often show a halo around the heads of saints, but in descriptions she found of luminosity, it is the entire body of the holy person that appears surrounded by *light.* One person, in testimony for considering Maximilian Kolbe (1894–1941) for sainthood, reported that during a religious conversation Kolbe was "transfigured in a diaphanous form, almost transparent, and surrounded by a halo of light" (p. 29). Treece compares this to *light* around people of other religions. In the Jewish religion, there is a Shekinah (meaning "glory") *light,* a sign of God's presence. Moses had this *light* around him when he came down from Mount Sinai with the Ten Commandments (Exodus 34:29–35). Baal Shem Tov saw the Shekinah *light* at times. In Islamic art from the sixteenth to the nineteenth century, holy people and the prophet are depicted as surround by flames, similar to the halo concept in Christian art.

Similarly, tales about Hindu, Buddhist, and Sufi saints often contain references to divine *light.* The Hindu term for this *light* is *Brahmic splendor.* Treece also notes that in 1899 Muslim and Christian Lebanese people reported a *light* around a grave where a holy monk of the Maronite rite had been buried without being embalmed and without a coffin. His body was dug up and found incorrupt, but no time period was specified. The monk, Charbel Makhlouf, eventually became the first Maronite saint, in 1977. Treece also discusses human auras and mentions the studies of Shafica Karagulla, which I previously reviewed in chapter 8.

Of course, Christ had this luminous phenomenon happen to him in an event referred to as the Transfiguration (Matthew 17:1–3; Mark 9:2–4). In both accounts, Moses and Elijah appeared beside Jesus and his clothes shone whiter than any snow seen on earth. The observers were three apostles: Peter, James, and John.

My explanation of luminosity would be that simple auras are only visible to gifted or trained people, whereas the luminosity of holy people is often witnessed by those around them. I would interpret the latter as the *light* coming from Union with the person's Spirit and not as the aura of the astral body or mental body.

7. Immunity to Fire/Heat

Thurston titles his chapter on immunity to fire and heat "Human Salamanders," using the latter term to refer to a mythical creature resembling a lizard that can withstand fire. Thurston explains that a few saints had this ability, but he gives other examples of the ability not within a religious context.

An example of a saint with such an ability is St. Francis of Paula {Paola} (1416–1507), who allegedly held a red-hot piece of iron in his hand. Other feats of his include purportedly entering a lime kiln, holding some red-hot charcoal in his hand, and putting his arm into boiling oil. St. Francis also had other mystical gifts. For example, in 1564 he supposedly was denied entry into a boat to cross the Strait of Messina. He placed his cloak on the water and sailed across, his companions following in the boat. Franz Liszt titled one of his compositions *St. Francis of Paola Walking on the Water*. Francis is the patron saint of boatmen and mariners. He was canonized in 1519, only twelve years after his death, which is considered a short time.

While noting these examples of saints, Thurston also indicates that certain Spiritualist mediums have this immunity, as do firewalkers among indigenous peoples and in non-Western societies. Thurston's example of a firewalker is a bishop in India. The man who demonstrated the ability was a Muslim. He had hundreds of people follow him through the bed of burning coals, and at one point he said that no more should go through the firelit path. Several who tried at that point were severely burned. Thurston also mentions another, nonreligious person referred to as a fire-eater who allegedly put hot coals, even melted lead, into his mouth, and touched other parts of his body with white-hot metal, and was not injured. Thurston specifically states that this person was not in a trance state.

Thurston notes that the Spiritualist D. D. Home was able to hold red-hot coals without being injured and could impart this ability to people who were willing to take the coals from his hand and hold them for a period of time. Home sometimes performed this feat in front of aristocratic admirers. If anyone was injured, it would have ruined his career. He could even remove a piece hot coal (actual coal, not wood coals) from a blazing fire.

8. Incendium Amoris

In one sense, *incendium amoris* is the opposite of immunity from fire/heat. Some holy people or mystics are able to generate high amounts of internal heat. These people attribute it to the love for God that they feel inside themselves. To temper the heat, they may apply cloths dipped in cold water or simply go outside in the winter without a coat. Some may drink large quantities of cold water. Those who touch them can feel the heat.

The biography of Suor Maria Villani of Naples (1586–1670) was published only four years after her death. She drank up to 45 liters of water a day, around 3.5 gallons. A hissing sound, like water being converted to steam, was made when she drank the water. After her death, her body, which prior to death appeared emaciated, dry, and dark, became fresh-colored and lifelike. Some of the blood removed from her remained liquid and incorrupt three years after her death. Nine hours after her death, a doctor had difficulty removing her heart because it was so hot. There was a wound in her heart (as she had predicted earlier in her life), and the wound was cauterized, as if it had come from a spear of fire. A doctor who was treating Padre Pio reported that the thermometer he was using broke from the expansion of the mercury past the highest temperature (108 degrees Fahrenheit) it was capable of recording. Treece reports that a backup bathhouse thermometer recorded Padre Pio's temperature at 125.5 degrees Fahrenheit. Most doctors agree that a temperature above 106 degrees Fahrenheit may cause permanent brain damage.

9. The Odor of Sanctity

The odor of sanctity occurs fairly frequently in mystics while they are living and can persist long after the person has died. In ADCs, it is often a friendly smell associated with a deceased person. A widow may sense the presence of her deceased husband's pipe tobacco or his workshop, with a pleasant, not offensive, association. A widower may smell his deceased wife's cologne or perfume. In either case, it is often just a gentle reminder of warm times together or that the person continues some type of afterlife existence. The person who detects the odor is often alone, but, if with other people, these others may not detect the odor.

Pious people may generate a pleasing odor to many people, both when the saintly person is living and after he or she has died. The scent is sometimes similar to flowers, but others describe it as a celestial odor, utilizing terms like *indescribable sweetness* and saying that the fragrance cannot be compared to any earthly scent. It often has a strong and favorable emotional effect on the person sensing the odor. If it is of a particular flower, the smell may be out of season for that flower. In some cases, the smell may occur in a place, such as in the pious person's cell in a monastery or convent, rather than from the physical body itself, or it may be in the clothes after they are removed, in other personal effects, or in the mattress on which the person slept. The odor may persist for many years, even if the items in the cell have been removed and replaced, and also in the tomb or crypt in which the person is buried. For some who visit the room in which the holy person lived, the odor may cling to the visitors' clothes.

According to Treece, Buddhist lore in Japan sometimes includes a pleasing fragrance associated with a holy person. She also notes that Paramahansa Yogananda's *Autobiography of a Yogi* and other religious sources discuss this fragrance but report that some activities regarded as paranormal can be spiritually useless and merely for entertainment, display, or self-aggrandizement, hindering progress toward Union with the divine. Of course, if the person emitting the fragrance is deceased, it is difficult to imagine that he or she is doing it to impress anyone.

Treece lists various places and circumstances wherein a pleasing odor may be associated with a holy person:

1. A live, visible, sanctified body
2. The stigmata wounds or blood of a saint
3. Apparent communication from a live saint who is not present (either by some form of projection or signaling and indivisible bilocation)
4. An object or place strongly associated with a living saint who is not present, as if his or her odor lingers or penetrates deeply
5. The deaths of some saints
6. An object or place strongly associated with the dead saint, including the grave
7. Apparent communication by a dead saint or in regard to a dead saint without link to any material object or visible body
8. Visible after-death appearances by saints
   (p. 219)

10. Incorruption of Physical Body After Death

The next three sections are primarily related to the corpses of deceased saints. I, as well as Thurston, consider that physical incorruption (no decay) of the body after death, the absence of rigor mortis in the hours or days after death, and fresh blood coming from a deceased body months or even years after burial are separate topics. There seems to be less emphasis on the holy people to whom these phenomena occur as being mystics, but some of the people were previously mentioned, such as St. Catherine of Genoa (1447–1510). In these cases, the bodies Thurston discusses were not embalmed. He does report some alternative natural processes, for example, mummification, which can account for some of the phenomena, but usually the alternate explanation will apply only to special situations that are not applicable to these saints. My discussion here will also include topics previously mentioned, such as a frequently encountered pleasant odor coming from these incorruptible bodies and, in some rare cases, a warmer than ambient temperature body.

In his discussion of incorruption, Thurston explores conventional decomposition of the body. Normally, signs of decomposition are evident within two weeks of death, with some exceptions, such as a very cold temperature. However, he does note that in some places people's bodies are not buried underground but are placed in crypts. After a number of years, the space is emptied and then reused. In a small percentage (much less than 1 percent) of those crypts, the body is found incorrupt. This is not mentioned by Thurston, but possibly the incorrupt bodies were of people who had led saintly lives but were never recognized as having done so by the church. Thurston notes that in a few instances, the remains, possibly in a sealed casket, appeared incorrupt but then decomposed very rapidly when exposed to air.

Not all preservation is necessarily incorruption. For instance, Thurston explains that a revolution that took place in Paris in 1830. During a riot, a number of people were killed and then immediately buried, most with no wrapping, some in canvas, and only a few in coffins. Ten years later, it was decided that they should be reburied. None of them were corrupt. In a few of them, some features were distinguishable due to saponification and the formation of adipocere (the word is a combination of the Latin words for *fat* and *wax*). The word was invented at that time to indicate that fat may be saponified into a wax, usually in a moist setting, and then, like drying, prevent further decay. Thurston speculates that this may have happened to the bodies of some of the saints described as incorrupt, but certainly only to a small fraction of the total number of incorrupt bodies of saints.

Thurston discusses some other natural explanations for incorruption. He mentions mummies found in Peru that received no preservatives like those in Egypt. Parts of Peru are very dry. When tissue becomes desiccated (loses moisture), that condition prevents decay by microorganisms. He also mentions a corpse preserved from putrefaction when it was found in guano (bat dung). In Mediterranean countries, dried remains of nonsainted people are often hundreds of years old. A number of preserved bodies were found in the vaults of one St. Michan's church, but its location is not specified. Although mummies may have some of the features of the person when they were living, mummies are generally very rigid, unlike the suppleness (soft and flexible) displayed by many incorrupt bodies of saints. This will be discussed further in the next section.

The oldest case of incorruption Thurston provides is that of St. Ambrose's (ca. 396) description of the discovery of the body of St. Nazarius. He had been beheaded, and his head was incorrupt and had a sweet fragrance. Thurston does not mention the condition of the remainder of the body or even if a skeleton was next to the head.

An example of how the early history of the church can be confusing is that, according to *Wikipedia*, St. Nazarius was allegedly converted by St. Peter himself but is also listed as the possible son of St. Perpetua, who died around 203—two incompatible time lines. In either case, he would have been dead for centuries when St. Ambrose found his body. Thurston also lists some famous English saints whose bodies were allegedly incorrupt, but the examples were often a millennium or so ago, so the documentation may not be as reliable. Although he was not a direct witness, the Venerable (St.) Bede (ca. 673–735), author of *The Ecclesiastical History of the English People*, recounts from other witnesses that the body of St. Cuthbert (634–687) was found incorrupt in his sepulcher eleven years after his death.

Examples of some reasonably recent cases of incorruption, obviously of bodies found fewer years after the saint's death, are St. Madeleine Sophie Barat (1779–1865) and St. Bernadette Soubirous (1844–1879). Madeleine is not considered a mystic, and Bernadette's claim to mysticism is that she had visions of the Virgin Mary who became Our Lady of Lourdes. Madeleine was disinterred 28 years after her death. Her coffin was partly decayed and covered with mildew, making it unlikely that her body had been mummified by dehydration, but her body was incorrupt. When the body of Bernadette was exhumed in 1909, it was described as brown and with eyes sunken, but otherwise incorrupt. Her funeral garments were damp, and she was placed in a new coffin. When she was exhumed again ten years later, she exhibited some further decay but was not a skeleton. Those who exhumed her were able to make a cast of her face.

Thurston also mentions one case in which he was a witness of an incorrupt body of a deceased priest when the coffin was opened. The priest was Fr. Paul Mary Pakenham, a Passionist priest, who died at a young age in 1857. In 1894, it was decided to move his body to a new cemetery. Thurston said that Pakenham had a lifelike expression on his face as if he were sleeping peacefully.

A number of Russian Orthodox Church remains have been found incorrupt, so it is not solely a Roman Catholic phenomenon. The Orthodox Church considers incorruption of the cadaver to be an important condition for canonization. Incorruption does not just happen to people in religious communities. A married woman named Blessed Anna Maria Taigi, who was uneducated but greatly respected by her local community, died in 1837 at age 68. Her remains were inspected 31 years later. The doctor who prepared the report about the body felt she could have died two or three days earlier.

Another unusual phenomenon in connection with incorruption is the emission of an oily fluid. For instance, the remains of Spanish nun Blessed Maria Anna Ladroni, who died in 1624, were inspected in 1731 and were found to be soft and flexible, emitting a remarkable perfume and an oily fluid that also saturated her clothing, as attested to by a number of professors of medicine. They dissected her, and the oily fluid impregnated all of her tissues. The deeper the incision, the greater the fragrance. Thirty-five years later, her body was no longer flexible but was not completely decayed. Maria Anna had been buried near others whose bodies were subject to normal decay.

Two cases of incorruption were not mentioned by Thurston or Treece, but I have read about them and verified the information in *Wikipedia* (2016). One case demonstrates a very long time for a body to remain incorrupt. In the Middle Ages, people often died crossing rivers. Thus, people who built bridges (civil authorities often would not build them) were often considered to have a calling from God. St. Benezet (French for "Benedict"; 1163–1184) heard voices telling him to build a bridge although he was a simple shepherd. He planned and began the construction by himself at age fourteen over the Rhône River at Avignon, but when alleged miracles began to happen at the construction site he began to receive assistance. This led to an organization called the Bridge Builders Brotherhood. About the time the bridge was completed, he died. His body was placed in a coffin in a small chapel on the bridge. Almost five hundred years later, in 1669, part of the bridge was washed away; his coffin was rescued; and his body was found incorrupt. Similarly, the grave of St. Germaine Cousin of Pibrac (1579–1601) was opened in 1644, and her body was found to be incorrupt. A shepherdess who had a disease and was mistreated by her family, she had very little to eat but shared that small amount with the poor people of her area.

11. Absence of Rigor Mortis

As explained, many incorrupt bodies were soft and flexible. This section will primarily emphasize absence of rigor mortis (or cadaveric rigidity) between death and burial. Thurston reports that he has found at least 50 cases in which a holy person's recently deceased body had a complete absence of rigor mortis. In some of these cases, the person was not a saint or being considered for sainthood but still lived in a religious community. Another phenomenon, of a mysterious moisture that sometimes occurs in conjunction with the lack of rigor mortis, will also be discussed.

There may be variations as to how many hours after death rigor mortis begins. According to a *Wikipedia* article on rigor mortis, it usually commences within three to four hours of death, reaches a peak in about twelve hours, and then dissipates after 48 to 60 hours. It is a natural physiological reaction in muscle tissue that normally cannot be prevented in human bodies. A process is employed to prevent it in edible farm animals, and it is frequently sped up or occurs sooner in warmer conditions. Since rigor mortis ends at some point, perhaps the flexibility in bodies that are incorrupt is not that amazing, although even after rigor mortis is completed, limbs may not be as supple as they were when the body was living. Putrefaction often begins soon after rigor mortis has ended.

Thurston discusses the possibility that in some cases the holy person may have been in an ecstatic trance and was only thought to have been dead. However, ecstatic trances usually will not last for three or four days, a typical waiting period before burial. A number of these holy people's bodies were not buried for three or four days and remained flexible during that entire time. Such is the case of St. Francis, the alleged first stigmatic, who was also sometimes listed as the first person whose corpse did not exhibit rigor mortis. However, Thurston found a similar description in the life of St. Raynerius of Pisa (1117–1160), whose biographer states that the limbs of the cadaver were flexible and showed no signs of stiffening. Although these bodies may not have had an odor of sanctity, some had no offensive odor for four days in the heat of summer in addition to remaining flexible. Although not identifying her illness, Thurston mentions a nun who died in 1848 whose limbs were stiff and immovable during her illness but then became supple and flexible after her death. The body of a lay-brother who had a gangrenous necrosis resulting in the contraction and knotting of his limbs prior to death straightened out and became pliable after he died, and the various visible wounds of the gangrene on his body disappeared.

In some cases, a combination of other previously discussed phenomena may occur in addition to the absence of rigor mortis. For instance, when Spanish Dominican St. Louis (Lewis) Bertrand (1526–1581) died, a brilliant *light* flashed from his mouth, illuminating his cell for ten to fifteen seconds. He was known for his preaching and had spent part of his life in Colombia. A perfume came from his dead body; heavenly music was heard in the church where he was awaiting burial; and many witnesses saw a *light* being emitted from the uncovered parts of his body.

12. Blood Prodigies

Just as Thurston used an alternative definition of the word *salamander*, his title for the topic of blood prodigies is apparently an alternative definition. Typically, the word *prodigy* implies an exceptionally bright talented child, but it may also mean an event so extraordinarily rare as to inspire wonder. A blood prodigy is when blood flows from a dead body long after it is expected; this may occur in conjunction with incorruption and the odor of sanctity. According to one of Thurston's medical references, blood usually thickens and ceases flow within eight hours of death. He does mention a condition called hypostases, or the accumulation of uncongealed blood, but this may only happen for a few hours or days and not for months or years after death.

Franciscan nun St. Catherine of Bologna (1413–1463) was buried in the ground without a coffin within hours of her death. There was a fragrance around her burial plot, and some miraculous medical cures occurred there. After 18 days, her body was dug up. Though dirty, it was incorrupt. It was placed in a sepulcher. A few days later, the sepulcher was reopened. Observers found St. Catherine's body bathed in a "sweat," possibly the same moisture discussed in the previous section. One man pulled on a piece of skin on her foot, after which red blood flowed out as if she were still alive. Three months later a cup of blood flowed from her nostrils. Her body is still on display at her convent.

Other cases, names, the time period after death, and other features of blood prodigies include the following:

- St. Peter Regalatus, blood flow 36 years after death when finger was severed.
- Geronimo Batista de Lanuza (d. 1624), 36 days, legs surgically severed.
- St. Nicholas of Tolentino (1246–1306), large flow of blood when arms cut off incorrupt body 40 years after his death. Thurston describes the evidence of the flow as not that reputable, but there is little doubt that the arms continued to exude a red fluid on occasion during the seventeenth century, more than 300 years after St. Nicholas's death. The fluid could not be confirmed as real human blood.
- St. John of the Cross (1542–1591; author of a book on mysticism), blood flow when fingers cut off body nine months after death.

13. Inedia

Inedia is the ability to live without eating any food or eating well below what would be considered normal consumption. For example, while Moses was on Mount Sinai receiving the Ten Commandments, he allegedly neither ate food nor drank water for forty days (Exodus 29:28). In chapter 10, on spirit intrusion, there was a section about the Magnus of Strovolos, Stylianos Atteshlis. His designated successor, Kostas, claimed that he had lived for an entire year with almost no food when he realized he could energize his etheric double directly from *light*. Perhaps that is what the people I will be discussing in this section are doing, but they are not familiar with these terms to describe what is happening to them.

Thurston discusses an English woman who ate little (e.g., a half pint of milk in three weeks), had some unusual abilities, was paralyzed, and eventually became blind. Her name was Mrs. Croad, and she was born in 1840. Her medical problems resulted from a number of injuries (attributed to falls) after she was married at age 19. After one of those falls, she began having epileptic seizures and convulsions. She became bedridden in 1866. With her fingers, she could "see" what was on a photograph. She could also communicate with deceased friends. She informed some people that her husband had died at sea, which was confirmed when the news arrived. Her father was also a seaman, and she knew when he was in danger. She also knew when visitors would be arriving. Thurston also discusses several other people who could read with their hands or had other senses that were misplaced, like smelling with the chin.

Treece lists detailed examples of two 20th-century inedics, both of whom were reparatory sufferers (people who offer to suffer in place of others). One is a Portuguese woman, Alexandrina de Costa (1904–1955). When she was twelve, a farmer she was working for tried to rape her, but she got away. Two years later, that farmer and two other men broke into her home, where her sister and a friend were sewing. She jumped out a second-story window and was seriously injured but managed to grab a piece of firewood, crawl up the stairs, and beat the man off. Her spine was broken, and she became paralyzed. At first, she believed and prayed she would be healed, but she finally accepted her condition. In 1931, she had her first ecstatic experience and felt that Christ had called her to be a reparatory sufferer. In 1938, she became an inedic. Until her death in 1955, she neither ate any food (except a Eucharist wafer) nor drank any water. She was investigated for a 40 day period to verify her inedia. A pleasant odor was also noted around her.

Thurston has numerous other examples of inedia collected from various medical journals and several countries. One was a woman named Maria Furtner (d. 1884) from Bavaria who did not eat anything for 40 years. Although she was Catholic, her abstinence from food did not seem to have any religious overtones. A Swiss physician described the abdomen of another inedic, Apollonia Schreier, as looking like her viscera were removed, but otherwise she was not emaciated. She had no excretions during a three-week study of her eating habits in a hospital. Another person Thurston lists is a Jewish girl in Russia who ate no food and drank next to nothing for 21 months and was not extremely emaciated. Finally, Thurston mentions some studies in which Indian fakirs (people who perform feats of magic or endurance) apparently enter a state of quasi hibernation by being buried in a container underground for months without air or food.

Thurston also discusses other Catholics who were reported to be inedics. Many of them have not been declared saints but were considered very holy when they were living. The following is a list of them, the years they lived (or just the year of death), and the length of time they allegedly went without any food and often with no water, with the possible exception of Communion (now often called Eucharist), which often relieved their bodily weakness. For those without any year specified, the fast may have been for Lent only. A number of them were previously mentioned as ecstatic, as stigmatic, or as having symptoms of hysteria.

- St. Catherine of Siena (1347–1380)
- Blessed Mary of Oignies (early thirteenth century), weeks at a time
- St. Lidwina of Schiedam (1380–1433), 28 years
- Venerable Domenica del Paradiso (d. 1553), 20 years
- Blessed Nicholas von Flue (d. 1487), perhaps the only man in the group, 19 years
- Blessed Elizabeth von Reute (d. 1420), 15 years
- Anne Catherine Emmerich (1774–1824)
- Mother Agnes of Jesus (seventeenth century)
- Domenica Lazzari (d. 1848), 12 years
- Louise Lateau (1850–1883), 12 years, worked hard on farm but bedridden for last seven years
- Teresa Higginson (1844–1905), also needed very little sleep
- Marie-Julie Jahenny (1850–1941)
- Theresa Neumann (1898–1962), 35 to 40 years, also stigmatic, would lose weight when she bled on Fridays but would regain weight without eating by the next Friday

14. Multiplication of Food

In contrast to living without eating, this section is a discussion of some holy people who seemed able to multiply food in order to feed others. In a sense, it is a Christlike ability, as Jesus, in the Gospels, on several occasions allegedly increased a small number of loaves of bread and fish in order to feed thousands of people. According to those accounts, fragments picked up after the people ate were greater than the amount with which they began. There are no fragments in the cases reported by Thurston and no weight or volume measurements, simply a mention that the given food supplies lasted for an extraordinarily long time.

For St. Andrew Fournet's consideration for sainthood, one nun reported this incident to the Congregation of Rites for Sainthood. In about 1824, Fr. Fournet was informed by his cofounder that the nuns of her religious order (approximately two hundred members at the time) could not attend their annual retreat (about ten weeks in the summer) because there was not enough grain to feed them and no money to purchase more grain. Fr. Fournet said she needed to have more faith and told her to invite the nuns to the retreat. They came, and the amount of grain the nuns had expected to last only one week lasted for the entire ten weeks—and the pile of grain they began with never seemed to decrease. On another occasion, another nun estimated the amount of grain as eight bushels, but after Fr. Fournet prayed there were sixty bushels.

While in most cases the multiplication of food is for those with desperate need, a Fr. Angiolo Paoli (1642–1720) was holding a picnic for some well-to-do friends who had previously assisted him financially. A decanter of wine remained half full even after providing wine to a dozen people. He performed a similar feat for twenty-five people from a single decanter, and on another occasion fed a number of beggars from a few scraps of bread.

Thurston mentions, without much detail, a number of saints who allegedly multiplied food. Those names came from the previously cited Treatise on Beatification and Canonization by Prosper Lambertini. More than one gift is probably the norm rather than the exception. Thurston also cites later cases of food multiplication from sainthood investigations, but he admits that the evidence, while not merely a legend, may be historically inadequate.

15. Supernatural Energy

Supernatural energy was not investigated by Thurston, but it is discussed by Treece, who holds that it is the most common bodily phenomenon among mystics. For a number of holy people, they carry on vigorously during the day but almost never sleep, often absorbing themselves in prayer throughout the entire night. This appeared to be the case with a number of holy people who were previously mentioned, such as Mother Cabrini. However, Treece does note that some of them were physically disabled and thus not vigorous, but sleeplessness is still uncommon.

In addition, Treece mentions that Hindu yogis often speak of ways to energize the body with special breathing techniques and by practicing yoga. A number of Jewish mystics are also noted as sleeping very little and consuming small amounts of food.

Treece postulates two possibilities for these energy observations. "Either sanctity and its prayer life changes the body so drastically that food and sleep are no longer necessities, or the prayer states of holiness open the sanctified person to an exterior, numinous source of energy" (p. 91). My concept of human spiritual nature would probably more closely align with the second possibility. However, with regard to incorruption of the physical body after death, I would agree that there must be some alteration to the physical body.

Among those Treece lists with supernatural energy are St. John Vianney; St. John Bosco; Blessed Jacques Laval (1803–1864); Blessed Anna Maria Taigi (1769–1837), who was not a nun and who had seven children; and Praxedes Fernandez (d. 1936), widowed mother of four children. Treece also delves into some detail on the life of the previously mentioned Padre Pio. He had tuberculosis and appeared frail around 1917–18, but he appeared stocky later in life, living on 300 to 400 calories per day while losing up to a cup of blood daily from his stigmatic wounds and never becoming anemic despite eating no meat. Several other holy people, as youths or as adults, also had tuberculosis or other debilitating illnesses that would ordinarily reduce their ability to work but that, in these cases, did not do so. For example, St. Maximilian Kolbe had tuberculosis and worked hard with little food or sleep. He died at Auschwitz after being placed in an underground unlit bunker without food or water with nine other prisoners. He had volunteered to take the place of another prisoner, who had a family. After two weeks, he was the only one still conscious, but he was then murdered by a chemical injection.

St. Andre Bessette (1845–1937) almost died at birth. He was frail and had numerous ailments all his life. Because of his poor intellectual skills, he could not become a priest, only a brother who did maintenance work. He even survived the influenza of 1918 and also lived through double pneumonia at the age of 86. He ate sparsely and slept very little. He was known as a healer of others and is best known for building the Oratory of St. Joseph in Montréal, always attributing the healings in his presence to the intercession of St. Joseph rather than to himself. He lived to age 91. Treece notes what I discussed earlier: that many shamans had illnesses that led them to find their calling to be a shaman. However, many of them recovered from their illnesses, while Bessette and others had poor health their entire life.

Treece comments that the ill health of many mystics may be the result of their choosing to be reparatory sufferers, that is, taking on the burdens of others, including their physical illnesses. She mentions one writer who knew of two Protestants who felt called to be reparatory sufferers (alternative term: *vicarious atonement*). Treece notes this characteristic among Hindu holy people. Judaism also has tales of just men who suffer for others. Treece also mentions that the previously cited Agnes Sanford warns against judging suffering as a sign of a neurosis. Some inedics or other mystics who are disabled may be reparatory sufferers "engaged in a much more cosmic drama then personal illness" (p. 176).

16. Bilocation

Bilocation is not discussed by Thurston, but it is delved into by Treece. This is not just something that happened a "long time ago, far, far, away." Padre Pio (St. Pius of Pietraclina), who died in 1968, was known to bilocate on numerous occasions. Essentially, a person is considered to bilocate when he or she is undeniably seen a distance away from his or her actual location. Since Padre Pio never left his monastery in the last 50 years of his life, if he was seen elsewhere it had to be by means of bilocation.

Pio explained himself as being in two places as a "prolongation of personality," or else he said that he was able to observe distant locations, what some recent investigators refer to as "remote viewing." This would be similar to what NDErs claim they can do during the NDE. If an NDEr simply thinks of a place she would like to be, she immediately feels that she arrives there, but the person at the remote location does not sense her presence. In after-death communication, a living person does sense the presence of a deceased person. However, since the bilocator is seen at the remote location, the bilocator must be inducing a vision in the viewer.

Although some are visions only, there are also indications that the viewer can speak to and touch the bilocator.

Treece goes into detail about some of Padre Pio's bilocations, which are always in the context of his spiritually assisting another person. One case shows that he also had a paranormal form of knowledge. One day Mary, the mother of Jesus, conveyed a message to him, saying that he had the responsibility for the spiritual direction of a child. Right after Mary conveyed this message, Padre Pio bilocated to a child named Giovanna who was being born as her father was dying. Many years later she visited his monastery, and he told her (without her giving any details of her life) that he was present in her room the night on which she was born and her father died.

Treece closes her section on bilocation with a quotation from St. Martin de Porres (1579–1639). He had many mystical gifts and was the son of a nobleman and a black woman in Peru. In response to a question, he replied that if God could multiply loaves of bread, he should be able to multiply Martin.

17. Observation

One item I have noticed is that education or intelligence is not apparently a factor in becoming a mystic or saint. St. Teresa of Avila held a position of authority and authored a book on the mystical life. She and St. Catherine of Siena (classified as a doctor of the church) led movements for reform within the church. In contrast, St. Joseph of Cupertino, St. John Vianney, and St. Andre Bessette were considered mentally slow, and St. Germaine Cousin and a number of nuns previously mentioned were uneducated peasants.

18. Speculative Explanation

I would like to propose one possible general explanation for the unusual mystical phenomena presented in this section. When Isaac Newton developed his famous laws of physics, they involved the mass of an object. The planets revolving around the sun can be explained with his laws. Albert Einstein (1879–1955) applied a minor correction factor to the mass of an object when using Newton's equations. Einstein concluded that Newton's law applied to the resting mass of an object. Einstein proposed that the mass of an object can increase if it is moving very rapidly. His correction factor is to divide the resting mass of an object by the square root of one minus the velocity of the object squared divided by the velocity of light squared ($\sqrt{1 - v^2/c^2}$), where v is the velocity of the object and c is the velocity of light. Since the velocity of light is extremely high, the correction factor is impossible to measure at ordinary speeds. This correction factor explains why a physical object with mass cannot reach the speed of light. As an object approaches the speed of light, its mass would approach infinity, and thus it would take an infinite force to further increase its velocity. Einstein did not disprove Newton; he simply provided a correction factor that is negligible under the conditions that Newton was assuming. He limited the domain of applicability of Newton's law.

I propose that when mystics and saints are deeply in the realm of Spirit, a correction factor must be applied to the physical world around them. Among items that this would include would be the law of gravity, the nature or generation of light, decomposition of the physical body, and the necessity of food or the multiplication of it. Since there is a wide range of physical phenomena associated with mysticism, this correction factor probably cannot be described with a mathematical equation.

E. Spiritually Transformative Experiences

1. Introduction

The concept I have developed regarding multiple spirit bodies residing within a human physical body is derived from and supported by various sources. There is an Eastern concept for explaining mystical experiences, although a different term is used. For this discussion, I will reference a book written by Yvonne Kason, MD, titled *Farther Shore: Exploring How Near-Death, Kundalini and Mystical Experiences Can Transform Ordinary Lives* (2000, rev. ed.). Kason had an NDE and employs the term *spiritually transformative experience* (STE) for the experience in the subtitle of her book and for other, related experiences. She frequently adds the letter *P* to "STE" (resulting in "STEP") for the word *peak*, for the most significant of these experiences.

Kason's general model is that of a kundalini experience. This is a term from the yogic tradition in India. A full kundalini experience has many similarities to mystical experiences. I will go into more detail later, but the traditional explanation for a kundalini experience is that there exists a dormant coiled-up energy or serpent at the base of the spine that, when awakened, can travel up the spine to the top of the head. A full encounter with the *light* ensues when the kundalini energy reaches the crown chakra, passing through the other chakras on the way. Reaching the crown chakra is sometimes referred to as a state of samadhi. The Buddhist term is *nirvana*. A commonly used term for this is *enlightenment*. An extremely small number of people may reach a *sahaja* state, in which the kundalini remains permanently in the crown chakra. A person who reaches this state can be aware of external realities while existing in a perennial state of mystical Union. This contrasts with many mystics who appear to be unaware of the external world.

Some people experience some energy flow in their spine without its going all the way to the head; this could be called a partial kundalini experience or kundalini awakening. While a gradual awakening is more common, some people have a totally unexpected full kundalini experience. This type of experience is more likely to occur in people who are involved in spiritual practices such as meditation, intense prayer, deep absorption, or concentration. Some people with fully awakened kundalini can activate it in other people. Kason believes "that once a kundalini pathway to the brain has been opened it never shuts down completely, and is much easier to reopen" (p. 144). In an earlier section of this chapter, I referred to a mystical experience as a Union of a person's soul with the divine. The meaning of the word *yoga* is "Union" or "to bind together."

Although this explanation of mysticism and encounters with the paranormal may seem different from my own concept that an NDE and mystical experiences involve a person's own Spirit, both concepts are spiritually based and nonreductionist. The chakras are part of our spiritual makeup, and the Eastern concept includes spirit bodies residing within the physical body, so I maintain that an energy flow would involve one or more of the spirit bodies, not simply a flow through the spine.

I maintain that Kason's book is a good summary of ancient concepts and modern research. I will condense her explanation of kundalini and other STEs. One of her principal sources is Gopi Krishna (1903–1984), who began having these experiences in the 1930s and who studied ancient texts to determine the cause of his sensations. He wrote numerous books on the topic; his most well-known one is *Kundalini: The Evolutionary Energy in Man*. Note that the Hindu religion is polytheistic. One of the gods is Krishna. When I use the name Krishna later in this section, I am referring to Gopi Krishna and not to the god. Although not mentioned by Kason, the term *Krishna consciousness* does refer to the god. Krishna predicted that as part of evolution, a higher number of people would begin to experience kundalini activity and its accompanying paranormal phenomena.

2. Kason's NDE

Kason is from Canada. Her 1979 NDE began during her medical residency, when she was assisting in a medical evacuation. A winter storm caused the plane in which she was traveling to crash-land on a partially frozen lake. Even before the plane crashed, she felt a "sense of peace, love, and the presence of God" (p. 6), and "everything was proceeding according to some divine plan and that there was nothing to fear" (p. 7). While in the water, she felt her consciousness leave her body and could observe her physical body struggling in the water. Then,

> I felt like I was being embraced by a universal, loving, and omnipotent intelligence. This was not an intellectual knowledge; it was a certainty that went to the very core of my being. The presence of this loving intelligence enveloped and overwhelmed to me. It was the most profoundly beautiful, blissful experience I have ever had in my life. I knew that everything was enfolding as it should. (p. 9)

While in the water, she tried to get on the ice but then heard an inner voice say that she should swim to shore. Obeying this voice is probably what enabled her to survive.

When she returned to work after a month of recovery and explained the above experience to her colleagues, most of them told her she was having hallucinations. However, one person informed her she had had a mystical experience.

3. Psychic Abilities

Shortly after Kason returned to work, she was going to visit a friend named Susan. While driving there, she had a vision of a brain coated with pus. When she arrived at Susan's home, she asked Susan how she was feeling. Susan replied that she had a headache. That symptom was consistent with Kason's vision that perhaps Susan was in an early stage of meningitis. When additional symptoms began that were consistent with frequent symptoms of meningitis, Susan went to her doctor and asked to be checked for meningitis; this ended up being the proper diagnosis. Kason felt that this was an example of the psychic experiences that began happening in her life after her NDE. Since then, she continues to have strong intuitive feelings and dramatic instances of clairvoyance and clairsentience. She also has a richer dream life and periods of luminosity.

The yoga term for psychic abilities is *siddhis*. These frequently occur after a kundalini awakening or another mystical experience. Many of the aftereffects of NDEs or paranormal phenomena associated with mystics are siddhis. These experiences are part of a long-term process of spiritual transformation. However, some people may have these psychic abilities as children and do not necessarily have an STE occur first. Kason's transformation actually began in 1976. She had her NDE in 1979 and continues to experience ongoing kundalini activity. At the same time, she maintains a well-adjusted, balanced life. While not explaining her religious views, Kason does frequently use the word *God* and recommends that people who are confused about their STEs read sacred scriptures of their own. It is not necessary to become a Hindu to believe in the reality of kundalini experiences.

Kason provides a list of various psychic experiences that occur during the process of spiritual transformation. These experiences include the following: "(1) abstract intuition [knowing the solution to a problem without taking the logical steps]; (2) astral travel; (3) automatic writing; (4) clairsentience; (6) clairvoyance; (7) psychic or spiritual healing; (8) out-of-body experiences; (9) past-life recall; (10) precognition; (11) psychometry [the ability to receive intuitive information about a person or an object by touching either the person or the object with one's hands]; (12) communication with spirit guides; (13) telekinesis; (14) telepyrokinesis [the ability to mentally start fires]; (15) telepathy; (16) trance channeling" (pp. 91–94). All of these abilities could be classified as being in the realm of the paranormal.

If a person is unaware that these things may happen after an STE, the incidents can be unsettling and confusing. For instance, clairsentience is the ability to sense a nearby person's agitated emotional state, which may result in physical symptoms. If the clairsentient person is unaware that he is attuned to another person, he may think the impressions are from his own body due to illness.

Kason warns that a person who begins to have these experiences has to be cautious. The person may become self-inflated, hold that psychically received information is always correct (it could be the result of wishful thinking from within the mind), and lack judgment as to when and with whom to share the information. In most cases, psychically received information should be balanced with normal discriminating intelligence.

Yogis hold that siddhis can be impediments to reaching the goal of enlightenment. This assertion can be difficult to evaluate. When discussing NDEs, it was often mentioned that a person found her purpose in life during the NDE. Perhaps a person develops the ability to heal others, and that is her purpose (rather than reaching a state of enlightenment). Kason also notes that some people may use psychic abilities to harm others.

4. Creativity and Spiritual Transformation

Regardless of whether it comes from kundalini awakening or from one's Spirit, Kason and I agree that inspired creativity comes from the spiritual realm. She mentions some individuals known for their creative minds who may not have been thought of as mystics but who nevertheless had indications of spiritual transformation.

- St. Hildegard of Bingen (1098–1179) experienced what she called a "reflection of the living light" (p. 117). She wrote beautiful music, poetry, plays, and books on natural history and medicine, and was also known for her artwork (she is classified as a polymath).
- Johannes Brahms (1833–1897) reported that he would formulate a desire to compose something that would uplift humanity and

then, when he was in an inspired mood, the finished product was revealed to him, measure by measure. He was not religious.

- Albert Einstein (1879–1955) wrote in *The World As I See It*, "I maintain that the cosmic religious experience is the strongest and noblest insightment to scientific research" (Kason, p. 118).

A person named Edward, whom Kason knew, had a desire to paint and would enter an altered state of consciousness (ASC; a trancelike state) when painting. He cannot paint commissioned work; the creative urge must come from his innermost self. His paintings are from nature but have an otherworldly luminosity. Edward frequently feels rushes of energy in his spine. Several other people who discussed their creative urges also felt they entered ASCs.

5. Characteristics of STEs

Kason cites William James's characteristics of religious experiences, but in reality he was analyzing STEs. His characteristics include (1) ineffability; (2) a noetic quality; (3) transiency; and (4) passivity. The term *ineffability*, previously mentioned in regard to NDEs, refers to an experience that is difficult to explain to another person who has not had one. The word *noetic* implies knowledge or understanding, not simply a feeling. The experience is transient in that it lasts only briefly in real time and its sense of wonder cannot be reproduced in memory. *Passivity* implies that the person is overwhelmed and does not feel in control of the process, but her life is modified afterward.

While earlier I mentioned several types of mystical experiences (e.g., the varieties listed by Sir Alastair Hardy in his RERU study), Kason also has a list of various types of STEs she has encountered in her study: (1) unitive experiences; (2) ecstatic or bliss episodes; (3) mystical visions; (4) expansive episodes; (5) spiritual rebirth; (6) illumination; and (7) dissolution experiences (p. 35-36).

6. Further Description of Kundalini

Kundalini energy is generally symbolized by *light* or fire. In the Tibetan Buddhist tradition it is called a *candali* or *Dumo fire*. A similar experience is described by various shamans and other religions. In the Christian tradition, the first instance of the Holy Spirit coming to the apostles was in the form of parted tongues of fire (Acts 2:1–4). NDE researcher P. M. H. Atwater discerns similarities between NDErs and Christians who claim an encounter with the Holy Spirit. Some of the "gifts" of the Holy Spirit can be compared to the aftereffects of any type of STE, including kundalini awakening. Although he did not specify these as from the Holy Spirit, the apostle Paul, in 1 Corinthians 12:28, speaks of some people in the early church as being prophets, some as teachers, some as performing miracles or healings, some as helping others, some as giving guidance, and some as speaking in tongues.

Christians often use the phrase *descent of the Holy Spirit*, which can be thought of as a downward flow of energy. Kason provides an example of a woman named Jyoti who described an experience that began when she heard a buzzing sound and when a *light* from above poured into the top of her head. The room seemed to glow, and four figures in white robes appeared. As the experience continued, she felt herself in a white swirling tunnel with a red sphere at the end of the tunnel. This description has similarities to an NDE, except that she was not near death.

Signs of a kundalini awakening include any of the following:

- Sensations of energy, heat, or *light* that rush up the spine and rise through the body toward the head and that sometimes involve intense sensations of sexual energy or spontaneous inner orgasms
- A perception of inner sound often likened to ringing, buzzing, the rushing of wings, or the roar of a waterfall [Moody mentions unusual sounds as one of the phases of an NDE.]
- Perception of intense white *light* or all-pervasive luminosity (p. 29)

In the classical awakening of kundalini, these physical and perceptual symptoms culminate in a profound mystical experience that can include Union with the divine, spiritual revelation, creative insight, prophetic or psychic visions, or a profound expansion of consciousness. Elsewhere, Kason lists cranial pressure as a possible symptom.

Kundalini operates in the following manner, according to Kason's interpretation of Krishna's writings. When kundalini is activated, a higher quantity and a more potent and refined form of *prana* is produced.

Prana, an energy of the yogic tradition, is similar to the kahuna idea of mana. It provides a fuel for the body. Prana is produced by the body from food but is also in the air we breathe. Several of the inedics previously discussed mentioned breathing in energy in order to survive without food. There is also a more potent fuel for transforming the brain called *ojas*. Ojas is normally in the sexual organs, but when kundalini is awakened, ojas is transmuted to a finer form and travels through the spinal cord to the brain. It activates a previously dormant region of the brain known as the *brahma randhra*, and then new brain functions develop, such as those previously listed as psychic experiences. Its specific region in the brain has not been identified. Although an individual can do activities to increase the chances of an awakening, according to Kason, the "Higher Power, God, or The Absolute drives the spiritual transformation through its loving, creative aspect" (p. 140).

7. Difficulties in Kundalini Awakening

There are numerous difficulties that can appear if this kundalini energy is not properly aroused. While the letter *E* in the acronym STE usually stands for "experience," it can also signify "emergence." In some cases, the phenomena encountered during kundalini awakening can become an "emergency." Some of the unexpected symptoms can appear similar to a psychosis. It was several psychiatrists familiar with kundalini who were able to insert a new diagnostic category into the *DSM-IV* called "Religious or Spiritual Problem." This was done so that some religious and spiritual issues are not pathologized.

Although the energy flowing up the spine was previously discussed, there are allegedly three possible channels. If the meditation procedure or posture is incorrect, the energy can flow through a side channel and create undesirable side effects. This happened to Krishna, as apparently his meditation caused the energy to flow up the right side, the *pingala*, which is associated with the sun and heat; consequently, he became very hot. He altered his meditation to emphasize the left side, the *ida*, which is associated with the moon and cold. This balanced his flow of energy so that it traveled up the central channel, the *sushama*, and he underwent an effulgent kundalini experience. This demonstrated to him that the body, mind, and spirit need to be equally prepared for awakening.

The various difficulties that are encountered after an initial STE can be divided into three broad categories: physical, psychological, and spiritual/paranormal. Some of the physical symptoms associated with STEs, especially kundalini, are as follows:

- Kriyas and sensations of pranic activity (jerking motions of various parts of the body, but not a seizure since there is no loss of consciousness)
- Undiagnosable body pains and chakra sensations
- Metabolic changes (one way to correct these is to eat smaller but more frequent meals)
- Changes in sleep patterns
- Changes in sexual energy (which can cause difficulty for one's partner)
- Energy fluctuations
- Yogic phenomenon (a spontaneous urge to assume yoga positions) (p. 179)

Kason notes that even if the person experiencing an STE follows good nutrition and other healthy practices, he or she may still end up dying from the same illnesses that other people die from. "It is a mistake to presume that intensive spiritual practices, positive thinking, or repeated affirmations make one immune to the biological laws of nature" (p. 198).

Kason divides psychological symptoms of kundalini into positive and negative changes. The positive ones include the following:

- Maturation of the personality
- Spontaneous abandonment of self-destructive habits (such as consuming illegal drugs and alcohol)
- Reevaluation of jobs
- Reevaluation of relationships
- Resolution of psychological blocks
- Setting healthier interpersonal boundaries
- Absolute belief in the existence of a higher power
- Loss of the fear of death
- Being inspired by the memory
- Increased humanitarianism, love, and empathy

- Increased altruism
- Increased morality
- Decreased materialism
- Increased spiritual focus and deeper spiritual insights
- Increased intuitiveness
- Increased creativity
- A belief in the reality of one's spiritual experiences (pp. 201–3)

Kason prefers to use the term *challenging* rather than *negative* when describing symptoms. The challenging psychological symptoms of STEs include the following:

- Anxiety
- Confusion
- Mental dulling
- Fixation with experiences
- Despair that the STEP has ended
- Rebound depression and lassitude
- Decreased capacity to love
- Fear of losing control
- Fear that one is dying
- Fear of going insane
- Fear of possession
- Fear of the Devil
- Inexplicable mood swings
- Cyclothymia (mild bipolar disorder)
- Intensification of unresolved psychological issues
- Emotional distress
- Gender identity crisis
- Poor ability to control increased sexual urges (pp. 205–8)

Relatedly, Kason does not mention it as part of psychological issues, but earlier she comments that "shadow" tendencies that everyone has, such as anger, fear, guilt, shame, and selfishness, are often thrown from the subconscious to the conscious mind in people undergoing STEs.

Just as there can be positive and challenging psychological symptoms after an STE, the same applies to spiritual/paranormal symptoms. Spiritual and paranormal symptoms can be divided into five broad categories: "(1) the mystical and the spiritual; (2) kundalini; (3) the psychic and paranormal; (4) changes in dream life, and (5) changes in visual perception" (p. 216). They are more likely to appear in people involved in spiritual practices and are more marked during or after STEs.

Under the category of mystical and spiritual, some of the positive symptoms are, in effect, demonstrating that a person is undergoing transformation. These include "bliss, Union, higher guidance, divine inspiration, [and] expansions of consciousness" (pp. 217–18). Kason considers higher guidance to be the most common one. The voice she heard during her NDE saying that she should swim to shore is an example.

There are only two negative spiritual symptoms listed, namely, negative visions and evil presences. For visions, they are obviously sightings of alleged devils, demons, or evil spirits, but an evil presence is simply something felt and not seen. The two cases of such presences that Kason mentions both occurred at night and then left when the person turned on a light and began to pray. She also recommends positive affirmations, such as affirming the presence of the Divinity in oneself. In chapter 8, I discussed that one of our spirit bodies is termed an astral body. In the yogic tradition, there are also levels within an "astral plane," where spirits of various types may reside. The lower astral planes may include demonic presences. It is speculated that people undergoing spiritual transformation may be more open to these lower levels, while primarily being open to beneficial realms of various types. Others conjecture that people who have distressing NDEs may be visiting these lower astral planes. Kason warns that people should not experiment with dark forces in any manner.

Kason classifies the negative psychic symptoms of STEs as disorders. These include "painful clairsentience [tapping into the physical or emotional pain of a nearby person], excessive clairvoyance, intrusive past-life memories, horrific visions [similar to negative spiritual symptoms], possession, channeling disorders, and psychic assault or telepathic invasion" (pp. 230–32). Kason notes that these can also result from "dabbling with occult powers" (p. 236). She adds that religious traditions have emphasized that psychic gifts are by-products of spiritual development and should not be striven after for their own sake. To clarify, not everyone who has psychic experiences is undergoing spiritual transformation.

Kason lists various strategies to cope with psychic disorders. Although she lists these as strategies for psychic disorders, I believe they would also assist with negative physical and psychological symptoms. The coping strategies include "adapting a more grounding lifestyle [temporarily suspending meditation, concentration, yoga, or tai chi, and doing more physical exercise]; visualize your chakras retracting and closing; visualize a protective bubble; cleansing negative energy; remove yourself from negative environments; mitigate horrific visions; attune yourself to God only; and pray for protection" (pp. 236–38).

With regard to changes in dream life as a result of a STEP, Kason reports that some people spontaneously develop "lucid dreams—the ability to be consciously aware of the dream while it is going on and to alter or influence the path the dream is taking" (p. 239). STErs may also notice synchronicities in dreams, may receive answers or solutions to problems in dreams, and may dream in color. The changes in visual perception often mean that the person is seeing finer and more beautiful details in scenes of nature. These would be classified as positive changes rather than difficulties.

When any of the previously discussed ranges or spectrums of symptoms becomes a crisis, the person may be thought to be psychotic. Kason refers to such individuals as being in a "healing crisis," and she says that they do not indicate that anything is necessarily wrong with them. In many cases the individual realizes that any voices heard or visions are not real, unlike schizophrenics who cannot distinguish between inner and outer reality. Kason presents the following table to distinguishes a spiritual emergency from a psychosis (table 5, p. 248).

TABLE **7.1.** Contrasts between a Spritual Emergency and Psychosis

Spiritual Emergency	Psychosis
Challenged by experiences	Overwhelmed by experiences
Great difficulty functioning	Unable to function

Thought processes clear	Thought processes incoherent or contain loose associations
Transient grandiose ideas	Delusions of grandeur
Difficulty separating inner and outer realities	Unable to distinguish inner and outer realities
Aware at some level that experiences are part of an inner process	Has paranoid delusions and projects cause of experiences onto others
Fears losing control	Is out of control
Exhibits mildly unusual behaviors	Exhibits inappropriate behaviors including outwardly destructive acts, self-destructive acts, disorganized behaviors, fixed obsessions
Able to tolerate negative visions	Overwhelmed by horrific visions
Can ignore voices heard	Overwhelmed by voices heard
Fairly appropriate emotional responses	Inappropriate emotional responses
Difficulty making discerning judgments	Unable to make discerning judgments
Moral and ethical values remain intact	Moral and ethical values may be lost

When people are having these challenges, they often have the following predisposing factors, which need to be corrected or adjusted. The factors are as follows: "1. Out of balance lifestyle; 2. Extremely intensive spiritual practices; 3. Extremely intensive concentration; 4. Inadequate psychological 'housecleaning'; 5. Unblocking unresolved psychological issues from perceived past lives [some psychologists who do not believe in past lives still considered the memories as meaningful symbolic metaphors.]; 6. Excessive greed and desire for wealth; 7. Excessive ambition and lust for power; 8. Fixation on psychic gifts; 9. Unresolved conflicts with the God concept; 10. Turning to the dark side; 11. Unresolved spiritual guilt; 12. Terminal illness; 13. Hereditary factors" (pp. 259–67). The first two are the most common.

8. Some Explanations of and Conclusions about STEs

Kundalini experiences provide a possible (but probably unprovable) explanation for how NDErs can remain healthy when their NDEs are caused by suffocation, with potential long-term oxygen deprivation. Suffocation may activate the kundalini mechanism, and the energy stream may protect the brain from oxygen deprivation, preventing permanent brain damage.

It is easy to see a comparison between the *incendium amoris* of some mystics and Gopi Krishna's body becoming hot when the energy was not traveling up the middle channel of his spine. Krishna seemed distressed by the situation, but Padre Pio seemingly considered his own being hot as an inconvenience but not distressful. It would be interesting to research the lives of numerous mystics/saints to see if they reported energy in their spine. The documents presenting research into the lives of saints are generally written in Latin.

Kason's conclusion from her study of kundalini is "that we are fundamentally spiritual beings living in a multidimensional universe. Further, the purpose of our physical existence on earth is to provide an opportunity for our souls to learn spiritual lessons and grow" (p. 152). She would like to see the day when society promotes the lifestyle factors needed for healthy spiritual growth.

F. Classical Mysticism

1. Introduction

Evelyn Underhill's (1875–1941) *Mysticism: A Study in the Nature and Development of Spiritual Consciousness* was first published in 1911 (the 1961 edition is used as a reference here). The book has two parts: "The Mystic Fact" and "The Mystic Way." The person who is on the Mystic Way may be thought of as going from the World of Becoming to the World of Being. Underhill was a mystic and thus wrote from an insider's perspective. Her book is the most well-known writing on the subject. She notes that writings by scholars of mysticism are usually attempting to discuss a place they have never been. She does not mention her own mystical experiences but mainly reviews writings and experiences of famous mystics. Some information comes from people who are not necessarily thought of as mystics. For instance, Dante Alighieri (1265–1321), the author of *The Divine Comedy*, may be thought of as a poet, but the spiritual journey he describes is a poetic equivalent to many mystic experiences. Underhill frequently quotes him.

Underhill sometimes uses quotations but does not specify the author. Perhaps in her day many readers would recognize a well-known phrase without the author's name. For example, one of the phrases she uses is, "The heart has its reasons which the mind knows not of," which was earlier expressed by Blaise Pascal (1623–1662). He was a famous mathematician (the originator of Pascal's triangle), scientist/physicist (studying hydrodynamics), and inventor (of an early calculator). In 1654 he had a mystical vision and thereafter devoted most of the rest of his life to theology and metaphysics. He wrote this vision down and carried it with him. It was found after his death and is titled *Memorial*. He claimed the vision was the result of a carriage accident, and thus he may have had an NDE. His most famous spiritual writing, often classified as a masterpiece of mystical writing, is titled *Pensees* (*Thoughts*). He led an ascetic lifestyle, a common practice for many mystics.

In her part titled "A Mystic Fact," Underhill discusses mysticism in relationship to psychology, theology, magic, allegory, and philosophy. "In theological language, their [mystics'] theory of knowledge is that the spirit of man, itself essentially divine, is capable of immediate communion with God, the One Reality" (p. 24). She notes that although all mystics may arrive at the same destination, there are many aspects and descriptions of the various stages that may appeal to one temperament or another. She uses the analogy that all of them may have been to the same country but may speak different languages. She maintains that apprehension of that other world is humanity's most sublime end.

Underhill employs various terms to describe the unceasing desire for the who or the what with whom or with which the final Union is made. The most common terms, or its qualities, are "Absolute," "Real," and "Reality." Other terms (almost always beginning with capital letters), in addition to simply "God," include the following:

- All
- Good or Goodness
- Beauty or Beautiful
- True
- Absolute Truth

- Absolute Beauty
- The Perfect or Perfection
- The One
- Perfect One
- Pure Being
- Pure Love
- Divine Love
- Divine Companion
- Divine Embrace
- Divine Transcendence
- Divine Wisdom (Sophia)
- Eternal Wisdom
- Eternity
- Source
- That Which Is
- Object
- Infinite
- Uncreated Light
- Indwelling Light
- Beatific Vision

Two terms may seem a contrast to those just listed, "Divine Dark" and "Abyss." Some of the terms may have been emphasized by just one particular mystic. For instance, Plotinus (205–270) frequently employed the term *the One*. Meister (German for "Master") Eckhart (Eckhart von Hochheim, 1260–1327) and St. John of the Cross refer to it as *the All*. I may switch between these terms, using whichever ones I think appropriate when expressing my opinion and not be reiterating the term used by Underhill.

Underhill comments that many mystics gain insight about the Absolute from the mysteries of nature. Their cycles have "this power of unleashing the human soul" (p. 191). Mystics may describe their system to reach Union, but they never describe the result. "No direct description of spiritual experience is or can be possible to man. It must always be symbolic, allusive, oblique" (p. 126). Studying about mysticism is not the same thing as being a mystic who achieves Union. Mystics' messages and methods to reach Union are timeless. The Mystic Way is a long-term process for reaching the final stage. Underhill does not mention people who seem to have spontaneous mystical experiences, such as NDEs.

2. The Mystic Fact

Underhill mentions mystics in numerous religions including Judaism (kabbalism), paganism, Islam, and infrequently Zen Buddhism and the Hindu yogic tradition. Historically, she goes back as far as Heraclitus (ca. 535–475 BCE) and Plato (423–347 BCE). According to Underhill, the vast majority of mystics of the great religions remained faithful to the religion they belonged to before their mystical pilgrimages. She was a Christian and a convert to Catholicism, so she may have emphasized Christian mystics. Perhaps, because she was a Christian, Underhill maintains that a church does not have to be in conflict with mystical views of the spiritual world. Many contemporary self-styled New Age mystics would probably disagree with that view. As she says, mystics who reject religion often develop pantheistic viewpoints and seldom exhibit the richness of the unitive life. She provides no explanation for that determination. Underhill maintains that mysticism is about spiritual life and should not be confused with "occultism, dilute transcendentalism, vapid symbolism, religious or aesthetic sentimentality and bad metaphysics. [Instead, it is] the expression of the innate tendency of the human spirit toward complete harmony with the transcendental order" (preface).

Since the term *Ego* is often used in describing mysticism, Underhill simply states that Ego is the normal self-conscious subject writing or reading her book. This would include performing activities referred to as "subliminal," which are actually unconscious parts of the Ego. This may also be thought of as the Self. She notes that the sense world is only Self's projection. Thus, "the evidence of the senses, then, cannot be accepted as evidence of the nature of ultimate reality: useful servants, they are dangerous guides" (p. 6). Her argument would be that what mystics encounter is as likely to be reality as input from the senses. However, an argument may be that mystics' perceptions are subjective whereas sense perceptions are generally the same in all people. She might counter that mystic perceptions are identical; it is only when translating the experience to our normal sense world that dissimilar expressions are employed. A mystic is striving to escape the bondage or barriers of the sense world so that the Absolute may flow in. Mystics deny that knowledge is limited to sense impressions, processes of the intellect, or normal consciousness.

Underhill mentions a perception that may have been considered unusual at the time she was writing. The perception was reported by a visionary named St. Martin. He said he heard flowers and saw notes that shone. Underhill also mentions, without specific names, other mystics whose senses were "fused into a single and ineffable act of perception, and color and sound are known as aspects of one thing" (p. 7). This unusual feature resembles synesthesia (confused sense impressions), which occurs in some individuals after an NDE. However, some mystics simply hold that in heavenly music is how they encounter the Absolute. Underhill maintains that music and poetry, with their qualities of beauty and rhythm, are unlikely to contribute to physical evolution. Therefore, they must be contributing to the spiritual/mystical aspect of humans, which is the crown of human evolution.

3. Psychology of Mysticism

In technical language, the mystic is proceeding from one level of consciousness to another, that is, from the ordinary realm to the transcendental realm. "Its [the mystic's soul] life is enhanced, the barrier of personality is broken, man escapes the sense world to the apex of his spirit, and enters briefly into the more extended life of the All" (p. 74). According to Underhill, the attainment of this higher consciousness must be actively sought. Mystics in contemplation may appear passive, but they are actually in a state of intense activity. While the mystical state may be thought of as a "higher" consciousness, it is actually reaching the "depths" of the soul.

Underhill considers there to be two major aspects of Reality that a mystic seeks to discover. In one, the mystics consider themselves to be part of Divine Life and thus connected to all of living reality in the immanent universe. An example of this might be the Franco Zeffirelli 1972 film made about the life of St. Francis of Assisi that was titled from terms the saint used, namely, *Brother Sun, Sister Moon*. Other mystics consider themselves to be connected to the utterly Transcendent, or God, and not connected to the temporal world at all.

In seeking these ends, mystics most often encounter opposites. To find the *light*, they must experience darkness; to find good, evil; to find joy, sorrow; and to find life, death. The purification and dark night can be painful steps that alternate with the pleasurable steps. The soul, in its ascending spiral toward reality, must experience sunshine and shade. However, with regard to transcendence and immanence, Underhill says these are not antithetical but rather that they consolidate and enrich each other.

In discussing psychology, Underhill reviews behavior from the standpoint of emotion, intellect, and will. While modern psychologists may use the first two terms, the word *will* has been rarely discussed by reductionist-based behaviorists over the last 50 years. Underhill believes will is important because desire for the mystical goal is not an intellectual effort. The intellect is analytical, not exploratory. The passion for the Object comes from the heart ("the innermost sanctuary of personal being" [p. 117]), not from the intellect. Ultimately, the quest transcends the emotional, intellectual, and volitional life of ordinary people. The desire to meet the Absolute has been discussed by philosophers, poets, and religions for centuries but can never truly be explained other than as the innate tendency of the soul toward its Source. In addition to the desire, the individual on a mystic path must have "an appropriate psychological makeup, ... capable of extraordinary concentration, and exalted moral emotion, a nervous organization of the artistic type" (p. 91). Mystical achievement "is at once an act of love, an act of surrender, and an act of supreme perception" (p. 84). While many people in the modern world speak of freedom in a political or economic sense, to a mystic it means more that each human has free will and can make choices in his or her life.

Underhill notes that artists, poets, composers, and inventors are also able to reach the creative aspects that manifest through contact with Cosmic Life. This is in agreement with the contention of my book. Some mystics report that their writings were composed through automatic writing. The person would become very uncomfortable if he or she ignored the urge to write. Mystical poet William Blake reported that some of his memorable writings ("Milton" and "Jerusalem") were dictated to him. In many works, the conscious self cooperates with the subliminal self. An example of a famous work that came from rapid, deep insight is *Messiah*, which George Frideric Handel composed in 24 days.

4. Mysticism and Theology

Underhill employs the terms *emanations* and *immanence*. Holders of the emanation theory of reaching the Absolute believe it is a long journey of multiple steps. Believers of the immanence theory hold that the ultimate goal is within the self ("The Kingdom of Heaven is within you" [Luke 17:21]). Underhill states that the latter theory can sometimes degrade into pantheism. Overall, theology plays only a small part in a mystic's quest.

5. Mysticism and Symbolism

Symbolism has already been discussed briefly, but Underhill considers there to be three great classes of symbols for transcendence of the sense world, each of which appeals to a different temperament. These are: (1) a craving to be a pilgrim or wanderer in search of a lost home; (2) the craving of the heart for a perfect mate (a mystical marriage); and (3) the craving for inward purity and perfection. The ultimate goal of Union remains the same; only the descriptions differ. Each of these, in turn, may be affected by the transcendent/external view or the immanent/internal view.

As Underhill contends, "The homeward journey of man's spirit, then, may be thought of as due to the push of the divine life within, answering to the pull of the divine life without" (pp. 132–33). Thus, although the goal is usually portrayed as people's quest for God or the Absolute, in reality the Absolute is just as much seeking each person. It is Reality's quest for the unwilling self. God needs each person as much as each person needs God. It is a mutual desire. That is why the parable of the prodigal son (Luke 15:11–32) is one of the Christian mystics' favorite parables. The Father is as much seeking Union with each person as the person is seeking to separate himself from the material world and find Union with the Father. This relationship is also described in the famous poem of Francis Thompson (1869–1907), "The Hound of Heaven," and by many prominent mystics.

For those seeking a perfect mate, the Song of Songs (Song of Solomon) is considered an allegory of the spiritual life. The term *Divine Companion* may be employed by people of this temperament. There are often four stages for this process: betrothal, the marriage, the wedlock, and the fruitfulness of the soul. These have nothing to do with sexuality.

Those involved in the search for inward purity and perfection often note moral changes or moral transcendence within themselves as their spiritual consciousness grows. In Underhill's words, "He has seen the Perfect; he wants to be perfect too" (p. 90). It is not sentimental or affective piety. Those of this temperament often use the symbols of alchemy to describe their quest. A "Philosopher's Stone" is an example of a perfect and incorrupt substance. A mystic must turn his imperfect self into spiritual gold in order to meet God. However, this perfection is not just moral perfection but also a transmuting of one's life to a new form. The final stage is the fusion of the human spirit and the Divine Spirit. In addition to those classes of symbols, Underhill notes that mystics may represent their goal as a place (my examples of a beautiful garden for NDErs), a person (Beatrice for Dante), or a state (not explained by Underhill; a possible example is the Upper World of shamans).

6. Mysticism and Magic

Underhill states that during periods of "true mystical activity we find an outbreak of occultism, illuminism, or other perverted spirituality" (p. 149). Among these, she includes the Gnostics, Brethren of the Free Spirit, Manichean and Quietist heresies, the Rosicrucians, Christian kabbalists, and Theosophy. However, later she does cite as legitimate some of the writings of Madame Guyon (1648–1717), who was often associated with the Quietists.

Underhill maintains that there are two fundamental attitudes toward the unseen. On one side, mysticism shades off into religion; on the other, religion shades off into magic. "No deeply religious man is without a touch of mysticism; and no mystic can be other than religious, in a psychological if not theological sense of the word" (p. 70). The difference between the two is that magic/occultism wants to get while mysticism wants to give. Both types impart to their followers powers unknown to ordinary people, but "the ends to which the powers are applied differ enormously" (p. 70). In mysticism, the will is united with the emotions to transcend the sense world. "In magic, the will unites with the intellect in an impassioned desire for supersensible knowledge" (p. 71). The latter may come from a desire to help others by acquiring knowledge, but it may also involve power. It includes praying for rain or the healing of a disease. The true mystic simply wants to reach the Absolute (passion for love for love's sake) but may have these other abilities (control of weather, healing) as an incidental talent. Practitioners of magic want to know, whereas true mystics desire to be. They are not self-seeking or in the pursuit of supernatural joy or transcendental satisfaction. The mystic obtains satisfaction because she does not seek it.

7. The Mystic Way

Underhill lists several stages or classifications along the Mystic Way. These are the awakening of the self, the purification of the self, the illumination of the self, introversion (divided into recollection and quiet and contemplation), ecstasy and rapture, and the dark night of the soul. A final section is on the unitive life; this is not a stage but rather a description of how life is different after unity is reached. However, these stages are a typical format or composite portrait, and each person is on an individual path that may not include some of the above and may include others—or the order may vary. There is no set time period for each stage. As mentioned earlier, NDErs may enter at the illumination stage, and some may experience illumination immediately after their awakening. Eastern religions (which to Underhill would include Sufism) speak of one further stage of annihilation, or reabsorption of the individual soul into the Infinite. She prefers to describe it for Christians as the transformation of the self in God and thus as serving God by engaging in activities to assist fellow humans.

A term that Underhill frequently uses is *orison*. The dictionary definition is simply "prayer," but Underhill implies a more profound form of absorption or communication than simply rote prayers or petitions. Orison has no form; it is not articulated. The final stage of the mystic is sometimes referred to as the orison of Union.

A number of mystics have described their methods as travel, usually upward travel. St. John Climacus, a seventh-century saint of the Eastern Church, titled his writing *The Ladder of Spiritual Ascent*. Underhill considers mysticism as "an ordered movement towards ever higher levels of reality, ever closer identification with the Infinite" (pp. 81–82). Some mystics think of this ascension as a slope rather than as distinct stages.

a. The Awakening of the Self

This first stage on the Mystic Way is not an ordinary religious conversion involving acceptance of theological beliefs. Instead, it is a shifting of consciousness from lower to higher levels to an object brought into view. It is "an alteration in the self's attitude to the world" (p. 177). Once a person is conscious of Reality, he cannot evade it. Most people to whom this happens already have common religious views. To some, the changes are gradual and increase in lucidity without a crisis of any kind to precipitate the increase. More frequently, though, the change is abrupt and follows a crisis. Underhill mentions St. Paul's conversion and notes that many mystics felt a period of restlessness and mental stress in their lives prior to their conversion. This conversion often involves three characteristics: "a sense of liberation and victory; a conviction of the nearness of God; a sentiment of love towards God" (p. 179). When this happens, a number of people seek assistance from a spiritual advisor. Many advisors are helpful, but perhaps some potential mystics do not find a competent advisor and are hampered in their journey.

b. The Purification of the Self

Purification or purgation means much more than eliminating what might be called a sinful life. It implies getting rid of the elements of normal experience that are part of the old illusion of the prime importance of the physical world and that are not harmonious with the new Reality. A person's heart must be free of desire, free from the fetters of the senses, and set entirely on Pure Good. The self must be purged of any attachment that stands between itself and goodness. Chief among these may be pride and self-centeredness. A number of mystics have taken to fasting or engaging in other mortifications to remove desires of the flesh. These are part of the alternate phases of pleasure and pain.

Purification is divided into two phases: detachment and mortification. Detachment is in turn divided into poverty, chastity, and obedience. Poverty is detachment from all finite things, immaterial as well as material. True mystics can claim nothing as their own, can have no conflicting interests, and can seek nothing less than God. Things that conflict with purification can include riches, habits, religious observances, friends, or any desire. Detachment is a mental, rather than a material, state. These distractions dissipate the energy required to meet the goal. Most Catholic religious orders, such as the Franciscans, Dominicans, and Jesuits, require their members to take vows of poverty, chastity, and obedience.

c. Illumination

The topic of illumination is interesting, because many NDErs begin at this phase. Underhill considers it to be the most exalted form of catharsis on the path to the Transcendent; it is temporary consciousness that they are in a God-centered world. The person who is illuminated has a loving and joyous relationship with the Absolute, but still his individuality remains separate, distinct, and intact. The person has pierced the veil and no longer needs to believe in this other reality; he knows it exists. "To say that God is Infinite is to say that He may be apprehended and described in an infinity of ways" (p. 238).

Underhill maintains that all real artists are sharers in the illuminated life. After an initial experience of illumination, the hunger for the Absolute becomes even greater. This new reality apprehended by the heart is often best conveyed to others in artistic form. Underhill mentions the music heard by many of those illuminated but then states that true Union can never be described by using any form or image. However, the best analogies often have a rhythm to them, such as music or poetry. "The mystery of music is seldom realized by those who so easily accept its gifts. Yet of all the arts music alone shares with great mystical literature the power of waking in the response to the life movement of the universe: brings us—we know not how—news of its exultant passions and its incomparable peace. Beethoven heard the very voice of Reality, and little of it escaped when he translated it for our ears" (p. 77).

There are three main characteristics that appear as a result of illumination, each characteristic not necessarily appearing in each person. The first characteristic is an apprehension of the Absolute or a sense of the presence of God, albeit less than full Union. The person may seem to see, feel, and think all at once and be in orison. The effect of the temperament of the person is especially evident in the form the Absolute takes in this illumination phase.

The second characteristic is an enhanced view of the world, a mental lucidity in which all of creation is transfigured. There is a cleansing of the doors of perception as people enter higher levels of consciousness and they are freed from domination by the senses. The third characteristic is that there is an extension of consciousness as a result of the dialogue with another intelligence, and this may result in voices, visions, and automatic writing. In addition, the illumined person may experience peace, but a peace "not of idleness, but over ordered activity" (p. 264).

d. Voices and Visions

Underhill goes extensively into voices and visions, which may easily be confused with malevolent hallucinations associated with abnormal behavior. Many mystics warn against attributing too much significance to these and accepting them as the voice of God, but they also emphasize that they cannot be ignored or avoided. Voices and visions may be the "effort of the self to translate something impressed upon its deeper being" (p. 269).

While voices and visions are the most common form, the impressions can be from other senses. Some of these have previously been discussed under the subhead "Physical Phenomena," such as sweet perfumes and tastes, sensations of touch, and inward fire. They may include "radiant appearances of our Lady" (p. 269) and thus may be a possible explanation for alleged apparitions of the Virgin Mary at various sites such as Lourdes and Fatima. When these nonphysical sensations occur, they leave the individual better off—physically, mentally, and spiritually—which is opposed to those sensations connected to mental illness. For instance, the voices may bring calm to a person in turmoil or doubt. Nevertheless, mystics who generally experience enhanced visions or voices may occasionally experience frightful ones. A number of saints have had visions of Satan.

The voices heard may be of three types: a difficult-to-define, inarticulate voice; an articulate voice, but one recognized as being only within the mind; and an exterior voice heard by the outward ear. These correspond to the three types of visions: intellectual, imaginary, and corporeal. These voices may bring fresh or eternal truths and are not rearrangements of thoughts. They are clearly understood and cannot be misinterpreted, a similar point noted by many NDErs when they have conversations in the transcendental realm. In some mystics, the voices seemingly take the form of a dialogue between the mystic's soul and Divine Reality. A number of mystics had had voices and visions as children before they began on their path to unity.

St. Hildegard of Bingen reported that her revelations came to her in "an instant." She would sometimes begin a statement with words that sounded like those of an Old Testament prophet: "Thus saith the Living Light" (p. 276). Likewise, one of St. Bridget of Sweden's (1303–1373) books came to her in "a flash." St. Teresa of Avila's reform movement was guided by her voices. Underhill also mentions the voices that guided St. Joan of Arc (1412–1431), for which she was burned at the stake as a heretic by religious representatives controlled by her enemies. I have often wondered why the Absolute would care who was ruling France. Perhaps the Absolute sometimes responds to the desire of an individual, for example, Joan's yearning to have a French king, while at other times the choice is made by the Absolute. It is acceptable to make these intuitions subject to analysis by the conscious mind, but they are best not ignored. Conceivably, the voices or visions could be expressing the desires of the emotional aspect of the person and not come from Divine Wisdom and thus be untrustworthy.

A more controversial topic than voices and visions is the aspect of the mystical gift of automatic writing. A similar concept was discussed in the chapter on NDEs. This is more than having an irresistible impulse to write and then having to consciously think of what to write. In true automatic writing, the hand of the person becomes the agent of another personality. Automatic writing may take two forms: one in which the person listens and writes down what she hears, or one in which the writing instrument is totally controlled by the hand without the involvement of the surface mind. Although called automatic writing by Underhill and many others, a modern term for it is *channeling*, much of the product of which is of questionable value. An example of the hearing variety is that St. Catherine of Siena dictated some of her writings while in a state of ecstasy. Those writings, characteristic of subliminal energy, appeared "dissociated from the criticism and control of normal consciousness" (p.

294). William Blake credits his writings to his "celestial friends." After their altered state of consciousness, some mystics were astonished at what they had written. Some wrote at immense speed. Madame Guyon had this ability. One scribe could not rewrite in five days what she had written in one night. Once, a part of her writings was lost and she rewrote it. The original was then found and was determined to be identical, word for word, to the original.

e. Introversion

Although Underhill is mainly describing higher levels of consciousness as she proceeds through her description of the mystic process, on introversion she discusses the various thought processes but does not indicate their relative importance. While voices and visions are communication to the mystic, contemplation is withdrawal of attention from the external world, an emptying of all that is unreal, in order to perceive the nonmaterial world. It is an imageless apprehension (supernatural intercourse) between the soul and the Absolute, between Lover and Beloved. During introversion, "A mysterious fusion of divine and human life takes place" (p. 304). It is meeting God without an intermediary. As I interpret it, voices and visions are not part of this communication but serve to provide guidance to the mystic.

Mystics need to discipline their minds to be able to concentrate or focus their attention. There may be brief flashes of insight, but steady progress to higher levels of consciousness requires training of the will and progressive concentration, as do other forms of genius. Thus, many mystics read the guidance provided by previous mystics or have a spiritual advisor who is familiar with the process. The process of contemplating may begin by simply focusing attention on a physical object, be it a natural object, such as a tree, or a human-made object, such as a picture or statue. According to Underhill's description, after a while the barrier between the object's life and one's own will melt away, beyond what normal surface intelligence discerns. Some people may be born mystics, but that does not make the task of contemplation less difficult for them. After practice, the person may spontaneously enter a contemplative state. In this supersensual activity, messages from the senses or reason need to be refused in order to make the journey to the invisible at the center.

Full contemplation is associated with the Unitive Way. When a person has reached full contemplation, he is capable of temporary, but not permanent, Union with the Absolute. If all knowledge of the external world is lost, the person may enter a state of trance, where personality is lost as it merges with Reality. A mystic may enter involuntarily states of rapture or ecstasy, but these are actually different from contemplation. While it may be mentioned in other states, the concept of eternity—no past or future, but only the ever-present now—is most noticeable in contemplation. It is also in contemplation that the term *Divine Dark* is often mentioned, but this is not the same as the *dark night of the soul*, which will be discussed later.

f. Ecstasy and Rapture

Ecstasy comes at the point where the concentration of interest on the Transcendent is so complete that the person becomes unconscious of the external world. It is contemplation carried to its highest pitch and a necessary prelude to unification, but it can be difficult to determine the difference between ecstasy and Union. The person describing either state is using metaphors that are enigmatic. Psychologically, it is sometimes referred to as complete monoideism, the absorption of the self into one idea. For the mystic, though, it represents an exalted act of perception. Consciousness escapes the limitations of the senses. This phase is evident in mystics of all religions and in shamans. There are three noticeable aspects of the ecstatic state: physical, psychological, and mystical.

Some of the physical changes are that the body becomes rigid, even cataleptic, and the breathing rate is reduced. In this manner, a state of ecstasy may mimic the symptoms of some brain disorders or mental illnesses, such as epilepsy or schizophrenia, in which the rigid state is referred to as catatonia. Thus, by itself, ecstasy is no guarantee of spiritual value. In addition, there is often complete anesthesia for pain when pricked or burned. In some cases, the symptoms of the pricking or burning may appear when the mystic returns from ecstasy, but in other cases there is no evidence of injury. Thus, the value of ecstasy is only in the inward grace that comes to the true mystic. However, even some of the great mystics have had periods of psychopathic ecstasy, especially during periods of poor health. The symptoms of catalepsy were so severe in some mystics that they were assumed to have died. If the changes occur gradually, the state is called ecstasy, but if they occur suddenly it is called rapture. Ecstasy usually occurs when the mystic voluntarily begins contemplation. Rapture may often be involuntary, and the mystics perceive themselves as unable to prevent it.

Rapture often begins with the appearance of an idea, such as a word or symbol of the Divinity from the person's religion, for example a crucifix for a Christian. In either case, the person may be described as being in a trance. Ecstasy occurs in virtually all mystics, but rapture occurs in only a few. Rapture is "an indication of disharmony between the subject's psychophysical make-up and his transcendental powers" (p. 376). Levitation may occur in either ecstasy or rapture, but it is more commonly associated with the latter. Some mystics in rapture do have sense impressions that are diminished, for example, they hear as if from a distance away.

g. The Dark Night of the Soul

The phrase *dark night of the soul* was originated by St. John of the Cross to describe an extended period in which, after the mystic seems to have developed a regular relationship with the Absolute, there is misery, emptiness, darkness, stagnation, and the loss of orison. This dark night is one of the oscillations between states of pleasure and pain. The previous pain stage was a purgation/purification. The dark-night stage is difficult, as the person has already been with the *light* and is concerned that God has deliberately (possibly permanently) withdrawn his presence. The self may begin to question the path of forsaking the desires the natural world has to offer. This stage may last for months or years. St. Teresa described it as feeling like she was suspended in midair, unable to reach either the earth or heaven. The frightful voices and visions that were previously mentioned are part of the dark night of the soul. Eventually, miseries and disharmonies of the dark night give way to rays of *light*.

h. The Unitive Life

According to Underhill, the standard description of the Unitive Life is that "man's will is united with God" (p. 376). The lives of individuals to whom this happened need to be investigated. They are our ambassadors to the Absolute, as they are no longer separate from it. They may live in the world, but they are not of it.

As previously discussed, there are two broad categories that accomplished mystics used to describe this ineffable relationship after Union. Those who hold that the Absolute is impersonal and transcendent describe the process as deification, the transmutation of the Self in God. The holders of the immanent concept view it as a communion of their soul with God, the previously cited spiritual marriage.

Within either category, the mystic notes that his life is now in conjunction with the interests of the Infinite. Although aligned with the Infinite, the mystic feels he has complete freedom to choose how he will bring beneficial changes to fruition by assisting humanity in charitable works or creative endeavors. Reaching the destiny of Union allows a mystic to be. His accomplishments are the fulfillment of a desire to love others after experiencing so much love from the Absolute. Mystics also seem to have a childlike gaiety and to demonstrate playfulness and joy. Songs or other music composed by mystics are about joy and love.

G. Mystical Experiences and Spirit

Another possible tile for my book would be *The Spectrums of Spirituality*. I would now like to provide evidence that there is a spectrum of levels in the Upper World that affects our view of the nature of this other reality. The similarities within the spectrum, despite disparate outward circumstances, demonstrate that these are human spiritual experiences and not figments of the imagination. The differences reveal these to be individual experiences within a common framework that provide for the spiritual growth of each individual; that is, what is the most desirable for one person may not be appropriate for another person. These experiences also demonstrate that the transcendental world needs to be expressed in myths, metaphors, allegories, or symbolic language.

Although this section will not provide a complete explanation of the Spirit, I will explain how my concept of Spirit relates to mysticism or other STEs and to a spectrum of spiritual levels in the Upper World. While throughout this book I have offered my opinions or interpretations, I will do so here more frequently.

In the first chapter of this book, I explained that I am using an eclectic approach. That is, if one aspect of some psychological approach appears to fit my findings, I use it, even if all aspects of that approach do not fit. In particular, the one I find useful here is Max Freedom Long's concept that if an individual's High Self does not have the necessary power, authority, or knowledge for a desirable task, it can go to higher levels above it. Or the High Self may be informed that the task is not in the long-term spiritual interest of the person, and thus the individual should not complete the undertaking. Long also specifies that all High Selves are connected to all others in the great company of High Selves. What are some of these higher levels?

To review some additional background material that relates to this concept of spiritual levels, recall that in chapter 5, on NDEs, I previously mentioned that when the apostle Paul wrote that he knew someone who went to a "third heaven," (2 Corinthians 12:2), he was possibly speaking about his own NDE or STE in his encounter with the *light* on the road to Damascus. If he went to a third heaven, he implies that there is more than one level within the concept of heaven. Although not mentioned much by Christians, the term *seventh heaven* has meaning in Jewish and Islamic eschatology. It specifically references the highest level of heaven and, thus, indicates at least seven levels.

Although all of the levels of spiritual beings are not mentioned in either the Old Testament or the New Testament, the Jewish and Christian religions do refer to various levels of spiritual beings. Actually, the ancient Greeks knew of these levels, and Dionysius the Pseudo-Areopagite (late fifth or early sixth century CE) divided these beings into three levels with three in each level and referred to them as the Celestial Hierarchy. The highest level consists of Thrones, Cherubim, and Seraphim. The intermediate level includes Dominions, Virtues, and Powers (Authorities). Principalities (rulers) are grouped with Angels and Archangels at the lowest level. Each level has its own function, and "high" and "low" do not relate to importance. The most common ones are Angels and Archangels, and the "highest" levels are Cherubim and Seraphim (Isaiah 6). Cherubim are a high level of spiritual beings that do not have physical bodies. First Peter 3:22 mentions Angels, Authorities, and Powers. Underhill describes the stages of mysticism as an ordered movement through higher *levels* of reality. Gopi Krishna describes kundalini as evolutionary and maintains that an increasing number of people are likely to be having kundalini experiences. This appears to be true, in the form of NDEs. Humanity in general is slowly proceeding to higher levels of understanding, what is sometimes referred to as the evolution of consciousness. How does this relate to mysticism/STEs?

The previous sections on mysticism and NDEs included many different descriptions of spiritual contact with an indescribable majesty. Many of the descriptions are, of course, ineffable, and metaphors must be employed to describe them. However, some of these metaphors can be subdivided. For instance, some mystics have described themselves as seemingly connected to either nature or all of humanity. I would contend that nature has its own High Self (i.e., Mother Nature or Gaia). In a mystical experience, a person first has a more complete connection to her own Spirit, and then her Spirit can connect to either the High Self of nature or to the company of High Selves of other people. Underhill also mentions the power of nature influencing mystical experiences, saying that many poets, musicians, and scientists often have a mystical bent because they are attuned to their own spiritual nature. The psychiatric group CPR cites Einstein as having a mystical-like vision of the world, especially with his analysis of light. Other mystics feel they are more connected to God or higher spirits rather than to nature or other humans. In this case, they are connected through their own Spirit to beings within the Celestial Hierarchy, possibly to God.

Likewise, although NDErs have different descriptions of the transcendental world, such as meadows, mountains, and flowers, these are natural variations that make the NDEr feel comfortable through a connection to nature. Other NDErs encounter various *beings of light*, and some have perceived the supposed secrets of the universe without being allowed to bring this information back with them. To me, these variations, while reflective of the individuality of the NDEr, also indicate that there are various levels in the afterlife.

Similarly, the rigorous training (learning to contemplate) that mystics undertake is simply learning to establish solid contact with their own Spirit. Each person has a Spirit, but the thinking self is not necessarily in frequent communication with its own Spirit. Long's concept that people must go through their low self to contact their High Self coincides with Underhill's view that reaching the Absolute is not an intellectual undertaking but a matter of the heart or emotional desire. Shamans also do this in their training in order to go to the Upper World. A frequent "method" for shamans to reach the Upper World is a ladder, and a number of mystics have described the steps to advanced mysticism as a ladder.

Another contrast within descriptions of mysticism is that of transcendent or immanent types of experiences. In these cases, I would describe an immanent encounter as one in which the mystic is aware that she has connected through her own internal Spirit. In the Bible, the ultimate statement of the immanence concept is, "The kingdom of heaven is within you" (Luke 17:21). For a transcendent encounter, I would interpret it as simply an awareness of something above oneself without awareness that one's own internal Spirit is involved. This unawareness is virtually always present with regard to the various spiritual components of humans. A person never realizes that a decision was made by her emotional or mental body. And, in fact, virtually no decision is ever 100% emotional or mental. Emotions and the mind always have input into any decision.

H. Other Comparisons and Contrasts among STEs

There are other similarities and differences related to these STEs that do not relate to a spectrum within the concept of Spirit but that do indicate commonality. For instance, one contrast seems to be Kason's concept of a kundalini experience versus Underhill's description of a mystical experience. NDEr Kason did have the spinal sensations, as did neuroscientist and spiritual investigator Mario Beauregard, author of *The Spiritual Brain*. Beauregard's experience is what propelled him to become a neuroscientist. Although the end results appear to have similarities, there seem to be differences in how to reach those levels.

There also seem to be major differences between training methods to reach higher spiritual levels. Eastern concepts of meditation often include no thought, perhaps similar to what Underhill describes as the practice of Western Quietists. However, Underhill believes that Western mystics must participate in active contemplation. This is not a quieting of the mind to the internal spiritual world but only to the senses. The body and the mind must be prepared for awakening to Spirit. However, as is clear in Kason's interviews with Westerners and numerous people who have had spontaneous kundalini experiences, some of these happened during or after periods of intense concentration.

The difference in some descriptions of STEs may be a matter of the phase of mysticism a person is in at a particular moment. Kason speaks of early awakenings, as does Underhill. Thus, these neophyte experiences are much different from those experienced by an advanced-stage mystic, but they may still be referred to as mystical experiences. Some NDErs encounter with the *light* appears to be more of an illumination stage, whereas other NDErs appear to have achieved the Unitive stage.

Another interesting variation in these STEs regards unpleasant experiences. Underhill discusses purification and the dark night of the soul, possibly stages ensuring that the individual desires to proceed further toward Union. Kason speaks about difficulties and challenges that a person may undergo as part of the kundalini experience. She further divides these up into physical, psychological, and spiritual/paranormal difficulties. The physical ones seem unique to kundalini, with the exception that being abnormally hot may be similar to the *incendium amoris* described by Thurston. The positive kundalini psychological symptoms were similar to the aftereffects of an NDE, such as frequent psychic experiences. The challenging symptoms described by Kason had some similarities to unpleasant phases that mystics encounter. Because the nature of the kundalini experience is dissimilar to Western mystical experiences, as previously mentioned, these challenges seem to remind the person that there can be incorrect procedures that can result in making the ultimate goal of a kundalini experience more difficult to attain. NDErs who are unable to discuss their internal transformation as compared to the former outward world in which they were living, and to which they have returned, have a much more difficult time integrating the NDE without assistance from others who have encountered a similar situation.

Some NDErs also have distressing experiences that may be similar to the dark night of the soul, but the difficulty in expressing them in other than symbolic terms makes comparison formidable. Kason does mention negative spiritual symptoms, such as visions of demons and evil spirits, that even saintly mystics have encountered. Thurston and Underhill also note mental disorders, as well as poor physical health, in numerous mystics.

I imagine that all of the other authors and NDErs discussed in this chapter would agree with Underhill's and Kason's contention that God or a higher power is as much seeking to be in Union with the person as the person desires to be in Union with God, even if the person had no spiritual beliefs at the time of the initial encounter. In contrast, shamans were often more interested in using their contacts with the Upper World for gaining practical information rather than achieving personal transformation.

Underhill and Kason both discuss how life is much different after reaching a period of living in almost continuous Union. Kason calls this the *sahaja* state. For instance, some mystics may receive inner guidance when in an ecstatic state, but a person in continuous Union can receive this guidance at any time without entering a trance state. It can be difficult to discern the effects of an occasional state from those of a continuous one.

A number of these authors discuss various triggers for STEs, although they do so in slightly different contexts. Hardy mentions "at the moment" triggers, such as being out in nature or hearing a beautiful piece of music. Kason's triggers coincide more with circumstances in a person's life at the time, such as meditation practices. Thurston mentions that a religious object, such as a crucifix, could induce rapture (and possibly levitation), but these are for individuals who have frequent mystical experiences, rather than an initial and/or singular incident like Hardy describes. Underhill notes that the mystical quest may begin after some personal tragedy in the person's life. NDErs have nearly died, which could be a tragedy, but the person may be a "seeker" at the time of the NDE, similar to Underhill's concept of a pilgrim being on a journey about which she is unaware. While many of Hardy's sample population had singular experiences, Kason holds that a person who has one STE is likely to have others. Many NDErs feel close to the spiritual world after their NDE, but they rarely have an STE as profound as the NDE unless they have a second NDE.

Numerous people are confused when STEs occur, especially when they are unfamiliar with these types of experiences or are skeptical of their reality. Kason classifies herself as a counselor for people who have STEs. I have already mentioned that some psychiatrists are interested in these experiences, partly for educating other psychiatrists that STEs are not pathological problems that must be treated as disorders that need to be cured. The branch of psychology/psychiatry that deals with these experiences is referred to as transpersonal psychology, implying something beyond the self. A psychiatrist who simply dispenses medications for alleged neurochemical deficiencies is not a person who should be consulted after an STE. I previously discussed the topic of spiritual emergence and emergency in the section on Kason's study, and in a religious context I briefly discussed spiritual advisors.

I. Paradoxes

In his book *The Big Book of Christian Mysticism*, author Carl McColman (2010) identifies numerous paradoxes within mysticism. He discusses mysticism as being an experiential religion versus one based on authority, doctrine, and rules. Some of his paradoxes are similar to my contrasts, but they are related to mysticism only. Since he addresses these from a religious perspective, he refers to the goal as a relationship with God. Most of these explanations are from McColman, but a few are mine.

1. Mysticism is the quest for God, but God has to find you. God is not a formula that follows a predictable pattern and certainty.
2. Mysticism is about experience but cannot be limited to experience. It is about knowing God rather than knowing about God from reading the Bible, but any human experience can be an illusion and not a genuine mystical experience.
3. Mysticism may involve a life-transforming experience, such as an NDE, but insignificant events can also result in profound changes to a person's life. A person does not "fail" if her goal is Union but she does not reach it.
4. A person cannot earn a mystical experience, but she can reject God's grace and ignore His calling.
5. Mysticism is the "flight of the alone to the Alone" (Plotinus's expression), but Christ is present when two or three are gathered in His name (Matthew 18:20). McColman emphasizes the

importance of belonging to a church community, even if fellow members are not interested in mysticism.

6. Seek the *light*, but embrace the dark. Dark is not understood here to be evil; instead, it is mystery that remains hidden. The Greek root of the word *mysticism* is the same as the word *mystery*.

7. Delight in God, but accept suffering. The latter gives people a newfound appreciation for God's presence.

8. God is both just and merciful. Perhaps this can be compared to NDErs who, during a life review, observe how they have hurt others and were disconcerted by their own behavior but sense a forgiving presence beside them.

9. Follow the Christian tradition, but embrace wisdom from other traditions, though a blend can lack identity. A person should not judge other people's spiritual paths.

10. A person should love God's creation but not love the world. It is acceptable to love the natural world but not to become too involved with human creations, such as possessions, especially those that show pride rather than necessity.

11. Look forward to Union with God, but live in the moment. If a person lives in the moment, she will not be disappointed if a Unitive experience never happens.

12. Pray methodically instead of using prayer that cannot be reduced to a method. This is similar to the question of whether a person should use recitative/methodical prayers, such as the Lord's Prayer, as opposed to spontaneous expressions (nonmethodical prayers).

13. A person should become like a little child (Matthew 18:3) but love God with all his heart, soul, and mind (Matthew 22:37). The latter represents a more mature, questioning mind. An individual may still love God in this manner while adopting an uncomplicated child's mind.

14. The Ultimate Mystery is silent, but mystics still try to express it through words. "All words fail. But even the words that failed need to be spoken" (p. 116). If no mystic ever attempted to write about mysticism, I would not have been able to demonstrate how mysticism fits in with my concept of spirituality. During this writing, I have gained a great respect for various spiritual literature that

involves metaphors, allegories, and symbols and that provides a better understanding of biblical parables. Though not biblical, in "The Rime of the Ancient Mariner" by Samuel Taylor Coleridge (1772–1834), forgiveness is expressed by the falling of an albatross from the neck of a sailor after he expresses a blessing.

J. Paranormal Phenomena

Each of the investigators of STEs in this chapter, as well as NDErs, report paranormal phenomena. For example, Hardy, Kason, and Underhill discuss that people with STEs believe that they know things innately. However, those experiencing an STE maintain that it is proper to evaluate later what they knew by using sense-based information or rational thought. NDErs also experience knowing, either during the NDE or as an aftereffect. For NDErs, this often is in the form of telepathic communication with a *being of light*. If the NDEr postulates a question in her mind while in the presence of the *being of light*, she immediately knows the answer nonverbally. Long speaks about the High Self employing a mental process referred to as "mentation," or knowing something without using a logical thought process to reach a conclusion. There are two varieties of this type of knowing. One is simply receiving information by a method other than the senses, and the other is perceiving the solution to a specific problem. Kason refers to the latter as abstract intuition.

Another commonality of the three principal researchers discussed is that each found people with STEs who felt they had a purpose and would often receive guidance, primarily in the form of voices, visions, or psychic impressions, such as clairvoyance or clairsentience. Most NDErs feel they came back for a purpose, but they often have difficulty understanding that purpose, although they may perceive what that purpose was later in their life. Perhaps disseminating a person's specific purpose by exploring incorrect choices is itself one of life's general purposes. There can also be short-term purposes in a person's life that are part of an overall goal. Some NDErs are also able to discern an inner guidance. Perhaps all of them have this inner guidance but are not necessarily aware of it. This inner guidance is their own Spirit, although it may manifest in different ways, such as conversing with an angel that is always with them or receiving a job offer when they had not expected to change occupations.

Kason provides a list of common psychic or spiritual healings that happen around people who have kundalini experiences. I maintain that many of these happen to people with any STEs. Hardy's research was mainly on the religious experience itself and not on aftereffects, so healings were only mentioned in several instances in which the experiencer alone felt healed. Some mystics, such as Padre Pio, were known for having healing abilities and numerous other paranormal abilities. However, some of the mystics who became saints (and saints who are not classified as mystics) often had their investigation for sainthood begin after numerous healings around the funeral ceremony or the location where that holy person was buried, thus demonstrating that paranormal events can occur around a mystic—even after he or she has passed on.

Although recovery from a physical illness or disease may be the easiest form of healing that can be verified, recovery from mental disorders and addictions are also quite frequent. In today's world, there are numerous counseling centers for people with alcohol and drug addictions. The counseling process may take years, as the counselor attempts to find the basis for the addiction and self-destructive behavior. The counseling may continue even after the behavior has been discontinued but the desire remains. When people receive a healing in the presence of a mystic or a person who had any STE, the healing is often instantaneous and permanent, provided the person takes reasonable steps to prevent relapses.

Although I have only briefly mentioned the Christian concept of the Holy Spirit in this book, these healings often occur when a Holy Spirit—infused Christian prays for a person. For instance, in chapter 8, on Eastern concepts, I mentioned Kathryn Kuhlman. At her services, she would call out after receiving a spiritual message (an ability referred to as *discernment*) that someone in the building, even sometimes specifying that person's location in the building but not a name, was cured of a specific illness, either physical (e.g., cancer, heart disease, disability) or nonphysical (e.g., addiction, release from abuse-related trauma). Only a small fraction of the people in attendance received healing, and the person receiving the healing did not have to be a Christian. At times, an attending person who was accompanying someone to the service whom they hoped would receive a healing (e.g., someone in a wheelchair or with cancer) would receive an unexpected healing while the sick person did not. This could call into question the idea that faith is required to receive a healing. I maintain that these healings can happen in any person in the presence of a person who had an STE, and that the gift of healing others is that STEr's special calling.

Precognition is an interesting paranormal event, because it involves time. STErs identify free will, as well as futures, as already "cast in stone." For instance, a person may choose a lifelong destiny or purpose before coming into the physical body. It is best to follow that destiny rather than try to create a new one. Long specifies that seeing the future is one of the specific abilities of the High Self. Atteshlis notes that the ability is only in relation to the "crystallized future," which I would interpret as situations in which a free choice by a human has been made. Events may be leading to one future, but if a human seriously chooses a different future (and conveys that information to his Spirit), the future for that individual can be altered. There are, of course, futures for groups of individuals (e.g., an organization, a city, or a nation).

Luminosity is certainly a factor discussed by all of the authors covered in this chapter, although possibly in different manners. Kason, NDErs, and Underhill all specifically mention luminosity as something STErs observe, and Long specifies it as a property of the High Self. Thurston and Treece note that this *light* can be seen by other people; it is not just an internal impression of the mind. Perhaps *light* being manifested in the area near a mystic is similar to the *light* around dying people and hearing the "celestial" music that the dying and NDErs often hear. In these instances, possibly the spiritual music (and *light*) is so powerful that it penetrates the barrier between the spiritual and the physical. The other option is that some people within the presence of a dying person are just more spiritually attuned.

Some of Thurston's examples of the paranormal only seem to occur within a specific religious context. For instance, why would anyone other than a Catholic have stigmata? I opine that stigmata may be part of a continuing purification or a temporary regression back to the purification stage. Most stigmatics reach ecstasy, so it is not an early stage purification from which the stigmatic never proceeds. The fact that many stigmatics also have dissociative factors in their lives may also be an issue in manifesting stigmata, or the person may have a somatoform/conversion disorder in which a mental problem is transferred to a physical condition.

Telepathy is listed by Kason as a psychic experience. While I agree that it is paranormal, it could also involve communication between the spiritual entities in humans other than the Spirit; that is, one astral body could possibly communicate with another astral body. However, if the communication is with a deceased person or a *being of light*, then it does involve Spirit. While it involves Spirit, communicating with a deceased person is probably marked by a less complex level of relationship of a person to Spirit than are many STEs. It does not usually involve a major transformation in a person's life, unless the person is a hard-core materialist who suddenly realizes there is something beyond the physical world.

The list of psychic experiences cited by Kason and the list of physical, psychological, and spiritual/paranormal effects when undergoing an STE quite frequently parallel the changes noted by Atwater in relation to aftereffects of an NDE. Such overlays include abstract intuition, healing abilities, and precognition. This is not surprising, since an NDE is an STE that occurs under the circumstance of being near death.

K. A Modern Mystic

The following discusses the interesting life of a man who had characteristics of a nonreligious mystic. He may have had an NDE, but he wrote his story before that term was developed. Since his abilities began when he was a child, it is difficult to notice a sudden personal transformation that many adult NDErs report after their NDE. I will discuss how the phenomenon he exhibited closely parallels views of people who have STEs.

Although he is not well-known, Jacques Lusseyran (1924–1971) had an NDE, I believe, or a spiritually transformative experience (STE). He may have been a natural-born mystic. His autobiography is titled *And There Was Light*. It was originally published in 1963 (as a translation from French) and was republished in 1987 by Parabola Books, which publishes books by the Society for the Study of Myth and Tradition.

Lusseyran was born in Paris to well-educated parents. Even as a child, Lusseyran had a special relationship to *light*. He said he could "eat the sun" and that darkness was *light* in a new form and rhythm. He had to wear glasses when young. At age seven, after a visit to his grandparents and their beautiful garden in the country, he said to his mother that he would never see the garden again. At school three weeks later, another child bumped him. He lost his balance and fell; he hit the sharp corner of the teacher's desk; and his glasses went deep into his right eye and tore it away. His left eye was less severely injured, but sympathetic ophthalmia caused loss of sight in that eye. He lost consciousness. Although Lusseyran did not recall, I think the pain may have resulted in an NDE. Perhaps his natural mystical bent simply came to the surface.

Afterward, he said,

> I began to look more closely ... from an inner place to one further within ... for light was there. ...

> I found light and joy at the same moment, and I can say without hesitation that from that time on light and joy have never been separated in my experience. I have had them or lost them together.

> I saw light and went on seeing it though I was blind. (pp. 16–17)

Lusseyran was excited about being a prisoner of *light*. He saw not only *light* but also all the colors of the rainbow. He could recognize people by the color they generated in his mind. He also found that his emotions could affect his new "vision." He could know where almost every object in a room was, but if he became angry or impatient, he also became confused about the location of those objects. If he became too competitive in a game, he went into a fog or felt surrounded by smoke. If he became jealous or unfriendly, he felt like he was in a black hole.

Similar to what many other blind people report, Lusseyran found that his other senses became more acute. However, I believe he had additional sensations. For instance, as he writes, "Little by little, my hands discovered that objects were not rigidly bound within a mold. It was form they first came in contact with, form like a kernel. But around this kernel objects branched out in all directions" (p. 28). For example, if he walked by a tree, he could tell its height and shape. My interpretation is that he could detect the aura of objects, a topic discussed in an earlier chapter. Lusseyran also believed that people really "hear" from inside themselves, that sound vibrates inside the head, chest, and throat. One day he detected a change in the tone of his math teacher. One week later, he found that his teacher's wife had left him. He could also detect "moral smells."

Lusseyran considered blindness to be a temporary impediment and recommended against schools in which everyone is blind. I believe our modern term for participating in regular activities is *mainstreaming*. He did not have trouble making friends with classmates. For this, he feels grateful to his mother and believes she "gave birth to him a second time," because she did not shelter him from his disability. He met another blind child who was miserable because his parents had prevented him from participating in many activities. One of his interesting statements is, "Blindness is an obstacle, but only becomes misery if folly is added" (p. 30). When Lusseyran compared himself to others who were blinded, he was referring to people who become blind after being able to see. Some of his comparisons may not apply to people born blind and who thus have no concept of vision.

Some of the ways Lusseyran processed information are similar to the methods used by other blind people, but others resemble phenomena encountered by NDErs. Recall that many NDErs undergo a panoramic life review similar to watching a film on a screen, but usually with the emotions of the moment when the incident occurred. Lusseyran said many blind people have an increased ability to memorize, but his method was different. As he writes,

> I remembered well, but above all I visualized. It was an enchantment to watch the appearance of all the names and figures on the screen inside me, and then to see this screen unfolding like an endless roll of film.
>
> This screen was not like blackboard, rectangular or square, which so quickly reaches the edge of its frame and has to give way to a useless piece of wall or a door which loses its meaning as soon as it is closed. My screen was always as big as I needed it to be. Because it was nowhere in space it was everywhere at the same time, and to manage it I only had to call out "Attention." The chalk on the inner screen did not turn to powder like other chalk. It was stronger and more

supple, being made of the substance called "spirit." Let us not quibble over words. Call it matter or essence. In any case it is a reality closer to us than words can tell, a reality to be touched, manipulated in shape. And when such treasures are unveiled how can a child fail to be consoled for the loss of his sight. (p. 42)

Among the abilities he acquired was that for questions about intangibles (things not explained), he could respond much quicker than sighted people, because he did not have to "darken the outside world and light up the world of the mind" (pp. 42–43). All names, figures, shapes, letters, and numbers had a color. "Nothing entered my mind without being bathed in a certain amount of *light*. To be more precise, everything from living creatures to ideas appeared to be carved out of their primordial *light*. In a few months my personal world had turned into a painter's studio" (p. 43). Maps with shapes appeared in his mind. If he was walking around Paris with friends and the group got lost, his friends would always ask him for directions back. He could also do mathematics on his screen. Once, he was asked to give a long talk on a subject, and for this he had prepared many notes. His teachers took his notes away from him, but then he realized his notes were on his screen and he could easily recall them.

Lusseyran was a very good student at school. Students in today's world may have difficulty fathoming the subjects in his curriculum. He particularly loved the study of mythology. His heroes were poets and gods, and he especially liked Apollo. After school on Saturdays, his father would take him to hear one of the large symphony orchestras in Paris. He could distinguish which conductor was in charge of any concert, and he "wept with gratitude every time the orchestra began to sing" (p. 93). Although Lusseyran did not employ the term, he had synesthesia, as each tone produced a different color in his mind. The orchestra flooded him with colors of the rainbow. Some people develop synesthesia after an NDE, as previously discussed. However, as much as he enjoyed listening to music, he had difficulty speaking it (i.e., playing an instrument).

Up to now, I have been describing how Lusseyran interacted with the world. Much of the remainder of this review has to do with actual events in his life, particularly after Germany invaded France in World War II.

Following the invasion, the radio and newspapers were controlled by the Germans. It was such a circumstance that enabled his abilities to shine forth. Prior to the invasion, he had been learning how to speak German. He began university studies shortly after the invasion in 1941, at age 17, majoring in literature. He states that he did not like psychology because it was only concerned with outward manifestations and not with the rich inner life he experienced. One psychologist who was an exception in Lusseyran's opinion was Henri Bergson, who taught that we each have an inner world.

The German occupation of Paris became personal to Lusseyran. He had a friend named Jean, and Jean had a close relationship to a man named Weissberg, who was a friend of Jean's father for many years. The Germans came and took Weissberg away because he was a Jew. Another friend of Lusseyran was also arrested.

Shortly after the incidents above, Lusseyran developed the measles. He had an interesting perspective on his illness. As he described, "In the first hours of fever it became obvious that my system was purging itself of a poison and spewing out foreign bodies. But the poison was moral as much as it was physical, of that I am sure" (pp. 157–58). When the fever left him, he had a surge of energy and a resolve to oppose the occupation. He began to wake up at 4:30 a.m. and say a prayer including the phrase, "By myself I know how to do almost nothing, but if you [God] will it I am capable of almost everything. Most of all give me prudence" (p. 162).

Lusseyran and a number of his fellow students decided to form a resistance movement. At his first meeting, 52 people showed up and he was put in charge. In his group, all were under age 20. Nationwide, 80% of Resistance members were under age 30. After that initial meeting, the group would not have more than three people meet together, except in emergencies. His particular group eventually reached 600 members, and only one in ten was approved for membership. His group called themselves the Volunteers of Liberty. Their primary function was to gather information and let other French people know what was really happening (control of the press and radio by the Germans meant that information was suspect). Most members in his group were participating in the Resistance while continuing their university studies.

Lusseyran's specialty was recruiting. He was chosen for this because the others claimed he had a sense of human beings. He never had to write down a name or phone number (he eventually knew 1,000 of them), because he used his screen for memory. If other members were thinking of asking another person to join, they would watch the person for several weeks, and if they believed he or she could be trusted, they would bring the proposed member to Lusseyran after he summoned the person. Many of the French people were rather apathetic about the German occupation, so one quality Lusseyran wanted to see in a recruit was confidence in the ultimate outcome of the group's efforts. During his work for the Volunteers of Liberty, he felt the following: "Around me it [the note of confidence] drew a magic circle of protection, a sign that nothing bad could happen to me. The *light* which shone in my head was so bright and so strong that it was like joy distilled. Somehow I became invulnerable" (p. 176).

However, Lusseyran was arrested on July 20, 1943. It turned out that the man who betrayed him was a medical student named Elio. Three months earlier, Elio had come with another person without Lusseyran's being aware that a recruit was coming; thus, Lusseyran did not go through his normal questions and procedures that enabled him to detect infiltrators. While in captivity, he found that Gestapo members did not respect courage, but he wrote about something for which they did have respect:

> Was it something more indispensable, more at the core of things? It was a fact that when I managed to forget their presence, when I forgot everything except what I found in the depths of my being, in the innermost sanctum of my inner world, in the place which, thanks to blindness, I had learned to frequent, and where there is absolutely nothing but pure light—when this happened the SS did not wait for my answers; they changed the subject. (p. 251)

While in prison, he found that if he concentrated on his inner life he would not even realize he was in prison.

At times, I wonder if this betrayal was not foreordained so that Lusseyran could do his best work later, in the Buchenwald concentration camp, where he was sent six months later. Of the 2,000 Frenchmen sent there with Lusseyran in January 1944, he was the only one of about thirty who survived. He did receive some good advice from another prisoner upon his arrival at Buchenwald. He was told not to say he was a student at the University of Paris, as intellectuals were usually executed immediately. He was able to say he was an interpreter of French, German, and Russian, although he did not know Russian at the time he made this statement. People who had "useful" occupations had a better chance of survival. Since he was blind, he was not put into a forced-labor camp.

As a blind person, Lusseyran was placed in a barracks with other "invalids." They were given only half the meager rations of normal prisoners. Numerous people were dying every day. Lusseyran developed pleurisy, dysentery, and erysipelas, and was even deaf for two weeks. He was carried to a "hospital," largely a place for dying, as there were no medications or treatment there. Very few left the hospital alive.

He was able to survive by a "celestial stream" and by not refusing "God's help." After he left the hospital, he was referred to as "the man who didn't die," and he would sometimes be taken by other prisoners to people who needed encouragement to live. Other prisoners even stopped stealing his bread or soup. He learned he could survive by not living for himself and by finding joy in the midst of fear.

The Buchenwald camp was liberated in April 1945. Lusseyran taught French literature in the United States and died in an automobile accident on a trip back to France in 1971. The final three sentences of his book were two truths that he said he found: "The first of these is that joy does not come from outside, for whatever happens to us it is within. The second truth is that light does not come to us from without. Light is in us, even if we have no eyes" (p. 312).

The following is a list of comparisons of some of the abilities of Lusseyran to those of people who have had any type of STE and consequently exhibited some spiritual insights or paranormal phenomena:

1. Lusseyran had numerous types of *"light"* experiences despite being blind.
2. He had synesthesia (confused senses, especially common with music and light impressions).

3. He could observe an unending screen (similar to NDErs) that he used for storing real information.

4. He possibly survived on an unsustainable amount of food, closely paralleling inedics.

5. He placed an emphasis on moral values, resolving to use his abilities in service to others.

6. He likely had a sensitivity to auras of objects and of other people.

7. He had the ability to detect major changes in people's lives by inflections in their voices.

8. He grasped the idea that various myths represent the spiritual aspects of human development translated into common language.

9. He perceived that psychology needs to be more concerned with people's inner, or spiritual, lives.

10. He relied upon prayer.

11. He realized that when he was within his inner sanctum or in connection to Spirit, he could deflect harm from outside influences; this is similar to the shaman's concept of a Power Animal providing protection.

12. He employed language that a mystic may use, such as "depths of my being" and "celestial stream."

13. He could respond quicker than sighted people because he did not have to darken the outside world to light up the world of the mind. I contend that this could be compared to a person living in sahaja state, in which kundalini remains permanently in the crown chakra, as explained by Kason.

Max Freedom Long said that the kahunas thought the High Self was only attached to the physical body and to the low and middle selves but that it primarily resided outside of them. Earlier in this chapter I mentioned the evolution of consciousness. I maintain that what is happening is that the High Self or Spirit is further penetrating into the physical body and our other spiritual bodies. When this happens, a person no longer feels that information is coming from outside herself but is simply part of her normal thought process, similar to not knowing if a decision was made by the mental or emotional body. In many cases, to the outside world, these thoughts may seem paranormal, but in reality they are part of our spiritual evolution. While many shamans and mystics have to enter a trance state in order to receive information from their Spirit, many modern people, such as Lusseyran, can do this without entering a trance.

L. Parables

Although not mentioned by the principal authors reviewed in this section, another form of describing the transcendental world that may be more familiar to Westerners (specifically, Christians) is in the parable, that is, a teaching from the Gospels employing symbolic language. Although parables were used by Jesus for other purposes, I will emphasize parables concerning the kingdom of heaven (or kingdom of God) and how it functions. The majority of the descriptions of what the kingdom of heaven is like are from parables in Matthew 13, but there are a few others, or repetitions of the ones in Matthew, in the other synoptic Gospels. These parables also appear to indicate that Jesus's disciples were given additional information to explain the parables. In Matthew 13:3–23 (also in Mark 4:3–20 and Luke 8:5–15), there is the parable of the sower and the seed. In the parable, Jesus first states that seed falls in various places. His disciples then ask him why he speaks in parables. He replies,

> Because to you it is granted to know the mystery of the kingdom of heaven, but it is not granted to them. For to him who has shall be given and it shall increase to him; but to him who has not, even that which he has shall be taken away from him. This is the reason I speak to them in figures, because they see and yet cannot perceive; and they hear and yet they do not listen, nor do they understand. ... For the heart of this people has become hardened, and they hear with difficulty, and their eyes are dull; so that they cannot see with their eyes and hear with their ears and understand with their hearts; let them return, and I will heal them. (Matthew 3:13–15, LT)

After that, he explains that the seed is the Word of God, and he describes what happens to the seed that fell in various places.

The following is a list of some of the other parables about the kingdom of heaven, which I only summarize:

1. Matthew 13:24–30, 36–43. A sower sows good seed, but an enemy puts tares among the good wheat. The landowner decides to let them grow together and to separate the seeds at harvest and burn them. Jesus also gives further interpretation to his disciples when asked. The good seeds are the sons of the kingdom, and the tares are the sons of evil, sowed by Satan. The reapers are angels who will separate the good from the bad at the end of the world.

2. Matthew 13:31–32 (and Mark 4:31–32, Luke 13:19). A small mustard seed grows and becomes a large tree.

3. Matthew 13:33 (and Luke 13:21). A small amount of leaven leavens a large quantity of flour.

4. Matthew 13:44. A man finds a hidden treasure in a field, so he sells everything he owns and then buys that field.

5. Matthew 13:45. A merchant is seeking a good pearl. When he finds one, he sells everything he owns to buy that pearl. To me, Matthew 13:44–45 most clearly represents the description of mysticism provided by Underhill; that is, that Union is the pearl of great price.

6. Matthew 13:47–50. A net is thrown into the sea and gathers many fish, some of which are kept. The bad ones are thrown away. Similar to tares, the angels will throw the bad souls into the furnace of fire at the end of the world.

7. Matthew 18:23–35. A king forgives the debts of a servant who could not pay the debt, but that servant does not forgive a smaller amount from a fellow servant. The king finds out and puts the unforgiving servant into prison.

8. Matthew 18:1–6 (and Matthew 19:14, Mark 10:13–16). While not strictly a parable, these verses mention Jesus's telling the people that they must become like little children to enter the kingdom of heaven. This is similar to avoiding a purely intellectual approach to the Absolute.

9. Matthew 20:1–16. A vineyard owner pays the workers who only work one hour the same wages as he pays those who had worked all day for an agreed-to wage. This parable can explain why some people seemingly receive God's grace (Union) without much effort whereas others have to exert more effort.

10. Matthew 25:1–13. Ten wise virgins bring extra oil for their lamps while ten foolish ones do not bring extra oil.
11. Matthew 25:14–30. Three servants are given talents (coins). The servants who receive five and two talents double their amounts by trading and are rewarded, whereas the one who receives only one talent hides that talent and is admonished, with that talent taken away from him.

These parables appear similar to the allegories and symbolic language used by mystics to describe the Absolute or the transcendental world.

M. Siddhis

In the section on STEs, I briefly mentioned the Eastern concept of *siddhis* (pronounced "sid-hees" or "cities"), often referred to in the West as psychic phenomena. One of the better explanations of siddhis (derived from a word meaning "perfection") and their relationship to spiritual practices is from a book by Dean Radin, PhD, titled *Supernormal: Science, Yoga, and the Evidence for Extraordinary Psychic Abilities* (2013). His aim is to demonstrate that the claims of the paranormal were addressed over 1,600 years ago in a classic text titled *Yoga Sutras* (the word *sutra* means "thread") by a yogi master (or seer) named Patanjali who lived 1,600 to 2,000 years ago. Note that the exact years he lived are not known, as many of his concepts may not have been written down until years or centuries after his death and may have been revised or added to over the years by his followers.

The foreword for this book is written by Deepak Chopra, MD, author of numerous books in the controversial field of Eastern understanding of the paranormal. Chopra cites research that demonstrates that when people are presented with facts that contradict their long-held beliefs, they tend to ignore the facts. Of course, skeptics and debunkers often cite that same research when seeking to explain why people believe in religion or psychic phenomena. This topic from a skeptic's viewpoint is covered extensively in the book *The Believing Brain: From Ghosts and Gods to Politics and Conspiracies—How We Construct Beliefs and Reinforce Them as Truths* (2011) by Michael Shermer. I maintain that many scientists who defend the assumptions of physicalism, despite significant evidence of the supernormal, are not much different from religions that believe in a document alleged to have been developed without errors over thousands of years. Radin quotes one scholar of religion who sees the refusal of both science and mainstream religion to take the paranormal seriously as an indication that "the paranormal is our secret in plain sight" (p. 49). Radin holds that some debunkers of the paranormal who did thoroughly investigate it simply left the material unpublished, or were refused publication rather than the publisher admit that his materialistic assumptions were incorrect. "There is social pressure in the scientific community to publish results that conform to mainstream beliefs and expectations, and equally strong pressure to withhold results that might be perceived as strange or questionable" (p. 127). The existence of siddhis does not fundamentally conform to mainstream beliefs. Other scholars believe that Eastern studies of the paranormal have the advantage of not stepping on the province of God. Some fundamentalists maintain that anything paranormal that is not from God is from the Devil.

Radin prefers the term *supernormal* to *paranormal*; the former was coined by Frederick Myers, who was previously discussed in chapter 4. In the glossary of his book, he defines supernormal as "aspects of nature that are not yet well understood; superior to normal, but not supernatural" (p. 324). These abilities are attainable through advanced meditation, repetition of mantras, the use of drugs, or natural talent. Other techniques encompass "ecstatic dancing, drumming, praying, chanting, sexual practices, fasting, or ingesting psychedelic plants and mushrooms. In modern times, techniques also include participation in extreme sports, floating in isolation tanks, use of transcranial magnetic or electrical stimulation, listening to binaural-beat audio tones, and neural feedback" (p. 7). Later, he adds contemplation of sacred symbols. This may explain why some Christian mystics can enter an ecstatic state when simply contemplating a cross. For some people, siddhis begin after an NDE or an STE. Myers believes that siddhis will someday be considered completely normal. Radin notes that these alleged abilities have been used by scam artists throughout history.

Siddhis generally begin to appear when a person has reached a state called samadhi. Meditation is often considered the most effective means to reach this unified state. Samadhi is employed to describe both the technique for reaching unifying consciousness and the state of ecstatic Union. There are several levels of samadhi. Samadhi is often classified as the final step of an eightfold path to enlightenment. Radin compares the ecstasy of Union to a drug high.

> The ecstasy associated with the experience of samadhi might sound superficially similar to the momentary high achieved by smoking crack or shooting heroin. But while narcotics can blast the mind into a euphoric stupor, it doesn't take long before that route becomes horrifically grim, to say nothing of fleeting and a considerable drain on society. By contrast, the mind trained to sustain samadhi is focused, calm, and crystal clear, and the accompanying happiness doesn't fade or cost anything. (p. 99)

As evidenced by the difficulties Gopi Krishna encountered (as described in the writing of Kason), Radin cautions that meditation, when overdone, can "lead to introversion, depression, or spiritual hedonism" (p. 7). However, these consequences seem much less severe than addiction to drugs to become high.

The word *yoga* is derived from an ancient word meaning "combine, connect, join, or unify." While many Western psychic abilities are considered to be spontaneous and not under conscious control, siddhis can be controlled by an advanced practitioner of yoga. Radin considers Tibetan Buddhism practices to be an advanced form of meditation, with results similar to yoga. Radin does not consider postural yoga to be a form of yoga that leads to advanced mental states. He further states that

> the connection between the mystical and the miraculous in the context of this book is that yoga is a path for practical mystical development, and that path *explicitly includes* the development of miraculous phenomena, or more precisely, of super-marvelous phenomena that *appear* to be miraculous. Walking on water, manipulating matter with a mind, and foreseeing the future are all said to be produced through gaining expertise in mystical states. (p. 52; italics original)

These siddhis can be developed by the yoga path, while many religions and much of the general public maintain they are God-anointed gifts.

Tibetan Buddhists and advanced yoga practitioners both maintain that their students need to attain these abilities but that they should not get distracted by them, through pride and arrogance. When I have read similar statements throughout my years of study, I understand that the main context is that the person needs to continue moving toward enlightenment and not be enamored by a particular siddhi. However, it is possible that if one of the abilities is healing, that person's purpose in life may be to be a healer—and proceeding to higher levels is not part of his purpose. Assisting others is often considered an important aspect of spiritual development beyond simply reaching enlightenment. Healing must be done without selfish motives or the creation of sensationalism.

Radin discusses some of the issues of neuroscience, which I will review later. He notes that correlating two items does not prove that one causes another. Thus, activity of the brain as evidenced by MRI or PET scans does not prove that the brain causes thought. The "hard problem" in the philosophy of the mind is how subjective experiences can arise from inanimate matter. Or, stated another way, how does an insentient universe create sentient beings? Although there may be a neural pattern for mystical experiences, it does not prove that the neuron activity is the cause of the mystical experience. It may be the result.

Radin briefly mentions medical miracles. He comments that doctors will refer to these as "spontaneous remission." For some obscure illnesses, there may have been a misdiagnosis, but Radin cites one case from the *British Medical Journal* in which x-rays showed extensive lung damage, regardless of whether the diagnosis of a fatal form of sepsis was correct. The patient's lungs became normal within two days after several prayer sessions by her friends. In addition, this patient was expected to be permanently blind in one eye due to intraocular bleeding that was diagnosed by an ophthalmologist, who classified her eventual complete recovery of sight as unique.

Radin lists approximately 25 siddhis, but these primarily break down into three main abilities. These are as follows:

- Exceptional mind—body control
- Clairvoyance or nonsensory knowledge that is beyond the constraints of space and time
- Psychokinesis, or mind directly affecting matter

Some abilities are rather unusual and are capable of being a subset of the three above (not having been previously mentioned). One is "invisibility," or the literal disappearance of a body from view. Clairvoyance may include knowledge of the outer universe (other planets or other solar systems on a macroscopic level) and knowledge of the inner universe, that is, microscopic objects (atomic level or cellular level in living things). Another is the ability to influence others through a field effect. For instance, one sutra reads that in the presence of a person firmly situated in nonviolence, all hostilities desist. An additional ability is invulnerability, which I would compare to a shaman under the protection of his Power Animal.

Other abilities listed by Radin have been frequently mentioned in regard to mystics. These include levitation, living without food or water (inedia), incendium amoris (inner fire), bilocation, not being harmed by fire, and the ability to change the weather. Some of these abilities, especially those in the area of mind—body control, may be learnable without esoteric practices or considering them to be "spiritual" abilities. While "most esoteric practices explicitly warn against demonstrating these skills in public" (p. 121), these admonitions may not apply if they are learned through concentration techniques or are derived from a natural talent, as mentioned previously. For instance, Radin cites a Dutch athlete named Hof who holds the record for sitting submerged in ice water for 100 minutes and for performing other feats of "inner fire." Similarly, some Tibetan monks are known to be able to evaporate to dryness a wet towel placed on the monk's bare back while he meditates in the snow. The underlying mechanism that allows this ability to work is not known, but Hof did employ a *tummo* meditation practiced by Tibetans to develop his ability. Radin also cites a study done in the 1980s on an Indian sadhu named Prahlad Jani. He claimed to have not eaten anything for eighty-one years. He was observed continuously in a hospital for ten days, and while he neither ate nor drank anything, no changes (such as weight loss) were noted in his physiology. It is believed that a person can absorb energy (called prana) from the air; this ability is sometimes referred to as *breatharianism*. Inedia in mystics was previously discussed.

One ability that can be supernormal and that is not mentioned elsewhere in this chapter or in Radin's book is dream interpretation. Sigmund Freud even wrote a book on this topic. Several incidents of dream interpretation figure prominently in the lives of two patriarchs in the Old Testament. Both of them had at least two major reported incidents of dream interpretation, and in both cases it is classified as a God-given ability. For example, in Genesis 40:8, a butler and a baker who worked for the pharaoh reported their dreams to Joseph. "And Joseph said to them, Behold the interpretation belongs to God." Later, the Egyptian magicians and wise men were unable to interpret the pharaoh's dream, so the butler informed the pharaoh of Joseph's ability to interpret dreams. The pharaoh actually had two separate dreams, but each conveyed the same message, which Joseph correctly interpreted.

What is interesting is that one of prophet Daniel's interpretations included revealing to the king what the dream was before interpreting it. Normally, the person who interprets a dream needs to be told the dream. The Chaldean magicians and astrologers reported that "there is no man who can show it [the dream and its interpretation] before the king except the gods whose dwelling is not with men born of flesh" (Daniel 2:11, LT). The dream was revealed to Daniel in a vision, which he credits to God.

> Then was the mystery revealed to Daniel in a night vision. And Daniel blessed the God of heaven. Daniel answered and said, Blessed be the name of God forever and ever; for wisdom and might belong to him; ... He reveals the deep and secret things; he knows what is in the darkness and the light is with him. To thee, O God, of my fathers, I give thanks, and I praise thee, who has given me wisdom and might, and hast now made known to me what we desired of thee; for thou hast made known to us the king's matter. ... Daniel answered in the presence of the king, and said, The mystery which the king has demanded to know, can no wise man, sorcerers, nor the magicians, nor the astrologers reveal to the king; But there is a God in heaven who reveals mysteries, who has made known to the King Nebuchadnezzar on his or what shall be

in the latter days. Your dream and the visions of your head
upon your bed are these. (Daniel 2:19–20, 22–23, 27–28, LT)

The king was ready to kill the magicians who could not reveal or interpret the dream, but Daniel asked mercy for them not to be killed, as he would interpret the dream.

Although Radin does not mention dream interpretation, performing any siddhi may be in violation of the warning that these abilities are not to be done for public display. According to Radin, this is true even if the person attributes the ability as coming from her teacher (guru) or God. Also note that Daniel specified that the *light* was with him when he had his vision of the king's dream. The *light being* with someone is an indication that her Spirit is involved in the process. In another dream of the king at some later unspecified time, the same king told the dream to his magicians, astrologers, and soothsayers, but they were unable to interpret it (Daniel 4:7). The question that might arise is, why did he first ask the magicians instead of asking Daniel first?

The king stated that Daniel was able to interpret his dreams because "the spirit of the holy gods is in you" (Daniel 4:18, LT). An interesting fact about the first interpretation is that it involves two separate abilities. Knowing the dream without its being told to Daniel would involve nonsensory knowledge. The actual interpretation involves precognition of future events. The pharaoh and the king each had a dream, so they were actually seeing into the future, but neither could interpret the symbols in the dream. Dreams involve much symbolism, as do many visions by mystics and other information a person receives from his Spirit. Modern studies of dreams indicate that many people have premonitory dreams but do not recall them upon awakening, or do not attempt to or cannot interpret them. The dreams are often of mundane things that may happen in the next day or two and are not necessarily significant. Recall that learning to remember and understand significant dreams is important in the training of shamans. Another alleged ability of Daniel was that he could solve riddles (Daniel 5:16), although no examples are given. Riddles are common in mythology, and people who could solve them were held in high esteem in their respective societies.

Centuries ago people would say that any siddhi is a God-given ability, but my interpretation is that these abilities flow naturally from a person who has a deeper contact with her Spirit. In a later chapter, I will discuss a writer who traced the origin of the word *genius*. At one time, a majority of humans felt that creativity was the province of the gods or of God who chose to reveal information to a select number of people. I do not think it is a select number, but rather that each person has amazing possibilities if functioning in accordance with his or her Spirit. Marianne Williamson, in her book *A Return to Love* (1992), made the following comment: "Our deepest fear is not that we are inadequate. Our deepest fear is that we are powerful beyond measure. It is our Light, not our Darkness, that most frightens us." Another quote from the same book conveys another inspirational theme related to light: "As we let our *light* shine, we unconsciously give other people permission to do the same."

Radin spends considerable time presenting data on successful complex laboratory studies of clairvoyance, telepathy, precognition, and psychokinesis. LeShan would consider such studies unnecessary and meaningless, because the artificial constraints of a laboratory remove these abilities from the Realm of Meaningful Behavior. Tibetan monks believe that clairvoyance is among low-level abilities that are often natural talents but that can be improved upon by meditating. Even people who achieve samadhi may only be 80% accurate in their clairvoyant abilities. Scientific studies of these particular siddhis are only slightly better than chance, but they involve may trials. Radin himself may consider these studies to be demonstrating a siddhi in public. However, most people who take part in the studies are not aware that they have any of these abilities and, thus, are not trying to prove their superiority. Nevertheless, studies in this area indicate that for all of these abilities, the likelihood that the results are attributable to chance is in the range of a million to one to a billion to one.

Another ability mentioned by a researcher whom Radin cited could be the most important in understanding human behavior but be the least spectacular and also difficult to classify with the other three previous siddhi classifications. This is the "destruction of defiling impulses" (Radin 2013, 282). I would classify addictions and some other problem behaviors discussed in chapter 10, on spirit intrusion, as defiling impulses. Addictions and other serious behavioral problems are sometimes eliminated in people who have NDEs or STEs. Contrary to this, some people have addictive behaviors begin after their NDE or STE. My explanation for these seemingly contradictory results would be that the *light* encountered in NDEs or STEs is a temporary state of samadhi that can force out some undesirable entities. However, during an NDE or STE, the spirit body's relationship to the physical body may become fragmented (possibly from the medical situation or accident that caused the NDE) and allow intrusion by some entities. For instance, imagine a soldier unfamiliar with spirituality who is nearly killed in battle, hospitalized, and given an anesthetic, all conditions that increase the likelihood of intrusion. He then has an OBE and comes back to a situation in which he is confused about his role in life. This is especially true if the experience is only an OBE type, in which the soldier did not experience the *light* but has a new perspective on the world that is difficult to process with his previous understanding from living in a society in which a materialistic view prevails. The soldier may wonder how he can be alive and simultaneously be away from his physical body. Some people in situations that cause fragmentation, such as the soldier's injury, develop addictive behaviors or become depressed/suicidal. Another way to view this situation is that the soldier, as a result of his NDE, may become more empathic, not realizing that his own "boundaries" have expanded. Thus, he may accept other people's emotions as his own and begin using alcohol or drugs to protect himself from others' pain.

N. Conclusions

There are multiple roads to Union with the Absolute (or its various other names, including God). The Absolute represents a higher or the highest level of a spiritual hierarchy or spectrum, but all of these can only be reached if a human first contacts his own Spirit, although the person may be unaware of this pathway. The Absolute cannot be described by language from the Realm of Sensory Experience; hence, it is described with metaphors, allegories, parables, or symbolic language. Paranormal abilities may develop as a result of deep contact with Spirit or the spiritual spectrum above Spirit.

In the next chapter, I unite the diverse concepts that have been presented in this chapter and in previous chapters.

Chapter 12

DISCUSSION

A. Introduction

In this chapter, I will elaborate on my concept of Spirit. In addition, I will give my explanation of another spirit form within each person (i.e., in addition to Spirit). In chapter 1, I explained how various chapters in the Bible refer to soul and spirit as separate entities within each human. I use *spirit* in the biblical sense (in reference to humans and not the Spirit of God), written as *Spirit*, to distinguish from alternate uses of the term. The form called Spirit may have multiple functions. It can act as protector and healer and is also responsible for creative functions in humans. It has previously been introduced by the names High Self and Inner Self-helper (ISH). This spirit form also has access to spiritual beings above itself, such as the angelic hierarchy or the Holy Spirit, that is, beings who do not have physical bodies. Thus, Spirit is the passageway by which mystics reach Union with the Absolute.

My explanation of *soul* is as previously presented. Soul and Spirit have different functions; these usually work together and complement each other. In some cases, the soul entity may be displaced or influenced by an intrusive entity. Spirit intrusions are more likely if a person experiences trauma resulting in soul loss or soul fragmentation. In this chapter, I explain that the soul no longer fully penetrates the physical body and, thus, that a spirit intruder can attach itself through the opening by which the soul fragment departed. I also point out the serious problems that have arisen from the reductionist concept that mental illness is caused by neurochemical imbalance. Moreover, I describe other theories of human behavior, both secular and spiritual. Seeing as many different fields of science have unsuccessfully attempted to explain how consciousness can arise from purely chemical processes in the brain, I then disclose how my spiritual concept can explain the nature of consciousness.

B. Spirit and Protection

In chapter 11, I partially explained Spirit in relation to mysticism and near-death experiences (NDEs). In sum, I contended that Spirit has numerous abilities of its own but can also request assistance from spiritual levels above itself. The first ability I discuss is a protection mechanism. In chapter 5, I discussed the Third Man factor. In his book of the same title, John Geiger presents numerous cases in which a typically visible entity came to the assistance of a person or people who were in danger of death from atypical circumstances. Although Geiger mentions angelic intervention as one possible explanation for the survivals, he also considers hallucinations. I would like to present further evidence that these appearances are angelic and related to Spirit. In some cases, Spirit may be able to act on its own.

As noted in chapter 11, on mysticism, angels are part of the celestial hierarchy. While usually considered to be pure spirits without bodies, angels, I maintain, are able to temporarily manifest a physical body. Deceased humans also sometimes appear to other humans with a temporary physical body. At times, this body may appear diaphanous; a living person can pass a hand through it. At other times, it can appear solid and have an effect on material objects. Dr. Elisabeth Kübler-Ross, most famous for her book *On Death and Dying*, had a deceased former patient of hers appear to her a few months after the patient died. Kübler-Ross was about ready to give up her work assisting people through the death process, but this patient convinced her of her work's importance. Kübler-Ross asked this "ghost" for her signature and was able to obtain it. If the deceased spirit body of a human can affect matter (e.g., hold a pen and sign a paper), then, I argue, an angel should be able to do likewise. Mystics who can bilocate are another example of the spirit form having the appearance of a physical body.

In his book, Geiger includes several instances of protection in the form of the voice of a deceased person. Similar accounts were found in the writings of the Guggenheims. Although I maintain that there is an existence after death, it is possible that, for protection, the Spirit aspect of an endangered human may mimic the voice of a familiar deceased person, as the person needing assistance is more likely to respond to a known voice than to an unknown voice. In the Guggenheims' book, there are also examples of voices of unknown origin.

I conceive that there are many similarities between an angelic, or Third Man, assistance and the shamanic concept of a Power Animal. Indigenous peoples often understand life in natural terms. Thus, animals act as their protectors rather than abstract angels. Just as mystics have to portray a relationship with a higher being in symbolic language, indigenous peoples use animal symbols to designate their protectors. Recall that the Power Animal is not an individual wolf, bear, or eagle but, rather, the species of wolf, bear, or eagle.

The occurrence of spiritual or angelic rescue raises the question of why some people are rescued when others are not. I would suspect that when a person is about ready to come into a physical body, she may have already made decisions about life, such as to achieve special purposes or how long she might live. If a person is "destined" for a long life but an accident happens that threatens physical death, then that person may receive spiritual assistance in order to achieve the original purpose.

C. ISH Therapy as Protection and Healer

I surmise that the Inner Self-helper that assists patients who have dissociative identity disorder (DID) in achieving integration is Spirit in another form. In this form, it collaborates with a therapist as an advisor. The parallels between Spirit and the ISH are numerous. I will explain how the ISH, and its assistance in therapy, agree with my general concept of Spirit. Among these agreements are the following:

1. The ISH often has no body form. Neither do the alternate personalities (APs). However, in some cases, the ISH may assume a body form so that the patient does not hear a disembodied voice, which may be confused with the unfriendly AP voices often heard.

2. The ISH does not have the typical problems of an AP; it is only helpful.

3. The ISH is present even before therapy begins; it is not iatrogenic. In addition, it may not have a "birth date" as the APs may have;

the ISH should be the same age as the birth personality. Based on the ISH's having memories of abuse prepartum, this indicates that the ISH is present from conception, not just postpartum.

4. The ISH is usually described as genderless, although in some functions it may appear to have a gender.

5. The ISH can seek advice from Higher Helpers. The ISH may seemingly be absent from the therapy process for a period of time while seeking advice from Higher Helpers. When the ISH returns, it may have new insights into the therapy process. The Higher Helpers consider themselves to be under the guidance of a Supreme Being.

6. The ISH often communicates by visions, automatic writing, or an inner voice. For mystics, these communication methods indicate an advanced relationship with the Absolute, a term they employ. This Absolute would be one of the highest levels of the hierarchy that a mystic can reach, but the ISH may communicate to the patient without intervention from levels above itself.

7. Although materialist therapists are reluctant to discuss this, there are often parapsychological phenomena happening in the lives of DID patients. Any "predictions" generally involve only the patient.

8. One therapist claimed that the patient's ISH could be in communication, probably telepathically, with the therapist's ISH. This would enable the therapist to have more insight into the therapy process. This would be an example of Long's concept that the High Selves of all humans are connected. Another example of this would be that in one DID group therapy session, the ISHs of each patient were able to communicate rationally with each other.

9. The ISH is not always attuned to the physical body and its condition. This is probably because it resides in a spirit body that is only attached to the physical body. This may also be why it does not respond to cultural demands, such as obedience to authority. However, as I explained in the partial explanation of Spirit in chapter 11, Spirit, as part of evolution, may be further penetrating the physical body.

10. The ISH is often considered to be rational (alternative descriptions: logical, methodical, mature, legalistic, serious, introspective) and unemotional. The emotional part of human nature is the result of a separate spiritual entity, the emotional or astral body.

11. The ISH will often use symbolic pictures or words to describe itself or the therapeutic process. Similarly, mystics must use symbolic language to describe their encounter with the Absolute.

12. Physical healings are often encountered when Spirit is active.

13. One therapist considered the ISH to be the source of love, appreciation, truthfulness, coping ability, and artistic talent. These would not often be thought of as "rational." I suspect that these are qualities not from the ISH itself, but rather a description of connections to levels above itself. Artistic talent and creativity as connected to Spirit will be discussed later.

While this may not contribute to a further explanation of Spirit, one therapist reported that it (i.e., the ISH, or hidden observer) could not have significant power for action or else there would be no need for therapy, because the ISH would have "cured" the person. I maintain that this agrees with the general concept that humans have free will. If the ISH could simply correct the consequences of child abuse, then a perpetrator of child abuse would not observe adverse consequences of his actions. thus, there would be no internal incentive to correct his behavior to one of love and respect?

Psychiatrist Ralph Allison states that helper personalities may be selected by the ISH for specific purposes. For instance, a helper personality may assume control of the physical body and drive the patient to a hospital after a hostile AP attempts suicide or encourages the host personality to attempt suicide. While most hostile APs have major "issues" (drug abuse, anger, or violent tendencies), carryovers from the physical body in which they previously lived, perhaps these helper personalities are simply confused or have self-imposed unfinished business from their previous body and do not have a specific agenda or desire to harm the body in which they are now residing. The ISH can recognize confusion or other such issues within that disembodied spirit and may be able to program this AP to be helpful.

D. Spirit and Creativity

In chapter 3, I proposed that various types of creativity may be the result of a special relationship with a person's own Spirit. I provided some examples, such as Tesla's unusual mental abilities, Ramanujan's mathematical formulas, and some famous musical compositions. I attribute these abilities, within mystics, to their relationship to their Spirit through contemplation.

Spirit may operate in a functional mode or an inspirational mode. The functional mode would include the protection or therapeutic/healing aspects previously discussed. The inspirational mode would include creative works in any field, such as mathematical equations or scientific formulas, musical compositions, poetry, and themes for books. It should be noted that these inspirational activities require competency in the subject matter. People with only minimum mathematical ability are unlikely to suddenly receive a complex mathematical expression, such as a mathematical formula in "pure" mathematics or one that describes the physical universe. Similarly, an NDEr or a person near a dying person who hears beautiful music from no physical source is not likely to be able to convert it to an exemplary composition if she is not a trained musician. In addition, the music heard may only be a theme and may require complex orchestration by the composer. Likewise, an interesting manner of explaining a life lesson in a novel requires writing skills beyond the creation of a commendable theme.

The following are some additional examples of unexpected creativity. The first comes from neuroscientist David Eagleman's book *Incognito: The Secret Lives of the Brain* (2011). Eagleman writes,

> So who, exactly, deserves the acclaim for a great idea? In 1862, the Scottish mathematician James Clerk Maxwell developed a set of fundamental equations that unified electricity and magnetism. On his deathbed, he coughed up a strange sort of confession, declaring that "something within him" discovered the famous equations, not he. He admitted he had no idea how ideas actually came to him— they simply came to him. William Blake related a similar experience, reporting of his long narrative poem *Milton*: "I have written this poem from immediate dictation twelve or

sometimes twenty lines at a time without premeditation and even against my will." Johann Wolfgang von Goethe claimed to have written his novella *The Sorrows of Young Werther* with practically no conscious input, as though he were holding a pen that moved on its own.

And consider the British poet Samuel Taylor Coleridge. He began using opium in 1796, originally for relief from the pain of toothaches and facial neuralgia—but soon he was irreversibly hooked, swigging as much as two quarts of laudanum [opium in alcohol] each week. His poem "Kubla Khan," with its exotic and dreamy imagery, was written on an opium high that he described as a "a kind of reverie." For him, the opium became a way to tap into his subconscious neural circuits. We credit the beautiful words of "Kubla Khan" to Coleridge because they came from his brain and no one else's, right? But he couldn't get hold of those words while sober, so who exactly does the credit for the poem belong to?

As Carl Jung put it, "In each of us there is another whom we do not know." (pp. 7–8)

I claim that the "other" is our own Spirit. Blake's and Goethe's experiences illustrate examples of automatic writing.

English psychiatrist Anthony Storr investigated the topic of sudden creativity in one chapter of his book *Feet of Clay: Saints, Sinners, and Madmen: A Study of Gurus* (1996). A number of other chapters of his book deals with an unusual mix of characters, from cult leaders such as Jim Jones, David Koresh, and Bhagwan Shree Rajneesh to other people such as St. Ignatius of Loyola and Carl Jung. Storr's examples of sudden insight into the solution for a problem were from two mathematicians.

Carl Friedrich Gauss (1777–1855) had been struggling unsuccessfully for two years to prove a mathematical theorem. [Then Gauss wrote,] Finally, two days ago I succeeded, not on account of my painful efforts, but by the grace of God. Like a sudden flash of lightning, the riddle happened to be solved. I myself cannot say what was the conducting thread which connected would I previously knew with what made my success possible. (p. 176)

Storr notes that Gauss must have had religious beliefs in order to attribute his insight to God. Similar insights have occurred to agnostics; these attribute their insight to the subconscious mind.

Mathematician Henri Poincare had a similar sudden insight after his endeavors to solve problems related to Fuchsian functions. During a geological excursion in which he was not even thinking about mathematics, he had a sudden insight into a novel solution. Physicist Erwin Schrödinger developed his famous wave equation, one of the foundations of quantum mechanics, while recovering from tuberculosis. Storr notes that some "solutions" that came in this manner were erroneous but that most corresponded to reality.

Storr comments that these inspirations correspond well with Graham Wallas's (1858–1932) description of the creative process. According to his process, there are four stages: preparation, incubation, illumination, and verification. The illumination stage is when Spirit is bringing the solution to the problem to the conscious mind. *Illumination* is an excellent term, as it brings into play the connection of Spirit to *light*, especially as evidenced by NDEs. Later in this chapter, I will discuss the exclusively human concept of intentionality, in which answers are not provided unless sought. The conscious mind brings the intention, and the superconscious mind (Spirit) provides the answer.

The concept of Spirit and creativity in connection to an "outside" source can be compared to the ancient Greek concept that artistic talent comes from the Muses. The Muses' mythological origin is uncertain, but usually they are perceived as the daughters of a god or a king and are thought to be keys to prosperity and a good life. Originally, there were thought to be three Muses, but eventually there were nine, one Muse for each of the following: epic poetry, love poetry, song or lyric poetry, hymns, comedy, tragedy, history, dance, and astronomy. The last of the list may be thought of as any science or mathematics. Some famous writers, including Dante Alighieri and William Shakespeare, have called upon a Muse to inspire them in their writings.

In 1994, a film was made about Ludwig von Beethoven titled *Immortal Beloved*. According to the film, a document using those words was found in Beethoven's personal effects after his death, and the film postulates that this immortal beloved was a secret lover of Beethoven, who never married. The film speculates that this secret lover was his brother's wife. While that is possible, although disputed by most scholars, I am convinced that the immortal beloved could more easily have been a spiritual "source" that was providing Beethoven's music to him, a source to which he simply listened and then wrote down what he heard. Most people do not use the word *immortal* to describe a fellow human being, but some may employ that term in reference to the spiritual world.

I inquired into an English translation of the fourth movement (choral part) of Beethoven's Ninth Symphony. Below is one stanza of it:

> Joy, a wondrous spark divine,
> Daughter of Elysium,
> Drunk with fire now we enter,
> Heavenly one, your holy shrine.
> Your magic powers join again
> What fashion strictly did divide,
> Brotherhood unites all men
> Where your gentle wings spread wide.

I believe that in this excerpt it is possible to see many connections to the concept of Spirit and the spiritual levels above it as presented in this book: joy, a divine spark, and entering a holy shrine. *Elysium* is an ancient term (from Greek mythology) for a modern heaven; *fire* represents light; *magic powers* imply paranormal events; *brotherhood* intimates that all humans are connected (on a Spirit level); and wings are often a symbol for protection provided by heavenly beings (God or angels). I am not sure if Beethoven used his exact words, but the Ninth Symphony is based on a revised Friedrich Schiller (1759–1805) poem written about twenty years earlier. The original poem by Schiller in 1785 was titled "Ode to Freedom," but in 1803 it was revised to "Ode to Joy." The words must have resonated with Beethoven's view of life. Continuing on this theme of a beloved, a person may refer to another person as his beloved. In the Gospel of John there are several references to "the disciple whom Jesus loved," or the Beloved Disciple (John 13:23; 19:26–27; 20:2; 21:7, 20–24). These references appear only after Lazarus is referred to by his sisters Mary and Martha as "the one whom you [Jesus] love" (John 11:3, LT). Some biblical scholars speculate that the Beloved Disciple was John himself. The Gospel of John is often separated from the other synoptic Gospels. Although the Gospel of Matthew contains the most parables about the kingdom of heaven, John's Gospel is often considered the most mystical of the four Gospels. In the Old Testament, the book that most closely describes Union in symbolic language is the Song of Solomon. The term *beloved* is frequently employed. In addition, the name David means "beloved."

E. Spirit as Compensation

Another area in which I believe Spirit may be active is savant syndrome. The word *savant* generally means "a learned person," but the archaic *idiot savant* implies a developmentally disabled person with a great ability. In modern usage, people with savant symptom are typically considered to suffer from a condition within autism spectrum disorder (ASD).

A savant's IQ is generally above the IQ of someone for whom the technical definition of *idiot* (an IQ of 0 to 25) applies. I maintain that Spirit intervenes in the lives of select people to give them special abilities in order to compensate for deficiencies in standard mental skills. I will most frequently employ the term *savant* when discussing people with these abilities. Savant syndrome is classified as an Axis II mental disorder by the *DSM*, but a large percentage of people considered to be savants do have Axis I mental disorders. Much of my information comes from the book *Extraordinary People: Understanding "Idiot Savants"* by Darold A. Treffert, MD (1989). He reviews many historical writings in the field and also describes his encounters with a number of savants during his psychiatric residency.

The most well-known savant ability is in the field of music. Other famous savant abilities include lightning calculation, calendar calculation, and memory abilities of various types. Many savants have more than one of these abilities, a prodigious memory being a common secondary ability. Other savants will also be discussed, such as those with artistic abilities.

Treffert found that the highest percentage of savants were children diagnosed with early infantile autism, although only 10% had special abilities. The second-largest group was childhood schizophrenics, and the third group was those with organic brain damage from injury or illness. He estimated that seven out of 100,000 children have savant syndrome, and the ratio is about three to four males for each female. Some children who later display savant abilities may be born with congenital or prenatal problems, or be born prematurely, but others may develop savant syndrome later if organic brain damage occurs in early childhood. Some disabilities are so profound that the savant cannot dress or feed himself. A number of savants also have epilepsy.

Savant syndrome is often classified as an aspect of autism, as most savants display symptoms typical of autism. Many of them will have temper tantrums or episodes of rage if something out of the ordinary happens. They are often withdrawn socially and, other than rage, display few emotions.

1. Musical Savants

For those savants with musical abilities, although the notes they play are correct, their music is usually described as mechanical and expressionless. Most musical savants have perfect pitch, the ability to identify a single note. If the first time he hears a piece of music an error is made, the savant may always reproduce that error. Many savants can improvise, but only a few can compose. Although Treffert does not mention this, many savants can only begin with the first note of a musical composition. They cannot begin in the third part of a symphony, for example. They may become distressed if they cannot complete a piece of music.

One well-known musical savant was known as Blind Tom. He was the son of a slave who was purchased in 1850. At age four, Blind Tom played a Mozart sonata after hearing the daughter of the slave owner (Col. Bethune) play it. At one time, he knew five thousand compositions. He earned a considerable amount of money when Bethune took him on a concert tour. He toured until Bethune died almost fifty years later, at which time he lost his abilities. Other savants have also lost their ability when someone close to them dies.

While most musical savants often play back after hearing instrumental music, Leslie Lemke (1952–) can play on a piano a song he only heard from the voice of the singer. Another musical savant had paralysis on his right side but could still play the piano one-handed. Ellen Boudreaux (1957–) is a blind musical savant who, in addition to her musical talents, has the ability to visualize objects in her environment and avoid walking into them.

2. Calendar and Lightning Calculators

Calendar calculators are typically those that can tell you the day of the week for any date requested, past or future. Some of them can only do this for a certain span of years, but for others the span seems unlimited. Two gifted calendar calculators were identical twins named George and Charles. They were born three months premature, and one was more proficient than the other. In addition to their low intelligence, they were destructive, displayed tics and convulsions, and rocked and swayed almost continuously. Also lightning calculators, they could do the following:

- Report the factors of large nonprime numbers
- Repeat 300-digit numbers read to them
- Immediately number many items dropped on the floor (once they did it for 111 matchsticks)

One researcher, Steven B. Smith, wrote about mental calculators, both prodigies and those with disabilities, and concluded that they "made numbers their friends." One slave named Thomas Fuller, who had a serious mental handicap, was born in Africa in 1710 and was able to multiply nine-digit numbers. He could also give the correct answer to how many seconds were in x number of years plus months plus days. This calculation would take him several minutes to do. Another lightning calculator, named Jedediah Buxton (also in the 1700s), could give answers to math calculations that were twenty-eight digits long, but such calculations often took him five hours. He once took two and a half months to calculate 2^{139}. He could stop calculating for a period of time and then resume where he had left off.

One high-functioning autistic (Asperger syndrome) savant in England named Daniel Tammet (1979–) has received much publicity in recent years and has been studied because he is able to describe what is happening in his head as he performs some of his abilities. He has written three of his own books and also wrote the foreword to Treffert's second book, *Islands of Genius* (2010). Perhaps Tammet is best known for calculating pi to 22,514 digits in his head. He does not calculate it in the normal sense, but the next digit appears to him as a color. In addition, all numbers up to 10,000 have their unique shape, color, texture, and feel. He has participated and was placed high in the World Memory Championships. His first book was titled *Born on a Blue Day* (2006), because to him Wednesday is blue. He was able (as a challenge) to learn the Icelandic language in a week.

3. Mnemonists (Unusual Memories)

Some savants have no ability other than a fantastic memory. The words *memory* and *mnemonics* are derived from the Greek goddess Mnemosyne. She was mother of the nine Muses. The term *echolalia* is used to describe a mnemonist's abilities, implying a direct repetition of every single word.

Though memory savants can remember reams of data, most of that information is insignificant. For those who can remember a long story or poem, there may be little understanding of the content. Some other items remembered, in addition to the proverbial phone book, include the following:

- The weather on every day in the savant's life
- Every hymn in a hymnal
- Bus schedules for a large city
- Historical information about famous people
- Census data, such as a list of all towns with a population over a specific number, or county seats for every county in the United States
- Lengthy conversations on radio or TV heard years earlier (but some savants only remember visual, not auditory, information)
- License plate numbers

It is possible that every person retains the information of every life incident without conscious recollection. The life-review segment of an NDE may also reflect this. Memory savants are simply able to recall it.

4. Artistic Abilities

Artistic prowess is much less common than the other savant abilities mentioned. One handicapped artist named Nadia could do ballpoint pen drawings of animals and human figures after seeing a picture only once. She has incredible manual dexterity, unlike the majority of developmentally disabled children. Nadia has the ability to make art objects drawn in two dimensions appear as if they were three-dimensional. She lost her ability when she learned to speak at school, but her mother died at the same time, so the specific reason for the ability loss is unknown.

A Scottish man named Richard Wawro (1956–) employs a rather unusual implement for his drawings—oil-based crayons, which he does not even sharpen. Wawro has such poor eyesight that his face is only inches from his paper when he draws. Another artistic savant, Alonzo Clemons of Colorado, has received much notoriety for his art, sculpting wax with only his hands and an awl. His pieces, generally horses, have generally sold from $300 to $3,000, but one piece sold for $45,000. He has completed small pieces in as short a time as twenty minutes. When asked where he obtained his ability, he replies that it is a "gift from God" or says, "God gives talent." Clemons was born with normal intelligence and indications of artistic ability, but then he incurred a brain injury from a fall when he was three years old. His IQ is estimated to be 40 to 50. While not listed by Treffert, once a TV news report on similar abilities mentioned a savant who had the talent to fly once over a city and then draw a complete a map of the entire city.

5. Other Abilities

Treffert also mentions several instances of ESP. One savant knew when his parents were unexpectedly coming to pick him up at times when normally he would ride a bus home. Another was able to pick up conversations heard outside the normal range of hearing. This range is apparently well beyond the normal, as Treffert also cites extraordinary sense perceptions—tactile, olfactory, and auditory. A third savant knew when her sister would phone, and another knew the time of day to the minute without looking at a clock.

One researcher of savants commented that in many cases teachers attempt to eliminate the savant's (mental) defects rather than training the talent.

6. Attempted Explanations

Treffert reviews a number of published explanations for these abilities. He mentions compensation of one ability or sense for deficiency in another. For example, some blind people have unusually acute hearing, a compensation for sightlessness, as the brain processes nonvisual input. Unlike my perspective, his explanation is only physical.

These are only attempts at explanations. For each small group of savants for whom one explanation appears valid, there are numerous other savants for which that explanation is totally invalid. Since Spirit often intervenes when injury or death is imminent, I maintain that the Spirit is able to provide meaning in the lives of some people who will not enjoy normal mental fulfillment.

F. The Soul Aspect of Humanity

Previously, I presented several explanations of the various spiritual aspects of humans. For instance, I explained Max Freedom Long's concept of the low self, the middle self, and the High Self derived from his study of the kahunas. Karagulla and Kunz wrote about an etheric body, an astral/ emotional body, a mental body, and a self. Atteshlis (from the writings of Markides) employed the term *psychonoetic body*. Shamans explain that there is a lower world and a Upper World, and that illnesses may be caused by soul loss. In DID therapy, I discussed the ISH and how DID patients seem to have a completely distinct spiritual entity able to take control of one physical body at different times. Something similar happens with spirit intrusion, but it only influences behavior and does not have complete control as in DID. During an NDE, a spirit form is able to leave the physical body and observe the physical world or encounter a transcendental world. I maintain that my concept of more than one spiritual entity residing in a human physical body can explain the seemingly diverse descriptions of various spiritual forms. My concept of Spirit explains the High Self, the ISH, and related aspects. I will now put forth my concept of soul, that is, the other spiritual entity, distinct from Spirit.

While Long's High Self was useful for explaining many aspects of Spirit, I have more difficulty with his properties of the low self and middle self. I prefer Kunz's model in conjunction with terms used by Atteshlis. His idea of a psychonoetic body is a combination of Kunz's astral/emotional body and the mental body. Together, these are "soul," that which departs the physical body during an autoscopic NDE. At death, this soul permanently leaves the physical body. At that time, it is expected to meet its own Spirit and leave the earth plane. If for reasons of addiction or unfinished business the soul does not encounter its Spirit, it becomes an earthbound spirit and can intrude upon another person's life.

In DID, one soul or psychonoetic body (the alternate personality) has nearly completely replaced the soul of the host or birth personality. Depending upon the circumstances in the patient's life, different souls may take control and implement their own agendas (hostile APs) or assist the patient (helper APs). In spirit intrusion, the intruding soul may only influence behavior but not completely control it. In cases of severe addiction, the control may approach that of an AP, as in an alcoholic's recalling past behavior only when similarly intoxicated. The combination of the diverse therapeutic methods for spirit intrusion is to have an earthbound spirit join its Spirit (i.e., go toward the *light* or join deceased relatives who are already in the *light*), which it should have joined at the moment of death. In the case of DID, the patient has had one of the spirit intruders for an extended period of time and cannot function normally if it leaves, so therapy is more complex.

Shamans maintain that many illnesses are due to soul loss. I hypothesize that this idea conforms well with my concept of soul. In soul loss, part of the original soul has departed or fragmented, and an earthbound spirit has attached itself. While I have emphasized procedures that persuade the intruding spirit to depart and join its own Spirit, shamans recall the original soul that is meant to occupy that physical body. If the original soul fully occupies the body, there is no place for an intruding spirit. Fiore emphasizes that simply commanding an intruding spirit to leave may cure the patient but may leave the spirit to wander in the netherworld to attach to another person.

G. Memory

When a person has an OBE, that person is able to later recall those events. Since I maintain that it is the soul that is out of body, memory must be formed and stored therein. When the soul returns to the physical body, these memories may be transferred to the brain, but they are not removed from the soul. When retrieving information from memory, the soul and brain generally work together. When a person with Alzheimer's disease or dementia is about to die, that person's memory often returns. The term for this is *terminal lucidity*. I would assert that this happens because the soul begins to dissociate itself from the physical body and, thus, memory retrieval is from the soul and is not hampered by a deteriorated brain.

H. Trauma and Soul Loss

The concept that the severe trauma of sexual child abuse can cause DID is well established. I maintain that less severe trauma may also cause soul loss or fragmentation and resultant spirit intrusion. I will briefly review some of the factors causing soul loss listed earlier in this book. The list provided by Fiore (1987) is perhaps the most comprehensive.

In Fiore's therapy sample, intrusion typically occurs in a vulnerable person who has a psychic opening. The most frequent cause is substance abuse, which may include prescription drugs, especially painkillers (including opioid drugs). After spirit intrusion occurs, the person loses the ability to make a choice without concerted effort. Fiore and McAll also encountered spirit intrusion resulting from occult practices. Most spiritual literature over the centuries has cautioned against occult practices, often referred to as *black arts*.

My book has frequently mentioned some activities that could be considered occult practices, with potentially beneficial or detrimental effects. For example, when a mystic takes up automatic writing, the message is coming from his Spirit. An individual may "volunteer" to have messages come through to him, but the message could come from a disembodied spirit rather than from his own Spirit. Likewise, if a person is in danger, an unexpected protective message may come from a deceased relative or from Spirit. But if a person seeks a message from "a spirit," that spirit may not be the friendly type. To determine from where an automatic writing message came, it may be necessary to examine the person's life. If the message is inspirational, it may be from Spirit; if a person has symptoms of spirit intrusion, then I would suspect that the message should be disregarded. That is why I am very cautious about people who claim to "channel" messages.

I maintain that many minor traumas that result in soul loss can correct themselves. For example, in chapter 5, on NDEs, in the section titled "A Unique Journey," I described how near-death experiencer (NDEr) George Ritchie observed the spiritual bodies of several sailors opening up when they fell unconscious from excessive alcohol consumption, which resulted in disembodied spirit intrusion. Although intoxication is not usually classified as trauma, in terms of the functioning of our spirit entities making up a human being, it is traumatic, as it disconnects the psychonoetic body from the physical body, allowing some of the fragmented soul to "leak" away. If there are no disembodied spirits around the person, the soul can repair the opening that occurred and there will be no long-term consequences. It just so happens that in the case of the drunken sailors, there were numerous disembodied spirits lurking around the tavern and seeking opportunities to fulfill their desire for the effects of alcohol. Even if a disembodied spirit has entered a sailor—if that intoxication was an unusual event and if the spirit cannot find fulfillment of its desires in future intoxication—it could depart from the body it has temporarily joined, although Fiore identifies a case in which the disembodied spirit did not leave even after a period of four years of the host's not drinking. And although the spirit body of the sailor opened up, this disembodied spirit will only be a spirit intruder and not cause the problems that an alternate personality causes unless the person already has DID.

Although I disagree with many scientists who base their conclusions on neurochemistry, brain images, and behavioralism, these researchers have made great strides in identifying various traumas. In World War I, soldiers who were in major combat, with or without physical injuries, often had psychological difficulties. At that time, the condition was referred to as "shell shock." Similar difficulties occurred in World War II, but the new term was "combat fatigue." In the Vietnam War, the situation was comparable, but a number of the soldiers began using hallucinogenic drugs—and the aftereffects of drug addiction and trauma both have analogous symptoms.

I believe that psychiatrists have developed an excellent term to describe the effects of combat: posttraumatic stress disorder, or PTSD. But by employing the adjectival form of the word *trauma*, the effects have now been separated from military situations and recognized as occurring under numerous other traumatic circumstances.

The aftereffects of PTSD include many of the symptoms of spirit intrusion or soul loss/fragmentation, such as suicidal tendencies or the inability to concentrate. In recent years, the effects of traumatic brain injury (TBI) have been studied extensively as a result of improvised explosive device (IED) attacks on US soldiers in Iraq and Afghanistan. Scientists have also begun studying TBI in National Football League players, college football players, and even much younger athletes in order to learn the effects of concussions from head injuries. The researchers in this field have come to realize that the effects of TBI are compounded when the recovery period is too short. TBI is also worse in younger people for the reason I explained earlier—the soul is not fully bonded to the physical body. Although I am mainly concentrating on the mental effects of trauma, pathologists have studied the brains of football players who suffered numerous concussions during their playing years. He did his studies after these players had died, often as a result of suicide. There are definite physical changes resulting from concussive trauma, and the name given to it is chronic traumatic encephalopathy (CTE). I maintain that simple physical changes happen as a result of a concussion, but the changes are compounded when soul loss or fragmentation occurs, as the reduced amount of soul is less able to heal the damaged brain. Alcohol and/or hallucinogenic drugs may compound the effects of the trauma. However, the use of alcohol and drugs may not have begun until after the initial brain trauma.

The case of sports injuries is different from psychological PTSD. In sports injuries, the cause is physical TBI. In the military, the cause can be physical or psychological trauma, such as being near people who die, even those among the enemy. Military people stationed in the United States have developed symptoms of PTSD from guiding drones to kill other people. I believe that all of these incidents of trauma indicate soul loss or fragmentation, often in conjunction with spirit intrusion. In addition, when a soldier is traumatized in battle, it is possible that spirits intruding into the soldier's energy body are enemy combatants who lived in another country. Spirits do not recognize available energy bodies as "friend" or "foe."

Fiore fathoms that intrusion may happen in a hospital. I maintain that the reason for this is that a sick person has her soul more loosely connected to her physical body. However, a sick person in a hospital is very unlikely to attract an addictive disembodied spirit if that sick person has no addiction tendencies. This concept of vibrating analogously may not apply in the case of children who undergo trauma. Some type of trauma often got the person to the medical situation that occasioned the NDE. But instead of calling it a posttraumatic stress disorder (PTSD), Morse (1992) refers to it as a posttraumatic bliss syndrome. I believe this is because the person encounters her own Spirit and does not allow entry of a spirit intruder.

While I have emphasized trauma's involvement in soul loss or fragmentation, there are other types of events that can affect the soul and, in turn, behavior. In chapter 8, I discussed the chakras and how they are associated with endocrine glands. In recent years, there have been numerous findings showing that various chemicals, particularly organic chemicals such as pesticides, can serve as "endocrine disruptors." These chemicals can attach to receptor sites in the gland and affect its proper function. The most common entry of such chemicals into the body is through contaminated water supplies. While some industrial chemicals may cause problems due to their volume, problems from other chemicals may be the result of those chemicals' original function. For instance, if medications are flushed into the water system, they may survive through the waste treatment process and enter the river stream only to be input to another water supply miles downstream. Medications and pesticides may be active in concentrations as low as one parts per million or billion. Although it can be difficult to prove how human behavior is affected by these chemicals, the behavior of fish is affected at these extremely low levels.

Improper endocrine function is equivalent to soul fragmentation, and the effects of such soul fragmentation can include physical or behavioral changes. The effects can be either a reduction or increase in the gland's proper hormone release. In either case, there are abnormal quantities in the location that the hormone is supposed to affect. Most pesticides are designed to affect the chemical processes in plants, insects, and fungi, but some of those functions are similar in humans and other animals. For instance, some early insecticides called organophosphates were classified as cholinesterase inhibitors. Cholinesterase is necessary for the functioning of a neurotransmitter that is present in both insect and human nervous systems. This class of chemical was originally developed as a possible military "nerve" agent, but it is much less frequently used as an insecticide in the United States today because of environmental restrictions created on account of the fact that these chemicals are toxic to agricultural workers or consumers of sprayed crops. Heavy metals can also have very deleterious effects in various parts of the body, on memory, and on behavior. These environmental factors may be affecting children in utero.

I also speculate that having a child exposed to frequent ear-piercing music could result in trauma and soul fragmentation, thus allowing entrance by a spirit intruder. I comment on this to indicate that there may be multiple causes of soul fragmentation that appear unrelated to affects normally thought of as "spiritual" behavior.

One symptom of spirit intrusion and soul fragmentation not previously identified may be that an individual does not appear to learn from his poor choices. An example may be the effects of alcohol on driving a vehicle. A person who has drunk too much alcohol on one occasion and who subsequently drives a vehicle may come close to an accident and thus be very careful in the future or arrange for a nondrinker to drive the vehicle. Often, an alcoholic believes that a near accident is a fluke that will not happen again, which leads him to continue to drive under the influence of alcohol. In such cases, the individual's understanding is altered by the intruding spirit. Also, children who have been abused have much more difficulty learning from their incorrect choices, because the intruding spirit makes such learning difficult.

I. Soul Fragmentation and Creativity

For a number of years, researchers into creativity have noted a frequent connection between creativity and mental illness, especially depression and addiction. A significant number of famous writers had depression, and many of them committed suicide: Ernest Hemingway, Sylvia Plath, and Virginia Woolf, to name a few. I speculate that many of these creative people often received guidance from their Spirit, which is usually more active in people with mental illness.

Depression is often cited as the most common mental illness, but some researchers specify bipolar disorder as the most pervasive mental disorder. Although I have discussed how seemingly wonderful a relationship with a person's own Spirit is, in reality an individual can accomplish much more if her multiple spiritual components are functioning together as one unit. It is possible that people on the manic side of bipolar disorder are receiving uncontrollable assistance from their own Spirit, as the person cannot coordinate that input with functions of their emotional and mental bodies. Another way to describe this is as follows. Therapist Kason notes that some people have difficulties when their kundalini rises to their crown chakra when the other chakras have not been properly developed. I have already explained how some people may have spiritual "emergencies" if unprepared for encounters with their own Spirit. Gopi Krishna described difficulties arising from his intense meditation until he realized that he was arousing his kundalini. I conjecture that the manic phase of bipolar disorder is one of these encounters. Some bipolar people only experience mild manic symptoms, and this is classified as hypomania. While the mystic often learns to channel supernatural supplies of energy into worthwhile efforts, the manic may lose everything to gambling or a business venture while feeling invulnerable and tireless.

Mental illnesses do not necessarily begin on a certain day or even in a certain year, a problem in formal diagnosis. In 2001, the film titled *A Beautiful Mind* was made about the life of the winner of the 1994 Nobel Prize in Economics, John Forbes Nash Jr. (1928–2015). The film is based on an unauthorized biography of the same title by Sylvia Nassar. Nash was a paranoid schizophrenic. According to the film, his really bizarre symptoms began sometime after he wrote the papers that became the basis for his Nobel Prize, in the early 1950s. Although Nash's Nobel Prize is in economics, he studied mathematics. His theory describes people's decisional behavior mathematically (market economics). A majority of Nobel Prizes in Economics are for complex mathematics rather than financial analysis. Nash exhibited eccentric behavior before his diagnosis of schizophrenia. He was first admitted to a psychiatric hospital in 1959. The Nobel committee waited a few years before awarding Nash the Nobel Prize (shared with some other mathematicians/economists), as they were worried that Nash might demonstrate bizarre behavior as he was receiving his prize. Nash has said that his paranoid delusions have not necessarily disappeared, but now he can recognize them as delusions.

J. The Etheric Body

Kunz identifies the etheric body as the spirit entity that most "densely" inhabits the physical body. How does the etheric body relate to other spiritual entities? I maintain that it is the entity that regulates the physical body's mechanisms. It cannot depart from the body. When discussing the effects of abuse, Dr. Colin Ross (1989) comments that neurochemicals can affect behavior but should not be considered the cause of the behavior. To actually heal an abused patient, some form of psychotherapy is necessary to relieve the trauma and remediate neurochemical production.

The etheric body has electrical and chemical properties that interface with the physical body and thus mediate the effect that trauma has on the emotional body. In other words, as a result of abuse, the emotional body is first traumatized, consequently sending abnormal signals to the etheric body, which in turn produces incorrect neurochemical levels that result in abnormal behavior. The only proper way to correct the situation is to normalize the emotional body, which will then correct the signals to the etheric body and, in turn, to the physical body, by correcting the neurochemical imbalance. The emotional body is always processing information in conjunction with the mental body, the two together forming the psychonoetic body, and thus psychotherapy must address mental and emotional issues resulting from the trauma. Prescribing neurochemical medications can often make the situation worse because the trauma induces a new homeostatic level of neurochemicals. In the case of trauma not caused by abuse, such as TBI, it is simpler to imagine therapy as retrieval of a lost or fragmented soul or as removal of an intruding spirit.

The etheric body addresses the question raised by some scientists that if a person has a purely spiritual soul, then how can that spiritual aspect affect physical matter and behavior? The etheric body is an intermediary between the psychonoetic body (or soul) and physical matter. The etheric body has no "executive" functions. It converts signals from the soul to chemical and electrical signals the physical body can understand. It is analogous to a software program.

Although I have said that the etheric body cannot depart the physical body except at death, in the case of nonessential gland failure the etheric body does depart that gland. Either can happen first: the etheric body controlling a gland may be slowly departing. When totally departed, the gland ceases functioning, or if a gland is damaged beyond repair, the etheric body will depart that gland. I use the term *nonessential* because some gland secretions can be replaced by pills or injections, as with the thyroid and pancreas.

Another way to imagine the etheric body or the soul (a combination of the emotional and mental body) is to view it as a field. Most people have seen pictures of iron filings placed on a piece of paper above a magnet. The filings line up in a pattern resembling two earlobes. The farther from the center of the magnet, the fewer the filings that are caught up in the field. The magnetic field determines the direction of the filings, and the density of the filings indicates the strength of the field at that particular point.

The various spirit bodies are like fields that penetrate the physical body at various strengths. If the strength of the field is at normal level around a gland, then the gland is functioning normally. If the field weakens, then the physical gland slowly becomes less functional—and completely nonfunctional when the field strength drops to zero. The chakras are minor fields within the etheric body, and each chakra is related to and regulates a specific gland. Rather than viewing the decreasing strength of a chakra as a lower-strength field, to a person like Kunz, who could view the chakras, the chakra indicates reduced strength by turning at a reduced speed (recall that the word *chakra* means "wheel").

K. A Two-Way Street

While I concede that the psychonoetic body affects the etheric body and then body chemistry, note that there is an exchange between the two. If a person is in an accident and the physical body is injured, this in turn affects the person's emotional state. The person may have some choice in how she reacts to the accident. Likewise, when I attribute some abnormal behavior to spirit intruders, I mean that the condition of the physical body can affect entry of spirit intruders. Again, I go back to Ritchie's description of the opening of the sailor's protective cocoon of *light* around his body after he fell unconscious from drinking too much alcohol. The soul is affected by substances, injury to the brain, vitamin or mineral deficiencies, or infectious diseases. The condition of the physical body definitely affects soul loss; in fact, it may be the primary cause. One of the major nonphysical causes of soul loss may be involvement in occult practices.

L. A Neglected Topic

Atteshlis uses the term *elementals* and gives the most descriptive explanations for how elementals affect behavior. The term *thought forms* is mentioned in Max Freedom Long's analysis of the kahunas, and Kunz also uses it. I consider the terms *elementals* and *thought forms* to be identical. Atteshlis does not explain the origin of the term, but I suspect that elementals are so called because they have only a singular nature, whereas humans have a complex nature, consisting of an etheric body, an astral or emotional body, a mental body, and a Spirit.

The composition of an elemental may be similar to an astral body. How do these elementals affect behavior? Atteshlis comments that earthbound spirits are attracted to people who "vibrate analogously." I conjecture that these earthbound spirits, whose behavior is greatly influenced by elementals, are attracted to living people who have similar elementals. One of the principles of the spiritual world is that "like attracts like," unlike the physical world in which opposites attract (magnetism, electric charges). Spiritual attraction is similar to dissolving one substance in another to form a solution. Polar materials dissolve other polar materials, and nonpolar materials dissolve other nonpolar materials.

An example of this attraction to similar behavior from earlier in this book comes from Ritchie's observation of deceased spirits quarreling and fighting among themselves on a plain in an afterlife. I conjecture that these spirits were attracted to each other by similar elementals they had created when living. Ritchie describes them as being held there by an "absorption with self," again from when living. This raises the possibility that after death we are not sent "somewhere" but, instead, choose where we will go in accordance with our behavior while living and the elementals we have created.

This concept of vibrating analogously may not apply to soul fragmentation in children. If a child is injured or abused, an earthbound spirit may enter the child. If abuse is the cause of the soul fragmentation, the malevolent spirits around the abuser may attach themselves to or enter the child, regardless of the child's vibrations. Since children, especially preschool ones, are often around the home, they may also be more susceptible to earthbound spirits of deceased relatives, who often linger around the family.

M. Characteristics Exhibited by People Who Have Had Spiritually Transformative Experiences

I have already discussed unusual abilities of people who have had an NDE, a mystical experience, or a spiritually transformative experience (STE.) While the term to be mentioned here was not in use when most of my sources were written, I believe that people who have had an STE generally exhibit a much higher level of *emotional intelligence*. The first prominent use of this term was by writer Daniel Goleman in his book of that title (1995). Goleman provides the following list of emotionally intelligent behaviors in the *Harvard Business Review* (1998):

1. Self-awareness—the ability to know one's emotions, strengths, weaknesses, drives, values, and goals and to recognize their impact on others while using gut feelings to guide decisions.
2. Self-regulation—involves controlling or redirecting one's disruptive emotions and impulses and adapting to changing circumstances.

3. Social skill—managing relationships to move people in the desired direction.
4. Empathy—considering other people's feelings, especially when making decisions.
5. Motivation—being driven to achieve for the sake of achievement.

Although these are learned capabilities, some people learn them much more quickly, either by normal observation or as the result of an STE.

I believe many of these characteristics fit in with the descriptions of people who are operating in a good relationship with their Spirit. Goleman states that children who exhibit emotional intelligence are more likely to be successful as adults, and not just financially. NDE researcher Dr. Melvin Morse feels that childhood NDErs act much more mature than other children. Note that the phrase "using gut feelings to guide decisions" probably indicates a person in tune with messages (probably unconscious) from his own Spirit.

One other characteristic often resulting from an NDE that I would like to elaborate on is "gratitude," or being thankful. Just as composers hear music from nowhere, music that in reality is from their own Spirit (who may have received it from a Muse), messages from a person's Spirit may simply inform a person how his life can be better. A recent book by John Kralik (2010) titled 365 Thank Yous illustrates this principle. Kralik was in financial trouble and was having many personal relationship problems. One day he was hiking in the mountains and thinking about what a "loser" he was. Then he heard a voice say, "Until you learn to be grateful for the things you have, you will not receive the things you want." He had no idea where the voice came from, but he sat down to think about it. He decided that every day he would say thank you to someone, either in person or with a note or card. He felt his life began to turn around as a result of implementing the suggestion from a voice.

Although it may seem unrelated to Kralik's message, Morse (1992) conveys the story of a child NDEr who, during the NDE, heard voices singing in a garden but only saw one man. The man said he had messages for people on the other side of the glass wall (i.e., for those in physical bodies). He said that those people had problems and that he had messages that would help them. However, he said they would not stop worrying about their problems long enough to let his messages come through. Perhaps by being in a quiet place out in nature, Kralik was able to hear the message intended for him, not only listening to it but also actually putting the suggestion into action. Another example of the importance of gratitude is that mystic Meister Eckert once said that if a person's only prayer in life was "Thank you," that would suffice. Although saying thanks to other people is a good start, spiritual gratitude is more than showing common courtesy to other people. In explaining McAll's therapy method, I stated that he often held a Eucharistic service for a deceased person. The word *Eucharistic* is derived from the Greek word meaning "thanksgiving." I have previously used a number of quotes by Thornton Wilder. This sentence is an interesting way of describing gratitude. "We can only be said to be alive in those moments when our hearts are conscious of our treasures." Found under Wilder in brainyquote.com

Some of the apostle Paul's writings help distinguish characteristics from abilities in spiritually transformative experiencers (STErs). Paul denotes gifts or abilities that he believed were found in Christians who were graced by the presence of the Holy Spirit. These abilities are listed in 1 Corinthians 12:4–11 (LT).

> Now there are diversities of gifts, but there is only one Spirit. And there are diversities of ministries, but there is only one Lord. And there are diversities of powers, but it is the one God who works all things in all man. But the manifestation of the Spirit is given to every man as help to him. For to one is given by the Spirit the word of wisdom; to another the word of knowledge by the same Spirit. To another faith by the same Spirit, to another gifts of healing the same Spirit; to another the working of miracles; to another prophecy; to another of the means to distinguish the true Spirit; to another different languages; to another the interpretation of languages. But all of these gifts are wrought by that one and same Spirit, dividing to every one severally as he will.

In Galatians 5:22–23, Paul denotes various fruits of the Spirit: "But the fruits of the Spirit are love, joy, peace, patience, gentleness, goodness, faith, meekness, self-control, there is no a law against these."

There is some overlap between Paul's gifts and the abilities I have listed for people who live in close rapport with their own Spirit. There are also differences because Paul's abilities are within a religious context, but these and others, like creativity, gratitude, and living in the moment, are often viewed from a secular standpoint. I maintain that Paul's diversity of gifts and fruits of the Spirit are a limited number of examples rather than an exhaustive list of all possibilities.

While not an ability, gift, or fruit, the importance of living in the present moment and not dwelling on past regrets or fantasizing about how wonderful life could be in the future is something that mystics emphasize. This does not imply that a person cannot plan for the future; it is simply means that joy must be found in the moment.

N. Soul Loss, Spirit Intrusion, and Mental Health

In chapter 10, on spirit intrusion, I discussed numerous cases of healings. A majority of the illnesses healed would be classified as abnormal psychology or mental-health problems. I maintain that a majority of mental-health problems are caused by soul fragmentation / spirit intrusion or elementals / thought forms. In this section I will connect predominant mental-health problems to my concept of spirit intrusion.

Most mental illnesses have a "spectrum" of influence, resulting from how much the spirit intruder can take control of the birth personality. It is interesting that the form that involves the most soul loss, dissociative identity disorder (DID), is the one in which a complete cure may be achieved without the use of medication. Lengthy periods of therapy can be reduced by using another aspect of human spiritual nature, the Inner Self-helper (ISH). Interestingly, psychiatrist Colin Ross has determined that if a patient with DID is treated and cured, the patient is usually cured of all the other mental illnesses. I maintain that the curing of DID comes about when the birth (or original) soul is completely restored into the physical body and all discarnate spirits are forced out.

I will now discuss the hearing of unpleasant voices as an indicator of spirit intrusion. Many people hear voices that have a positive influence or provide protection, but those are from a person's own Spirit or deceased relatives. The unpleasant voices result when soul fragmentation causes the person to tap into the realm of deceased spirits who have not entered the realm of *light.* Many people who hear these derogatory, demanding, or questioning voices are classified as schizophrenics. Psychical researchers over a century ago proposed that the brain is not the source of consciousness but that it acts as a "filter" to sort out incoming messages from the mind. According to my concept, consciousness, or the mind, is a human's spiritual components working together—etheric body, astral body, mental body, and Spirit—to constitute thoughts. These components can be influenced by deceased spirits, such as when soul fragmentation occurs and these components cannot filter out incoming messages from deceased spirits or elementals. Soul fragmentation results in the spiritual components losing their filtering ability. Even if the voices heard are not derogatory, there can be such a quantity of voices speaking on different subjects that a person cannot understand what is being said. Similarly, in patients with DID, it is very common for alternate personalities (APs) (who are the spirits of deceased humans), when in control of the physical body, to speak disparagingly toward the host personality.

Schizophrenia is a multisymptom diagnosis, and there are symptoms other than voices that are also an indication of soul fragmentation or spirit intrusion. For example, Ritchie observed spirits on a wide, flat plain arguing, fighting, and cursing among themselves. Schizophrenics may be tapping into these spirits, but the voices from those spirits are directed at the schizophrenic rather than at other spirits. Although these spirits are "attached," the spirits can be imagined as those residing on Ritchie's "physical plain."

One occult term for the unpleasant afterlife is *the lower astral plane.* One of the levels of heaven would be the upper astral plane. Distressing NDEs may be visits to the lower astral plane. In addition to Ritchie, who described encountering this plain during his NDE, numerous other NDErs have seemingly visited hell or a very distressing environment. Though not suffering directly, they observed spirits in an anguished state, and this was frightening. These fighting spirits on a plain are a symbolic manner of describing a poorly chosen afterlife to which the person was attracted through his thought pattern while living. Although here I suggest that the voices heard by schizophrenics may be from spirits in the lower astral plane, the spirits may simply have never left the earth plane and may have attached themselves to a living person for reasons previously discussed.

In chapter 11, the topic of multiple levels of heaven was reviewed. Similarly, there are multiple levels of the afterlife in the underworld. The mythology of the ancient Greeks recognized this; the lowest level was referred to as Tartarus. The names Hades and Tartarus are used as "locations," but they are actually the names of the primordial deities who preside over their respective domains. Since these states are not physical, one level is not physically located at a lower level—but the spirits at lower levels appear more tormented.

An example of a possible level of Hades and how it is related to the manner a person lived her life on earth (elementals the person was attracted to) is provided by Atteshlis (Markides, 1991). One of Atteshlis's abilities was being able to "visit" many levels of the possibilities for an afterlife that a soul may enterin an afterlife, such as the domains of Hades or Tartarus, but also heaven. He reported that one man who was a miser during his life was observed by Atteshlis as constantly counting his "money." The man would carefully be counting but then become briefly distracted, lose count, and have to begin counting again and again. I conjecture that this is similar to one of Ritchie's scenes of the afterlife and that it would not end until the man whom Ritchie had observed looked around to see one of the *beings of light* in the background that could assist him in departing his self-imposed imprisonment.

O. Schizophrenia

In addition to hearing voices, some of the other symptoms of schizophrenia depend upon which subtype each case falls within. Schizophrenics experience three main types of symptoms: positive, negative, and disorganized. Positive symptoms (distortions of reality) include hallucinations and delusions. Negative symptoms (deficiencies from normal behavior) include emotional flattening, poverty of speech, asociality, apathy, and anhedonia (the inability to experience pleasure). Disorganized symptoms include bizarre behavior and disorganized speech, for example, completing a sentence on a different subject from that in the beginning of the sentence.

The various subtypes of schizophrenia include paranoid, disorganized, catatonic, undifferentiated, and residual types. Those who suffer from the paranoid type often have delusions of persecution or grandeur and can attract followers for cult activities. These delusions may be caused by the voices the schizophrenic is hearing. A person with the catatonic subtype will often assume a rigid posture (immobility in an odd posture) for hours but may become very violent and active when not in a stupor. The undifferentiated is a catchall for symptoms that do not fit the other subtypes. Those in the residual subtype have less prominent symptoms. Many schizophrenics do not present the full symptoms of that disorder until adulthood, but they may exhibit bizarre childhood behavior prior to adult diagnosis.

As is the case for many mental illnesses, researchers into schizophrenia often try to find correlations between the frequency of schizophrenia and many variables. These attempted correlations include environmental factors; physical factors in the brain and neural development; substance abuse or physical abuse early in life; geographical factors, including birth in a foreign country; and, of course, family history. There are some clear indications that the likelihood of getting schizophrenia increases with genetic similarity, with the highest correlation being between identical twins. However, that correlation is less than 50% If it were purely genetic, it should be closer to 100%

In addition to schizophrenia itself, there are two other related illnesses within the schizophrenia spectrum. These are schizophreniform disorder and schizoaffective disorder. Schizophreniform disorder entails experiencing a brief form (less than six months) of psychotic symptoms. If the schizophrenia symptoms proceed to remission, schizophreniform disorder is the diagnosis, but if the symptoms continue, the person receives a schizophrenia diagnosis. Schizoaffective disorder is diagnosed if the person has schizophrenia symptoms in conjunction with a mood disorder.

In addition to these Axis I schizophrenic spectrum disorders, there are also Axis II diagnoses, of schizoid personality disorder and schizotypal personality disorder. People with Axis II disorders have chronic interpersonal difficulties and a problem with a sense of self but are not psychotic. These patterns often emerge during childhood and become established with time, normally lasting a lifetime. Although some Axis I disorders may show up in childhood, a person with an Axis I disorder may eventually overcome that condition, such as giving up substance abuse or overcoming depression. The Axis II personality disorders are as follows: paranoid, histrionic, narcissistic, antisocial, avoidant, dependent, and obsessive-compulsive.

The most stigmatized of these may be antisocial personality disorder (APD), because numerous serial killers, such as Ted Bundy, had this diagnosis. In this diagnosis, the person has no guilt concerning any of his actions. I once read of a serial killer whose only regret was that he had not killed the person who testified against him. Although people with APD may not feel guilty or have regrets, they may "socialize" their behavior and know that society does not condone their attitude. Because of this, sociopaths learn to mask their true attitude of disgust for other people. However, people with APD can be charming. Criminals who have swindled other people out of large amounts of money may be diagnosed with APD.

Some of these diagnoses have large gender differences in their occurrence. Women are much more likely to be diagnosed as having histrionic or borderline personality disorders and receive one of these diagnoses prior to concluding they have DID. Men are much more likely to be diagnosed as having narcissistic personality disorder or APD.

P. Gender Identity

In the section on spirit intrusion, I discussed the case (from DID literature) of a young man who was prepared to have surgery to become a woman, as he felt like a woman and had many feminine characteristics. He went to a doctor with a spiritual background who performed a religious ceremony involving the invocation of the Holy Spirit. Afterward, the man no longer felt like a woman and did not have the surgery. Fiore contends that homosexuals have such a proclivity on account of an intruding spirit of the opposite sex, although she does not give any examples of cures. McAll claims to have cured homosexual behavior by holding a religious service for a deceased partner. A majority of people with DID have APs that are the opposite gender of the host personality.

Although gender identity disorder (GID)—also called gender incongruence or gender dysphoria, with its sufferers often referred to as transgendered—and homosexuality are different, I maintain that both are the result of an intruding spirit that most likely entered at a young age, definitely before puberty. There are multiple events that may occur in early childhood that may result in such spirit intrusion. Among these are birth difficulties; early injuries, especially to the brain; and surgeries. Some people with DID reportedly had their first alternate personality enter prepartum (in utero). Those who claim they were born that way may be correct, but it is still a case of spirit intrusion, not of genetics.

I recall once reading that children who are autistic are more likely to have been anesthetized for surgery than nonautistic children. There are indications, such as anhedonia, that autism is a result of soul fragmentation and that surgery is one of many possible mechanisms for soul fragmentation. I have also read that there is a possible correlation between a mother's health and autism in her child. Women who take selective serotonin reuptake inhibitors (SSRIs) during certain stages of pregnancy have a statistically higher likelihood that the child will develop autism or depression. Although GID and autism are totally different, I maintain that both are related to soul fragmentation and that both may have similar causes but different resulting behavior.

I would argue that GID is a variation of homosexuality or vice versa. If a man has the spirit of a woman attached to him, that spirit may desire to have sexual relations with a man and thus the man would be classified as a homosexual. If the spirit of the woman has no desire for sexual relations, that would be a transgender issue. In DID-caused abuse, there is frequently an AP of the opposite sex—and APs are spirit intruders. Since there are many other causes of soul fragmentation and spirit intrusion other than abuse, having a child with autism or homosexuality is not an indication of abuse. Recall that earlier I specified that children are more likely to attract random spirits or ancestors, unlike adults, who attract spirits with similar elementals. That the spirit intrusion in those with GID occurs prior to puberty is important. An adult alcoholic heterosexual male who has the spirit of a deceased female alcoholic attached to him is unlikely to become gay. Generally, the spirit of a deceased person has one primary reason for remaining earthbound, and if that reason is to satisfy its desire for alcohol, it may have no desire for sexual encounters of any type. However, the APs in people with DID often have a full range of human desires, but other APs may fulfill only one function.

I hypothesize two other findings that support the concept of an intruding spirit of the opposite gender causing homosexuality on account of that spirit's having some unresolved sexual desire from its physical life.

One finding is that homosexuals often act like people of the opposite sex. Gay men often seek jobs that were traditionally considered women's occupations, although in modern Western society such boundaries often no longer apply. Likewise, lesbians often have jobs that were more traditionally male occupations, such as in athletics or the military. Perhaps homosexuals are better able to recognize another person with a spirit that has sexual desires. There is a term, *gaydar*, used for the ability of gay people to recognize other gays, possibly sensing the desires of the attached spirit.

A second finding is that homosexuals appear to be overrepresented in some creative occupations. There are a number of famous writers, poets, and composers who were homosexual. The creative impulse is often the result of the person's Spirit being more active in people with spirit intruders. And being homosexual does not necessarily make a person more creative; there are numerous homosexuals in ordinary occupations.

Of course, my assertion that gender identity behavior is a result of spirit intrusion raises a number of side questions. If the spirit intruder had sexual difficulties in his or her own life, and those difficulties were the result of spirit intrusion, what happened to the secondary intruder after the primary intruder died? Is its real attachment to the spirit of the primary intruder or to the physical body? If to the spirit, is there a multiplier effect? When the person to whom the primary intruder was attached dies, are the primary and secondary intruders now both earthbound spirits? In one DID case, a spirit indicated he was following a female AP around. When the AP took control of another female person with DID, that following spirit indicated he would enter the body of a man who was having sexual relations with a female AP, which made him believe he was having sex with the spirit he was following around. Although this is only one case, it indicates that one spirit can be attached to another spirit, not just to a physical body, and then detach itself to enter temporarily into another physical body.

Although abuse by a parent is perhaps the most frequent cause for spirit intrusion, abuse by other persons may have similar consequences. The writer Adeline Virginia (née Stephen) Woolf (1882–1941) was raised in a large blended family (her mother, Julia, was widowed) that included half-brothers with the last name of Duckworth (Julia's surname in her first marriage). These half-brothers sexually abused Virginia and her sister. Virginia, who had numerous psychiatric problems her entire life, indicating soul fragmentation / spirit intrusion, eventually committed suicide. Several other children in her blended family were homosexuals, which I argue is a result of rampant sexual abuse in that household, which caused soul fragmentation / spirit intrusion. Verbal abuse or neglect may also result in soul fragmentation, but sexual abuse may increase the probability that the consequences are manifested in sexual behavior. While in this section I have emphasized trauma after birth, endocrine disruptors and neurochemicals taken by the mother during pregnancy may affect the gender of the child *in utero*.

I consider that the spirit that enters before puberty becomes fairly solidified and comfortable in its new role. Hence, having sex with people of the same gender as the physical body into which the spirit intruded is easily accepted. Removal of this type of spirit intrusion would be fairly complex. A person who is classified as bisexual still has his or her natural sexual proclivity but also is influenced by a spirit intruder. Spirit intruders can become more powerful if their desires are met. Men who regularly have sexual relations with their wives, but who then follow a spirit intruder's desire for gay sex, often drift into a predominance of gay sex.

Q. Organ Transplants

Elsewhere, I have shown that paranormal abilities may appear in people whose crown chakra has been activated by kundalini. Chakras, discussed in chapters 8 and 11, provide an alternative explanation for unusual types of behavior. To explain how chakras may affect behavior, I will review some findings by researchers into the aftereffects of heart transplants. The title of the article reviewed is "Changes in Heart Transplant Recipients That Parallel the Personalities of Their Donors," by Pearsall, Schwartz, and Russek (2002). In addition to discussing behavior, their article raises the issue of whether memory resides strictly in the physical brain or if the brain retrieves memory-related information that is stored elsewhere. NDE and DID research indicates that memory may not be in the brain. The information in this article also raises the issue of where a person's decisions about likes, dislikes, attractions, and fears arise.

The authors of the article interviewed heart (or heart and lung) transplant recipients and their family and friends, as well as organ donors' family and friends, to see if changes in behavior in the recipients paralleled the behavior of the donor. The researchers found parallels in food, music, art, and sexual, recreational, and career preferences, in addition to perceptions of names and sensory experiences. They collected their information before the donors and recipients met. The authors propose that the changes may be due to cellular memory, but later I propose a different interpretation. The researchers present their information in specific and sporadic cases. Thus, they were unable to calculate the percentage of patients who reported personality changes. The following are summaries of some of the cases they present in their article.

1. A boy who died at age 18 loved poetry and music and had written in his diary about his impending death, indicating foreknowledge. The choice to be a donor was his and was not something done afterward by his parents. One of the songs he had written was titled, "Danny, My Heart Is Yours." The recipient of his heart was an 18-year-old female named Danielle. She felt she could finish the phrases of some of the donor's songs, and she took up guitar lessons after her transplant, the instrument the donor played. Note that some of these names and circumstances closely parallel a case discussed in chapter 5, on NDEs, concerning a recipient who, during surgery, traveled out of body to the site of the donor's dead body and heard words similar to the above song title, albeit not in a song.

2. The donor was 16 months old, and the recipient was seven months old. At the age of five, the recipient had not met the donor's father, but in a crowd, he left his parents' side and went up to the donor's father and called him Dad. The donor had cerebral palsy on the left side, and the recipient had stiffness and shaking on his left side that he had not had prior to the transplant.

3. The donor was a 24-year-old lesbian and a landscape artist. The recipient was a 25-year-old man whose girlfriend said he was a better lover after the transplant, because he now had a female understanding of her emotional needs. He also now

carries a purse, likes to shop, and goes to art museums, where he especially likes to view landscape paintings.

4. The donor was a 17-year-old African American student who was randomly shot to death on his way to a violin lesson; playing classical music was his passion. The recipient was a 47-year-old white foundry worker who developed a new desire to listen to classical music. Previously he had never asked any African American coworkers over to his home, but he regularly did so after the transplant.

5. This is the most interesting case for my concept of GID. The donor was a 19-year-old woman who owned and operated a vegetarian food restaurant and was described by her mother as "man crazy." The recipient was a 29-year-old woman who, prior to her transplant, was a meat lover and a militant lesbian. After her surgery, she became a dedicated vegetarian. She now thinks that sex with men is terrific and no longer has interest in sex with other women. The modern materialistic explanation for being gay or lesbian is that the person was born that way and it cannot be changed. This case questions that view.

Although Pearsall et al. found other similarities in organ transplant situations other than the heart, the association was much greater for heart transplants. Although these researchers attribute the connection to possible memory stored in the heart cells, I conjecture that the heart chakra of the donor also follows the physical heart. The memories and desires are stored in the chakra.

In chapter 10, I discussed soul fragmentation. According to Baldwin (2003), fragmentation of the soul often occurs during organ transplants, as a fragment follows each individual organ. Thus, these fragments are widely distributed. In the cases cited by Pearsall, the influences from these fragments that follow the heart were experienced as simple desires (often beneficial) by the heart transplant recipients, but they were not the type of debilitating influences for which psychiatric therapy is sought.

R. Brain Imaging

I am very skeptical of images of brain activity performed by positron emission tomography (PET) or other modern brain-mapping techniques purporting to contribute to the understanding of mental illnesses. However, when schizophrenics are hearing voices, brain mapping does indicate that speech areas (rather than hearing areas) of the brain are more active. Thus, they could be sensing internal voices, but which I maintain are from a spiritual realm. In addition, I do not have any problem with brain mapping that indicates that people who have had traumatic brain injury (TBI) have areas of the brain that indicate inactivity relative to uninjured people. An indication of injury is much different from attributing behavior to an uninjured brain.

My skepticism regarding brain mapping is supported by an article titled "Neuroscience Fiction" by Gary Marcus (2012). He reports that a graduate student named David Poeppel analyzed a number of peer-reviewed and published studies on active areas of the brain during speech perception. Poeppel concluded that none of the studies agreed; there was total inconsistency among the conclusions. These inconsistencies may be due to the maps' being partly dependent on software that interprets the raw data, and thus the type of software will affect the conclusion. The bright colors seen on brain maps are software-generated and are not what sensors are detecting. Many scientists have begun to question whether these brain scans have any research value. Three books addressing this issue of the implications of brain imaging have been published in the last several years. These are titled *Neuromania: On the Limits of Brain Science* (2011) by Paolo Legrenzi and Carlo Umilta, *Out of Our Heads: Why You Are Not Your Brain, and Other Lessons from the Biology of Consciousness* (2010) by Alva Noe, and *Aping Mankind: Neuromania, Darwinitis, and the Misrepresentation of Mankind* (2011) by Raymond Tallis. The last-mentioned book will be discussed later in this chapter.

The view that the activity of a person's brain is exclusively responsible for that person's behavior is purely a reductionist conclusion. The video media particularly like these aesthetically pleasing studies, as they can show colored diagrams of these software-enhanced brain scans. The diagrams that I consider invalid are ones that have determined that sexual perpetrators receive a brain "reward" when they molest a child that nonperpetrators do not receive. Therefore, the perpetrators cannot control these behaviors. Supposed reward scenarios are also alleged to apply to gamblers and to alcohol and drug abusers. There is a possibility that they do feel rewarded, but this is the result of spirit intruders or elementals that the addict or perpetrator has attached, or created herself, and are not genetically based. Some defense attorneys argue that some people should not be found guilty because they are "victims" of their brain's reward system, but people need to be held responsible for their own behavior even if influenced by a spirit intruder.

S. From General to Specific

I have discussed my general hypothesis of spirit forms and how some of the information presented throughout this book supports the hypothesis that each spirit form has different functions but all work together for a complete human being. When I originally presented the information, I often treated it only as findings related to my contention rather than showing how each item fit into the general hypothesis. There were also some thoughts that it was too early to present as connections to my hypothesis. In this section I will go over various chapters and connect them together. Specifically, I will discuss findings about NDEs, DID, Eastern concepts of spirituality, shamanic practices, and spirit intrusion therapy, showing how each fits into my general hypothesis of multiple spirit forms, thereby making connections among all areas of my inquiry. Some comments may be speculative, but these are warranted by evidence.

1. NDEs

I have divided NDEs into two types: autoscopic and transcendental. These epitomize the division of soul and Spirit into two separate forms with disparate functions. These roles are more easily divisible during unconsciousness.

An autoscopic NDE (or OBE) is representative of the soul's (psychonoetic body) temporarily departing the physical body. In this discussion, I will generally use the term *psychonoetic body* as an indication that it has a form, somewhat in the shape of the physical body, instead of *soul*, with its possible religious implications. The word *psychonoetic*, from the findings of Atteshlis, implies a combination of emotion and rational thought processes, that is, the combination of astral and mental bodies from Eastern concepts of human spiritual nature. When the departure of this psychonoetic body takes place, hearing and vision are able to function, even more vividly than when the individual is physically conscious. This vividness is certainly unexpected from a physical viewpoint, as delirium generally results in reduced and distorted sensory input. In fact, the senses are no longer impeded by injuries to the physical eyes or ears. Thus, blind and deaf people can see and hear when out of their body during an autoscopic NDE. The same functionality probably applies to taste and smell, but during an OBE most people do not put much emphasis on those senses. The sense of touch seems to be absent, as most NDErs report that they readily pass through physical objects. An NDEr in the transcendental realm does not "hear" spoken words but telepathically understands messages with perfect clarity from spiritual beings of various types. During an autoscopic NDE, some NDErs are able, by thought transference, to discern concerns that attending medical personnel may have in their own life.

Since an autoscopic NDEr can see, hear, and remember what she saw or heard, this implies that memory is actually a function of the psychonoetic body, since the memory occurs without entering through the body. When sense information enters through the physical body, brain malfunctions, such as Alzheimer's disease, prevent the information from being recorded. The brain does work in conjunction with the psychonoetic body; thus, the act of touching a neuron in the body during open, but conscious, brain surgery may bring a memory to the surface. In attempting to explain memory, some students of the paranormal compare it to reception by a television set. The program is not in the television set itself but is part of an external source. Although the psychonoetic body is internal, it is where memory is stored (and not recognized by theories of physicalism). A person with Alzheimer's disease has a partially malfunctioning receiver.

Although an autoscopic NDE may seem related to the earth plane, the concepts of time and space contradict normal earth-plane logic, as they are irrelevant when dealing with most various spiritual forms in humans. Thus, during an autoscopic NDE, the psychonoetic body may travel anywhere on earth simply by thinking where he might like to be, such as with a family member, even if that family member is in an unknown location. Most NDErs report arriving immediately at the desired destination, but some felt they were traveling, although at an unearthly rapid speed. While some leave their body and travel through walls, many NDErs perhaps are unaware of that ability and simply remain near the ceiling in the corner of the room in which the medical incident that caused them to "die" occurred. Not being able to travel through walls is simply a limitation of the thinking process employed from residing in a physical body. Also, the person may not have thought about visiting family or was simply interested in the actions being done by medical personnel to his physical body.

I have mentioned several times that a person's Spirit is attached to the psychonoetic body and physical body. One possible method to describe the "tunnel" through which many NDErs pass is to imagine it as the link through which the psychonoetic body travels to Spirit, which is often represented as *light*. Recall that anything in the transcendental or spirit world can only be discussed in symbolic terms. The "tunnel" in NDEs or the kundalini traveling up the spinal cord are two symbolic ways to represent a merging with or deeper connection to Spirit.

The most common aftereffect of a transcendental NDE (or various other STEs) is simply the person's first becoming aware of her own Spirit. The individual to whom this happens is virtually never the same, although there can be difficulties. Some of the difficulties can be explained by using Kason's kundalini model from chapter 11. If a chakra has not been trained or prepared for an encounter with the kundalini, there may be physical and psychological effects. Practitioners of various spiritual paths, such as the Mystic Way, have most likely properly prepared their chakras for this encounter with Spirit. If a person is not properly prepared, difficulties can arise, such as energy surges.

Some of these difficulties have arisen simply because our materialistically oriented society dismisses connections to spiritual influences as a notion that needs to be corrected. For instance, the view of a materialistic-oriented psychiatrist may be the result of a schizophrenic's explaining that "God" told him to injure another person or himself. But if that psychiatrist's paradigm included spirit intruders, therapists would not construe delusional voices to be the jabbering of a confused brain claiming to be God. Instead, they would construe them as messages from an unfriendly spiritual world.

The transcendental world described by NDErs, in addition to the love, joy, and peace experienced, may appear ineffable and thus thought to be illusory by people oriented only to materialism. There are two possible explanations for this alleged loss of reality. The first is that the transcendental world can only be described symbolically. Each NDEr may have her own idea of what heaven or paradise would be like, or a situation in which she would be most comfortable, and this is how it is the NDEr must portray it with earthly terms. The second explanation is the concept of spiritual levels above Spirit. When I wrote chapter 5, on NDEs, I only briefly introduced Long's concept that the High Self can contact spiritual levels above itself. I covered this topic in greater detail in chapter 11, which is about mystical experiences. Once an NDEr has entered the world of his own Spirit, he may proceed to any of these levels. Of course, any of these levels would still be represented symbolically; one person's description of an angel may disagree with another person's description of the same. However, deceased relatives are not symbolic and typically appear as they looked when about age thirty—and without any infirmities their physical bodies may have had while living.

While most NDErs consider their NDE to be one of the most wondrous and transformative experiences of their lives, it often becomes just another memory. Other NDErs believe that they have established a lifelong relationship with the force they encountered during their NDE and that it influences them daily. This would correspond to a deep and permanent connection to Spirit. The Eastern term for this is *sahaja state*. A Western-oriented Christian may think of it as a relationship with the Holy Spirit.

Several NDErs and hospice care workers who have been around people close to death note that humans are spiritually connected with each other. The cancer survivor Anita Moorjani observed during her NDE that not only are all humans interconnected but also that all humans are to a lesser extent connected to all living things. An analogy sometimes used to describe this is threads in a woven tapestry. These connections may be greatest to relatives, spouses, and long-term friends, but thinner threads extend to all of humanity, even to animals and the inanimate world. Recall that Kunz could see an aura around crystals; while not as fluid or changing as the aura around living things, it definitely was observable. Thus, human auras could connect to those inanimate auras. Note that any such threads have no physical properties and are not limited in length or quantity. Although it may not apply to inanimate objects, Long's concept of the High Self includes the notion that all High Selves are connected.

A similar thread possibly connects a human psychonoetic body to the physical body. Several NDErs observed a thread going from their out-of-body position back to their physical body. Occult literature often alludes to a "silver cord," connecting a spirit body to the physical body. This term is also used in reference to death in Ecclesiastes 12:6–7 (LT): "Remember him before the silver cord is cut off and the golden bowl is broken and the pitcher is broken at the fountain or the wheel is broken at the cistern. Then the dust shall return to the earth as it was; and the spirit return to God who gave it."

I am not sure what the references to the breaking of a golden bowl, a pitcher, or a wheel imply. Shared or empathic experiences and end-of-life experiences (ELEs) are interesting in that they illustrate that being in the presence of a dying person can occasionally send the healthy observer into the transcendental realm. Other features could indicate that the dying person has a short spiritual insight into the afterlife world before his final departure from the physical body.

Distressing NDEs, but not simply the confused type, are difficult to explain by using my theory of multiple spirit forms in each human. I will speculate that everything in nature seems to have an opposite (magnetic poles, electric charges, left–right, cold–hot, good–evil), so perhaps a dark distressing world is a necessary complement to the world of *light* found in many STEs. The New Age explanation for distressing NDEs is that the person has gone to the *lower astral plane*. Although I have generally contended that many "evil spirits" are simply earthbound human spirits, my hypothesis does not dismiss the possibility that they are satanic beings that have never been in a physical body, that live in darkness, and that desire to bring humans to their world. My preferred definition of *sin* is to "miss the mark" or not to live in harmony with agreed-upon purposes and goals before being born, although the purposes are fluid and adaptable throughout life. The word *Satan* is derived from a similar root word for a spiritual being who attempts to make a person "miss the mark." It is also possible that distressing NDEs are kundalini energy entering into chakras that have not been prepared properly. A third possibility is that a distressing NDE is the purgation stage or "dark night of the soul" phase of a mystical experience.

A fear-death experience (FDE), rather than requiring any injury happen to the physical body, demonstrates that people only have to think they might die to initiate the experience. Although people who have only a transcendental NDE may not recall being out of their body, I maintain that they most likely have loosened the attachment of the psychonoetic body to the physical body. This loosening probably applies to other spiritual experiences, such as mystical experiences and shamanic journeys. Although I have used the term *loosening* here, it may be considered a type of dissociation, but it is only temporary and not pathological as in DID.

Most NDErs who had a life review felt the review was for learning purposes and did not feel judged. Many NDErs seem like they have lived ordinary lives. The incidences seen in their life review show how they could have acted much better. I did hear once about an NDEr who was an enforcer for organized crime and had killed a number of people, but this is unusual. This enforcer did have a positive NDE and changed his life so he could be of service to other people.

Some of this book has dealt with child abuse and its effects on the lives of the victims. I sometimes wonder if observing yourself doing serious abuse to a child is simply a case of "I should have done better" or if there could be more serious consequences. Of course, many perpetrators of child abuse were themselves abused when they were children and thus were influenced by spirits not of their choosing.

2. Dissociative Identity Disorder

The various APs found in DID are the psychonoetic bodies or earthbound spirits of deceased humans. From their previous lives, they bring their own unfulfilled desires, which they seek to fulfill using the physical body of a person whose own psychonoetic body (i.e., the birth or original personality) has departed (via soul loss or soul fragmentation), generally the result of severe abuse during early childhood. Although the spirits may have a primary agenda when entering another physical body (e.g., to satisfy an addiction), they do bring memories and traits from their life or lives in a previous physical body or bodies. Thus, if the AP was nearsighted, had hypertension, had various allergies, or was diabetic, those characteristics will be present in the body it now occupies. The same applies to psychological traits from life in another body, such as anger, and capabilities such as artistic talent and speaking in foreign languages. The cases in which various APs switch hands quite readily, for example, indicates an ability that would be very difficult for a person who was faking her diagnosis. This spirit also brings along memories, but if it were in several previous bodies, the memories may seem inconsistent, such as remembering life in two different cities at the same age, two high school graduations, and two marriages at the same time. Verification of the spirit's previous life or lives would be very difficult to obtain. Some APs are able to acquire information of other APs, to "remember" that information, and to report it as their memory, although the activity of the memory did not occur when the person in question was in control of the body. A few of the earthbound psychonoetic bodies may be simply confused and can be programmed by the Spirit to assist the person with DID.

Prebirth memories and feelings indicate that our spirit bodies are definitely present prior to birth. One child felt that her first split (formation of an AP) occurred in utero when her father kicked her mother. According to my concept of spirit forms, this is readily believable, but many therapists would consider it an instance of false memory syndrome (FMS). In my book, I have explained that other types of trauma, such as concussions or viewing a person being killed, may also cause spirit intrusion. However, a person's intent may be a factor. Some pregnant women may be seriously injured with no psychological impact on the child in utero, but the same type of injury as a result of intent to cause harm to the mother or the child may cause typical effects of trauma. This does involve some speculation, as an in utero child whose mother was injured may be regarded as physically normal at birth. However, spiritual effects and possible intrusion may be noticeable later in life. Although behaviorally normal children often have imaginary playmates or companions, a higher percentage of people with dissociative identity disorder (PwDID) have them. These could represent spiritual companions that comfort and assist the child who is being abused.

A person with DID may still have some spirit intruders that do not completely control the physical body. These intruders can exert their influence on the birth personality or on one of the APs, or act like an AP but have only one minor function. Lowered sensory awareness, or dulling of the senses, may be the result of incomplete penetration of the physical body by either the birth personality or the APs.

In the studies I reviewed, the numerous diagnoses that DID patients were given before proper diagnosis by the therapist indicate that various presenting personalities displaying themselves to diverse therapists evinces a prime underlying basis for most mental illnesses, which are the result of soul fragmentation and spirit intrusion. One personality may present itself as depressed, another as seeking alcohol or drugs, and another as having myriad phobias. These alternate diagnoses disappear if the hierarchically superior DID is treated to completion.

I would like to reemphasize that early childhood abuse results in much greater soul fragmentation because a child's spirit bodies are not as firmly connected to the physical body. Thus, DID as a result of childhood abuse may represent 90-plus percent of the instances of soul loss and nearly complete personalities, whereas adolescent and adult trauma results in only attached spirits with less influence. While DID represents greater soul fragmentation, it is considered to be curable (by using complex psychotherapy), but many other mental illnesses with less soul fragmentation are presently considered to be lifelong illnesses. Of course, my argument is that these less severe mental illnesses would be curable if a spiritual therapy were employed rather than having the reductionist prescribe psychopharmaceuticals with their inherent and often debilitating side effects.

DID does occur more frequently in families. Rather than consider it genetic, as the reductionist proponents interpret this fact, I agree with DID therapist Ross that the most likely parental child abuser is a person who was abused during childhood. Discarnate spirits are inclined to remain around the home. One survey revealed that 20% of APs were deceased relatives.

I have already emphasized the similarity in nature between the ISH encountered in DID and Spirit. The ISH is more attuned to therapy than is the creative end of the abilities of Spirit. The ISH is able to communicate with the ISH (or Spirit) of other people or with spiritual levels above itself (one therapist referred to assistance from levels above the ISH as Higher Helpers), indicating each human's connections to all of humanity. This would confirm the view expressed by several NDErs that any action an individual does to or for another person, beneficial or harmful, he does to himself.

In the chapter on DID, I also discussed hypnotism as it is often employed by DID therapists. However, Crabtree (1985) presents some interesting details about hypnotism, independent of its therapeutic value. His "lower phenomena," which include suggestibility and insensitivity to pain, are often encountered in stage presentations for entertainment. One possible explanation for these lower phenomena in anyone could be direct control by a hypnotist of a hypnotized person's etheric body, bypassing normal thought processes. This explanation would also apply to seminars on smoking cessation or weight reduction.

What Crabtree classifies as "higher phenomena" is close to what I have categorized as paranormal. These phenomena include establishing mental rapport between two people and several types of clairvoyance, including seeing at a distance (remote viewing), seeing into the body (medical intuition), and seeing back through time (retrocognition). An additional ability is induced ecstasy, such as visions of the afterlife and afterlife communication. These abilities would all involve the Spirit aspect of the person that is to be involved in these higher phenomena.

Similarly, Ross notes the close connection between ESP and dissociation. My inquiry into spirit bodies residing in the physical body confirms this connection. Ross further notes that the ESP–dissociation linkage is a double threat to reductionist dualism. ESP is a subdivision of the paranormal. Rudimentary ESP, such as telepathy, may simply involve conveying messages along the "threads" that connect us to people we have known—and ultimately to everything in the universe—whereas advanced paranormal events, such as levitation, precognition, and inedia, involve the Spirit level of these spirit bodies.

3. Eastern Concepts of Spirituality

In one sense, the ideas presented in this field of study are the partial basis for my overall concept, so obviously the ideas and overall concept should be in agreement. However, I would like to emphasize some particular points.

When Kunz was observing people's spirit bodies, she had to focus intently and could only do so for a few hours. This could indicate the use of her own Spirit, which according to Long requires its own form of vital energy; thus, it can be temporarily depleted. People with DID can only engage their ISH (Spirit) for about twenty minutes. This is a much shorter time than Kunz was able to engage hers. DID itself indicates a problem with vital energy, as suggested by the incidence of lowered sensory awareness. A person engaging his Spirit must be able to focus and concentrate. Atteshlis also emphasizes this, and most mystics have this ability to focus, sometimes entering a trance state. Shamans are also able to focus intently. Kunz was also sensitive or allergic to some medical drugs, or could take lower doses than normally prescribed for the same effect. Many NDErs exhibit similar phenomena.

Kunz notes that the etheric, astral, and mental bodies all disintegrate after death. I surmise this may be true for a normal death and direct transition to the afterlife. My general explanation has been that the combination of astral and mental bodies (collectively called the psychonoetic body or soul) does not make this transition if it becomes earthbound for the various reasons previously described, such as addictions. An alternative explanation for an afterlife would be that the "self" (Kunz's term for Spirit) is encountering spiritual levels above itself. My book is eclectic and involves some speculation and thus, alternatives are readily possible. The reader of this book may be able to fathom other spiritual explanations. Kunz did not describe any attached spirits in the mentally ill people whom she observed, but none of them had normal spirit bodies; that is, their auras appeared distorted. There were often vital energy problems in people with mental illnesses, indicating soul fragmentation.

Kunz comments that when a person goes to sleep, her astral body exits through her crown chakra. Various spiritual theorists agree that in sleep part of our spiritual makeup leaves the body. Long maintains that the lower self contacts the High Self during sleep. This is why dreams are symbolic, as everything at Spirit level cannot be physically described. As portrayed by Kunz, these various spiritual bodies are in a constant dynamic state with each other and also with other people, animals, and even the etheric forms of the inanimate world. This would agree with the tapestry model of threads connecting self and universe as recounted by some NDErs.

4. Shamanism

In chapter 9, on shamanism, I provided evidence that there are strong similarities between shamanic concepts of life and what NDErs believe they have learned about the meaning of life. Among these common similarities are the following:

- The calling to be a shaman can be likened to an NDEr's coming back for a purpose.
- Ritual dismemberment during shamanic initiation is similar to a distressing NDE.
- During training, some shamans are filled with *light* and develop various abilities as in the transcendental part of an NDE.
- Shamans and many indigenous peoples feel a close connection to their ancestors, like NDErs who communicate with their ancestors during their experience.
- Shamans have the ability to travel out of body at will, and NDErs often have a spontaneous OBE during their NDE.
- Shamans have the ability to observe the past and future, and NDErs frequently do the same, either during their NDE or afterward.
- Guardian spirits, spirit helpers, and Power Animals are similar to angels, guides, and spirit beings encountered during an NDE.
- Shamans believe in the importance of certain dreams, and some NDErs feel that their dream life is enhanced after their NDE.
- The many different types of encounters with the afterlife during an NDE is an indication of more than one heaven, as recognized by many shamans.
- The concept of a circle to a shaman can be likened to the idea of reciprocity as expressed by many NDErs.

- Shamans and NDErs both agree that when our physical bodies are no longer useful, we continue our existence in an afterworld.
- Shamans readily concede that their view of earthly life is based on a soul/spirit or spirits concept. The various and diverse phenomena that occur during an NDE can be more easily understood from a soul/spirit perspective.

In addition to illustrating the connection between shamanism and NDErs' views, I endeavored to demonstrate that some modern techniques that therapists use to assist people with psychological/psychiatric problems closely parallel the shamanic technique of psychopomp healing (soul retrieval). For example, although the therapists do not mention NDEs, their techniques assist people by guiding an alleged "possessing" spirit to the *light* or to deceased ancestors, similar to an NDE encounter in the transcendental realm of an NDE.

5. Spirit Intrusion

The following are some specific comments on the subject of spirit intrusion and release from chapter 10, and on interrelationships among the various therapies or with other subject matter in various chapters, such as NDEs, shamanism, and DID. This section will illustrate how these therapeutic methods support my overall concept that human beings have several levels of spirits (etheric, astral, mental, and Spirit) as part of our nature. I will also point out some contradictions among the therapeutic methods that have not been previously noted, as well as provide some unique perspectives about human spiritual nature not usually discussed within the boundaries of religion.

a. Atteshlis and Oesterreich

The term *psychonoetic body* comes from Markides's writing about the late Cypriot healer named Atteshlis, who believes that problems with elementals (thought forms) cause more problems than intrusion by earthbound spirits. Since Atteshlis presents no general symptoms of a person with elemental problems, it is impossible to directly apply his methods for therapeutic purposes. My interpretation is that elementals may be predecessors to some mental disorders, such as addiction. For example, moderate use of alcohol may not involve any elementals. As consumption increases, various elementals may be created in the person in response to the reason he was overconsuming alcohol, such as a reaction to peer pressure. However, earthbound spirits can detect these elementals and remain in the vicinity of the drinker. Then, when the heavy drinker becomes unconscious due to becoming drunk, the protective aura opens up (soul fragmentation occurs), at which time the spirits can enter or attach to the drinker and then remain there as the spirit's desire for alcohol is temporarily being satisfied. In advanced cases of spirit intrusion, as described by Martin (1976), a spirit form from the dark hierarchy of nonhuman entities may assume partial or almost complete control of the living human. Frequently, addicts report that they require the substance to relieve tension. This tension is likely caused by the demands of the intruding spirit.

Atteshlis reports that he had a spirit helper named Fr. Dominico who would sometimes assist him in his spiritual work or even in everyday difficulties. Although this spirit helper had a name, I would not necessarily associate him with a real human who once lived. In such cases, the helper may simply be a spiritual resource that is an aspect of Spirit that happens to have a name. This could be compared to spirit guides encountered by NDErs. Ireland-Frey has a spiritual advisor named Master Ching. In addition to a personified individual spirit helper from which advice could be sought, a number of therapists I have reviewed had groups of spirit assistants who would aid them. For instance, Modi specifically mentions angelic assistance, and Wickland implied assistance from the spiritual world that he termed a "Mercy Band." Baldwin's term for these assistants is "warrior *angels of light*," and for Ireland-Frey they are called "bright beings."

Atteshlis does claim that evil voices originate from elementals and not from the spirits of deceased humans who have not transitioned to the world of *light*. He does say that mystics enter the realm of angelic elementals, which I might consider the same as the hierarchy of upper-level spirits, from angels to Seraphim.

Oesterreich (1966) mentions several types of possession, such as somnambulistic (trance with amnesia) and lucid, but he does not always distinguish between the two when discussing incidents related to intrusion. He does note "voluntary" possession, such as that displayed by shamans in some indigenous societies when entering an altered state of consciousness (ASC), but I would proffer that this voluntary possession is actually an active aspect of Spirit and not any intruding spirit from outside the individual. He states that music is often played to induce voluntary possession, which would agree with principles of shamanism described by the anthropologist Harner in chapter 9. Oesterreich also mentions that during this phase, a shaman who is voluntarily possessed and in a trance state is often insensitive to pain or heat, a phenomenon also noted by Eliade (1964) and found in some Christian mystics. A voluntarily possessed person may have healing abilities as well.

Oesterreich was a researcher, not a therapist, but he confirms findings in chapter 9 that many shamans have more excitable personalities than the general population, which may be hereditary—and there may be consequences for refusing their destiny or calling to be a shaman. He also notes that there can be "white" shaman, who are helpful, and "dark" ones, who may use their powers to harm others or exclusively for their own benefit. He agrees that shamans lead ordinary lives when not involved with their shamanic endeavors.

Oesterreich also confirms many concepts presented in this book for causes of spirit intrusion or methods for spirit removal. He states that early Christians believed the souls of deceased humans could affect the living. McAll (1982), the English psychiatrist, supports this when he mentions that early Christians held several religious services for the souls of the deceased, but he notes that one service with caring concern is more important than several routine ones. Oesterreich also mentions a multigenerational family intrusion, which would also agree with McAll's findings concerning one family in which the effects lasted over a century.

Oesterreich claims that some spirits can be induced to depart by fulfilling the spirit's desire, but that would appear to contradict most addiction therapy, as having its desires fulfilled causes the spirit to become more deeply entrenched. However, in another case, he mentions that yielding to the spirit's urgings results in a deteriorating physical condition. A purported spirit intruder that occurs in the Middle East, called a *Zar*, may leave if offered fine clothes and jewelry. Thus, it could be an alter ego of the person involved and not related to actual spirits. Finally, Oesterreich agrees with Fiore, Martin, McAll, Modi, and Baldwin that occult practices may lead to numerous spiritual difficulties. Martin notes that one person lost his "occult" ability to read minds after his exorcism. He had developed the ability from his training to be a psychic.

I have a comment on what might be considered occult practice, namely, contacting the dead or mediumship. Most monotheistic religions are against the practice, and with good spiritual reasons (beyond concerns that the person could become a victim of fraud). In Luke 16:19–27, Jesus tells the parable of a formerly rich man who, after death, is in a place of torment while Lazarus, a former beggar in front of the rich man's house, is comfortable beside Abraham (in heaven). The rich man desires to inform his brothers not to lead a hedonistic life and ignore the less fortunate. The rich man is told there is a barrier between himself and the living. The parable does not specify that there is a barrier between those in heaven and the living. I believe that there is contact by NDErs with deceased relatives, and after-death communication (ADC) may come from the deceased and be passed to the living, but it is best if the communication is initiated by the deceased. A widow or widower who receives communication from his or her deceased spouse is not involved in occult activity. Even the medical profession has statistics showing that this happens to over 50% of surviving spouses, but medical professionals usually attribute it to wishful thinking or a grief-induced hallucination.

While McAll advocates prayers for the spirits of the deceased, Oesterreich reports that one intruding spirit claimed that prayers would not benefit the spirit. Milingo (1984) found the spirit of a deceased aunt who had died 28 years earlier. This aunt described herself as living in a world of darkness where prayers would not do her any good. Milingo does not report any behavioral problems in the living sister through whom the deceased sister spoke, so I am not sure if this is a case of spirit intrusion. This also appears similar to traditional spiritualism, but virtually all Spiritualists (if they are in contact with the deceased) report a wonderful life on the "other side of the veil" for everyone. Spiritual mediums claim they have no control over which spirit visits during their alleged contact with deceased spirits. Thus, only the spirits that are having a wonderful time on the other side may come through, although Milingo did contact the aunt discussed above who was in a less desirable afterlife.

According to Oesterreich, the ancient Greeks considered possession to be more divine than diabolical. There were a number of mystery schools in Greece, and he mentions one called the Pythoness school. Allegedly, priestesses (oracles) would inhale vapors to induce ecstasy, which I maintain would be to assist them in contacting Spirit. Many shamans employ hallucinogenic substances to enter ASCs. The Greeks referred to this as the priestess speaking for Apollo. Socrates and Plato had a high regard for these mystery schools. Perhaps the most famous Greek mystery schools were at Delphi and Eleusis. A recent film, *Minority Report* (2002), employs this concept of oracles. the story line projects a future in which some people are trained to have the ability to enter an ASC. In the movie, priestesses ("precogs") could prophesy upcoming crimes, and a "precrime" police unit could intervene before the crime was committed. The unit had to be shut down when one unscrupulous person was using the precogs' information for political purposes. The film was loosely based on a short story by prominent author Philip K. Dick (1928–1982), whose writings often include monopolistic corporations, authoritarian governments, and ASC.

Oesterreich mentions that some intrusions occur during illness, which would agree with Fiore's theory that a weakened body makes a person more susceptible. Oesterreich does note that the intrusion is more common in women, but he never broaches the possibility that this gender discrepancy may be due to rates of childhood abuse. I might also conjecture that the spirit intruders in males are often more violent than those in women.

Although at times Oesterreich seems to consider spiritual causes of intrusion, he also notes that exorcisms are effective because the victims no longer believe themselves possessed. In other words, exorcisms are a consequence of the placebo effect and not the actual removal of an intruding spirit.

b. Fiore, Wickland, Crabtree, and Van Dusen

Fiore's primary list of reasons why a spirit remains earthbound is fairly comprehensive and agrees with many of the other therapists discussed. These reasons are as follows:

1. Ignorance, confusion, or fear (especially of going to hell)
2. Obsessive attachment to living persons or places

3. Addiction to drugs, alcohol, smoking, food, or sex
4. Sense of unfinished business
5. Desire for revenge

An example of unfinished business is Wickland's (1924) contention that spirit bodies are goal directed, and death does not necessarily interfere with seeking to complete an earthly goal. This is especially true if the cause of death is a sudden accident, a murder, or war. Long-term care for an illness may result in a person's amending or abandoning her original goals in the anticipation of death.

Fiore confirms that people who commit suicide are likely to remain earthbound and carry their depression into another person. They also carry their abilities, addictions, attitudes, and beliefs with them, as these are ingrained into each person's psychonoetic body. Ritchie describes a young man who committed suicide and whose spirit was apologizing to the living for his mistake. This indicates that the spirit of the person who committed suicide was still earthbound. Physicist Fred Alan Wolf has an interest in various paranormal happenings and altered states of consciousness. He comments that he once dreamt himself into a state in which he visited the "astral plane of suicides," where he experienced the desolation and gloom of the postsuicidal spirits. The term *astral plane* is employed by various New Age groups to indicate different levels in the afterlife and was previously discussed.

In some Asian countries, suicide may be committed as a part of restoring family honor and may be considered valorous. Since the reasoning is different, the consequences may be different. Suicide bombers in the Middle East may not be depressed, but their view of life is likely to keep them earthbound after their suicide. The belief that the bomber's purpose is to bring his form of justice to the world (even if based on religious interpretations) is a materialistic concept of the real world. While it is easy to understand how a spirit like this could become earthbound, Wickland holds that dogmatic principles of all kinds can result in the same thing. Perhaps, it is because they have a predetermined, but false, expectation of what life will be like after death.

A significant number of therapists (McAll, Atteshlis, Modi, Baldwin, and Wickland) note that intruding spirits that are reluctant to leave can be forced to enter a spiritual realm that is away from humans but not yet within the *light*. In this spiritual realm, the spirits can be educated to understand the problems they have created while living in a physical body. Knowledge of this realm may have led some religious denominations to speculate on an afterlife level called purgatory. Fiore also notes that electroshock therapy may remove an intruder, though the intruder remains earthbound and could intrude into another person.

In chapter 5, in the section on distressing NDEs, I mentioned that Rommer (2000) speculates that NDErs who travel to the lower astral plane could describe that visit as an LTP (less than positive) NDE. I am not a student of what the lower astral plane consists of, but on that plane could be spirits of deceased people that are not necessarily earthbound but that also have not gone to the *light*. In some cases, it appears that an NDE (whether heavenly or distressful) may result in these entities departing from the NDEr (which would result, for example, in an alcoholic's losing the desire to drink). It may be that the *light* beings encountered by the NDEr escorted the attached entities to the realm of *light*. Note that I have argued that the *light* the NDEr encounters is his own Spirit (High Self, ISH), and therefore the attached entity would have to be led to her own Spirit. Each person's Spirit can cooperate with other Spirits. That is, the NDEr's Spirit may "discuss" the situation with the entity's Spirit and agree to have the entity depart the NDEr. Long (1948) refers to this as the "company of High Selves." However, an alternate explanation is that the NDEr who has the distressing NDE reassesses his life and simply chooses to give up the self-destructive path he has been on. Distressing NDEs may happen to people who are not on a self-destructive path.

Fiore and other therapists would appear to associate addictions primarily with substance abuse, because the two are frequently related. Fiore confirms that activities that cause unconsciousness may result in spirit intrusion. This would thus include various types of trauma and substance abuse. However, addiction is much broader, and it includes nonsubstances such as in gambling or Internet addiction. All addictions involve elementals, which may or may not require a physical substance. I would also include sexual addiction, especially to pornography, which is becoming ever more pervasive thanks to the ease of obtaining pornography on the Internet. Numerous serial killers of women have claimed they were addicted to pornography. It is possible that religious guilt may compound any problem; that is, the person may incorrectly believe that God no longer loves him because he disobeyed a commandment. Forgiveness may be an early stage in the desire to remove or negate the influence of elementals.

Those who become child abusers after viewing pornography are virtually impossible to cure with standardized addiction therapy. The recidivism rate for child molesters who view child pornography regularly and abuse children, and who have been imprisoned and subsequently released, is one of the highest for any crime. Child molesters are often targets of violent behavior by other prisoners. Ariel Castro, the Cleveland-area man who kept three women imprisoned in his home, one for over ten years, stated that he had been abused as a child and was addicted to pornography. He committed suicide in prison shortly after his sentencing. Pornography is the ultimate materialistic view of life in that it assumes that one person lives exclusively to give pleasure to another person.

Fiore states that every homosexual patient whom she has treated had a domineering spirit of the opposite gender. She also contends that having one spirit intruder makes a person susceptible to further intrusions, but that may primarily be for substance abuse or similar proclivities. Homosexuals are not necessarily more open to intrusions by earthbound spirits seeking to satisfy their former addictions.

Fiore also mentions spirit intruders involved in obesity. I recall once reading of a therapist who interviewed a number of obese patients. The majority of them claimed to hear voices urging them to eat. Unrelatedly, Fiore notes one spirit intruder who had no function but who was pursuing another spirit intruder. When the latter spirit departed, the other intruder followed it. Baldwin discusses a case of a man losing his attraction to a woman after an intruding spirit was removed from her. His real attraction was to the intruding spirit. DID therapists have also noted connections between APs that do not seem related to the client.

The therapy of Wickland is not likely to be duplicated, because it requires an assistant with an unusual ability (his wife could function as a medium). Wickland reports that one of his wife's spirit guides was a Native American, and Wickland states Native Americans rarely become earthbound. He was writing almost a century ago, when there were more shamans in their society to function as psychopomps to assist the spirits in completing their transition to the *light*. Komianos's method of applying an electric shock to select acupuncture points closely approximates Wickland's electric shock method.

Wickland maintains that he verified the identity of an intruding spirit as having a real human life, but that may be unusual. Fiore felt she could try to identify the former real existence of a spirit intruder but did not believe it was a worthwhile use of her time. I previously commented that verification may be difficult, because the spirit may have been an intruder into several people prior to the current intrusion and, subsequently, confuse/combine memories from each intrusion. Wickland asserts that one intruding spirit could speak a foreign language that the patient did not know. Milingo was the only other therapist who mentions finding spirits other than those in DID patients that could speak foreign languages.

Wickland also states that if the intruding spirit was killed in an accident, the body of the person the spirit entered may have pains similar to those that caused the spirit to separate from its former body. Modi and Baldwin also found pains in a client that were similar to the injury that had caused the intruding spirit to die. While these pains are often physical, McAll discusses a psychological trait that was passed on in the case of one woman who was afraid of water (hydrophobia). It was determined that her uncle had died in the *Titanic* disaster. When a committal service was held for the uncle, the hydrophobia was eliminated in the niece.

Wickland also believes that a majority of crimes are committed under the influence of spirits. I might say that many theft crimes related to the perceived need to purchase drugs are instigated by the cravings of the spirit intruder, but the spirit intruder may not actually be involved in planning the crime. My opinion is that domestic violence incidents are often directly initiated by intruding spirits who, in many cases, are influenced by a demon or dark-force entity.

The hypnosis/relaxation method of Crabtree also demonstrates the importance of suitable family connections while here on earth if a transition to heaven is to occur at death. His concept of a group mind affecting behavior can be compared to elementals.

Van Dusen confirms much of the findings previously discussed concerning voices. While many people associate voices with schizophrenia, some of Van Dusen's patients who heard disparaging voices were alcoholics or had brain damage. McAll encountered a woman with anorexia who heard voices. I discussed that obese people hear voices encouraging them to eat more. The tormenting and obscene remarks made by these voices appear similar to Ritchie's description of spirits fighting among themselves and insulting each other in an undesirable afterlife. These voices were very antireligious and were described by Van Dusen as lower members of a hierarchy, which would agree with Martin's depiction of various levels of evil spirits in control of a possessed person. Modi and Baldwin also note the hierarchical nature of dark-force entities.

c. Christian Therapists (McAll, Basham, Milingo, and Martin)

McAll states that if a living person is an intruder that affects the behavior in another person's life (almost always family), then that intrusion is likely to continue after the death of the intruder. Although one of his cases was a grandmother who had psychological problems when alive, it is quite common for a voice heard by a DID patient to be that of the deceased parental abuser. Abuse, especially sexual, tends to establish connections between the abuser and victim, and the connection does not end at the death of one or the other. While in several places in this book I have noted that all human beings are interconnected, that connection is often through Spirit, but when psychonoetic bodies are connected through abuse, the consequences are not benevolent. The adult person generally initiates the connection, sometimes through parental "hovering" rather than abuse, but this also results in behavioral consequences.

McAll notes that while it is assumed that a person needs to forgive the dead if they have intruded into her life, it is also important for the dead to forgive the living. Although a spirit may be responsible for not immediately proceeding to the *light* (or to the spirit's deceased ancestors), the individual intruded upon may bear some responsibility for the undesirable connection by having left himself open to intrusion through such things as addiction or occult practices. Martin referred to "victim's consent" in possessions. Perhaps this is tantamount to Atteshlis's concept that people who attract spirits often vibrate with the pattern that attracts the spirits. Thus, some persons with spirit intruders are active participants and not innocent victims. A modern term that arose from addiction therapy and various twelve-step programs is *enabler*. An enabler is a person that allows addictions to persist by preventing the addict from experiencing the consequences of his addiction. Dr. Allan

Hamilton kept a child's spirit from progressing to join the child's ancestors, and this resulted in a physical medical (not psychological) consequence for Hamilton. Thus, he was not an innocent victim, but rather he enabled the child's intrusion into his life.

McAll includes a number of cases of physical illnesses that were cured by employing his therapeutic method of addressing the issues of living and deceased ancestors. This may be the result of the attached spirit's draining vital energy from the body. When a person's energy level is lowered, any type of physical illness may occur. Perhaps physical illnesses can be compared to the anhedonia experienced by many people with DID, as the APs are depleting the host's emotional energy rather than her physical energy.

McAll also points to the dangers of automatic writing. While I agree that simply willing a spirit to take control of your hand may result in spirit intruders, I maintain that some inspirational literature has come from the person's own Spirit through automatic writing. Thus, that practice is not always harmful, but caution is mandated.

McAll comments that one woman's voices began after she was anesthetized. Fiore notes that anesthesia could result in spirit intrusion. Possibly, some anesthetics open up the protective aura that humans naturally have around themselves. This may be only one particular anesthetic, or the severity of the illness may be a factor, as all anesthetics are unlikely to cause spirit intrusion. Some effects of anesthesia may be individualized. I have read of several cases of NDEs precipitated by a dentist using nitrogen oxide (NOx) as an anesthetic. Obviously, only a small percentage of people anesthetized using NOx are affected by it; otherwise its use would be curtailed. The particular patient noted by McAll also had difficulty adapting to living after the removal of the voices that came after anesthesia, as she had become dependent on those voices for advice in everyday situations. Similarly, many DID patients have difficulty adjusting to life when a stressful situation arises and the patients no longer have an alternate personality handling the situation.

McAll was unique among the therapists discussed in chapter 10 in noting the importance of a committal service to preventing family intrusions. He was also the only therapist to describe the behavioral effects in families in which one person had an abortion, stillbirth, or miscarriage. Collectively, I will refer to these as fetal deaths. Perhaps, this demonstrates that it is not the mother's intention that could cause the problem, but it could be the soul (psychonoetic body) of the deceased prepartum child that has not made a complete transition to the *light*. While there are numerous studies that allegedly demonstrate no physical or psychological effects upon a woman who has an abortion, there are probably no studies that discuss the children born after fetal deaths. In some cases, the potential mother's attitude may be a factor in the behavior of the child born after a fetal death. If the potential mother thought of the child as simply a piece of tissue, she would have no longings for the child, and the spirit of the child may leave the family alone. However, a woman who was reluctant to have the abortion but who was pressured to do so may experience longing for the child, keeping the child closer to the family to have a later effect. While grouped as a fetal death, a miscarriage or stillbirth is more likely to result in grief, which I believe could be equivalent to a committal service.

A materialistic position would be that any effects of an abortion would be primarily to the mother who had the abortion. However, a spiritual analysis that does not recognize spatial distances might suggest that children born to prospective fathers could just as easily have difficulties in life, related to the spirit of an aborted child's intrusions into the father's later children. And the father may not even have known that he had conceived a child or that the mother had chosen to abort.

A question may arise about the effect of the large increase in abortions after Roe v. Wade in 1973. Although proving a cause-and-effect relationship—in this case, the behavior of children born after a fetal death—with statistics is difficult, I reviewed two areas of possible breakdown in American society beginning in 1973. One is the number of people sent to prisons. I emphasize state prisons, since many in federal prisons may be incarcerated for tax fraud or immigration issues, which are not related to crimes against other people. The number of inmates in state prisons was in a steady decline (~4% per year) from 1960 to 1972, which includes the turbulent 1960s, but thereafter began a dramatic increase, from 1973 until the great economic decline in 2008. Of course, there were a number of illegal abortions prior to 1973.

The second great indicator of social decline is the number of child abuse cases. In Illinois, which did not allow legal abortions until 1973 (some states had allowed them prior to 1973), the number of reported incidents of child abuse was under a thousand per year. Beginning in 1973, the number of reported cases began to increase by double-digit percentages each year, reaching over a hundred thousand by the late 1980s. I could only find data on a national level prior to 1976, but beginning then, and for a number of years afterward, the increase was similarly dramatic.

I speculate that the numerous social problems in Russia (primarily alcoholism), and other countries governed by communism, may be caused by the huge numbers of abortions in those countries. At one time, the average Russian woman might have numerous abortions in her lifetime, as abortion was the principal means of birth control. Of course, abortion in Russia is often considered a simple medical procedure with no consequences because communism is based on the materialistic paradigm that humans have no spiritual aspects. Some Americans who have adopted unwanted Russian infants have found serious psychological problems in those children as they grow up. I speculate that those children were the ones born after the birth mother had had a previous abortion. A meaningful analysis would require that the rate of psychological problems be compared to children whose mothers had not previously had an abortion.

One of McAll's cases involved a girl named Dorothy who was healed of anorexia after praying for her aborted sister. Dorothy reported she had heard her sister calling to her for years but had not told her parents of this. I suspect that many voices heard by schizophrenics or anorexics are spirits of the dead, and many of those voices may be from aborted children or from other deceased people.

Therapist Gwendolyn Awen Jones has written about the effects of abortion in her book *A Cry from the Womb* (2004). She had two abortions before realizing the consequences of her actions. She claims that even an early stage fetus is aware of and responsive to the needs of the mother-to-be. Jones maintains that if a woman does not want the child, she can have a serious inner conversation (Spirit to Spirit) with the fetus, explain the circumstances for not wanting a child at that time, and ask the child to leave. That child will nearly always depart (i.e., make a complete transition to the *light*), and there will be none of the consequences that there are for medically induced abortions.

While he does not comment on abortion, the British psychiatrist Guirdham (1982) states explicitly that the immortal spiritual aspect he calls the psyche of a person arrives at the moment of conception, which he implies happens during intercourse. Some people might argue that conception does not truly occur until the sperm enters the egg or when the fertilized egg is implanted into the uterus. This view of conception came from Guirdham's medical practice and not from a religious interpretation, the latter of which many opponents of abortion claim as their basis for opposing abortion.

One social commentary claimed that crime did not increase in the United States during the 1990s as much as expected because the children aborted in the 1970s had not grown up to become criminals. I am not sure how the commentary concluded that only future criminals were selectively aborted. I agree that the amount of crime was not proportional to the number of arrests and imprisonment. However, a large number of the prisoners were sentenced for drug use, which could be a possible aftereffect of intruding spirits resulting from an abortion in the family.

Basham was the only other therapist besides Atteshlis to mention animal sounds emanating from a person with spirit intruders. Oesterreich frequently remarks on animal sounds emanating from a person with a spirit intruder, but not within the context of therapy. In one of Oesterreich's cases, a person with a monkey intruder had an extraordinary climbing ability. Basham prefers the term *afflicted* over *possession*, the latter being a word I have also avoided using. However, Basham reports that the spirits would sometimes identify themselves as Satan or as demons, two other words that I have generally refrained from using. Basham would undoubtedly disagree with me that these could be deceased human spirits. He thought they were only imitating deceased people, but this does indicate that some of the spirits he encountered had human characteristics, such as a desire for food. A purely spiritual being, such as Satan, should not have a desire for a physical substance. In my analysis of the terms *demons, unclean spirits*, and *evil spirits* in the Bible, I correlated the behavior of one person who had DID and was under the influence of a psychiatric drug to that of a man described in the Bible as having a "legion" of evil spirits. Some of the evil spirits in Martin's exorcisms could be analogous to the hostile APs in people with DID.

Basham discusses "overindulged carnal desires" to emphasize human desires that have gone awry after being influenced by spirit intruders. Thus, he identifies the cause, rather than the result, when he references the term *gluttony* instead of stating the person is obese. Similar to the other Christian therapists McAll and Milingo, Basham has an ability called discernment, which helped him in identifying spirits that would not name themselves. The Christian healer Kathryn Kuhlmann has a similar ability. She can either "call" a disease that would be healed if people in the audience with that disease claimed their healing or discern a location in the auditorium where numerous healings might be taking place. For Basham and Milingo, epilepsy is a disease involving spirits, but psychiatrist Guirdham feels that the physical symptoms of epilepsy are more the body's attempt to thwart the intruding spirits and less the spirit's act of causing the symptoms.

Basham did encounter "parapsychological" phenomena when one spirit knew the intimate details of another deliverance minister's life. Martin also discusses this happening to a priest while conducting an exorcism. Martin further describes superhuman strength in an allegedly possessed person during an exorcism, such as breaking the restraints holding the person down. Perhaps more paranormal than parapsychological is the drop in temperature around possessed people. Guirdham has observed similar paranormal episodes. While much of the paranormal I have presented in this book is a result of operating with one's own Spirit, and is primarily employed to assist other humans, it is likely that evil forces that obtain a high degree of control of the afflicted person may have some paranormal abilities that are employed for harming people.

Milingo comments that most native Africans, including himself, seem to be more aware of spirits than Westerners are. Perhaps this is because many Africans are only a few generations removed from tribal societies with shamans in their midst. Many Africans, similar to people of indigenous societies, believe that the Western God is removed from their daily problems, whereas their family spirits are concerned about them and can help keep them safe and healthy.

Milingo's method of conducting religious ceremonies for people afflicted with the spirit intruders somewhat resembles that of McAll, but Milingo may have hundreds in attendance at his services while McAll often has only the immediate family present. However, the behavior of the people being healed by Milingo more closely resembles that of Basham and was not as severe as those behaviors described by Martin.

Fiore feels that if an intruding spirit is not removed in one session, she could come back to it later. Milingo thinks it best not to disturb a spirit only to fail to send it away. Fiore induces the intruding spirits to leave voluntarily, whereas Basham and Milingo hold that the spirits have to be forced out. Milingo discusses an unusual case of speaking to a deceased sister through a living sister. This more closely resembles traditional spiritualism, as there was no indication of spirit intrusion and consequent behavioral changes in the life of the living sister.

d. Guirdham and Jewish Concepts of Spirits

Some of Guirdham's information is difficult to compare to that of other therapists discussed in chapter 10, since he employs his own terminology. His term *psyche* appears similar to my term *Spirit* when he states that the psyche can directly perceive true information without sensory input. He also believes each human has multiple spirits as part of their natural composition.

Guirdham maintains that some of the visions seen by the mentally ill are not hallucinations but are the materialization of "discarnate entities." My theory would be that they are most likely deceased humans, but they could be other malevolent spiritual entities. Guirdham comments that epileptics often observe discarnate entities prior to a seizure. He further notes that Dostoyevsky, a known epileptic, would have periods of bliss prior to a seizure. I would argue that Spirit is coming to the epileptic's assistance prior to his upcoming stress. Epileptics are often creative people, as the epileptic becomes familiar with interacting with his Spirit. One of the difficulties in evaluating creativity among epileptics is that there is a historical record of famous people who have epilepsy. Whether the millions of ordinary people who have epilepsy are more creative, this is impossible to measure, as there is no method for evaluating their creativity. As previously discussed, alcoholics and people with depression are often considered creative.

Guirdham claims that evil is a force in itself and not just the absence of good. Disease can be a manifestation of the force of evil. Respectable members of society can transmit evil, either actively or passively. People near human transmitters of evil often become depressed. This phenomenon is comparable to Karagulla's concept that some people are "sappers," that is, they can drain energy from others.

Martin mentions that a familiar spirit's facial features would become distorted when the exorcist said the name Jesus. Howard Storm's NDE initially began as a distressing situation, as he was surrounded by malevolent spirits who taunted him. Although he described himself as an atheist at the time of his NDE, he had attended church as a youth. When he began to repeat the words of a simple child's song ("Jesus Loves Me"), the acrimonious spirits around him began to back away and eventually departed. His NDE then turned into a pleasant one. After Storm recovered, he eventually became a minister. One of the Jewish concepts pertaining to this is that some dybbuks may be functionally useful for a person.

e. Additional Factors Therapists (Sagan, Modi, Baldwin, Ireland-Frey, and Komianos)

These therapists have all found behavioral issues related to past lives in conjunction with spirit entities. As a group, they agree that physical healings may frequently happen when entities are induced to depart the client. After removal of an entity, clients often feel more energy (both physical and emotional), as entities borrow some energy from the client.

Sagan provides the information that spirits were addressed in ancient Indian and Chinese texts, so the presence of spirits was known in earlier civilizations. Sagan does not specify how the ancient texts proposed to remove the spirits. I believe that Sagan coined the term *soul fragmentation* and explained the soul as being composed of astral substance that may become fragmented at death or after trauma. Astral "mist" is normally returned to the undifferentiated astral world to be recycled later into other astral bodies. However, if this mist has unresolved issues and remains in its organized pattern, it will attempt to resolve those issues, such as an unfulfilled desire for alcohol. I employ the term *mist* here to avoid the term *material*, since the substance is not like earthly minerals. In one sense, this mist is ineffable; that is, our language does not have proper words to describe it. The same is true for the composition of an etheric body. It is also recycled into an undifferentiated etheric world, to be used in a later etheric body. Thus, soul fragments are not inherently evil, but their presence may result in poor choices by the person under their influence. While Baldwin agrees that earthbound entities are not inherently evil, when in conjunction with dark-force entities they may cause the person in whom they reside to engage in actions classified as evil. Atteshlis claims that the form of elementals cannot be eliminated, but if their energy is depleted they cannot function. If, as Sagan claims, elementals are composed of astral mist, then I would expect that elementals are eventually returned to the undifferentiated astral world and recycled.

Sagan is the only therapist who found that consumption of junk food or anything that decreases mental acuity increases the entity's control over the client. He describes the entities as functioning as parasites that can focus on one particular emotion in the client. He classifies his therapeutic process as assisting the client to observe the entity and its activity. The client may even choose not to remove the entity. Freedom of choice is one of the gifts with which humans (creatures with an individual Spirit) have been bestowed, but the gift comes with the responsibility to choose wisely. While most of the therapists discussed in this chapter sought to find the time and circumstances for the entry of an entity, Sagan had the client attempt to understand the reason for the attachment. My own explanation of the difference between circumstances and understanding is that for an alcoholic the circumstances for the initial intrusion may be "when I was drunk," but the reason for the drinking may lead to an even deeper understanding, which might help prevent future occurrences of a drinking bout.

According to Sagan, since many behavioral patterns are caused by simple fragments that a client may observe, to some extent they appear different from the seemingly complete spirits that some of the other therapists could engage in conversation. DID therapists speak of personality fragments and not complete personality. Regardless, these various therapists seem to achieve the same results; that is, undesirable symptoms are relieved from the client.

Whereas many of the other therapists I reviewed seem to indicate that people with earthbound deceased human entities are common in the population, Sagan, without specifying a percentage, believes that the body has numerous barriers to prevent a fragment from attaching itself. However, he does agree that alcohol and drugs (especially illegal drugs and pain or anesthesia medications that affect the nervous system), which breach the body's defense system, are more likely to result in a fragment attaching itself. Thus, the unintentional circumstances that resulted in intrusions described by Modi, Baldwin, and Ireland-Frey seem less likely to occur.

While most therapists have simply developed this spirit-release process as an extension of other types of common therapy, Sagan refers to a therapist as a trained connector or clearer for removing an entity. This connector must be "in touch with a particular frequency of spiritual light" (Sagan, 1997, 176), with guides or angels assisting in the process. I have already discussed the individual spiritual assistance upon which some therapists may call for guidance, as well as groups of spiritual assistants that some therapists may request for the removal of an intruding entity.

Modi went to medical school in India. Although yoga may have come from there, it is not something that every person in India does—nor do all Indians know about the etheric and astral body information I have discussed. Perhaps Modi is familiar with the terms *etheric body* and *astral body*, but she would use terms such as *aura* and *energy field*, broad terms that I believe would include both the etheric and astral bodies. She chose to employ Western names, such as *demons* for undesirable nonhuman spirits, and *angels* for friendly *beings of light*.

While some of the therapists previously discussed mention trauma as the possible source of entities, Modi considers trauma to be extremely important; she even suggests that trauma can cause soul fragmentation, a term she employs. However, Modi considers the soul to be the human spiritual component that reincarnates, whereas in my concept it is the Spirit that would reincarnate (if humans do indeed reincarnate). To Modi, trauma can occur prenatally, occur during birth, and be from a previous lifetime. Generally, soul fragmentation results in spirit intrusion, as a fragmented soul will result in openings in the energy shield. However, a person with a fragmented soul may feel disconnected and empty even if an entity has not yet attached itself. Modi was the only therapist to note that a fragment may remain at the age at which fragmentation took place. From reading about DID, it appears to me that alternate personalities (APs) also do not age. Similar to several other therapists, Modi believes that earthbound entities may bring the pain from an incident that occurred in the entity's previous body and that trauma may result in psychological/psychiatric or physical symptoms.

Modi and several other therapists employed hypnotism or deep relaxation to speak with the intruding entities. Any time a client is hypnotized, the idea of suggestion on the part of the therapist is an issue. The therapists I have discussed who employ hypnosis claim they are asking open-ended questions and not leading the client toward a desired answer. Although Crabtree discusses higher-level phenomena in hypnosis (well beyond the antics of stage hypnotism), the ability to see spirit forms during hypnosis is not considered a standard finding by trained hypnotists. Perhaps a hypnotist who does not believe in spirits would never think to ask the question of a hypnotized subject if the former could observe a spirit around the latter.

Modi's list of conditions that open people to intrusion is much broader than other therapists' and includes loud music and video games. Her list of reasons as to why the spirit is remaining earthbound includes past-life connections and interference by Satan. With her many years of practice, she was able to quantify the types of spirits, such as relatives or strangers, who are attached to her clients. While Modi claims that electroshock therapy only temporarily relieves conditions, Wickland and Komianos use different types of electric shock in conjunction with verbal therapy to force an entity out of the body—and it is possible that in cases such as this the spirit may not return.

While Baldwin accepts the decision of some clients not to have an entity removed, Sagan feels that the entity has more influence if it is not removed after being discovered. Baldwin introduces the topic of a lifescript as part of the reincarnation process. A person may have several checkouts or possible times of death in his lifescript. Baldwin has numerous methods that lead these entities to the *light*. After the departure, he holds a sealing-light meditation to protect the energy body from future intrusions. Fiore employs a similar procedure.

Baldwin does relate soul fragmentation to easier access by various entities. In addition to having an earthbound entity, abuse perpetrators most likely harbor a dark-force entity (DFE). These DFEs appear to be part of a hierarchy, as also found by Modi. Baldwin and Modi hold that these DFEs can be led to the *light*, as they were former angels. However, this is a purely metaphysical claim, one that cannot be verified. Similarly,

Baldwin found entities classified as extraterrestrials, and Modi found entities she classified as being from another dimension. Again, these claims are virtually impossible to verify. Modi and Baldwin are the only two therapists to find devices, such as clamps, that DFEs had inserted into patients to carry out the former's purposes.

Baldwin notes that some people can be affected by occult practices performed by someone who is against them. This practice may also result in fragmentation in the practitioner. Of course, many occult practices, such as using a Ouija board, simply involve one person. Nearly all therapists found behavioral difficulties related to occult practices.

Baldwin admits that he employs his concept of entities as a working hypothesis without scientific proof. This is true for all of the therapists discussed in this chapter, and thus also for my book. Some of these therapists have also found the "nesting" of entities. This may be an earthbound entity inside another earthbound entity, or a dark-force entity inside an earthbound entity.

Ireland-Frey gives a better explanation of the range of influence an entity may have, from a minor influence to full-out possession. She agrees with DID therapists that outside confirmation of child abuse needs to be found. Ireland-Frey claims that it could be the spirit of the deceased abuse victim that is describing the views the victim held while alive and that the host may not have been abused. DID therapists have found that alternate personalities (or the host personality) are often consummate liars. These therapists agree that entities should not be exorcised, as they may intrude into another person. Several of these therapists maintain they can release an entity from a person, even one that is not in the room with the therapist. According to Ireland-Frey, a surrogate is chosen, and through the surrogate the Higher Self of the remote client is asked if the release procedure can be performed. I believe these advisors may be an aspect of the therapist's own Spirit.

Komianos cites many of the other therapists I have reviewed in this chapter. He has an interesting method for removing the entities: by applying an electric shock to an acupuncture point. He normally converses with an entity in a hypnotized client before applying the shock. Wickland applied the shock first in order to have the entity enter a surrogate. He then proceeded to converse with the entity in the surrogate, who was in a trance at the time. Many of Komianos's indicators of entities are similar to other therapists'. Komianos has a unique finding: that several women were able to become pregnant after removal of an earthbound entity. He agrees with other therapists who have noted that entities often express physical and emotional reactions in the client after an entity has been discovered. Komianos has also found nonhuman entities, and these induce more severe conditions in a client than an earthbound entity does.

f. Final Comments on Spirit Intrusion

While some of the therapists discussed in chapter 10 may have made the process of therapy appear simple, their therapeutic procedures may actually be complex and time-consuming. However, these methods should involve less time than current psychotherapeutic methods that are not based on spirit intruders. Although the spirits may be persuaded to depart, the elementals—if the spirits were initially attracted to elementals—may remain, and the patient will be more vulnerable to intrusions of the same type, such as addictions. The spiritual methods described seemingly eliminated numerous physical illnesses in addition to psychological problems. If a regular physician is not having success in treating some of the diverse physical illnesses mentioned by therapists in chapter 10, the physician may want to suggest use of one of these spiritual methods.

If I had to suggest one area that may recognize the most benefit from the application of therapeutic concepts discussed here, that area would be therapy for prisoners. I believe that this could also greatly reduce the recidivism rate of ex-convicts. Another area for application is all children who have been removed from a home for probable abuse. These children should be reviewed for intrusions. In addition, all addiction therapies should consider these findings on spirit intrusions.

While only the Native American healer named Lake mentioned his wife assisting a child with autism, I believe the shamanic concept of soul retrieval may greatly aid in therapy for autism spectrum disorder (ASD) and also attention deficit hyperactivity disorder (ADHD), although no therapist discussed those particular disorders in chapter 10. A number of these therapists were practicing before ASD and ADHD received widespread attention. Psychiatric drugs have certainly not contributed to curing either disorder; in fact, they have probably made them worse per the study by Whitaker (2010). McAll particularly notes childhood behavioral issues.

T. The Aftermath of Biological Psychiatry

In chapter 10, on spirit intrusion, I reviewed the book *Pseudoscience in Biological Psychiatry* (1995) by psychiatrist Colin Ross and psychologist Alvin Pam. They present valuable evidence showing that many behavioral problems arise from abuse/trauma and that attempting to correct brain neurotransmitters with pharmaceuticals will not solve the underlying causes of a problem. Ross and Pam are concerned with the effectiveness of treatment, but a more recent book addresses whether psychiatric drugs may be doing more harm than healing in regard to mental illness. This book is titled *Anatomy of an Epidemic: Magic Bullets, Psychiatric Drugs, and the Astonishing Rise of Mental Illness in America* (2010), by investigative reporter Robert Whitaker. Whitaker has no personal attachment to this issue, but his research is a continuation of some earlier investigations into the abuse of psychiatric patients in research settings. In fact, he was originally a believer that new generations of psychiatric drugs were improving the conditions of the mentally ill.

A century ago, the mentally ill were placed in state mental hospitals, sometimes for life. One alternative that was tried in the 1940s (and discarded as worthless) was frontal lobotomy. The man who developed the procedure (Antonio Egas Moniz) received the 1949 Nobel Prize in Physiology. President John F. Kennedy's sister Rosemary underwent the procedure in 1941 and was left permanently incapacitated. Later, after a first-generation antipsychotic drug named Thorazine was introduced (in 1954), which was only tested on 150 people, psychiatrists came to believe they had discovered the biological causes of mental disorder. Through sophisticated public relations efforts financed by the pharmaceutical industry, many Americans have been convinced that pharmaceuticals can correct mental disorders. A large number of mental hospitals were closed, and the patients were transferred to community-based health systems where the drugs could be administered. Whitaker maintains that deinstitutionalization had more to do with the passing of the bills instituting Medicare and Medicaid, and their financial incentives, than with Thorazine or other drugs.

Whitaker claims that if psychiatrically prescribed drugs are actually healing people, the number of mentally disabled people should be decreasing, but in reality the number has been growing rapidly. In 1955, 1 in every 468 Americans was hospitalized for mental illness. In 1987, when Prozac was introduced, there were 1.25 million people on supplemental security income (SSI) and Social Security disability income (SSDI); that number is now 3.97 million, or 1 in 76 Americans (2009 data or earlier). Comparing a hospitalization rate with a disability rate is somewhat tenuous. The rise in children being treated for mental illness has grown even more dramatically. Whitaker asks why a product that is effective in assisting people to lead normal lives has led to a mind-boggling rate of increase in mental illness and resulting disability. He believes psychiatric drugs are fueling this epidemic. The idea that drugs for mental illness can be dispensed like insulin for diabetes is a fallacy.

In the twenty-first century, Americans take it for granted that drugs have been proven safe and effective; that was not the case back in the 1950s, when drugs only had to be shown not to be harmful. Effectiveness of the medication was not added as a requirement until 1962. Even with that requirement, the difficulty with many pharmaceuticals, especially drugs for psychiatric disorders, is in measuring the effectiveness and the improvements in behavior. The evaluator may judge the patient's being more socially acceptable to the hospital staff as more important than ultimate benefit to the patient. In addition, the studies of effectiveness were often of short-term duration, thus resulting in scientific myopia. Also, it is a formidable task to evaluate allegedly behavioral benefits versus the numerous side effects, which are different for each drug and which often result in the patient's abruptly ceasing to take the medications. In most studies, the rehospitalization rate is often lower in patients who are administered placebos.

1. Neurotransmitter Functioning

The concept of cures for mental illnesses arose from the idea of receptors by which chemicals can fit into cells (neurons), thereby serving as a magic bullet. This idea was originally developed for infectious diseases, but it also applies to neurotransmitters. Thus, the terms *antidepressant* and *antipsychotic* followed from *antibiotic*, and these medicines were promoted as disease fighters. Similarly, some early psychiatric drugs were the result of investigations into anesthetics that affect the central nervous system. Antianxiety drugs are not simply sedatives. Psychiatric drugs allegedly work by normalizing the chemical messengers that are generated at the synapses between neurons.

Researchers concluded that depression is caused by too little of the neurotransmitter serotonin in the synapse between neurons. The condition is corrected—or so it is said—by increasing the amount of serotonin. One type of antidepressant blocks the enzyme that metabolizes serotonin, and a second type blocks the reuptake of serotonin, preventing a deficit. The latter type is referred to as an SSRI, or selective serotonin reuptake inhibitor, the most well-known among these being Prozac. In addition to serotonin, neurotransmitters that affect psychopathology include acetylcholine, norepinephrine, dopamine, glutamate, and gamma-aminobutyric acid (GABA). Drugs that purportedly correct the levels of neurotransmitters in psychotic patients are referred to as neuroleptics. In contrast, hallucinations that are caused by overactive dopaminergic pathways and antipsychotics, such as Thorazine, slow down the system by blocking or binding the receptors. The levels of these neurochemicals (or their metabolites) can be measured in the cerebrospinal fluid.

Whitaker notes that about 25% of people who are not depressed have low serotonin and that some people with high levels of serotonin can still be depressed. The National Institute of Mental Health (NIMH) in the 1970s concluded that serotonin levels are not associated with depression. Likewise, schizophrenia does not appear related to dopamine levels. Thus, the biochemical theory of mental illness is unsubstantiated and false, or else the medications simply mediate the illness, not the direct cause.

Attempts to normalize brain chemistry with medications actually result in an abnormal condition. For instance, antidepressants affect the normal removal of serotonin from the synapse, which then results in an aberrant level of serotonin. An individual's level of a neurochemical is kept in balance by homeostasis. In contrast, artificial methods interfere with the process, leading the homeostasis mechanisms to break down. The effects can be permanent perturbations in neurotransmitter functions and consequent side effects. There were probably no chemical imbalances prior to psychiatric medications (or ones not yet understood), but there is an imbalance after the introduction of these medications. The effects are especially pronounced if the medication is stopped abruptly, which is not unusual given the serious side effects of some of these medications. Psychiatric drugs have one of the lowest compliance rates (percentage of pills actually used) of any type of drugs, which is due to their severe side effects.

2. Depression and Bipolar Disorder

Whitaker, who lives in the Boston area, attended a local meeting of the Depression and Bipolar Support Alliance (DBSA). He noticed that many of the attendees were overweight, one of the side effects of a particular antidepressant medication. Some individuals began with one medication and eventually ended up on a "cocktail" of drugs for the side effects, such as anxiety. While some of the attendees felt the medications greatly improved their lives, more felt personally ruined, unemployable, and reliant upon SSI or SSDI. For example, one person began with only mild depression, but the first antidepressant drug that individual took resulted in that person's becoming bipolar. Psychiatrists argue that this is the normal progression of the illness, but more people became bipolar after taking medications than did those who went unmedicated.

A translation of the ancient Greek word for the disorder now referred to as depression is *melancholy*. In the 1930s and 1940s, depression only affected about one in a thousand people, these generally over age thirty-five. A Swedish physician found that 50% of people with one episode of depression never had a second attack and that another 30% only had two attacks. In other words, depression was fairly rare, and was generally terminated in spontaneous remission.

Depression is now often referred to as unipolar disorder. Bipolar disorder was originally called manic depression. Medications can result in a much more rapid altering between the two states, referred to as cyclothymia. Psychiatrists have also expanded the definition of various mental illnesses. For instance, only two days of an elevated mood can result in a diagnosis of bipolar.

A number of medications for treating depression rarely perform better than a placebo. After publication of Whitaker's book, Leslie Stahl of the CBS News program *60 Minutes* interviewed Irving Kirsch of Harvard

University, and he claimed that except in cases of severe depression, most antidepressants are not any better than placebos. Several studies done in other countries have shown that nonmedicated patients show a greater reduction in symptoms than do medicated patients. Standard test procedures involving placebos as controls lose some of their value with psychiatric medications because those with serious side effects know they are not taking a placebo. Psychological therapy, such as cognitive therapy, often has better results than medications.

Since the introduction of SSRIs in the late 1980s, the amount of disability due to bipolar disorder has greatly increased. As Whitaker reports, the side effects of SSRIs "include sexual dysfunction, suppression of REM sleep, muscle tics, fatigue, emotional blunting, and apathy. In addition, investigators have reported that long-term use is associated with memory impairment, problem-solving difficulties, loss of creativity, and learning deficiencies" (p. 170). Some of the deleterious effects observed in brain tissue studies of those on medications appear to be irreversible. In addition, the medications to treat bipolar disorder may result in obesity, cardiovascular problems, or diabetes.

Early trials of Prozac, a drug used to treat depression, generally demonstrated it to be ineffective. Prozac's manufacturer, Eli Lilly, persisted and was able to convince regulators that the high number of test subjects who committed suicide or became psychotic was a result of the disease, not the result of Prozac. There were numerous other side effects, such as hallucinations, hostility, confusion, and tremors. The Food and Drug Administration (FDA) quickly received more complaints about Prozac than they had received about any other drug. Eli Lilly's persistent manner in seeking FDA approval for Prozac, despite Prozac's ineffectiveness and serious side effects, became the model when applying for future FDA approval of psychiatric drugs. Xanax, a drug for anxiety disorders, and risperidone and olanzapine, drugs for schizophrenia, were also approved by the FDA despite their not being better than a placebo and their causing serious side effects, up to and including death. Xanax is very addictive.

Prior to Prozac's FDA approval, only 1 in 250 children under age 19 was taking an antidepressant. By 2002, the figure was 1 in 40. Whitaker lists various deceptions employed by Eli Lilly to obtain FDA approval of Prozac. By most standards, it should not have been approved, because, in a majority of cases, it was no better than a placebo—but especially not for children. While preparing for one trial, the children were placed on a placebo for a week, and those who got better were excluded from the main study. After a week, only those who seemed to adapt well were enrolled for the remainder of the study. These two deceitful practices lowered the placebo response rate and increased the drug response rate. Despite these practices, Prozac was barely shown to be effective. In England, most SSRIs were banned for children under age 18. The side effects of SSRIs include physical, mental, and emotional difficulties. Numerous patients worsened after taking SSRIs.

An earlier medication for depression was lithium (with various compounds containing it, as the active ingredient). Like with other drugs, a few people who take lithium may benefit in the short term, but the long-term prognosis for recovery is greatly reduced. Prior to lithium, perhaps one in ten thousand people was bipolar. Today, the incidence is as high as one in fifty people who is bipolar. Without drugs, 85% of bipolar patients achieve social and occupational functionality, but only one-third of those administered drugs do so.

Although Whitaker does not mention this, sometimes a person who is simply bereaved over the recent death of a loved one will be given an antidepressant. Bereavement is a natural process, and administering an antidepressant is unlikely to have a beneficial effect. If the bereavement process appears to be too long, counseling may be helpful. Bereavement can become pathological, but it cannot be cured with psychotropic medications.

3. Schizophrenia and Anxiety Disorders

Whitaker investigated the long-term outcomes of schizophrenic patients prior to the introduction of neuroleptics, such as Thorazine in 1954. He found that only about 10–30% of patients required long-term hospital stays; the remainder were discharged from the hospital and functioned in the community. However, other studies were in the 50% or less recovery range. In contrast, only about 30% of neuroleptics were relapse-free, and virtually none of them improved better than the nonmedicated patients. The prognosis for schizophrenic patients in foreign countries is often better than in the United States because those patients frequently do not have access to psychiatric medications.

The difference between short-term and long-term recovery results was demonstrated by one study of sixty-two young schizophrenics cited by Whitaker. The study was not funded by a drug company. At the end of two years, the group not on antipsychotics were only slightly improved compared to the medicated group. After four and a half years, 39% of the nonmedicated group were in recovery and 60% were employed, while the figures for the medicated group were 9% in recovery and few employed. After ten years, the recovery figures were 40% in the nonmedicated group and 5% in the medicated group. The conclusions from this study were as follows:

- There is no good evidence that antipsychotics improve long-term schizophrenia outcomes.
- There is evidence that drugs may worsen the long-term outcomes.
- There is no biological explanation of why drugs make patients more vulnerable to psychosis over the long term.
- Long-term recovery rates are higher for unmedicated patients.
- Drugs can induce global brain dysfunction, as evidenced by tardive dyskinesia, which involves involuntary and purposeless movements and which is usually uncorrectable after the medication is stopped.
- MRI scans show that for those administered drugs there are morphological changes in the brain in addition to cognitive impairment.
- These results are the opposite of what were expected.

In 1955, there were 267,000 people with schizophrenia in mental hospitals, or 1 in every 617 Americans. Today, there are an estimated 2.4 million people receiving SSI or SSDI because they are ill with schizophrenia or some other psychotic disorder, a disability rate of 1 in every 125 Americans.

Some patients think antipsychotic medications turn them into zombies. The technical descriptions of this state include chemical anhedonia, psychotic depression, or neuroleptic dysphoria. Other frequent side effects include muscle spasms and tremors, in some cases resulting in permanent tardive dyskinesia or tardive psychosis. These side effects are thus classified as iatrogenic (doctor-caused) illnesses. One foreign physician referred to neuroleptics as psychosis-inducing agents. If the patients are on a "cocktail" of drugs, such results are termed *polypharmacy psychiatric drug illness*. The cost for some of these polypharmacy patients can be over $10,000 per year, even if generic drugs are prescribed. Most of these patients have to remain on disability in order to have their costs covered by Medicare. Psychiatric medications are a $40 billion a year business, and one of the fastest-growing areas of medical expense.

The result of treatment of anxiety disorders with medication is not any better than that of depression or psychotic disorders. The anxiety drugs typically prescribed bring very short-term improvements (about one week's worth), but in the long term there is often impairment of psychomotor and cognitive functioning, amnesia, insomnia, seizures, headaches, hallucinations, depersonalization, and possibly permanent brain damage. For example, Valium was first introduced in 1963, and shortly thereafter numerous people on Valium were admitted to mental hospitals and emergency departments for complications. SSRIs are also being employed for social anxiety disorder, and as many as 13% of the population may be affected by this "disorder." Whitaker comments that people with this trait were formerly thought of as shy, but according to psychiatrists they are now mentally ill.

4. Medicated Children

One of the worst tragedies is the number of children who are treated with psychiatric drugs. Almost no children were given psychiatric drugs prior to 1980. Then, psychiatrists "discovered" that children regularly suffer from mental illnesses. ADHD was not listed in the *DSM* until 1980, and now 3.5 million children are being treated for it. No neurochemical imbalance has ever been found for the cause of ADHD despite numerous searches for one, yet millions of children are prescribed medications to cure it or at least to control the symptoms. Whitaker notes that children on Ritalin are emotionally flat, lack spontaneity, exhibit no curiosity, and are devoid of humor. Ritalin may control a child's classroom manageability, but it does not result in improved academic performance. In fact, it interferes with higher-order cognitive functioning. Many undesirable symptoms actually increase after several years on the medication and may result in oppositional defiant disorder symptoms. The side effects, up to and including death, are too numerous to mention all of them, but they include bipolar disorder (11 percent). Thus, a significant number of those currently diagnosed as having ADHD could end up becoming bipolar. Children come to believe not in the soundness of their own bodies or in their ability to learn and control their behavior but in magic pills that make them a good boy or girl.

There was a 40-fold increase in bipolar disorder in children in the United States from 1995 to 2003, but this is not exclusively due to SSRIs, as the number includes children taking Ritalin, which is generally considered a stimulant that usually has the opposite effect in children. Of children diagnosed as bipolar, 84% had been exposed to psychiatric drugs. By contrast, children in the Netherlands rarely become bipolar, because they rarely receive prescriptions for antidepressants or stimulants. Mood stabilizers and atypical antipsychotics prescribed for pediatric bipolar disorder are neither safe nor effective. In 1987, before Prozac, for example, there were only 16,200 psychiatrically disabled youth on the SSI rolls; this was less than 6% of all disabled youth. Twenty years later, there are over half a million mentally ill children on the SSI rolls; this is over 50% of the total. Some 2- and 3-year-old children are being given psychotropic drugs, and 1 in 15 Americans has a serious mental illness by the time he becomes an adult, many of these illnesses iatrogenically caused. I read even higher figures elsewhere (Holland, 2015): that in the United States, 1 in 4 college students; 1 in 4 adult women; and 1 in 7 adult men is on a psychiatric medication.

Statistics on children are necessary for evaluation of the consequences for society, but each case represents a tragedy in the affected family. One child was anxious about going away to camp and occasionally wet her bed. Her parents took her to a psychiatrist. One tricyclic antidepressant led to a cocktail of drugs; she stopped taking them because of the side effects, underwent withdrawal psychosis, and ended up a schizophrenic. Another child referred to his drugs as "medical bondage." Children with minor behavioral problems are being groomed to be on psychiatric medications for life. A high percentage of children receiving antipsychotic medications for minor behavioral issues are on Medicaid.

5. Reductionist Ideology in Conjunction with Money

As Ross and Pam (1995) note, the belief that all mental illnesses arise from biological imbalances is called reductionism. This belief is often referred to as the "medical model." Also reductionists are the materialists who claim that NDEs are solely the result of interpretations of brain activity and are not spiritual. I maintain that it is this materialist/reductionist mind-set that has led to such an epidemic of mental illnesses and to the disabling of millions of people through drug-based treatment.

Whitaker explains that some alleged early successes with psychopharmacological drugs such as Thorazine failed to result in a revolution in the curing of mental illness. A group of "antipsychiatrists" received publicity in the 1960s, after which alternative psychological concepts abounded. Their view was popularized by the Ken Kesey book and film *One Flew Over the Cuckoo's Nest*. There was also a philosophical split between Freudian psychoanalysts and psychiatrists supporting the medical model. In the 1970s, the percentage of medical school graduates going into psychiatry dropped from 11% to 4% The use of prescription psychiatric drugs also dropped in the 1970s.

The *DSM-II*, which was issued in 1967, still reflected the Freudian model. In 1980, the *DSM-III* was published, and it reflected the new medical model. And since only psychiatrists could prescribe drugs, it limited the scope of psychologists. The president of the American Psychological Association classified the *DSM-III* as a political position paper rather than as a scientifically based classification system. While all medical organizations are concerned with the economic interests of their members, the American Psychiatric Association (APA), publisher of the *DSM-III*, adopted marketing practices similar to any trade organization. The APA developed public service spots on television and on a cable TV program, and promoted select in-depth newspaper articles. Through these various media, psychiatrists claimed they could heal sick minds with molecular psychiatry and psychic engineering. They claimed that psychiatric illnesses are diseases similar to heart disease and cancer. The claim to cure people of mental illnesses with medications is another form of promissory materialism. The *DSM-IV*, issued in 1997, listed 32 more disorders than did the *DSM-III*, which expanded the scope of the APA's influence and now included as treatable some conditions that were long considered to be within the range of normal human behavior, such as shyness. The *DSM-5* was published in 2013. Although it seemingly reduced the number of disorders, it did this by grouping several disorders into a spectrum of one overall disorder, for example, autism spectrum disorder ASD). I do not object to employing groups, since I maintain that most mental disorders are variations of one cause: spirit intrusions.

Reductionist-based psychiatrists contend that psychiatric illnesses are real and that their pharmaceutical treatments are effective. The proponents of this movement are often "thought leaders" or "key opinion leaders" from top academic medical schools. These leaders are often consultants to pharmaceutical companies (sometimes disparagingly referred to as Pharma), sit on the advisory boards, and are part of a well-compensated speakers' bureau. While accepting money from drug companies, they claim that their views are unbiased. However, the recent policy of most medical organizations is that a presenter of a paper must state if he or she has a financial interest in the product being discussed. At one conference, a speaker claiming that antidepressants were a disaster was booed by the audience, indicating acceptance of the medical model. He also asked whether fifty thousand psychiatrists could be wrong and then answered his own question with "yes."

The interests of Pharma and psychiatrists have become closely aligned. Prior to 1980, Pharma could only put up exhibits at APA meetings, but afterward they could pay to put on "scientific symposiums" that included excellent audiovisual content. One cynic suggested that the APA change its name to the American Psychopharmaceutical Association. The alleged psychopharmacological revolution is a business enterprise more than a medical enterprise, ignoring the long-term consequences of drug manufacturers' products. Criticisms of psychiatric drugs, such as a note of their serious side effects, are rarely published, as Pharma threatens to withdraw advertising if the article is published. For example, one researcher who wrote about the side effects of psychiatric medicines had his invitation to speak at an upcoming conference withdrawn. Another psychiatrist was offered a major post at a university, but after criticizing neuroleptics, the offer was rescinded.

About the time of publication of the *DSM-III*, the biological psychiatrists captured control of the National Institute of Mental Health (NIMH) when the director of the APA's public affairs became head of

NIMH. The NIMH often issues press releases with inconsequential matters and ignores important information about the consequences of psychiatric drugs. Reports concerning the better results for schizophrenia in less developed countries never specify that the improvement is the result of drug avoidance. "In order to sell our society on the soundness of this form of care, psychiatry has had to grossly exaggerate the value of its new drugs, silence critics, and keep the story of poor long-term outcomes hidden" (Whitaker, p. 312).

The National Alliance for the Mentally Ill (NAMI) is an organization of families affected by mental illness. It receives money from the pharmaceutical industry and, like NIMH, has become completely enamored with the medical model. In addition, the supporters of the medical model received fortuitous assistance when the Church of Scientology began a campaign against electroshock and psychiatric drugs. Psychiatrists could now aggregate all criticisms of the psychiatric drugs as nonsense coming from an unpopular group.

The state of Illinois has been having many financial problems in recent years. As part of a study on the expenses incurred by the state of Illinois, my local newspaper, *The State Journal-Register*, published the salaries of the highest-paid state employees ($300,000+), excluding employees of the university systems. Eight of the top ten salaries went to psychiatrists, but those were top-level administrators rather than doctors formally conducting therapy. However, administrators usually are paid a certain percent above those they supervise, so there may be therapists making near those top-level salaries. Psychiatrists are no longer in the lower tier of physician compensation.

Since becoming interested in this topic, I have collected some incidents of improper or off-label use of psychiatric drugs. For example, the manufacture of Zyprexa was fined over $1 billion by the state of Texas in 2013 for persuading doctors to prescribe that drug for uses not approved by the FDA. The US attorney general is also suing this company on behalf of the other states. Although theoretically the drug companies are not responsible for illegally obtained prescription drugs, the number of deaths from overdoses of drugs has increased for eleven straight years. About 60% of those deaths are from prescription drugs, mostly painkillers that are opioid-based, such as OxyContin and Vicodin. Some patients will obtain prescriptions from two or more separate doctors, whereas other patients may obtain the drug to sell to other addicts at a much higher price than the prescription price. A second variety of drug that is addictive and overdosed, with consequent deaths, is antianxiety medication such as Xanax. There have been numerous other fines against Pharma for using their influence to persuade doctors to use pharmaceutical drugs for off-label conditions. Many of these are for nonpsychiatric disorders, but this reflects the same unethical attitude by Pharma.

6. Alternatives, Trauma, and a Word of Caution

Whitaker discusses several countries around the world that are developing programs for the mentally ill that do not involve drugs. He concludes as follows:

> We need to talk about what is truly known about the biology of mental disorders, about what the drugs actually do, and about how the drugs increase the risk that people will become chronically ill. If we could have that discussion, then change surely will follow. Our society would embrace and promote alternative forms of non-drug care. Physicians would prescribe the medications in a much more limited, cautious manner. (p. 359)

It also should be noted that neither I nor Whitaker is a psychiatrist. We are dealing with overall effects. If one particular patient is a threat to society or to himself, then some drugs may have to be temporarily administered to that person. Even some of the psychiatrists whom I cited earlier are not against all medications, but if they do not see an improvement within a month or if they observe significant side effects, they consider alternatives.

In Whitaker's examples of specific patients, several reported conditions in their lives prior to taking their antidepressant drugs that have been described as possible sources of soul loss / spirit intrusion, namely, being molested as a child or using illegal drugs. Children in foster care or in trouble with the law are often diagnosed as bipolar when they were simply brought up in a dysfunctional home. Whitaker reports that one-third of people had used marijuana or other illegal drugs prior to their first episode of bipolar disorder or a psychotic episode. Whitaker does not have any statistics on the frequency of illegal drugs or the percentage of people who are not bipolar and had taken the same amount of illegal drugs; however, Dutch investigators reported that marijuana use is associated with a fivefold increase in the first diagnosis of bipolar disorder.

6. A Medical View on Pharma Practices

Some professional people may question the qualifications of an investigative reporter, but two former editors of *The New England Journal of Medicine*, the late Arnold S. Relman (1923 - 2014) and Marcia Angell, both of whom were associated with Harvard Medical School, wrote an article titled "America's Other Drug Problem" in 2002 in *The New Republic* about the dominating influence of the pharmaceutical industry in all of medicine, not just the field of psychiatry. In 2009, Angell wrote an article/ book review titled "Drug Companies & Doctors: A Story of Corruption." Relman and Angell (2002) state that "It [the pharmaceutical industry] has also, with the acquiescence of a medical profession addicted to drug company largesse, assumed a role in directing medical treatment, clinical research, and physician education that is totally inappropriate for a profit-driven industry" (p. 27). They maintain that there is little indication of true competition in the industry, which tries to avoid head-to-head comparisons.

According to Whitaker, the 1980 publication of *DSM-III* was crucial for psychiatric drugs, and Relman and Angell state that from 1960 to 1980 all drug costs, as a percent of gross domestic product (GDP) were steady, not just psychiatric medications, but by 2000, costs had almost tripled. Since that article in 2002, drug costs are now included by law in most insurance plans and Medicare/Medicaid, and costs for all drugs have risen substantially as these third-party payers have "deep pockets." There was even a provision put in the 2003 Congressional bill that Medicare Part D could not negotiate prices with Pharma.

Pharma claims that the high prices reflect the high cost of research and development (R&D), but Pharma often spends more on marketing and influencing federal (more than one lobbyist per member of Congress) and state governments than they do on R&D. They also create and fund "supposed grassroots organizations... to promote drug company interests" (p. 39). At one time, Pharma was not allowed direct-to-consumer (DTC) advertising, but it is now allowed. It is not unusual to watch television news or programs in which a majority of the advertisements are for drugs. The amount now spent on DTC advertising is about the same as spent on advertising in medical journals and other professional media.

Relman and Angell also point out that much of the original basic drug research on the molecular basis of disease was performed at university medical schools at public expense. The medical school is allowed to patent the taxpayer-funded discovery and license it to a drug company. In the field of psychiatry, I have tried to demonstrate that there is no molecular basis of disease (also referred to as an unproven chemical imbalance theory, which is the reductionist assumption), but I am not claiming that for all illnesses. Pharma is not considered an innovative industry but rather makes practical applications of the basic research. Much of the research now done by Pharma is for "me-too" drugs in which Pharma uses minor variations to extend patent protection on current "blockbuster" drugs, those with sales over one billion dollars per year. Pharma claims that less than one in 5,000 drugs originally identified ever gets to market and this is why Pharma spends its money on me-too drugs. As Relman and Angell contend "Drug companies apparently see no contradiction in manipulating existing laws and regulations to stave off competition from generic and foreign manufacturers of and lobbying for even more governmental protections while at the same time using free-market rhetoric to demand less government involvement in the pricing and the marketing of drugs" (p. 28). They believe Pharma's estimate of $800 million per drug to bring to market is an imaginary number as it includes items like opportunity costs and other questionable costs. The 2016 number is two billion dollars, but one bogus number is as good as another.

Relman and Angell point out that for twelve years beginning in 1990, the FDA approved 1,035 drugs but only 23% were significant improvement over products currently in the market, and only a few of those were new molecular entities. They believe that testing for efficacy should be a comparison with a previous drug, including safety and side effects, rather than merely with a placebo. "Physicians are led to believe that the newest, most expensive brand-name drugs are superior to older drugs or generics, even though there is seldom any evidence to that effect..." (Angell, 2009, 10). Furthermore, Whitaker pointed out that unfavorable research results are often not published in medical journals and Angell confirms this point. In 74 trials of antidepressants, 37 of 38 with positive results were published, but 33 of 36 with negative results were either not published or published in a form that conveyed a positive outcome, such as emphasizing a favorable secondary effect.

Earlier, I mentioned Whitaker's comment about how testing for Prozac was done in the way to maximize favorable results, and the conditions during testing may not be the case when the drug is actually prescribed. Relman and Angell point out that Pharma now contracts out most of these efficacy tests, but Pharma specifies all the conditions for the tests and interprets the results. They also comment that "Virtually every research intensive medical center in the country now has contractual ties with one or more drug firms, usually involving subsidies or collaborations with particular research programs and faculty" (p. 33). Pharma has often donated an endowment for a permanent faculty position at numerous medical schools, especially prestigious schools whose faculty are key opinion leaders. These donations threaten objectivity by those medical schools. Pharma supports many continuing medical education (CME) programs which have become more of a sales pitch for specific products than the expected unbiased professional education on a disease. In many cases, the CME is presented by a third party and may seem to be unbiased, but the agenda for those programs are prepared by a drug company. The American Medical Association (AMA) issued guidelines on accepting gifts, but the guidelines are considered voluntary and often not monitored. Pharma is also able to obtain data from drugstores on what individual doctors are prescribing which medication.

The trivial variations in blockbuster drugs mentioned earlier often enable the drug company to extend their patent protection for the product, as allowed by the Hatch-Waxman Act of 1984, despite the fact that patents are intended to be useful, novel, or not obvious. In addition to the patent, the FDA grants exclusive marketing rights for products it approves. Pharma uses various stratagems to extend this exclusivity, such as minor variations in the formulation to prevent generic companies from entering the market. Other strategies include flimsy legal pretexts, such as new uses, dosage forms (one example was a weekly formulation to replace daily), combinations of drugs, and even the coating of the pills. The Hatch-Waxman Act also allows drug makers an extra thirty months protection if they sued a generic manufacturer attempting to enter the market and more than one lawsuit may be filed. Pharma also receives additional protection if the product is switched to over-the-counter status. In some cases, they will even pay the maker of a generic product not to enter the market. the FDA Modernization Act of 1997 allows the drug companies an six extra months patent protection if they test their drugs on children. In one case, a drug company extended its patent by filing for a separate patent for a metabolite of the original product. The original product becomes that metabolite after it is swallowed, so it is not new. Another company switched to an isomer rather than a metabolite. Eliminating these avenues of insignificant changes to a drug may result in incentives to find truly original improvements in treating diseases.

The Prescription Drug User Fee Act of 1992 allows Pharma to pay FDA to speed up processing of applications for a drug. This has made the FDA more dependent on the industry it regulates and has resulted in more frequent withdrawals from the market due to the death of the users. There are advisory committees for each specialty area of pharmaceuticals, and many members of those committees have financial connections to drug companies.

Two of the three books Angell (2009) reviewed were specifically about psychiatric drugs, which are alleged to improve disorders, but which have more subjective symptoms than many other illnesses. She mentions three specific medical school psychiatrists who received large consulting fees, speaking fees, or owned stock in drug companies. Theoretically, these doctors were required to report any remuneration from drug companies, but often they did not or underreported the amount. Some psychiatrists may have articles published with themselves listed as the authors, but the pieces were actually written by drug companies. These faculty members often point out their value to the medical school, which often hold equity interests in companies that sponsor research at that university. Drug companies are theoretically not allowed to market a drug for off-label use, but they often pay academic authors to write articles applauding these off-label uses. This is particularly easy for psychiatric drugs since similar symptoms often are parts of multiple disorders. The fines imposed for off-label marketing are usually small compared to the additional revenues from the off-label uses (Angell, 2009).

She also comments that *DSM* is "the product of a complex of academic politics, personal ambition, ideology, and, perhaps most important, the influence of the pharmaceutical industry" (p. 9). There is not much evidence for the various disorders. One of the books she reviewed describes how shyness went from a rare "social phobia" in *DSM-III* to become "social anxiety disorder" in *DSM-IV* that is a common and a severe medical condition.

Doctors often give seemingly minor illnesses serious sounding names. For instance, heartburn is now gastro-esophageal reflux disease. Angell humorously points out that the strategy of drug marketers is to successfully convince "Americans that there are only two kinds of people: those with medical conditions that require drug treatment and those who don't know it yet" (p. 8).

Angell concludes that, "It is simply no longer possible to believe much of the clinical research that is published, or to rely on the judgment of trusted physicians or authoritative medical guidelines. I take no pleasure in this conclusion, which I reached slowly and reluctantly over my two decades as an editor of *The New England Journal of Medicine*" (p. 10). I believe these two articles give great support to Whitaker's findings.

8. Conclusions of This Section

It is unlikely that psychiatrists would have made their errors in understanding the true nature of mental illness if it were not for their unproved reductionist assumptions. Textbooks about abnormal psychology will often include a historical review about the inhumane and deplorable conditions and practices under which "lunatics" in "insane asylums" lived in many Western countries a century or two ago. When considering the number of people whose lives have been ruined by psychiatric drugs, I wonder if there has been much improvement with modern neurochemical psychiatric methods. Today, many patients end up living in chemical asylums rather than physical asylums.

Although I advocate a spiritual understanding of mental illness, I do worry that misguided religious views may become popular and that alleged faith healers will attempt so-called exorcisms and charge large fees to rid a person of "evil spirits." Even worse than attempting to remove spirits as a source of revenue is a child's fearfulness when adults seemingly compel "demons" to depart from the child. While some people may be partly responsible for the spirit intruders within them, it is best not to assess blame for the situation, which may have arisen in childhood or from accidents and illnesses, and then simply to cure the problem with one of the multiple methods I discussed in chapter 10, on spirit intrusion. Other possible methods of therapy include revising psychotherapy or updating shamanic practices of soul retrieval to address spirit intrusions. Another possible method for controlling, if not curing, mental illnesses may be music therapy. I have previously discussed how David was able to quell the evil spirit in King Saul by playing a harp.

U. Alternative Theories—Secular

While I have criticized materialism/reductionism, a number of recent writers have seen through the façade of materialism without any reference to spirituality or the paranormal. Some of these writers even classify themselves as atheists. One of these writers is Raymond Tallis, author of *Aping Mankind: Neuromania, Darwinitis, and the Misrepresentation of Humanity* (2011). He is a retired English medical doctor and has written and published articles in this field for 20 years. In this book, he references 31 of his own writings. Tallis classifies himself as a humanist. He says he "escaped the intellectual, emotional and spiritual prison of religious belief" at age 15 (p. 10). However, as he writes, "It does not seem to me a very great advance to escape from the prison of false supernatural thought only to land in the prison of a naturalistic understanding" (p. 10). While Tallis states that he rejects "supernatural" explanations for the manner in which life on earth has progressed, he uses the term *creationism* as an example of a supernatural explanation, as if that were the only nonphysical explanation. I will also present my theory of how a spiritual concept can be compatible with evolution and show how it accounts for consciousness and behavior. Although not all are professed, a large number of proponents of neuromania and Darwinitis whom Tallis denigrates are well-known atheists, such as Richard Dawkins and Daniel Dennett.

1. Human Differences

Tallis's overall view is that standard neuroscience and evolutionary theory are not able to explain consciousness, behavior, culture, and society. He contends that humans are a difference of kind rather than of degree as compared to other primates, and that human uniqueness cannot be accounted for in biological terms as simply another evolutionary adaption. Darwin also believed that humans were just a degree of difference away from primates. Tallis's view is that human consciousness is not simply brain-based and that certain evolutionary steps, to be described later, account for difference of kind. The brain may be a necessary condition for consciousness, but it is not a sufficient condition for it.

Neuromania is the concept that human behavior is determined by the firing of neurons in the brain as viewed by modern brain-imaging techniques. One example of neuromania that Tallis criticizes is literary writer A. S. Byatt's claim that the poetry of John Donne (1572–1631) is appreciated by readers because it stimulates particular neuronal pathways. Tallis refers to this as "neuroaesthetics," something that has also been introduced into painting, music, and other arts. One psychologist maintains that the appeal of music falls into six categories and that each of these serves an evolutionary function that causes certain neurons in the brain to ignite. Similarly, a person enjoys reading Shakespeare because of the work's impact on pertinent neurons. However, neuroaesthetics cannot distinguish one form of pleasure from another. Tallis correctly describes this type of explanation as ideological pseudoscience. Neuromania has also crept into law (neurojurisprudence), ethics, philosophy, and theology, each employing the prefix neuro-. Some politicians even believe that social policies should be based on neuro-evolutionary thought. My opinion is that those policies would probably be justification for the policies they have already been promoting, not a breakthrough in social improvement. However, Tallis maintains that humans do have the ability to work together to improve the conditions of our existence. He also holds that neuromania is simply an updated version of phrenology, the nineteenth-century idea that bumps on a person's head are indications of personality. Neuroscientists look past what makes us distinctly human.

766

Humans would probably not have come to predominate over animals had our ancestors only been looking for pleasurable brain experiences.

While Tallis is a confirmed believer in evolution, Darwinitis is taking evolution to an extreme by denying "the distinctive features of human beings—selfhood, free will, that collective space called the human world, the sense that we *lead* our lives rather than simply *live* them as organisms do. ... Such views may have consequences that are not merely intellectually derelict but dangerous" (pp. 8–9; original italics). Tallis refers to these extreme evolutionary beliefs as *biologism*, a variation of scientism. As he writes, "The pseudo-neurosciences may actually cause real damage to human institutions and actual human beings" (p. 306). When philosophy becomes neurophilosophy, it no longer is a separate source of knowledge (epistemology) and understanding that can be acquired by conceptual analysis, but instead it has subordinated leadership in understanding to the supposed superiority of scientism.

One aspect of Darwinitis is evolutionary psychology, the concept that selfish genes determine human behavior. These genetic traits were allegedly introduced by natural selection. Evolutionary psychologists maintain that humans believe they are making free choices, but the choices are actually genetically determined. The experience of free will is only an illusion. Our genes determine how we think, and most decisions are made by unconscious cognition, or *neurodeterminism*.

One of the consequences of evolutionary psychology and neuromania is that each person no longer has free will and thus bears no personal responsibility for his actions ("My brain made me do it," even if not insane). As Tallis writes, "Biologism takes away rights and responsibilities" (p. 314). A correlation of brain differences between an abnormal and a normal brain does not prove that the abnormality is the cause of the undesirable behavior. Tallis maintains that free will is a metaphysical question that cannot even be addressed by an empirical science. For example, free will cannot appear on a brain scan. And if free will does not exist, then the concept of the self, or "I," does not exist, because it cannot be found in the brain. However, this "I" or self does exist at a given time and over time, and can consider an explicit past and a future. Only humans can fear the future. Neural impulses, being purely physical matter, can neither contemplate a past or future nor have appearances. Analysis of brain patterns cannot provide humans with values, meaning, purpose, culture, and morality. Tallis places great emphasis on free will and intentionality. Simply because some actions are not freely chosen does not mean that no actions are freely chosen.

Materialist views always deny or marginalize intentionality. Through intentionality, the human brain (mind) is not passive, as in animals, but actively constructs the outside world.

> There is nothing elsewhere in nature comparable to intentionality. It will prove, as we shall see, to be the key to our human differences: our subjectivity; our sustained self-consciousness; our sense of others as selves like us; first- and second-person being; our ability to form intentions; our freedom; and our collective creation of a human world offset from nature. (p. 105)

Just as free will is a metaphysical question, "morality is a human construct and is therefore not amenable to explanation in biological terms" (p. 320). Thus, humans are a difference of kind from animals and not of degree, as maintained by reductionists.

2. Tallis's Theory

Tallis presents his idea of how humans became a difference of kind from other primates. He maintains that when primates were able to assume an upright position, this enabled the hand to turn consciousness upon itself; thus, self-awareness arose. The body upright, the hand developed the opposable thumb, which enabled the thumb and fingers to be used as proto-tools. The sense of touch then became magnified in the hand, which now works closely with vision. Whereas some animals may use natural objects as tools, only humans use tools to make more complex tools. The hand is also able to make gestures. Tallis uses these developments as an example of the butterfly effect, when a small initial difference may result in massive differences over a long period of time.

Tallis holds that we can only employ human thought to understand matter (e.g., technology) because humans

> approach nature from an outside whose seed is intentionality. It [technology] is built up as an expanding space of possibility,

a first-person plural reality, constructed through the joined endeavors of the human race, and expanded since the first hominids first awoke to their own existence. Such conscious exploitation of the laws of nature lies beyond description in terms of material causes and the material effects: it cannot be described in terms of biological tropisms or instincts or drives as proxy for intermediate material causes. (p. 260)

While generally agreeing with Tallis, I would maintain that "beyond … material causes" is the spiritual nature of humans, which is a step well beyond the spirit forms that live in animals.

Tallis states that specialized neuroscientists, such as neurosociologists, sometimes claim to uncover truth that belongs to common sense. An instance of this is that "if a child is treated badly, it may grow up to lead a catastrophically adult life" (p. 278). This is simply another statement about the effects of trauma (and subsequent soul loss), one of the principal focuses of my book. What Tallis considers common sense (and he is supported by neuroscience) has apparently not influenced many members of the American Psychiatric Association or the Pharmaceutical Manufacturers Association, who believe that the effects of trauma can be corrected with pharmaceuticals. I would classify this incorrect concept as an example of Tallis's earlier statement that pseudoneuroscience may cause real damage to actual human beings.

3. Brain Scans

In an earlier section on brain imaging, I noted the difficulties of evaluating brain imagery. Tallis also discusses a number of researchers who question the validity of brain imaging devices, such as fMRI and PET, especially for higher cognitive functions in the frontal cortex. The same areas of the brain may appear more active during many different types of thoughts, so an activated area says nothing about an individual thought. It is possible that an emotionally painful experience could produce a similar neuronal discharge as a blissful experience. Neuromaniacs believe that a correlation between a neuronal discharge in the brain and a conscious thought is a cause, when it is only a correlation. "[E]xperiences are distinct from nerve impulses but are the effect of them. … [For example,] nerve impulses are the means by which light energy is changed into *experience* of light energy" (p. 89). Nerve impulses are not a sufficient condition to experience light. Thus, there can never be a true science of consciousness. In the language of LeShan (1984), neuroscience is a nomothetic science while consciousness is an idiographic science. Tallis also notes that electrochemical energy of nerve impulses is similar regardless of the color perceived. In addition, neuroscientists know that the prefrontal cortex is associated with more complex thoughts, but there is nothing special about the nature of the prefrontal cortex that would make it more likely than other neurons to participate in more complex thoughts.

Tallis quotes a writer named Andrew Scull, who expresses the following: "The neuroscientific findings that are so proudly proffered reflect simple simulated experiments that in no way capture the intricacies of everyday social situations, let alone the complex interactions over time that make up human history" (p. 282). Tallis maintains that we should be very afraid when technologists "seek biomedical and genetic means to enhance the moral character of humanity" (p. 327). I maintain that the previous discussion of the destructive effects of many psychiatric drugs is an example of the unintended consequences of such biomedical intervention.

4. Darwinitis

Many supporters of evolution believe that humans are like animals in many respects and that, therefore, humans must be just like animals in all respects. In contrast, Tallis maintains that "we appropriate the biological givens and subordinate them to distinctively, uniquely human ends" (p. 149). Humans do things deliberately and not as instinctual responses. That humans share 98% of their genes with chimpanzees is not relevant. Humans share 50% of their genes with bananas. Humans share no whole chromosomes with chimpanzees. Some instinctual behavior may appear complex but remain as instinct. In contrast, complex human institutions are not related to basic instincts.

For centuries, many writers have noted the gap between brain activity and consciousness. The most focus has been given to the synapses between neurons where the neurotransmitters are active. Tallis maintains that by strict evolutionary standards, consciousness should not exist. Tallis emphasizes the difference between human and animal consciousness. I would classify animals as conscious beings, although not self-conscious. Sleep is a "state of consciousness" but is much different from waking consciousness. One theoretical physicist (Brian Pippard) notes that there is nothing in the laws of physics that could predict that a complex structure would arise that is aware of its own existence. Computers are not conscious or self-aware and can only process information, not meaning.

5. Neurotheology

Although my book is not about religion per se, I have used the religious view that humans have a spiritual aspect that resides in the human body. While he is an atheist, Tallis, I believe, has more respect for religious views than do many neuromaniacs. Neurotheologists believe that activation of certain neuronal pathways creates what they believe to be a false impression that the person in question is in contact with a deity. People with temporal lobe epilepsy sometimes have intense mystical experiences and become obsessed with religious spirituality. One researcher believes that the seizure simply activates a portion of the lobe he calls "the God module," which does not relate to any actual deity. In contrast, when higher-level brain function is activated by Spirit, the result may be paranormal abilities. Neurotheologists do not believe in anything classified as paranormal.

Tallis dislikes the approach that belief in a deity is neuronally based. A research study Tallis cites attempted to demonstrate what alleged factors are typically displayed in the regions of the brain activated by "beliefs." Tallis notes that everyone has some type of belief. "[B]rain scans cannot distinguish between everyday factual beliefs and the most profound ideas human beings have ever had" (p. 329). This type of study diminishes human believers of any subject, including science and evolution. Some studies also maintain there is a God gene. Tallis maintains that the notion of a "gene for" that applies to human behavior needs to be discarded. He further states,

> The suggestion that the God might be a tingle in our heads, rather similar to epileptic seizures, or religiosity a propensity to have such tingles, is to misconceive the nature of religious belief. We must distinguish between religious experiences (of well-being, of joy, of terror, of shame, of expanded awareness)

and the translation of those experiences into, say, a revelation of God with certain characteristics. Isolated brains or, even less, bits of brain, do not have the wherewithal to make this translation, which depends on many things. (p. 331)

The idea of an eternal Supreme Being cannot be connected to simple nerve impulses.

Continuing on this theme, Tallis relates,

Perhaps it is not an atheist's place to second-guess the mind of God but I don't think he would like being hard-wired very much. At any rate, he would be right to treat the notion with divine suspicion. The implication that our vision or intuition or experience of God is simply a good idea from an evolutionary point of view somewhat diminishes the Almighty. It makes him merely a useful notion to help one small part of the universe (we human beings) ensure the replication of their genetic material. What a come down for the author of everything to become a product of a tiny part of something! Patronizing, or what? Darwinizing the idea of God makes prayer and the holding of theological beliefs a mere organic function, a bit like secreting urine. If you naturalize belief in God, then it is very difficult to see how God can remain as a supernatural Being with all those characteristics we have ascribed to Him. (p. 333)

A creature must be self-conscious to be aware that it will die and conceive of the idea that there may be an afterlife. On the other hand, "[e]volution ... has nothing to do with love, mercy, or even common decency" (p. 334), feelings and behaviors typically associated with the belief that humans are spiritual beings.

As a result of skepticism of neuromania, some atheists and theists could join forces.

To naturalize religion is to naturalize even those parts of humanity that are most remote from the natural world. It is the supreme expression of a devastating reductionism that disgusts even an atheist like me. In defending the humanities, the arts, the law, ethics, economics, politics and even religious belief against neuro-evolutionary reductionism, atheist humanists and theists have a common cause and, in reductive naturalism, a common adversary: scientism. (p. 336)

The fallacies of scientism have been one of the main themes of my book, and therefore I agree with much of Tallis's criticisms. However, Tallis sees his interpretation as an extension of natural evolution, whereas I believe it may be a guided and purposeful process.

6. My Theory of Human Development

While my few paragraphs of Tallis's evolutionary theory may not do him justice, I will use his ideas as a starting point from which to explain my own integration of spirituality and evolution. I have already mentioned that through time the aspect I call Spirit is further penetrating the physical body. That is partially why individuals may experience contact with their Spirit without realizing it. Some people experience sudden insight from outside themselves, whereas others simply experience a profound rational thought.

I also allude to the idea that animals may be watched over by a "group soul," but in actuality this is a form of Spirit that has responsibility for more than one physical body, that is, herds or colonies. A distinct human species arose when each individual was imbued with her own individual Spirit, but at first this Spirit was barely connected to the physical body. I cannot say when this happened; it may have been a million years ago, 250,000 years ago, or 100,000 years ago. There may have been several branches of primates that were test species for the integration, but only for one, which we call Homo sapiens, did the integration take hold. In the modern world, the primary (and perhaps only) evolution taking place is the evolution of consciousness, as Spirit further incarnates into the human physical body. This further incarnation primarily affects the mental body. Human capacity for rational thinking has greatly expanded throughout the centuries as a result of further integration of Spirit into the physical body. There have always been people who are farther along on this path, promoting ideas that may take centuries for others to realize.

7. Conclusions of This Section

While throughout my book I have criticized scientism for its inability to explain paranormal phenomena, even those without a spiritual viewpoint can see the inherent fallacies of scientism in explaining human behavior. These fallacies include the following concepts:

- Neuronal activity alone can result in consciousness.
- Neurons determine human behavior; therefore, there is no free will or personal responsibility.
- There is no "I" or Self.
- The behavior of ancient ancestors or even prehuman animals that enabled them to survive now has a major influence on current human behavior.
- Human appreciation of culture and art is the result of the discharge of pleasurable neurons.
- Behavior promoted by religion or a belief in God is based on neurons or genes that helped ancestors with those beliefs to survive.
- Humans are gifted chimps and, thus, human use of tools is no different from animals using tools.
- The similarity of human genes to primate genes demonstrates that humans are only a difference of degree from primates.
- Genes can be selfish and only concerned with their own replication.
- Computers will someday equal human intelligence (promissory materialism).
- Morality can be biologically determined.

Since the reductionist theory has so many misconceptions, it needs to be replaced with a view that lacks those misconceptions and explains consciousness, the self, spiritual beliefs, morality, and paranormal and abnormal behavior. Spirit forms residing in the human body can explain all of these.

V. Alternate Theories—Secular II

A very interesting person in the study of human psychology is Abraham Maslow (1908–1970). I was rather surprised that Tallis never mentioned him. Like Tallis, Maslow was classified as a humanist, having received the American Humanist Association award for Humanist of the Year in 1967. At the end of his life he became interested in transpersonal psychology, which is often involved in mystical experiences and what Maslow called "peak experiences." While an STE may occur once in a lifetime, a person may have peak experiences more frequently. Maslow felt that Freud neglected human aspirations and godlike qualities. Humanistic psychologists generally dismiss behaviorism as irrelevant to the study of humans, since early behaviorists principally performed much of their research on animals. However, behaviorists would claim that humanistic psychologists have difficulty developing testable hypotheses for their claims. Maslow was performing his research before the term *evolutionary psychology* came into vogue.

Maslow is famous for his main concept that goes by two names. One name is eponymous with his paper "A Theory of (Human) Motivation" (first formally presented in 1943), and the second is the hierarchy of needs. The first four needs of this hierarchy are often referred to as deficit, or *D*, needs. These are physiological needs, safety needs, belonging needs, and esteem needs. The fifth need is classified as a being, or *B*, need. Maslow refers to these needs as a hierarchy because until the lower ones are satisfied, an individual generally will not be concerned about the next level. The physiological needs are things like food, water, clothing, shelter, and homeostasis. Safety needs would include health, a home in a safe environment, and economic safety. Belonging needs would include relationships such as with friends, family, intimates, and community. Esteem needs are divided into two levels. The lower level is the respect of others, such as recognition, reputation, and dignity. The higher esteem need is self-respect, the need to feel confident, competent, achievement, independence, and freedom. All of these are called deficit needs, because if a person does not have them he feels the desire to find them, often unconsciously. However, once a person fulfills that need, it fails to become a motivating force. Maslow felt that all of these deficit needs were "instinctoid," that is, similar to an animal's instincts, though on a grander scale.

Maslow's writings mostly emphasize the Being Needs, metaneeds, or what he called Self-actualization, sometimes also referred to as full humanness. Maslow would probably dismiss the current form of evolutionary psychology because it does not recognize free will or Being Needs. However, he could view his theories as an evolutionary step toward an advanced level of humanness rather than as a step backward into animal behavior, as most believers in evolutionary psychology present the concept.

To raise children who are more interested in metaneeds, Maslow placed more emphasis on parents providing for the deficit needs of a child than on genetics. For developing self-esteem in a child, Maslow thought it important to provide reasonable challenges for the child and not simply to praise the child for expected good behavior or provide for every wish. Maslow held that undesirable behavior results when basic needs are not met.

Unlike behavioral or evolutionary psychologists, both of whom prefer not to use terms like *values*, Maslow would use value words, or what he termed "fusion words," such as *mature*, *evolved*, *stunted*, *functioning*, and *graceful*. He felt that people are not innately evil, sinful, or cruel, but rather that they develop such traits when one of their basic needs is not met. Even most animals are not hostile unless their safety needs or physiological needs (e.g., food) are not met.

In *Towards a Psychology of Being*, Maslow listed the following characteristics and B-values of self-actualized people (Maslow, 1999, 32, 93–94).

Characteristics

1. Superior perception of reality
2. Increased acceptance of self, of others, and of nature
3. Increased spontaneity
4. Increase in problem centering
5. Increased detachment and a desire for privacy
6. Increased autonomy and resistance to enculturation

7. Greater freshness of appreciation, and richness of the emotional reaction
8. Higher frequency of peak experiences
9. Increased identification with the human species
10. Changed (the clinician would say "improved") interpersonal relations
11. More democratic character structure
12. Greatly increased creativeness
13. Certain changes in the value system

B-values (the following are direct quotations)

1. Wholeness (unity; integration; tendency to oneness; interconnectedness; simplicity; organization; structure; dichotomy-transcendence; order);
2. Perfection (necessity; just-rightness; just-so-ness; inevitability; suitability; justice; completeness; "oughtness");
3. Completion (ending; finality; justice; "it's finished;" fulfillment; *he looks* and telos; destiny; fate);
4. Justice (fairness; orderliness; lawfulness; "oughtness");
5. Aliveness (process; nondeadness; spontaneity; self-regulation; full-functioning);
6. Richness (differentiation; complexity; intricacy);
7. Simplicity (honesty; nakedness; essentiality; abstract, essential, skeletal structure);
8. Beauty (rightness; form; aliveness; simplicity; richness; wholeness; perfection; completion; uniqueness; honesty);
9. Goodness (rightness; desirability; oughtness; justice; benevolence; honesty);
10. Uniqueness (idiosyncrasy; individuality; noncomparability; novelty);
11. Effortlessness (ease; lack of strain, striving or difficulty; Grace; perfect, beautiful functioning);
12. Playfulness (fun; joy; amusement; gaiety; humor; exuberance; effortlessness);

13. Truth; honesty; reality (nakedness; simplicity; richness; oughtness; beauty; pure, clean, and unadulterated; completeness; essentiality);

14. Self-sufficiency (autonomy; independents; not needing other than itself in order to be itself; self-determining; environment transcendence; separateness; living by its own laws)

I maintain that a person more engaged with her Spirit demonstrates more of these Being Needs.

W. Alternative Theories—Spiritual, the Binary Soul Doctrine

I will now discuss a spiritual concept of humans that employs many of the writings I have evaluated. The author of this concept reaches a different, but interesting, conclusion. Psychologist Peter Novak developed a Binary Soul Doctrine (BSD), that is, the concept that humans have more than one spiritual element. The BSD hypothesis is that humans have two souls, and Novak quotes the Bible on "soul" and "spirit" being two separate spiritual entities that reside in humans, as I did in chapter 1. The title of his book is *The Lost Secret of Death: Our Divided Souls and the Afterlife* (2003). Like I do, Novak employs the writings of Max Freedom Long and the concepts of the kahunas. He also discusses NDEs in detail to support his doctrine.

1. Religious and Psychological Support for Two Souls

While modern Christianity rarely emphasizes two separate spiritual aspects of humans, Novak frequently quotes from Gnostic Christianity. The Gnostics were around for about the first two centuries of Christianity, but they were eventually considered heretics and disappeared. Various Gnostic Gospels were rediscovered in Nag Hammadi, Egypt, in the 1940s. Novak's quotations were frequently from the Gnostic Gospels of Philip, Thomas, and Truth.

In addition to the Christian Bible, Novak reviews the world's major religions (Hinduism, Buddhism, Islam, Judaism) and concludes that they, as well as past ancient cultures the world over, also support the concept of a binary soul. Novak explains the concept of two souls, including their names, in the above religions and cultures, but I will not go into his details except to make a brief comment on Judaism.

According to Novak, the Old Testament word generally translated as "soul" is *nephesh* (used 451 times), and the word translated as "spirit" is *ruah* (used 271 times). Novak's hypothesis of two souls then proceeds to more modern times, mentioning Freud and Jung's discovery of the unconscious mind and modern neuropsychological findings, namely that each side of the brain seems to have different functions. The earliest book in this field is titled *Left Brain, Right Brain*, written by Sally Springer and George Deutsch (1981). Novak holds that this modern split-brain research on the functions of each side of the brain (left and right hemispheres) closely matches, but expands upon, Freud and Jung's concepts and that of the two souls of the diverse religions and cultures listed above. For example, the kahunas used the terms *uhane*, which Long calls the low self, and *unihipili*, the middle self, as discussed in chapter 2.

2. Functions of Each Soul

According to split-mind research, the functions of the left side of the brain, our rational intellectual consciousness, *ruah*, and Long's middle self (which controls the right side of the physical body) are mainly recognizing distinctions and differences between things. The left side considers itself objective. It has an independent free will and takes initiative but only possesses short-term memory. In addition, it is separate, active, autonomous, logical, "masculine," verbal, and a decision maker.

The functions of the right side of the brain, our emotional subconscious, *nephesh*, and Long's low self include focusing on patterns, similarities, and relationships between things; containing memories; and communicating by images, symbols, pictures, and metaphors. The right side of the brain is also subjective, dependent, nonverbal (although it perceives content), passive, reactive, instinctive, responsive, and "feminine." The subconscious does not see options or choices but accepts all input as equal. It is like a person who is hypnotized and does whatever the hypnotist suggests without questioning it. Novak writes, "While we are alive, these two compliments are always intertwined, never allowing us to experience one or the other in a pure and undiluted state. ... Each defines the other, and it is not possible, in the universe of the living at least, to have one entirely without the other. To separate these external pairs is to violate the very nature of reality" (p. 49).

3. Separation of the Two Souls at Death

Novak's interest in the subject matter of what ensues after death began with some after-death communication from his deceased wife. She committed suicide soon after the birth of their daughter.

How does Novak employ these separate brain functions to explain religious and paranormal phenomena? It is simple: at death of the physical body, or in some cases a period of time after death, the two souls separate and each proceeds to have its own afterlife. For instance, some phenomena reported by NDErs can be explained by what one soul thinks/observes/feels, and other phenomena by what the other split-off soul thinks/observes/feels. When the two souls are in the physical body, they operate together, although the conscious, thinking soul usually predominates, at least when awake. In the afterlife, one soul can go to heaven or hell while the other reincarnates.

Some religions or cultures think that one soul is more valued than the other and, thus, that the less valued soul simply disappears when the person dies. According to Novak, religions such as Hinduism and Islam believe that the rational conscious self is more important, whereas Christianity believes the unconscious emotional self is more important. As he writes,

> After death, the two souls (conscious and subconscious) divide and the conscious part would be like a computer that was able to recognize, identify, classify, and distinguish a million different things, but could never realize that it, itself the subject perceiving all these objects was there as well. ... The conscious half would lose everything it used to receive from the unconscious; although it would still possess free will, it wouldn't have the slightest clue what to do with it, remembering nothing, feeling nothing, and seeing nothing but random, meaningless chaos. ... Without the unconscious's subjective, emotional perspective, the conscious mind would not feel related or connected to its environment in any way. It would feel completely isolated and uninvolved. In fact, without the unconscious, it would not experience any feeling or emotion whatsoever. Objective to the end, the conscious would then just be a bodiless, identityless, emotionless,

historyless, uncomprehending point of pure, living awareness. (pp. 43–44)

Without a memory, the conscious would exist in the spirit realm until it decided to reincarnate, but it would then have no memory of its previous incarnations and would often repeat the same mistakes.

Separated from the conscious, the subconscious would experience its own disparate life without input from the conscious.

> Meanwhile, the unconscious would experience purely internal awareness, sensing everything subjectively, and could never glimpse anything "outside its own skin." Everything it saw and experienced would be a reflection of its own contents. ... The unconscious would lose all ability for objective thought, logical analysis, and discriminative reason, along with all ability to make new choices. However, it would still possess emotion and memory, it would still be reactive and responsive, and it would still see connections and patterns and relationships. ... The unconscious would at least contain a memory of the person he used to be. (pp. 44–45)

The unconscious would review and reexperience its memories, feelings, and self-judgments and react emotionally to them. If the self-judgments from memory were favorable, then the unconscious would think it was in heaven, but if they were self-condemning, it would think it was in hell. These views would come from within itself and not from any judgment from without. It would not have any decision-making ability to make changes.

4. Explaining Paranormal Phenomena

I formerly described how heaven, hell, and reincarnation can be explained by the BSD doctrine, but there are other stages of an NDE that can also be resolved by the BSD. The darkness perceived in a tunnel is attributed to the conscious aspect. Novak states that in the darkness many NDErs feel no emotions. Novak believes that the dark stage of an NDE occurs when the conscious mind is no longer connected to the subconscious and therefore is objective and emotionless, using logical thought for detailed perception. The person also has free will, but without any memory or meaning the choices are limited. The memories are in the now detached subconscious.

In the next stage of an NDE, perceiving or being in the *light*, the person feels much emotion and feels connected to other people and the universe. The NDEr sees patterns and meaning without details. However, the separate subconscious has very little reasoning or decision-making power. There is less verbal capacity; communication is telepathic, ineffable, and often understood as metaphors. These are typical properties of the subconscious. Novak contends that these two stages, the darkness and the *light*, are not happening in sequence but are simultaneously occurring in separated souls.

In chapter 5, on NDEs, in the section titled "A Unique Journey," I describe people in the afterlife trapped in their addictions. Novak believes these are subconscious souls that are unable to understand that they cannot have their former physical appetites satisfied but that only remember behavior associated with the addictions. They proceed on unchanged because they lack objective analytical reasoning. In addition, initiative is part of the conscious mind, and thus those bewildered spirits are unable to take any action (volition) to remove themselves from their environment, an option that is available if they look at the friendly spirits in the background willing to give assistance.

Novak also discusses soul retrieval by a shaman, a subject I discussed in chapter 9. He does not specifically state which soul needs to be retrieved, but he believes that most people who have had their souls retrieved are able to experience an improved emotional life. Based on this, he maintains that partial soul division is already occurring in most people multiple times prior to death. At times he refers to this soul division as dissociation, but I believe clinical dissociation is a much more severe mental illness than is the more commonplace soul division.

5. Problems in This Life as a Result of Soul Division

Novak then discusses how we believe our society ignores the subconscious, or the emotional side of our life, and how people need to integrate it with the conscious mind before death so that separation does not happen after death. He states that at birth, we are whole and undivided, but as we grow, our intelligent cerebral left brain takes dominance over our emotional right brain mind. He argues that several stories in the book of Genesis are metaphors for this split. In particular, the stories of Cain and Abel, Isaac and Ishmael, and Jacob and Esau represent these divisions.

Novak also explains his theory of how Jesus Christ can live in us and lead us to self-integration, even if a person does not acknowledge Christ or the Christian religion. He uses quotations from both the New Testament and the Gnostic Gospels. By Christ's resurrection, his soul is conjoined to everyone else's. He can accept our emotional pain and prevent a separation while alive, and thus prevent separation after death. However, in order to receive Christ's assistance, a person must lead a life of personal integrity and self-honesty.

6. Critique of BSD

I have presented the BSD and have shown why Novak believes that it explains many spiritual phenomena. Now, I will divulge why I judge that it has major deficiencies. In chapter 5, on NDEs, I explained my own concept that the transcendental realm of an NDE is a personal encounter with a person's own Spirit or High Self. At that time, the High Self may be contacting spiritual levels above itself, such as angels or divine beings. I do not believe the experience with the *light* is just the subconscious experiencing favorable self-judgment.

I suppose that every person with a psychological theory handpicks information that fits his theory, ignoring contradictory evidence. When Novak interprets the peace felt when leaving the body as not an emotional peace, I would disagree. I believe that departing the painful physical body, even for just a short time, is an emotional peace.

When Novak describes a realm of darkness, he means the tunnel. Like so many other individual phases of the NDE, this only occurs in about 25% of cases and appears to me to be a temporary transition phase rather than a place where people could remain after death. Although many describe it as a dark narrow tunnel with a *light* at the end, others felt that the tunnel was bright and that other beings were in the tunnel with them. Hieronymus Bosch's painting titled *Ascent of the Blessed* (alternative title: *Ascent to the Empyrean*), drawn in about 1505, demonstrates this. Novak also interprets the tunnel as floating in a void, but I interpret it as moving, usually rapidly, toward a place where NDErs feel they must reach the *light* at the end of the tunnel.

Novak uses the well-known fact that time is often irrelevant during an NDE (e.g., a full life review takes a few seconds) to make the claim that the dark phase and the *light* phase are occurring at the same time. Novak never discusses the autoscopic phase as part of an NDE. The autoscopic phase does occur in real time. It is only in the transcendental realm that time is meaningless. He does discuss OBEs, but in another context. I interpret the data of the autoscopic phase as such: the tunnel is a transition, and the transcendental realm is generally proceeding in a sequential manner.

Another difficulty I have with Novak's concept is his handpicking of data. I did not review all of the religious interpretations, as stated earlier, but he listed the two souls in Hinduism as Atman and Jiva. Those two words are from a native Indian language. In chapter 8, on Eastern concepts of spirituality, I discussed the English words for various souls from Theosophy, whose concepts generally came from India. Theosophists had four souls, the etheric body, the astral body, the mental body, and the Self. When I investigated information on Atman in *Wikipedia*, I found that the description most closely resembled the Self, or what I call Spirit, and not the conscious and subconscious.

I also question the use of certain biblical quotations that Novak utilizes to indicate that we should integrate our two souls. He cites Ephesians 2:14, which refers to making the two into one. When I read that passage, it appears to me that Paul is making Gentiles equal to Jews in sharing the message of salvation in Jesus Christ, which has nothing to do with making two souls into one that functions as a unit.

Novak maintains that our moral sense or balance is part of our subconscious. I have difficulty when anyone says that society's problems are the result of the misprogramming or repression of our subconscious. How does one determine that the subconscious was misprogrammed? How is our emotional life completely separate from our animal instincts? Animals fight and often kill members of their own species in order to protect their territory, never mind the fact that they have to kill other animals if they are carnivores. Why can't our rational mind be programmed to control some aspects of our subconscious rather than infer that the subconscious was repressed or misprogrammed?

Novak uses the kahuna concept of the low self and middle self of Max Freedom Long, but Long believed it was important that the rational middle self be in charge rather than the low self, which desires instant gratification. My own suggestion of how to improve the connection between the conscious and subconscious minds would be through good music and artistic pursuits rather than psychological training.

I am also contending in my book that a soul division occurs at the time of death. In chapter 10, on spirit intrusion and release, I mentioned a number of therapists who appeared to heal people of psychological problems by convincing them to join deceased relatives in a *realm of light*. Thus, I believe there is a separation in some people at death, but this is a separation of a person's ordinary thought from his High Self or Spirit. This thought pattern is the person's soul, and when it rejoins its own Spirit, it no longer is causing misbehavior in the person undergoing therapy. I also believe that this separation is much less frequent than in Novak's analysis.

7. Final Remarks on BSD

Novak believes that he solves "the greatest riddle known to man," that is, what may happen after death.

Novak states, and expresses worry, that his writings will be classified as just another New Age book. It does not help his case that his publisher mostly publishes New Age books. Novak's book is unlikely to be accepted by many Christians because he employs Gnosticism as a frequent reference. I do applaud him for his alternative theory to what usually happens at death and how such things can be prevented. Novak believes that with so many contradictory afterlife possibilities, people will conclude that none of them can be valid and that therefore there is an absence of life after death. However, it may be good to have alternative spiritual concepts, rather than just one versus the materialist paradigm.

X. A History of Genius, and Its Connection to Spirit

Darrin McMahon's book *Divine Fury: A History of Genius* (2013) complements my concept of Spirit and traces how it has evolved. The word *genius* today simply means a person with high intelligence, but perhaps one with creativity and insight. However, this is much different from the ancient concept of genius and its intimate connection to the divine.

While *genius* often meant the truly eminent, such as Mozart or the quintessential Einstein, *genius* also implies power to divine the secrets of the universe and the "profound religiosity associated with genius and the genius figure" (pp. xii–xiii). Einstein had a mystical intuitive approach to solving problems and desired to understand how God had created the world. It is also interesting that some of his findings involved light, but this was seemingly physical light. He was also considered eccentric, a quality found in many other accomplished geniuses.

1. Derivation of the Word

When writing *Diving Fury*, McMahon was a historian at Florida State University but is now at Dartmouth, and his book is extremely well referenced. Except toward the end of the book, his idea of genius is exclusively focused on Western civilization. According to McMahon, the word *genius* itself was first used by the Romans and implied a guardian spirit that accompanied a person from birth throughout life and that connected the person to the divine, similar to my concept of Spirit. The word *genius* comes from a Latin verb meaning "to generate, father, or beget." In surviving records, it was first used by a Roman playwright named Plautus (ca. 254–184 BCE), to describe a divine power or life force or energy similar to the mana of the Polynesians mentioned in chapter 2. It was linked to generative or reproductive capacity; sometimes a horn or a snake may have acted as a totem for genius.

> Just how and when, precisely, the free-flowing life-force of the early Italian *genius* became a personal spirit and individual protector of the sort invoked by Ovid and Horace is not altogether clear, though it is easy enough to imagine the general progression: a power initially associated with procreation, and believed to course through the body of the paterfamilias, was gradually envisioned not just as the divine energy of the one who maintained the family, but as divinity itself, accompanying, watching over, and protecting all man from the moment of their birth. ... The *genius*, an individual's "companion" (*comes*) and spiritual double, is

aware of, and responsible for, and differences that shape human personalities and determine their fates. ... It was also natural to conclude that this god—who might soar through the heavens to intercede with the divine forces of the universe—was also resident within us. ... The relationship between this divine companion and one's inborn nature was close (pp. 22–23). [Later, McMahon would add,] With his *genius*, the individual was in the presence of a force other than himself that was greater than himself, a divine expression of his nature that linked him to the gods. All men had a *genius*. (p. 25)

Later it would sometimes become merged with the term *ingenium* (or "genius within"), meaning our inborn nature, disposition, or talent. A Roman author commented that there can "be no great *ingenium* without a touch of madness" (p. 23). Another writer named Apuleius (ca. 125–ca. 180) drew a correlation between the Greek *daimon* and the Roman *genius*.

2. Two Transformations

McMahon identifies two broad transformations over many centuries that led to the modern concept of the genius. The first of these is the "withdrawal of God" and the "dismissal of a range of spiritual companions—spirits and angels, prophets, apostles, and saints—who had long served human beings as guardians and mediators to the divine" (p. xviii). Thus, to a great extent, I am receding to this former interpretation but from a new perspective and with an interpretation of old, but recently explored, information, such as shamanism, and with much new information, such as NDEs arising from resuscitation technology.

McMahon's second broad transformation is related to the belief in equality, although some classes of people were excluded from the equality granted to others. He reports that Jefferson "spoke of a 'natural aristocracy,' composed of individuals of talent, creativity, and intelligence, that might replace the old aristocracy of birth and blood" (p. xx). According to McMahon, genius has always been a relationship but our relationship with it has changed over the centuries.

3. The Greeks and the Romans

McMahon notes that the ideal for ancients was never to create something original without precedent or pattern. God or gods were believed to have created the universe, and thus genuine originality was impossible. Humans were to recover what already existed. For instance, the word *discover* really means to uncover what was already there. *Invent* implies accessing an inventory of existing knowledge. The word *royalties* derives from the belief that a king was God's representative on earth and was entitled to collect on behalf of the true Creator. A human who created something was flirting with danger in that she was challenging the gods.

> It is largely for that reason that the ideal of creativity only began to emerge as a modern value in the eighteenth century, and that in earlier times imagination was viewed with deep suspicion as a faculty to be controlled and even feared. ... It could only be where the Creator's existence was called into question that human creativity could fully emerge (p. 5). ... The Prometheus myth is an archetype of the dangers, as well as the temptations, of usurping divine creativity and knowledge. (comment under painting of *Prometheus Bound*, opposite p. 40)

McMahon maintains that the history of the word *genius* began with Socrates (ca. 470–399 BCE). Socrates reported that he had a familiar divine sign that came to him as a voice since his childhood. McMahon states that while Socrates taught by the power of his intellect, or rational thinking, he also "recognized the existence of mysterious forces, and obeyed them" (p. 7). The belief in a *daimon* was widely shared by ordinary people. The word used by Socrates to describe this voice was *daimonon* (or *daimon*, or *guardian spirit*). This same word is used in some Bibles based on translations from Greek to Latin as *daemon* and then to English as *demon*, but I maintain that Socrates's "voice" is from his Spirit. Socrates reported that the voice never urged him to act, and thus he did not become involved in politics. The prominent citizens of Athens felt he was introducing a strange god. He was subsequently put on trial for heresy and corruption of youth and was condemned to death. Socrates reported that his daimonon approved of his drinking the hemlock and never held him back.

Plato (ca. 429–348 BCE) was a pupil of Socrates and frequently commented on *daimones*, believing them to the messengers between gods and people. Poets were often thought of as mediums revealing divinely inspired messages, but often from a Muse rather than a daimon. They told stories of gods and heroes. In fact, the word *poetry* is derived from the expression "to create," that is, the creation of the gods through human agents. Poets were often compared to prophets. The word *prophet* implies "one who speaks for another," in other words, one who reveals the thoughts of God. Plato wrote that poets would often enter a trance or a state of ecstasy, a topic previously discussed with regard to shamans. In a trance, the poet's mind was not his own. The word *ecstasy* literally means "standing outside of oneself." At various mystery schools in Greece, priestesses or oracles would also be in ecstasy when making their prophecies. Plato argued that some poets can be irrational and their ideas abused in a political setting. Socrates's principal accuser was a poet.

The title of McMahon's book *Divine Fury* comes from the Latin term *furor divinum*, or *divine madness*, a term used by Plato. The first three forms of madness are for poetry, prophecy, and religious ecstasy, but the greatest is the divine madness for love. However, in Plato's case, his concept is a lover of truth, the highest form of wisdom, and is achieved through human reason. The word *philosophy* means "love of wisdom."

Another term that was used in reference to a genius was *charisma*. Although now often indicating an outgoing personality, the word actually means "a divine favor or grace, a gift of the gods" (p. 26). In Greek, the apostle Paul's term for the gifts of the Holy Spirit is *kharis*, or *charism*. German sociologist Max Weber would use the term to indicate "a certain ineffable something, a quality of the personality or soul, that created the illusion that one was touched by supernatural, superhuman, or exceptional powers" (p. 26). Similarly, Cicero referred to a *divinum quiddam*, a mysterious power that some people held.

4. Genius from Early Christianity to the Renaissance

McMahon begins discussing the Christian era with the martyrdom of St. Polycarp (69–155 CE), who refused to swear by the genius of Caesar (Marcus Aurelius). Other legends say Polycarp simply refused to burn incense to him. While not necessarily employing the term *genius*, Christians did believe that various powers were gifts (charisms) of the one true God and that martyrs were models of transcendence.

Martyrs during the Roman persecution, or saints later, were considered to be conduits to the divine or human mediators who embodied ideals each person should seek. "Saints were privy to a higher order of knowledge and understanding: they could relay messages and dispatch wisdom, utter prophecies, petition miracles, and disclose truths with an epiphanic power" (p. 41). The bones of martyrs or saints were, and still are, called relics and are held to be of special importance. When the bones of two martyrs were "translated" (moved) from the place where they were found to a new home, demons allegedly fled from people along the route. The new home, in effect, became a *genius loci* (a place of genius) of sacred power. Rather than use the term *genius*, Christians would seek the assistance of a patron saint, after whom they would be named. "The saint was the genius's heir, watching over people and places alike and protecting their human charges from birth until death" (pp. 36–37). The day a saint died is of special importance, in that it is the day of his or her "birth" into heaven (*dies natalis*).

In addition to saints, Christians had another source of mediation between themselves and God. These were the angels, and they functioned as guardians similar to a genius for Greeks and Romans. St. Jerome stated that each person has a guardian angel from birth. The saints were believed to be guarded by a higher order of angels. However, caution was urged as evil forces could disguise themselves as angels, similar to the idea of evil *genii*.

McMahon moves rapidly toward the end of the Middle Ages, discussing a rather obscure Florentine named Marsilio Ficino (1433–1499). Ficino is classified as a Neoplatonist. He translated the works of Plato into Latin. His final book is titled *Three Books of Life* (1489). Plato emphasized the *furor divinus* as being powered by love, but Ficino emphasized that the daimon was the rational part of the soul. "The genius of the highest man, in other words, was his own rational soul, guided directly by God" (p. 53). Ficino also agreed that "melancholy was the natural counterpart to the supernatural impetus of divine illumination" (p. 55). However, he believed that divine madness came exclusively to melancholics, a concept with which my theory of Spirit would disagree, because Spirit can be accessed under numerous circumstances. Also, some Christian writers at that time thought that melancholy made a person more susceptible to the influence of evil forces. It was about the time of the Renaissance that contributors to this subject began to ponder if humans could create, invent, or conceive by themselves, and not simply recover or imitate the creations of God.

5. Modern Era

Different interpretations were posited in the northern Protestant countries. Writers there began to discount the concept of mediators, "displacing the souls, saints, and spirits who had come before" (p. 60). This helped give rise to the modern concept that the *ingenium*, or genius within, is the genius of humanity itself.

René Descartes (1596–1650) is known for two areas of study, mathematics and philosophy. His most famous statement is, "I think, therefore I am." He began "positing that existence of a new mechanical world of cause and effect in which there would be no room for genii at all" (p. 68). Both he and Voltaire (1694–1778) said that they had never seen a genie, and therefore genii did not exist. They stated that Socrates was a great thinker, independent of to whom or to what he attributed his concepts. These ideas are the basis for McMahon's comment in the introduction of his book that God had to withdraw from human affairs for human genius to appear. The individual genius became a new creation, a man of genius (*l'homme de genii*). This was an exception to the notion of the equality of all (or most) humans that was also beginning to take shape at this time. In the eighteenth century, a woman wrote that souls and geniuses have no gender, but her view was generally ignored. According to my concept of Spirit, it has no gender. However, it could function differently in each gender.

Anthony Ashley Cooper (1671–1713), the 3rd Earl of Shaftesbury, in an essay titled "Advice to Authors," relayed an unusual viewpoint:

that great writers are mirrors that allow us "to comprehend the secret language of the soul. ... *Geniuses*, in effect, become our *genii*, serving as our guides and better selves, our guardian protectors and moral spectators, who help us to negotiate the mysteries of the self and of the world" (p. 77). What I call Spirit, in many of its manifestations, such as music scores heard by composers rather than actively developed, often speak to the soul of many humans.

An atheist writer named Denis Diderot (1713–1784) attempted to describe the *furor poeticus* that may overtake a genius in her imaginative moments, but his description appears more mystical than physical. Other writers would refer to it as an *enthusiasm*, with its modern terminology, but the word originally meant "from God" (*en theos*). As McMahon explains it, "Commentators on genius retained and reasserted, often despite themselves, a language replete with allusions to possession, transcendence, rapture, and special revelation, even as they denied the existence of possessing demons or the possessive power of divinely conferred gifts" (p. 88).

Two people who are often referred to as geniuses are Sir Isaac Newton (1642–1727) and Wolfgang Amadeus Mozart (1756–1791). Since Mozart began to compose at such an early age, that ability must have been present at birth. As a result of his dying a pauper, the idea arose in the nineteenth century of a suffering or misunderstood genius. An Italian poet named Torquato Tasso (1544–1595) was committed to a "lunatic's cell," and many considered him to be a martyr to genius. He most likely was bipolar. Eugène Delacroix (1789–1863) made a famous painting in 1839 of Tasso in his cell. Of course, the idea that mental instability is connected to genius goes back to the Greek concept that geniuses often had a melancholic temperament. As McMahon comments, "If genius was a gift, it was also a curse" (p. 139). Newton's crypt is in Westminster Abbey, resting place of saints. In effect, he became a secular saint.

Historians have often debated whether significant changes in society are determined by great men (*grands hommes* in French) or by social forces. During the French Revolution, a number of great men were cited for their contributions to ideas prevalent in the Revolution. Among these were Voltaire, Jean-Jacques Rousseau (1712–1778), Benjamin Franklin, and Descartes. Though never implemented, a proposal was made during the Revolution to create a new calendar with a "festival of the genius." Geniuses were thought more easily to originate in a society with liberty, equality, and democracy.

McMahon reviews numerous concepts of genius in the late nineteenth and early twentieth century. One writer (Edgar Zilsel) in 1918 titled his book *Die Geniereligion* (*The Religion of Genius*). He found it "particularly troubling in light of the fact that the genius religion possessed no stable moral ground. Their genius was revered for the alleged 'depth' of his person and the profundity of his work, regardless of its content or moral consequences" (p. 195). Many other writers accepted moral transgressions as natural for a genius, seeing that creativity was amoral.

6. Geniology

In a chapter titled "Geniology," McMahon discusses the concept of trying to measure genius. Early attempts in the late eighteenth to the early nineteenth century were based on physiology, such as phrenology (the word means "knowledge of the mind"). Others who attempted to measure brain volume or weight held that geniuses had larger or heavier brains. Ultimately, though, none of these methods to relate genius to physical measurements proved valid.

A medically trained Italian psychologist named Cesare Lombroso happily repeated the story that the Italian philosopher Giambattista Vico had derived his genius from a childhood fall, later observing that "it has frequently happened that injuries to the head and acute diseases ... have changed a very ordinary individual into a man of genius" (p. 170).

I make note of this, as NDE researcher Melvin Morse commented that people who had NDEs as children were often very creative and accomplished much as adults. Thus, the people Lombroso mentioned as having had injuries and acute diseases may have had an NDE. Lombroso further noted that many geniuses lived long lives but also that "it was not uncommon for geniuses to be born of criminal parents" (p. 172). This would apparently refute the idea that geniuses became geniuses by way of genetics.

In chapter 8, on Eastern concepts of human spirituality, I mentioned that one of the people who saw auras (Dora Kunz) became head of the Theosophical Society in the United States. I also mentioned that one of

the founders of Theosophical Society was Helena Blavatsky. McMahon
discusses some writings of Blavatsky, in which she said,

> The philosophers of old were near the truth that our modern
> wiseacres, when they endowed man with a tutelary Deity, a
> spirit whom they called genius. ... What distinguished the
> greatest men "was the imprisoned Spirit, the exiled 'god'
> within." That notion, she insisted, retained its basic truths. In
> "every manifestation of genius," Blavatsky continued, "in the
> warrior or the Bard, the great painter, artist, statesman or
> man of Science," one could discern "the undeniable presence
> of the celestial exile, the divine Ego." (pp. 185–186)

Kunz employed the term *self* for what Blavatsky called "Spirit" or
"divine Ego."

7. Post–World War II

Since World War II, the concept of areas in which a genius may arise
has expanded well beyond arts and sciences. Athletes, coaches, actors,
musicians, and corporation heads are often described as geniuses. Many
Americans are more into applied and practical genius rather than truly
creative ideas. McMahon lists a number of self-help books that have
been published in recent years that claim they can turn a person into a
genius or a more creative person. He then comments, "But if genius is
everywhere, the genius is nowhere" (p. 235). McMahon also mentions
an article that commented, "Organized research does not depend upon
individual genius; it is a group activity" (p. 236). A Nobel Prize is usually
shared, and the people who share the prize are often team leaders who
depend on many subordinates for ideas that result in receiving a Nobel
Prize. McMahon does discuss the concept of geniuses being celebrities.
However, fame is not genius, but it can be a good marketing strategy
that is affected by modern electronic media.

8. Conclusions of This Section

There are several main points about genius that have frequently shown
up over the centuries. I will attempt to relate these and other factors to

my concept of Spirit. This concept of mind can easily relate to McMahon's early discussion of genius as the following:

- An individual's "companion"
- A spiritual double
- The relationship between a divine companion and one's inborn nature
- A force other than oneself
- Being linked the person to the gods

These ideas closely resemble my idea that Spirit is one part of our spiritual component that functions as the following:

- High Self (and through it access to higher spiritual levels)
- Third Man factor (primarily physical protection)
- Inner Self-helper (psychological protection and healing)
- Mystical Union
- Realm of *light* during NDEs

In his discussion about the Third Man factor, Geiger (2009) states that some people employed the term *companion* in reference to the Third Man. Geiger also discusses Julian Jaynes's concept of the bicameral mind during ancient times in which the right side of the brain was an authority or a God-side figure that gave commands by way of visual and auditory hallucinations. Earlier in human evolution, this is how Spirit may have operated, but now Spirit's goal as it further interacts with our physical body is to have humans understand concepts and not simply respond to commands. Socrates's daimon illustrates this, as it could speak to him (not necessarily authoritatively) but also encouraged logical dialogue to reach conclusions.

In one sense, some modern people have come full circle in that they can "know" something without the use of logical steps. This is different from knowing something "from authority," as referenced by Jaynes. Long (1948) spoke about the High Self using a process called mentation to know things without an intermediate logical thought pattern. Some NDErs who entered the transcendental realm felt they somehow understood how everything works together, though they may not remember it when returning to their bodies.

Another idea that has been discussed over the centuries is whether genius could be related to madness (mental illness). The ancient Greeks thought genius often appeared in people with melancholy/depression. As explained in an earlier section, I do not believe melancholy directly results in more ideas that are thought to be creative. Rather, people with any type of mental illness (including alcohol and drug addiction) are more likely to be working with their Spirit as part of therapy, and this connection may result in greater contributions to insight about human behavior. Mental illness seems more prominent in people in the field of the arts, rather than the sciences, although some scientists can be eccentric. The saints who were revered and thought to have more influence with God (e.g., more effective prayers or healing powers) were often mystics. I maintain that mystics were more in communication with their own Spirit and that this Spirit had more access to spiritual realms above itself.

An additional topic about genius over the centuries is whether it is inherited and naturally occurring or more affected by the environment. Even if considered to be natural, there could be further discussion of genius as a gift of nature or a gift from "heaven" (from the gods or God). I would interpret the data from my research to indicate that many people who are considered geniuses have an inherently closer relationship to their Spirit. Intention can also be a factor; a person may simply motivate him- or herself to understand something better, and the answer will come from Spirit in response to the desire.

A final note about genius is its relationship to moral character. Although NDErs often do not feel judged for past actions, they do believe that treating other people with love and respect in the future is very important. Mystics often point to their relationship with God to impel them to treat their fellow humans better. This is my viewpoint and interpretation of moral values in relation to spirituality. While creative ideas may come through Spirit, which possibly may have come from spiritual levels above Spirit, as Spirit has further entered our physical bodies it may no longer relate to a God that promotes love. While a person's Spirit may be the source of its true ego, a person whose Spirit is more integrated into its body can more easily relate to his little ego and begin to feel more important than and superior to fellow human beings.

While I have emphasized the importance of being aware of our own Spirit, actual behavior involves all of our spiritual components. A person's etheric and astral bodies may have developed cravings from improper training or spirit intrusion. A person's behavior can be determined by those cravings and result in harming other people. These cravings do not necessarily stop a person from achieving creativity through her Spirit. People nowadays do not feel an inspiration as coming from a spiritual source, unlike in centuries past. Also, what a person judges as moral behavior can be partly determined by the society in which she lives, especially if the viewpoints are controlled by political media.

Creativity is now considered to be part of nature because our Spirit is more integrated with our physical body. Consequently, it seems to lose its relationship to a spiritual world. With this change, moral views sometimes come from a different perspective than what a God or gods say is prohibited. Many indigenous societies centuries ago, though living in harmony with nature, considered anyone not in their own tribe to be an enemy. Modern society has expanded its view of who we consider to be our friends due to this integration of Spirit, though we may still find a different basis for disliking other human beings as a group.

Y. Consciousness

Consciousness is one of the great dilemmas facing standard science, as is those who view life from a spiritual basis. The basic question for those supporting physicalism is, how can a thought process be explained from the basic laws of chemistry and physics? In general, in this section I will be dealing with human consciousness, but many of the principles may apply to diminished levels of consciousness in animals.

One of the essential issues of consciousness is how a human creates a picture or representation in her mind. A person may say he "sees" an object in his head, but that object was first light reflected off the object before the light entered the eye, which converted it to a combination of electrical and/or chemical signals to the brain, which then translated into an image in the brain. The mind also has the ability to create these images when there is no object in the line of vision.

Even people with the materialistic viewpoint have attempted to address the subject of consciousness, but I will not endeavor to summarize their multiple explanations. Instead, I will review Pim van Lommel's explanation of NDEs and consciousness in terms of quantum mechanics (QM) in his previously cited book *Consciousness Beyond Death* (2010). Materialists may partially use QM in their explanations of consciousness, but they disagree with van Lommel's contention that consciousness does not end with the death of the physical body. Van Lommel is a medical doctor, and his explanation is a summary of others' interpretations of the philosophical implications of QM. He maintains that materialism is a prevailing paradigm that has become prejudiced and dogmatic. He was educated with these reductionist and materialistic explanations of life but was able to overcome them. Science must be more accepting of alternative explanations if older concepts do not explain the available findings. Science proponents argue that one of their strengths is "respect for evidence," but few scientists actually have that respect for authentic paranormal evidence that contradicts their current paradigm.

While I agree with van Lommel's concept of similarities between QM and NDEs, I consider QM to be a model or metaphor and not a direct explanation. QM is a theory developed by physicists to explain the behavior of matter at atomic and subatomic distances. I am not convinced that QM concepts are directly responsible for human behavior at distances of human interactions. It is possible that the etheric body does interact with the physical body in a manner that involves QM principles. As van Lommel notes, QM was developed in regard to the coherent and closed systems of inorganic matter, while biological processes are incoherent and open systems.

One of the properties of QM is referred to as *entanglement*. If two particles are entangled and one electron is forced to alter its spin, the other will automatically alter its spin so that the two entangled electrons remain with opposite spins. (A frequent example is a pair of electrons with opposite spin. Spin does not necessarily imply rotation about an axis but is a fundamental property of matter that has two opposites, arbitrarily assigned values of $+\frac{1}{2}$ and $-\frac{1}{2}$.) This alteration will occur instantly regardless of the distance between two electrons. Some researchers have speculated that this "instantly" can even be faster than the speed of light. Einstein referred to this as "spooky action at a distance." Van Lommel draws a comparison between this phenomenon and a life review in which a person is interconnected to other people with whom he previously interacted.

The timelessness of reviewing one's past life as if in the present moment is also related to another principle of QM called *nonlocality*. The ability of an NDEr who is experiencing an OBE to travel instantaneously to any person she thinks about is also an example of nonlocality. The NDEr can also experience thought transfer with these other, nonlocal people, alive or deceased, demonstrating a connection between the two. Speaking theoretically, as probably no experiment can be designed to verify it, some physicists believe nonlocal space may be responsible for consciousness.

Another finding of QM is called the *uncertainty principle*, a concept proposed in 1927 by physicist Werner Heisenberg (1901–1976) and now accepted by most physicists. At ordinary dimensions, a person may specify the location of an object observed. Light is reflected from an object, and this enables the object's location to be determined. At a subatomic level, the light that is reflected actually moves the object. (Note that this movement is of the distance in the nanometer or a much shorter distance.) Thus, its location after the light reflects is different from before the light struck the object. The "error" in describing the location or momentum of the object can be specified mathematically employing a term called Planck's constant. Thus, its new location is "uncertain." According to van Lommel, some prominent physicists have claimed that if observing an object alters the results of an observation, then consciousness can create physical reality. I have difficulty with that claim. For instance, van Lommel employs the term "fundamentally altering the observed object" (p. 237). I doubt that observing something and moving it a nanometer would amount to a fundamental altering of the object, and I also question if consciousness and observation are identical.

Quantum physicists also speak about the duality of nature, such as light sometimes acting as a particle and sometimes as a wave but not doing both at the same time. This dual nature is also referred to as complementarity of nonlocal space. The wave nature of matter would fit in well with the spiritual concept of humans, as ideas I have previously discussed, such as chakras, are viewed as having a vibration/wave nature. Both light and sound (e.g., beautiful music), two vibrations or waves, are encountered frequently during NDEs. According to van Lommel, at death consciousness no longer has a particle aspect (the brain) but exists as a wave function in nonlocal space.

These waves are often described as probability waves. Van Lommel states, "In quantum physics the information is not encoded in a medium but is stored nonlocally as wave functions in nonlocal space, which also means that all information is always and everywhere immediately available" (p. 244). Consciousness is nonlocal, and the brain is a relay station for these wave functions. Brain activity is the result of consciousness and not the cause of it. Van Lommel admits he does not have an explanation for how this relay from nonlocal space to the brain occurs, but he speculates it may be due to quantum spin coherence and also involves DNA acting as antennae for nonlocal communication. I would argue that it is through our spiritual components, the psychonoetic body and etheric body, that this relay takes place. During most NDEs, the brain is not being used, so enhanced levels of consciousness are possible. Van Lommel even claims that "consciousness is nonlocal and functions as the origin or basis of everything, including the material world" (p. 266). In this sense, nonlocal consciousness may correspond to the highest level that mystics encounter, which I would maintain is one level of the spiritual world, while ordinary waking conscious is not operating at the highest level.

Van Lommel also mentions the theory developed by anesthesiologist and consciousness researcher Stuart Hameroff and physicist Roger Penrose. Their theory is that small structural components in neurons called microtubules could be a location where quantum phenomena occur—and that these microtubules account for consciousness. Although Hameroff classified himself as a nonbeliever, when he stated at a conference that these quantum sites (the microtubules) could account for paranormal phenomena, his idea was severely criticized by scientists. According to van Lommel, "Penrose has argued that on theoretical grounds that consciousness cannot be produced by the brain" (p. 271). Penrose also speculates that computers can never fully replicate consciousness.

In addition, van Lommel discusses memory, one major function of consciousness, as being comparable to a hologram. Despite some researchers alleging that touching one neuron can activate a memory and thus that the memory must have been in that neuron, other researchers have shown that removing an area of the brain where a memory was believed to reside (or the brain cells die) does not fully erase that memory. All memories are stored in nonlocal space, which uses the entire brain. It should be noted that if part of the brain is removed, then the memory may be less clear than if the full brain is involved. This is comparable to how a hologram operates.

He delves further into the concept of consciousness not being present in the brain and why NDE studies support that concept. He notes that NDEs often occur when there is no measurable activity in the cerebral cortex and brainstem, such as during cardiac arrest. Oxygen deficiency cannot be an explanation, because NDEs, in the form of fear-death experiences or empathic NDEs, happen without oxygen deficiency. Since van Lommel relates consciousness to NDEs and indications that there is an afterlife, he refers to it as endless or continuous consciousness. He also maintains that it explains other types of topics discussed in chapter 7, on ELEs, such as deathbed visions, after-death communication, and perimortem experiences (knowing that a person not in the vicinity has died).

Van Lommel reviews the idea of a collective unconsciousness in flocks of birds or schools of fish. This would correspond to my earlier proposal that a beehive may have a "group soul," which is actually a form of Spirit, while each human has his or her own individual Spirit.

Van Lommel provides an example of entanglement of consciousness, although he does not provide a reference to the research or mention how many people participated in the study. The research was performed on two people who were closely connected (entangled), such as parent and child. The test subjects were separated in Faraday cages, which prevent any communication by electromagnetic information transfer. One subject was stimulated with a flash of light, which caused an evoked potential that could be seen on an EEG. The potential immediately showed up on the EEG of the unstimulated person. This may be compared to finding that mothers often know when one of their faraway children is injured. Other studies using fMRI in place of EEG have found similar results.

Z. Conclusions of This Chapter

Nineteenth-century physics was based on "common sense" and how the world rationally operated. QM and paranormal phenomena share one aspect; neither one follows the rules of common sense. Communicating with someone, alive or deceased, without the use of the physical body's five senses is obviously "nonsense." But that and other paranormal events, such as levitation, knowledge of the future, curing of abnormal behavior (various severe mental illnesses) with psychotherapy rather than psychiatric medications, and hearing music without a physical source are not common sense, but they happen—and theories based on physicalism will never be able to explain them. Only a spiritual theory of the world, consciousness, and human behavior can account for the real world of the abnormal and paranormal.

Chapter 13

CONCLUSIONS

A. Introduction

My overall objective has been to demonstrate that many aspects of human behavior can best be explained with a model showing that more than one spiritual form resides within the physical body. Each of these forms has separate functions, but they all work together for a complete human being. These forms generally depart the body at physical death, but some of the forms may partially or temporarily depart while the person is alive. These latter departures may be voluntary or the result of trauma, either physical or psychological, or a combination of the two. This concept is in fundamental contrast to the currently prevailing materialistic supposition that consciousness and behavior are dependent upon the neurochemicals active in the brain and that events considered paranormal do not occur. For the two main spiritual forms, I have chosen to employ terms from the Western tradition, mainly *Spirit* and *soul*, but I recognize similarities of these terms to those of various non-Western traditions.

B. The Spirit Form

The form I call Spirit is only attached to our physical body (the theory of Long [1948]), or in Eastern parlance is a finer part of the aura and further away from the physical body, but I speculate that as part of human development over millennia, this form is penetrating the body to a greater extent or becoming denser and moving closer to the physical body, resulting in higher levels of consciousness (sometimes classified as superconsciousness), which culminate in greater understanding of art and technology. When Spirit is operational in a person, insight may be expressed as a "knowing" without having to proceed through rational "proofs," although the logical steps to support the proof may then follow.

Various types of spiritually transformative experiences (STEs) increase this penetration of Spirit into the physical body. STEs, such as transcendental near-death experiences (NDEs) and mystical experiences (Union), are temporary deep penetrations of Spirit into the physical body, but some people may have a continuous deep connection while seemingly in a normal or ordinary state of consciousness. This is a contrast to past generations of people, for whom a trance state was often necessary to achieve this connection. The Spirit form cannot ever leave the physical body except at death.

I have previously described how this Spirit may serve to protect a person from harm (e.g., the Third Man factor or a power animal), to assist in psychotherapy (e.g., the Inner Self-helper [ISH]), to rapidly heal the physical body (as has happened to numerous near-death experiencers [NDErs]), or to act as a resource for creative expression in artistic or scientific/mathematical fields. Another term for Spirit is High Self. Some of these activities may be the Spirit operating alone, or Spirit may seek assistance or guidance from various spiritual levels (a spectrum or hierarchy) above itself. This Spirit form closely parallels what Christians refer to as an active Holy Spirit, the third person of the Trinity. Some Eastern religions view what I describe as a more intense connection to Spirit as a force arising from the base of the spine to the crown chakra (kundalini). Many spiritual encounters with Spirit are expressed in symbolic language, and thus kundalini is another symbolic way of representing this intense connection. The nature of the Spirit world is usually elucidated in symbols, metaphors, parables, myths, or allegories, as words are never adequate (i.e., they are ineffable). The converse is not necessarily true; symbols and myths can represent numerous concepts not related to Spirit. One common symbol of Spirit is *light*. While in this *light*, a person may hear ethereal music. Composers of the highest order are often able to tune into this music (perhaps not sensing any *light* but possibly sensing love and joy, two of the *light's* most common features) and translate it into famous compositions. On rare occasions, people in ordinary consciousness may sense this *light* around a person who is in the *light*.

When this Spirit form is active, various types of paranormal events may occur. Paranormal, or psi, events are difficult to study by the standards of empirical science, which are based on the mechanical model of nineteenth-century physics. Paranormal events are in the Realms of Consciousness and/or Meaningful Behavior, a different metaphysical system, but one that has similarities to a quantum model in which space, time, distance, location, and physical properties are not relevant and the concept of death is not applicable. There are also strong indications that the Spirit of each human is connected to the Spirits of all other humans.

C. The Soul Form

While the Spirit form does not leave the physical body except at death, the soul form may partially or nearly completely leave the body while still living, often as a result of trauma. Physical trauma is a rather broad classification including severe injury, especially traumatic brain injury; serious infectious diseases; shock; seizures; environmental toxins (which may include some anesthetics or medications that induce a long-term coma); or substance abuse. Child abuse may be the most serious form of trauma, as it usually involves both physical and psychological trauma. My analysis suggests that the spiritual form that departs during trauma is a combination of the astral/emotional body and the mental body, collectively called the psychonoetic body. In children, this psychonoetic body is less penetrated into the physical body and is more easily, but temporarily, severed. This psychonoetic body is what I maintain has been referred to as the human soul, although in some descriptions the soul more closely is thought of as what I refer to as Spirit. When the psychonoetic body leaves the physical body temporarily, such as during an out-of-body experience (OBE) (e.g., an autoscopic NDE), sense impressions are directly made on the psychonoetic body and are then transferred back to the brain when it returns. The physical brain is not the source of consciousness, but consciousness originates in the spiritual forms that use the brain. Conversely, materialists would maintain that "mind" is an epiphenomenon of brain activity.

In the language of shamanism, partial departure of the psychonoetic body or soul is called *soul loss*, but a better descriptive term is *soul fragmentation*. At the time of death, a fragment with unfulfilled desires may not enter the *light*, that is, its own Spirit. Therefore, this fragment has not left the physical earth plane (is earthbound) and may enter the soul field of a person who has also experienced soul fragmentation, as fragmented souls usually have elementals that act as magnets for earthbound spirits with similar elementals. This soul fragment (often called a [noncapitalized] spirit, as in *spirit intrusion*) is generally only attached to the body of a person and will depart if the original soul is recovered, that is, if the fragmentation is repaired and returns to normal status. This fragment may also be led to the *light* by some therapeutic methods, religious practices, or a simple commitment ceremony. While not a form of trauma, various types of occult activities may result in soul fragmentation. This is likely because they compromise the cocoon of protection around people that acts as a shield warding off spirit intruders. This cocoon normally prevents the psychonoetic body from becoming fragmented. Referring to an attached soul is much different from the Spirit being attached. An attached soul is an intruder into the normal psychonoetic or soul field, while an individual's own Spirit is intended to be connected to only one physical body.

While soul fragmentation often results in spirit intruders, some of the same trauma that results in soul fragmentation may bring about an encounter with one's own Spirit, such as happens in a transcendental NDE. An autoscopic NDE would indicate that the soul has temporarily left the body. However, I have not read of any cases in which an intruding spirit attempted to or actually did enter the body of an NDEr. Apparently the body is protected from spirit intruders during an NDE but may not be protected when substance abuse causes temporary soul fragmentation and partial departure. One therapist (Atteshlis) noted that the physical body must be protected from spirit intruders when experimenting with out-of-body experiences, but this protection seems to automatically occur in NDEs.

Primarily in chapter 10, but also elsewhere, I presented various types of therapies that appeared to remove spirit intruders or restore a person from behavioral indicators of soul fragmentation, which are generally classified as mental illnesses. However, spirit intruders may also increase the likelihood of physical illnesses (often considered psychosomatic or conversion disorders), probably because they use the body's energy. These therapies are rather diverse, including spiritually oriented psychotherapy, such as that practiced by Fiore and Crabtree; holding religious practices for troubled ancestors (McAll); the rather unusual spiritual method (use of electricity) of Wickland and Komianos; and the shamanic method of soul retrieval. These, in conjunction with the methods of standard psychotherapy employed by therapists of patients who have dissociative identity disorder (DID), indicate that a majority of mental illnesses can be totally cured, rather than temporarily relieved of symptoms, without the use of pharmaceuticals. Medications often have serious side effects and frequently turn a mild disorder into a disabling condition. Psychotropic medications cannot correct the results of trauma and consequent soul fragmentation. In fact, many medications aggravate the fragmentation.

Several therapists have found evil spirits or demons that are not fragmented human souls. These demons are also part of a hierarchy, just as there are realms of helpful spirits. Behavior can also be affected by thought forms/elementals.

Although many types of abnormal behavior can be corrected by psychotherapy, I have certainly not dismissed physical causes of soul fragmentation. Traumatic brain injury is obviously a physical event, as is substance abuse. The latter is interesting in that it can be a cause or an effect. An otherwise moderate consumer of alcohol may choose to imbibe too much, and the subsequent alcoholic stupor can result in his losing the protective cocoon around himself, which allows earthbound spirits to enter the psychonoetic field. Thereafter, he is likely to become an alcoholic with much less choice to stop drinking. Likewise, many illegal drugs, especially ones classified as psychedelic or hallucinogenic, have a similar effect of opening the protective cocoon and allowing spirit intruders to enter. While not capable of causing psychedelic highs, ordinary substances like lead and other heavy metals, or numerous organic chemicals (especially those that affect the nervous system), may result in chemical brain injury and significant behavioral changes. Even if this chemical brain injury results in soul fragmentation, the behavior cannot be changed by psychotherapy or the spirit-removal techniques I discuss unless the chemical brain injury is corrected first, which may not be possible. In addition to foreign chemical substances causing behavioral problems, malnutrition may cause behavioral problems from vitamin or mineral deficiencies in calorically sufficient food.

D. Interactions of Spirit Forms

The etheric body regulates physical body functions and can be compared to the autonomic or involuntary nervous systems. It may only completely depart at death, but it may begin to disintegrate days or hours before death. It does not make decisions but mediates input from the psychonoetic body. Thus, if the psychonoetic body becomes fragmented as a result of trauma, it may send confused signals to the etheric body, which then sends inappropriate neurochemicals to the physical body. Attempting to correct a neurochemical imbalance by outside intervention (e.g., neuroleptics) usually will not correct the imbalance and often makes the situation worse on account of the interference with the process of homeostasis. Trauma and the resulting fragmentation caused the deviation from the original homeostasis point.

The spiritual model I have presented is the best explanation of why some people with fragmented souls, as evidenced by mental illnesses, are often creative. Bipolar disorder and substance-abuse disorder are the two primary mental illnesses that often seem to result in creative ideas. The Spirit form is attempting to correct the fragmented soul situation, and the person concomitantly receives creative ideas from Spirit. In addition, the negative stereotypes of being mentally ill may be an incentive for the affected people to prove themselves. While the etheric body at death disintegrates into undifferentiated etheric "mist" and the astral body disintegrates into undifferentiated astral "mist" (both capable of being recycled), the Spirit form is itself essentially divine (Underhill) and never disintegrates.

E. Concerns and Historical Context

I have already expressed concern about unqualified members of religious groups trying to remove evil spirits from people, especially children, using the old and misunderstood religious model of evil spirits. A second major concern is that numerous people who have achieved a high level of contact with their Spirit may use that ability for power or control over others rather than service to others. Being of service to others is a message conveyed by NDErs and many world religions. Morality does not necessarily follow Spirit, evolving into a deeper penetration into the physical body. Or, the scientist does not see the effects of her findings because they are only viewed from a reductionist perspective.

Although scientists claim that evidence supports their materialistic view that behavior is entirely brain-based, I maintain that history supports the view that I have presented. Shamans have been employing their view of human nature to keep people reasonably healthy for at least 20 millennia. I agree with Raymond Tallis that for centuries philosophical inquiry was a form of knowledge and was able to reach many correct conclusions about human nature without scientific proof. Neurophilosophy and other proponents of neurons determining human behavior need to be discarded. Scientism reaches incorrect conclusions because it ignores evidence, particularly evidence of the paranormal. Scientism also follows the incorrect reductionist assumption that behavior is caused by an imbalance in neurochemicals, rather than the neurochemicals being imbalanced due to trauma. Although I do not see a connection between dark matter and dark energy and the paranormal, it does seem strange that many scientists speculate that the universe is made up of 70–95% dark matter and energy, terms for forces they do not understand. If they can speculate on that, why can they not consider the possibility of spiritual forces interacting with matter (the physical body)? I believe that Judaism, early Christianity, ancient Greek religions, and Eastern religions all hold the view that humans have more than one spiritual form residing in the body and at least one of these forms permanently survives death.

There are two final aspects that I would like to reemphasize. One is that since all humans are connected on a Spirit level, there is no separation between ourselves and other people, even with the animal and plant kingdoms, since these kingdoms have their own form of Spirit, albeit one that is not individualized. The second is that people would not have to be taught self-esteem if each person realized that he or she had his or her own Spirit.

I can only present evidence for the concept of two or more separate spiritual forms in each person and for the idea that each form by itself or in combination affects many aspects of human behavior. My theory is evidence-based, but it may be a different interpretation of the evidence than is commonly presented. Each individual reader needs to make an assessment of the evidence, based on experiences in his or her own life, and should not depend on an opinion of some expert scientist who is actually a believer in scientism and thus not open to all possibilities. I trust all readers to evaluate the evidence and then to decide for themselves.

ABBREVIATIONS AND ACRONYMS

ADC	After Death Communication (plural ADCs)
ADHD	Attention Deficit Hyperactivity Disorder
AEVR	Average Evoked Visual Response
AI	Artificial Intelligence
AMA	American Medical Association
AP	Alternate or Alter Personality (plural APs)
APA	American Psychiatric Association
APD	Antisocial Personality Disorder
ASC	Altered States of Consciousness
ASD	Autism Spectrum Disorder
ASPR	American Society for Psychical Research
BPD	Borderline Personality Disorder
BSD	Binary Soul Doctrine
CES	Cranial Electrotherapy Stimulation
CME	Continuing Medical Education
CPR	Committee on Psychiatry and Religion
CTE	Chronic Traumatic Encephalopathy
CTM	Computational Theories of Mind
DBSA	Depression and Bipolar Support Alliance
DDIS	Dissociative Disorder Interview Schedule
DES	Dissociative Experiences Scale
DFE	Dark Force Entity (plural DFEs)
DID	Dissociative Identity Disorder
DIS-Q	Dissociation Questionnaire
DSM	Diagnostic and Statistical Manual of Mental Disorders (various editions)
DTC	Direct-to-consumer (advertising)
ECT	Electroconvulsive Therapy
EEG	Electroencephalogram
ELE	End-of-Life Experience (plural ELEs)

EMG	Electromyography
ELO	Empathic Life Overview
ER	Encyclopedia of Religion
ESP	Extra Sensory Perception
FDA	Food and Drug Administration
FDE	Fear-Death Experience
FMS	False Memory Syndrome
GABA	Gamma-Aminobutyric Acid
GID	Gender Identity Disorder
HHs	Higher Helpers
HSP	Higher Sense Perception
IANDS	International Association for Near Death Studies
ICD	International Classification of Diseases
IED	Intermittent Explosive Disorder
IIC	Internalized Imaginary Companion
ISH	Inner Self-helper
ISIS	Inner Space Interactive Sourcing
ISSTD	International Society for the Study of Trauma and Dissociation
LT	Lamsa Translation (of the Bible)
LTP	Less than Positive
MADD	Mothers Against Drunk Driving
MPD	Multiple Personality Disorder
MRI	Magnetic Resonance Imaging
NAB	New American Bible (translation of the Bible)
NAMI	National Alliance for the Mentally Ill
NDE	Near-Death Experience (plural NDEs)
NDEr	Near Death Experiencer (plural NDErs)
NIMH	National Institute of Mental Health
NIV	New International Version (translation of the Bible)
NJKV	New King James Version (translation of the Bible)
NOS	Not Otherwise Specified
OBE	Out of Body Experience
OSC	Ordinary State of Consciousness
PBP	Pseudoscience in Biological Psychiatry
PDE	Pre-Death Experience (plural PDEs)
PDNOS	Personality Disorder Not Otherwise Specified
PET	Positron Emission Tomography

PwDID	Person (or People) with Dissociative Identity Disorder
QM	Quantum Mechanics
R&D	Research and Development
REM	Rapid Eye Movement (during sleep)
RERU	Religious Experiences Research Unit
RSV	Revised Standard Version (translation of the Bible)
SIDS	Sudden Infant Death Syndrome
SPR	Society for Psychical Research
SRT	Spirit Replacement Therapy
SSC	Shamanic State of Consciousness
SSDI	Social Security Disability Income
SSI	Supplemental Security Income
SSRI	Selective Serotonin Reuptake Inhibitor
STE	Spiritually Transformative Experience (plural STEs)
TADD	Teens Against Drunk Driving
tDCS	Transcranial Direct-current Stimulation
TDE	Temporary Death Experience
TLE	Temporal Lobe Epilepsy
TMS	Transcranial Magnetic Stimulation
VER	Visually Evoked Response
WCEI	Weighted Core Experience Index

Appendix B

SPECIFIC INCIDENTS OF CHILDREN'S NDES

Case numbers are from Morse (1990). Patient numbers are from Morse (1992), no names.

Case No. 1. Gender and age at time of NDE: Boy, 11
Interviewed: seven years later.
Medical circumstances: no heartbeat for 20 min., had pacemaker inserted.
NDE description/aftereffect: OBE; could see his own body because it was like there was a *light* bulb inside himself. Watched doctors perform resuscitation, accurately described it, and their conversation; one minute he was seeing the backs of doctors and then after the electric shock he was looking up at the doctors. He told them that they sucked him back into his body. Feels like he is more serious about life has a purpose here on earth, not interested in partying and drinking, and not afraid to die.

Case No. 2. Gender and age at time of NDE: Boy (Chris), 10
Interviewed: his mother states what he said immediately after resuscitation. He was given a number of medications, which possibly resulted in him not remembering it later on.
Medical circumstances: kidney transplant but bacterial infection from that surgery entered his heart and later heart valve surgery was required.
NDE description/aftereffect: climbed a staircase to heaven but knew if he went too far he would not return. Met his little brother who had died earlier. Returned because his parents would be alone if he died.

Case No. 3. Gender and age at time of NDE: Boy (Dean), 16
Interviewed: two years later.

Medical circumstances: cardiac arrest during kidney dialysis.

NDE description/aftereffects: wide tunnel with no walls; met a being wearing a white gown; not Christ but sent from Christ, possibly an angel. Returned to body. He also had a NDE at age 10 after nearly drowning; encountered a bright *light* and had life review, which is unusual for children. Not as rebellious as before his NDE.

Case No. 4. Gender and age at time of NDE: Boy (Kurt), 7

Interviewed: hours after resuscitation.

Medical circumstances: muscular dystrophy/pneumonia.

NDE description: the boy died soon after his heart stopped; he watched doctors revive him. Also saw angels and Jesus and knew that when he died he would be in a world without pain.

Case No. 5. Gender and age at time of NDE: Girl (June), 8

Interviewed: several years later.

Medical circumstances: drowning; no heartbeat but administered CPR for 45 minutes; full neurological recovery in six weeks.

NDE description: saw herself underwater and later the resuscitation procedure. In tunnel and then in heaven; asked by a man if she wanted to stay but when she said she wanted to be with her family she returned to her body.

Case No. 6. Gender and age at time of NDE: Girl (Michelle), 8

Interviewed: several weeks after recovery.

Medical circumstances: diabetic coma; highest blood sugar ever encountered at that hospital.

NDE description/aftereffects: at first reluctant to discuss but after drawing pictures she did explain the pictures. Behind her were a bunch of doctors in white, who gave her choice to return if she pushed one button or not return if she pushed the other button. She did have some fear of the doctors in white. Later in life she is more serene and calm, a vegetarian and friend of animals, and does not fear death.

Case No. 7. Gender and age at time of NDE: Boy (Mark), 9 months

Interviewed: unclear: at one point Morse said the boy told his parents about his experience at age 3; elsewhere, it was at age 7 when he told his parents, but Morse also says the boy began to forget the experience beginning at age 5.

Medical circumstances: bronchitis, cardiopulmonary arrest for 45 minutes, but the doctors were working on him during that time; full recovery and normal growth afterward.

NDE description/aftereffect: saw doctors working on him; saw grandparents (alive) crying in the waiting room; crawled through tunnel with unidentified assistance and saw bright *lights*. He told his parents a person can double jump in heaven. He did not want to return to Earth but did so anyway. Morse believes a person can remember an NDE that happens at that age.

Case No. 8. Gender and age at time of NDE: Girl (Cindi), 17

Interviewed: two weeks later.

Medical circumstances: cardiac arrest/chest pains, after use of cocaine; two hours to resuscitate.

NDE description/aftereffect: OBE; also entered a room with a door and knew that if she opened the door she would not return. Deceased grandfather came to her and told her to go back. Her doctor had arrived to speak to her and said she had to fight to survive. She may have interpreted her doctor's voice as that of her grandfather.

Case No. 9. Gender and age at time of NDE: Girl (Linda), 13

Interviewed: not specified but sounded like short time afterward.

Medical circumstances: asthma attack/cardiopulmonary arrest, blue from lack of oxygen when found by her father.

NDE description: OBE, but not distinct as if moving in and out of body; peaceful feeling.

Case No. 10. Gender and age at time of NDE: Boy (Daniel), 6

Interviewed: not specified, but was comatose for two weeks afterward.

Medical circumstances: car/bicycle accident; head trauma.

NDE description/aftereffect: watched being loaded into ambulance; observed tunnel with bright *light*; saw three men with the rainbow bridge behind them that stretched across the sky; then back in body. Daniel was a little afraid of the men.

Patient No. 1. Gender and age at time of NDE: Girl, 9
Medical circumstances: high fever, had to be packed in ice which is when NDE began.
NDE description: tunnel with someone in tunnel to help her; then *light*, field with flowers, gorgeous horses and a *light* presence beside her. Horses were over a fence, and as she was climbing a fence a voice asked what she was doing there. When told she had to go back she threw a tantrum. Went back through tunnel.

Patient No. 2. Age at time of NDE: between sixth and seventh grades,~12
Medical circumstances: waterskiing accident, arm severely injured when caught in rope and also dragged underwater. Almost died from loss of blood, shock.
NDE description: OBE, life review, warm *light* and peace, not concerned about her physical body being dragged behind boat.

Patient No. 3. Age at time of NDE: 9
Medical circumstances: big wave on beach carried person to deep water, nearly drowned.
NDE description: tunnel, beautiful garden, life review, a *light* figure NDEr thought of as God.

Patient No. 4. Age at time of NDE: 4
Medical circumstances: fell down stairs onto cement floor in cellar.
NDE description: OBE, dark cellar turned very bright and then saw a bright *light* behind him/her.

Patient No. 5. Gender and age at time of NDE: Girl, fifth or sixth grade, ~11
Medical circumstances: leg infection; later went to hospital but NDE occurred before going to hospital.
NDE description: looked down through peephole (later thought of this as a tunnel), saw greenery and stone wall, then a beautiful

woman and long dress who picked her up, laughed with her, and hugged her.

Patient No. 6. Gender and age at time of NDE: Girl, 16
Medical circumstances: during surgery.
NDE description: Being that radiated unmeasurable love; glad to be
    dead but then told she had an unfinished mission in life. Became
    a nurse but is not sure she is doing what she is supposed to do.

LINDBERGH'S GHOSTLY PRESENCES IN HIS OWN WORDS

Full Quotation from *The Spirit of St. Louis* by Charles Lindbergh (1953), Pages 389-391

While I'm staring at the instruments, during an unearthly age of time, both conscious and asleep, the fuselage becomes filled with ghostly presences—vaguely outlined forms, transparent, moving, riding weightless with me in the plane. I feel no surprise at their coming. There's no suddenness to their appearance. Without turning my head, I see them as clearly as though in my normal field of vision. There's no limit to my sight—my skull is one great eye, seeing everywhere at once.

These phantoms speak with human voices—friendly, vaporlike shapes, without substance, able to vanish or appear at will, to pass in and out through the walls of the fuselage as though no walls were there. Now, many are crowded behind me. Now, only a few remain. First one and then another presses forward to my shoulder to speak above the engine's noise, and then draws back among the group behind. At times, voices come out of the air itself, clear yet far away, traveling through distances that can't be measured by the scale of human miles; familiar voices, conversing and advising on my flight, discussing problems of my navigation, reassuring me, giving me messages of importance unattainable in ordinary life.

Apprehension spreads over time and space until their old meanings disappear. I'm not conscious of time's direction. Figures of miles from New York and miles to Paris lose their interest. All sense of substance leaves. There's no longer weight to my body, no longer hardness to the stick. The feeling of flesh is gone. I become independent of physical laws—of food, of shelter, of life. I'm almost one with these vaporlike forms behind me, less tangible than air, universal as aether. I'm still attached to life; they, not at all; but at any moment some thin band may snap and there'll no difference between us.

The spirits have no rigid bodies, yet they remain human in outline form—emanations from the experiences of ages, inhabitants of a universe closed to mortal men. I'm on the border line of life and a greater realm beyond, as though caught in the field of gravitation between two planets, acted on by forces I can't control, forces too weak to be measured by any means at my command, yet representing powers incomparably stronger that I've ever known.

I realize that values are changing both within and without my mind. For twenty-five years, it's been surrounded by solid walls of bone, not perceiving the limitless expanse, the immortal existence that lies outside. Is this death? Am I crossing the bridge which one sees only in last, departing moments? Am I already beyond the point from which I can bring my vision back to earth and men? Death no longer seems the final end it used to be, but rather the entrance to a new and free existence which includes all space, all time.

Am I now more man or spirit? Will I fly my airplane on to Europe and live in flesh as I have before, feeling hunger, pain, and cold, or am I about to join these ghostly forms, become a consciousness in space, all-seeing, all-knowing, unhampered by materialistic fetters of the world?

At another time I'd be startled by these visions; but on this fantastic flight, I'm so far separated from the earthly life I know that I accept whatever circumstances may come. In fact, these emissaries from a spirit world are quite in keeping with the night and day. They're neither intruders nor strangers. It's more like a gathering of family and friends after years of separation, as I've known all of them before in some incarnation. They're as different from men, and yet as similar, as the night's cloud mountains were to the Rockies of the West. They belong with the towering thunderheads and moonlit corridors of sky. Did they board my plane, unseen, as I flew between the temple's pillars? Have they ridden with me through sunrise, into day? What strange connection exists between us? If they're so concerned with my welfare, why didn't they introduce themselves before?

I live in the past, the present, and the future, here and in different places, all at once. Around me are old associations, bygone friendships, voices from ancestrally distant times. Vistas open up before me as changing as those between the clouds I pass. I'm flying in a plane over the Atlantic Ocean; but I'm also living in years now far away.

Lindbergh, Charles A. (1953), *The Spirit of St. Louis*, Charles Scribner's Sons, New York

Appendix D

NATIVE AMERICAN
SPIRITUAL VIOLATIONS

Listed by Native American Healer Medicine Grizzlybear Lake (1991) in *Native Healer: Initiation into an Ancient Art*, p. 197-199. Minor grammar and punctuation corrections made.

1. Human beings are not supposed to have sex in Nature; upon the mountains, in the woods, on the desert, in meadows, on or near the ocean, nor in creeks, lakes, and rivers. *Reason:* Such places are the residents of good and bad spirits; they do not like to be contaminated by "human's" smell and activity.

2. It is against the law to molest, kill, or experiment upon animals, birds, snakes, bugs, trees, plants, fish, and human beings needlessly. *Reason:* Such entities are the Great Creator's property. They have been placed on Earth for a purpose and function. Humankind does not have the right or authority to destroy or molest the Creator's property without just cause and restitution.

3. It is against the Creator's Law for menstruating women to walk, hike, swim, or bathe in Nature, or have sex while on their menses. *Reason:* Nature is purifying the women mentally, physically, and spiritually. As a consequence, toxins and negative energy are being discharged, and they can contaminate others and Nature. By the same token, the women are being replenished with positive spiritual power. A woman should therefore isolate herself, purify herself, center herself with a cosmic forces, rejuvenate herself, and not just burst her power socially, physically, mentally, or spiritually.

4. It is against the Creator's Law for humans to have unusual sex acts. *Reason:* Humans were originally "souls" at one time. They broke their Creator's Law when they left the spirit world and took over the bodies of animals in order to experience sex. Humans are expected to be humanlike and develop their soul toward spiritual purity. Thus, animal type sex acts are considered impure and unnatural for humans. Violations of this Law can cause mental, physical, and spiritual sickness.

5. It is against the Creator's Law to murder, rape, torture, or commit suicide. *Reason:* Human beings are the property of the great Creator and therefore sacred. Humankind does not have the right or authority to abuse the Great Creator's property.

6. Human beings are not supposed to participate in prayer, sacred ceremonies, rituals, or healing while under the influence of alcohol, sex, or menses. *Reason:* Spiritual power is pure and must therefore be treated with respect, purity, and clarity.

7. It is against the Creator's Law to use witchcraft or to make bad prayers, bad thoughts, bad wishes, or use evil power against others. *Reason:* The great Creator made everything in the universe, including human beings and powers. He established the law and order amongst the created. The first Law of the Land was respect for all living things, including the Earth, Universe, and humankind. The use of evilness abridges the Law of Respect and causes harm to others.

8. Human beings must always be "clean" whenever they hunt, fish, or gather herbs. This means a clean body, no sex, no alcohol, nor women on their menses. *Reason:* Natural foods and plants have power. Human beings should always "pray" to the entity before taking its life and explain why it is being used. Humans must be cleaned mentally, physically, and spiritually whenever praying and using this power. In this way, the spiritual powers of the entity will be transferred to the human being with the physical properties. Nature's powers strengthen our souls and enrich our

health. Negative powers contaminate our soul and weaken our health. Abuse of "powers" causes sickness to the violator.

9. Human beings should not waste their life on drugs, alcohol, selfishness, or idleness. *Reason:* Every human being was placed on this earth for a purpose and reason. The Creator wants all human beings to discover their purpose in life and carry out their function. Humans are sacred and should therefore not waste their life. To do so will cause sickness, natural life will shorten, and death may occur.

Lake, Medicine Grizzlybear, 1991, *Native Healer: Initiation into an Ancient Art.* Theosophical Publishing House, Wheaton

Appendix E

A DISCUSSION OF APPLICABLE BIBLE QUOTES

In Chapter 10, I presented one *Bible* quotes relating to evil spirits, unclean spirits, or demons to uncontrollable personalities in a person with DID. In this appendix I relate other healings in the Bible that relate to these spirits, regardless of actual appellation. The purpose of this appendix is to demonstrate that evil spirits, unclean spirits, and devils and demons may be interchangeable words and that removal of them often results in physical healings, as well as mental health healings. I will present this information in titled sections, followed by a short explanation. Of 28 Gospel passages quoted, five were told by three evangelists, four were told by two evangelists, and five were reported by one only. It is interesting that the Gospel of St. John never mentions healing of people with evil spirits. The only use in John of similar terms is that after Judas accepted a piece of bread from Jesus at the Last Supper, John reports that Satan entered or took possession of him (13:27). Luke confirms Satan's entry but states that the entry occurred when Judas went to the chief priests about the betrayal and not at the Last Supper (22:3). After the betrayal, Judas committed suicide. In Chapter 12, I provided an explanation of the reason John rarely speaks of possession. Other than the Gospels, there are only three other passages that mention possession by spirits: one in the standard Old Testament, one in the Apocrypha, and one in Acts of the Apostles.

The actual quotes are taken from the New International Version (NIV) of the *Bible*. Terms like "evil spirits" or "demons," that are employed in several other translations, such as the New King James Version (NKJV) (which is identical to the Revised Standard Version [RSV]), the Lamsa translation (which comes from Ancient Eastern Manuscripts), and the New American *Bible* (NAB) are also listed. The New English Bible almost exclusively uses "possessed by devils." I used my own judgment to determine when the passages were describing the same situation.

I have organized the terms to describe evil spirits into the tables below, with the terminology below each translation. The abbreviations employed are: "ES" refers to Evil Spirits, "US" refers Unclean Spirits, and "DP" refers to demon-possessed or possessed by demon(s). The demons are the spirits themselves, while "demon-possessed" refers to the person the demons enter. Poss. is short for possessed, Pr. short for Prince.

1. Healing of many, including demon possessed:

	NIV	NKJV/RSV	Lamsa	NAB
Matthew 8:16	DP	DP	Lunatics	DP
Mark 1:32-34	DP	DP	Insane	DP
Luke 4:40-41	Demons	Demons	Demons	Demons

Matthew: When evening came, many who were demon-possessed were brought to him, and he drove out the spirits with a word and healed all the sick.

Mark: That evening after sunset the people brought to Jesus all the sick and demon-possessed. The whole town gathered at the door, and Jesus healed many who had various diseases. He also drove out many demons, but he would not let the demons speak because they knew who he was.

Luke: When the sun was setting, the people brought to Jesus all who had various kinds of sickness, and laying his hand on each one, he healed them. Moreover, demons came out of many people, shouting, "You are the Son of God!" But he rebuked them and would not allow them to speak, because they knew he was the Christ.

In these healings, the unusual aspect is that the demons identified Jesus as the Christ, but He did not desire that, so He forbade them to speak. This is, to some extent, the opposite of the Barlow et al. article in that the demons were identifying the expeller rather than the expeller identifying the demons. Basham and Martin reported that the demons identified themselves.

2. Mute man speaks after the demons depart, house divided lesson:

Matthew 12:22-28
_____ NIV _____
DP/Beelzebub(Pr. Demons)/Satan
_____ NKJV/RSV & NAB _____
Demoniac/Demons/Beelzebub/Pr. Demons/Satan
_____ Lamsa _____
Lunatic/Beelzebub(Pr. Dem.)/Satan

Mark 3:20-30
_____ NIV & NKJV/RSV & NAB _____
(Jesus) Possessed by Beelzebub(Prince of Demons/Satan)
_____ Lamsa _____
Beelzebub is with him (Jesus)(Prince of Demons)/Satan

Luke 11:14-20
_____ NIV & NKJV/RSV & NAB _____
Demon/Beelzebub(Prince of Demons)/Satan
_____ Lamsa _____
Demon/Beelzebub(Prince of Devils)/Satan

Matthew: Then they brought him a demon-possessed man who was blind and mute, and Jesus healed him, so that he could both talk and see. All the people were astonished and said, "Could this be the Son of David?" But when the Pharisees heard this, they said, "It is only by Beelzebub, the prince of demons, that this fellow drives out demons." Jesus knew their thoughts and said to them, "Every kingdom divided against itself will be ruined, and every city or household divided against itself will not stand. If Satan drives out Satan, he is divided against himself. How can his kingdom stand? And if I drive out demons by Beelzebub, by whom do your people drive them out? So then, they will be your judges. But if I drive out demons by the Spirit of God, then the kingdom of God has come upon you."

Mark: Then Jesus entered a house, and again a crowd gathered, so that he and his disciples were not even able to eat. When his family heard about this, they went to take charge of him, for they said, "He is out of his mind." And the teachers of the law who came down from Jerusalem, said, "He is possessed by Beelzebub! By the prince of demons he is driving out demons." So Jesus called them and spoke to them in parables: "How can Satan drive out Satan? If a kingdom is divided against itself, that kingdom cannot stand. If a house is divided against itself, that house cannot stand. And if Satan opposes himself and is divided, he cannot stand; his end has come. In fact, no one can enter a strong man's house and carry off his possessions unless he first ties up the strong man. Then he can rob his house. I tell your the truth, all the sins and blasphemies of men will be forgiven them. But whoever blasphemes against the Holy Spirit will never be forgiven; he is guilty of an eternal sin." He said this because they were saying, "He has an evil spirit."

Luke: Jesus was driving out a demon that was mute. When the demon left, the man who had been mute spoke, and the crowd was amazed. But some of them said, "By Beelzebub, the prince of demons, he is driving out demons." Others tested him by asking for a sign from heaven. Jesus knew their thoughts and said to them: "Any kingdom divided against itself will be ruined, and a house divided against itself will fall. If Satan is divided against himself, how can his kingdom stand? I say this because you claim that I drive out demons by Beelzebub. Now if I drive out demons by Beelzebub, by whom do your followers drive them out? So then, they will be your judges. But if I drive out demons by the finger of God, then the kingdom of God has come to you.

There are many interesting points in this healing. One is the association of physical problems with possession. This is still true. Conversion disorders, which are frequent in people with DID, may include physical effects, such as temporary blindness. Why the evangelists used demons, devils, Satan, and Beelzebub almost interchangeably is not known. Mark does not even mention the healing. It is difficult to explain who the prince of "earthbound spirits" is if demons are earthbound spirits. The name Beelzebub means "lord of the flies" and is taken from Baal, a god of the enemies of the Jewish people. Mark's narration is unique in all translations in that the teachers of the law say that Jesus is actually possessed by Beelzebub, not just using the power of Beelzebub.

3. Daughter with evil spirit is cured at a distance at mother's request:

	NIV	NKJV/RSV	Lamsa	NAB
Matthew 15:21-28	DP	Poss. by Demon	Insanity	Tormented/Demon
Mark 7:24-30	ES/Demon	Poss. by US	US/demon	US/Demon

Matthew: Leaving that place, Jesus withdrew to the region of Tyre and Sidon. A Canaanite woman from that vicinity came to him, crying out,

"Lord, Son of David, have mercy on me! My daughter is suffering terribly from demon-possession." Jesus did not answer a word. So his disciples came to him and urged him, "Send her away, for she keeps crying out after us." He answered, "I was sent only to the lost sheep of Israel." The woman came and knelt before him. "Lord, help me! she said. He replied, "It is not right to take the children's bread and toss it to their dogs." "Yes, Lord," she said, "but even the dogs eat the crumbs that fall from their masters' table." Then Jesus answered, "Woman, you have great faith! Your request is granted." And her daughter was healed from that very hour.

Mark: Jesus left that place and went to the vicinity of Tyre. He entered a house and did not want anyone to know it; yet he could not keep his presence secret. In fact, as soon as she heard about him, a woman whose little daughter was possessed by an evil spirit came and fell at his feet. The woman was a Greek, born in Syrian Phoenicia. She begged Jesus to drive the demon out of her daughter. "First let the children eat all they want," he told her, "for it is not right to take the children's bread and toss it to their dogs." "Yes, Lord," she replied, "but even the dogs under the table eat the children's crumbs." Then he told her, "For such a reply, you may go; the demon has left your daughter." She went home and found her child lying on the bed, and the demon gone.

Mark uses evil spirits and demons interchangeably. These passages emphasize the importance of faith in healing. The evangelists differ on the woman's nationality.

4. Jesus heals a son at father's request after Jesus's disciples are unable to heal the son:

	NIV	NKJV/RSV	Lamsa	NAB
Matthew 17:14-21	Demon	Epileptic/Demon	Epileptic/Demon	Lunatic/Demon
Mark 9:14-29	Spirit Poss.	Dumb Spirit/US	US/Epileptic	Poss. Spirit/US
Luke 9:37-42	Spirit/ES/Demon	Spirit/US	Spirit/Demon/US	Spirit/Demon/US

Matthew: When they came to the crowd, a man approached Jesus and knelt before him. "Lord, have mercy on my son," he said. "He has seizures and is suffering greatly. He often falls into the fire or into the water. I brought him to your disciples, but they could not heal him." "O unbelieving and perverse generation," Jesus replied, "how long shall I stay with you? How long shall I put up with you? Bring the boy here to me." Jesus rebuked the demon, and it came out of the boy, and he was healed from that moment. Then the disciples came to Jesus in private and asked, "Why couldn't we drive it out?" He replied, "Because you have so little faith. I tell you the truth, if you have faith as small as a mustard seed, you can say to this mountain, 'Move from here to there' and it will move. Nothing will be impossible for you."

Mark: When they came to the other disciples, they saw a large crowd around them and the teachers of the law arguing with them. As soon as all the people saw Jesus, they were overwhelmed with wonder and ran to greet him. "What are you arguing with them about?" he asked. A man in the crowd answered, "Teacher, I brought you my son, who is possessed by a spirit that has robbed him of speech. Whenever it seizes him, it throws him to the ground. He foams at the mouth, gnashes his teeth and becomes rigid. I asked you disciples to drive out the spirit, but they could not." "O unbelieving generation," Jesus replied, "how long shall I stay with you? How long shall I put up with you? Bring the boy to me." So they brought him. When the spirit saw Jesus, it immediately threw the boy into a convulsion. He fell to the ground and rolled around, foaming at the mouth. Jesus asked the boy's father, "How long has he been like this?" "From childhood," he answered. "It has often thrown him into fire or water to kill him. But if you can do anything, take pity on us and help us. If you can'?" said Jesus. "Everything is possible for him who believes." Immediately the boy's father exclaimed, "I do believe; help me overcome my unbelief!" When Jesus saw that the crowd was running to the scene, he rebuked the evil spirit. "You deaf and mute spirit," he said, " I command you, come out of him and never enter him again." The spirit shrieked, convulsed him violently and came out. The boy looked so much like a corpse that many said, "He's dead." But Jesus took him by the hand and lifted him to his feet, and he stood up. After Jesus had gone indoors, his disciples asked him privately, "Why couldn't we drive it out?" He replied, this kind can come out only by prayer."

Luke: The next day, when they came down from the mountain, a large crowd met him. A man in the crowd called out, "Teacher, I beg you to look at my son, for he is my only child. A spirit seizes him and he suddenly screams; it throws him into convulsions so that he foams at the mouth. It scarcely ever leaves him and is destroying him. I begged your disciples to drive it out, but they could not." "O unbelieving and perverse generation," Jesus replied, "how long shall I stay with you and put up with you? Bring your son here." Even while the boy was coming the demon threw him to the ground in a convulsion. But Jesus rebuked the evil spirit, healed the boy and gave him back to his father.

These passages demonstrate a relationship of seizures/convulsions to spirits/demons and also a connection to a physical problem. They also show the importance of faith in healing. The symptoms during removal more closely resemble those of Basham than of most other therapists discussed because the spirit shrieked when departing.

5. Jesus gives authority to drive out evil spirits/demons to disciples:

	NIV	NKJV/RSV	Lamsa	NAB
Matthew 10:1	ES	US	US	US
Mark 6:7	ES	US	US	US
Luke 9:1-2	Demons	Demons	Demons	Demons

Matthew: He called his twelve disciples to him and gave authority to drive out evil spirits and to heal every disease and sickness.
Mark: Calling the Twelve to him, he sent them out two by two and gave them authority over evil spirits.
Luke: When Jesus had called the Twelve together, he gave them power and authority to drive out all demons and to cure diseases, and he sent them out to preach the kingdom of God and to heal the sick.

These passages indicate that a spiritual power can be given to drive out evil spirits and cure illness, a power few churches employ today. Jesus was not the only one with that power. Not everyone has the power to drive out evil spirits by command, but non-Christians can achieve something similar by using other methods, including conversations with the spirit and persuading it to depart.

6. Evil spirit speaks and identifies Jesus, who speaks with authority:

	NIV	NKJV/RSV & NAB	Lamsa
Mark 1:23-27	ES	US	US
Luke 4:33-37	ES/Demon	Spirit of Unclean Demon	US/Demon

Mark: Just then a man in their synagogue who was possessed by an evil spirit cried out, "What do you want with us, Jesus of Nazareth? Have you come to destroy us? I know who you are -- the Holy one of God!" "Be quiet!" said Jesus sternly. "Come out of him!" The evil spirit shook the man violently and came out with a shriek. The people were all so amazed they asked each other, "What is this? A new teaching -- and with authority! He even gives orders to evil spirits and they obey him."

Luke: In the synagogue there was a man possessed by a demon, an evil spirit. He cried out at the top of his voice, "Ha! What do you want with us, Jesus of Naxzareth? Have you come to destroy us? I know who you are -- the Holy one of God!" "Be quiet!" Jesus said sternly. "Come out of him!" Then the demon threw the man down before them all and came out without injuring him. All the people were amazed and said to each other, "What is this teaching? With authority and power he gives orders to evil spirits and they come out!" And the news about him spread throughout the surrounding area.

"Evil spirit" and "demon" are used interchangeably by Luke. A healer must use power and authority to force departure, as these passages illustrate. Jesus did not attempt to lead any demons to find the Light within themselves, as several therapists claimed they could do.

7. Man not following along with disciples could also drive out demons in Jesus's name:

	All Translations
Mark 9:38-40	Demons
Luke 9:49-50	Demons

Mark: "Teacher," said John, "we saw a man driving out demons in your name and we told him to stop, because he was not one of us." "Do not stop him," Jesus said. "No one does a miracle in my name can in the next moment say anything bad about me, for whoever is not against us is for us. I tell you the truth, anyone who gives you a cup of water in my name because you belong to Christ will certainly not lose his reward.

Luke: "Master," said John, "we saw a man driving out demons in your name and we tried to stop him, because he is not one of us." "Do not stop him," Jesus said, "for whoever is not against you is for you."

These passages show that followers of Christ can be a diverse group.

A person can use the power of Jesus' name without being a follower of Jesus, but non-Christians are less likely to believe the name of Jesus has any influence.

8. Where evil spirits go:

	NIV	NKJV/RSV	Lamsa	NAB
Matthew 12:43-45	ES	US	US	US
Luke 11:24-26	ES	US	US	US

Matthew: (Jesus speaking) "When an evil spirit comes out of a man, it goes through arid places seeking rest and does not find it. Then it says, 'I will return to the house I left.' When it arrives, it finds the house unoccupied, swept clean and put in order. Then it goes and takes with it seven other spirits more wicked than itself, and they go in and live there. And the final condition of that man is worse than the first. That is how it will be with this wicked generation."
Luke: Identical to Matthew except that last sentence does not appear.

These are very interesting verses. Matthew definitely implies that evil spirits can return to the person they left. This is most likely if the person does not give up the practices with which the spirits were associated. Upon its return, the evil spirit may bring others with it. This could support the contention that a person who has one obsessing spirit may easily pick up others. In the section on Christian deliverance, I explained that Basham interpreted the passage as meaning that a person's life has to be filled with positive Christian attitudes after removal of a spirit to prevent the spirit's return. Atteshlis posits that this passage concerns elementals.

9. Healing of mute man:

	NIV & NAB	NKJV/RSV
Matthew 9: 32-34	Demons/Prince of Demons	Demoniac/demon

	Lamsa	
	Devils/Pr. Devils	

Matthew: While they were going out, a man who was demon-possessed and could not talk was brought to Jesus. And when the demon was driven out, the man who had been mute spoke. And the crowd was amazed and said, "Nothing like this has ever been seen in Israel." But the Pharisees said, "It is by the prince of demons that he drives out demons."

This passage is very similar to that in Matthew 12:22 - 28, which is discussed in 3 above.

10. Same power used in physical healings seems to drive out evil spirits:

	NIV	NKJV/RSV	Lamsa & NAB
Luke 6:17-19	ES	US	US

Luke: He went down with them and stood on a level place. A large crowd of his disciples was there and a great number of people from all over Judea, from Jerusalem, and from the coast of Tyre and Sidon, who had come to hear him and to be healed of their diseases. Those troubled by evil spirits were cured and the people all tried to touch him, because power was coming from him and healing them all.
Luke states that some kind of power is used in healing people with physical problems and those troubled by evil spirits.

11. Mary Magdalene had seven demons come out of her:

        All Translations
Luke 8:2   Evil Spirits/Demons

Luke: After this, Jesus traveled about from one town and village to another, proclaiming the good news of the kingdom of God. The Twelve were with him, and also some women who had been cured of evil spirits and diseases: Mary (called Magdalene) from whom seven demons had come out.

Perhaps Mary's well-known actions of love and humility later was a result of the freedom she felt after having the demons removed from her by Jesus.

12. Ability to cast out demons can be taught if Jesus' name is used:

        All Translations
Luke 10:17   Demons

Luke: The seventy-two returned with joy and said, "Lord, even the demons submit to us in your name."

Submitting by the demons would be the response to the use of power and authority of Jesus' name. NDEr Howard Storm was able to drive away beings who were tormenting him during his distressing NDE by invoking the name of Jesus.

13. A seemingly pure physical ailment can be caused by a spirit:

	NIV & NAB	NKJV/RSV	Lamsa
Luke 13:10-13, 16	Spirit/Satan	Spirit of Infirmity/Satan	Adversary

Luke: On a Sabbath Jesus was teaching in one of the synagogues, and a woman was there who had been crippled by a spirit for eighteen years. She was bent over and could not straighten up at all. When Jesus saw her, he called her forward and said to her, "Woman, you are set free from your infirmity." Then he put his hand on her, and immediately she straightened up and praised God. ... Then should not this woman, a daughter of Abraham, whom Satan has kept bound for eighteen long years, be set free on the Sabbath day from what bound her?"

Luke specifies spirit only, and not evil spirit, but definitely says the spirit caused a person to be a cripple. In this instance, there were no unusual noises or indications of the departure. This passage does not necessarily imply that everyone who is crippled has a spirit.

14. Fortune-telling ability can develop as a result of a spirit:

	NIV	NKJV/RSV	Lamsa	NAB
Acts 16:16-19	Had a spirit	Spirit of divination	Possessed of a spirit	With an oracular spirit

Acts: Once when we were going to the place of prayer, we were met by a slave girl who had a spirit by which she predicted the future. She earned a great deal of money for her owners by fortune-telling. The girl followed Paul and the rest of us, shouting, "These men are servants of the Most High God, who are telling you the way to be saved." She kept this up for many days. Finally Paul became so troubled that he turned around and said to the spirit, "In the name of Jesus Christ I command you to come out of her!" At that moment the spirit left her. When the owners of the slave girl realized that their hope of making money was gone, they seized Paul and Silas and dragged them into the marketplace to face the authorities.

Although McAll, Fiore, and Basham show that spirit intrusion can result from involvement in occult activities, this passage demonstrates that an intruding spirit is responsible for the psychic ability. The passage does not explain the circumstances under which the spirit entered her.

15. Certain music can keep intruding spirit from gaining control:
<u>All Translations</u>
1 Samuel 16:14-23   Evil Spirit

Samuel: Now the Spirit of the Lord had departed from Saul, and an evil spirit from the Lord tormented him. Saul's attendants said to him, "See, an evil spirit from God is tormenting you. Let our lord command his servants here to search for someone who can play the harp. He will play when the evil spirit from God comes upon you, and you will feel better." So Saul said to his attendants, "Find someone who plays well and bring him to me."

One of the servants answered, "I have seen a son of Jesse of Bethlehem who knows how to play the harp. He is a brave man and a warrior. He speaks well and is a fine-looking man. And the Lord is with him. Then Saul sent messengers to Jesse and said, "Send me your son David, who is with the sheep." So Jesse took a donkey loaded with bread, a skin of wine and a young goat and sent them with his son David to Saul.

David came to Saul and entered his service. Saul liked him very much, and David became one of his armor-bearers. Then Saul sent word to Jesse, saying, "Allow David to remain in my service, for I am pleased with him." Whenever the spirit from God came upon Saul, David would take his harp and play. Then relief would come to Saul; he would feel better, and the evil spirit would leave him.

This is a very intriguing passage. For one, it says that God sent the spirit to Saul. The music did not remove the spirit permanently but more or less kept it at bay. Many of the cases of spirit intrusion discussed in this book have periods when the spirits would assume control or influence, but much of the time the spirits are silent. Some people may think that music therapy is a relatively new use of music, but this passage demonstrates that it was employed about 3,000 years ago.

I conclude that the various terms employed in the Bible such as evil spirits, demon possessed, unclean spirits, Satan, and other variations of those words were generally indications of what in modern society are mental illnesses, many of which may be healed without use of psychiatric medications. I do not know if music therapists have delved into curing mental illnesses, but perhaps more research in that area is justified. Music therapy has been used for many other situations, such as assisting the mentally disabled and persons with neurological problems, including Parkinson's disease.

SELECT PREVIOUSLY PUBLISHED ARTICLES AND LETTERS OF THE AUTHOR

Probable Childhood NDE in a Now Famous Scientist

While reading a book review of some famous women in science, I came across one woman I had not previously encountered. The book review stated that she had nearly died as a child so I looked into her life on Wikipedia. Her name is Mary Anning (1799 - 1847), and her fields of endeavor were geology, paleontology and fossil collecting. Her discoveries included many famous or first time skeletons of fish. Her father was a cabinet maker who died when she was 11. The family was very poor, and eight of her ten siblings died at an early age.

Wikipedia outlines the incident in which she nearly died, and the description leads me to believe she may have had an NDE, although it can never be proved.

> On 19 August 1800, when Anning was 15 months old, an event occurred that became part of local lore. She was being held by a neighbor, Elizabeth Haskings, who was standing with two other women under an elm tree watching an equestrian show being put on by a traveling company of horsemen when lightning struck the tree killing all three women below. Onlookers rushed the infant home where she was revived in a bath of hot water. A local doctor declared her survival miraculous. Her family said she had been a sickly baby before the event but afterwards she seemed to blossom. For years afterward members of her community would attribute the child's curiosity, intelligence and lively personality to the incident.

Two well-known living NDErs, Dannion Brinkley and Dr. Tony Cicoria, had their experiences as a result of lightning, but they were adults when it happened.

Anning lived her entire life in Lyme Regis in Dorset County in England where there are marine fossil beds on the cliffs along the English Channel. There would be landslides during the winter, and she would collect fossils before they were washed out to the sea and nearly died in 1833 during a landslide. She earned income by selling many of the fossils. Anning had very little education and was snubbed because her religion was Congregationalist and not Anglican (which she became later), and women were not accepted into the Geological Society of London. She was considered very religious. When she wrote articles, they had to be published by men, who rarely gave her any credit. It would not surprise me if Charles Darwin read some of those articles. However, in 2010, the Royal Society included Anning in a list of the 10 British women who have most influenced the history of science.

Mary died of breast cancer. Writers on NDEs in children often emphasize their creativity. I believe it is also necessary to realize that NDErs are often able to rise above the circumstances of their lives.

Published in *Vital Signs,* the Newsletter of the International Association for Near-Death Studies, Summer 2015

A NDE Described in a Short Story Whose Author Was Shot in War

Ernest Hemingway was seriously injured during World War I and included a fictional near-death experience (NDE) in his 1929 novel *A Farewell to Arms.* I came across a fictional NDE written by a less prominent author named Ambrose Bierce (1842 - 1914). He was a Lieutenant in the Union Army and a topographical engineer (map maker) rather than a leader of troops. He was shot with a glancing blow to the temple area of his head in 1864 in Georgia as part of Sherman's March to the Sea and probably had a NDE in order to write his unusual stories. He was able to return to the war three to four months later. After the war, he moved to San Francisco and wrote short stories that were published in magazines from 1872 to 1886. Later, he became a journalist and wrote and edited for William Randolph Hearst who gave

Bierce more national attention. He is often classified as a satirist and considered a nonconformist. His most famous complete book is titled *The Devil's Dictionary* and it was compiled from selected newspaper writings of his. He mysteriously disappeared on a trip to revolutionary Mexico in 1913/1914. Although not well-known today, Bierce was either admired or reviled by many other writers during his life.

The short story that I believe is a description of a NDE titled "An Occurrence at Owl Creek Bridge," which is in Alabama. It includes both an out of body experience (OBE) and transcendental aspects as narrated during wartime. In this tale, a southern slave owner and planter named Peyton Farquhar is in the process of being hanged by the Union for hindering their military efforts. As Peyton is falling with a rope around his neck he begins to feel the pressure of the rope on his neck. He then believes he falls into Owl Creek after the rope is broken. The following are some of the descriptions in the story that appear to be similar to a NDE.

- As he came to the surface of the water he was "blinded by the sunlight" (p. 309).
- His physical senses became "preternaturally keen and alert" (p. 309). For example, "He looked at the forest on the bank of the stream, saw the individual trees, the leaves and the veining of each leaf — saw the very insects upon them: the locusts, the brilliant-bodied flies, the gray spiders stretching their webs from twig to twig. He noted the prismatic colors in all the dewdrops upon a million blades of grass. The humming of the gnats that danced above the eddies of the stream, the beating of the dragon-flies' wings, the strokes of the water-spiders' legs, like oars which had lifted their boat — all these made audible music. A fish slid along beneath his eyes and he heard the rush of its body parting the water" (p. 310).
- He sees the soldiers on the bridge begin shooting at him but they either missed or the shots entered through the water and did not harm him.
- "Objects were represented by their colors only; circular horizontal streaks of color — that was all he saw. He had been caught in a vortex and was being whirled on with a velocity of advance

- and gyration that made him giddy and sick. In a few moments he was flung upon the gravel at the foot of the left bank of the stream"... (p. 311).
- As he reached shore, "He dug his fingers into the sand and threw it over himself in handfuls and audibly blessed it. It looked like diamonds, rubies, emeralds; he could think of nothing beautiful which it did not resemble. The trees upon the bank were giant garden plants; he noted a definite order in their arrangement, inhaled the fragrance of their blooms. A strange, roseate light shone through the spaces among their trunks and the wind made in their branches the music of aeolian harps. He had no wish to perfect his escape — was content to remain in that enchanting spot until retaken" (p. 312).
- He felt he traveled at night to arrive at his home. He sees his wife and extends his arms to clasp her. At that time he "feels a stunning blow to the back of his neck; a blinding white light blazes all about him with a sound like the shock of the cannon — then all is darkness and silence" (p. 313)!

Farquhar was then dead with a broken neck and dangling from the bridge. His escape was entirely his imagination that occurred in the instant from the time he first felt the presence of the rope on his neck until the time his neck broke. He did not really have an OBE. I believe Bierce may have had an OBE and experienced the *light* either at the time of being shot or on his way to medical treatment many miles away on an open flatbed railcar in order to portray so accurately many of the findings of modern NDE research. However, many NDErs do not believe it all ends in darkness and silence. While an encounter with light has long been associated with religious or mystical experiences, time speeded-up, hearing ethereal music, desiring to remain on the other side, preternaturally keen senses and a vortex, comparable to a tunnel, are relatively new findings for occurrences near death.

The compiler of the stories classified the narratives into horror stories, those during war, and tall tales. A number of the horror stories involve haunted houses, ghosts and after death communication, all indicators of a post-mortem existence.

Bierce, A. (1970). An Occurrence At Owl Creek Bridge (pp. 305 - 313). In: *The Complete Short Stories of Ambrose Bierce* (compiled by E. J. Hopkins). Garden City: Doubleday & Company, Inc.

Hemingway, E. (1929/1995). *A Farewell to Arms*. New York, NY: Scribner Paperback/Simon & Schuster

Published in *Vital Signs*, the Newsletter of the International Assoc. for Near-Death Studies, Fall/Winter 2015, Nos. 3/4. Published title is: Who's NDE Is the War Shot Author Really Writing About?

End-of-Life Experience of Famous Artist J. M. W. Turner

To the Editor,

The International Association for Near Death Studies (IANDS) occasionally views the area of end-of-life experiences (ELEs) as confirming many of the topics found in near-death experiences (NDEs). I recently came across an ELE when reading about a 2014 biographical film, *Mr. Turner,* that received four Academy Award nominations and numerous awards and wins from foreign film associations, for example best actor (Timothy Spall) at the Cannes Film Festival. It was a dramatic foreign film and probably received few screenings in the United States. The film concerned the last 25 years of the life of eccentric English landscape artist J. M. W. Turner (1775 – 1851), after the death of his father. In his day, he was known as the "painter of light," well before Thomas Kinkade (1958 – 2012) trademarked the term for himself. Turner was not religious, but his last words before dying were, "The sun is God." Some NDErs claim the "light" in their NDEs is brighter than the sun, but I see a comparison to Steve Jobs saying "Oh, wow!" three times as he lay dying.

References

Lowe, G. (Producer). & Leigh, M. (Director). (2014). *Mr. Turner* (Motion picture). New York, NY: Sony Pictures Classics

Published in the *Journal of Near-Death Studies*, 33(3). Spring 2015

Best-Selling Book with NDE Becomes Major Motion Picture

In her 2015 book, *Miracles from Heaven,* and the 2016 film of the same title, Christy Wilson Beam (played by actress Jennifer Garner) narrates the story of the miraculous healing from serious and painful digestive disorders of her then nine-year-old daughter Annabel (Anna) after Anna's near-death experience (NDE) in 2011. The disorders were pseudo-obstruction motility disorder (considered incurable but manageable) and antral hypomotility disorder, for which she underwent several surgeries by a specialist and then was taking medications that took two pages to list all of them. The primary drug for the illness, cisapride, has side effects which had to have frequent blood monitoring and only a few doctors in the country can prescribe it so Christy and Anna had to travel from Texas to Boston Children's Hospital every few months. Other medications were a proton pump inhibitor, a laxative, antibiotics, probiotics, anticonvulsants, pain medication, and an antidepressant. Sometimes she had to be fed intravenously

Anna's NDE came as a result of falling thirty feet into the hollow interior of a tree. It took rescuers several hours to remove her from the tree, but there were only minor bumps and bruises from the fall. Considering she fell headfirst, the fall could have been fatal in and of itself. In the film, Anna visited a beautiful garden during her NDE, but in the book she sat on the lap of Jesus and then had a guardian angel beside her during the time she was alone, but conscious, in the tree after her NDE. Due to the presence of the angel, she did not become hysterical while alone in the dark interior of the tree and she had to put on a harness in order to be lifted out. The family was religious (Baptist) and the family and their church prayed for her to heal, but their prayers were not answered until the NDE happened. She was told that God had a plan for her life.

Before her NDE, Anna had expressed a desire to die in order to be free of her extreme pain and to be with Jesus. Immediately after the NDE, she stopped taking her pain medication, which were on an as needed basis. Her previously distended abdomen appeared normal, but she was weaned off some of the other medications as her parents were afraid of what might happen if they stopped them abruptly. Anna became very physically active immediately after her NDE and is now symptom-free from the previous life-threatening disorders and takes no medications.

It is sometimes more difficult to notice NDE aftereffects in children, but when holding a pool party at her home after her NDE, Anna requested that a lonely girl at school be invited rather than some popular classmates who spoke disrespectfully of some other children. Also, Anna envisions her future occupation as one in which she can be of service to other people. In the film, but not the book, Christy Beam quotes Einstein that a person can believe nothing in life is a miracle or that everything is a miracle. She was speaking not only of Anna's healing but also of the kindness the family received from numerous people during the days of Anna's multi-year illness, such as neighbors and church members who would watch the Beam's other children when they had to rush Anna to the emergency room.

Beam, C.W. (2015). *Miracles from Heaven: A Little Girl, Her Journey to Heaven, and her Amazing Story of Healing*. New York: Hachette Books

Submitted on May 8, 2016 for publication in *Vital Signs*, the newsletter of the International Association for Near-Death Studies

Book Review: *The Ultimate Journey: Inspiring Stories of Living and Dying* (2000)

Edited by James and Sean O'Reilly and Richard Sterling

Travelers' Tales is a series of books that that take "travel" in the broadest sense; besides country and regional guides, specialized women's journeys, and travel stories that focus on food or humor, this series looks at spiritual exploring—of which *The Ultimate Journey* is one volume. The editors created this book by gathering 43 writings, already published elsewhere, from authors as diverse as NDE researchers Melvin Morse and PMH Atwater, physicist Fred Alan Wolf, novelist-essayist Barbara Kingsolver, and actor Dirk Bogarde—all writing about what they learned from their various contacts with death.

There are five main subdivisions in the book: mysteries, encounters, rituals, shadows, and blessings. Of direct relevance to NDEs, besides the selections from Atwater and Morse, is a chapter by Diane Culbertson. Diane had two NDEs (at ages 5 and 20) and in each saw a man dressed in white. In her second NDE, Diane told him, "You must be my angel." Fifteen years later she was shown some old family photographs. The man dressed in white was her mother's uncle. The mother had only met him twice when she was a young child; he died in France in World War I, well before Diane was born. Diane's mother had never discussed the uncle with her.

Several of the selections may be classified as nearing death awareness, which many people consider closely related to NDEs.

In these days of multiculturalism and diversity, the variety of tales in this book are a treasure that would amaze and challenge many thinkers, but would perhaps seem not so startling to NDErs (and those of us nonexperiencers familiar with the topic) because by now we take some of these concepts matter-of-factly. These cross-cultural selections are not analyses of entire cultures; rather they are stories of individuals in other lands. For example, one woman described visiting a cemetery in Mexico with a family on the Day of the Dead. In another selection, an African shaman (now living in the US) told the story of unusual phenomena that occurred during his grandfather's death, when the shaman was still a young child. In a primitive situation where there was no medical review, the grandfather is said to have died in a village away from home, so the local medicine man placed a hyena's tail in the dead man's hand, which revived him and allowed him the strength to get up and walk back to his own village. There his family held a going away meal so he would have food for his afterdeath journey. He then officially died.

Another story had to do with an experience at Buchenwald concentration camp. Jacques Lusseyran, a French resistance fighter, was captured by the Nazis and sent to the camp, where he fell ill and was put into the camp hospital—from which almost no one ever left alive. Though blind from the age of eight, he behaved in the hospital with such optimism, that whenever someone became discouraged about living, the person would be taken to talk with Jacques who would give them hope.

In another story, a physicist says he dreamt himself in to a parallel universe that had many levels, but he knew one of the levels was the astral plane of suicides.

Therese Schroeder-Sheker describes the Chalice of Repose project, in which music is played to dying people. She explains its origins in the Middle Ages, and then describes her own application of the concept.

Though *Ultimate Journey* is not exclusively about NDEs, most people with an interest in NDEs will find it contains many important lessons on what death has to teach us.

Published in *Vital Signs* (Vol. 21, No. 1), the Newsletter of the International Association for Near Death Studies

November 9, 2010

Letter to the Editor
The State Journal-Register (Springfield, IL)

Dear Editor:

In the Obituary column on Tuesday for Richard A. Luttrell, it mentioned that he had been on Dateline in 2000. Although I never met Richard, I still remember that story on NBC's Dateline program. In battle, he shot and killed a Viet Cong soldier during his service there in 1967-68 and on the soldier he found a photo of the soldier with a young girl, presumably the soldier's daughter. Richard took the photo with him.

Many years later, probably in the early 1990s, someone who knew of the photo convinced him to ask the Vietnam embassy if they would print the photo in the main Vietnam newspaper to see whether anyone knew the identity of the soldier in the photo. There was no response for a long period of time, but then it turned out that someone used a copy of the newspaper as wrapping material in a package sent to a small village. The person who received the package looked at the paper and recognized the dead soldier. Richard made several trips to Vietnam to meet the now grown daughter of the soldier he killed. It is interesting coincidence of how death brought these two together. Richard seemed contrite about the girl having to grow up without a father and I believe she forgave him for killing her father.

Dan Punzak

SOURCES

INDEX

Sufism 599, 637
Suggestability/Suggestion 221, 288, 433, 496, 505, 722
Suicidal Ideation 464
Suicide 37, 57, 68, 92, 100, 105, 110-111, 121, 124, 128, 133-134, 140, 142, 155, 168-169, 171, 189, 213, 219, 226, 231, 242, 246-248, 253, 272, 296, 300-301, 319, 411, 419, 441, 449, 452, 458, 460-461, 471, 484, 500, 512, 532, 539, 542, 549, 553, 555, 562, 584, 674, 679, 693, 710, 730, 732, 751, 780
Sullivan, Robert 143
Summit, Dr. Roland 553-554
Sun 405
Sunlight 356
Suor Maria Villani of Naples 601
Superconscious 25
Superconscious Self-Awareness 423
Superconsciousness 227, 803
Superhuman Strength 530, 534, 739
Supernatural 584, 590, 597, 667, 765
Supernatural Aid 379
Supernatural Apparition 394
Supernatural Beings 401, 586
Supernatural Energy 612-613, 696
Supernatural Intercourse 642
Supernatural Music 187, 190
Supernatural Power 573
Supernatural Rescue 56, 101, 192
Supernatural World 572
Supernormal Events 50
Supernormal Reality 667, 671

Supersensible Knowledge 636-637
Supersensual Activity 642
Superstition 580
Supplemental Security Income (SSI) 758, 750, 753, 755
Suppressed Memories 451
Suppression 498-499
Suprahuman Spirits 478
Supraliminal Self 49, 235
Supreme Being 246, 678, 772
Supreme God 403
Surface Mind 641
Surgery 446
Surrogate Experience/Pain 122-123
Surrogates 745
Survival Mechanisms 286
Survival of Death 291, 519, 809
Sushama 623
Susto 375-376
Sutherland, Cherie (1992, 1993, 1995, 1996) 58-59
Sutras 670
Sweat Lodge 379, 381, 384, 395
Sweating 379
Swedenborg, Emanuel 74-75, 301, 536, 575
Swedenborgian Churches 575
Swelling 534
Swiss Alpine Club 75
Sylvian Fissure 187
Symbolic After-Death Communication (ADC) 294
Symbolic Resurrection 395
Symbolism 635
Sympathetic Ophthalmia 657
Synchronicity 237, 322, 340, 627

BOOK REFERENCES

A Beautiful Mind. (2001). Universal Pictures.

Abanes, R. (1996). *Journey into The Light: Exploring Near-Death Experiences.* Grand Rapids, MI: Baker Books.

Adams, M. A. (1989). Internal self helpers of persons with multiple personality disorder. *Dissociation,* 2(3): 138-143.

Allison, R. w/ T. Schwarz. (1980). *Minds in Many Pieces.* New York: Rawson, Wade Publishers.

Amatuzio, J. (2002). *Forever Ours: Real Stories of Immortality and Living from a Forensic Pathologist* . Novato, CA: New World Library

Amatuzio, J. (2006). *Beyond Knowing: Mysteries and Messages of Death and Life from a Forensic Pathologist* Novato, CA: New World Library.

Andorfer, J. C. (1985). Multiple personality in the Human Information-processor: A Case History and Theoretical Formulation. *J. Clin. Psych..* 41(3, May): 309-24. PMID 3998154

Atwater, P. M. H. (1988). *Coming Back to Life: The After-Effects of the Near-Death Experience.* New York: Dodd, Mead & Co. Reissued in 2001.

Atwater, P. M. H. (1994). *Beyond the Light: What Isn't Being Said About Near-Death Experience.* New York: Birch Lane Press

Atwater, P. M. H. (1999). *Children of the New Millennium: Children's Near-Death Experiences and the Evolution of Humankind.* New York: Three Rivers Press/Random House. Reissued in 2005 as *The New Children and Near-Death Experiences.*

Atwater, P. M. H. w/ D. H. Morgan. (2000). *The Complete Idiot's Guide to Near-Death Experiences.* Indianapolis: Alpha Book/McMillan. Reissued and revised in 2007 as *The Big Book of Near-Death Experiences.* by Hampton Roads Publishing

Baldwin, W. J. (2003). *Healing Lost Souls: Releasing Unwanted Spirits from Your Energy Body,* Charlottesville, VA: Hampton Roads Publishing.

Barlow, D. H., G. G. Abels, & E. B. Blanchard. (1977). Gender Identity Change in a Transsexual: An Exorcism. *Arch. of Sexual Behavior,* 6(5):387-95.

Basham, D. (1972). *Deliver Us From Evil,* Grand Rapids, MI: Chosen Books/Baker Publishing.

Beahrs, J.O. (1983). Co-consciousness: A Common Denominator in Hypnosis, Multiple Persoanlity, and Normalcy. *Am. J. Clin. Hypnosis.* 26(2, Oct): 100-13. PMID 6678534

Beauregard, M., & O'Leary, D. (2007) *The Spiritual Brain: A Neuroscientist's Case for the Existence of the Soul,* New York, NY: HarperCollins.

Belanger, J. (2003). *Dybbuk - Spiritual Possession and Jewish Folklore,* Found on website: http://www.ghostvillage.com/legends/2003/legends32_11292003.shtml (accessed, Sept. 2016)

Bentov, I. (1988). *Stalking the Wild Pendulum: On the Mechanics of Consciousness.* Rochester, VT: Inner Traditions/ Bear and Company.

Berman, E. (1981). "Pram lamentis," or she's a young thing and cannot leave her mother. *Family Process,* 20: 449-451.

Blackmore, S. (1993). *Dying to Live: Near-Death Experiences.* Buffalo, NY: Prometheus Books.

Blanke, O., S. Ortigue, T. Landis, & M. Seeck. (2002). Stimulating illusory own-body perceptions *Nature.* 419 (6904): 269–270.

Blanke O., T. Landis, L. Spinelli & M. Seeck. (2004). Out-of-body Experience and Autoscopy of Neurological Origin. *Brain.* 127 (2): 243–258.

Bliss, E. L. (1980). Multiple Personalities. *Arch. Gen. Psych.* 37: 1388-1397

Bliss, E. L. (1983). Multiple Personality, Related Disorders, and Hypnosis. *Amer. J. Clin. Hypnosis.* 26: 114-23

Bliss. E. L. (1986). *Multiple Personality, Allied Disorders, and Hypnosis.* New York: Oxford University Press.

Bowman, E. S. S. Blix & P. M. Coons. (1985).Multiple Personality in Adolescence: Relationship to Incestual Experiences. *J. Amer. Acad. Child Psychiatr.* 24: 109-114.

Brandt (1988). Unable to relocate original source.

Brassfield, P. A. (1983). Unfolding Patterns of the Multiple Personality Through Hypnosis. *Am. J. Clinical Hypnosis.* 26: 146-152.

Braun, B. G. & R. G. Sachs. (1985). The Development of Multiple Personality Disorder: Predisposing, Precipitating, and Perpetuating

Factors. In Kluft, R. P., (ed.). *Childhood Antecedents of Multiple Personality.* Washington, D.C.: American Psychiatric Press

Braun, B. G. (1984). Hypnosis Creates Multiple Personality. *Int J Clin Exp Hypn.* 32(2, Apr):191-7.

Brende, J. O. (1984). The Psychophysiological Manifestations of Dissociation. *Psychiatr.Clin.of North Amer.* 7: 41-50

Brother Sun, Sister Moon (1972). Paramount Pictures.

Burpo, T. w/L. Vincent. (2010). *Heaven is for Real: A Little Boy's Astounding Story of His Trip to Heaven and Back,* Nashville, TN: Thomas Nelson.

Bush, N.E. (2009). Distressing Western Near-Death Experiences: Finding a Way through the Abyss. Chapter 4 (pp. 63-86.) in Holden, Greyson, and James.

Cardena, E., S. J. Lynn,& S. Krippner, Eds. (2000). *Varieties of Anomalous Experience: Examining the Evidence,* Washington, DC: American Psychological Association.

Carlisle, A. L. (1986). Multiple Personality and Criminal Behavior. In: B. G. Braun (Ed.). *Proceedings of the Third International Conference on Multiple Personality/Dissociative States.*

Carlson, E. T. (1984). the History of Multiple Personality in the United States: Mary Reynolds and Her Subsequent Reputation. *Bull. History Medicine.*58: 72-82

Carlson, E.T. (1986). The History of Dissociation Until 1980. In J.M. Quen (Ed.). *Split Minds/Split Brains: Historical and Current Perspectives.* New York: New York University Press.

Carroll, L. (1865). *Alice in Wonderland* (numerous editions available)

Carter, C. (2010). *Science and the Near-Death Experience: How Consciousness Survives Death,* Rochester, VT: Inner Traditions.

Castle, K. & S. Bechtel. (1989). *Katherine It's Time: An Incredible Journey into the World of a Multiple Personality.* New York: Harper & Row

Caul, D. (1984). Group and Videotape Techniques for Multiple Personality Disorder. *Psychiatric Annals.*14: 43-50

Chamberlain, D. (1998). *Babies Remember Birth.* Los Angeles: Jeremy P. Tarcher.

Chaneles, S. (1987). Growing Old behind Bars: The Aging of Our Convict Population Brings with It Special Needs and Problems

That Few of Our Prisons Are Ready to Handle. *Psychology Today*, Oct.: 46+.

Cohen, T. (2006). *The Day I Died: Remarkable True Stories of Near-Death Experience*, London: John Blake Publishing.

Comstock, C. (1985). Inner Self Helpers or Centers: What Is It They Do and How Do They Do It?, *Paper Presented at the 2nd International Conference on Multiple Personality/Dissociative States,* Chicago

Comstock, C. (1987a) . The Concept of a Birth personality and Center to Expedite Treatment, *Paper presented at the 4th International Conference on Multiple Personality/Dissociative States,* Chicago

Comstock, C. (1987b). Internal Self Helpers or Centers, *Integration*, 3(1), 3-12.

Condon, W. S., W. D. Ogston, & L. V. Pacoe. (1969). Three Faces of Eve Revisited: A Study of Transient Microstrabismus. *J. Abnormal Psych.* 74 (5, Oct.): 618-20

Coons, P. M., V. Milstein & C. Marley. (1982). EEG Studies of Two Multiple Persoanlities and a Control. *Arch Gen Psychiatry.* 1982;39(7):823-825.

CPR [Committee on Psychiatry and Religion]. (1976). *Mysticism: Spiritual Quest or Psychic Disorder?* (Vol. IX, Publication No. 97). New York, NY: Group for the Advancement of Psychiatry.

Crabtree, A. (1985). *Multiple Man: Explorations in Possession and Multiple Personality,* New York: Praeger

Crabtree, A. (1993). Puzzling Over Possession: Comments on Dissociation Articles on Possession. *J. Dissociation.* 6(4): 254-59.

Crisp, P. (1983). Object Relations and Multiple Personality: An Exploration of the Literature. Psychoanalytical Rev. 70: 221-34.

Davis, S. T. (2010). *Butterflies Are Free to Fly: A New and Radical Approach to Spiritual Evolution.* In Chapter 32 "Compassion," kindle edition, Location 6184

Delacor, J-B, (1974), *Glimpses of the Beyond: The Extraordinary Experiences of People Who Crossed the Brink of Death and Returned.* (Trans. E. B. Garside). New York: Delacorte Press.

Eadie, B. (1992). *Embraced by the Light,* Placerville, CA: Gold Leaf Press.

Eliach, Y.(1982). *Hasidic Tales of the Holocaust* (1982). New York: Avon.

Eliade, M. (1964). *Shamanism: Archaic Techniques of Ecstasy* (1994, 4th edition). Princeton, NJ: Princeton University Press.

Ellenberger, H. F. (1970). *The Discovery of the Unconscious: The History and Evolution of Dynamic Psychiatry,* New York, NY: Basic Books

Ellwood, G. F. (2001). *The Uttermost Deep: The Challenge of Near-Death Experiences,* New York: Lantern Books.

Encyclopedia of Religion. (2005). Dybbuk. Second Ed., Vol. 4. Detroit: Macmillan Reference, Thomson Gale Publishing

Evans-Pritchard, E. E. (1937). *Witchcraft, Oracles and Magic among the Azande,* London: Oxford University Press.

Evergreen Study, The. (Lindley, J.H., S. Bryan, and B. Conley) (1981). Near-death experiences in a Pacific Northwest American Population: Anabiosis 1: 104-125.

Fagan, J. & P. P. McMahon. (1984). Incipient Multiple Personality in Children: Four Cases. *J. Nerv. and Mental Disease.*172: 26-36. PMID 6690651

Farr, S. S. (1993). *What Tom Sawyer Learned from Dying,* Charlottesville, VA: Hampton Roads.

Fenwick, P. & E. Fenwick. (1997). *The Truth in the Light: An Investigation of Over 300 Near-Death Experiences,* New York: Berkley Books.

Fenwick, P. & E. Fenwick. (2008). *The Art of Dying,* London/New York: Continuum Books.

Fine, C. G. et al. (1985a and 1985b). Unable to laocate. Probably papers presented at conference

Fiore, E. (1987). *The Unquiet Dead: A Psychologist Treats Spirit Possession,* Garden City, NY: Dolphin Book/Doubleday & Co.

Flynn, C. P. (1982). Meanings and Implications of NDEr Transformations: Some Preliminary Findings and Implications. Anabiosis: J Near-Death Stud, 2, 3-13.

Fraser, G.A. (1987), The Central ISH: The Ultimate MPD Inner Self Helper. *Paper presented at the 4th International Conference on Multiple Personality/Dissociative States,* Chicago

Gallup, G., Jr., & W. Procter. (1982). *Adventures in Immortality.* New York: McGraw-Hill.

Galvin, J. A., & A. M. Ludwig. (1961). A Case of Witchcraft. *J. Nerv. Ment. Dis.,* 133:161.

Garfield, J. (1986). *The Life of a Real Girl.* New York: St. Martin's Press.

Geiger, J. (2009). *The Third Man Factor: Surviving the Impossible,* New York, NY: Weinstein Books.

Ghost (1990). Paramount Pictures

Goldman, A. (1988). *The Lives of John Lennon,* New York: William Morrow.

Goleman, D. (1995). *Emotional Intelligence: Why It Can Matter More Than IQ,* New York, NY: Bantam Books.

Greaves, G. B. (1980). Multiple Personality 165 Years After Mary Reynolds. *J. Nerv. Ment. Dis.* 168: 577-596

Grey, M. (1985). *Return from Death: An Exploration of the Near-Death Experience,* London: Arkana

Greyson, B. & C. Flynn, Eds. (1983).*The Near-Death Experience: Problems, Prospects, Perspectives.* Springfield, IL: Charles C. Thomas Publishers

Greyson, B. & N. E. Bush. (1992). Distressing Near-Death Experiences. *Psychiatry.* 55 Feb (1):95-110. PMID: 1557473

Greyson,B. & M. B. Liester. (2004). Audiorty Hallucinations Following Near-Death Experiences. J. Humanistic Psychology. 44: 320-36.

Greyson, B. (1993). Near-Death Experiences and the Physio-Kundalini Syndrome. *J. of Religion and Health.* 32: 277-90.

Greyson, B. (2000): Near-Death Experiences, Chapter 10 in Cardena, Lynn and Krippner.

Greyson, B., E.W. Kelly and E.F. Kelly (2007). Unusual Experiences Near Death and Related Phenomena, Chapter 6 in Kelly et. al.

Grof, S. and J. Halifax. (1977). *The Human Encounter with Death.* New York: Dutton.

Gross (1986). Unable to relocate original source.

Grosso, M. (1983) Jung, Parapsychology, and the Near-Death Experience: Toward a Transpersonal Paradigm, *Anabiosis: J. Near-Death Studies,* 3, 3-38

Gruenewald, D. (1978). Analogues of Multiple Personality in Psychosis. *Int. J. Clinical and Experimental Hypnosis.* 26: 1-8.

Guggenheim, B. & J. Guggenheim. (1995). *Hello From Heaven!* New York: Bantam.

Guirdham, A. (1982). *The Psychic Dimension of Mental Health.* Wellingborough: Turnstone Press

Hamilton, A.(2008). *The Scalpel and the Soul: Encounters with Surgery, the Supernatural and the Healing Power of Hope.* New York: Tarcher/Penguin.

Hardy, A. (1979). *The Spiritual Nature of Man: A Study of Contemporary Religious Experience,* Oxford: Oxford University Press.

Harner, M. (1990, Third Edition). *The Way of a Shaman.* HarperSanFrancisco.

Harris, (2008). *Glimpses of Heaven: True Stories of Hope and Peace at the End of Life's Journey.* Grand Rapids, MI: Revell/Baker Publishing.

Hawksworth, H. w/Ted Schwarz (1977). *The Five of Me.* Chicago: Henry Regnery Company

Hieronymus Bosch (~1506), *Ascent into the Empyrean* (painting)

Holden, J. M., B. Greyson, & D. James. (2009). *The Handbook of Near-Death Experiences: Thirty Years of Investigation,* Santa Barbara, CA: Praeger Publishers

ICD, International Statistical Classification of Diseases and Related Health Problems Geneva, Switzerland: World Health Organization

Immortal Beloved (1994). Columbia Pictures.

Ireland-Frey, L. (1999). *Freeing the Captives: The Emerging Therapy of Treating Spirit Attachment,* Charlottesville, VA: Hampton Roads Publishing.

ISSTD, International Society for the Study of Trauma and Dissociation (2011): Guidelines for Treating Dissociative Identity Disorder in Adults, Third Revision, *J. of Trauma & Dissociation,* 12:2, 115-187

Jaynes, J. (1976). *The Origins of Consciousness in the Breakdown of the Bicameral Mind,* Boston, MA: Houghton Mifflin/ Mariner Books.

Jorn, N. (1982). Repression in a Case of Multiple Personality Disorder. *Perspectives in Psychiatric Care.* 20: 105-110

Josephus, F. (1843). *The works of Flavius Josephus: The Jewish war.* Vol. II, Book VII, Chap. VI. Philadelphia: Grigg & Elliot.

Jourdain, R. (1997). *Music, the Brain and Ecstasy: How Music Captures Our Imagination,* New York: Quill.

Karagulla, S. & D. v.G. Kunz . (1989). *The Chakras and the Human Energy Fields,* Wheaton, IL: Theosophical Publishing.

Karagulla, S. (1967). *Breakthrough to Creativity: Your Higher Sense Perception,* Santa Monica, CA: DeVorss and Co.

Kason, Y. (1994). *Farther Shores: Exploring How Near-Death, Kundalini and Mystical Experiences Can Transform Ordinary Lives,* Toronto, CN: HarperCollins Canada.

Kelly, E. F., E. W. Kelly, A. Crabtree, A. Gauld, M. Gross, & B. Greyson (Eds.). (2009). *Irreducible Mind: Toward a Psychology for the 21st Century*, Lanham, MD: Rowman and Littlefield.

Kelly, E.W. (2009). F. W. H. Myers and the Empirical Study of the Mind-Body Problem. Chapter 2 in Kelly et. al.

Kenny, M. G. (1985). *The Passion of Ansel Bourne: Multiple Personality in American Culture*. Smithsonian Series in Ethnographic Inquiry, Vol. 5.

Keyes, D. (1981). *The Minds of Billy Milligan*. New York: Random House.

Kluft, R. P. (1984). An Introduction to Multiple Personality Disorder. *Psychiatr. Ann. 7*: 19 - 24.

Kluft, R. P. (1985). *Childhood Antecedents of Multiple Personality Disorder*. Washington, D. C.: American Psychiatric Assoc.

Komianos, A. N. (2011). *Rapid Entity Attachment Release: A Breakthrough in the World of Spirit Possession and Replacement*, Corfu, Greece: Hypnoscopesis Publishing.

Kralik, J. (2010). *365 Thank Yous: The Year a Simple Act of Daily Gratitude Changed My Life*, New York, NY: Hyperion Books

Kubler-Ross, E.(1969). *On Death and Dying*, New York, NY: Macmillan Publishing.

Kunz, D. v.G. (1991). *The Personal Aura*, Wheaton, IL: Quest Books.

Lake, M. G. (1991). *Native Healer: Initiation Into an Ancient Art*. Wheaton, IL: Quest Books.

Larmore, K., A.M. Ludwig, & R. L. Cain. (1977). Multiple Personality - An Objective Case Study, *Brit. J. Psychiat.*, 131: 35-40

Lauridsen, M.(1997). *Lux Aeterna (Light Eternal)*, musical composition

Legrenzi, P., & C. Umilta. (2011). *Neuromania: On the Limits of Brain Science*. (F. Anderson, Trans.), Oxford: Oxford University Press

Lerma, J. (2007). *Into the Light: Real Life Stories about Angelic Visits, Visions of the Afterlife, and Other Pre-Death Experiences*. Franklin Lakes, NJ: New Page Books/Career Press.

Lerma, J. (2009). *Learning from the Light: Pre-Death Experiences, Prophecies, and Angelic Messages of Hope*. Franklin Lakes, NJ: New Page Books/Career Press.

LeShan, L. (2000). *The World of the Paranormal: The Next Frontier* (rev. ed.). New York, NY: Helios Press.

Loewenstein et al. (1986). Unable to relocate original source.

Long, J. w/P. Perry. (2010). *Evidence of the Afterlife: The Science of Near-Death Experiences,* New York, NY: HarperCollins

Long, M. F. (1948). *The Secret Science Behind Miracles,* Santa Monica, CA: DeVorss & Co.

Ludwig, A. M. J. M. Brandsma, C. B. Wilbur, F. Benfeldt, & D. H. Jameson. (1972). The Objective Study of Multiple Personality. Or Are Four Heads Better Than One? *Arch. Gen. Psychiatry.* 26(4, April): 298-310.

Lundahl, C. & H. Widdison. (1997). *The Eternal Journey: How Near-Death Experiences Illuminate Our Earthly Lives,* New York: Warner Books.

Lusseyran, J. (1963/1987). *And There Was Light.* (E. R. Cameron, Trans.). New York, NY: Parabola Books

Mahler, G. (1894), *Resurrection Symphony (Symphony No. 2),* musical composition

Malz, B. (1977). *My Glimpse of Eternity.* New Carmel, NY: Chosen Books (Guideposts Edition).

Marcus, G. (2012). Neuroscience Fiction. *The New Yorker.* Nov. 30.

Markides, K. C. (1987). *Homage to the Sun: The Wisdom of the Magus of Strovolos,* New York, NY: Arkana/Penguin.

Markides, K. C. (1990) . *The Magus of Strovolos: The Extraordinary World of a Spiritual Healer,* New York, NY: Arkana/Penguin.

Markides, K. C. (1991). *Fire in the Heart: Healers, Sages, and Mystics.* New York, NY: Arkana/Penguin.

Martin, M. (1976). *Hostage to the Devil.* New York: Reader's Digest Press.

Maslow, A. H. (1999, 3rd Edition, originally published in 1968). *Toward a Psychology of Being,* New York, John Wiley and Sons.

McAll, K. (1984). *Healing the Family Tree (rev. ed.).* London: Sheldon Press

McColman, C. (2010). *The Big Book of Christian Mysticism: The Essential Guide to Contemplative Spirituality,* Charlottesville, VA: Hampton Roads Publishing

McMahon, D. M. (2013). *Divine Fury: A History of Genius,* New York, NY: Basic Books.

Mesulam, M. M. (1981). Dissociative States with Abnormal Temporal Lobe EEG. *Arch. Neurology.* 38: 176-181

Methvin (1989) . Unable to find original source.

Milingo, E., M. McMillan, Ed. (1984). *The World in Between: Christian Healing and the Struggle for Spiritual Survival,* Maryknoll, NY: Orbis Books.

Miller, S.D. (1989). Optical Differences in Cases of Multiple Personality Disorder. *J. Nervous and Mental Disease,* 177(8), 480 - 486.

Modi, S. (1997). *Remarkable Healings: A Psychiatrist Discovers Unsuspected Roots of Mental and Physical Illness,* Charlottesville, VA: Hampton Roads Publishing.

Moody, R. (1975 or 2001, 25th anniversary ed.), *Life after Life.* New York: HarperOne (original by Mockingbird Books).

Moody, R. (1977). *Reflections on Life after Life.* New York: Bantam/ Mockingbird Book

Moody, R. w/ P. Perry, (2010). *Glimpses of Eternity: Sharing a Loved One's Passage from This Life to the Next,* New York, NY: Guideposts.

Moody, R. w/ P. Perry. (1988), *The Light Beyond: New Explorations by the Author of Life after Life.* New York: Bantam.

Moorjani, A. (2012). *Dying To Be Me: My Journey from Cancer, to Near Death, to True Healing.* Carlsbad, CA: Hay House, Inc.

Morgan, A. J., R. D. Hales, & S. D. Miller. (1986). Refractive Errors in Cases of Multiple Personality Disorder. In B.G. Braun (Ed), *PROCEEDINGS OF THE THIRD INTERNATIONAL CONFERENCE ON MULTIPLE PERSONAUTY/DISSOCIATIVE STATES,* (p. 126.)

Morse, M w/ P. Perry, (1990). *Closer to the Light: Learning from the Near-Death Experiences of Children,* New York: Villard Books.

Morse, M w/ P. Perry, (1992). *Transformed by the Light: The Powerful Effect of Near-Death Experiences on People's Lives,* New York: Villard Books.

Morse, M. w/ P. Perry (1994). *Parting Visions: Uses and Meanings of Pre-Death, Psychic, and Spiritual Experiences,* New York: Villard Books.

Morse, M. w/ P. Perry. (2000). *Where God Lives: The Science of the Paranormal and How Our Brains Are Linked to the Universe,* New York: Cliff Street Books/HarperCollins.

Myers, F.W.H. (1903/2005). *Human Personality and Its Survival of Bodily Death,* Mineola, NY: Dover Publications/Courier Corp.

Nagy, T.F. (1986). Patient Use of a Daily Log in Diagnosis and Treatment of MPD, *Paper presented at the 3rd International Conference on Multiple Personality/Dissociative States,* Chicago

Nash, M. R. & S. J. Lynn. (1986). Child Abuse and Hypnotic Ability. Imagination, Cognition, and Personality. 5: 211-218.

Nathan, D. (2011). *Sybil Exposed: The Extraordinary Story Behind the Famous Multiple Personality Case..* New York: Free Press.

Nature. (2008). 454:(14, Aug), 828

Nelson, K. (2011). *The Spiritual Doorway in the Brain: A Neurologist's Search for the God Experience.* New York: Dutton.

Nelson, K. R., M. Mattingly, A. L. Sherman, & F. A. Schmitt. (2006). Does the Arousal System Contribute to Near Death Experience? *Neurology.* 66(7, April): 1003-1009.

Noe, A. (2010). *Out of Our Heads: Why You Are Not Your Brain, and Other Lessons from the Biology of Consciousness,* New York, NY: Hill and Wang.

Novak, P. (2003). *The Lost Secret of Death: Our Divided Souls and the Afterlife,* Charlottesville, VA: Hampton Roads.

Noyes, R., Jr., P. Fenwick, J. M. Holden, & S. R. Christian. (2009). Aftereffects of Pleasurable Western Adult Near-Death Experiences. Chapter 3, pp. 41-62, In Holden, Greyson, and James.

Noyes, R. Jr. (1982). The Human Experience of Death or, What Can't We Learn from Near-Death Experiences?, *Omega,* 13(3), 251 - 259.

Noyes, R. Jr. & R. Kletti. (1976a). Depersonalization in the Face of Life-Threatening Danger: A Description. *Psychiatry,* 39(1), 19 - 27. PMID: 1257352

Noyes, R. Jr. & R. Kletti. (1976b). Depersonalization in the Face of Life-Threatening Danger: an Interpretation, *Omega,* 7(2), 103 - 114.

Noyes, R. Jr. & R. Kletti. (1977a). Depersonalization in Response to Life-Threatening Danger, *Comprehensive Psychiatry,* 18 (4): 375-84. PMID: 872561

Noyes, R. Jr. & R. Kletti. (1977b). Panoramic Memory: a Response to the Threat of Death, *Omega,* 8(3), 181 - 194

Noyes, R. Jr. (1972). The Experience of Dying. *Psychiatry,* 35 (May 1971), 174 - 184.

Noyes, R. Jr. (1980). Attitude Change Following Near-Death Experiences, *Psychiatry*, 43(August), 234 - 242.

Noyes, R., Jr., Hoenk, P. R.,Kuperman, S., & Slymen, D. J. (1977). Depersonalization in Accident Victims and Psychiatric Patients, *J. Nerv. Mental Disorders*, 164(6), 401 - 407.

Nuland, S. B. (1997). *The Wisdom of the Body*, New York, NY: Alfred A. Knopf.

O'Neill, J. J. (1944). *Prodigal Genius: The Life of Nikola Tesla*, New York, NY: Tartan Books/Ives Washburn, Inc.

Oesterreich, T. K. (1921/1966). *Possession: Demonical and Other*, (D. Ibberson, Trans.). New Hyde Park, NY: University Books.

Osis, K. & E. Haraldsson (1961) *Deathbed Observations by Physicians and Nurses*

Osis, K., and Haraldsson, E. (1977). *At the hour of Death*, New York, NY: Avon Books.

Pearsall, P., G. E. R. Schwartz and L. G. S. Russek (2002). Changes in Heart Transplant Recipients That Parallel the Personalities of Their Donors. *J. Near-Death Studies*.20(3).

Peck, M. S. (1983). *People of the Lie: The Hope For Healing Human Evil*, New York: Touchstone/Simon & Schuster.

Pitbaldo, D. & J. Densen-Gerber. (1986). Pattern-Evoked Potential Differences among the Personalities of a Multiple: Some New Phenomena. *Proceedings of the Third International Conference on Multiple Personality/Dissociative States.*

Plato, *The Republic* (numerous editions available)

Putnam, F. W., R. J. Loewenstein, E. J. Silberman, & R. M. Post. (1984) Multiple Personality in a Hospital Setting. *J Clin Psychiatry*. 45(4, Apr): 172-5. PMID: 6715291

Putnam, F. W., J. J. Guroff, E. K. Silberman, L. Barban, & R. M. Post. (1986). The Clinical Phenomenology of Multiple Personality Disorder: Review of 100 Cases. *J. Clin. Psychiatry*. 47(6, June):285-93. PMID: 3711025

Radin, D. *(2013). Supernormal: Science, Yoga, and the Evidence for Extraordinary Psychic Abilities* New York, NY: Random House/ Deepak Chopra Books.

Raiders of the Lost Ark (1981). Paramount Pictures.

Rawlings, M. S. (1979). *Beyond Death's Door.* Nashville, TN: Bantam Book/Thomas Nelson Publishers.

Rawlings, M. S. (1993). *To Hell and Back: Life After Death - Startling New Evidence,* Nashville, TN: Thomas Nelson Publishers.

Restak, R. (1984). People with Multiple Minds. *Science Digest.* June: 76-77.

Riley, R. L. & J. Mead. (1988). The Development of Symptoms of Multiple Personality Disorder in a Child of Three. *Dissociation.* 1(3): 41-46.

Ring, K. & C. J. Rosing. (1990). The Omega Project: An empirical study of the NDE-prone personality. *J. Near-Death Studies.* 8(4): 211-239.

Ring, K. (1980). *Life at Death: A Scientific Investigation of the Near-Death Experience,* New York, NY: Coward, McCann & Geohegan.

Ring, K. (1984). *Heading Toward Omega: In Search of the Meaning of the Near-Death Experience,* New York: Quill/William Morrow.

Ring. K. and E. E. Valarino. (1998). *Lessons from the Light: What We Can Learn from the Near-Death Experience.* New York: Insight Books/Plenum Press.

Ritchie, G.G. (1978). *Return from Tomorrow.* New York: Chosen Books (Guideposts Edition).

Robertson, N. (1988). *Getting Better: Inside Alcoholics Anonymous.* New York, NY: William Morrow & Co.

Rodman, J. S, (1979). *The Kahuna Sorcerers of Hawaii, Past and Present,* Hicksville, NY: Exposition Press.

Rogo, D.S. (1987). *The Infinite Boundary: A Psychic Look at Spirit Possession, Madness and Multiple Personality.* New York: Dodd, Mead and Company

Rommer, B. R. (2000), *Blessing in Disguise: Another Side of the Near-Death Experience.* St. Paul: Llewellyn Publications.

Ross, A. A., G. R. Norton & K. Wozney. (1987). Multiple Personality Disorder: An Analysis of 236 Cases. *Can. J. Psychiatry.* 34(5, June): 413-18.

Ross, C. & A. Pam. (1995). *Pseudoscience in Biological Psychiatry: Blaming the Body.* New York: John Wiley & Sons.

Ross, C. A. (1997). *Dissociative Identity Disorder: Diagnosis, Clinical Features, and Treatment of Multiple Personality Disorder* (2nd ed.). New York: John Wiley & Sons.

Sabom, M. (1982). *Recollections of Death: A Medical Investigation,* New York, NY: Harper & Row.

Sabom, M. (1998). *Light & Death: One Doctor's Fascinating Account of Near-Death Experiences,* Grand Rapids, MI: Zondervan Publishing House.

Sacks, O. (2007). *Musicophilia,* New York: Borzoi books/Knopf/Random House.

Sagan, C. (1979). *Broca's Brain: Reflections on the Romance of Science.* New York: Random House.

Sagan, S. (1997). *Entity Possession: Freeing the Energy Body of Negative Influences,* Rochester, VT: Destiny Books.

Schenk, L. & D. Bear. (1981). Multiple Personality and Related Dissociative Phenomena in Patients with Temporal Lobe Epilepsy. *Am. J. Psychiatry.* 1311-1316

Schreiber, F.R. (1973). *Sybil.* Chicago: Regnery

G. M. Schreckenberg, H. H. Bird. (1987). Neural plasticity of musculus in response to disharmonic sound. *The Bulletin* (New Jersey Academy of Science). 32: 77-86.

Schwartz, P.G. (1988) A Case of Concurrent Multiple Personality Disorder and Transsexualism. *Dissociation.* Vol. 1 (2, June): 48-52

Scialli (1982). Unable to relocate original source.

Science (23 February 2007). 315: p. 1061)

Shelley, W.B. (1981). Dermatitis artefacta induced in a patient by one of her multiple personalities. *Brit. J. Dermatology.* 105:587-589.

Shepard, K. R. & B. Braun. (1985). Visual changes in Multiple Personality. *Proceedings of the Second International Conference on Multiple Personality/Dissociative States.*

Shermer, M. (2011). *The Believing Brain: From Ghosts and Gods to Politics and Conspiracies---How We Construct Beliefs and Reinforce Them as Truths,* New York: Times Books.

Shermer, M. (2014). *Scientific American.* October

Siegel, R. K. (1980), The Psychology of Life After Death. *Amer. Psychol.* 35(10): 911-931.

Siegel, R. K. (1981). Life After Death. In O. Abell and B. Singer (Eds.), *Science and the Paranormal: Probing the Existence of the Supernatural,* New York, NY: Charles Scribner's Sons.

Springer, S., & G. Deutsch. (1981/2001). *Left Brain, Right Brain: Perspectives from Cognitive,* W. H. Freeman/Worth Publishers.

St. Clair, M. (1997). *Beyond the Light: Files of Near-Death Experiences,* New York, NY: Barnes & Noble.

Storr, A. (1996). *Feet of Clay/Saints, Sinners, and Madmen: A Study of Gurus,* New York, NY: The Free Press/Simon & Schuster.

Strassman, R. (2001). *DMT: The Spirit Molecule, A Doctor's Revolutionary Research into the Biology of Near-Death and Mystical Experiences.* Rochester, VT: Park Street Press.

Strauss, R. (1889). *Death and Transfiguration,* musical composition

Tallis, R. (2012). *Aping Mankind: Neuromania, Darwinitis and the Misrepresentation of Humanity,*(1st ppb. ed.). Durham and Bristol, Eng.: Acumen.

Tammet, D. (2006). *Born on a Blue Day,* London: Hodder and Stoughton, Ltd.

Taylor, W. S. & M. F. Martin. (1944). Multiple Personality. *J. Abnormal and Social Psychol.* 39(3): 281-300

The Amazing Grace (2006). FourBoys Films

Lilly, J. C. (1972/1985). *The Center of the Cyclone: An Autobiography of Inner Space.* New York: Random House.

The Diagnostic and Statistical Manual of Mental Disorders (DSM). Several editions cited, *DSM-III, DSM-III-TR, DSM-IV* and *DSM-5.*

Thurston, H. (1952). *The Physical Phenomena of Mysticism,* (J. H. Crehan, Ed.). London: Burns Oates and Washbourne, Ltd.

Torem et al. (1986). Unable to relocate original source.

Toufexis, A. (1988). Why Mothers Kill Their Babies. *Time Magazine.* June 20.

Tavris, C. (2011). Multiple Personality Deception (book review). *Wall Street Journal.* Oct. 29.

Treece, P. (1989). The *Sanctified Body,*New York, NY: Doubleday & Co.

Treffert, D. A. (1989). *Extraordinary People: Understanding "Idiot Savants,"* New York, NY: Harper and Row.

Treffert, D. (2010). *Islands of Genius: The Bountiful Mind of the Autistic, Acquired and Sudden Savant,* Philadelphia: Jessica Kingsley Pub.

Trost. (1988). Article in *Wall Street Journal.*

Ubell (1986). Unable to relocate original source.

Underhill, E. (1911/1961) *Mysticism: A Study in the Nature and Development of Man's Spiritual Consciousness,* New York, NY: E. P. Dutton.

Van Dusen, W. (1974). *The Presence of Other Worlds*. New York: Harper & Row.

van Lommel, P. (2010). Translator: L. Vroomen. *Consciousness Beyond Life: The Science of the Near-Death Experience*. New York: HarperCollins.

Verdi, G. (1874). *Requiem* musical composition

Verny, T. (1981). *The Secret Life of the Unborn Child*. New York: Delta Book.

Voien, B. & D. Schafer. (1986). Alcoholism and Unconscious Abuse-The Traumatizing Environment. Paper Presented *The Third International Conference on Multiple Personality/Dissociative States*.

Weber, R. (1991). Foreword (p. ix-xviii) in Kunz (1991), *The Personal Aura*.

Weiss, B. L. (1988). *Many Lives, Many Masters*, New York, NY: Fireside/ Simon & Schuster.

Weiss, J. E. (1972). *The Vestibule*, Port Washington, NY: Ashley Books.

Whinnery, J. E. (1997) in Greyson, Kelly and Kelly, 2010, p. 379.

Wickland, C. (1924) *Thirty Years Among the Dead*. Los Angeles: National Psychological Institute.

Wilbur, C. B. (1984). Treatment of Multiple Personality. *Psychiatr. Ann.* 14: 27-31.

Wilbur, C. (1979). *People Magazine*

Wilder, T. (1927). *The Bridge at San Luis Rey* (1955 ed.). New York, NY: Harper & Row.

Wilder, T. (1938/2003). *Our Town*, New York, NY: Harper Perennial Modern Classics.

Williamson, M. (1992). *A Return to Love*. Quotes also found in quotationspage.com under Williamson

Young (1985). Unable to relocate original source.

Zaleski, C. (1987). *Otherworld Journeys: Accounts of Near-Death Experience in Medieval and Modern Times*, Oxford: Oxford University Press.

Printed in the United States
By Bookmasters